C. Michael Myers
4200 Factoria Blvd. SE Apt. B10
Bellevue, WA 98006-1953

W9-AZH-614

Who's Who
IN ANCIENT EGYPT

Available from Routledge worldwide:

Who's Who in Ancient Egypt
Michael Rice

Who's Who in the Ancient Near East
Gwendolyn Leick

Who's Who in Classical Mythology
Michael Grant and John Hazel

Who's Who in World Politics
Alan Palmer

Who's Who in Dickens
Donald Hawes

Who's Who in Jewish History
Joan Comay, new edition revised by Lavinia Cohn-Sherbok

Who's Who in Military History
John Keegan and Andrew Wheatcroft

Who's Who in Nazi Germany
Robert S. Wistrich

Who's Who in the New Testament
Ronald Brownrigg

Who's Who in Non-Classical Mythology
Egerton Sykes, new edition revised by Alan Kendall

Who's Who in the Old Testament
Joan Comay

Who's Who in Russia since 1900
Martin McCauley

Who's Who in Shakespeare
Peter Quennell and Hamish Johnson

Who's Who in World War Two
Edited by John Keegan

Who's Who IN ANCIENT EGYPT

Michael Rice

London and New York

First published 1999
by Routledge
11 New Fetter Lane, London EC4P 4EE

Simultaneously published in the USA and Canada
by Routledge
29 West 35th Street, New York, NY 10001

Routledge is an imprint of the Taylor & Francis Group

Typeset in Sabon by Routledge
Printed and bound in Great Britain by
TJ International Ltd, Padstow, Cornwall

British Library Cataloguing in Publication Data
A catalogue record for this book is available from the British Library

Library of Congress Cataloging in Publication Data
A catalog record for this book has been applied for

ISBN 0–415–15448–0

Contents

Preface

Anyone who presumes to compile a work such as *Who's Who in Ancient Egypt* will find himself somewhat in the position of C. G. Jung when he felt obliged to write *Septem Sermones ad Mortuos* (*Seven Sermons to the Dead*) as a consequence, it seemed to him, of finding his house infested with the spirits of the dead, demanding instruction. Though the spirits of the dead have their place in Egyptian royal legend, for they were said to be the forerunners of the historic dynasties of kings, it is they who are the instructors in this case, summarily demanding inclusion. The compiler is merely the scribe, sitting meekly with legs crossed, awaiting the opportunity to set down the record of their lives at their dictation, a self-effacing servant of Thoth.

Who's Who in Ancient Egypt attempts to identify the most celebrated of the sons and daughters of Egypt, whose attainments forged its unique civilisation. But it also seeks to record the names of less august figures, whose lives may throw a modest but particularly focused shaft of light to show what it may have been like to live in Egypt at the height of its power and prosperity, or in one of its not infrequent periods of hardship and disorder. Some have been included because their lives or careers illumine an aspect of the Egyptian experience which may be unfamiliar or unusual. In general, the *Who's Who* records those Egyptians whom the visitor to Egypt or to an Egyptian collection in one of the great museums which house so considerable a quantity (though still only a tiny fraction) of the work of Egyptian artists and artificers, might be expected to encounter.

Because of their concern to perpetuate their names, a procedure essential if eternal life was to be achieved, it must surely be that we know many more of the inhabitants of Ancient Egypt than we do of any other ancient culture of comparable antiquity. *Who's Who in Ancient Egypt* cannot in the nature of things pretend to be exhaustive; at best it can only be representative. It can only record a sadly limited number of entries; but how many 'Third Prophets of Amun', '*wab* priests', 'Sole Companions' or 'Singers in the Temple before the God', worthy though they doubtless were, might non-professional readers be expected to accept? But there must be many who fulfil the criteria indicated above who have, for one reason or another, not been given space here; if so, the compiler, not himself a professional Egyptologist, would be pleased to hear of them, possibly for inclusion in future editions.

The entries in *Who's Who in Ancient Egypt* are listed in an English-language alphabetical order. The Egyptians did not, in any strict sense, employ an alphabet, at least until late times. The sequence which is conventionally adopted for the hieroglyphic characters which stand for individual letters is entirely different from the alphabetical order familiar to a European reader; to adopt such a sequence would be perverse and probably deeply confusing. The hieroglyphic script was perhaps the most elegant ever produced, certainly amongst the most complex and subtle; it was reserved mainly for monumental inscriptions and the most important documentary uses. Its two companions, hieratic and demotic, were successfully developed for more everyday use; the last-named was effectively a form of 'speed writing'.

The transcription of Egyptian names presents another hazard. Since the Egyptians did not as a general rule write vowels, and their language involved several consonants that an English speaker, for example, does not use, cannot tell apart, or might not even recognise as meaningful consonants. Scholarly transcriptions are complicated, artificial and scarcely pronounceable. The rendering of Egyptian names in a book such as this must therefore be a matter of compromise – a compromise which in all probability is not completely consistent. Names which when transliterated into a European language would start with an 'A' for example, would in Egyptian be written with the group which formed the compound of the name and which an educated Egyptian would know would be articulated as if it began with the sound which English renders as 'A'. In common with general Egyptological practice today, names have been rendered in a fashion which corresponds more precisely to the Egyptian original than to the Greek, popular in earlier scholarship: thus 'Amenhotep' rather than 'Amenophis', though, of course Amenhotep itself is an Anglicisation. Similarly, it adopts usages such as 'Khnum-Khufu' for the king associated with the Great Pyramid, rather than the name by which he was known to the Greeks, 'Cheops'. 'Chephren' and 'Mycerinos' are to be found in association with *their* pyramids in their correct names of 'Khafre' and 'Menkaure'. In such cases, however, what may still be the more familiar, alternative name is shown in parenthesis. In the case of Late Period kings, particularly from the Twenty-Seventh Dynasty onwards, the Greek forms have generally been employed, as by that time their usage had become widespread outside Egypt.

The influence of Greek writers and their versions of Egyptian names is particularly evident when dealing with the familiar names of the Egyptian gods. Most of those which are in common use today derive from Greek transliterations. These have become so established that it would be pretentious in this context to insist on *Djehuty* rather than Thoth (or *Djehuty-mes* rather than the familiar royal name, Thutmose), on *Heru* rather than Horus, *Aset* than Isis, *Asar* or *Wesir* for Osiris. In all these and other similar instances the names of the gods appear in their familiar, Graecised forms.

The substance of the entries themselves has been drawn from a wide range of published sources; a number of these are now of some age, as Egyptologists of earlier decades seem often to have been more interested in the lives of individual Egyptians than in the social, economic and historical forces which determined the character of their society and which have tended more to occupy the attention of contemporary scholars. In some cases there are anomalies and variations, a consequence of the influence of a particular researcher's native tongue, when expressed in English. In general, the form of the names given here conforms with the principal source or original of the entry; if the original transcription has not always been retained it is because of a more recent, widespread acceptance of a revised form.

The principal publications consulted are listed in the Bibliography and in the individual entries; amongst the most productive sources are museum and exhibition catalogues and books which review specific collections. These, because they are often intended for public information as well as for the use of scholars, frequently contain valuable material relating to the lives and careers of individual Egyptians.

Most of the entries in *Who's Who in Ancient Egypt* are supported by bibliographical references. In a number of cases objects – statues or inscriptions for example – which bear on the subject of the entry may be identified by the museum in which they are exhibited. With some of the subjects, the more assertive of the kings for instance, the sheer number of their images surviving precludes any meaningful selection; indeed, a choice would often be invidious. In the case of lesser known subjects, however, it may be helpful to have the existence of a relevant artefact noted; wherever possible the museum accession number of the object concerned is identified. A summary of the relevant museum holdings referred to in the entries is given in Index 3.

It should be noted that numbered references refer to pages in the publication concerned, with the exception of Breasted 1906 and Kitchen 1986, where the numbers relate to one or more paragraphs.

Cross references to entries in the *Who's Who*, and to those in the Glossary, are capitalised. The names of non-Egyptian subjects, other than those who were recognised as kings of Egypt, are enclosed in square brackets.

Acknowledgements

The obligations of the author of a work such as this present are multiple and various. First, to the legions of scholars who have excavated, studied, translated, drawn, photographed, conserved and commented on the products of the three thousand and more years covered by this book.

Then to those who have helped in the book's production, bringing it to fulfilment.

To my friend Andrew Wheatcroft who proposed my name as the compiler of the *Who's Who* and in doing so gave me one of the most agreeable assignments of my writing career, and to Routledge for accepting his proposal and inviting me to undertake it.

I am especially indebted to Jacqueline Pegg, of the Institute of Archaeology, University College London, who has been invaluable in checking chronologies, relationships and a multitude of facts, and ensuring that wherever possible the conventionally accepted form of transliteration of names has been used. I am equally grateful to Professor John Tait, Edwards Professor of Egyptology at UCL, who introduced Jacqueline to me. I am deeply grateful to Sandra MacKenzie Smith, herself a dedicated Egyptophile, who has been invaluable in editing the various disks on which *Who's Who in Ancient Egypt* was compiled. It goes without saying (though of course I am saying it) that any errors surviving are entirely mine.

Encountering the Ancient Egyptians

Who's Who in Ancient Egypt is, in the words of the memorable description of the London Telephone Directory, 'a book about people'. Specifically, it is a summary rendering of the lives of a selection of the people who lived in (or in some cases visited) the Nile Valley during a period of something over 3,000 years, from the end of the fourth millennium (*c.* 3100 BC) until approximately 200 AD.

Inevitably, the result is the product of a highly selective process; those whose names appear are, not surprisingly, the men and women of whose lives records exist in one form or another. Generally, such records may be expected to speak of those individuals who achieved enough in their lifetimes or who were of a sufficiently exalted rank to ensure that some sort of memorial was set down in stone, if the inscription was intended to be monumental, or on the papyrus on which Egyptian writing was preserved for more transient or simply less expensive records. Sometimes the only record of a life will be contained in another's memorial.

The recording and preservation of an Egyptian's name was of great importance because if the name survived then the individual's vital essence, the life force which animated him or her, would continue to exist, if not for all eternity (the Egyptians were unsure about this) then at least for 'millions of years'. The names of those who appear here have achieved this prerequisite of lasting identity; this present record will merely serve to provide another element of insurance for them, in the perpetuation of 'the name'.

This having been said, it will be clear that most of those whose names are recorded in this volume are, one way or the other, the élite of the dead of Ancient Egypt. Many of those whose names are known owe their posthumous identity to the happenstance of archaeology; indeed it may be said that with the exception, generally speaking, of the very greatest of the inhabitants of the Valley whose names might be inscribed in or on the superb monuments with which they were identified, the *post-mortem* celebrity of most of them is the product of the painstaking work of generations of Egyptologists. It is to these scholars that the Ancient Egyptians, if they are enjoying the benefits of survival after death which by the remembrance of their names they hoped to ensure, are properly indebted.

Then again, some of the most influential of the Ancient Egyptians who left an enduring impression on the development of their country are unknown by reason of having lived in pre-literate times. This is a sadly unjust situation, for many of them must have been men (they tended mainly to be men, as far as we know) of exceptional ability; they were the leaders of the societies which existed in the Valley before the Kingship. They were the initiators of the most remarkable of all Egyptian innovations, which brought about the unification of the Valley and the creation of the first nation state in the history of the world. As the beginning of writing nears, in the latter part of the fourth millennium BC, obscure marks on pottery or other media may conceal a name which is lost, for the means have not been found to decipher them. Such markings may conceal the identity of some of the men whose genius gave rise to the most august civilisation that the world has ever seen or, judging by the experience of the last two thousand years in particular, is ever likely to see.

It is strange how the *idea* of Egypt has persisted in the consciousness of the people who lived around, or who drew their sense of the proper order of things from, the lands bounded by the Mediterranean Sea. The sea was not itself particularly important to the Egyptians, who broadly speaking disapproved of it and mistrusted it; the river was quite a different matter, but they might be prepared to admit (though it would not seem especially important to them) that the sea was the one of the principal routes by which those people unfortunate enough not to have been born in the Valley drew their understanding of some of the eternal truths which it was the Egyptians' purpose to preserve.

They would have been deeply surprised to find that the Judeo-Hellenistic cast of much of the scholarship of quite recent times was fixed on the idea that the Egyptians were obsessed by death. This is an entire inversion of the truth; the Egyptians, throughout most of their history, rejoiced in life, in all its aspects and, if they were obsessed by anything, it was by its perpetuation. The records of the lives of those who lived in the Valley which are noted here, will demonstrate the truth of this contention abundantly.

But nonetheless, all the world knows that the vast preponderance of evidence of life in Ancient Egypt and of the achievements and apprehensions of its people, is drawn from tombs, the 'Houses of Millions of Years' in which this inventive and optimistic people expected to spend their afterlife. Each Egyptian age had its distinctive funerary monument. With the first appearance of the Kingship – the most important single development in the history of the Two Lands – massive brick-built *mastabas* house the bodies of the Great Ones (the high officials and nobles of the first rank) and their servants, whilst the kings are interred in immense brick-built funerary palaces. Then, in the Old Kingdom, the mastabas are stone-built and the kings – and some of the more favoured of their relatives – are provided with pyramids, the archetypal Egyptian form. In the Middle Kingdom a variety of funerary styles appear, notable for the refined elegance of their architecture. In the New Kingdom immense palaces were built to commemorate the lives of the greatest in the society, and valleys near Thebes were honeycombed in attempts, most of them quite futile, to protect the dead from the predatory attentions of their descendants.

Who, then, are the people presented in *Who's Who in Ancient Egypt*, who created this most complex and richly endowed of all ancient civilisations? Certainly there are ranks of kings, queens, princes, great ministers, high priests and dignitaries holding offices of great status, power and antiquity who had no doubt of their importance in sustaining the order of the universe; but there are also musicians, soldiers, sculptors, painters, limners of papyri, officials of modest attainment, singers, shipwrights, architects, builders, artisans, doctors (many of them engaged in highly specialised areas of practice), farmers, children, a throng of individuals who lived their lives as members of our species have always lived their lives, since our strange choice of living in complex societies. These were the people who provided the dynamic for Egypt's phenomenal history and who together represented its unique corporate genius.

The number of inhabitants of the Nile Valley during the period represented by this volume has been computed at 5.25 billion (Strouhal 1989; 1992: 256), assuming a generation at twenty years and averaging the population at 3 million over the (approximately) 3,500 years involved. Estimates of the population at given periods have been prepared, based on estimates of cultivable areas and yields (Butzer 1976). These suggest that in Predynastic times the population totalled 350,000. By the time of the 'Unification', *c.* 3150–3100 BC, it had risen to 870,000. During the Pyramid Age, in the Old Kingdom, around 2500 BC, the figure was perhaps 1.6 million. During the Middle Kingdom, *c.* 1800 BC, the numbers would have increased to 2 million, whilst at the height of the New Kingdom the population may have risen to 3 million, and in Ptolemaic times from 2.4 million at its commencement to 5 million at its end (Strouhal 1989; 1992: 134–5, quoting Butzer 1976).

Looking at the history of Ancient Egypt through the lives of even so small a sample as it is possible to consider here, gives a particular and interesting cast to that history itself. Certain factors become apparent which may not be immediately discernable in more conventional historiography. Thus the role of women in Egypt is clearly far more important than in any other early society. Women were not confined to the home or the harem as in many later societies; they occupied places in society which often went far beyond their domestic or familial responsibilities, sometimes, even, assuming the kingship itself. One in eight of the biographies in *Who's Who in Ancient Egypt* are of women; no other society of comparable antiquity would be able to provide the same statisitic – or anything like it.

The Egyptians were diligent and committed autobiographers, the first people indeed to develop the genre. To be sure, many of the inscriptions and texts on which this present work draws are merely formulaic, the pious repetition of the deceased's fine qualitites: concern for the poor and needy, management of resources in times of stress for the benefit of the community, protection of the widow and orphan. But as often, the record of a man's (or woman's) life will suddenly reveal an incident or achievement which lifts the subject out of the merely conventional into the individually real and significant.

We know the Ancient Egyptians directly by the portraits of themselves which they left behind them. They were the world's first portraitists, and the quality of the finest of their work has never been surpassed. It has become one of the conventions of Egyptology to insist that the statues in stone, wood and metal, and the splendid repertory of paintings of the Egyptians in antiquity are invariably idealised, not to be regarded as naturalistic in any sense that would be understood today. But this is not so; even a superficial familiarity with the contents of the world's great museums will demonstrate that when they wished to do so, the Egyptians could produce work of a naturalism and individual power fully comparable with the work of the greatest Renaissance masters. Of course, there *are* many youthful, sleek, elegant and well exercised bodies abounding; slender, perpetually youthful figures, bright with expectation and the promise of fulfilment, in this life or the next. Indeed it may be confidently asserted that there are probably more such from Egypt than ever graced any human society. But then the sudden recognition of a living man or woman, carved to perfection in the hardest stone or painted with verve and absolute confidence, with the imperfections and the majesty of humanity fully realised, can bring the living presence of the individual, though dead perhaps for four thousand years and more, instantly into the present day.

Similarly, the consideration of the lives and careers of the individuals portrayed here indicates how flexible was Egyptian society, and how it was possible for a man of humble origins, by ability or simple good fortune, to rise to the highest ranks of that society. Equally it is plain that, in general, privilege was not permanently vested in a family which had once held office (even the crown), but generation by generation the status of such families would be expected to decline, unless that movement was arrested by the appearance of another especially talented or resourceful member.

What really makes the Egyptians of antiquity seem quite different from those peoples who have come after them was, first, the quality and character of their achievements, and second, the sense of transcendence which pervades their works and often the record of their lives. There has never been any people quite like them. It is their inheritance which our modern world enjoys and equally regards with astonishment. How did they move great blocks of stone, or cut and assemble them with such exquisite precision? How did they sculpt wonderful likenesses of the kings in the most intractable of stones? How did they organise what must have been armies of workers, craftsmen and supervisors ('Overseers of All the Works of the King') to build the immense monuments which they strewed across the Two Lands with such prodigality? One of the most ancient and most powerful of all the entities which are collectively called 'the gods' was Ptah, the Artificer, Lord of All. The architects and artists recorded here were truly spoken of as 'sons of Ptah'.

Then, it may reasonably be asked, from whence did the Ancient Egyptians who achieved these marvels, come to the Valley which was to be their home? The question is necessary for it appears that until around the seventh millennium BC the Valley was void of permanent or settled inhabitants. It is a question which has proved to be surprisingly difficult to answer. On the evidence of their language, which belongs to the great family of languages embraced by the term Afro-Asiatic (in the past called Hamito-Semitic), they had strong associations with East Africa, to the south of the Valley and with the people of the Saharan steppelands, as once they had been, to the west. The desert people, infused with drifts of transhumant migrants from the Sinai peninisula and moving down through the Levantine coast, contributed the Semitic linguistic elements, though these are not as significant as the other strains, in early times. Each of these groups repays a little further consideration.

The African component in the Egyptians' historic collective personality and in the influencing of every department of their lives was probably the most important and the most enduring. It derived in large part from the presence from very early times of bands of hunters who followed the great herds of wild cattle which moved northwards from East Africa, perhaps from the area now known as The Mountains of the Moon, into the Nile Valley. The inheritance of the cattle people was very great and appears, in various guises, throughout Egyptian history. The king, when the principal personality in the evolving unitary state came to be recognised by titles that we render as 'king', was hailed as 'Mighty Bull' and his people were 'The Cattle of God'. The gods and goddesses themselves and all manner of cult and religious customs hark back to these doubtless 'primitive' wandering hunters; primitive is, however, a term which must be used with caution, certainly when dealing with matters Egyptian. One of the most ancient of all the evidences of funerary cults comes from the very distant past in the extreme south, from Tushka in Lower (Northern) Nubia, where burials have been excavated dating from the *twelfth millennium* BC which were surmounted by the skulls of the wild bull, the aurochs, *Bos primigenius*, which roamed the Valley until it was exterminated by the kings of the New Kingdom, ten thousand years later.

Another people with a profound cattle tradition also contributed substantially to the Egyptian gene pool. These were the hunters of the Sahara, one of the most remarkable and most mysterious of the peoples who appeared in the Mediterranean region and in lands contiguous with it, after the end of the last Ice Age. These people also followed the herds and later domesticated the cattle. They left behind, on rocky overhangs and in shelters deep in what is now the most inhospitable desert, a repertoire of brilliant paintings of astonishing quality, which show forms and subjects which are similar to those which are later to be found in Egyptian art. It may be that the later Egyptian reverence for the West and the nostalgia which they seem to have harboured for a westward land of lost content, is drawn from some sort of collective memory of the rich pasture and grazing lands of the Sahara before the extreme desiccation of the past six thousand years began.

In later periods, certainly during the times of Egypt's greatness, the influence of the Semitic-speaking congeries of tribes which lived on Egypt's eastern and northern boundaries was greater, just as the threat which they were seen to pose to Egypt's security represented an ever-present danger to the country's archetypal – and long enduring – tranquility.

Throughout history, humans have generally demonstrated little enthusiasm for moving from wherever they found themselves comfortably ensconced until a climate change forced them to remove themselves or until other peoples, whose own ancestral lands had been affected by adverse conditions, pressed on them, forcing them to find somewhere else to go, often to the misfortune of yet another people. From about eight thousand years ago the climate began to change dramatically throughout the Middle East, forcing many of the peoples of the region to find themselves new homelands. In the case of Egypt – as it was to become – the Valley was virtually empty of human inhabitants; it was a paradise for the animals who lived on its richly endowed river banks unthreatened until humankind entered what might very well be regarded as the prototypical Eden.

From the west, the people of the Sahara drifted towards the east; they probably already knew of the Valley's idyllic character from following the herds. Those who similarly drifted up from the south, from deeper Africa, undoubtedly did; when and how the two groups met and began to coalesce, we do not know. Most of the very early evidence of human habitation on the Nile banks has been lost after millennia of agricultural exploitation of the rich alluvial deposits on which the people always based their livelihood, and by the rising of the Nile's levels which laid down the alluvium. What is certain, however, is that the earliest populations of the Valley were directly ancestral to those who created the civilisation of Egypt, when its first evidences appear, approximately 7,500 years ago.

Egypt's was overwhelmingly an agricultural economy, powered by the river which was country's life-blood; her people, even if they were part of the central administration, attending the King, the High Priests or the great magnates, always identified with the land and the life with which the river and the gods had so abundantly endowed it. The decoration of their tombs, from the earliest to the latest times, celebrated the Egyptian countryside and the animals with which they shared it. The fact that the people of Egypt were so rooted in the land and that the prosperity of Egypt was so bound up with a riverine and agrarian economy, is fundamental to an understanding of Egyptian society and of the particular directions in which it developed.

By historiographical convention Egyptian history is divided into a sequence of chronologically based blocks: the two broadest divisions are between the Predynastic and the Dynastic periods, the one relating to pre-literate times, before the introduction of the kingship, and the other, after approximately 3150 BC, when the kingship becomes the characteristic and dominant form of Egyptian political organisation. Within these two broad divisions are a number of more sharply focused periods, which will be explained here in their turn.

The first Predynastic culture to be identified in Egypt is that which was originally recognised at El-Badari (see BADARIAN), a site in Upper Egypt. The Badarians were agriculturalists and domesticated goats and sheep. They maintained some sort of contact with the Red Sea, for shells from there have been found in their graves. They were exceptionally skilled potters, producing a fine ware, burnished a deep red with black tops, effected by inverting the vessel in the fire; a similar ware was produced in Nubia until quite recent times. Badarian pottery is most remarkable for the exceptional thinness of its fabric and its equally exceptional hardness. Such results could only be produced consistently by very skilful potters, able to control the firing of high temperatures very precisely, who were working in a long and secure tradition.

The Badarians buried their dead in the desert, in shallow graves, the excavated material forming a mound over the burial. This was to remain a constant feature of the Egyptian way of burying the dead, though, as we shall see, it was dramaticaly transformed, especially in high-status burials in the early dynasties, two thousand years and more after Badarian times.

The Badarian culture first appears around 5500 BC; it was followed by the first to be associated archaeologically with the important Predynastic site at NAQADA, which is situated in the stretch of the river which was always to have a special importance to the development of Egypt, especially in relation to the kingship; this phase of the Egyptian Predynastic, *c.* 4000–3500 BC, is also referred to as the Amratian, after the site of El-Amra.

It is generally accepted that there was a connection between Naqada I and the preceding Badarians. The Naqadans, however, appear to have evolved a more sophisticated material culture; their pottery is quite different and is notable for the elaborate engraved scenes, infilled with white, which decorated the surfaces of the vessels. This development represents the first appearance of one of the glories of Egyptian art, draughtsmanship; it is tempting to suggest a connection with the artists of the Sahara, who were also superb draughtsmen, of a somewhat earlier time, but such is speculation.

The third Upper Egyptian Predynastic culture, Naqada II (also known as the 'Gerzean', *c.* 3500–3100 BC), reveals that very rapid advances were being made in all aspects of Egyptian life, material culture, art and technology. Once again, pottery provides many of the clues to the changes which were taking place. Naqada II pottery is quite different, both from Naqada I and from the Badarian. It is generally a buff ware richly decorated with scenes depicting animals, the river, landscapes, and a curious device of three, sometimes more, little triangular hills, an anticipation of what was to become the most characteristic of all Egyptian forms.

The people of Naqada II seem to have maintained some form of contact, or perhaps shared a common origin with, the people of south-western Asia, far away at the head of the Arabian Gulf. It is very remarkable that at this time Egypt and the region of western Iran which was later to be known as Elam share a significant number of themes in art and design motifs which are too numerous merely to be the result of chance. Elam, though it was culturally distinct with its own language, was part of the wider Uruk culture, which had its origins in southern Mesopotamia and which was approximately contemporary with the Naqada II horizon in Upper Egypt. It seems certain that the influence of a people, either from western Asia or who were themselves deeply influenced by its culture, made a very particular series of contributions to the development of the historic Egyptian personality in late Predynastic times. How this was effected is still enigmatic. One slight hint may be provided by the fact that lapis lazuli was much prized by the Egyptians, in the period immediately before that which is identified as the Unification; lapis in antiquity came only from one principal source, Badakshan in northern Pakistan. The distances which the merchants traded the stone from its source to its eventual market in the Nile Valley were immense, but the route ran through south-western Iran and it may be that contact was established in this way.

But this surely does not explain the whole of the phenomenon, particularly the remarkable fact that the badge in which the early kings displayed their most sacred name, the ***serekh***, signifying their appearance as the incarnate HORUS, was based on an architectural motif which originated in south-western Asia, probably in Elam, in the second half of the fourth millennium. The same architectural motif, of walls built with repeated recessed panelling, was also to be adopted as the invariable decoration of the great mastaba tombs (built in mud-brick, a very un-Egyptian substance, as it turned out) in which the great magnates were buried and which appear, quite dramatically, at the beginning of the First Dynasty. Some authorities have seen the prototype of the mastaba tomb in the temples built in the southern Mesopotamian cities, at sites such as Uruk, Ur and Eridu from about 3500 BC. Recently, evidence of what appears to have been an actual western Asiatic presence in Egypt in late Predynastic times has come from the Delta, in the north of the country. There, what is unmistakeably a temple building of the type which originated in Uruk in southern Mesopotamia around the middle of the fourth millennium, has been found, with examples of the highly individual decorated cones which were used to brighten the surfaces of the otherwise rather barren mud-brick architecture of the Sumerians. This suggests something like a settled community in northern Egypt at this very early time which had strong Mesopotamian connections – to put it no higher. It is a most intriguing mystery – for which no doubt there is a perfectly rational explanation which, for the time, has escaped us.

A glance at the map of Ancient Egypt will show that these three important type-sites, el-Badari, el-Amra and Gerza, as well as Naqada itself, are all clustered in the southern reaches of the Nile Valley. The recognition of this apparent coincidence of location is of crucial importance in understanding one of the essential characteristics of the civilisation which rose and flourished so abundantly in the Valley: Egypt's heartland always lay in the south. Whenever, in later times, the integrity of Egypt was threatened or her institutions became wearied and in decline, it was to the south, to Upper Egypt, that she returned for revivification and renewal.

Throughout the country's history a cardinal principle about the nature of Egypt, promoted from the earliest times of the kingship, was that there were two kingdoms, south and north. The king, when he came to be recognised as the supreme, even universal sovereign, was a dual king, Lord of the Two Lands, as

Egypt was always described. However, though there is ample evidence of a system of local government in southern Egypt, probably a form of chieftaincy from which the kingship ultimately derived, there is no comparable evidence for the north. It must be said, however, that the state of preservation of the northern (Delta) sites is nowhere as good as that which characterises sites in Upper Egypt; inevitably, the depredation of northern sites has influenced markedly and perhaps incorrectly, the analysis of their historical significance.

The Valley was notionally divided somewhat to the south of the modern capital, Cairo, close to the city which the Greeks called Memphis. To the north lay the Delta, where the Nile divided into branches, to flow into the Mediterranean. This was marshy country, later found to be ideal for the raising of cattle. It, too, had Predynastic cultures, identified by sites at Ma'adi, Merimde and El-Omar. There is evidence that the Delta Predynastic cultures actually predate those in the south; they obviously received some of their influences from still further north, from Palestine and the Levant (possibly from the north-western outreaches of Mesopotamian culture too) but they never exercised the same weight of influence themselves on the development of the historic Egyptian personality.

At some time during the thirty-second century before the present era, all the ideas and innovations which had been fomenting in the south began to coalesce. The focus for this extraordinary phenomenon appears to have been located in the city of Hierakonpolis, deep into Upper Egypt. There, a dynasty of chieftains who identified themselves with a Falcon as their badge and probably as their eponym, determined upon a singular and very bold enterprise, the political unification of the whole Valley, south to north, under their direct rule. No other portion of the world, up to this time, had experienced so profound a change in what were already millennia-old systems of social organisation. Even Egypt up to this time had been a fairly typical example of a well developed, pottery-making but otherwise still basically neolithic society, probably organised into chieftaincies along the river banks. The local chiefs, some of whom probably exercised considerable personal power, were perhaps already identified as divine or semi-divine beings, an aspect of Egypt's African inheritance. They seem often to have been associated with animal powers, or sometimes with more abstract forms, which symbolised their chieftaincy. In the very last decades of the Predynastic period shadowy figures can be discerned, whose names are generally unknown or uncertain, who seem already to possess some of the status and even the regalia which came to be associated with the kingship in historic times. One of the latest was identified by the badge of the SCORPION, which may also have been his name. Others are less certain still, IRYHOR and KA for example; even the existence of the first of these has been questioned, but this view has not gone unchallenged.

But it was the task of a young prince of Hierakonpolis to attempt to bring all these diverse chieftaincies, representing a variety of local customs and cultic practices, into a centralised, corporate whole. According to the officially promoted legend, this exceptional young man was named MENES (a term which in fact may mean something like 'The Unifier') or NAR-MER, a name which is represented by early hieroglyphic signs of catfish and chisel, who was always credited as the first king of the the unified Two Lands. In fact, Nar-Mer was probably the last of the Predynastic kings and it is to his successor, probably his son, that the credit really belongs for launching the process which ultimately was to result in the unification of the Valley. His name was AHA, 'The Fighter'. He was evidently still young when he succeeded, for he is said to have reigned for sixty-four years and to have died hunting hippopotamus.

It is at this point, around 3150 BC, that Egyptian history really begins. From this time onwards, until the depredations of Rome and the malice of the newly emerging Christian authorities finally destroyed the remnants of Egyptian civilisation in the first millennium of the present era, king followed king in a long, sometimes glorious, sometimes confused succession. The first two dynasties of Egyptian kings represent the Archaic Period, which lasted from *c*. 3150 BC to *c*. 2750 BC. It was a period absolutely fundamental to Egypt's subsequent three millennia of history and to its immeasurable contribution to the history of the world. In the complex process of the emergence of the historic Egyptian persona, the king is revealed as the Great Individual, the very reason for the existence of the Egyptian state and, in effect, its soul.

There is something deeply mysterious about the kings of the earliest dynasties, particularly the First. The very names of the kings are strange, though they they are certainly Egyptian, but Aha, DJER, DJET, DEN and the rest have a harsh, barbaric quality about them, unlike the generally euphonious, theophoric formulations of the names and titles of their successors over the many centuries in which kings ruled Egypt. But, barbarous or not, these men laid down the essential character of the country which was to prevail throughout the entire history of Egypt. In doing so, they gave names to the fundamental structure of what as to become an immensely complex society, which provided the matrix from which all nation states in the West have developed ever since.

The First Dynasty was a time of great advances in the organisation of the society. In every department, in government, state ceremonies and rituals, in architecture, art and technology, immense developments occurred which were to sustain Egypt's growth far into the future. The nearly three hundred years during which the First Dynasty survived were crucial to all of the Nile Valley's subsequent history. The driving impulse of the kings seems to have been the imposition of a coherent system of rule throughout the length of the Valley; though their essential motivation came from Upper Egypt, the intention was to unify the land from the first cataract to the sea, far to the north. This was always to be regarded as the true extent of the land of Egypt, and for many centuries (if indeed they ever changed) the Egyptians had but little interest in foreign countries, other than to ensure that they did not threaten the security of the Valley.

The Egyptians' own view of the founding dynasty was singularly ambivalent. They honoured the early kings greatly and long maintained cults in their honour, in some cases for the length of Egypt's history, yet all their tombs were destroyed by fire, apparently set deliberately. This was an appalling fate for an Egyptian, whose immortality also depended on the survival of his mortal remains. Could it have been something to do with the very un-Egyptian practice of the sacrifice of retainers which prevailed in First Dynasty royal burials and in those of the high officers of state?

The First Dynasty is also the occasion for the appearance of one of the determining characteristics of the Egyptian state: an extensive and complex bureaucracy. At its head were the king's immediate coadjutors, the bearers of already ancient offices which were denoted by richly inventive titles. The holders of these titles were the élite of Ancient Egypt, the Seal-Bearers, a term which implied nobility. The Second Dynasty, though it survived almost as long as the First, is much less well-documented; this may be because the programme of unification which the kings tried to impose did not achieve unquestioned acceptance by the smaller local loyalties which they sought to replace. It was only in the reign of the last king of the Second Dynasty that something like the unification of the entire Valley was achieved.

This was the work of one of the most remarkable of Egypt's kings, Khasekhem, who later changed his name to KHASEKHEMWY. His memory, too, endured throughout the centuries; he was said to be of gigantic stature, and the shadow which he cast on Egypt was commensurately great.

It appears however, that Khasekhemwy had no surviving son. His wife (who may also have been his daughter) NEMAATHAP was his heiress, and she brought with her the succession to the throne. This was an experience which was frequently to be repeated in Egyptian history; indeed, the succession was always considered to be through the female line, at least in the earlier centuries, during the Old Kingdom. The eldest daughter of the king, or his principal queen was the incarnation of the goddess Isis (just as he was the reincarnation of the god Horus) and Isis' name was represented by the hieroglyph of the throne. By contact with the throne at his coronation the king became a living god.

Nemaathap was venerated as the ancestress of the Third Dynasty. She had two sons who became kings: first, SANAKHTE or Nebka and then the great DJOSER NETJERYKHET.

Netjerykhet was the first king in Egypt to be commemorated by a pyramid tomb, the stupendous Step Pyramid complex raised to his glory and perpetuity in Saqqara, by the genius of his minister and architect, IMHOTEP. The enterprise of building this monument of nearly one million tons of finely dressed stone was unparalleled anywhere in the world and the pyramid form, adapted by later generations of kings, was to give Egypt its most enduring symbol. It is not difficult to apprehend why Imhotep came to be acknowledged as the prototype of the supreme, creative Egyptian genius: truly, the son of Ptah.

The Third Dynasty was another period of exponential advance, not only in technique and the adaptation of materials, but also in more philosophical concerns, of which the principal was the divinity and status of the king. This was undoubtedly inspired by Netjerykhet, who stands for all time as the archetype of the god-king. Heliopolis was an important centre for the royal cult and the observation and worship of the stars seems to have been particularly significant.

A princess was again the conduit through whom the kingship passed to the next family to possess it. HETEPHERES I, the daughter of King HUNI, the last king of the Third Dynasty, married SNEFERU and inaugurated the Fourth Dynasty, which forever will be identified as the Pyramid Age. Sneferu was another remarkable creative genius, establishing monuments on an immense scale and of a diversity of character which is most extraordinary. His achievements actually surpass those of his more celebrated son, KHNUM-KHUFU, to whom is attributed the building of the Great Pyramid at Giza. Sneferu built three, possibly even four pyramids, and to do so excavated, cut and laid *nine million tons* of stone, all in his own lifetime. Khnum-Khufu and his successors built the pyramids which stand on the Giza plateau, and in doing so created between them the most renowned group of monuments anywhere in the world, of any age. But the achievement of Sneferu, though less celebrated, outshines them by far.

The later history of the Fourth Dynasty, however, was marred by dissension in the royal family. As it reached its end, once again the kingship passed through the female line to the next family to hold it. The Fifth Dynasty of Egyptian kings presided over a period of unexampled prosperity for Egypt, a supremely tranquil time of peace and the enjoyment of the life which the gods had given to those who were fortunate enough to live in the Valley. Now it could be truly said that all was for the best in the best of all possible worlds with, perhaps for the first and only time anywhere on earth, the people (or at least the more fortunate of them) able to live their lives in absolute harmony with the world around them. The Fifth Dynasty's principal glory, however, must be the revelation of the PYRAMID TEXTS, the most ancient corpus of ritual texts in the world, which decorate the interior walls of the pyramid of the last king of the Dynasty, UNAS, and which appear throughout the subsequent Sixth Dynasty.

The Egyptian kingdom, however, like many of the political institutions which were to follow it, was the victim of its own success. The Sixth Dynasty, continuing the placid way of its predecessors, began to manifest signs of fracture and stress which were eventually to bring down the edifice which had been built up over the previous thousand years.

The problem was twofold: first, the increasing power of the temple institutions which were growing ever richer and more avaricious; and second, the influence of the great magnates whom the kings, from the late Fourth Dynasty onwards, had felt it necessary to endow with much of their own wealth, to ensure their loyalty. In many cases this had had the effect of creating competing dynasties in the country who saw themselves effectively as independent princes and who maintained a state to match. In the case of the Sixth Dynasty the problem was compounded by the hundred years-long life of one of its latest kings, PEPY II, when the administration atrophied and the power of the magnates grew unchecked.

There now followed a period of political uncertainty (called by Egyptologists the First Intermediate Period), of which the loss of the central, royal authority was the most immediate manifestation. A succession of generally weakened monarchs, often with more than one reigning simultaneously in various parts of the country, tried to sustain some sort of authority; a few succeeded in doing so and, for the majority of the people, life probably continued much as it had always done. It was by no means an entirely barren time in the life of Egypt; trade flourished and literature became one of the art forms which was to add significantly to Egypt's cultural inheritance, particularly under the Ninth and Tenth Dynasties which came from Heracleopolis. But the fabric of Egypt came apart, with rulers in the north maintaining some sort of tenuous control whilst infiltrators from beyond Egypt's desert frontiers began to penetrate the Valley. Meanwhile, in the south, where Egypt's heart beat still steadily, a family of princes was preparing itself once more to attempt to reunify the Valley.

This, after long years of struggle, they succeeded in doing. But Egypt had changed; the king now was a god by custom as it were, no longer the incarnate ruler of the universe. The kings of the Eleventh Dynasty, the first of the period which Egyptologists call the Middle Kingdom, were rather austere, certainly dedicated men, of whom NEBHEPETRE-MONTUHOTEP II was the most outstanding, as he was the longest reigning. The king now became the Great Executive, himself directing the affairs of the country which, in the latter part of the Old Kingdom, had become the responsibility of an increasingly diverse and influential bureaucracy. In the Twelfth Dynasty, founded by a man who had been Vizier to the last of the rulers of the Eleventh Dynasty, the power of the provincial nobles was finally broken, not for centuries to threaten the royal authority again.

The Twelfth Dynasty was one of the high points of the historic Egyptian experience. Its kings were amongst the longest reigning of all of Egypt's sovereigns; they extended Egypt's influence far beyond its historic, god-given frontiers, a process which was to pay a dangerous dividend in centuries far into the future. They also left behind them one of the longest enduring myths associated with once-living men, the myth of the more-than-human king who controls the fates and who exercises powers which are more than mortal. This was no new dimension for the god-kings of Egypt, but for the world which was to come after them there were two kings in particular whose lives and legend provided much of the source of the later myths: the wonder-working king who directs not only the destinies of his people but is possessed of still greater powers. The kings who bore the name 'SENWOSRET' (which the Greeks rendered as 'Sesostris') are the archetypes of this formidable invention; their fame endured throughout Egypt's history into Greek times and on into the present day. From their lives and the myths which accreted around them descend Sarastro in *Die Zauberflöte* and, with a change of gender, Mme Sesostris in *The Waste Land.*

The Twelfth Dynasty was another of the times when the arts in Egypt flourished exceedingly. Sculpture takes on a new life and architecture, though not as monumental as during the Old Kingdom, has a grace and elegance which is unsurpassed.

But the longevity which characterised the reigns of the kings of this dynasty and the peace and security which they brought to the Two Lands led in time to something like complacency. This in turn introduced what was to be a frequently recurring problem, the succession devolving either on elderly heirs or on distant relatives who, in the nature of things, could provide little continuity with their predecessors.

The alien infiltrations which had occurred during the years after the end of the Old Kingdom now began to threaten the stability of the entire Valley. The Thirteenth Dynasty was amongst the most disrupted of all Egypt's lines of kings; few of the rulers survived long enough to leave substantial evidences of their reigns behind them. Invaders now appeared in the north of the country and established an independent kingship, outwardly Egyptian in many of its forms but actually alien to all that the Egyptians held sacred.

At least, this was the official line pursued by royal propagandists when the native-born Egyptian kingship was restored. In fact the 'Hyksos' kings, so-called from a corruption of the term 'rulers of foreign lands' (in Egyptian, *Hekaw-khasut*) attempted to follow Egyptian customs carefully and to respect Egyptian preconceptions and attitudes. This did not prevent them from being execrated throughout the centuries remaining, when Egypt was once more a great and powerful nation.

Again, salvation came from the south. Thebes, hitherto a relatively unimportant provincial centre other than during the Eleventh Dynasty, was now fated to become for centuries the greatest city in the world. This came about with the rise of a family of Theban princes, who represented the Seventeenth Dynasty of kings and who began the task of driving the Hyksos invaders back into their northern reaches, ultimately expelling them from the land of Egypt. A new line was proclaimed, descended directly from the Seventeenth Dynasty, to form the Eighteenth, perhaps the most sumptuous and celebrated of all Egypt's later rulers.

Egypt now set out on a completely new course in its history; for the first time it became an Empire, the greatest and most powerful nation in the world, asserting itself above all of its neighbours, the thrones of its kings elevated above all the thrones of the world. This era, a paradoxical one for a land which had always valued its containment from the rest of humankind, was heralded by the appearance of a phenomenon which was to become one of the marks of the dynasty: a succession of powerful queens who, sometimes ruling on their own account, left an indelible impression on the character of the times over which they presided. Often, by reason of the relatively early demise of some of the kings, their queens acted as regents, ruling during the minority of a son; sometimes they shared the sovereignty with the king, giving a particular air of grace to the otherwise often monumental quality of Egyptian architecture, for example, or to the lesser and applied arts.

Three great queens stand at the threshold of the Eighteenth Dynasty. They were followed by others who were as influential; it has already been observed that women always played an important part in the public as in the domestic life of Ancient Egypt. Women were not secluded in the later fashion of Near Eastern societies, but appeared with their menfolk on terms of equality. Some occupied great offices in the temple administrations; others were queens ruling in their own right. In the New Kingdom, as this period is described, women were especially significant in the nation's life and it is by no mere chance that the queens of the Theban family now coming to power are particularly dominant.

This was a time of entirely unprecedented wealth and power for Egypt. It became the greatest power in the Near East in material and military terms, and its kings became the exemplars of the supreme autocrat, ruling by divine authority. In fact the administration of Egypt continued in place, with the ranks of civil servants and those employed by the huge temples which rose up majestically beside the Nile growing ever more numerous, powerful and rapacious.

The architecture of the New Kingdom period is enlightening, in that it demonstrates in stone much of the principles which governed the Egyptian world-view. The kings of Egypt had always manifested a tendency towards the colossal; the pyramids are not the expression of a society uncertain of its place in the world. But in the New Kingdom size and massivity seem to have been pursued largely for their own sake; it was as though Egypt sensed the need to assert itself in a world which was changing around it, though the phenomenal 'eye' which Egyptian artists of all disciplines always possessed ensured that even the largest buildings displayed the sense of proportion and order which is the true mark of the Egyptian aesthetic genius.

For this was the reality which Egypt now encountered: no longer was she *sui generis*, unique and unchallenged. Other lands and peoples, perhaps inspired by her example, now claimed a status to which before only Egypt had presumed. Partly this was the result of the invasion by the Semitic-speaking foreigners, partly the result of greater contact between peoples around the Mediterranean; but life in the Valley would never be quite the same again.

Egypt's great days were far from over, however. The tremendous flood of riches which poured into the country, by way of conquest, tribute and trade, raised the splendour of the royal state to a condition never before seen. Even quite modest people, the lesser servants of the court and temples and those who served them, could now prepare for eternity on a scale which their ancestors could not have envisaged, as though the heirs of a Tudor merchant could plan for their future security by a carefully devised and generously endowed retirement plan. The Egyptian's retirement plan, however, was, as near as it might be, forever.

The kings of the New Kingdom extended Egypt's influence far beyond the Valley and the traditional frontiers of Egypt. The kings (and the occasional queen) were skilled diplomatists and, when they had to be, implacable warriors. But it is the arts of peace, as at all times in Egypt, which really prevail throughout the New Kingdom.

Though men like THUTMOSE III, who was as great a king as ever sat on Egypt's thrones, are to be found in the annals of the Theban family, their celebrity pales beside that of two far lesser members of the dynasty. The first of these equivocal figures is AMENHOTEP IV-AKHENATEN, the son of the magnificent AMENHOTEP III. Akhenaten was responsible for the admittedly brief period in which the old gods of Egypt were obscured and a newcomer, the Aten, raised supreme above Egypt's ancient, and by this time complicated pantheon. Akhenaten's religious reforms did not really change the traditional role of the temples in Egyptian society (except ultimately perhaps to strengthen them and so contribute to the decline of the kingship and of Egypt's ancient paramountcy) but he did introduce a sea-change in the arts of Egypt, especially the relatively minor arts.

But the supreme irony of this period late in the lifetime of the Eighteenth Dynasty was the succession to the throne of a nine-year-old boy, whose very existence was long doubted but who was to become the most renowned of all Egypt's kings. The discovery of TUTANKHAMUN'S virtually intact tomb in the Valley of the Kings was one of the most dramatic events, other than the two World Wars, of the twentieth century. From the little tomb in which his mummified body lay (and, much battered, still lies) came the recognition of what it had meant to be a king of Egypt, even a very small one, and in a period of marked decline.

The Eighteenth Dynasty came to a relatively tranquil end with the assumption of the kingship by a professional soldier, HOREMHEB, who had served the previous kings in high office. He imposed order on a society which, after the rule of the rather epicene members of the dynasty in its decline, had become seriously depleted. He had no direct heir, however, and passed the thrones to another soldier, who founded the Nineteenth Dynasty; he was to adopt 'RAMESSES' as his throne-name and in doing so inaugurated a line of kings who, if they did not all share his bloodline, adopted his name. Of these the most famous was his grandson, RAMESSES II, the son of the distinguished SETI I whose accomplishments and perceptions seem to have been exceptional even for an Egyptian king. By the standards of the Egyptian kingship in the previous centuries of its existence, the Nineteenth Dynasty was *parvenu*; it does not appear to have had any royal connections in its lineage, though the family was important, probably noble, from the north-west of the country. Ramesses II, however, though he manifested a concern for the perpetuation of his own image on a scale and frequency bordering on the manic, and insisted on his divinity beyond the prevailing conventions of the kingship, was an effective administrator who took to the business of ruling as to the manner born – as indeed he was. But the monuments with which he so prodigally covered the Valley are impressive principally because of their scale; though some lack that singular combination of qualities which Egyptian architecture at its best presents – monumentality combined with grace, often with elegance – much of the sculpture of Ramesses' time preserves the finest qualities of the work of Egypt's sculptors at its height.

Ramesses lived long, dying in the sixty-seventh year of his reign. The problem of a long-living king was a familiar one in Egypt, but no lasting solution had been found to it. Ramesses was succeeded by his thirteenth son, MERENPTAH, already an elderly man; he reigned only for nine years, to be followed by a succession of short-lived rulers, in some cases with a very dubious entitlement to the kingship.

The Twentieth Dynasty, which now succeeded to the kingship, was at pains to emphasise its connections with its immediate predecessors with whom, indeed, it may have had some familial relationship. It demonstrated this concern by adopting the throne-name 'Ramesses' for nine of its members who occupied the kingship, as it turned out, increasingly uneasily.

The first to assume the name, RAMESSES III, is often regarded as the last great native-born king of Egypt. His reign was fraught with difficulties, not the least of which was an invasion in the north by a confederation of Egypt's enemies, known collectively as 'the Sea-Peoples'. Ramesses defeated them and reigned for thirty years. He died, it is thought, as the consequence of an assassination attempt.

His successors seldom even approached his authority over what had become an increasingly fractious kingdom. The power of the temples increased ominously, to the degree that their wealth and the extent of the country that they ruled challenged, if it did not actually exceed, that of the king.

At the death of the last Ramesses, the eleventh in the line, Egypt sundered, entering a long period when the two principal regions of the country were separated, sometimes splitting into even smaller divisions. In the south, the power of the High Priests of Thebes encouraged them to adopt royal prerogatives. In the north, the Twenty-First Dynasty ruled a diminishing area; this period, extending over much of the next three hundred years, represents what Egyptologists define as the Third Intermediate Period.

This is amongst the most confused and obscure phases in the history of Egypt; it came to an end with a succession of small states being established in the north of the country, often under the control of princes from Libya, a people for whom the Egyptians had little affection or respect. Sometimes they managed to extend their influence to parts of the south, including the area of the ancient capital, Memphis; frequently they really controlled only a small part of the Delta.

These petty rulers were finally swept away by an invasion from the far south, from Nubia, whence came a family of African kings who set out, with piety, determination and considerable military and administrative skills, to restore the rule of the gods in Egypt which, in their view, had been disgracefully abandoned. The most powerful of these kings from Kush was PIANKHY, who effectively conquered the whole country; he was recognised as undisputed King of Upper and Lower Egypt.

The Kushites ruled for a little under a century, forming the Twenty-Fifth Dynasty. They were succeeded by a native Egyptian dynasty which originated in the ancient northern city of Sais.

The Saitic kings, during the hundred and fifty years that their dynasty survived, did much to recall the days of Egypt's splendour, through a deliberate harking back to the forms of the Old Kingdom in the arts, especially in sculpture and architecture. The cities which they built were magnificent, and Egypt entered its last period of great prosperity under their rule, at least until the time of the Greek Ptolemaic dynasty, nearly four hundred years later. The country was increasingly opened to foreign traders, of whom the Greeks and the Jews were probably the most significant. These incursions, especially those of the Greeks, were to have important lasting effects.

The Saites fell; Egypt underwent another invasion, this time from the newly emergent Persian Empire, which had become the dominant power in the Near

East. The Persians were not entirely confident in their rule of Egypt, however, despite the support of sections of the indigenous population. After the restoration of native Egyptian rule, culminating in the reign of the last true Egyptian king, NECTANEBO II, the Persians returned briefly, to be expelled finally by ALEXANDER THE GREAT in 332 BC.

Alexander was hailed by the Egyptians as 'Saviour'. Though he only spent about six months in the country, after his coronation in Memphis, his presence was to be felt for hundreds of years to come, even, it might be said, until the present day. His creation of the city of Alexandria, on the country's Mediterranean coast, was a decision which was to have the most profound influence on the subsequent history of the world. From Alexandria there flowed a tide of intellectual and scientific innovation and speculation which marked the end of the ancient world and inaugurated – for better or worse – its modern successor.

After Alexander's death in 323 BC, PTOLEMY, one of his companions and a most competant general, seized control of Egypt, in the turmoil of the disputed succession to Alexander's empire. He proclaimed himself king in 305 BC and thus inaugurated the last of the dynasties, albeit a foreign one, to reign over Egypt. Ptolemy and his son, PTOLEMY II, were admirable rulers, imposing a generally firm but equitable control over the country. Gradually, however, the quality of the Ptolemaic kings deteriorated catastrophically, some of the generations producing monsters of cruelty and lust who outdid the most decadent Roman Emperors in imaginative infamy. The dynasty came to its end with CLEOPATRA VII, whose defeat and melodramatic death opened the way to the Roman conquest of Egypt. Henceforth the most ancient and august of kingdoms became a province of the Roman Empire, administered as the private domain of the emperors. But they belong more to the history of Europe than to that of immemorial Egypt.

Rome however, like Greece before it, opened Egypt to the new world which was emerging in Europe and the Levant. The myth of Egypt grew over the centuries, giving life to the Renaissance and the Enlightenment. Although Egypt's greatness was now long past, the myth accreted and today still exerts its almost uncanny power, standing for a time, however fancifully, when man was closer to the gods and to the fulfilment of a richer human destiny.

Egypt has the quality, unique amongst all the great civilisations of antiquity, that demands explanation, not merely description and analysis. Its origins remain largely obscure, despite two centuries of careful exploration and sometimes less careful speculation. It is as though on one day towards the end of the fourth millennium BC, the old neolithic societies were still in place along the length of the Nile's banks, whilst on the next day the complexities and splendours of the civilisation which was to excite the wonder of the world for thousands of years, began to unroll. There is little evidence of experiment or change in the course of the Valley's history, even in its earliest years, any more than there is evidence of experiment or failure in the production of the works of art which flowed from the country's artists and craftsmen.

The leading figures of this time, too, stand absolutely assured, their titles, modes of dress, the structure of the administration which they led and the works which they achieved coming into being seemingly fully realised; there is no real formative stage in the development of Egyptian culture, no primitive beginnings from which the society can be seen to grow. It is a genuine mystery, and whilst there must be some rational explanation, allowing the conscientious humanist to discard the wilder theories of extraterrestrial intervention and the like in the seeding of Egypt, the mystery remains.

The inhabitants of the Nile Valley five thousand years ago fulfilled an exalted and extraordinary destiny. It was they who, seemingly instinctually, recognised, identified and named the great archetypes which became the marks of sophisticated, complex societies, and which determined the lives of those living in such societies for many hundred years, and indeed still influence the world of the present day. The list of those archetypes which we owe to Egypt is formidable: the nation state, the kingship, the Divine King, Order and Truth, the Creative Force, monumental stone buildings, the pyramid, the Hidden God, the power of the stars. All of these were first defined in Egypt, and once having been named and acknowledged they assumed their own independent existence, to be similarly acknowledged when, in time, they appeared in other, later cultures. This is the true mystery of Egypt and the reason why the culture which arose so swiftly and perfectly on the Nile's banks still excites the minds of so many people living today, in lands far distant from the Valley and long after Egypt's high destiny was fulfilled.

The most arresting quality of the Ancient Egyptians themselves, especially those who lived in the Valley during the earliest centuries, is this air of certainty, of absolute, blissful assurance. The Egyptians had no need to assert themselves, no need to prosyletise, no need to convince anyone of the superiority of their vision of the world: they simply seem to have known that such was the case. With it, all the Egyptians of antiquity were the most humane of peoples, and despite their supreme confidence in themselves and the immense achievements of their culture, in scale, quantity and perfection of form and craftsmanship, they are the most approachable of all the peoples of the past. To a degree quite unlike any other ancient people, their bequests to the world which came after them still live; it may be said with truth that the Ancient Egyptians, through their assiduous perpetuation of their names and likenesses, and the abundant power of the multitudinous creations which they left behind them, are still among us.

Further reading

Baines, J. and Málek, J. (1980) *Atlas of Ancient Egypt*, Amsterdam and Oxford.
Edwards, I. E. S. (1993) *The Pyramids of Egypt*, 5th edn, London.
Grimal, N. (1992) *A History of Ancient Egypt*, trans. Ian Shaw, Oxford.
Rice, M. (1997) *Egypt's Legacy*, London.
Shaw, I. and Nicholson, P. (1995) *The British Museum Dictionary of Ancient Egypt*, London.
Trigger, B. *et al.* (1985) *Ancient Egypt: A Social History*, Cambridge.

The Egyptian kingship

The supreme achievement of the people of the Nile Valley in the late fourth millennium BC was the vision, ultimately brought to reality, of the political unity and coherance of the entire Valley, from the First Cataract to the Mediterranean. The river itself was the catalyst which gave life to this unprecedented and audacious concept, which had no parallel in any other part of the world at the time. The Valley was an entity by reason of the common way of life which the river made possible for its people as riverine agriculturalists. The bounty of the river was common to all; from it all drew their means of living at a level of prosperity probably otherwise unknown in the late Neolithic world.

The river gave generously but it could also withhold its bounty. The cycle of the seasons induced a sense of the regularity of nature and of the advantage of order. To ensure the fertility of the land required a degree of organisation, discipline, technique and social responsibility not to be found in any other part of the world at the time.

From the Valley people's recognition of their common destiny, expressed through their sharing of the Valley's unique resource, emerged in due time the political construct which was its logical, perhaps inevitable, outcome: the nation state. It is perhaps unlikely that anyone, even an Egyptian of the sort of genius with which the Valley seems at this time to have been quite disproportionately endowed, ever articulated such a concept so specifically. Nonetheless, the creation of the nation state was the irresistible consequence of the processes which came surging up out of the Valley people's collective unconscious at this time.

It may be said (though such a suggestion is unlikely to go wholly unchallenged) that early Egypt's unique contribution to the human experience was the recognition and naming of the archetypes which go to make up an ordered human existence. Of such archetypes the most enduring and universal was undoubtedly the concept of the kingship.

It cannot be said with absolute certainty when the kingship first emerged in Egypt. The historiographical and Egyptological convention is to define the historical period in Egypt, beginning around 3150 BC by identifying a series of 'Dynasties' into which the rulers of the unified country are grouped. Such dynastic groups may or may not be directly related familially; frequently they were, and certainly in the earliest periods the succession seems usually to have been in the direct line.

It is assumed that the original political structure of the Valley was a network of greater and lesser principalities or chieftaincies, each with its ruling family, customs and tutelary divinities. Certainly, in historical times the Valley showed a pronounced tendency to fragment into local centres of control whenever the central authority of the kingship weakened, as happened not infrequently over the course of the next three thousand years. Equally, there was always a degree of competition amongst the entities whom we call 'the gods', with otherwise quite obscure local divinities, through the vagaries of politics and the rise to power of a family of regional magnates, achieving the status of national, even perhaps, universal divinities: a situation not unknown in later, less illustrious cultures than Egypt's.

The kings of the First Dynasty established the capital of the notionally united country at the point where the two principal divisions of the country, Upper and Lower Egypt, the southlands and the north, met, near the modern capital of Cairo, at the city which the Greeks knew as 'Memphis'. From the earliest times the kings seem to have claimed sovereignty over the entire Two Lands, though the actual process of unification took a long time to be realised.

The arrival of the First Dynasty of kings marks an absolute change in the nature, organisation and iconography of Egypt. There are some indications in the Predynastic period of the forms which later will come to be regarded as immemorially Egyptian, but the differences between Egypt in the times before the kings and Egypt during dynastic times are far greater than any similarities which can be identified. The creation of the Egyptian kingship was so momentous an event that the world was never entirely to be the same after it, for the naming of the archetypes had identified and released them into the common consciousness of humanity. From this time onwards, from the the end of the fourth millennium BC, the pattern established in Egypt was to be repeated in many regions of the world, the product not of diffusion but of a similar response to similar social needs and opportunities and the demands of each people's collective unconscious.

Certain conventions began to surround the king, evidently from the very earliest days of his recognition. He assumed special ROYAL NAMES, in addition to his own birth name. Initially three, later five in number, these were of profound significance, each with its own deep resonances. He wore or carried special regalia, including a diversity of CROWNS with considerable symbolic significance. All of these marked him out from the generality of humankind.

In no case was the king of Egypt's essential difference from all other men more pronounced than in the singular fact that he was a god; indeed in the early centuries he was presumed to be *the* god, the Master of the Universe, by whose will the sun rose, the Nile flooded and the stars turned in their motions. It was a breathtakingly audacious concept and it has to be seen for the paradox that it represents, that the most intensely creative people of antiquity, capable of raising superb monuments and of devising one of the most subtle and complex societies of which we have knowledge, invested the Chief Officer of their state with the quality of divinity despite what must sometimes have been the all-too-obvious evidences of his human nature.

The King of Egypt was the entire centre of the life of Egypt; he was the reason for Egypt's existence, and the Two Lands were the heavenly mansions brought down to earth because of him. Everything that could secure the life, prosperity and health of the king contributed to the perpetuity of Egypt. If the king lived, Egypt lived.

The king was god because he was the incarnation of the archetypal god of kingship, Horus; he was Horus because he was king. There has been much misunderstanding of the adoption of the persona of Horus by the King of Egypt. In later times, after the kingship had been in existence and had flourished for a thousand years, Horus was represented as the son of Osiris, a latecomer into the Egyptian corporation of divine entities, but who came to symbolise the king-after-death. But there was a much more ancient Horus who was perpetually reincarnated in the living body of the king.

At his coronation, a wonderful event full of allusive panoply and the interplay of a multitude of different forces, the king assumed the DOUBLE CROWN and rose from the throne a god. The throne was personified by the goddess Isis, who in later times was identified in consequence as the mother of Horus. But Horus the king was immensely more ancient than his alleged parentage by Osiris and Isis; as with some of the most ancient of Egypt's gods, he must probably be seen as self-begotten, from before time. At a particularly beautiful moment in the coronation, all the birds of the air flew off to the four corners of the earth to proclaim the return of the Horus-King. On this occasion the role of Isis was crucial in conferring the divine kingship on the reincarnated Horus by contact with her lap; the importance of the daughters of the king, who conveyed the kingship from one generation to the next, is a reflection of Isis' part in the divine transmission of the kingship to earth.

Even at the beginning of the First Dynasty, when the lineaments of the royal Egyptian culture were being laid down, the king was Horus; indeed his great royal style was 'The Horus *X*' and throughout Egyptian history the Horus-name was the most sacred that the king possessed. It was the source of his power, as king and as god.

The king was not merely the equal of the gods; at certain occasions he was their master and they deferred to him. Always they were to be found in his train, attendant on him on the great occasions of state, when to mortal eyes they would be impersonated by the great officers of the kingdoms and the High Priests of the temples, though they were believed only to perform their offices as surrogates of the king himself. The king was the supreme priest of Egypt, himself performing a perpetual round of ceremonies, consecrating himself to himself. It was a melancholy fact, however, that the power and prestige of the King of Egypt was eventually to be undermined by the power of the clerical bureaucracies which rose out of the temple servants originally appointed to serve and glorify the king. The corrupting influence of religious bureaucracies, first manifested in Egypt, was to become a familiar if no more welcome experience for the societies which were to follow Egypt, down to the present day.

It is one of the most singular characteristics of the emergent Egyptian state which began to coalesce around the person of the king in the latter part of the fourth millennium BC that, from the outset, he was surrounded by a court of state bureaucrats, with well defined roles and titles of considerable complexity. Many of those who served the king and who are known, for example from the great MASTABA tombs in which they were buried, bore titles which it is hard to believe were invented summarily but which rather must have had a far greater antiquity, reaching back to some structure which existed before the accepted appearance of the monarchy. This is another of the many enigmas which are associated with the origins and formative influences of the Egyptian state.

The kings of Egypt are the first true individuals known to history. Despite the sparseness of the surviving records there is no doubt of the power and achievements of the early kings. Whilst the king was, in a profound sense, 'The Great Individual', he was also the soul of Egypt, through whom Egypt lived.

As time went by, so the nature of the Egyptian kingship underwent adaptation and change. For the whole course of the Archaic Period and the Old Kingdom the king enjoyed a unique and absolute paramountcy, when he was regarded as an immanent divinity. The very success of the institution, however, was its undoing. As the kingship became involved in more and more elaborate state enterprises, of which the building of pyramids was but one example of many, the king came to depend more and more on his partisans, in the court and the temple. The employment of short-term expediencies, beloved of all politicians in every generation with no concern for those who would follow them, was a device first practised by the Egyptian monarchy in the closing decades of the Old Kingdom, to secure the loyalty of the great magnates by bestowing on them more and more royal lands and showering them with privileges and exemptions which eventually were to cripple the state.

That the kingship was the archetypal Egyptian political institution, however, was unmistakeably confirmed at the restoration of a coherent political structure in the Valley which was the particular triumph of the kings of the Eleventh Dynasty and their immediate predecessors, so skilfully built on by their successors in the Twelfth Dynasty. The Middle Kingdom restored the power of the kingship after the pressures which it underwent at the end of the Old Kingdom, though it was subtly altered; the king was a god but, more important, he was the Chief Executive of the Two Lands. He was as formidable in this role as he had been in the early centuries of the kingship when his divinity was his dominant nature, to the exclusion of all other considerations.

So immense was the span of Egyptian history, in all its forms enduring for more than three thousand years, that its institutions, including the kingship, altered as the world outside the Valley altered; sometimes influences percolated into the Valley which provoked dramatic change, as when Semitic-speaking peoples or Africans from the south ruled the country. These altered states could be greatly beneficial to much of the historic Egyptian persona as, for example, the kingship mutated into a prototypical oriental imperial monarchy, resulting in the splendour and rich diversity of the New Kingdom, which endured in its own right for half a millennium.

The Egyptian kingship was a unique institution, the first of its kind anywhere on earth. The kings were always represented as being more than mortal and, as the Lands' presiding genius, the earlier generations of the kings perhaps achieved a more enduring set of consequences, of more lasting worth, than any other group of individuals known to history.

Further reading

Clayton, P. A. (1994) *Chronicles of the Pharaohs*, London.
Frankfort, H. (1948) *Kingship and the Gods*, Chicago IL.
Hoffman, M. (1980) *Egypt Before the Pharaohs*, London.
Kemp, B. J. (1989) *Ancient Egypt: Anatomy of a Civilization*, London.
Rice, M. (1990) *Egypt's Making*, London.
Spencer, A. J. (1993) *Early Egypt: The Rise of Civilisation in the Nile Valley*, London.

The gods of Egypt

The non-human, supranatural entities known collectively in Egypt as *netjer*, a word customarily translated as 'god', are perhaps best understood as forces of nature, even as powers beyond nature, rather than the more conventional idea of them as anthropomorphised beings or as theriocephalic emanations. Some of them were indeed represented in human or humanoid form, others manifested themselves as animals, birds, insects or reptiles, but these forms concealed rather than revealed their true nature.

Many of the *netjeru* had their origins in remote times when they were identified with particular parts of the Nile Valley; some of them retained these associations throughout Egyptian history whilst others became national gods. These were identified with the king or with what were considered to be particular departments of divine responsibility: the sun and the moon, truth and order, creation, or the vital essence which informs all living things.

Some of the great gods were already powerful at the dawn of Egyptian history. These included ATUM, the spirit of creation; RE, the sun-god; THOTH, the god of wisdom and the moon; HATHOR and ISIS, forms of the great goddess; NEITH, a warrior goddess from the north; PTAH, the supreme creative force; SET, originally the god of the south, later the god of the desert and storm, later still the personification of malignancy and destruction. This last role arose from his supposed part in the murder of his brother, OSIRIS (in fact a relatively late arrival in the Egyptian pantheon, who is attested towards the end of the Old Kingdom, though older gods in the Abydos region were sometimes thought of as Osiris' forerunners) and his conflict with Osiris' son, HORUS.

Behind even the greatest and most ancient of these entities was the veiled presence of 'He whose Name is Hidden', a mysterious, all-powerful being to whom even the mightiest of the gods deferred; the most ancient Horus in his Falcon manifestation was said to perch upon the battlements of this god's celestial palace. This Hidden One, however, was never revealed during Egypt's lifetime, though AMUN was, at least according to one of the several theogonies which the Egyptians maintained, sometimes acknowledged as 'Hidden'.

Before the Fourth Dynasty, the Pyramid Age, when for reasons which are unclear a change in religious orientation took place, Egypt seems principally to have followed stellar cults, identifying certain stars and constellations for particular regard. There is no doubt that the stars played an important role in determining the orientation, for example, of the massive architectural and engineering projects which characterise the Old Kingdom. Architects used the stars to establish true north and to align their buildings to the cardinal points with astonishing precision; they also were capable of locking an entire building on to a particular star, doubtless to allow its light to shine directly into the sanctuary on nights of special festivals. It is thus entirely consonant with the Egyptian mind to have drawn down the configuration of those constellations which were especially important to them and to have replicated their positions in the Valley, a suggestion which has raised as much controversy as it has interest. Much Egyptian thought was devoted to uniting the two realms of earth and sky, just as the early kings sought to unify the notional 'Two Lands' into which Egypt was always said to be divided.

When the kings of the First Dynasty began their programme of unifying the Valley, creating a nation state out of a jigsaw puzzle of disconnected principalities, some of the gods are said to have been 'born'. The introduction of systems of worship and observance for the 'new' gods suggests that the First-Dynasty kings were as innovative in the recognition of the divine powers as they were in the secular management of the state.

In the early days of the kingship, in the Archaic Period and the early Old Kingdom, the gods and the observances directed towards them were the exclusive concern of the king. He was their equal, indeed, except for the very greatest, their ruler, as the Incarnate Horus. Later, his position was somewhat reduced, but the gods were still his companions and supporters.

The nature of the society's attitude to the gods changed, as did so much else, after the end of the Old Kingdom. Then Osiris, possibly originating in Western Asia, emerged as a god of redemption, becoming assimilated with local gods in Abydos and eventually himself becoming the principal divinity of that part of Egypt. Gradually the cult of Osiris became general; for the first time the people were able to approach the gods and something like corporate worship appeared. Osiris offered the possibility of redemption and eternal life to all, not merely to the king and his closest coadjutors, as originally was the case. It was, however, not a generalised system of ritual to which all had access until much later in Egypt's history, when influences from outside began to change the indigenous Egyptian forms, in cult practices as in other aspects of life in the Valley.

The gods were served by priests, of different grades and functions. In the early centuries all Egyptians of standing were expected to serve as priests in the temples, for an agreed period each year; this represented more of a social obligation than evidence of a religious vocation. Later, as the perquisites of the temple hierarchies grew, the priesthood became increasingly professional. Many of the most rewarding of the temple benefices became hereditary fiefs. Nonetheless, the king was notionally the High Priest of every cult, the temple priests merely his surrogates. However, each major temple community was directed by a High Priest whose power was often very great. Some of the High Priesthoods, such as that of Ptah of Memphis, Re of Heliopolis and Amun of Thebes (though Amun was something of a parvenu divinity, only coming to national prominence after the rise of his city and its princes in the Middle Kingdom) were the greatest political figures in the state; eventually, the power of some of them was to rival, if it did not exceed, the power of the kings.

Religion in Egypt was not originally concerned with considerations of morality or behaviour. Its practice, in so far as it related to the divinities, was the responsibility only of the king and his immediate officers. Its concern was to ensure the security and well-being of the Egyptian state and of its personification, the king. The individual initially was of no significance in the scheme of things. Gradually, however, the idea of the gods controlling human destiny, from which originally they were remote, gained acceptance and the great temples became places of immense wealth, power and prestige as they conducted the round of ceremonies held in honour of the gods for the benefit of the people.

The Egyptians were not very much given to philosophical speculation. Ruled by an immanent divinity, most of the great and perplexing questions which have occupied the minds of later peoples would have seemed irrelevant to them; the truth was always with them. Certainly, concepts such as truth, justice and the honourable treatment of one's fellows were deeply ingrained and were clearly passed on to subsequent cultures. Later cultures, when considering the complexity and apparent contradictions of Egyptian religious 'beliefs', have inevitably tended to view them through the filter of their own belief systems and religious prejudices. Much of what is thought to be known about the beliefs of the Egyptians is based on relatively late sources, many of them Greek; it is not easy to discover the archetypes which expressed the essential nature of the people's convictions in the centuries during which Egyptian belief systems were developing.

The great temple priesthoods evidently did offer what are probably best recognised as parables or mythologies, which were designed principally to explain origins – of the cosmos, of Egypt, of the kingship – and, in a peculiarly powerful fashion, to convey a sense of the mystery of creation. At least three distinct 'theologies' (a word which is really too formal in its meaning to be very helpful here) existed simultaneously. These were identified with Heliopolis, emphasising the role of the sun and Re as the symbols of the Divine Kingship; with Memphis and the creator god Ptah; and with Hermopolis and the god Thoth. At Abydos much later, after the rise of the Theban princes in the Middle Kingdom, the cults of Osiris became very important. Until it was later superceded to some degree by the cults of Amun, the cult of Osiris then became something like a national religion; with its ideas of personal salvation and the suffering and dying god, it clearly had a considerable influence on other societies and peoples long after Egypt had ceased to be the dominant power in the Near East.

The nearest that the Egyptians got to articulating a philosophical principle in relation to one of the divine entities was expressed in the person of a very ancient *netjer* who, paradoxically, was represented as a young girl. This was MA'AT, in whose name the king was said to live. Ma'at was Truth, Justice and, most important of all, Order. The primary reason for the perpetuation of the monarchy was that the king was the custodian of Ma'at. By his existence in Ma'at and, as the rubric went, by ensuring his 'Life, Prosperity, Health', the prosperity of Egypt (and hence of the universe) was ensured.

Ma'at features in the most beautiful of all the creation myths devised by the Egyptian sages. When the Creator decided to initiate the process of creation his first act was to raise Ma'at to his lips and to kiss her. Equally poetic, it may be felt, was the myth which had the process of creation begun by the lonely cry of a waterfowl in the marshes.

As the years went by and Egypt grew old, the nature of the gods inevitably changed too. Foreign divinities were brought into the pantheon and the Egyptian gods began to take on the common nature which most ancient societies attributed to all the multitudinous divinities who plagued or comforted them. The king remained a god, even a great god, but he was no longer the sovereign of the entire universe. The process of democratising the gods began with the introduction of Osiris to the company of the gods and, it might be said, has continued ever since.

In the last centuries of Egypt's history the myth of Egypt began to gain widespread currency, and newly emergent societies around the Mediterranean and far beyond, began to speculate about the nature of the Egyptian experience and of the Valley people's apprehension of the divine. Then the Egyptian gods, even the relatively debased ones who appeared as the ancient world neared its end, acquired a quality of mystery and potency in the minds of impressionable people, newly civilised (to the extent of living in cities) and beginning to question the often confused and disreputable colleges of gods to which they had become subjected.

The latest manifestation of the divine powers which emerged in the Nile Valley was the appearance of a bearded, patriarchal High God, a conflation of Osiris and the sky gods of the north such as Zeus, and of the immensely ancient figure of the divine mother nursing her divine child; Isis cradles Horus on her lap. This expressed in visual form the divine origins of the Egyptian kingship, and it became the most appealing icon of the newly arrived cult of Christianity, though celebrating a divine figure whom the ancient Egyptians themselves would have found deeply improbable.

In the centuries after the effective end of Egypt's history, her gods have continued to haunt the imaginations of peoples in lands of which the Egyptians themselves can have had no knowledge. No corporation of divinities, or of the principles which may be thought to give expression to the divine, has ever remotely approached the Egyptian in power and mystery. The Egyptians first gave names and identity to the great archetypes which are represented by the *netjeru*, and in doing so, gave them perpetual life.

SOME OF THE PRINCIPAL GODS OF EGYPT

Amun (alt. Amon)

'The Hidden One', a god of the Theban region who eventually became the principal divinity of the royal lines and the nearest approach to a national god of Egypt. The Temple of Amun in Thebes was one of the most powerful religious foundations, especially in the later periods, eventually threatening the royal power.

Andjeti

A god of the Delta with whom OSIRIS, who was first associated with the Delta town of Busiris, was assimilated.

Anhur

A god identified as the creative power of the sun, later recognised as a god of war.

Anubis

A very ancient divinity, originating in Abydos. He is represented as a wolf or jackal; he was associated especially with mummification, the practice of which was the responsibility of his priests.

Apis

A manifestation of Ptah incarnate in a bull with particular markings and physical characteristics, Apis was known in the First Dynasty. His cult became widespread in the Late Period, when the chosen bull (and his mother) were given lives of great luxury in the temple at Memphis and, at death, sumptuous obsequies at Saqqara.

Ash

A god of deserts, of great antiquity, sometimes identified with Set, particularly in the south.

Aten

The personification of the sun's rays, proclaimed by AMENHOTEP IV-AKHENATEN as the supreme god of Egypt. After the king's death Aten was overturned by the priests of Amun, a return to whose worship was demanded by them, signalled by such events as the renaming of King Tutankhaten, Akhenaten's eventual successor, as TUTANKHAMUN.

Atum

'The Undifferentiated One', 'The All', the original creator of the cosmos who, after lying inert in the abyss, appeared on the primordial mound, 'The Divine Emerging Island', to initiate the process of creation. Finding himself alone he masturbated and from his sperm produced the first generation of gods.

Bes

A dwarf god, popular in later times, who was invoked for luck and who facilitated childbirth.

Buchis

A sacred bull, associated with Montu at his cult centre at Armant (Hermonthis); the bull was an incarnation of Re and Osiris.

Bastet

A cat goddess, worshipped at Bubastis, a Delta town named in her honour.

Geb

The earth god and father, by the goddess NUT, of Osiris, Isis, Set and Nephthys. Initially he divided the sovereignty of Egypt between Set and his nephew Horus, gods of the south and north respectively, but eventually gave dominion over the whole land to Horus.

Hapy

The god of the Nile, portrayed with bisexual secondary characteristics.

Hathor

An ancient cow goddess, associated with Isis, and in whose form queens were frequently depicted.

Heh, Hehet

Frog divinities, representing the element water who, with others of their kind, produce the egg which is placed on the 'Divine Emerging Island'. Heh was also the god of eternity, represented anthropomorphically.

Horakhty

A manifestation of Re as the dawn light appearing on the eastern horizon. In New Kingdom times the Great Sphinx at Giza was thought to be an image of the god Horus and was identified with Horakhty.

Horus

A very ancient sky divinity from the south, the son of Osiris and Isis according to a relatively late myth, who avenged his father's murder by Set, becoming King of Upper and Lower Egypt. All subsequent kings of Egypt were revered as incarnations of Horus. There were many local manifestations of Horus throughout Egypt.

Isis

Sister-wife of Osiris and mother of Horus. Queens were identified with Isis and, especially in the early dynasties, the succession to the throne often passed through the female line by marriage to the heiress. Isis was represented astronomically by the constellation Sirius (Egyptian *Sopdet*).

Khentiamentiu

An ancient god of the necropolis of Abydos, 'The Foremost of the Westerners' with whom Osiris was assimilated and whose form, swathed in mummy cloths, he adopted. Like Anubis, with whom Khentiamentiu shares a number of attributes, he is also manifest as a dog or jackal.

Khepri (alt. Kheper)

The scarabeus beetle which was regarded as the manifestation of the sun god. Its practice of laying its eggs in a ball of dung came to symbolise regeneration, and the hieroglyph derived from it signified 'becoming'.

Khnum

The ram-headed god of Elephantine who was responsible for fashioning the *Ka* of the royal child at the moment of conception, on his potter's wheel.

Ma'at

Truth, divine order; the goddess in whose name the king was said to rule, and by whom he was bound to rule justly.

Mefnut

A lioness goddess.

Mertsager

A snake goddess, revered as the 'Lady of the Peak' and associated with the pyramid-shaped mountain which rises over the Valley of the Kings at Thebes. Her name means 'She who Loves Silence'.

Meshkent

The goddess of childbirth.

Min

'Lord of Coptos', often represented as though one-armed and usually ithyphallic.

Mnevis

A god who manifested his presence in a selected bull (see also Apis, Buchis).

Montu

A warrior-god of the Theban region, manifest both as a falcon and as a bull. Montu was particularly reverenced by the kings of the Eleventh Dynasty, eventually being replaced by the ram of Amun as the principal divinity of the Thebaid.

Mut

A lioness-headed goddess whose temple was located at Asher (Thebes). She was sometimes represented as vulture-headed.

Nefertum

Horus as a child, born in the lotus flower and associated with the sun god.

Neith

An ancient warrior-goddess, resident in Sais in northern Egypt. From very early times she was symbolised by a device of crossed arrows.

Nekhbet

The vulture goddess of Nekhen in Upper Egypt and patron goddess of the south, one of 'THE TWO LADIES', with UADJET whose power protected the king. Some kings and a number of queens wore the double URAEUS of vulture and cobra.

Nephthys

One of the Heliopolitan Ogdoad, the company of eight primeval gods, the daughter of Geb and the consort of Set.

Nun

The personification of the primeval waters, the abyss, from which the earliest generations of gods were born. At night the sun journeyed to Nun on its voyage through the Underworld.

Nut

The sky goddess whose body symbolised the vault of the heavens. Every evening she swallowed the sun, Re, and every morning gave birth to him anew. She is frequently represented in the decoration of coffins.

Osiris

The ruler of the Underworld, identified with the king-in-death, who became Osiris. He was the father of Horus who avenged his murder by his brother Set. Osiris was regenerated that he might impregnate Isis; as a consequence he came to be worshipped as the god of rebirth and redemption. In time all the 'justified' dead became Osiris.

Ptah

The immensely ancient artificer god, Lord of Memphis, where his principal temple was established and hence especially identified with the royal house. He is depicted in human form, though wrapped in mummy cloths. He could also manifest himself in animal form, for example as a bull like Apis, Buchis or Mnevis.

Ptah-Soker-Osiris

A manifestation of Ptah combined with Osiris, particularly important in the region of Saqqara. Later Ptah-Soker-Osiris became transformed into the Graeco-Egyptian god Serapis, one of the archetypes of the bearded, patriarchal sky god.

Re (alt. Ra)

The sun god, from time to time regarded as the king of the gods, with whom the king was united at death.

Sekhmet

A lioness goddess, the consort of Ptah, she roamed the desert outside Giza. Because of an injury done to the eye of Re, her father, she determined to destroy the race of men and was only prevented from doing so by the subterfuge of making her drunk, so that she became unconscious and was carried back to heaven.

Selket

A scorpion-goddess who protected the coffin of the king.

Seshat

An ancient goddess, charged with responsibility for preparing all the divine records, hence for writing, architecture, the measuring of land on which a temple was to be built and, with the king, for determining the temple's axis.

Set (alt. Seth)

Originally the high god of the south of Egypt, Set became a god of deserts, of the storm and chaos. Later, he was regarded as the murderer of his brother, OSIRIS, and the antagonist of Osiris' heir, HORUS. Their conflict over the kingship of Egypt is one of the archetypal themes of Ancient Egypt.

Shesemuw

A god of wine and of the vintage, who also presided over the butchering of bulls.

Shu

The god of air and the sun; he was particularly associated with Heliopolis. He was said to be one of the first two divinities created by Atum.

Sobek

A crocodile-god, worshipped at Kom Ombo, who was especially popular in the Thirteenth Dynasty, when a number of the kings adopted Sobek's name as part of their titulary.

Soker

A god of the dead of Memphis; he was associated in late times with Osiris and Ptah to form the composite divinity Ptah-Soker-Osiris.

Taurt

A hippopotamus goddess, represented standing upright on her rear legs, who was particularly concerned with the supervision of pregnancy and childbirth.

Tefnut

A form of the lioness-goddess Sekhmet.

Thoth

The god of wisdom and the moon who was manifest both as an ibis and as a cynocephalus baboon. He it was who brought the arts of civilisation to men.

'The Two Ladies'

The godesses NEKHBET and UADJET.

Uadjet

The cobra-goddess of the north, the partner of NEKHBET who with her protected the king as part of his URAEUS diadem, sometimes forming with Nekhbet the double uraeus.

Wepwawet (alt. Upwaut)

A dog-god from Abydos, associated with graveyards. His name signifies 'Opener of the Ways' and it was believed that he conducted the dead to judgement.

Further reading

Hart, G. (1986) *A Dictionary of Egyptian Gods and Goddesses*, London.
Hornung, E. (1983) *Conceptions of God in Ancient Egypt: The One and the Many*, London.
Lurker, M. (1980) *The Gods and Symbols of Ancient Egypt*, London.
Quirke, S. (1992) *Ancient Egyptian Religion*, London.

Chronology

The dating of the reigns of individual rulers of Egypt and of the great events which determined the country's history is notoriously fraught with multiple complexities. Yet the chronology of Egypt is still the benchmark for all chronologies of the ancient Near East.

The history of Egypt spans the entire range of our species' recorded (that is to say, written) history. The earliest kings and their ministers recorded here are figures from the very dawn of history, 5,000 years ago. At this time, when Egypt first appears as a nation state, the accepted chronology may be 100–150 years out, in either direction. As the record moves on, the margin of error becomes somewhat lessened, but even in the time of the great conquering kings of the Egyptian Empire, the New Kingdom, scholars can still dispute dates vigorously. It is not until the seventh century BC that dates may, generally speaking, be regarded as absolute; by that time increasing literacy in societies with whom Egypt sustained contact meant that there were other records by which events and the reigns of kings might be tabulated.

Egyptian history is conventionally divided into blocks of time:

The *Prehistoric* is that which preceeds the invention of writing. The later centuries, immediately before the appearance of the kings whose names are known, are referred to as the *Predynastic*.

The first four hundred years (or thereabouts) of the country's history, represented by the first two dynasties of kings, is known as the *Archaic*; earlier studies sometimes called this division of Egypt's history the *Thinite* period, after the city where the first kings established themselves. It is also known as the *Early Dynastic Period*, borrowing terminology more usually applied to the early kingship in Western Asiatic archaeology.

The Third to the Sixth Dynasties comprise the *Old Kingdom*, in the eyes of most observers the high point of Egyptian civilisation; it is sometimes referred to as 'The Pyramid Age'. This was followed by the *First Intermediate Period*, comprising the Seventh to the Tenth Dynasties, when the central authority of the king was fractured, with competing kinglets controlling often very small regions of the Valley; order began to be restored by a family of princes from Thebes, initially controlling the south. Then, as the kings of the Eleventh Dynasty, they re-imposed royal control over all the country, and in doing so inaugurated a time of great achievement by the Egyptian state, the *Middle Kingdom*.

After the end of the Twelfth Dynasty, which equalled if it did not exceed some of the achievements and prosperity of the Old Kingdom, a time of division overcame Egypt, heralded by the Thirteenth Dynasty, with invaders from the north taking control of much of the country. The new rulers, the *Hyksos*, lasted for a century or so, latterly with native Egyptian dynasties controlling most of the south. This interruption in the cycle of the Egyptian dynasties is also known as the *Second Intermediate Period*. Eventually the Princes of Thebes, recognised as the Seventeenth Dynasty of Kings, expelled the Hyksos and founded the Eighteenth Dynasty.

This marked the beginning of the final period of Egypt's greatness, the *New Kingdom*, when the country achieved unexampled wealth and influence, becoming the greatest power in the Near East. For half a millennium, through the Eighteenth, Nineteenth and Twentieth Dynasties, the kings of Egypt raised monuments which still excite wonder and produced a flood of works of art of delicacy, elegance and, occasionally, grandeur.

After the decline of the Twentieth Dynasty the country once again fragmented, and the more than three centuries which follow are known as the *Third Intermediate Period*, embracing the Twenty-First to the Twenty-Fourth Dynasties.

A brief sunset period was granted to Egypt in the *Late Period*, covering the Twenty-Fifth to the Thirtieth Dynasties. An African Dynasty, the Twenty-Fifth, ruled for a little under a hundred years and tried to restore the dignity of Egypt and the worship of the ancient gods. The Twenty-Sixth Dynasty, represented by a family of princes from Sais in the north, continued this process and, in a time of relative tranquility, built handsome cities and fine monuments which consciously sought to recall the mighty days of the Old Kingdom. The benign rule of the Saite kings was ended by Egypt's absorption into the Persian Empire.

Finally, Alexander of Macedon appeared, and was hailed as the saviour of Egypt when he drove out the Persian invaders. He was succeeded by the dynasty of the *Ptolemies*, which started well and ended disastrously with Egypt falling prey to the Romans, on the suicide of Cleopatra VII in 30 BC.

***

Each entry in *Who's Who in Ancient Egypt* is provided with a chronological reference. In the case of the kings this can often be relatively precise; in the case of some private individuals, especially in the earlier periods, before *c.* 700 BC, it can only be approximate, related where possible to the known duration of a reign or an event otherwise documented.

The Egyptians themselves did not help matters for the contemporary reader in that time was reckoned in terms of regnal years, a convention which, curiously enough, is still maintained in the dating of British Acts of Parliament. To the Egyptian, time returned to the beginning on each occasion that Horus assumed the throne and the DOUBLE CROWN. Thus there are no absolute dates in Egyptian records, hence encouraging the creation of a substantial academic industry, in the attempt to provide a coherent sequence over the three thousand years that Egypt survived as a power.

The dates used in the entries have been drawn, very largely, from *The British Museum Dictionary of Ancient Egypt* (British Museum Press, London, 1995) which represents an up-to-date consensus of the country's historical chronology.

THE CHRONOLOGY OF THE DYNASTIES OF EGYPT

This chronology contains the principal rulers identified in the biographical entries. All dates given are BC, unless otherwise declared, and all before 690 are approximate.

The Predynastic Period, 5500–3150

Badarian Period, 5500–4000

Naqada I (Amratian) 4000–3500

Naqada II (Gerzean) 3500–3300

Naqada III, 3300–3150

Iryhor, 'Scorpion', Nar-Mer, Ka.

The Archaic Period, 3150–2686

Also known as the Thinite or Early Dynastic Period.

First Dynasty, 3150–2890

Aha ('Menes'), Djer, Djet, Den, Merneith, Anedjib, Semerkhet, Qa'a.

Second Dynasty, 2890–2686

Hotepsekhemwy, Raneb, Nynetjer, Weneg, Sened, Peribsen, Khasekhem/Khasekhemwy.

The Old Kingdom, 2686–2181

Third Dynasty, 2686–2613

Sanakhte, Djoser Netjerykhet, (Djoserti ?), Sekhemkhet, Khaba, (Qahedjet), Huni.

Fourth Dynasty, 2613–2494

Sneferu, Khnum-Khufu, Djedefre, Khafre (Bakare, Baufre), Menkaure, Shepseskhaf.

Fifth Dynasty, 2494–2345

Userkaf, Sahure, Neferirkare, Shepseskare Isi, Neferefre, Niuserre, Menkauhor Akauhor, Djedkare Isesi, Unas.

Sixth Dynasty, 2345–2181

Teti, Userkare, Pepy I, Merenre, Pepy II, Merenre II, Nitiqret.

The First Intermediate Period, 2181–2055

Seventh and Eighth Dynasties, 2181–2125

Numerous transitory kings, including Demedjibtawy, Hekare Abi.

Ninth and Tenth Dynasties, 2160–2025

Meryibre Akhtoy I, Nebkaure Akhtoy II, Wahkare Akhtoy III, Merikare, Neferkare.

Eleventh Dynasty (Thebes) 2125–2055

(Montuhotep I – 'Tepya'a'), Inyotef I, Inyotef II, Inyotef III.

The Middle Kingdom, 2055–1650

Eleventh Dynasty (all Egypt) 2055–1985

Nebhepetre Montuhotep II, Sa'ankhkare Montuhotep III, Montuhotep IV.

Twelfth Dynasty, 1985–1795

Amenemhet I, Senwosret I, Amenemhet II, Senwosret II, Senwosret III, Amenemhet III, Amenemhet IV, Sobekneferu.

Thirteenth Dynasty, 1795–post-1650

Many kings, frequently ephemeral, including Wegaf, Amenemhet V, Sobekhotep I, Sobekhotep II, Awibre Hor, Userkare Khendjer, Semenkhare Mermentifu,

Ibiya, Sobekemsaf I, Sobekhotep III, Neferhotep I, Sobekhotep IV, Merneferre Iy, Wepwawetemsaf, Djednefere Dudimose.

Fourteenth Dynasty, 1750–1650

'Seventy-six kings of Xois'.

The Second Intermediate Period, 1650–1550

The Hyksos period, when several dynasties ruled parts of Egypt contemporaneously.

Fifteenth Dynasty, 1650–1550

Salitis, Yaqub-Hor, Khayan, Apepi I, Apepi II.

Sixteenth Dynasty, 1650–1550

Seventeenth Dynasty, 1650–1550

Rahotep, Sekemre Wahkhau, Inyotef VI, Djehuty, Montuhotep VII, Sobekemsaf II, Sawadjenre Nebiryerawet, Userenre, Inyotef VII, Senakhtenre Tao I, Seqenenre Tao II, Kamose.

The New Kingdom, 1550–1069

Eighteenth Dynasty, 1550–1295

Ahmose, Amenhotep I, Thutmose I, Thutmose II, Thutmose III, Hatshepsut, Amenhotep II, Thutmose IV, Amenhotep III, Amenhotep IV-Akhenaten, Smenkhkare, Tutankhamun, Ay, Horemheb.

Nineteenth Dynasty, 1295–1186

Ramesses I, Seti I, Ramesses II, Merenptah, Amenmesse, Seti II, Siptah, Twosret.

Twentieth Dynasty, 1186–1069

Sethnakhte, Ramesses III, Ramesses IV, Ramesses V, Ramesses VI, Ramesses VII, Ramesses VIII, Ramesses IX, Ramesses X, Ramesses XI.

The Third Intermediate Period, 1069–747

Twenty-First Dynasty, 1069–945

Smendes, Amenemnisu, Pseusennes I, Amenemope, Osorkon I, Siamun, Pseusennes II.

Twenty-Second Dynasty, 945–715

Sheshonq I, Osorkon I, Sheshonq II, Takelot I, Osorkon II, Takelot II, Sheshonq III, Pimay, Osorkon IV.

Twenty-Third Dynasty, 818–715

Pedubastis, Sheshonq IV, Osorkon III, Takelot III, Rudamun, Iuput II, Peftjauawybast, Nimlot.

Twenty-Fourth Dynasty, 727–715

Tefnakhte, Bakenrenef.

The Late Period, 747–332

Twenty-Fifth Dynasty, 747–656

(Alara), (Kashta), Piankhy-Piye, Shabaka, Shabataka, Taharqa, Tanutamani.

Twenty-Sixth Dynasty, 664–525

(Necho I), Psametik I, Necho II, Psametik II, Apries, Ahmose II (Amasis), Psametik III.

Twenty-Seventh Dynasty (First Persian) 525–404

Cambyses, Darius I, Xerxes I, Artaxerxes I, Darius II, Artaxerxes II.

Twenty-Eighth Dynasty, 404–399

Amyrtaeus.

Twenty-Ninth Dynasty, 399–380

Nefaarud, Hakor.

Thirtieth Dynasty, 380–343

Nakhtnebef (Nectanebo I), Teos, Nakhthoreb (Nectanebo II).

Second Persian Period, 343–332

Artaxerxes III Ochos, Arses, Darius III Codoman, Khababash.

The Macedonian Dynasty, 332–305

Alexander III 'The Great', Philip Arrhidaeus, Alexander IV.

The Ptolemaic Period, 305–30

Ptolemaic Dynasty, 305–30

Ptolemy I Soter, Ptolemy II Philadelphus, Ptolemy III Euergetes, Ptolemy IV Philopator, Horwennefer (pretender), Ptolemy V Epiphanes, Ptolemy VI Philometor, Ptolemy VII Neos Philopator, Ptolemy VIII Euergetes II, Ptolemy IX Soter II, Ptolemy X Alexander I, Ptolemy IX Soter II (restored), Ptolemy XI Alexander II, Ptolemy XII Neos Dionysos Auletes, Cleopatra VII Philopator, Ptolemy XIII, Ptolemy XIV, Ptolemy XV (Caesarion).

The Roman Period, 30 BC–395 AD

Augustus, Hadrian.

Rank, title and office in Ancient Egypt

Egypt was an intensely hierarchic society, its social structure determined absolutely by the relationship of every part and every individual to the person of the king. It is a truism to compare the nature and form of Egyptian society by analogy with the pyramid; it was, nonetheless, unshakeably pyramidial, its apex occupied by the king in god-like isolation.

In theory at least, Egypt was a completely centrally directed society, law being determined by the will of the king and discharged on the basis of his word. In practice, complex and diffuse bureaucracies developed from the earliest times to manage the various departments of a society whose increasing sophistication demanded it. The bureaucracies were distinct in their functions and responsibilities, but all were interrelated through their dependence on the will of the king, to serve which was their reason for existence. Discrete organisations evolved which served the king directly, caring for his person and the immediate concerns of his family, state, prerogatives and fortune, for the government of the Two Kingdoms into which Egypt was notionally divided, for the worship of the gods and the management of their temples and estates, and for the army and the defence of Egypt's territorial integrity.

For the people of Ancient Egypt, from the king to the humblest peasant working in the fields or on the river's banks, the development of the central control of all departments of state made, on the one hand, for a stable and secure society and, on the other, for the eventual recognition of the individual's place in society and hence in the world-system of which Egypt was the embodiment. This concern for order is one of the distinguishing marks of Egyptian civilisation, and one of the factors which explain its unique survival.

That the sense of order (and organisation) which the existence of these control systems postulates is fundamental to the entire ethos of Egypt is evident from the fact that a bureaucracy of sorts existed *before* the presumed date of the commencement of the First Dynasty. Many of the great offices which recur throughout Egyptian history are in place in the reigns of the first kings who claimed to rule the whole Valley; it is now generally accepted that the kingship existed in the late Predynastic Period, and obviously the kings of that obscure time had at their disposal courtiers who carried out various of the functions later associated with the management of the notionally unified state and of the king's affairs.

Many of the most important offices in the state are notable for the vivid nature of their terminology. This was the case during the long history of Egypt, and it is also evident in the very early years of the Dual Kingship, after the establishment of the First Dynasty. This characteristic of the naming of offices suggests that they had a long history, before the invention of writing in the late fourth millennium made it possible to perpetuate them by some process other than custom and repetition.

Two of the most ancient titles in the Egyptian usage are rendered in English as 'Hereditary Prince' and 'Count'. These titles were awarded particularly to senior officials working in the provinces; the style 'prince' especially seems to have been attributed to favoured recipients with some generosity. The sons of kings were also styled 'prince', but despite the importance which women were frequently accorded, there was no special title which was equivalent to 'queen'. The chief wife of the king was described as 'She who sees Horus and Seth' and 'She who Unites the Two Lords'. Both of these titles obviously refer to the union of the disparate interests in the state, represented by the two ancient gods, perpetually at odds but perpetually united, who stood for the rule of the king on the one hand and on the other, the discord and chaos promised by the forces of disunity.

It was inevitable, given the nature of the Egyptian state, that the first individuals whose names are known, other than the kings themselves, should be the officials and courtiers most closely associated with them. Thus we find 'The Controller of the Two Thrones' and 'He who is at the Head of the King'. 'The Master of the Secrets of the Royal Decrees' was possibly the forerunner of the great official of later times in Egypt's history – certainly from the Old Kingdom onwards – who is given the name 'Vizier' in contemporary language. Another title, redolent of the mystery and intrigue of courts the world over, was 'He of the Curtain', one presumably who listens unseen to the king's audiences with others. Sometimes, He of the Curtain was also a judge.

Rank was always important to the Egyptians, and it was principally determined by the proximity of the subject to the king. 'Companion', even 'Sole Companion', were honorifics which were awarded to the king's associates, drawn from the members of his family and from the favoured courtiers who attended him. The variety and complexity of the titles which high Egyptian officials bore are comparable only to those employed, in much later times, in the Chinese and Byzantine empires. But Egypt, in this as in so much else, was undoubtedly the first to give them such importance, and those who created its royal and state administrations required no advice on their manipulation from those cultures which succeeded them. Even in the earliest times the various offices which made up the Two Lands' administration and the titles which were attached to those who exercised them, have a baroque quality which reveals that they had a long history before they were first written down.

An interesting feature of the early Egyptian system of identifying the élite of the society, those who stood close to the king and who discharged their duties as officials and courtiers directly under his glance, were known as 'Seal-Bearers'.

This term rapidly came to mean that anyone thus distinguished was noble, of the highest rank outside the immediate royal family.

The significance of the adoption of the seals by the emerging state to mark out its leading personalities around the king, arises from the fact that the earliest seals in Egypt, used for the identification of documents or recording the ownership of goods or products, are cylinder seals, that is to say they are tubular in shape and impress a continuous design when they are rolled out, for example, on clay. Such seals have their origin in Western Asia, specifically in southern Mesopotamia, where they appear in the latter part of the fourth millennium, that enigmatic time when so many innovations appear all over the ancient Near East and when Egypt seems to have absorbed influences from the East into its culture, by a process which is still unclear. It does, however, suggest that the original bearers of seals impressed the people of the Valley to the extent that the earliest kings accepted the seal as a mark of the highest status in the society.

As time went by, into the latter part of the First Dynasty, the great offices became more specific and more directly departmental. Thus the office rendered as 'Chamberlain' was responsible for all public functions undertaken by the king and for the management of his affairs. The 'Chancellor' attested from the early First Dynasty directed all the concerns of government with Egypt's wealth, the collection of taxes and the control of the Treasuries of the Two Lands. Theoretically, and sometimes in fact, there were two treasuries, one for each of the kingdoms, known as 'The White House' and 'The Red House', for Upper and Lower Egypt respectively; each had its dependent bureaucracy under officials who reported to the Chancellor, who in turn reported to the Vizier.

The Chancellor was responsible for the supervision of the 'Granaries of the Two Lands', an ancient institution which emphasises Egypt's essentially agrarian nature, its people dependent upon the product of the river's flood and the patient cultivation of the land. 'The Master of Largesse' was the official who distributed produce to the people in times of hardship and who rewarded, with collars of gold, for example, those whom the king wished to honour.

The Old Kingdom was the time of the most luscious flowering of the Egyptian enthusiasm for hierarchy and the minute differentiation of official duties. The king's closest adjutants provided the members of a body translated as 'Privy Council', the supreme advisory forum whose opinion the king could enlist when proceeding towards a decision which, theoretically at least, only he could make. The Privy Council was the distillation of the most powerful men in the Kingdoms, those who stood at the head of the various departments of state. The Privy Council was the medium through which all royal decrees were promulgated, hence its members were at the very heart of Egypt's government.

As the years went by, inevitably the character of some of the great offices changed. Those which had been identified particularly with the personal service of the king, began to assume a wider importance in the bureaucracy of the state as a whole, though still of course identified, as were all the country's officers, with the king. Thus the Royal Butler, an appointment which by its nature brought the official which held it in a close and trusting relationship with the king, was often entrusted with sensitive or delicate missions, particularly concerned with foreign rulers. Likewise the Royal or First Herald assumed responsibilities much wider than the title might be thought to imply. The Herald accompanied the king in war but he also acted as his mouthpiece, relaying decisions to the people and equally informing the king of the people's mood and their aspirations. He also played an important role in the organisation of the public ceremonies which were so dominant a feature in the daily life of the king and his closest associates. Later still, he was responsible for the direction of Egypt's relations with her neighbours.

Many of the senior officials in the government service were described as 'Overseers'. They were responsible for specific departments in the larger 'Ministries' under the control of one of the great officers. They would have charge of many lesser officials who carried out the complex business of the administration.

The most frequently encountered official category of Egyptian, in these pages as in Ancient Egypt itself, was that of scribe. The scribe was greatly respected and placed a commensurately high rating on his own importance. The scribes and their often extensive families made up the 'middle class' of Egypt in ancient times. All government officials were by definition scribes, but not all scribes were part of the government structure; some would be employed in the royal household, others in the households of the great provincial magnates, the nomarchs for example, whilst many others were engaged in the service of the temples. This last category of scribe might well be a priest, serving the god in a particular capacity and occupying a place in the intensely hierarchic gradings of temple personnel. These ranged from the High Priest, who presided over the entire concerns of the temple, which in some cases came in time to rival the power of the king himself; the Second, Third and Fourth Prophets, who were the senior clergy of the Temple; and to minor functionaries who, though their duties might be quite humble – cleaning the temple for example or ensuring that the god's clothes or daily rations were in order – nonetheless valued highly their employment in the temple, which provided an absolute security for life.

The scribe underwent a long and arduous education to fit him for his life's work; he may have begun by mastering the hieratic form of writing, a simplified system which enabled scribes to write at speed. Then he might move on to the hieroglyphs themselves, acquiring in the process a good scribal hand to transcribe them accurately and pleasingly. The scribe was trained to make careful notes of his superior's wishes and decisions and to minute them equally carefully; for this purpose the forms of rapid writing – originally hieratic and based directly on the hieroglyphs, and then in later times demotic, a still more simplified form of cursive script – would be employed. Many of the great officers of state and members of the royal family and the higher nobility were also literate and possessed scribal skills. In the case of the king's children and those of favoured nobles and officials they were educated in schools attached to the court, the *kap*, the 'nursery' in which they, together with the sons of foreign princes in later times, were trained for their eventual leading parts in Egypt's administration and that of its imperial possessions.

The army, and to a lesser degree the navy, also provided important career opportunities for young Egyptians. In the earlier periods the soldiery seems generally to have consisted of small bands of levies, often employing mercenaries, particularly from Nubia, who would be required from time to time to secure the frontiers. Similar bands would be in the employment of the nomarchs, who not infrequently praised themselves for the quality of the men they commanded, whose service was required in the dynastic and regional disturbances which periodically broke out.

The kings themselves were often great warriors; from the First Dynasty on they were portrayed fighting Egypt's enemies in an iconography which was retained throughout Egypt's history and which became a compelling act of propaganda, to remind subject or neighbouring peoples of the might of the king of Egypt and of the retribution which would be visited on anyone who ventured against his interests. Sekemkhet, Sneferu, Nebhepetre Montuhotep II, the kings of the Twelfth Dynasty, the princes of Thebes who drove out the Hyksos, Thutmose III, Amenhotep II, Horemheb and, supremely in terms of publicity even if it was not always wholly justified, Ramesses II – all were active in Egypt's wars. Under the king, the vizier was the Minister of War and directed the affairs of the army, especially in times of crisis. By the time of the New Kingdom, when Egypt was forced to recognise that it faced states beyond its frontiers which had pretensions to rival its power and authority, the army became a permanent feature of state administration; the basis of this development may be seen in the Middle Kingdom, when for the first time professional soldiers are known, the most senior of them recognised as important commanders.

General officers, including the 'Chief Commander of the Army', commanded divisions of the forces supported by adjutants who distributed their orders and ensured that they were carried out; often a king's son would occupy the post. 'Army Scribes' were responsible for recording the course of battles and for providing the administrative back-up to the forces in the field. Quartermasters provided the supplies, of food, fodder for the horses and equipment. The troops were organised into platoons of fifty men, with élite units undertaking much of the most challenging encounters with the enemy, keeping close to the king or the supreme commander; often these troops were mercenaries, and in this respect the Nubians were particularly highly valued as fighting soldiers. In times of peace the Nubians also provided much of the police force, the 'Medjay', a militia commanded often by their own officers and detachments of which were stationed in principal towns. The 'Chief of the Bowmen of Kush' was the title which denoted the commander of Egyptian forces in Nubia.

In the New Kingdom military ranks become a feature of the government system and of attendance on the king. Military activity had become more of a preoccupation in the state from the time of the Middle-Kingdom kings, and this trend increased as incursions of foreign interests into Egypt became a recurring problem. Other powers in the region began to threaten Egypt's security and the influence of professional warriors in the society grew in consequence.

With the introduction of the horse, in the middle of the second millennium, at the beginning of the Eighteenth Dynasty, warfare changed its character dramatically and the cavalry, and in particular the chariotry, became major arms of the Egyptian forces. The office of 'Master of the Horse' was established to control the recruitment, training, supply and command of the cavalry and chariotry; it was filled by a high-ranking courtier or member of the royal family. 'Charioteers' became notable figures and the king's charioteer in particular was highly honoured. 'Stablemasters' were responsible for the supervision of detachments of chariots and charioteers, though their military rank is sometimes unclear. The 'Chief Scribe of the Army' was responsible for recruiting, supply and the direction of records; the 'King's Scribe of Recruits' had control of the northern forts and coastal stations and thus was one of the officials responsible for ensuring the security of the Two Lands.

Throughout Egypt's history those who were entrusted with the building of the great temples, tombs and the monuments of the kings represented a very numerous, important and respected stratum of the society. The very highest officers in the state, the viziers and the king's closest relatives, were appointed as 'Chief of All the Works of the King'. Sometimes this was no doubt honorific, but more often it was a practical responsibility directed by men who were obviously highly trained and phenomenally skilful. Some of the greatest works in the history of civilised humankind come from their minds and hands; from Imhotep, the prototypical high executive with a creative energy reaching proportions of exceptional genius onwards, the architects and directors of public works produced what few would question were the richest contributions of Egypt's legacy to the world.

Even at a less exalted level, armies of builders, craftsmen, artists and specialists in every technical field crowd the multitude of Egypt's building sites. To be a member of one of the families in the towns which housed the builders of the temples and tombs was a sought-after status, jealously guarded. Many of these people, often classed as 'artisans' or 'workers', attained a high level of prosperity, as witnessed by their tombs, many of which were finely appointed.

The artists, sculptors, painters and scribes who prepared the glowing, resplendent papyri for royal or high official patrons, were often members of families which passed their skills from generation to generation. They were confident and proud men who, when the opportunity presented itself, left their names on their work, the first in the history of art to do so.

The base of the living pyramid which was Egyptian society, and on whom the entire structure stood, was provided by the *fellahin*, the peasants, farmers and fishermen who produced the wealth of Egypt. In the nature of the way the world has been managed, they are largely anonymous: as such, they do not appear here, but the history of Egypt's glorious centuries is very much their history, too.

Similarly, in the case of all of the officials, high and relatively low, they were supported by legions of lesser officials and assistants who discharged the detailed responsibilities of their offices. In an intensely centralised administration such as

Egypt developed from the earliest days of its existence as a nation state, the interlocking bureaucracies of government, royal household, provinicial administrations, temples and army were all united, at least in theory, in the person of the king, and were all directed towards the expression of his will and well-being. If the king flourished, Egypt flourished, and every official of whatever rank could find satisfaction in knowing that they played a part, however minor, in ensuring the life and prosperity of Egypt by their service.

Further reading

CAH I.2: 35–40.

Schulman, A. R. (n.d.) *Military Rank, Title and Organisation in the Egyptian New Kingdom*, Munich.

Strudwick, N. (1985) *The Administration of Egypt in the Old Kingdom*, London.

Ancient Egypt and Nubia

Showing the principal sites mentioned in the text

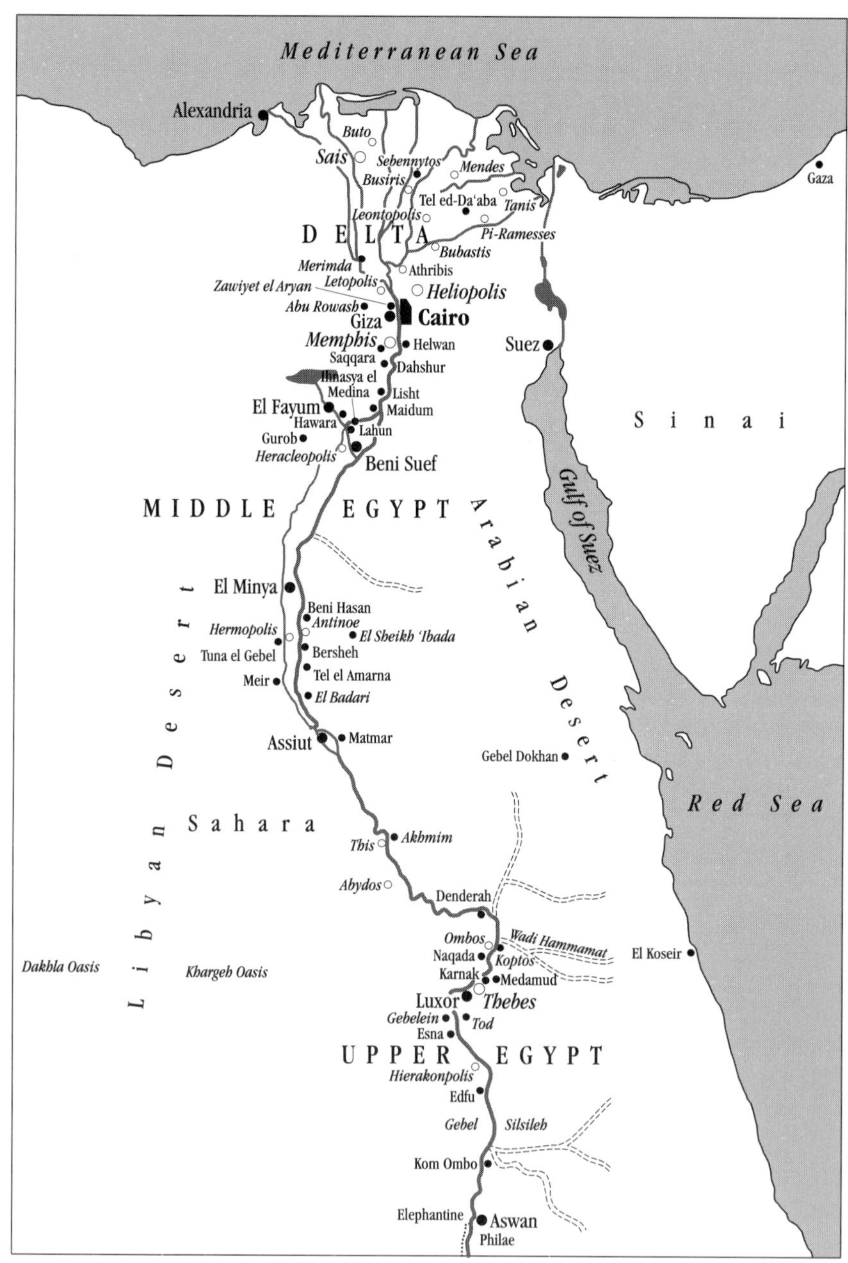

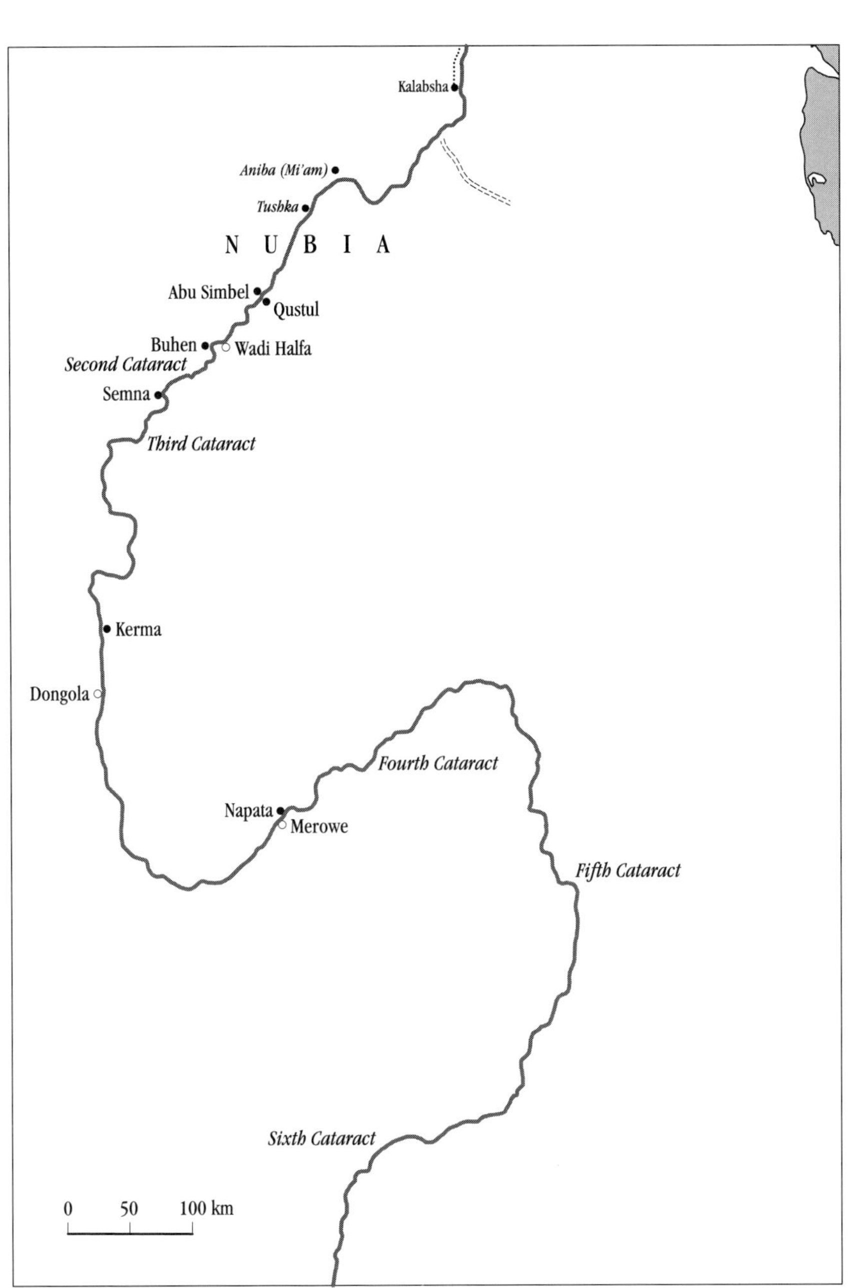

Kalabsha
Aniba (Mi'am)
Tushka
N U B I A
Abu Simbel
Qustul
Buhen
Wadi Halfa
Second Cataract
Semna
Third Cataract
Kerma
Dongola
Fourth Cataract
Napata
Merowe
Fifth Cataract
Sixth Cataract
0 50 100 km

Aakheperkare-senb, Scribe, Eighteenth Dynasty, New Kingdom, *c.* 1438 BC. The pyramids in Giza, Saqqara, Meidum and Abu Roash frequently attracted appreciative visitors during the reigns of the kings of later times. One such visitor was Aakheperkare-senb, the son of an important temple functionary, who left an inscription on the walls of the Meidum mortuary temple, ascribed to King SNEFERU of the Fourth Dynasty; Aakheperkare-senb's graffito is one of the reasons for the pyramid's attribution to the king.

Aakheperkare-senb was deeply impressed with what he saw. Giving the precise date of his visit ('the twelfth day of the fourth month of summer in the forty-first year of the reign of THUTMOSE III') he says that he found the pyramid 'as though heaven were within it and the sun rising in it'. He prays that the heavens may rain with myrrh and drip with incense upon its roof.

Fakhry 1961: 67–8.
Edwards 1985: 81.

Aba (alt. Ibi), Scribe, Twentieth Dynasty, date not known. A Scribe of horses during the Ramessid period, Aba was buried in an exceptionally large and palatial tomb in the Theban necropolis (TT 351).

PM I.1: 417.

Aba, Official, Twenty-Sixth Dynasty, Late Period, *c.* 664–610 BC. Aba was a high official, the steward of the God's Wife of AMUN in Thebes, NITIQRET. He came from the north and was a contemporary of King PSAMETIK I. He was buried in the Theban necropolis (TT 36).

PM I: 69.
Kitchen 1986: §353.

Abdi Kheba, Palestinian King, Eighteenth Dynasty, New Kingdom, *c.* 1352–1336 BC. The religious and aesthetic preoccupations of King AMENHOTEP IV-AKHENATEN, after his removal to the city of Akhetaten, encouraged many of the states beyond the northern frontiers, which were subject to Egyptian suzerainty, to rebel. The process of the disintegration of Egyptian authority was rapid and a number of Egypt's client rulers found themselves in a parlous situation. Some remained loyal, however, amongst whom was Abdi Kheba, the King of Jerusalem, who appealed to the Egyptian king for a modest contingent of troops, fifty men, to help him hold the land. Akhenaten ignored his pleas, as it appears he ignored the others which were directed to him.

Aldred 1988: 283.
W. L. Moran, *The Amarna Letters*, Baltimore, 1992.

Achoris, *see* **Hakor**

Agatharchides, Geographer and Historian, Ptolemaic Period, second century BC. Born in Cnidus, Agatharchides spent his career in Alexandria, at the court of PTOLEMY VI. He wrote a study of the successors of Alexander which was well received. He also produced a description of the Red Sea, in five books. His works are lost but DIODORUS SICULUS quotes a description of labourers washing out gold from crushed quartz.

Diodorus Bibliotheke III: 12–14. Loeb 1933–67.
Thompson, *Ancient Geography*.
S. M. Burstein, *Agatharchides of Cnidus: On the Enythrean Sea*, London, 1989.
P. M. Fraser, *Ptolemaic Alexandria*, 3 vols, Oxford, 1992.

Aha (alt. Hor-Aha), King, First Dynasty, Archaic Period, *c.* 3150 BC. Probably the first king of Egypt, Aha was the son or successor of NAR-MER. His mother may have been Queen NEITHHOTEP; alternatively she has been described as his wife. Aha is also most likely to be identified with MENES, the reputed unifier of the Two Lands.

According to MANETHO, Aha reigned for sixty-four years, presumably coming to the throne as a very young man. He was said to have died as the result of injuries sustained in a hippopotamus hunt, a story which is as likely as not, myth.

To Aha were ascribed many of the most important early achievements of the emergent monarchy. He is credited with campaigns in the north and south of the Valley, to bring about the Unification of the Two Lands. He also is said to have established temples to the gods of Egypt, thus inaugurating a practice which was one of the glories of the kingship over the next 3,000 years.

Aha is commemorated especially by what are customarily called 'labels', ivory plaques which appear to record outstanding events in the reigns of the early kings. One, the 'Abydos label', records the king's name, which is displayed in the formal surround of the *serekh*, the foundation of a temple to the goddess Neith, a shrine, the capture of a wild bull and a representation of boats sailing past towns on the banks of the Nile. Another seems to link Aha with Menes. He was the first Egyptian king to use the *nebty* name, honouring 'The Two Ladies' (the goddesses of Upper and Lower Egypt respectively) in his titulary: in his case the chosen name appears to have been *Men*.

During Aha's reign, architecture begins to be of a notable quality; in addition to the temples which he is said to have built, there is evidence of substantial funerary monuments, of a size and character markedly different from those of the preceding, late Predynastic period. The place of Aha's own burial at Abydos is really the first monumental funerary complex in the history of Egypt. A number of young people, presumably the king's retainers and servants and none of them above the age of twenty-five, were buried with him, to attend him in the afterlife. This custom was widespread during the First Dynasty.

The tomb of Aha's presumed mother (or wife), Neithhotep, also at Abydos, is a large and elaborate structure, which the king may himself have built for her. A remarkable tomb (3503) at Saqqara, probably the resting place of one of Aha's great ministers, has a model estate built inside it, showing granaries and other buildings of the sort which would have been in use in the king's time.

Emery 1954: 171; pls LVII–LXVI.
B. J. Kemp, 'The Egyptian First Dynasty Royal Cemetery', *Antiquity*, 41 (1967) 22–32.
Spencer: 63–5, pls 56–7.
B. Adams and K. M. Ciałowicz, *Protodynastic Egypt*, Princes Risborough, 1997: 63, fig. 44c.

Ahanakht, Nomarch, Ninth/Tenth Dynasties, First Intermediate Period, *c.* 2160–2025 BC. The nomarch of Hermopolis, during the reign of King

NEFERKARE, Ahanakht bore the title 'Overseer of the Western Desert'.

Kees 1961: 130.

Aha-nakht, Veterinarian, Twelfth Dynasty, Middle Kingdom, *c.* 1985–1795 BC. The veterinarian Aha-nakht's name appears amongst graffiti, identifying a number of medical practitioners of various disciplines working in the quarries at Hatnub. He was a *w'ab* priest of Sekhmet and is depicted in company with a more important physician, Hesy-shef-nakht. He is described as 'one who knows bulls'.

Nunn: 128–9.

Ahhotep I, Queen, Seventeenth and Early Eighteenth Dynasties, *c.* 1590–*c.* 1530 BC. The wife of SEQENENRE TAO II, who died in the campaigns waged to expel the Hyksos from Egypt, Ahhotep was one of the several powerful and determined women who exercised considerable influence in the New Kingdom, especially in the Eighteenth Dynasty, of which she was long revered as the ancestress. On Seqenenre Tao's death his son KAMOSE succeeded; it is not known for certain if he was the child of Ahhotep. Although Kamose was instrumental in carrying on the war against the Hykos after Seqenenre Tao's death, he did not long survive his father. After his death, Seqenenre Tao's son by Ahhotep, AHMOSE, was proclaimed king. He was too young to undertake the full responsibilities of the kingship and his mother acted as regent until he was sixteen. Ahhotep probably died in the early years of her son's reign; she was rewarded with divine honours and a long-surviving cult was established in her memory. Her son raised a stele in her honour at Karnak, praising her part in the expulsion of the Hyksos and describing her as 'one who pacified Upper Egypt and expelled her rebels'.

Ahhotep II was possibly the wife of King KAMOSE.

Urk. IV 21, 16.
A. Macy Roth, 'Ahhotep I and Ahhotep II', *Serapis* (1977–8) 31–40.
Saleh and Sourouzian: 118–26.
EMC.

Ahmose, King, Eighteenth Dynasty, New Kingdom, *c.* 1550–1525 BC. Ahmose was the first king of the Eighteenth Dynasty, hence the progenitor of a family which was to rule Egypt for more than two centuries and the founder of the New Kingdom which was to survive for half a millennium. He was the son of SEQENENRE TAO II and AHHOTEP, one of the formidable queens who frequently appear in the New Kingdom. When Ahmose succeeded, after the death of his elder brother KAMOSE, he was probably some ten years old and his mother was regent until he assumed his full powers, when he was about sixteen. He set about the expulsion of the Hyksos, who ruled the northern part of Egypt as the Fifteenth and Sixteenth Dynasties, which he achieved in the sixteenth year of his reign. The reign of Ahmose marked a return to the building of royal and temple monuments on a substantial scale. The quality of the craftsmanship is generally high, a characteristic which was to persist throughout the New Kingdom, even if the surviving works do not always match the best of the works of the Old and Middle Kingdoms. Egypt also resumed her contact with the world outside the Valley, a process which had been somewhat interrupted during the Hyksos period, and trade was maintained with Crete, Byblos and Nubia; lapis lazuli, from distant sources in Asia, began to reach Egypt once again.

Ahmose was honoured with a cult in his name throughout the Eighteenth Dynasty, a distinction he shared with his mother, Ahhotep. The oldest known royal *shabti* is ascribed to him. He is estimated to have been around thirty-five years old when he died.

Grimal: 193–202.
Shaw and Nicholson 1995: 18.
BM EA 32191.

Ahmose, Army Officer, Eighteenth Dynasty, New Kingdom, *c.* 1540BC. Ahmose was a native of Elkab in Upper Egypt and, like his father, Baba, was a soldier; Baba indeed served under the King SEQENENRE TAO II in the early campaigns against the Hyksos invaders. His mother, whose name is frequently joined to his, was Abana. Ahmose seems to have spent most of his career serving in the king's fleet; he left a detailed account of the fighting, on land and on the Nile, from a ship called *Appearing in Memphis*, led by the young king whose namesake he was. He fought at Avaris in the Delta, a stronghold of the Hyksos; he was present at the long seige of Sharuhen in Palestine, the capture of which effectively ended the Hyksos presence in Egypt. Twice he was awarded 'Gold of Valour' and was given numerous slaves by the king, captives secured in the battles in which he fought. He also served with Ahmose in putting down a rebellion amongst the people of Nubia in the south. Ahmose acquired two young warriors as slaves from this campaign and a gift of land.

Ahmose left the account of his exploits and the valiant and resourceful actions of his king in his tomb at his birthplace. His life spanned the reigns of Seqenenre Tao and King THUTMOSE I; he must have been a great age when he died when, as he said 'I rest in the tomb which I have made'.

V. Loret, *L'Inscription d'Ahmés, Fils d'Abana*, B d'E, Cairo.
Lichtheim 2: 12–13.

Ahmose-Meritamun, Queen, Eighteenth Dynasty, New Kingdom, *c.* 1525–1504 BC. Ahmose-Meritamun was married to her brother, King AMENHOTEP I, the second king of the dynasty which inaugurated the New Kingdom. Only one son appears to have been born of their marriage, who died in infancy.

James and Davies: 34–5; ill. 41.
Tyldesley: 60–2.
BM 93.

Ahmose Nefertiry, Queen, Eighteenth Dynasty, New Kingdom, *c.* 1570–1505 BC. Ahmose Nefertiry was one of the three exceptional women who so greatly contributed to the creation of the long-lasting imperial phase of Egyptian history, the New Kingdom. She was probably the daughter of KAMOSE, the king who did much to effect the expulsion of the Hyksos from Egypt, a task which was completed by his brother AHMOSE, to whom Ahmose Nefertiry was married.

The queen was closely associated with her husband in the work of rebuilding and consolidating the state which he undertook after the defeat of the Hyksos. It is clear from the many inscriptions which record their endeavours that Ahmose Nefertiry carried great authority during her lifetime.

Ahmose Nefertiry was the first royal lady to be given the title 'God's Wife of Amun', an office which was to become of great political significance in the south of Egypt, from Amun's principal shrine at Thebes. A number of queens and princesses followed Ahmose Nefertiry in the appointment, which in later times was to be identified with that of 'Divine Adoratrice'.

The queen was the mother of AMENHOTEP I into whose reign she survived. On her death she was accorded exceptional honours, eventually sharing a mortuary temple and perhaps a tomb with him. Her cult was long established and attracted particular devotion in the Theban necropolis, especially amongst the artisans who worked there. She is frequently depicted with her son, receiving the worship of devotees, in later ages.

It appears that Amenhotep I had no direct heir. He was succeeded by THUTMOSE I, whose claim to the throne was by right of his marriage to a daughter of Ahmose and Ahmose Nefertiry, who thus was responsible for the continuation of the line which the family had established.

M. Gitton, *Les Divines Epouses de la 18e Dynastie*, Paris, 1984.
Robins 1993: 43–5.

Ahmose-Pennekheb, Soldier, Eighteenth Dynasty, New Kingdom, *c.* 1550–1525 BC. Ahmose-Pennekheb served in the army of King AHMOSE, who finally drove out the Hyksos invaders from the north. He campaigned with the king in Palestine and Syria.

He may have been present at the fall of Avaris, the Hyksos capital, which was captured only after a prolonged seige.

Ahmose-Pennekheb was a contemporary of AHMOSE, son of Abana, and came from the same town as his near-namesake; he was also buried at Elkab. He was evidently long-lived; he died during the reign of Queen HATSHEPSUT, to whose daughter, Princess NEFERURE he was a tutor.

Breasted 2: §§17–25, §344.
CAH II.1: 295.
Grimal: 202.

Akhenaten (Amenhotep IV), King, Eighteenth Dynasty, *c.* 1352–1336 BC. The son of the magnificent AMENHOTEP III, Akhenaten was crowned as Amenhotep IV but in his fifth regnal year he proclaimed the supremacy of the Aten above all the other gods of Egypt (though he retained his own divinity), moved the capital to a new site, Akhetaten (now Tell El-Amarna) and assumed the name Akhenaten. His adoption of Atenism was not entirely unprecedented; in his father's reign the Aten was becoming significant and his mother, the redoubtable Queen TIY, was possibly an enthusiast for the reformed religion. Akhenaten's chief claim to significance – and some respect – in the history of Egypt resides in his influence on the country's art. Under his apparently direct guidance his sculptors, painters, architects and craftsmen produced a wholly new and, some would say fresh, approach to the creation of the stream of works which are associated with his reign and its aftermath (the 'Amarna Style'). One effect of the new approach to art was in the extreme, sometimes bizarre, informality of representations of the royal family, especially in the early years.

Akhenaten's own portraits are amongst the most remarkable ever produced by an ancient society. It is difficult to resist the impression that they indicate a considerable degree of neurosis prevailing in the circles around the king.

Akhenaten used to be described as a 'monotheist'. This is hardly the case and the term is less frequently applied today; however, some commentators have seen him as influencing the idea of the one god which, long after his lifetime, became identified with beliefs enshrined in the early books of the Old Testament. Whatever may have been Akhenaten's merits as a religious thinker, he was a disastrous politician. His evident neglect of Egypt's foreign relations and his apparent lack of support for her allies produced a parlous situation in the Eastern Mediterranean which only the general HOREMHEB, who eventually became king, and the early monarchs of the Nineteenth Dynasty, set to rights.

Akhenaten is remembered for his marriage to the spectacularly beautiful NEFERTITI, by whom he had six daughters, one of whom, Ankhesenpa'aten (later ANKHESENAMUN), was married to TUTANKHAMUN. There seems to have been a rift between the king and queen, however, and there has been some speculation about the nature of Akhenaten's relationship with his eventual but brief successor, SMENKHKARE.

The circumstances of Akhenaten's departure from the kingship and his death are unknown. The last recorded year of his reign is the seventeenth. He had a tomb prepared at Akhetaten and he, his mother Queen Tiy and at least one of his daughters, Meketaten, were buried there. It is possible however that King Tutankhamun, who succeeded him, had his mummy moved to Thebes and placed in a tomb in the Valley of the Kings, KV55. Akhenaten's memory was execrated by the priests of Amun when their orthodoxy was restored under Tutankhamun and, wherever they could effect it, his monuments were destroyed.

A. Aldred and A. T. Sandison, 'The Pharaoh Akhenaton: A Problem in Egyptology and Pathology', *Bull. Hist. Med.*, 36 (1961) 193–316.
Terrace and Fischer 26: 121–4.
Redford 1984.
Martin 1974–89.
Aldred 1988.
Reeves and Wilkinson: 116–21.

Akhpet, Scribe, Nineteenth Dynasty, New Kingdom, *c.* 1290 BC. Akhpet was Chief of the Embalmers of the Lord of the Two Lands at the beginning of the Nineteenth Dynasty; he was also named 'Truthful Scribe of the King who Loves Him'.

He was buried at Saqqara in a tomb which was built just beyond the mortuary temple of King TETI, the first king of the Sixth Dynasty. Akhpet's tomb was decorated with very fine reliefs and he was placed in a large pink anthropoid sarcophagus.

Comptes Rendu de l'Académie des Inscriptions et Belles-Lettres, Paris 1966: 467–8.
J. Leclant, *Bulletin de la Société Française de l'Égyptologie*, Paris, July 1966, 46, pls IIIa, IIIb.

Akhtoy I (alt. Khety), King, Ninth Dynasty, First Intermediate Period, *c.* 2160–2130 BC. Akhtoy was the governor of the Twentieth nome of Upper Egypt, centred on Heracleopolis (Egyptian Heneneswe, modern Ihnasya el-Medina) and he seized the throne in the period of anarchy which overcame Egypt after the end of the Old Kingdom. In the process he laid the foundations of the Ninth and Tenth Dynasties which are associated with Heracleopolis. Akhtoy took the throne name Meryibre; he set about imposing his will and some degree of order on the nomarchs, who had assumed virtually an independent status in the last years of the Old Kingdom. It was perhaps due to their influence that in later times his memory was reviled and he was branded as cruel and evil. He seems to have been acknowledged as king over most of Egypt, however, and the kings of his line undoubtedly regarded themselves as the legitimate successors of the Sixth Dynasty rulers.

After Akhtoy, kings came and went with some rapidity, seventeen of them reigning in about 120 years. However, the time when Heracleopolis was the capital of Egypt was by no means a sterile period in the country's history (literature particularly seems to have flourished) and although they were to be overthrown by a Theban dynasty, which ushered in the majestic achievements of the Middle Kingdom, Akhtoy's foundation of the Heracleopolitan kingdom provided some continuity between the coming age and the admittedly exhausted grandeur of the Old Kingdom.

According to MANETHO, Akhtoy went mad and was killed by a crocodile.

Waddell 1948: 61, 63.
CAH I.2: 464.
Hayes 1953: 143–4.
Grimal: 140–1.

Akhtoy II Nebkaure, King, Ninth Dynasty, First Intermediate Period, *c.* 2160–2130 BC. The fourth ruler of the Heracleopolitan line, Akhtoy II Nebkaure is probably the king remembered by the popular story of the Eloquent Peasant, a folk-tale which recounts the experiences of a peasant who, defrauded of his rights by a wealthy landowner, has justice done to his claim by the king's minister who enjoys hearing him present his case and in consequence requires him to retell it frequently, before presenting him to the king, who rewards him appropriately. The story of the Eloquent Peasant achieved great currency throughout Egyptian history and was a favourite text in the schools.

A. H. Gardiner, 'The Eloquent Peasant', JEA 9 (1923) 5–25.
CAH I.2: 464–5.

(Wahkare) Akhtoy III (alt. Khety III), King, Tenth Dynasty, First Intermediate Period, *c.* 2075 BC. Wahkare Akhtoy III was a long-reigning king at a time of unease and discontent in Egypt. He seems to have dealt with the Asiatics who were infiltrating the Delta and settled new colonies of Egyptians in the north-east of the country. The south continued to be troublesome also; with his ally TEFIBI, Akhtoy laid waste the ancient site of This and, mistakenly as he admitted, permitted his troops to plunder the tombs of the ancestors.

The engagement is recorded in the autobiography of ANKHTIFY in his tomb at Mo'alla.

He is credited as the author of the 'Instructions' to his son and successor MERIKARE, which are amongst the most celebrated and frequently reproduced of the literary works of the Heracleopolitan period.

CAH I.2: 466–7, 533–5.
Lichtheim 1: 97–109.
Grimal: 139, 141–7.

Akhtoy I, Nomarch, Tenth Dynasty, First Intermediate Period, 2160–2025 BC. The ruler of the nome whose capital was at Asiut, Akhtoy I was an assiduous conserver of his nome's resources, clearing and improving the canals and considerably extending the area of cultivable land. In the years of a low Nile, which could mean great hardship for the peasantry, he closed his nome's borders and distributed grain which he had stockpiled against such a calamity, to the consequent advantage of his people. He was evidently a formidable warrior and resolute in his support of the Heracleopolitan kings. He had been educated with the king's own children (he says that he learned to swim with the princes) and had been nominated as nomarch by the king himself. On his death was mourned by his people and the king alike. He was succeeded by his son, TEFIBI.

CAH I.2: 468–9.
Grimal: 144.

Akhtoy II, Nomarch, Tenth Dynasty, First Intermediate Period, *c.* 2160–2025 BC. When this Akhtoy II succeeded as Prince of the nome centred on Asiut his installation was attended by the king himself, MERIKARE, the successor of King Wahkare AKHTOY III, who sailed upriver attended by a large concourse of officials and courtiers.

Akhtoy of Asiut was the son of the nomarch TEFIBI, who ruled his nome with considerable success, despite the troubled times which Egypt was then experiencing.

CAH I.2: 467, 469.
Grimal: 144.

Akhtoy, Chancellor, Eleventh Dynasty, Middle Kingdom, *c.* 2055–2004 BC. The Chancellor of King NEBHEPETRE MONTUHOTEP, Akhtoy, son of Sitre, served his master diligently and long at the time when the king was reimposing royal rule over the Two Lands. He extended Egypt's control to Wawat (Lower Nubia). He travelled extensively in the south and was buried at Deir el-Bahri, near the king's own magnificent tomb.

CAH I.2: 480–3, 487.
Grimal: 157.

[Alara], King, Napatan Dynasty, Late Period, pre-*c.* 750 BC. Alara is the first known king of the Napatan dynasty which was ruling in Nubia from the late tenth or early ninth centuries BC. His brother was KASHTA, who was the father of the Kushite king who conquered Egypt, PIANKHY. It is possible that Alara had already conquered much of Lower Nubia, a process continued by Kashta and brought to a resounding and triumphant conclusion by Piankhy.

Kitchen 1986: 120–2, 320.
Grimal: 334–5.

Alexander III, surnamed 'The Great', 356–323 BC, King of Macedon. Great King of Persia and King of Upper and Lower Egypt: few men, if any, have had more written about them and few have remained more enigmatic than this son of PHILIP II of Macedon. During his extraordinary campaigns, directed principally against the power of the Persian Empire and his strange, almost dreamlike pursuit of DARIUS III, he advanced on Gaza after the victorious battle of Issos in the late summer of 332 BC. Egypt was surrendered to him without a battle by the Persian satrap, Mazaces. Alexander, perhaps influenced by the stories surrounding his birth, which suggested that his true father was the god Amun, set out on a journey to the god's oracle at Siwa. There he appears to have undergone some sort of mystical experience – to which he was in any case somewhat prone – which confirmed him in the belief that he was foreordained to assume the kingship of Egypt. He was greeted with acclamation by the Egyptians, who acknowledged him as their saviour, releasing them from the oppression of the Persians.

It was after his coronation at Memphis and his recognition as a god, the son of a god, that he began to lose touch with reality. He assumed the horns of Amun in numerous of his portraits, including the most widely distributed on the coinage of the successors to his empire. He undertook the proper functions of a king of Egypt, endowing temples at Karnak and Luxor, the evidence of which remains.

Returning to the Delta in 331 BC he gave instructions for the building of the Egyptian Alexandria; the city became the administrative centre of the country in the succeeding centuries and one of the most important trading and intellectual centres of the ancient world.

Alexander died in Babylon in June 323 BC. His mummified body, borne on a huge and richly appointed catafalque, was seized by PTOLEMY, one of his generals, who had determined to take control of Egypt. The body was taken to Memphis from where, in the reign of PTOLEMY II, it was transferred to Alexandria, to be installed in a splendid mausoleum.

W. W. Tarn, *Alexander the Great*, 2 vols, Cambridge, 1944.
Lane Fox 1973.

Alexander IV, King, Macedonian Dynasty, 317–310 BC. The son of ALEXANDER THE GREAT by his Bactrian wife Roxane, Alexander IV nominally succeeded the simple-minded PHILIP ARRHIDAEUS. He is shown as reigning as King of Egypt until 305 BC, when Ptolemy seized control of the Kingdom. In fact he was murdered in 311 BC, together with his mother.

Lane Fox 1973: 474.

Amasis (alt. Ahmose II), King, Twenty-Sixth Dynasty, Late Period, 570–526 BC. By reputation a rude and uncouth soldier, Amasis was proclaimed king by the soldiery serving under him. He was brought to power on a tide of intense nationalism which affected the nation after the misfortunes of his predecessor, APRIES. A state of civil war broke out between the Greek mercenaries employed by the king and the native Egyptians. From this Amasis emerged and, after the defeat of Apries at the battle of Memphis in 570 and his subsequent death, possibly at the hands of Amasis, assumed the full status of the kingship. Amasis was especially skilful in bringing the increasingly numerous groups of foreigners living in Egypt at this time under the state's control and into some sort of harmony with their neighbours. He developed the city of Naukratis in the Delta, which became one of the most important trading centres in the country, with a substantial Greek population, anticipating by more than two centuries the role of the Mediterranean coastal cities in the aftermath of ALEXANDER THE GREAT's conquest.

Despite having been remembered as a drunkard and buffoon, Amasis was a subtle and successful ruler, a fact to which the length of his reign testifies. He became the most powerful ruler in the Eastern Mediterranean, on good terms with the Greeks. He formed alliances with King Croesus of Lydia and with the equally ill-fated Policrates, the tyrant of Samos, to whom Amasis gave unavailing advice about not incurring the envy of the gods.

Amasis' death in 526 BC provided the Persians with the opportunity to invade Egypt, a course of action which they had long considered. The army of Amasis' successor, PSAMETIK III, was hopelessly defeated and Egypt became a province of the Persian Empire.

E. Edel, 'Amasis and Nebukadrezar II', GM 29 (1978) 13–70.
A. B. Lloyd, 'The Late Period', in Trigger *et al.* 1985: 285–6, 294.
Grimal: 363–4.

Amenaankhu, Painter, Twelfth Dynasty, Middle Kingdom, *c.* 1922–1855 BC. Amenaankhu was employed by DJEHUTYHOTEP, the splendid governor of the Hare nome, to decorate his tomb at El-Bersheh. The paintings which Amenaankhu produced for his patron are among the finest to survive from the Middle Kingdom. The design and decoration of the coffins of Djehutyhotep and his wife are also particularly fine and were probably the work of Amenaankhu.

P. E. Newberry, *El Bersheh, Pt. 1: The Tomb of Tehuti-Hotep*, London, 1896.
Terrace 1968.
——*The Entourage of an Egyptian Governor*, BMFAB 66 (1968) 5–27.

Amenemhat, Official, Thirteenth Dynasty, Middle Kingdom, *c.* 1786–1650 BC. Amenemhat's title, 'Overseer of the Storeroom of the Chamber of Fruits', does not sound especially elevated, particularly from a society which devised many complex and orotund dignities for its officers. Amenemhat honoured one Beb, described as a prince, and refers to Henu, who may have been Amenemhat's superior, on the funerary obelisk which he had prepared for himself. The adoption of an obelisk by a private person at this time was very unusual.

S. Birch, *Catalogue of the Collection of Egyptian Antiquities at Alnwick Castle*, London, 1880: 324–6, pl. vi.
Bourriau 1988: 66–7, no. 52.
Oriental Museum, University of Durham, no. 1984.

Amenemhat Nebuy, Temple Official, Twelfth Dynasty, Middle Kingdom, *c.* 1843–1787 BC. Amenemhat Nebuy ('Nebuy' was his given or family name, whilst Amenemhat was more formal) was Steward of the Temple Estates; his funerary stele was found at Abydos, where such evidences of piety were often deposited by Egyptians from all over the country. He is joined by his brother Sankh, the Overseer of Estate Workers, and other members of his family. Two of the servants pictured on the stele, who offer sustenance to the principals, are described as 'Asiatics', reflecting the incursions of people from Sinai and Syro-Palestine in the latter part of the Middle Kingdom.

Garstang, *El Arabah*, 33–4, pl. vi.
Bourriau 1988: 50, no. 39.
Fitzwilliam Museum E 207. 1900.

Amenemhe Sisete, Mayor, Thirteenth Dynasty, Middle Kingdom, *c.* 1725 BC. The 'Count, Overseer of Prophets', Amenemhe Sisete was the Mayor of Crocodilopolis

(Medinet el-Fayyum, ancient *Shedyet*), a member of a powerful family in the area. His father had been Mayor before him and his son inherited his office. He was the Overseer of the priests of the crocodile god Sobek, who was of considerable influence during the Thirteenth Dynasty.

Amenemhe lived during the reign of King NEFERHOTEP I.

Hodjash and Berlev 1982: no. 36, 81, 85.

Amenemheb, Army Officer and Oarsman, Eighteenth Dynasty, New Kingdom, *c.* 1479–1400 BC. The early kings of the Eighteenth Dynasty prided themselves on their prowess as sportsmen. AMENHOTEP II was an example; his ability as an archer was legendary and his reputation appears to be founded on truth. He specialised in particular in shooting from a fast moving chariot, no small feat.

Among his entourage was Amenemheb, who was a keen oarsman. On one occasion he was rowing in the king's barge when his energy attracted the king's notice. The king himself enjoyed the sport and was not above competing with Amenemheb. Prior to his service with Amenhotep II, Amenemheb had campaigned with the king's father, THUTMOSE III. During one of the Asiatic campaigns Amenemheb records that he went hunting with Thutmose; their quarry was elephant and it was claimed that one hundred and twenty of these noble beasts were killed. In one incident Amenemheb was said to have saved the king from injury or death by slashing off the trunk of an elephant which was attacking him. For this deed he was rewarded with gold.

Breasted 2: §§574–92; §§807–9.
CAH II.1: 336–7, 456.

Amenemhet I, King, Twelfth Dynasty, Middle Kingdom, *c.* 1985–1955 BC. Amenemhet was the founder of the Twelfth Dynasty. He had served the previous dynasty as Vizier; by a process which is unknown, he replaced MONTUHOTEP IV, the last king of the Eleventh Dynasty and was proclaimed King of the Two Lands.

He was a conscientious and able ruler and, like all great Egyptian kings, a dedicated builder. He reduced the already weakened power of the provincial nobles and instituted a tightly controlled central administration, which served his successors well. The dynasty which he founded was one of the most successful in Egyptian history and lasted for some two centuries. It is thought however that Amenemhet himself was assassinated in a harem conspiracy, having reigned for thirty years. He was succeeded by his son SENWOSRET I, to whom he was supposed to have given an oral testament from beyond the grave, 'The Instructions of Amenemhet I'. It is a deeply pessimistic document – perhaps unsurprisingly, in the circumstances of his extinction – but the same element of melancholy was to be evident in the portraits of some of Amenemhet's descendants.

Winlock 1947.
CAH I.2: 495–9.
Grimal: 158–61.

Amenemhet II, King, Twelfth Dynasty, Middle Kingdom, *c.* 1922–1878 BC. Amenemhet II reaped the benefit of the peace and prosperity of the reigns of his two predecessors, AMENEMHET I and SENWOSRET I, which had restored Egypt's position after the indecisive rule of the last kings of the Eleventh Dynasty and, by extending its influence to north and south, increased its wealth greatly.

Amenemhet encouraged trade and widening contact with Egypt's contemporaries. The 'Treasure of Tod', which is associated with the king, bears witness to the richness of the materials and the quality of the workmanship of objects produced for the benefit of the king and the court.

Winlock 1947.
F. Bisson de La Roque, G. Contenau and

F. Charpouthier, *Le Trésor de Tôd*, Cairo, 1953.
Grimal: 158–65.

Amenemhet III, King, Twelfth Dynasty, Middle Kingdom, *c.* 1855–1808 BC. Amenemhet succeeded his illustrious father SENWOSRET III, with whom he shared a period of co-regency, a procedure not uncommon in the family. In many respects their period as sovereigns marked the culmination of the Twelfth Dynasty's triumphant rule over Egypt. The country's international standing had seldom been higher, and Egypt enjoyed a degree of prosperity exceptional even for that prosperous land. His building projects were immense; one of these, his mortuary temple beside the pyramid which he built for himself at Hawara, was, according to STRABO, the origin of the legend of the Labyrinth.

Winlock 1947.
A. B. Lloyd, 'The Egyptian Labyrinth', JEA 56 (1970) 81–100.
Terrace and Fischer: 17, 85–8.
Grimal: 169–70.
Fitzwilliam Museum E.2. 1946.
BM EA 1063.

Amenemhet IV, King, Twelfth Dynasty, Middle Kingdom, *c.* 1808–1799 BC. This last king of the name was the least fortunate of the Twelfth Dynasty kings. He reigned only for about ten years; already the country was beginning one of its periods of decline. It is believed that his pyramid complex was south of Dahshur at Mazghura. Not for the first time Egypt was obliged to pay a high price for the tranquility which a series of long and peaceful reigns had produced. The Twelfth Dynasty faded into the Thirteenth, which was notable for the rise of an hereditary Vizierate, a concept which would have been anathema to Amenemhet I and his immediate successors, and for the rapidity with which kings came and went.

Grimal: 158–81.
Shaw and Nicholson 1995: 28.

Amenemhet, Scribe, Eighteenth Dynasty, New Kingdom, *c.* 1473–1458 BC. Amenemhet was a noble of Egypto-Nubian ancestry, one of the Africans educated at the Egyptian court in the *kap*, the 'nursery' for the sons of leading figures in the Egyptian dominions, and appointed to high office by the Queen HATSHEPSUT. He was described as a 'chieftain' and was an official and scribe.

Thomas 1995: 82 (181).
University of Pennsylvania Museum of Archaeology and Anthropology, E1098.

Ameneminet, Official, Nineteenth Dynasty, New Kingdom, *c.* 1279 BC. A contemporary of King RAMESSES II when he was Crown Prince, Ameneminet was one of Ramesses' closest companions and served him in a variety of important posts when he succeeded to the kingship. He was the son of the influential High Priest of Amun, WENNUFER, and his uncle was High Priest of Min and Isis at Koptos.

Ameneminet's official career began when he was appointed a Royal Charioteer and the king's Superintendent of Horse. He went on to become Royal Envoy to All Foreign Lands, a very high rank at the court; in this capacity he reported to the king directly on all issues affecting Egypt's relations with her neighbours, a department of state on which Ramesses placed great importance. Later still, he was Chief of Works and Commander of the Medjay Militia.

Kitchen 1982: 28, 44, 65, 126, 141.

Amenemnisu, King, Twenty-First Dynasty, Third Intermediate Period, *c.* 1043–1039 BC. Neferkare Amenemnisu was the son and eventual successor of King SMENDES and he succeeded to the throne on his father's death. He was destined to occupy it only for four years.

Little is known of the events of his reign; during it the formidable High Priest at Thebes, MENKHEPERRE, consolidated his position, securing his office for many years to come and augmenting its status *vis-à-vis* the royal authority.

Amenemnisu adopted Neferkare as one of his royal titles, a name which had seldom been used since the Old Kingdom, suggesting perhaps that he was concerned to bolster his position by appealing to the historic past of the kingship.

He was about sixty-six years old when he died; he was succeeded by PSEUSENNES I, who was probably his much younger brother.

Kitchen 1986: §218.

Amenemope, Viceroy, Nineteenth Dynasty, New Kingdom, *c.* 1279 BC. Amenemope was appointed Viceroy of Nubia during the later years of the reign of King SETI I; he continued in his office under Seti's successor, RAMESSES II. The principal concern of the Viceroy, apart from protecting Egypt's southern frontiers, was to ensure the security of the supplies of gold from the Nubian mines. The Viceroy was responsible for the direction of the last of the campaigns of Seti, against the rebellion of its dependency Irem. The twenty-two year-old Ramesses took part in the campaign, accompanied by his little sons, AMUNHIRWONMEF and KHAEMWASET. Amenemope erected stelae in honour of King Seti, one at the Viceregal capital at Shatt on Sai Island and the other at the new capital which he was building at what is now Amara West.

Amenemope died soon after Ramesses completed the building of a temple at Kalabsha, commemorating his Nubian forays. He was succeeded by Iuny.

Kitchen 1982: 28, 31, 40, 44.

Amenemope, Scribe, Twentieth Dynasty, New Kingdom, *c.* 1186–1069 BC. The son of Ka-Nakhte, Amenemope was the author of a set of 'Instructions' or wise sayings which are notable, in a genre which is frequently remarkable for its bombast, for a gentleness of spirit and the expression of concern for the unfortunate. Throughout the text the author urges moderation, good behaviour and understanding for others. The style of the text suggests that it was written in the Ramesside period, though the surviving copies are of later date.

Budge 1923: 9–18, 41–51; pls. 1–14.
——1926.
Lichtheim 2: 146–63.
BM Papyrus 10474.
EMB 6910, cat. no. 55.

Amenemope, King, Twenty-First Dynasty, Third Intermediate Period, *c.* 993–984 BC. Some confusion persists as to the order and indeed in the existence of some of the kings who ruled Egypt after the end of the New Kingdom, during the decline which followed the Ramesside kings of the Twentieth Dynasty. Amenemope was the fourth king of the Twenty-First Dynasty and is thought to have reigned for nine years, though one extant inscription appears to credit him with a forty-ninth regnal year.

Amenemope assumed the title of High Priest of Amun which, since he was king, was theoretically superfluous; however, the pretensions of the priesthood at this time and the serious inroads which they had evidently made into the royal power, probably justified this action.

Amenemope was buried in a small tomb in the dynasty's native town of Tanis; later, however, his mummy and funerary equipment were moved by King SIAMUN to a more imposing resting place in a tomb originally intended for Mutnedjmet, one of the queens of PSEUSENNES, who was removed to make way for him. He was buried in a particularly handsome yellow quartzite sarcophagus.

Kitchen 1986: §229.

Amenemopet, Vizier, Eighteenth Dynasty, New Kingdom, *c.* 1427–1400 BC. Amenemopet was a member of an influential family which provided the state with a number of high officials; his brother was SENNEFER who, like him, was Mayor of Thebes and was also buried in the Valley of the Nobles. Amenemopet was Vizier to King AMENHOTEP II; he was described as 'a tall, well built man'. His own tomb (KV 48) however, for reasons which are not known, was undecorated and was probably not completed.

Theodore M. Davies, *The Tomb of Siptah, the Monkey Tomb and the Gold Tomb*, London, 1908.
Reeves and Wilkinson: 184.

Amenemopet, High Priest, Nineteenth Dynasty, New Kingdom, *c.* 1269–1243 BC. The High Priest of Re at Heliopolis in the early years of the reign of King RAMESSES II, Amenemopet was a relative of Ramesses' close friend AMENEMINET who served the king in a number of high-ranking appointments. Amenemopet was followed in the High Priesthood of Re by Ramesses' sixteenth son, MERY-ATUM.

Kitchen 1982: 170.

Amenemopet, Jeweller, Eighteenth Dynasty, New Kingdom, *c.* 1320 BC. Living during the closing years of the Eighteenth Dynasty, Amenemopet was Superintendent of the Craftsmen of the King and Chief of the Goldsmiths. He probably died during the reign of King HOREMHEB. The reliefs in his tomb reflect the rather mannered art of the period, still influenced by the Amarna style; in one sequence Amenemopet and his wife, Neferetre, are shown making offerings to two human-headed birds, the form which the spirit was believed to assume after death, to permit it to fly from the tomb at will.

Staatliche Sammlung Ägyptischer Kunst, Munich.
Gl. 298: 109–12.
PM (J. Malek) 1981: 870.
University College London, no. 14467.

Amenemopet, Scribe, Nineteenth Dynasty, New Kingdom, *c.* 1213–1203 BC. This Amenemopet is remembered in a way which it is hard to believe would be his own first choice: a text on papyrus in the form of a letter from one HORI, who claims to be his friend but who nonetheless castigates Amenemopet as a failure in all that he attempts. He was apparently a travelling courier who might be expected to journey in particular to the Palestinian cities over which Egypt exercised suzerainty at this time.

It is possible, however, that the letter was an exercise in scribal training and Amenemopet a fictional character.

ANET 1969: 475–9.
A. H. Gardiner, *Select Papyri in the Hieratic Character from the Collections of the British Museum, vol. II*, 1942, London: pls XXXV–LXII.

Amenhirkhepshef, Prince, Twentieth Dynasty, New Kingdom, *c.* 1184–1153 BC. This Amenhirkhepshef was the son of RAMESSES III and was given a large tomb in the Valley of the Queens (QV 55). He is shown in a beautifully painted scene being presented to divinities by his evidently devoted father.

B. E. Shafer (ed) *Religion in Ancient Egypt: Gods, Myth and Personal Practice*, London, 1991: 15, 46, 52.
Grimal: 275.

Amenhirkhopshef (Amenhirwonmef), Prince, Nineteenth Dynasty, New Kingdom, *c.* 1279–1213 BC. The eldest son of RAMESSES II by his favourite wife, Queen NEFERTARI, Amenhirkhopshef was born when his father was still Crown Prince to *his* father, King SETI I. He accompanied Ramesses on his first military campaign to Nubia, when he was five years old. In the company of the Viceroy AMENEMOPE, he received tribute on behalf of his grandfather.

Amenhirkhopshef himself became a soldier, fighting in his father's campaigns. At some time his name was changed to Amenhirwonmef. He was appointed General-in-Chief of the Army and Crown Prince, but he died before his father, some time before the twentieth year of Ramesses' reign. He was buried in the Valley of the Kings at Thebes in a massive tomb constructed for the sons of Ramesses (KV 5).

Grimal: 256.
Kitchen 1982: 39, 40, 67, 102 (as Amonhirwonmef).
Reeves and Wilkinson: 144–5, 154.

Amenhotep I, King, Eighteenth Dynasty, New Kingdom (*c.* 1525–1504 BC). Amenhotep I was the son and successor of AHMOSE, the first king of the Eighteenth Dynasty, and of AHMOSE NEFERTIRY, his powerful mother. He was an energetic and forceful ruler, though records of his nearly thirty-year reign are relatively scant.

It is in foreign policy that he appears to have achieved most. Evidently determined to round off what his father had achieved and to remove the threat of Asiatic invasion from Egypt for ever, he pursued the enemy forces far into the north, possibly also to the east, where he may even have crossed the Euphrates. Similarly in the south, according to a statement by his successor, Egyptian forces penetrated as far as the Third Cataract, to remove the threat of Nubian attack.

His works of peace were intended to consolidate the Theban control of the throne. He undertook extensive building work in all his dominions, though many of his buildings were dismantled and the stone re-used by his succcessors, a practice from which few Egyptian kings were immune; Amenhotep did, however, restore the monuments of earlier kings, including the great tomb of King NEBHEPETRE MONTUHOTEP II of the Eleventh Dynasty, at Deir el-Bahri. By the time of his death the country was once again prosperous and his successors were able swiftly to achieve considerable advances which were, in part at least, the result of Amenhotep's work.

After his death he shared a mortuary temple, and possibly a tomb, with his mother, though the tomb's location is unknown. His mummy was recovered from the Deir el-Bahri cache.

He was married to Queen AHMOSE-MERITAMUN, but their only son appears to have died in infancy. He was succeeded to the throne by a senior army officer, THUTMOSE I, whose relationship with him, if any, is not known.

H. E. Winlock, 'A Restoration of the Reliefs from the Mortuary Temple of Amenhotep I', JEA 4: 11–15.
Shaw and Nicholson 1995: 28.
CAH II.1: 30–1.
BM 683.

Amenhotep II, King, Eighteenth Dynasty, New Kingdom, *c.* 1427–1400 BC. The second Amenhotep succeeded one of the greatest of Egyptian kings, THUTMOSE III. As a young man he was evidently the epitome of the dashing prince, active in sport and the hunt. Throughout his life he was much given to publicising this aspect of his activities.

Amenhotep II was one of the first kings of Egypt to grow up with horses. He was a keen equestrian all his life long; his father gave him charge of all the royal stables when he was still a boy. Amenhotep combined his enthusiasm for archery, gained in the hunting field, with his love of horses, and he became an outstanding exponent of mounted bowmanship. He was also a keen oarsman and was not above competing with one of his own officers, AHMOSE, who shared his pleasure in the sport. Not surprisingly, Amenhotep was a formidable warrior, but unlike his great father, he demonstrated a ferocity which not infrequently manifested itself in extreme cruelty. He adopted the very un-Egyptian practice of exposing the bodies of captured enemy princes on the walls of his cities. He undertook three principal campaigns in Syria.

During his reign Egypt evidently felt sufficiently confident to allow significant numbers of 'Asiatics', particularly Syrians, back into the country. They were important in the management of trade and in certain craft occupations in which they were especially proficient.

Towards the end of his long reign Amenhotep had to cope with risings in Nubia, a problem which was endemic in the Egyptian body politic and which in this instance continued into his successor's reign.

Amenhotep was buried in the Valley of the Kings (KV 35). When his tomb was opened in the last century it was found to contain the mummies of some of the greatest kings of the dynasty, including that of Amenhotep's own father. They had been placed there in the Twenty-First Dynasty in an attempt to thwart tomb robbers.

CAH II.1: 333–7, 410, 459–62.
Terrace and Fischer: 23, 117–20.
Luxor Museum J.129; cat. no. 88, fig. 53.

Amenhotep III, King, Eighteenth Dynasty, New Kingdom, *c.* 1390–1352 BC. The son of a non-royal wife of THUTMOSE IV, Amenhotep became king as a boy and, in the practice of his family which by his time was long established, his mother acted as regent during the first years of his reign. He was married early on to a non-royal person, TIY, the daughter of YUYA AND TUYU; this alliance was to have great importance in the events which marked the latter part and end of the dynasty of AHMOSE.

Few Egyptian kings, other than the great rulers of the Middle Kingdom, enjoyed so tranquil and prosperous a reign as Amenhotep III. At home, Egypt was at peace, her economy was sound, the people content; abroad, the reputation of Egypt had never been higher and a positive river of 'tribute' (viewed from the Egyptian standpoint) flowed into the country.

However, there were some disquietening signs beyond the frontiers which were to become actual threats to Egypt's security in the future. The very fact that Amenhotep's reign was so peaceful encouraged some of the new powers emerging in the Near East to cast covetous eyes on Egypt's riches.

Such considerations seem not to have disturbed Amenhotep unduly. He was, even for an Egyptian king, a prodigious builder. Those buildings which have survived are huge and dominating; some are not without elegance. The arts flourished exceedingly and the court was the recipient of some of the most magnificient works of art produced in Egypt since the Old Kingdom, a thousand years before. 'Magnificent' is a word which tends to recur in descriptions of Amenhotep III's occupation of the throne.

Amenhotep, at least in his earlier years, shared his family's enthusiasm for hunting. He was also concerned to make sure that his subjects and his client princes abroad should know of his exploits; the medium which he employed to publicise his successes in the field (and, from time to time, his royal marriages) was the large 'Commemorative Scarab', of which considerable quantities were made and distributed.

Amenhotep seems to have sustained a particular interest in theological debate. He was emphatic in the projection of his own divinity, but it is possible to detect the appearance of the cult of the Aten in his reign, which was to wreak such havoc with Egypt's traditional values in the next reign.

Towards the end of his life Amenhotep seems to have suffered from prolonged ill-health. His early portraits present him as a handsome prince; by his last years he is portrayed, with unusual candour, as fat and dropsical.

He was buried in the Valley of the Kings, in a suitably magnificent tomb (WV 22), after a long and splendid reign. He was succeeded by his son, who came to the throne as Amenhotep IV but is better known to history as AKHENATEN.

Hayes 1959: 231–59.
CAH II.1: 313–416.
A. Kozloff and B. Bryan, *Egypt's Dazzling Sun: Amenhotep III and His World*, catalogue, Bloomington and Cleveland, 1992.
Luxor Museum J.155; cat. no. 107, fig. 62 (Amenhotep III and Sobek).

Amenhotep IV, *see* **Akhenaten**

Amenhotep, Priest, Eighteenth Dynasty, New Kingdom, *c.* 1479–1425 BC. A senior temple official, Amenhotep was responsible for the control of much of the wealth of the Temple of Amun at Thebes. He was Overseer of the god's 'foreign lands', and the temple's gardens and granaries; he was also Chief of the Weavers. Amenhotep was mortuary priest of three kings, AMENHOTEP I, THUTMOSE I and THUTMOSE III.

Amenhotep came from a family of temple servants: his father and mother and both his grandfathers were employed in the Temple of Amun.

Hayes 1959: 172–3; fig. 94.
MMA 17.2.6.

Amenhotep, Royal Scribe and High Steward, Eighteenth Dynasty, New Kingdom, 1430–1350 BC. Amenhotep, son of Hapu, was celebrated throughout the remaining centuries of Egyptian history, long after his lifetime, as the exemplar of the wise counsellor and honourable servant of the king. He seems genuinely to have been a man of exceptional probity and talents. He enjoyed an outstanding career, as King's Scribe, Scribe of Recruits (a post with military responsibilities) and the ancient office of Overseer of All the Works of the King. This last appointment suggests that he was also an architect and thus responsible for the immense building projects which Amenhotep III commissioned.

On his death, at what was reputed to be a very great age, the son of Hapu was given the singular honour for a commoner of a mortuary temple in western Thebes, close by the temple dedicated to the perpetuity of the kings. Like theirs, Amenhotep's temple was to be endowed for all time and his cult flourished at least into the period of the Ramesside kings. He was especially revered as a sage, and many proverbs and sayings of wisdom were attributed to him. More than a thousand years after his death these were translated into Greek and he was worshipped as a god in Ptolemaic times.

Terrace and Fischer 1970: no. 25, 117–20.
D. Wildung, *Egyptian Saints: Deification in Pharaonic Egypt*, New York, 1977.
PM II: 118.
EMC JE 44861, 44862.
Luxor Museum J.4; cat. no. 117, figs 68–9.

Amenhotep, Royal Official, Eighteenth Dynasty, New Kingdom, *c.* 1400 BC. Amenhotep was the Overseer of the Royal Palace in Memphis, probably during the reigns of King AMENHOTEP II and his successor, THUTMOSE IV. He was provided with a finely carved block statue in highly polished black granodiorite, an exceptionally hard stone. The carving of Amenhotep's strikingly aristocratic features is particularly refined.

The statue was placed in the temple of Osiris at Abydos, a practice popular at the time to ensure the deceased a place in the train of the god.

BM EA 632.

Amenhotep, Vizier, Eighteenth Dynasty, New Kingdom, *c.* 1390–1352 BC. This Amenhotep was Vizier to AMENHOTEP III and thus the king's most important officer at the time when Egypt's richest and most magnificent court flourished. He was buried at Silsileh and for reasons which are unclear but which are probably to be associated with the fanaticism with which King Amenhotep's successor, Akhenaten, pursued any reference to the god Amun, his name, titles and representations were largely obliterated from his tomb. This vandalism even extended to the name of the deceased king, so it may be that Amenhotep the Vizier was not singled out for this treatment. The destruction of other mentions of the name of Amun is well documented throughout Egypt in the Amarna period.

R. A. Caminos, 'Amenhotep III's Vizier, Amenhotep, at Silsileh East', JEA 73 (1987) 207–10; fig. 1.

Amenhotep, High Priest, Twentieth Dynasty, New Kingdom, *c.* 1140 BC. The son of a High Priest of Amun-Re, RAMESSES-NAKHTE, Amenhotep also achieved the High Priesthood; he was one of those high temple officials who had undermined the kingship and whose influence led to the creation of what was virtually an independent ruling hierarchy based on Thebes, which was to result, ultimately, in the decline of Egypt. His period of office coincided with the reigns of the later Ramessids, Ramesses IX–Ramesses XI.

Amenhotep was High Priest at the time of the trials of the tomb robbers during the reign of Ramesses IX. He had himself portrayed in a relief at Karnak as of equal height to the king, a departure from customary Egyptian protocol. His arrogance was evidently such that he attracted many enemies. It is possible that he was 'suppressed' by PANEHESY in the reign of Ramesses XI.

Peet 1930.
W. Wente, *The Suppression of the High Priest Amenhotep*, JNES 25: 73–87.
M. Bierbrier, *The Late New Kingdom in Egypt*, Warminster, 1978.

Amenirdis I, Princess, Twenty-Third Dynasty, Third Intermediate Period, *c.* 747–716 BC. The careers of the princesses who carried the name Amenirdis in the latter part of Egyptian history provide revealing insights into the temple politics of the time. Ever since the extinction of the RAMESSIDE line, the temple administrations had been dangerously rich and powerful. In the Twenty-Third dynasty King TAKELOT III secured the appointment of his sister SHEPENUPET I as Divine Adoratrice of Amun at Thebes, a sort of high-priestesshood which carried with it considerable temporal power; it was analagous to the office of 'God's Wife of Amun' in the Eighteenth Dynasty. When the Kushite dynasty from Nubia conquered much of Egypt the kings were at pains to maintain Egyptian procedures, but also, as far as it was possible, to tie the temple administrations to their house. King PIANKHY arranged for Shepenupet to adopt his sister Amenirdis as her successor; for a time they ruled the region together.

Amenirdis I was married to SHABATAKA; eventually their daughter, SHEPENUPET II, succeeded her mother as Divine Adoratrice. Amenirdis built herself a mortuary chapel and tomb in the temple precincts at Medinet Habu.

Saleh and Sourouzian: 244.
Grimal: 335–54.
EMC JE 3420 (CG565).
BM EA 46699.

Amenirdis II, Princess, Twenty-Fifth Dynasty, Third Intermediate Period, 690–664 BC. Amenirdis II was the sister of King Taharqa. She was Divine Adoratrice in the reign of PSAMETIK I, sharing the office with SHEPENUPET II. They adopted Princess NITIQRET, Psametik's daughter, thus ensuring the dynasty's control of Thebes and the south.

R. A. Caminos, 'The Nitocris Adoption Stela', JEA 50: 70–101.

Amenmesse, King, Nineteenth Dynasty, New Kingdom, *c.* 1203–1200 BC. A shadowy figure, Amenmesse became king of Egypt for a brief period after the death of MERENPTAH, the eventual successor of RAMESSES II. Amenmesse was a grandson of Ramesses; his mother was Princess Takhat, and after the old king's near interminable reign most of the heirs in the direct succession had died.

Amenmesse seems to have been a competant administrator and was acknowledged, during his lifetime, as king by most of the country, though his power base was probably in the south. After his death, however, his memory was largely erased, the result of opposing parties in the dynastic intrigues gaining control of the central authority and the succession.

He was buried in KV 10. The tomb was unfinished and subsequently destroyed. His son eventually succeeded as King SIPTAH.

Grimal: 269.

Amenmose (alt. Amenmessu), Royal Scribe, Nineteenth Dynasty, New Kingdom, *c.* 1279–1213 BC. Amenmose was 'Royal Scribe of the Altar of the Two Lands', during the reign of King RAMESSES II. He is known from numerous statues and from an 'ancestor bust', commemorating his father, Pa-en-djerty, which was found in Amenmose's tomb in the Theban necropolis (TT 373). A similar bust of Amenmose's mother also survives.

His tomb shows Amenmose worshipping the cult statues of thirteen kings of Egypt.

PM I.1: 433–4; PM I.2: vxii.
Shaw and Nicholson: 152.
Luxor Museum J.147; cat. no. 230; figs 122–3 (bust of Pa-en-djerty).

Amenmose, Vizier, Nineteenth Dynasty, New Kingdom, *c.* 1200–1196 BC. Amenmose was the Vizier in the reign of King AMENMESSE who tried the case in which PANEB sought to malign his colleague and stepfather NEFERHOTEP, whose appointment he wished to acquire, as foreman of the workers in the Theban necropolis. Amenmose decided in Neferhotep's favour, and the inclusion of his name on Neferhotep's funerary stela may have been an act of gratitude. Unfortunately for Neferhotep the judgement was reversed and Paneb, evidently a thoroughly unscrupulous character, gained his objective and Neferhotep's position, after the latter's murder.

Paneb persuaded King Amenmesse to remove Amenmose from office.

G. A. Gaballa, 'Monuments of Prominent Men of Abydos, Memphis and Thebes', in J. Ruffle *et al.* 1979: 49.
A. Dodson, *Monarchs of the Nile*, London, 1995: 137.

Amenmose, Priest, Twenty-Second Dynasty, Third Intermediate Period, *c.* 945–715 BC. A specialist in the treatment of snakebites, Amenmose owed his skill to his training as a priest of the snake goddess Serqet (Selket). He worked at Deir el-Madina, where no doubt he attended the large numbers of workmen employed in the necropolis and dealt with the many snakes which infest the area.

Nunn: 135.

Amennakhte, Scribe, Twentieth Dynasty, New Kingdom, *c.* 1184–1153 BC. Amennakhte was an important official in the Theban necropolis, with special responsibilty for work on the royal tombs during the reign of RAMESSES III. He was much concerned with the workers' strikes which were a feature of the later years of Ramesses' reign; he seems to have contributed to the settlement of the disputes.

In all Amennakhte served four kings and lived to a ripe old age, founding his own dynasty. His will is preserved on a papyrus which also contains the plan of the tomb of RAMESSES IV.

W. Egerton, 'The Strikes of Ramesses III's 29th Year', JNES 10: 137–45.
Reeves and Wilkinson: 26.

Amenpanufer, Stone-Carver and Robber, Twentieth Dynasty, New Kingdom, *c*. 1124–1108 BC. At the end of the Twentieth Dynasty, when social conditions in Egypt were in some turmoil, there was an outbreak of tomb-robbing which gave the authorities considerable concern. In the reign of RAMESSES IX the trial took place of Amenpanufer, who confessed, in considerable circumstantial detail, to robbing the tomb of King SOBEKEMSAF II. He appears to have been the leader of the gang which perpetrated the robberies, but although an official enquiry was held, conducted at the highest level and involving the Vizier and the High Priest of Amun, it was inconclusive. Suspicion remains that highly placed officials may have been involved, including perhaps PASER, the Mayor of Thebes who initiated the enquiry by making accusations against his colleague PAWERAA, the Mayor of Western Thebes. The accused workers were punished, probably by impalement, the customary penalty for what was regarded as a particularly heinous act of sacrilege.

Papyrus Leopold II-Amherst: Capart, Gardiner and van der Walle, JEA 22 (1936) 171.
T. E. Peet, *The Great Tomb Robberies of the Twentieth Egyptian Dynasty*, Oxford, 1930.

Amentefnakht, General, Twenty-Sixth Dynasty, Late Period, 589–570 BC. Amentefnakht was buried in the ancient necropolis at Saqqara, which enjoyed something of a revival as a cemetery during Saitic times. His deep shaft-tomb was cut into the forecourt of the funerary temple of King UNAS of the Sixth Dynasty.

He lived during the reign of King APRIES. His tomb was intact when it was discovered; Amentefnakht was buried in a magnificent sarcophagus, carved from a single block of hard limestone. Curiously, it appeared that Amentefnakht was not properly embalmed but his corpse must have been placed in the coffin immediately after death. The coffin was anthropoid and made of a fine green slate. By the employment of a skilful engineering device, sand had been released into the tomb after the sarcophagus was lowered into it; it was this, no doubt, that ensured that it remained undisturbed. The excavator reported, however, that the coffin was filled with a 'pinkish liquid' which on analysis turned out to consist largely of water and embalming materials.

The general was buried without any amulets or ornaments. The handsome sarcophagus was the tomb's most notable feature, other than its occupant.

Amentefnakht was Chief of the Life Guard, Commander of the Recruits of the Royal Guard and 'Priest of the King'.

Z. Y. Saad, 'Preliminary Report on the Royal Excavations at Saqqara (1941–2)', *Annales du Service des Antiquities de l'Égypte*, 41: 381–403, figs 75–9, pls XXVI, XXVII.
——*Royal Excavations at Saqqara and Helwan (1941–5)*, Cairo, 1947: 2–11, figs 1–5, pls I, II.
A. Zaki and Z. Iskander, 'Materials and Methods used for Mummifying the Body of Amentefnekht', *Annales du Service des Antiquities de l'Égypte*, 42: 223–55.

Amenwah, Robber, Twentieth Dynasty, New Kingdom, *c*. 1100 BC. Amenwah, a worker from the artisan's village at Deir el-Medina, was accused of robbing the tomb of King RAMESSES III. He was discharged, however, for lack of evidence. In modern times his guilt was proven when the object from the king's burial which he had stolen was found in his own tomb.

Grimal: 287.

Amenwahsu, Priest, Eighteenth Dynasty, New Kingdom, *c*. 1550–1295 BC. Amenwahsu was provided with a very fine purple quartzite statue of himself, in an attitude of prayer, supporting a stele which shows the sun-god, Ra-Harakhty, sailing in his divine barque across the sky.

James and Davies: 35–6, ill. 44.
Shaw and Nicholson: 279.
BM EA 480.

Amenyseneb, Priest, Thirteenth Dynasty, Middle Kingdom, *c.* 1760–1755 BC. A priest in the temple at Abydos during the reign of King USERKARE KHENDJER, Amenyseneb was Controller of the Phyle, the monthly roster or 'watch' of priests serving in the temple. On his funerary stele he is accompanied by members of his family, other priestly colleagues and a variety of servants, mostly named and with their duties described. They include a brewer and a baker, thus ensuring a proper supply of food and drink for Amenyseneb in the afterlife.

Amenyseneb describes, on another stela which carries the cartouche of Userkare Khendjer, how he restored the temple of Osiris at Abydos. It was during the reign of King Khendjer that the so-called 'Bed of Osiris', a basalt figure of the god lying on a lion-bed, was placed in the tomb of King DJER, which was believed to be the god's own tomb.

K. Kitchen, JEA 47 (1961) 10–18, pls II, III.
Bourriau 1988: 60–1, no. 48.
University of Liverpool Department of Egyptology E 30.
MduL C11, C12, (as Imenyseneb).

Amunhirwonmef, *see* **Amenhirkhopshef**

Amyrtaeus, King, Twenty-Eighth Dynasty, Late Period, 404–*c.* 399 BC. The only Egyptian sovereign to be listed as the sole incumbent of his dynasty, Amyrtaeus deserved better of fate. He was a prince of Sais, from a family which cherished the independence of Egypt and deeply resented its occupation by the Persians. His grandfather, of the same name, had led a revolt against them in earlier times and in 404 BC the second Amyrtaeus brought the country into open revolt, after some years of active resistence to Persian rule. DARIUS II, the Great King of Persia, died in the same year and Amyrtaeus was proclaimed King of Egypt. Little is known of his reign, however, though he appears to have been acknowledged as king through the whole of the country. He ruled only for a few years and the circumstances of his death are not known.

Grimal: 371.

Anedjib (alt. Enezib), King, First Dynasty, Archaic Period, *c.* 2925 BC. Even in the general obscurity of the First Dynasty, the fourth successor of King AHA (excluding Merneith, though she may have been Queen Regnant, but this is still uncertain) left little trace of what was probably a fairly short reign. It may be that it marked a time of unrest, for the process of the Unification of the Two Lands on which Aha and his successors had set out, was not achieved without opposition from the diverse regions of the country. Anedjib seems, however, to have been particularly associated with Memphis (at least according to a somewhat later record), perhaps being the first king to reside in what was to become the most celebrated of Egypt's cities.

Anedjib was buried in a relatively modest tomb in Abydos, though it is notable for its wooden floor. He took over sixty of his retainers with him into the afterlife, however.

Emery 1949.
——1961: 80–4.
Spencer: 66, 83.

Anen (alt. Onen), High Priest, Eighteenth Dynasty, New Kingdom, *c.* 1390–1352 BC. The son of YUYA, the Master of the Horse and father-in-law of King AMENHOTEP III, Anen was one of the prominent figures in the Egyptian court at the time of its particular magnificence; he was, after all, the king's brother-in-law. He was Chief Seer (High Priest) in the Temple of Re at Karnak. He was also Second Prophet of Amun. To judge from the equipment which he is shown carrying on his one surviving statue, Anen may have been an astronomer.

He was buried at Sheikh Abd el Qurna, western Thebes, no. 120.

Scamuzzi n.d.: pl. XXXVI (as Onen).
Aldred 1988: 137, 166, 220.
CAH II.2: 79.
Museo Egizio, Turin 1377.

Anhernakhte, Army Officer, Nineteenth Dynasty, New Kingdom, *c*. 1279–1213 BC. In the latter years of the reign of King RAMESSES II Anhernakhte was Chief of the Bowmen of Kush, a senior army rank which denoted the military command of Nubia. He was also Fan-bearer on the Right of the King, a title of high honour. His name and titles are recorded on rock inscriptions on the island of Siheil. He was also named as Overseer of Southern Lands, a title often held by the Viceroys of Kush.

L. Habachi, 'The Owner of Tomb no. 282 in the Theban Necropolis', JEA 54 (1968) 107–13; figs 1–4.

Anhurmose, High Priest, Nineteenth Dynasty, New Kingdom, *c*. 1220–1203 BC. Anhurmose congratulated himself on his rise from comparative obscurity to the High Priesthood of the ancient royal centre of Thinis. The son of a middle rank official, he held his office in the latter years of King RAMESSES II and during the reign of King MERENPTAH.

Kitchen 1982: 145, 170.

Ani, Royal Scribe, Nineteenth Dynasty, New Kingdom, *c*. 1250 BC. Ani, whose titles included 'Accounting Scribe for the Divine Offerings of All the Gods' and 'Overseer of the Granaries of the Lords of Tawer' is remembered particularly for a superb recension of the Book of the Dead, the document which succeeded the Pyramid Texts and the Coffin Texts, which guided the souls of the dead through the perils of the afterlife, during the journey to judgement and, it was to be hoped, salvation (or 'justification', as the Egyptians expressed it).

Ani's Book of the Dead is one of the great triumphs of painted papyrus, a work of art of the very highest quality. Rather shamefully, however, for one in his profession, Ani's papyrus contains a considerable number of scribal errors.

R. O. Faulkner, *The Ancient Egyptian Book of the Dead*, London, 1972: 9, 13, 14.
BM EA 10470.

Ankh, Noble, Third Dynasty, Old Kingdom, *c*. 2667–2648 BC. Two seated figures, carved in hard stone, of the noble Ankh who was a leading figure in the reign of King DJOSER NETJERYKHET, demonstrate how far the technique of Egyptian sculptors had progressed in the relatively short space of time between the death of King KHASEKHEMWY and the accession of Djoser. In one of his statues, in the collections of the Musée du Louvre, Ankh sits placidly on his throne-like chair, smiling contentedly; the other, in Leiden – a particularly fine black granite piece – portrays him in a more formal persona, dressed in a priestly leopard skin, held in place by inscribed oval ornaments.

Vandier, Manuel 1: fig. 661; Manuel 3: 64, 2 n11, 126, n2.
Stevenson Smith 1946 (1949): 16–17, pl. 3 (as Nezem-Ankh).
C. Ziegler 1990: 21–3.
MduL A39.
Rijksmuseum van Oudheden, Leiden Inv. AST 18.

Ankhaf, Prince and Vizier, Fourth Dynasty, Old Kingdom, *c*. 2550 BC. An example of the Fourth Dynasty's practice of selecting the principal officers of state from the immediate family of the king, Ankhaf was probably the son of King SNEFERU by one of his lesser queens; an alternative parentage would make him the son of King HUNI and hence a half-brother of Sneferu. He was 'King's Eldest

Son' but this title was as frequently honorific as it was a literal expression of relationship. In the uncertain times which followed the death of KHNUM-KHUFU (CHEOPS) and the evidently disputed accession of DJEDEFRE, Khnum-Khufu's actual successor, Ankhaf was loyal to the direct line of succession represented by KHAFRE (CHEPHREN). His loyalty was rewarded with the Viziership, in which capacity he served Khafre. He appears to have died during this reign and was buried in one of the largest tombs on the Giza plateau.

Ankhaf is particularly remembered by an exceptionally fine portrait bust, now in the Museum of Fine Arts, Boston, which was found in his mastaba. It is one of the outstanding works from a period which was in so many ways the high point of Egyptian art. The bust is notable amongst funerary portaits of the time in being painted, the paint overlaid on a plaster surface. Ankhaf is represented as a man in vigorous middle age, with an expression of assurance and control which would make him well able to discharge the office of 'Overseer of All the King's Works'.

G. A. Reisner, *Giza Necropolis*, Cambridge, 1942: 46, fig. 8.
D. Durham, 'The Portrait Bust of Prince Ankhhaf', BMCA XXXVII (1939) 42–6.
MFA G 7510.

Ankhefenamun, Great Chamberlain, Twenty-First Dynasty, Third Intermediate Period, *c*. 1039–991 BC. The son of Nesyen-Amun, Ankhefenamun was Great Chamberlain to several kings of the early Twenty-First Dynasty at Tanis. He followed his father as Great Chamberlain and was also Royal Scribe (Chief Secretary) to King PSEUSENNES I. It was recorded that he died when he was 72 years, 5 months and 14 days old. His daughter was 'King's Nurse' and the husband of another important courtier, Sia, who was appointed mortuary priest to King Pseusennes on the latter's death.

Kitchen 1986: §222.

Ankhenmer, Royal Herald, Thirteenth Dynasty, Middle Kingdom, *c*. 1720–1650 BC. 'Prince, Mayor and Royal Acquaintance' are some of Ankhenmer's titles in addition to his principal office of Royal Herald. In later times the Herald was one of the great officers, with direct access to the king, to whom he was required to report the state of the kingdoms as well as acting as a royal chamberlain and Master of Ceremonies.

Bourriau 1988: 69–70, no. 55.
Liverpool Museum 1961, 178.

Ankhenesmeryre, Queens, Sixth Dynasty, Old Kingdom, *c*. 2321–2287 BC. Two sisters, both of whom were married to King PEPY I, the daughters of Khui, a noble from Abydos, bore the name Anhkenesmeryre. The elder sister was the mother of King MERENRE I, who briefly succeeded his father, and of the princess Neith. Ankhenesmeryre II was the mother of the immensely long-lived King PEPY II, who was married to the princess Neith, thus producing a complexity of relationships remarkable even in the Egyptian royal family. The brother of the two queens, DJAU, was vizier both to Menenre and Pepy II.

Stevenson Smith 1965 (1981): ill. 140.
J. Leclant, 'A la Quête des Pyramides des Reines de Pepy 1er', BSFE 113 (1988) 20–31.
Grimal: 83.
Brooklyn Museum 39.119.

Ankhesenamun (Ankhesenpaaten), Queen, Eighteenth Dynasty, New Kingdom, *c*. 1336–1327 BC. One of the daughters of AKHENATEN and NEFERTITI, Ankhesenamun (her name was changed after the restoration of the priests of Amun, following her father's death) was to play a melancholy role in the terminal phases of the rule of the family which descended from KAMOSE, AHMOSE and the powerful rulers of the earlier period of the Eighteenth Dynasty. She was married to TUTANKHAMUN and shared the nine years of his kingship in cheerful and affectionate companionship, to judge by the several scenes from their life together which have survived. After Tutankhamun's death in 1327 BC, Ankhesenamun was left in a perilous position. As the daughter of the king of Egypt she was the repository of the kingship, according to royal custom. There was no natural male heir, evidently, descended from Ahmose's line. Ankhesenamun was reduced therefore to sending a frantic message (the tone is unmistakeable) to the king of the Hittites, SUPPILULIUMAS, begging him to send her one of his sons, so that he might become King of Egypt; such a recourse was without precedent. On Ankhesenamun's repeated request Suppiluliumas obliged and despatched his son, the Prince ZENNANZA to her, but he was murdered on the journey to Egypt.

Ankhesenamun disappears from history, though it is possible that she was married off to the elderly AY who now became king.

In the tomb of Tutankhamun two foetuses, both female, were buried with him. They were perhaps the premature babies of Ankhesenamun.

Desroches Noblecourt 1963.
Aldred 1988.
Reeves 1990a: 124, 141, 155, 162, 184, 192, 199; ills 33, 140, 141, 165, 184, 198.

Ankh-Ka, Chancellor, First Dynasty, Archaic Period, *c.* 2950 BC. Ankh-Ka served DEN (Udimu), the fourth king of the First Dynasty after AHA, as Chancellor. He was also a regional governor, one of the first to be known by name. It is notable that even at this early date, great state officials already bear titles which were to survive throughout Egyptian history and which, even in Ankh-Ka's day, must have been of considerable antiquity.

Ankh-Ka was the owner of mastaba tomb no. 3036 at Saqqara.

Emery 1949: 71–81.
Lehner 1997: 80.

Ankhmahor, Vizier, Sixth Dynasty, Old Kingdom, *c.* 2345–2181 BC. A high-ranking official in the later years of the Old Kingdom, Ankhmahor was Overseer of the Great House and 'First Under the King'; he was also a Ka-Priest. His tomb at Saqqara, however, is comparatively modest in scale though it contains some highly individual scenes on its walls. Known, incorrectly, as 'The Tomb of the Physician', it depicts circumcision and scenes of mourning of great feeling. It also shows craftsmen, including dwarves, at work as jewellers, metalworkers and sculptors.

J. Capart, *Une Rue de Tombaux à Saqqarah, vol. 2*, Brussels, 1907.
A. Badawy, *The Tomb of Nyhetep-Ptah at Giza and the Tomb of Ankhmahor at Saqqara*, California, 1978.
Nunn: 126, 133, 169–71.

Ankhnesneferibre, Princess, 'Divine Adoratrice', Twenty-Sixth Dynasty, Late Period, 610–525 BC. A daughter of King NECHO II and sister of his short-lived but energetic successor, NEFERIBRE PSAMETIK II, Ankhnesneferibre's name ('Neferibre lives for her') proclaims her brother's affection for her. Psametik II ensured that Ankhnesneferibre was adopted by NITIQRET, the reigning Divine Adoratrice, eventually succeeding her in 584 BC and retaining the office until the Persian conquest in 525 BC. She was provided with a handsome schist sarcophagus, with a rather youthful representation of herself on its lid.

Grimal: 361.
BM 32.

Ankhpakhered, Priest, Twenty-Fifth Dynasty, Late Period, *c.* 680BC. One of a family of Theban priests, of whom several generations had served in the Temple of Amun. His 'block statue', showing him seated on the ground, wrapped in his cloak, anticipates the archaicising tendencies of the Twenty-Sixth Dynasty.

PM II: 152.
Saleh and Sourouzian: 247.
EMC JL 36993.

Ankhsheshonq (alt. 'Onkhsheshonqy), Priest, Ptolemaic Period(?), date uncertain. The priest of Re at Heliopolis, Ankhsheshonq, once travelled to Memphis to visit his friend, Harsises, the royal physician. Harsises welcomed him cordially, urging him to stay for an extended visit. He then told Ankhsheshonq that he and other courtiers were planning to kill the king. Ankhsheshonq tried to dissuade his friend but to no avail. Their conversation was overheard; Harsises and his co-conspirators were arrested, tried and executed. Ankhsheshonq was sentenced to a term of imprisonment for failing to report the treason.

While he was in prison Ankhsheshonq wrote a set of 'Instructions', a literary form long popular in Egypt, for his young son. The style is aphoristic; it is also humorous, surprising perhaps in the circumstances, and occasionally – and more to be expected – rather cynical.

S. R. K. Glanville, *Catalogue of Demotic Papyri in the British Museum. Vol. II: The Instructions of 'Onchsheshonqy.* British Museum Papyrus 10508, London, 1955.
Lichtheim 3: 159–84.

Ankhtify, Nomarch, Tenth Dynasty, First Intermediate Period, *c.* 2160–2025 BC. Ankhtify was the holder of many resounding titles and the incumbent of many of the great offices during a time of a much reduced royal authority, the Heracleopolitan Tenth Dynasty. He lived, in all probability, during the reign of King NEFERKARE, to whom he was evidently persistently loyal. According to the remarkably self-congratulatory inscriptions in his tomb at El-Moalla, he was Prince, Count, Royal Seal-Bearer, Sole Companion, General, Chief of Foreign Regions; he was nomarch of Edfu and Hierakonpolis and through an alliance with the Elephantine nome he established a powerful southern opponent to the rulers of Thebes. He records that he cared for the districts for which he was responsible in times of famine and distress. He was the leader of highly trained troops, who were feared by any forces who opposed them. He was, he observed, an honest man who had no equal, nor would any other man ever equal the achievements of his lifetime.

For a man of evidently such outstanding qualities Ankhtify was unfortunate in finding himself opposing the Theban prince INYOTEF, the ancestor of the Eleventh Dynasty, which was to bring about the reconstruction of Egypt under NEBHEPETRE MONTUHOTEP II at the beginning of the Middle Kingdom. Although Ankhtify was apparently defeated in battle by Inyotef, despite the exceptional fighting qualities of the forces which he commanded, he evidently survived to build himself and to occupy a rather graceful tomb at El-Moalla, in which the wonderful and heroic events of his life are recorded.

J. Vandier, *Mo'alla, la Tombe d'Ankhtifi et la Tombe de Sébekhotep*, Cairo, 1950.
D. Spaniel, 'The Date of Ankhtifi of Mo'alla', GM 78 (1984) 87–94.
Lichtheim 1: 85–6.

Ankhu, Vizier, Thirteenth Dynasty, Middle Kingdom, *c.* 1725 BC. During a time of considerable upheaval in Egypt, Ankhu seems to have represented a point of stability in the royal administration, serving in high offices over an extended period. He was active during the reign of King USERKARE KHENDJER when he is known to have restored the Twelfth

Dynasty temple at Abydos. He was Vizier to King SOBEKHOTEP III and was still in office in the reign of SOBEKHOTEP IV, when the Hyksos invaded Egypt and gained control of much of the north.

Ankhu appears to have had an extensive family, and a number of his descendants occupied important positions in the state; one such was Iymeru, also Vizier to King SOBEKHOTEP IV.

Breasted 1: §781ff.
Gardiner 1961: 153.
CAH II.1: 47–8, 51.

Ankhwah (previously Bedjmes), Ship Builder, Third Dynasty, Old Kingdom, *c.* 2686–2613 BC. Ankhwah is remembered by the survival of a statue in which he is shown seated and grasping his adze, a tool of considerable utility in his profession. This is one of the oldest statues in the round of a non-royal personage; it is the more remarkable in being carved in an exceptionally hard stone, a tribute to the skill of Egyptian sculptors even at so early a date.

Not all shipbuilders were thus commemorated in this way; one, admittedly from a much earlier time than Ankhwah, was given the honour of being buried amongst other sacrificed retainers around the tomb of Queen MERNEITH at Saqqara.

Spencer: 111.
Quirke and Spencer: 154, pl. 118.
BM 171.

Antef, *see* **Inyotef I, II and III**

Antefoker (alt. Intefoker), Vizier, Twelfth Dynasty, Middle Kingdom, *c.* 1985–1960 BC. Antefoker served the two first kings of the Twelfth Dynasty, AMENEMHET I and SENWOSRET I. The former had himself been Vizier in the previous reign, and Antefoker must have played an important part in the development of the administrative reforms which the king introduced on his assumption of the throne. The dynasty established itself at El-Lisht and Amenemhet built himself a pyramid there, using blocks from Old Kingdom burials. A necropolis for members of the royal family and the great officers of state was built nearby the king's pyramid. Here, unusually, Antefoker built only a cenotaph for himself, as he was actually buried at Thebes (TT 60).

There has been some speculation that Antefoker may have been implicated in the assassination of King Amenemhet. His mother, SENET (once thought to have been his wife), was buried on the hill of Sheikh Abdel-Qurna at Thebes and her son's name, titles and portrait have been excised from it, as if he had been execrated after his death; it is possible that the tomb was originally intended to be his. Senet's tomb was the earliest funerary monument to be built at Thebes and remained in isolation until some four hundred years after her death when the region became the most important necropolis in Egypt.

The tomb is the only one from the Middle Kingdom which has survived with substantial decoration. There are very fine depictions of harpists and flautists together with two singers, Didumin and Khuwyt, who entertain Antefoker.

A. H. Gardiner and N. de Garis Davies, *The Tomb of Antefoker, Vizier of Sesostris I and his wife Senet*, London, 1920.
L. Manniche, *Music and Musicians in Ancient Egypt*, London, 1991: 35–6.

Antinous, Imperial Favourite and God, Roman Period, d. October 130 AD. A Bithynian adolescent, the son of an official of the Empire, Antinous caught the attention of the resolutely homosexual Emperor, HADRIAN, remaining his companion until his mysterious death in the Nile. Antinous had travelled with the Emperor to Egypt and, perhaps as the result of an oracle, may have decided to offer himself as a sacrifice in the Emperor's stead. At any event, he was found drowned near Hermopolis. After his death Hadrian declared him divine, ordered temples built in his honour and established a cult for him with its own priesthood. Near the place of his death Hadrian created a city, Antinoopolis, which was celebrated throughout the Empire for the splendour of its buildings. Predictably it was largely Greek in inspiration and much of its ruins survived until the eighteenth century. It was sited at the modern town of El-Sheikh 'Ibada.

Hadrian commissioned countless statues of his lover. He appears to have been (or perhaps to have become) a rather hefty young man.

Lambert 1984.

Antiphilus, Painter, Ptolemaic Period, fourth/third century BC. A painter who was spoken of as a rival to Apelles (though not by Pliny, who considered him rather second-rate) Antiphilus was famous for the lightness and delicacy with which he executed his works. He ended his life at the court of PTOLEMY I where he was much prized.

Pliny the Younger (Gaius Plinius Caecilius Secundus) trans. L. Hutchinson, London, 1921–7: 35, 114, 138.
B. R. Brown, *Ptolemaic Paintings and Mosaics and the Alexandrian Style*, Cambridge MA, 1957: 88–92.

Antonius, Marcus (alt. Mark Antony), Roman General, Ptolemaic Period, 83–30 BC. One of the most powerful men in Rome in the final years of the Republic, Mark Antony was unfortunate in being a contemporary of CAESAR and OCTAVIAN. An able man of flawed character, Antony was given supreme command of Rome's eastern provinces. There he encountered the queen of Egypt, CLEOPATRA VII, and made her his mistress. He made her sons kings, proclaiming the elder PTOLEMY XV CAESARION, King of Kings. Political opinion in Rome, manipulated by Caesar's heir, Octavian, saw Cleoplatra as an enemy of Rome. Octavian turned against Antony and fought a great sea battle against his forces at Actium. The outcome was uncertain until Cleopatra suddenly withdrew her forces from Antony's support and fled back to Egypt. Antony, defeated, also sailed to Egypt, where both he and the queen killed themselves in 30 BC.

J. M. Carter, *The Battle of Actium: The Rise and Triumph of Augustus Caesar*, London, 1970.
E. G. Huzar, *Mark Antony*, Minneapolis, 1978.

Anu, Prince, Tenth/Eleventh Dynasties, First Intermediate Period, *c.* 2160–2125 BC. In his tomb in Asiut, in Middle Egypt, Anu installed some wall paintings generally typical of the period. However, an inscribed painting, with large clear hieroglyphs, is said to have been written by Anu himself.

Robins 1990: 36.

Apepi Awoserre (alt. Apophis, Apapy), King, Fifteenth Dynasty, Second Intermediate Period, *c.* 1555 BC. One of the more successful of the invading Hyksos kings, the semitic-speaking 'Rulers of Foreign Lands' who occupied much of northern Egypt in the period following the eclipse of the feeble Thirteenth and Fourteenth Dynasties, Apepi is known as one of the 'Great Hyksos'; he reigned for approximately forty years. He was a Hyksos king who embraced Egyptian ways most conscientiously, a patron of the arts and of learning.

It is possible that one of his daughters married the reigning prince of Thebes, whose family had maintained their position in the south throughout most of the Hyksos period. If this be so, then, ironically, Apepi would be one of the ancestors of the Seventeenth Dynasty which eventually drove out the Hyksos rulers.

Apepi evidently realised that matters did not bode well for the continuation of the Hyksos presence in Egypt. He is alleged to have sent a message to the King of Kush, to the south of Egypt, urging him to attack the Theban forces which were securing notable victories against the Hyksos and their allies. The message was intercepted, however, and the Kushites remained behind their frontiers. Eventually the Theban kings, SEQENENRE TAO II and his sons KAMOSE and AHMOSE, drove out the foreigners. By this time Apepi, who must have been an old man and had withdrawn to the north of the country, was dead.

T. Säve-Söderbergh, 'The Hyksos Rule in Egypt', JEA 37 (1951) 53–71.
J. van Seters, *The Hyksos: A New Investigation*, New Haven CT, 1966: 153–8.
Ryholt 1996: 307, 385–7

Apepi II-Aqenienre (Apohis II), King, Fifteenth Dynasty, Second Intermediate Period, *c.* 1550 BC. After the death of APEPI I the second of the name succeeded briefly to the Hyksos' throne. He seems to have had no authority in the south of the country, and such monuments as he left were mostly usurped from earlier kings, including two colossal statues of the Thirteenth Dynasty king SEMENKHKARE-MERMENTIFU.

Grimal: 192–3.

Aper-El, Vizier, Eighteenth Dynasty, New Kingdom, *c.* 1390–1352 BC. Aper-El was a high official in the service of King AMENHOTEP III; he was buried at Saqqara with his wife and his son, Huy, who was a general of chariotry.

He became vizier to the king and thus his highest ranking official. Despite this little is known of him other than that he was a 'child of the *kap*', the royal academy in which young foreign princes and others of good birth were educated with the royal children. It has been suggested that Aper-El's name indicates an Asiatic, possibly Syrian, origin.

A. Zivie, EA1: 26–8.

Apion, Scholar and Author, Roman Period, first century AD. Apion was the son of the philosopher Poseidonius. He was president of the philological academy at Alexandria. An arrogant and self-assertive man, he is remembered for a diatribe against the Jews, which drew a pained riposte from Josephus.

F. Jacoby (ed.) *Die Fragmente der Griechischen Historiker*, 1923: 616.

Apollonius, Minister, Ptolemaic Period, *c.* 285–246 BC. The Minister of Finance under PTOLEMY II PHILADELPHUS and his remarkable wife, ARSINOE II, Appollonius was responsible for much of the character of the royal administration which remained largely in place throughout the reign of the Ptolemies. He introduced a highly centralised and systematised governmental and fiscal structure which effectively made Egypt the personal property of the Ptolemaic kings.

Grant 1982: 40–1.
Bowman 1990: 117ff, 155ff.

Apollonius Rhodius, Writer and Librarian, Ptolemaic Period, *c.* 295–215 BC. Apollonius, called 'the Rhodian' though he was born in Egypt, was the Director of the Library of Alexandria, thought to have been founded by PTOLEMY I SOTER and greatly enhanced by PTOLEMY II PHILADELPHUS. He apparently retired to Rhodes (hence his nickname) in a fit of pique. However, he returned to Alexandria where he enjoyed great success, being appointed Librarian in succession to ERATOSTHENES. Apollonius was also the author of an epic poem in four books, the *Argonautica*, which was sharply disparaged by his teacher, CALLIMACHUS.

R. Seaton, *Apollonius Rhodius*, 1912.
Grant 1982: 40.

Appianus, Historian, Roman Period, first century AD. Appianus was born in Alexandria and was in the city during the Jewish revolt in 116 AD. He moved to Rome where he was favoured by

HADRIAN, subsequently achieving considerable status under Antoninus Pius. He wrote the *Romaika*, a history of the Roman wars in twenty-four books.

H. E. White, *Appian's Roman History*, 1912–13.

Apries, King, Twenty-Sixth Dynasty, Late Period, *c.* 589–570 BC. The son of king PSAMETIK II, Apries succeeded to the throne at what was both a time of opportunity and of challenge to Egypt.

Apries was a warlike king who had pursued his enemies far outside Egypt's frontiers. The largest threat to Egypt's security – and the security of the Near East as a whole – was represented by the Babylonian Empire, under NEBUCHADREZZAR II, but initially the Egyptians were successful in containing the Babylonians. They were particularly effective in securing and maintaining control of the sea-lanes in the eastern Mediterranean. The superior Babylonian land forces, however, gradually achieved supremacy on the ground; one of their victories was the capture of Jerusalem.

Late in Apries' reign the Egyptian garrison in Elephantine mutinied; at the same time he received a call for help from his ally, the ruler of Cyrene. Apries sent not Egyptian troops but Greek mercenaries, who suffered a humiliating defeat; a state of something approaching civil war broke out between the Egyptians and the Greeks. In 570 BC the army proclaimed their general, AMASIS, king. Apries confronted his sometime general in battle in 567 BC but was defeated and killed. To Amasis' credit, however, he ensured that Apries was eventually buried with the honours and reverence due to a King of Egypt.

W. M. F. Petrie and J. H. Walker, *The Palace of Apries (Memphis II)*, London, 1909.
B. V. Bothmer 1969: 58–9.
Grimal: 362–3.
Herodotus 2: 161–3.
Trigger *et al.*: 218ff.

Aristachus, Astronomer, Ptolemaic Period, early third century BC. Aristachus was born in Samos and studied in Alexandria; he was the teacher of Hipparchus. With him he greatly augmented the scientific understanding of astronomy, and he defined the motion of the earth around the sun and on its own axis. He wrote a treatise on the relative distances of the sun and moon from the earth.

T. L. Heath, *Aristachus of Samos*, 1913.

[**Arnekhamani**], Nubian King, Meroitic Period (= Ptolemaic Period), *c.* 218–200 BC. Arnekhamani was a contemporary of the Ptolemies and, in the manner of Nubian rulers, adopted the manner and forms of the Egyptian kingship, especially in its titulary and religious practice. His inscriptions at the Temple of Apedemak at Musawwarat es-Sufra are written in early Ptolemaic Egyptian. The king appears otherwise to have followed the worship of the gods of his ancestors and himself to have been portrayed in the regalia of a Meroitic king.

Africa in Antiquity, Brooklyn, 1978: 95–6, fig. 69.
Shaw and Nicholson: 37.

Arsinoe II, Queen, Ptolemaic Period, d. *c.* 270 BC. The daughter of PTOLEMY I SOTER and Berenice I, Arsinoe (whose name was that of her grandmother, Ptolemy I's mother, the probable mistress of PHILIP II of Macedon, who was conceivably Ptolemy's father) married first Lysimachus, one of Alexander the Great's successors. After his death she married Ptolemy Ceranus, who murdered her children. She fled from him after one day and came to Egypt where she married her brother, PTOLEMY II PHILADELPHUS and ruled with him, till her death.

She was a woman of great talent and powerful personality. She participated actively in government and was responsible for much that was successful in the early Ptolemaic period. She was deified during her lifetime; after her death she was proclaimed 'King [*sic.*] of Upper and Lower Egypt' by her brother.

Grant 1982: 195.
Hodjash and Berlev 1982: no. 127, 184–5.

Arsinoe III Philopator, Queen, Ptolemaic Period, *c.* 221–205 BC. The wife of PTOLEMY IV PHILOPATOR, of whose enthusiastic identification of himself with the god Dionysus she disapproved, was otherwise a commendable and supportive joint sovereign. She was acquainted with the goddess Isis, who visited her in dreams.

Grant 1982: 227, 229.

Artatama, Queen, Eighteenth Dynasty, New Kingdom, *c.* 1400–1390 BC. The daughter of the king of Mitanni, Artatama was married to King THUTMOSE IV. She was once thought to have been the mother of his son who became King AMENHOTEP III; it is now believed that the boy's mother was another of Thutmose's wives, an Egyptian, Mutemwiya.

Wilson 1951: 201.

[**Artaxerxes I**], King, Twenty-Seventh Dynasty, First Persian Period, 465–424 BC. The first king of this name came to the Persian throne after the assassination of his father XERXES and his brother, the Crown Prince Darius in 465 BC. The Persians had ruled Egypt uneasily, frequently resorting to brutal repression, since its conquest in 525 BC. For much of Artaxerxes' reign Egypt was in a state of rebellion, led by a Libyan prince, INAROS. The rebellion failed but Inaros' example, though he himself was captured and executed, lived on to inspire resistance against the Persians.

Grimal: 370–1.
E. Bresciani, 'The Persian Occupation of Egypt', *The Cambridge History of Iran, vol. 2: The Median and Achamenian Periods*, Cambridge, 1985: 502–28.

[**Artaxerxes II**], King, Twenty-Seventh Dynasty, First Persian Period, 405–359 BC. Artaxerxes was the son of Darius II; his given name was Arses. On the latter's death a prince of the Saite house, AMYRTAEUS, seized the Egyptian throne. Thereafter a succession of native Egyptian dynasties, though short-lived, opposed the Persians and often contrived to rule large parts of the country.

Artaxerxes took little interest in the affairs of this distant province of his empire. He had to face an Egyptian revolt in 401–399 BC, during which time Egypt was lost to Persia. As his long reign drew on various of the other provinces revolted, with the Persian satraps seeking to establish independent status for their satrapies. On his death he was succeeded by Ochos, who was proclaimed as ARTAXERXES III.

Kuhrt 2: 173–4, 683, 685, 687, 691, 695, 699.

[**Artaxerxes III**] (**alt. Ochos**), King, Twenty-Seventh Dynasty, Second Persian Period, 359–338 BC. After the death of ARTAXERXES II, the problems of the Persian empire became evident. Artaxerxes III devoted himself with some success to containing the rebellions which had marked the latter years of his predecessor's reign, including uprisings in Cyprus and Phonicia, and eventually determined on the reconquest of Egypt. By this time the country had largely disengaged itself from Persian rule under the kingship of NECTANEBO II.

The Persian attack, though led by Artaxerxes himself, was defeated. He regrouped, with the aid of numbers of Greek mercenaries, and set out on another invasion of Egypt. The Greeks were at this time the undisputed master tacticians of the ancient world, and their generals swiftly destroyed the Egyptian defences. Nectanebo realised that resistance was hopeless, and this last native Egyptian king fled southwards into Nubia taking, it was said, much of his treasure with him.

Artaxerxes responded to Egyptian resistance to Persian rule by what was alleged to be a harsh and tyrannical regime imposed over the country; but this may be exaggerated. He and all his family were, however, murdered by one of his generals, the eunuch Bagoas, in 338 BC. The way was now open for ALEXANDER III of Macedon to appear on the Egyptian stage.

Lichtheim 3: 41–4.
Kuhrt 2: 674–5.

Asha-hebsed, Courtier, Nineteenth Dynasty, New Kingdom, *c.* 1294–1270 BC. Originally in the service of King SETI I, by whom he was much favoured, Asha-hebsed was a Commandant of Troops and Royal Envoy to All Foreign Lands. He enjoyed the friendship and confidence of Seti's son King RAMESSES II, and he continued in high office in his reign.

Asha-hebsed was appointed First King's Cupbearer, confirming his close relationship with Ramesses. He was responsible for supervising the building works initiated by Seti in Sinai, and for the work originally undertaken for Ramesses' remarkable temple at Abu Simbel, where Asha-hebsed's involvement is commemorated by an inscription. He was entrusted by the king with the guardianship of his son, Prince MERY-ATUM.

It is possible that Asha-hebsed's family was not Egyptian, coming originally from Syria or Canaan.

Kitchen 1982: 28, 30, 66, 139.

[**Assurbanipal**], Assyrian King (= Twenty-Sixth Dynasty). Late Period, *c.* 668–627 BC. The King of Assyria, ESARHADDON, died on his way to attack Egypt in 668 BC. the King of Egypt took advantage of the Assyrian's death to launch a counter-attack against the Assyrians occupying Memphis, which they had captured in an earlier campaign. Assurbanipal, having taken the Assyrian throne, reacted swiftly and recaptured the city. He reacted harshly towards the Egyptian princes who had given evidence of support for TAHARQA. He executed a number of them but protected NECHO of Sais and his son PSAMETIK, who were destined to be Kings of Egypt.

Taharqa's nephew and successor, King TANUTAMANI, attempted to recover Memphis and to expel the Assyrians from the Delta, which was governed by petty rulers installed by the Assyrians. This time Assurbanipal's response was catastrophic for Egypt; he invaded the country and captured the sacred city of Thebes.

Assurbanipal was a scholarly king, whose great library at Nineveh was legendary. He collected the clay tablets which recorded the actions of his predecessors on the thrones of the Mesopotamian kingdoms.

CAH III.2: 143–61.
Kitchen 1986: §353.

Atet, Princess, Fourth Dynasty, Old Kingdom, *c.* 2613–2589 BC. Atet was the wife of the important Prince NEFERMAAT, vizier to King SNEFERU, who was probably his son. She was buried with her husband at Meidum and it is from her portion of the tomb that the famous, exceptionally vivid and well painted line of geese, now in the Egyptian Museum, Cairo, was recovered. The quality of the paintings in the tomb reflect the particular interest which Nefermaat and Atet took in the arts, in which her husband was evidently an innovator.

Petrie, *Meydum*, London, 1892.
Saleh and Sourouzian: 26.
EMC JE 34571 (= CG 1742).

[**Augustus Caesar (Octavian)**], Emperor, King of Egypt, Roman Period, 30 BC–14 AD. The inheritor of the Roman imperium, ultimately from his adoptive father Julius CAESAR, of whom Octavian, later to be known as Augustus Caesar, was the heir, was faced with a critical situation in the southern reaches of the Empire by the excursions of Marcus ANTONIUS and his infatuation with CLEOPATRA VII. After the battle of Actium, Marcus Antonius returned to Egypt, where he and Cleopatra both committed suicide. He had, in the heyday of his sojourn in Egypt, made Cleopatra's sons kings. The elder, CAESARION (whose very name was an invitation to subversion by the adherents of Caesar) had been proclaimed King of Egypt in his mother's lifetime. He was murdered on Augustus' instructions, thus extinguishing the line of the Caesars and perhaps of the royal Ptolemies as well.

Augustus maintained an interest in Egypt throughout his long life. He approved of the divinising of Egyptian rulers, and under his principate Egyptian cults, which had already been making significant advances over the previous century, accelerated in their attraction for all classes of Roman society.

Augustus was the first Roman to be depicted in the temples of Egypt as a sovereign, and he was given the full titulary of a King of Upper and Lower Egypt.

A. K. Bowman 1990: 34, 36, 65f.

Auta, Sculptor, Eighteenth Dynasty, New Kingdom, *c.* 1352–1336 BC. Auta was one of the artists who came to the fore in the reign of King AMENHOTEP IV-AKHENATEN. He is shown at work carving a statue of Princess BAKETATEN, probably the daughter of King AMENHOTEP III's old age. Auta is in his studio, attended by assistants and apprentices who are engaged in various tasks as he works on the princess's statue.

De Garis Davis 1905: pl. XVII.
J. Samson, *Nefertiti and Cleopatra*, London, 1985: 44–6.

Awibre Hor, King, Thirteenth Dynasty, Middle Kingdom, *c.* 1750 BC. Awibre Hor was one of the ephemeral kings who represent the middle and later periods of the Thirteenth Dynasty. King followed king in rapid succession, based on their capital at Dahshur. Control of the administration, such as it was in a time of chaotic conditions in the Valley, was in the hands of a succession of powerful viziers; the kings, in whose names notionally they ruled, were largely ciphers.

Awibre Hor is remembered principally for the very unusual wooden shrine which was found at what was evidently the site of his burial at Dahshur. The shrine contains a life-size figure of the king, who is represented as a naked man, stepping apprehensively from its protection. It is probable that the king was originally more decorously clothed, wearing a golden kilt. His statue is disturbingly lifelike, for unlike most royal statues which come from pillaged sites, his inlaid eyes are still intact.

Awibre Hor and his wife were buried in two shaft tombs near the pyramid of King AMENEMHET III at Dahshur.

J. De Morgan, *Fouilles à Dachour Mars-Juin 1894*, pls 33–5.
Stevenson Smith 1981: 179, ill. 170.
Saleh and Sourouzian: 117.
Lehner 1997: 181.
EMC JE 30948 (CG 259).

Ay, Courtier, later King, Eighteenth Dynasty, New Kingdom, *c.* 1327–1323 BC. Ay was the son of two of the most influential members of AMENHOTEP III's court, YUYA AND TUYU; their daughter, TIY, married the king and became his favourite wife, exercising a considerable influence over him and over their son, AMENHOTEP IV-AKHENATEN. Yuya ensured that his son was appointed to important offices in the king's entourage at an early age, including that of Master of the Horse.

It is possible that Akhenaten's wife, NEFERTITI, was the daughter of Ay; in any event his influence waxed during Akhenaten's reign. At some point Ay acquired the priestly title 'God's Father', which might have denoted a special (though not necessarily blood) relationship with the king.

After the death of Akhenaten and the eventual accession of TUTANKHAMUN, Ay set himself diligently to erase the memory of the king whom he had served and to restore the power of the priests of Amun. In this he seems to have been notably successful; Akhenaten was execrated as a heretic and the members of the royal family, whose names had been compounded with that of the Aten, were renamed by the substitution of Amun's name. When Tutankhamun died, and after an abortive attempt by his queen, ANKHESENAMUN, to secure a foreign prince to succeed, Ay secured the kingship, though he was not of the royal lineage. It has been suggested that he married Tutankhamun's widow who, as a king's daughter, would have carried the right of succession. In Tutankhamun's tomb in the Valley of the Kings, Ay is shown conducting the funeral rites, usually the responsibility of the deceased's son and heir.

Ay reigned for only four years. He had originally intended to be buried at Akhetaten and work had begun on the construction of a tomb there. It contained the only version known of the great Hymn to the Aten. Later, he commandeered for himself a tomb (WV 23) which was probably originally intended for Tutankhamun, near that of AMENHOTEP III and the mortuary temple at Medinet Habu. In his tomb he is shown in the company of his first wife, Tiy II. Of Ankhesenamun there is no trace.

K. C. Seele, 'King Ay and the Close of the Amarna Period', JNES 14 (1955) 168–80.
Aldred 1988: 298, 301.

B

Bak, High Priest, Nineteenth Dynasty, New Kingdom, *c.* 1279–1270 BC. King RAMESSES II made it a practice, especially in the early years of his reign, of appointing distinguished military or public servants to the various High Priesthoods which were in his gift. One such was the appointment of Bak, hitherto a Chief Charioteer of the Residence, as High Priest of Re in Heliopolis, one of the most prestigious and powerful pontificates in the Two Kingdoms.

Kitchen 1982: 170.

Baka, Baufre, Baefre, Bicheris, *see* **Bakare**

Bakare (alt. Bicheris, Baka, Baufre, Baefre), Prince (King ?), Fourth Dynasty, Old Kingdom, post–2566 BC. Bakare, identified in Manetho's list as 'Bicheris', was possibly an ephemeral successor of King KHNUM-KHUFU, at whose death, *c.* 2566 BC, there was dissent in the royal family and the succession was disputed. It is possible that he was a son of Khnum-Khufu's heir, DJEDEFRE. By some authorities Bakare has been given a brief reign between King KHAFRE and King MENKAURE.

If Bakare is synonymous with Baufre, then he may have been a son of Khnum-Khufu. He is described in a Twelfth Dynasty inscription as having been loyal to DJEDEFRE, one of Khnum-Khufu's sons, who was perhaps the direct ancestor of the kings of the Fifth Dynasty. A cult in Baufre's name was established in the Old Kingdom.

E. Drioton, 'Une liste de Rois de la IVe Dynastie dans l'Ouâdi Hammamat', *Bull. Soc. Fr. d'Egyptol.*, 16 (1954) 41–9.
CAH I.2: 172–6.
Grimal: 74.
Lehner 1997: 139.

Bakenkhons, High Priest, Nineteenth Dynasty, New Kingdom, *c.* 1310–1220 BC. Bakenkhons' career began under King SETI I; he was born *c.* 1310 and was first employed in the relatively modest post of stable lad at the Temple of Amun at Karnak. He joined the company of priests in the temple and then went on to serve King RAMESSES II throughout much of his reign. He rose through the ranks of the priesthood, becoming one of the Prophets of Amun.

Bakenkhons and the king were evidently near-contemporaries and he lived nearly as long as the king. He was one of Ramesses' building masters and built the eastern temple at Karnak for the king. Eventually he became High Priest (First Prophet) of Amun in Thebes and held the office for twenty-seven years.

Bakenkhons left a long inscription – carved on a handsome block statue of himself, looking both youthful and supremely confident – describing the course of his career, from its relatively modest beginnings to one of the most august offices in the land. He emphasises that he was kindly to his subordinates and he lists the projects which he undertook with them for the greater glory of the king whom he served. His reputation long endured, and the gateway to the temple which he built continued to be identified with him after his death.

He died when he was about ninety years old, in the last year of the king's reign. Before his own death Ramesses appointed Bakenkhons' son, ROMA-ROY, as High Priest in his place.

Breasted 3: §§561–8.
G. Lefebvre, *Histoire des Grands Prêtres d'Amon de Karnak jusqu'à la XXIe Dynastie*, Paris, 1929: 132–9.
PM I.1: 67.
Kitchen 1982: 28, 44, 126, 139, 171–4; pl. 53.
Staatliche Sammlung Ägyptischer Kunst, München Gl., WAF 38.

Bakenrenef (alt. Bocchoris), King, Twenty-Fourth Dynasty, Third Intermediate Period, 727–715 BC. The ruler of one of the splinter states in northern Egypt which emerged during the political confusion of the latter part of the eighth century BC, Bakenrenef was the son of TEFNAKHTE, a 'Great Chief of the Ma', who had proclaimed himself king from his family base at Sais in the Delta. Bekenrenef succeeded him and may have ruled from as far south as Memphis, outside modern Cairo. He was eventually defeated by SHABAKA, one of the kings of the Kushite (Nubian) dynasty, and was said to have been burned alive.

Grimal: 341.

Bakenwerel, Chief of Police, Twentieth Dynasty, New Kingdom, *c.* 1120 BC. The Chief of Police in Western Thebes, Bakenwerel was the commander of the Medjay, the Nubian militia in the region. He was one of the officials who investigated the robbery of the royal tombs in the reign of King RAMESSES IX.

Thomas 1995: 90, 189.
The Oriental Institute, University of Chicago, 14663.

Baket III, Nomarch, Eleventh Dynasty, Middle Kingdom, *c.* 2055–2004 BC. During the First Intermediate Period, after the end of the Old Kingdom, the central authority of the monarchy was greatly weakened and the provincial nobles, especially the nomarchs, the provincial governors, acquired extensive independence and, correspondingly, great power. One of these was Baket III, the Great Chief of the Oryx Nome. However, he seems to have seen which way the wind was blowing, and to have allied himself with the emergent line of Theban princes who were to form the Eleventh Dynasty of kings. In his tomb at Beni Hassan in Middle Egypt, a scene records the attack by soldiers, including non-Egyptians, on a fortress which is defended by Egyptians. This graphically demonstrates the situation which existed at the time when NEBHEPETRE MONTUHOTEP II was restoring the royal authority. Baket's strategy would appear to have paid off, as his son succeeded him as Nomarch on his death.

P. E. Newberry, *Beni Hasan, IV parts (Archaeological Survey of Egypt)*, 1st, 2nd, 5th and 7th Memoirs, London, 1893–1900: part 2, 5–7.

Baketaten, Princess, Eighteenth Dynasty, New Kingdom, *c.* 1350 BC. One of the daughters of AMENHOTEP III's old age, she is shown attending Queen TIY when the latter paid a formal visit to her son, AKHENATEN, in his new city of Akhetaten. She seems to have remained close to the old Queen during her remaining years.

CAH II.1: 313–416.
Aldred 1988: 182, 219.

Bawi, Vizier, Sixth Dynasty, Old Kingdom, *c.* 2280–2250 BC. There were in fact two viziers called Bawi – father and son. They came from Akhmim, the capital of the ninth Panopolite nome of Upper Egypt. Both were buried in rock-cut tombs in the mountain of El Hawawish, near the capital. The elder Bawi was vizier during the reign of King PEPY I, and his son served king PEPY II. A finely painted coffin belonging to the younger Bawi survives.

Kanawati 1980.
Ashmolean Museum.

Bay, Vizier, Nineteenth Dynasty, New Kingdom, *c.* 1194–1188 BC. An enigmatic figure, Bay is thought to have been an Asiatic, perhaps a Syrian. As the Nineteenth Dynasty, which had held such promise under SETI I and RAMESSES II, stuttered to its end, Bay emerged as the power behind the very insecurely settled throne. He was closely identified with the Queen TWOSRET, who was married to King SETI II and was the stepmother of his heir SIPTAH. Bay was portrayed, literally, behind the king; he was 'Great Chancellor of the Entire Land', a remarkable position for a foreigner to achieve. He built himself a tomb in the Valley of the Kings (KV13), which might have appeared presumptuous. It is suggested that Bay is referred to in an inscription which speaks of an Asiatic and his companions 'preying on the land'. Bay had, however, assumed an impeccably Egyptian name, Ramesse-Khamenteru.

After the death of her stepson, Queen Twosret proclaimed herself Queen Regnant. Her reign was short; Bay, too, disappeared. He did not occupy his tomb in the Valley, just as Twosret was thrown out of hers by her successor.

Papyrus Harris 1, 75: 2–6.
Breasted 4: §§397–8.
CAH II.1: 238–9, 241.
Gardiner 1961: 277–8.

Bayenemwast, Army Officer, Twentieth Dynasty, New Kingdom, *c.* 1153 BC. A conspiracy against the life of King RAMESSES III was instituted at the end of his life. It was promoted by a minor wife of the king, who sought to secure the throne for their son, PENTAWERET. The conspiracy involved a number of army officers, amongst whom was Bayenemwast, the Captain of the Nubian Archers. His sister was a woman of the harem who wrote to him, urging him to revolt against the king and to stir up sedition. The plot was discovered, and at the trial of the conspirators Bayenemwast was named as 'Evil in Thebes', a form of 'debaptising' designed to un-name the criminal and thus ensure that he did not survive in the afterlife; with his fellow traitors he was found guilty and sentenced to death.

A. de Buck, 'The Judicial Papyrus of Turin', JEA 23 (1927) 152ff.
G. Posner, 'Les Criminels Débaptiés et les Morts sans Noms', R d'E, 5: 51–6.

Bebi, Official, Fifth/Sixth Dynasties, Old Kingdom, *c.* 2494–2181 BC. Bebi bore the innocuous-sounding title, 'Son of the House', which in fact indicated that he was a sort of bailiff in the Revenue Department, responsible for bringing tax defaulters to justice. He was 'Supervisor of the Grain Storehouse and Overseer of Commissions'.

H. G. Fischer, 'Old Kingdom Inscriptions in the Yale Art Gallery', *Mitteilungen des Instituts für Orientforschung*, VII (1960) 299–315.
Scott 1986: 49, no. 22.
YAG 1937: 131.

Bek, Chief Sculptor, Eighteenth Dynasty, New Kingdom, *c.* 1350 BC. Bek was the son of Men, the Chief Sculptor to King AMENHOTEP III. When AMENHOTEP IV-AKHENATEN succeeded to the throne he appointed Bek to his father's position. Bek claimed that the king himself had instructed him in the manner in which his work was to be executed. In consequence he is credited with the development of the 'Amarna Style', the distinctive and often peculiar combination of the exceptionally mannered and the naturalistic. He is commemorated in a handsome stele, with his wife Taheret, now in the Egyptian Museum, Berlin. The stele is itself a very distinctive product, with the two figures contained within a naos but carved almost three-dimensionally. If, as would seem very possible, Bek himself carved the stele, this would be the oldest self-portrait known. Bek was succeeded as Chief Sculptor by THUTMOSE.

At Aswan a carving on a granite boulder shows both Men and Bek together, respectively honouring statues of Amenhotep III and Akhenaten.

L. Habachi, 'Varia from the reign of King Akhenaten', MDAIK, 20: 85–92.
Aldred 1968: 135, 214.
Frey 1982 (1992): 43.
W. Kaiser, 'Ein neues Werk der Amarnanzeit', *Jahrbuch der Stiflung Preussicher Kultrubesitz*, Bd It (1963) 133–6.
EMB, 1/63.

Bekh, Artisan, First Dynasty, Archaic Period, *c*. 3000 BC. An artisan with the name of Bekh was in the employment of King DEN, the fourth king of the First Dynasty. It is possible that he was sacrificed and buried with the king on the latter's death.

Bekh's name was inscribed on two copper adzes and also on an ivory label, in conjunction with the king's. This might suggest a status higher than that of a simple artisan.

W. M. F. Petrie, *Tombs of the Courtiers and Oxyrhynkos*, London, 1925: 4; pls xii 1, iii 1, 2.

Bener, Official, Twelfth Dynasty, Middle Kingdom, *c*. 1965–1920 BC. Bener was the Hall-Keeper to the Palace in the reign of King SENWOSRET I. He is commemorated by one of the earliest known *shabti* figurines, the small models of 'Answerers', placed in the tomb to carry out any disagreeable tasks which the deceased might be required to undertake on the journey to the afterlife.

Thomas 1995: 60, 154.
MMA 44.4.5.

Bener-ib, Queen, First Dynasty, Archaic Period, *c*. 3100 BC. Though the form of her name is disputed, this lady was probably the wife of the first king of the First Dynasty, AHA. A fragment of ivory from a box links her name with that of the king.

Emery 1961: 53.
Spencer: 79, pl. 57.
BM EA 35513.

Ben-Ozen, Royal Herald, Nineteenth Dynasty, New Kingdom, *c*. 1213–1203 BC. During the reign of King RAMESSES II it is noticeable that men with apparently Asiatic names are to be found occupying important offices. One such was Ben-Ozen who was Royal Herald during the reign of King MERENPTAH; it is perhaps ironic that Merenptah used to be described as the king of Egypt who presided over the Exodus, an event for which there is no evidence whatsoever.

Wilson 1951: 258.

Berenice I, Queen, Ptolemaic Period, d. 279 BC. The wife of PTOLEMY I SOTER, the founder of the dynasty, was evidently a woman of formidable character. With her husband, she was proclaimed divine by their son PTOLEMY II PHILADELPHUS, as set out in the Canopus Decree issued in 239 BC.

Grant 1982: 96, 195–6.

Bes, Nomarch, Twenty-Sixth Dynasty, Late Period, *c*. 664–610 BC. The governor of the Mendean nome in the Delta in northern Egypt in the reign of PSAMETIK I.

His block statue is notable for the tragic expression on the subject's face.

Bothmer 1961 (1969): 22, no. 20, pls 18–19. Museo Nationale Palermo, 145.

Bes, Mayor, Twenty-Sixth Dynasty, Late Period, 664–610 BC. The Mayor of Thebes during the reign of King PSAMETIK I Bes, the son of Amenemone, was Mayor of Thebes, an increasingly important office in the Late Period of Egyptian history. He was a Divine Father and Prophet, offices which his father had held before him, though he was not Mayor.

M-P. Foissy-Aufrère, 'Civilization Suivances et "Cabinetz de Curiositez" ', Édité par la Fondation du Muséum Calvet, Avignon: no. 88, *Cône Funéraire du Maire du Thébes, Bès*, Muséum Calvet, Avignon, A287.

Betrest, Queen, First Dynasty, Archaic Period, *c.* 2925 BC. This Queen, whose name is uncertain, is thought to have been the mother of King SEMERKHET, the penultimate king of the First Dynasty; she was therefore probably the wife of King ANEDJIB. It is significant that the mothers of kings are mentioned at this early period, suggesting that at the beginning of dynastic history the blood-royal, and hence the right to the kingship, was already considered to descend through the female line.

CAH I.2: 36.

Bint-Anath, Queen, Nineteenth Dynasty, New Kingdom, *c.* 1279–1213 BC. Bint-Anath, whose name acknowledges one of the goddesses of Canaan, was the eldest daughter of King RAMESSES II by one of his principal wives, Queen ISTNOFRET. She was born when Ramesses was still Crown Prince. Later, Bint-Anath is referred to as 'Princess-Queen'. She is recorded in inscriptions at the king's temple at Abu Simbel.

After the death of NEFERTARI Istnofret became Chief Queen and Bint-Anath was associated with her. When, comparatively soon after her appointment as Chief Queen, Istnofret died, Bint-Anath succeeded her. In the fullness of time she was accorded a splendid tomb in the Valley of the Queens.

Kitchen 1982: 40, 88, 99, 100, 191.

Bunefer, Queen, Fourth Dynasty, Old Kingdom, *c.* 2500 BC. Bunefer was the wife of King SHEPSESKHAF, one of the more intriguing figures of the Fourth Dynasty. When he died, after a reign of only four years, his funeral ceremonies were conducted by Bunefer. Such a procedure was highly unusual, the funerary rites normally being performed by a son or other close male family member. From this circumstance, it might be presumed that the relationship between husband and wife was especially close.

S. Hassan, *Excavations at Giza*, IV, Oxford and Cairo (1932–3) 119.

Butehamun, Scribe, Tomb Restorer, Twentieth/Twenty-First Dynasties, New Kingdom/Third Intermediate Period, *c.* 1070 BC. The outbreaks of tomb robbing at the end of the New Kingdom posed considerable problems for the bureaucracy of the royal necropolis. Butehamun and his father DJEHUTYMOSE, 'Scribes of the Necropolis', were leading officials in the necropolis, and Butehamun in particular undertook the restoration of the violated mummies of the kings and queens when they had been recovered. Their names are found in many contexts in the Valley of the Kings, and Butehamun is known to have been responsible for the restoration of the mummy of King RAMESSES III, his intervention being recorded on the king's replacement mummy-cloths.

Butehamun is shown incensing various past monarchs, on the lid of his outer coffin. This suggests that he was involved in the restoration of their burials also.

Butehamun bore a number of very unusual titles, which presumably reflected both his exalted status in handling the bodies of once-living gods and the responsibilities which he undertook in ensuring the security of their burials. These included 'Opener of the Gates in the Necropolis', 'Opener of the Gates of the Underworld' and 'Overseer of Works in the House of Eternity'.

Jansen-Winkeln, 'Coffin E5288', ZÄS (1995).
E.F. Wente, *Late Ramesside Letters*, Chicago, 1967: 59–61.
Reeves and Wilkinson: 203, 204–5, 206.
Museo Egizio, Turin.

C

[Caesar, Gaius Julius], Roman General and Dictator, Ptolemaic Period, d. 44 BC. An aristocratic Roman of consummate political skills and, for much of his career, remarkable good fortune, Caesar elevated himself from relative poverty and obscurity to a position of supreme authority over the entire Roman world. In his long-drawn rivalry with Pompey the Great he became involved in a series of long campaigns across the Empire. He gained control of Pompey's power base in Spain and then pursued him to Greece; Pompey fled to Egypt, where he was murdered in 48 BC. Caesar entered Egypt and became committed to the support of the Ptolemaic queen CLEOPATRA VII in her conflict with her brother, PTOLEMY XIII. He remained some months in Egypt, leaving Cleopatra pregnant with CAESARION (later Ptolemy XV) generally acknowledged to be Caesar's son.

Caesar's excursion to Egypt was to have lasting consequences for the independence of the country. Long subject to Roman influence, Egypt became a province of the Empire when Octavian (AUGUSTUS) occupied the country after the defeat of Marcus ANTONIUS at Actium and the suicide of Cleopatra in 30 BC.

J. Samson, *Nefertiti and Cleopatra*, London, 1985: 109–20.

Caesarion (Ptolemy XV), King, Ptolemaic Period, 47–30 BC. A quintessentially unfortunate figure, Caesarion was a son of CLEOPATRA VII, allegedly by Julius CAESAR; his ancestry could thus have hardly been more illustrious. His destiny was to be trapped between the ambitions of his mother and the power of Rome. Cleopatra's lover, Marcus ANTONIUS, had proclaimed Caesarion and his brother kings; Caesarion was crowned king of Egypt as Ptolemy XV in 44 BC. After Antony's defeat by the forces of Caesar's official heir AUGUSTUS CAESAR (Octavianus) in 31 BC, Caesarion, who might have served as a rallying point for those in Rome who were loyal to Caesar's memory as well as to the Egyptians (especially the Alexandrians with whom he seems to have been popular), was murdered by Augustus' order in 30 BC.

J. Whitethorne, *Cleopatras*, London, 1994.
Hughes-Hallett.
H. I. Bell, *Egypt from Alexander the Great to the Arab Conquest*, London, 1956.

Callimachus, Scholar and poet, Ptolemaic Period, 4th/3rd centuries BC. A most influential teacher, Callimachus was employed in the library of Alexandria and was court poet to PTOLEMY II PHILADELPHUS. He was a prolific writer, reputed to have produced some 800 works. His most famous work was *Aetia*, four books of elegies. Many of his epigrams survive.

R. Pfeiffer, *Callimachus*, 1949–53.
C. A. Trypanis, *Callimachus' Aetia*, 1958.

[**Cambyses II**], King, Twenty-Seventh Dynasty, Persian Period, 525–522 BC. Cambyses succeeded CYRUS II on the Persian throne in 525 BC, and one of his first acts was to march on Egypt, annihilating the Egyptian army at Pelusium. The king, PSAMETIK III, was later taken prisoner and sent in chains to Susa, an unheard of humiliation for a King of Egypt.

Cambyses has generally had a critical reputation, largely as a result of Greek propaganda when the Persians' erstwhile allies became their enemies; he also incurred the enmity of the priests when he reduced the subsidies from the state to which certain of the temples had become accustomed. Certainly there is no clear evidence for his supposed sacrilegious slaughter of the sacred Apis Bull as tradition insists; rather he seems to have been concerned to respect Egyptian beliefs and customs, a posture which would have been in line with Persian policy overall. There is a stele which depicts him, in the full regalia of a king of Egypt, worshipping the Apis. He was also notorious, perhaps with greater justification, for the loss of an entire army and its treasure in a gigantic sandstorm when it was marching to Siwa.

K. M. T. Atkinson, 'The Legitimacy of Cambyses and Darius as Kings of Egypt', *Journal of the American Oriental Society*, 76 (1956) 167–77.
Lichtheim 3: 36–41.
E. Bresciani, 'The Persian Occupation of Egypt', CHI II: 502–28.
A. B. Lloyd, 'The Inscription of Udjahorresnet', JEA 68: 166–80.

[**Chabrias**], General, Thirtieth Dynasty, Late Period, *c.* 380 BC. Chabrias was a Greek general serving in Egypt who had been instrumental in bringing King NECTANEBO I to the throne. The Persians were menacing Egypt at this time and succeeded in having Chabrias, whose generalship they feared, recalled to Athens.

Nectanebo's son TEOS was nominated as his heir, and in 361, having succeeded his father, he set out to oppose the Persians who now invaded Egypt. Chabrias had earlier served with him when he was Crown Prince, commanding the Egyptian navy. Teos was deposed, however, by his son, TJAHEPIMU, who secured the throne for his own son, NECTANEBO II. Teos fled from Egypt and Chabrias again returned to Athens.

Grimal: 375, 7, 8.

Chaeremon, Priest, Roman Period, first century AD. A priestly scholar living in one of the temples in the days when Rome controlled Egypt, Chaeremon is known from extracts from his works, quoted by Porphyry; the originals are lost. He was concerned to record the life of the priests of Egypt, emphasising their dedicated service to the gods. He is interesting in that he appears to be attempting to explain Egyptian traditions to a non-Egyptian audience.

Pieter Willem van der Horst, 'Chaeremon: Egyptian Priest and Stoic Philosopher', *Études Préliminaire aux Religions Orientales dans l'Empire Romaine*, 101 (1984) Leiden: 16–23.

Cheops, *see* **Khnum-Khufu**

Chephren, *see* **Khafre**

Cleomenes, Financier, Ptolemaic Period, *c.* 332 BC. Cleomenes was given charge of the financial administration of Egypt and responsibility for supervising the building of Alexandria. He was appointed governor of Egypt 332–1 BC and succeeded brilliantly. But after Alexander's death and having amassed a great personal fortune, he incurred the enmity of PTOLEMY I and was executed by him.

A. B. Bosworth, *Conquest and Empire: The Reign of Alexander the Great*, Cambridge, 1988.
CAH VII.1: 122–3.

Cleopatra VII, Queen, Ptolemaic Period, 51–30 BC. The most celebrated of the seven queens of the Ptolemaic dynasty who bore the name, Cleopatra VII succeeded her father PTOLEMY XII AULETES, ruling initially with her brother and husband PTOLEMY XIII, who expelled her from Egypt in 48 BC. She appealed (in both senses) to CAESAR in Rome, who effected her restoration. Ptolemy XIII was drowned in the Nile; another brother, PTOLEMY XIV, was appointed joint ruler with Cleopatra. In 47 BC Cleopatra bore a son, CAESARION, whom she insisted was Caesar's child and who was proclaimed king of Egypt as Ptolemy XV. Cleopatra bore her lover, Marcus ANTONIUS, twins, and in 34 BC Antony proclaimed Cleopatra 'Queen of Queens' and Caesarion 'King of Kings'.

Octavian Caesar (AUGUSTUS), Caesar's heir, represented Cleopatra as a threat to Rome and intrigued vigorously against her. After the battle of Actium in 30 BC, when Antony was defeated, like him Cleopatra committed suicide, rather than be taken in triumph to Rome.

Hughes-Hallett 1990.
J. Whitehorne, *Cleopatras*, London, 1994.
J. Samson, *Nefertiti and Cleopatra*, London, 1985.

Ctesibus, Engineer, Ptolemaic Period, third century BC. An engineer of genius, Ctesibus was credited with the invention of an accurate water-clock, a pump with a valve and plunger (he harnessed air pressure for his inventions); he also invented a catapult.

A. G. Drachman, *The Mechanical Technology of Greek and Roman Antiquity*, 1963.

[**Cyrus II**], Great King, The Achaemenid Empire, 559–530 BC. The accession of Cyrus the Great to the Persian throne signalled a period of danger to many of the states of the Near East, not least to Egypt. The ageing king of Egypt, AMASIS, sought to secure alliances against the Persian threat but was largely unsuccessful. Cyrus' son, CAMBYSES, effected the conquest of Egypt in 525 BC, culminating in the capture and probably execution of the king, PSAMETIK III. He is recorded as having died in August 530 BC.

Kuhrt 1995: II, 647–61.
CHI 2, *The Median and Achaemenian Periods*.

D

Dagi, Vizier, Eleventh Dynasty, Middle Kingdom, *c*. 2055–2004 BC. Dagi was descended from a family of provincial magnates and rose still higher to be Vizier to the founder of the Middle Kingdom and the Re-unifier of Egypt, King NEBHEPETRE MONTUHOTEP II. He was Chancellor, Royal Treasurer and the Superintendent of the the Pyramid City. As the king's principal Minister, Dagi must have been involved with Nebhepetre Montuhotep's campaigns to restore the unity of Egypt, which were brilliantly successful.

He was buried near his king's own burial place at Deir el-Bahri, in a richly appointed porticoed tomb (TT 103).

N. De Garis Davis, *Five Theban Tombs*, 28; pls XXIX–XXXVIII.
Winlock 1947: 44–5.
Hayes 1953: 162–3.

[Darius I], King, Twenty-Seventh Dynasty, First Persian Period, 522–486 BC. Though a Persian who took the throne of Egypt by conquest, Darius was always remembered with approval by the Egyptians for having scrupulously observed the immemorial customs and beliefs of the Two Lands; he observed the animal cults respectfully. He was a benefactor of the temples, building on a large scale, and reordered the administration, introducing a new legal code for the country, the result of sixteen years' deliberation by the commission appointed to carry out the task. He was, however, diverted from his concern for Egypt by the Persian defeat by the Greeks at Marathon, and despite his reputation for magnanimity, the Delta cities revolted. He was succeeded by XERXES, whose reputation, by contrast with that of Darius, was grim.

E. Bresciani, 'The Persian occupation of Egypt', CHI 2: 502–28.
J. H. Johnson, 'The Persians and the Continuity of Egyptian Culture', in *Achaemenid History VIII; Continuity and Change*, A. Kuhrt, H. Sancisi-Weerdenburg and M. Root (eds) Leiden, 1994.
Kuhrt 1995: II, 670–2.

[Darius II], King, Twenty-Seventh Dynasty, First Persian Period, 424–405 BC. The second Darius recalled the reign of his ancestor by adopting initially a policy of conciliation towards Egypt. The Persian predilection for seeking the goodwill of Jewish communities in their provinces was demonstrated by Darius in the case of the large and prosperous community in Elephantine. This expression of favour for a people whom the Egyptians regarded as foreign adventurers annoyed the more nationalistic among them. As a result, a revolt under the Saite prince AMYRTAEUS was launched in the year of Darius' death, giving rise to the short-lived Twenty-Eighth Dynasty.

The Jews were, by and large, loyal to the Achaemenids. However, they exposed themselves to criticism by insisting on sacrificing goats at the temple of Khnum in Elephantine. Arsames, the Persian satrap, forbad the practice.

E. Bresciani, 'The Persian occupation of Egypt', CHI 2: 502–528.

[**Darius III Codoman**], King, Thirty-First Dynasty, Second Persian Period, 336–332 BC. The third Persian Great King to bear the name Darius was the ill-fated opponent of ALEXANDER THE GREAT, who defeated the Persian army at the battle of Issos and hunted Darius until he was murdered by his own officers. Alexander invaded Egypt through Gaza and was proclaimed king and saviour of the country by the Egyptians, delighted at the Persians' expulsion from their land.

Lane Fox 1973.

Debhen (alt. Debehen), Noble, Fourth Dynasty, Old Kingdom, *c.* 2532–2503 BC. The actual status of Debhen, who lived during the reign of King MENKAURE, the builder of the Third Pyramid at Giza, is not known, but he was of sufficient importance for the king, on a visit to inspect work on his pyramid, to issue instructions for the building and equipping of Debhen's tomb nearby (LG 90). Fifty men were deputed by the king to work on its construction.

Although the decoration of his tomb is in a fragmentary state, enough remains to show that it was important in the history of tomb development. That Debhen was himself important is suggested by the fact that an inner wall in the tomb was lined with stone to give a better surface for the reliefs carved on it, the earliest example of this technique recorded. The most remarkable scene which it contained indicated the tomb's location on the Giza plateau; it shows men climbing a ramp to burn incense before a statue at a shrine on its summit. The tomb evidently contained a line of statues of Debhen. It is also notable for some of the earliest evidence of funerary ceremonies and priests participating in the funeral rites, which later became customary in the Old Kingdom.

Breasted 1: §§210–12.
Reisner 1942: 221, 310, 358–9.
Stevenson Smith 1946 (1949): 58, 166, 170–1, 190, 346, 358; pl. 47.

Dedia, Painter, Nineteenth Dynasty, New Kingdom, *c.* 1290 BC. Dedia was Chief of Draughtsman-Painters in Karnak, serving the Vizier, PASER, who was engaged in directing the construction and decoration of buildings commissioned by King SETI I. He supervised the decoration of the hypostyle hall at Karnak, one of the masterpieces of New Kingdom architecture. Seti's son, RAMESSES, who would eventually succeed Seti as king, was also closely involved, and Dedia would have worked to the prince's instructions likewise.

He was also responsible for the restoration of the monuments of earlier kings and queens of Egypt, including Queen AHMOSE NEFERTIRY, AMENHOTEP I and THUTMOSE III. A palette has been found which still retains colours and which may have belonged to Dedia.

Dedia came from a long line of professional artists; he was of the sixth generation of his family to work at Thebes. The family originally came from Syria or Canaan.

Kitchen 1982: 39.
Andreu *et al.* 1997: no. 63.
MduL C 50.

Dedu, Army Commander, Eighteenth Dynasty, New Kingdom, *c.* 1479–1425 BC. Dedu was a Nubian who commanded the Medjay, a militia force recruited from the Nubian tribes, who distinguished themselves during the struggle for the restoration of the Egyptian kingship in the

Seventeenth Dynasty and in the early years of the New Kingdom. Dedu served King THUTMOSE III; he was envoy to the tribes of the Western Desert, of which he was the governor.

During peace-time the Medjay acted as the police force of Egypt.

W. F. Edgerton, *The Thutmosid Succession*, Chicago IL, 1933.
D. B. Redford, *The History and Chronology of the 18th Dynasty of Egypt: Seven Studies*, Toronto, 1967.

[Deinocrates], Architect, Macedonian/Ptolemaic Periods, *c.* 330 BC. When ALEXANDER THE GREAT decided to build his new capital on the site which was to become Alexandria, he is said to have laid his cloak on the ground and to have instructed his architect, Deinocrates, to draw its outline and thus to determine the shape of the city-to-come. Grain was sprinkled around the cloak's edges and, to the horror of Alexander's entourage, birds flew down and consumed the grain and then flew away. Alexander reassured his followers however that his city was now carried up into the sky and so would endure for ever.

Deinocrates continued to supervise the design and construction of the city after Alexander's death.

R. D. Milns, *Alexander the Great*, London, 1968: 103.

Demedjibtowy, King, Eighth Dynasty, First Intermediate Period, *c.* 2181–2125 BC. Demedjibtowy was the last of the fragile kings to reign in Memphis after the end of the Old Kingdom. He was overthrown by the Heracleopolitan princes who eventually comprised the Ninth and Tenth dynasties.

CAH I.2: 198.

Demetrius, Landscape Painter, Ptolemaic Period, *c.* 163–4 BC. Demetrius, son of Seleukos, an Alexandrian, was an important influence in the development of a notable style of painting especially associated with artists in the City, of dramatic renderings of natural scenes. He was renowned as a *topographos* and moved to Rome where he introduced and popularised the form.

When PTOLEMY VI sought refuge in Rome whilst exiled from Egypt, Demetrius gave him shelter.

Diodorus Siculus, Biblioteka XXXI, 8.
Grant 1982: 179.

Demetrius Phalereus, Statesman and Scholar, Ptolemaic Period, *c.* 350–280 BC. A remarkably distinguished figure, Demetrius was to end his life ingloriously. At one time head of the Athenian state, to which he was appointed by the citizens, he was eventually deposed and fled to Egypt where he was well received by PTOLEMY I. It has been proposed that it was Demetrius who first suggested the idea of the Library to Ptolemy. However, he appears to have fallen out of Ptolemy's favour and was banished to Upper Egypt. There, it is said, he died from a snake bite.

CAH VIII.1: 55–6, 75–7.
P. Green, *Alexander to Actium: The Historical Evolution to the Hellenistic Age*, Berkeley CA, 1990.

Den (alt. Udimu), King, First Dynasty, Archaic Period, *c.* 2950 BC. By the time that Den came to the throne, the First Dynasty was well secured and the prosperity of the country was advancing with great rapidity. The quality of decorative and utilitarian objects as much as architecture, was now very fine, anticipating the highest standards achieved, for example, during the height of the Old Kingdom. It was also a time of innovation when many of the elements which were to become familiar parts of the rituals, titles and ceremonies associated with the kingship were first introduced.

In later times Den had a reputation as a

magician, who introduced some of the spells later assumed into the Book of the Dead, and also as a physician; MANETHO asserted that medical treatises said to have been written by the king, were extant in his day.

Den may have been a child when he succeeded; certainly he appears to have reigned for a long time and to have celebrated his jubilee. He was served by two notable ministers, HEMAKA, whose probable tomb at Saqqara produced a great mass of finely made artifacts, and ANKH-KA. Den was entombed at Abydos and even this aspect of his history was innovative, for his tomb possessed a granite floor, the first evidence of the use of stone in Egyptian architecture.

Petrie 1900.
Emery 1961: 73–80.
Spencer: 64–7, 93, 95; ills 45, 55, 66, 67.

Didia, High Priest, Nineteenth Dynasty, New Kingdom, *c.* 1260 BC. Didia was appointed High Priest of Ptah at Memphis by King RAMESSES II, probably succeeding his father, PAHEMNETJER, who was also Vizier. Didia was succeeded in turn by one who was perhaps the most memorable of Ramesses' sons, Prince KHAEMWASET, who remained in office until his death, around the fifty-fifth year of his father's reign.

Kitchen 1982: 170.

Diodorus Siculus, Historian, Roman Period, first century BC. A native of Sicily, Diodorus was an assiduous writer and produced a monumental history of the world, *Bibliotheke Historica*, the first book of which includes information about Egypt which Diodorus seems to have visited, if only briefly. He was responsible for the universal dissemination of the version of the Osiris-Isis-Set myth which attracted much attention in the world of late antiquity and was then passed on to later generations. He is not generally regarded as reliable an observer as HERODOTUS, though he provides some insights on the course of events in the centuries immediately after Herodotus' visit to Egypt in the fifth century.

C. H. Oldfather, *Diodorus*, 1933.
T. W. Africa, 'Herodotus and Diodorus on Egypt', JNES (1965) 254ff.

Djadaemankh, Official, Sixth Dynasty, Old Kingdom, *c.* 2200 BC. Djadaemankh was 'Overseer of the Offices of the Royal Administration'. He was able to secure an advantageous location for his burial, at Giza, close to the pyramid of King KHNUM-KHUFU.

Pelizaeus-Museum, Hildesheim, no. 12.

Djadjaemankh, Priest and Magician, Fourth Dynasty, Old Kingdom, *c.* 2613–2494 BC. A magician and Chief Lector Priest retained at the court of King SNEFERU, Djadjaemankh featured in a popular tale which had a long currency in Egypt. He was called in to lighten the king's mood when he was bored and depressed. He proposed that Sneferu should take a boating party to the lake, thus allowing him to watch the pretty, scantily clad girls who would make up the crew of the barge. During the outing one girl lost her turquoise pendant; Djadjaemankh separated the waters of the lake to recover it.

The story is related in the Westcar papyrus. The possibility cannot be entirely dismissed that the whole story is an engaging invention.

Lichtheim 1: 216–17.

Djar (alt. Djer), Official, Eleventh Dynasty, Middle Kingdom, *c.* 2055–2004 BC. Djar was Overseer of the Royal Harem during the reign of King NEBHEPETRE MONTUHOTEP II, the founder of the Middle Kingdom and the Re-unifier of Egypt. He was buried near the king's great tomb at Deir el-Bahri (TT 366).

Hayes 1953: 162–3.

Djari, Expert in Foreign Trade, Eleventh Dynasty, Middle Kingdom, *c.* 2112–2063 BC. At the time when the family of Theban princes was struggling to reassert royal authority over all of Egypt, INYOTEF II WAHANKH, one of the most successful of the early Eleventh-Dynasty kings, the grandfather of King NEBHEPETRE MONTUHOTEP II who eventually restored the unity of the Valley, had in his service Djari, described as an 'expert in foreign trade'. It is interesting that such an appointment could be made during a period of considerable stress in the country. It was a time when trade in the Levant, Western Asia and the Arabian Gulf was especially active; perhaps Djari had some part in the Egyptian end of such enterprises.

Clère and Vandier, *Stèles de la Première Periode Intermédiaire*, 18.
Kees 1961: 240.

Djau, Vizier, Sixth Dynasty, Old Kingdom, *c.* 2280 BC. An important official, the son of a noble family from Abydos, who served the two sons of PEPY I, MERENRE and PEPY II who became kings successively, Djau is an admirable example of the skilful, well placed noble who attained great influence and power in his lifetime by directing the royal civil service. Equally, through its alliance with him, the royal house had secured the loyalty and support of an important provincial noble family.

Djau was the brother of two of the wives of PEPY I, who were the mothers of his successors. The family prospered; one of Djau's sons, IBI, was appointed the Governor of the Twelfth Nome of Upper Egypt and seems to have established a form of dynastic succession for his heirs in the rule of the south.

Djau evidently maintained his links with his home province, setting up a foundation for the maintenance of his statue in the temple of Khentiamentiu at Abydos.

A. H. Gardiner, 'Was the Vizier Djau one of Six Brothers?' ZÄS 79 (1954) 95–6.

Djedefre (alt. Redjedef), King, Fourth Dynasty, Old Kingdom, *c.* 2566–2558 BC. When King KHNUM-KHUFU died there was dissent in the royal family and the succession was disputed. The Crown Prince, KAWAB, had died; his wife, HETEPHERES II married one of his brothers, Djedefre, who ascended the throne. Though the legitimacy of his claim has been disputed, Djedefre performed the funerary rites for Khnum-Khufu, the prerogative of a son and heir.

Djedefre planned his own pyramid and funerary temple to the north of Giza, at Abu Rowash. There, huge excavations still testify to what would have been the massive scale of his monuments if he had lived to complete them. It is likely, however, that his reign was cut short; the powerful princes ANKHAF and MINKHAF, both of whom were to be viziers, supported the rival branch of the family that brought KHAFRE to the throne. Hetepheres II made her peace with the new line and lived on to the very end of the dynasty, *c.* 2500 BC.

A memorial of the reign of Djedefre is one of the finest royal portraits to survive from the period which produced the greatest portrait sculpture in the long history of Egypt – a magnificent head of the king in quartzite. He was the first king of Egypt to adopt the style 'Sa-Re', Son of Re.

E. Chassinat, 'A propos d'une tête en gres rouge du Roi Didoufri', *Mem. Piot*, 25 (1921–2) 53–75.
J. Vandier, *Manuel d'Archéologie Égyptienne*, Paris 1954(?) 86.
Lehner 1997: 120–1.
MduL E12626.
PM III.1: 2.
Ziegler 1990: 21–5.

Djedkare Isesi, King, Fifth Dynasty, Old Kingdom, *c.* 2414–2375 BC. During his long reign, which may have been as much as forty years, Djedkare, the penultimate king of the Fifth Dynasty, was able to enjoy to the full the tranquil splendour of this latter part of the Old Kingdom period. The insecurities of the late Fourth Dynasty had largely been overcome and Egypt could enjoy a period of peace and considerable achievement in all departments of life. Djedkare's reign is notable for a number of inscriptions which record architectural projects and the king's pleasure in them.

He also encouraged long-distance expeditions, including, it is said, one to Punt. In the reign of PEPY II, the traveller HARKHUF records an expedition which, like his own, brought back a pygmy, the first known since the reign of Djedkare Isesi.

The king was served by several distinguished viziers and others in the increasingly complex administration which was growing apace in Egypt. Djedkare Isesi was buried in a pyramid to the south of Saqqara.

Breasted 1: §§264–7.
Grimal: 78–9.

Djedkare-Shebitku, *see* **Shabataka**

Djedkhonsuefankh, High Priest, Twenty-First Dynasty, Third Intermediate Period, *c.* 1000 BC. The High Priest (First Prophet) of Amun in Thebes. His relationship with the royal family is obscure, though he was undoubtedly a senior prince in addition to his ecclesiastical appointment. It is possible that he died a violent death, as the consequence of troubles in Thebes at the time.

A. Dodson, *Monarchs of the Nile*, London, 1995: 155.

Djedkhonsuefankh, High Priest, Twenty-Sixth Dynasty, Late Period, *c.* 664–610 BC. The Prophet (High Priest) of the important god, Montu of Thebes, who had been especially powerful during the early Middle Kingdom, it is probable that Djedkhonsuefankh lived during the reign of King PSAMETIK I.

Bothmer 1961 (1969): 4, no. 4, pl. 4.
MMA 07.228.27.

Djedneferre Dudimose, King, Thirteenth (?) Dynasty, Middle Kingdom, *c.* 1675 BC. Djedneferre Dudimose has been identified as the king of Egypt at the time when the Hyksos established their rule over much of the northern part of the land. MANETHO the historian thus described him, but it may be that he was confusing him with King SALITIS, who actually founded the Fifteenth Dynasty, the first of the Hyksos to rule in Egypt.

CAH II.1: 52–3.
Ryholt 1996: 156.

Djefai-nisut, Official, Third Dynasty, Old Kingdom, *c.* 2650 BC. Djefai-nisut was 'Overseer of Recruits', a military appointment which demonstrates how early many of the important, specialist offices and the titles that went with them had been established in Egypt in the early dynasties.

S. Hassan, *Excavations at Giza, Vol. 1*, Oxford, 1932: 64; fig. 116.
Kestner Museum, Hannover, 1935, 200.46.

Djehuty, General, Eighteenth Dynasty, New Kingdom, *c.* 1479–1425 BC. As soon as THUTMOSE III had rid himself of Queen HATSHEPSUT he returned to the profession of arms with which he had occupied himself whilst she ruled Egypt. He decided on a campaign into Asia and moved northwards. Amongst his senior officers was Djehuty, who distinguished himself at the seige of Joppa in Palestine. The story of what was said to be Djehuty's device to effect the city's capture, which anticipates the episode of the Trojan Horse, went into Egyptian legend, but it may have some basis in fact. Djehuty was made 'Resident', an appointment hitherto unrecorded, and amongst the prizes given to him by the king was a magnificent gold cup.

Djehuty's prowess and its reward are related in Papyrus Harris 500.

K. Sethe and W. Helck, *Urkunden der 18 Dynastie (Urk IV)*, Leipzig and Berlin 1901: 999.
PM I: 21ff.
Ziegler 1990: 43–5.
Andreu *et al.* 1997: no. 46.
MduL N 713 (gold cup).

Djehutyemhab, General, Twentieth Dynasty, New Kingdom, *c.* 1150 BC. 'The Great General of His Majesty's Army and Royal Scribe', Djehutyemhab was an important figure in his time, though it is not known for certain who was the king he served. His wife, Iay, was a Chantress of Wepwawet; in RAMESSES III's time the king made a gift to the temple of Wepwawet, which was under the charge of a General Djehutyemhab.

Scott 1986: 128–131m, no. 73.

Djehutyhotep, Nomarch, Twelfth Dynasty, Middle Kingdom, *c.* 1922–1855 BC. The hereditary governor of the Hare Nome in the reign of SENWOSRET III, Djehutyhotep was one of the most powerful and magnificent of the provincial magnates whose pretensions the king was ultimately to extinguish. Djehutyhotep, however, evidently survived long enough for him to build and occupy a splendid tomb at his capital El-Bersheh, which, among other vivid scenes, is famous for the representation of a colossal seated statue of Djehutyhotep, 6.8 metres high, being dragged by a team of 172 labourers from the alabaster quarries at Hatnub. Magnificent though the statue may have been, no part of it appears to have survived. According to an inscription it was carved by the scribe Sipa, son of Hennakhtankh; it has been estimated that the completed statue would have weighed fifty-eight tons.

Djehutyhotep's tomb contains some of the finest paintings to survive from the Middle Kingdom, their quality rivalling the best Old Kingdom work. The tomb was decorated by the artist AMENAANKHU, whilst the director of works, in charge of its construction, was Sep, son of Abkau. The coffins of the nomarch and his wife are especially remarkable, demonstrating great refinement of technique, colour and design. Djehutyhotep lived during the reigns of AMENEMHET II, SENWOSRET II and SENWOSRET III; it is likely that he died in the lifetime of the last-named.

P. E. Newberry, *El Bersheh I, The Tomb of Tehuti-Hetep*, London, 1896
F. Ll. Griffith and P. E. Newberry, *El-Bersheh II*, London, 1895: pls xii, xiii, xiv, xv.
Breasted 1: §§688–706.
PM VII: 381.
Terrace 1968.
Terrace, *The Entourage of an Egyptian Governor*, BMFAB 66 (1968) 5–27.
Lehner 1997: 203.

Djehutyhotep (alt. Pa-itsj), Nubian Prince, Eighteenth Dynasty, New Kingdom, *c.* 1473–1458 BC. During the reign of Queen HATSHEPSUT the Prince of Tehkhet in Nubia was one of the Nubian nobles who adopted Egyptian customs, to the extent of taking an Egyptian name, Djehutyhotep, and building a tomb for himself in the Egyptian style. The tomb was decorated with scenes of all the pastimes and entertainments which a well-to-do Egyptian would expect to occupy him in the afterlife. Djehutyhotep was no doubt 'a child of the *kap*', the academy in which young foreign nobles were educated in Egyptian ways.

T. Säve-Söderbergh, 'The Paintings in the Tomb of Djehutyhetep at Debeira', *Kush*, 8 (1960) 25–44.
B. Trigger *Nubia under the Pharaohs*, London, 1976: 115; fig. 40.

Djehutyhotep, Nubian Prince, Eighteenth Dynasty, *c.* 1360 BC. A contemporary of TUTANKHAMUN, Djehutyhotep was Prince of Mi'am (modern Aniba) in Lower Nubia. He is portrayed in his tomb at Debeira paying homage to the king with other

Nubian nobles; they are probably to be recognised as children of the *kap*, the royal nursery. They are exceptionally richly apparelled, and it is clear that the upper levels of Nubian society had become thoroughly Egyptianised by this time. Djehutyhotep and his companions are attended by a medley of racial types and a menagerie of exotic animals.

His brother Amenemhat was buried near him, beneath a pyramid.

G. Steindorff, *Aniba*, 2 vols, Gluckstadt and Hamburg, 1935, 1937.
S. Hochfield and E. Reifstahl (eds), *Africa in Antiquity*, 33; fig. 12.
Sudan National Museum, Khartoum.

Djehutymose, Scribe, Eighteenth Dynasty, New Kingdom, *c.* 1315 BC. Djehutymose, son of Hatiay and Iniuhe, was a scribe in the royal necropolis of Thebes. He was responsible for resealing the tomb of King TUTANKHAMUN after it was entered by robbers. He scribbled his name on a calcite jar in the king's tomb. The burial chamber and the antechamber were replastered and resealed, on this the second occasion on which the tomb had been entered illegally.

Djehutymose evidently made a speciality of the restoration of plundered royal tombs, as he left another note in the tomb of King THUTMOSE IV, in which he worked in the eighth year of the reign of King HOREMHEB. On this occasion he was acting as assistant to 'the King's Scribe, the Overseer of the Treasury, the Overseer of the Place of Eternity', MAYA. Djehutymose was described as 'the steward of the southern city' in the inscription which dates from Horemheb's eighth regnal year.

Reeves and Wilkinson: 108, 126, 193.

Djehutymose, Scribe, Twentieth Dynasty, New Kingdom, *c.* 1099–1069 BC. As the era of the Ramesside kings of the Twentieth Dynasty moved towards its conclusion, the internal political situation in Egypt deteriorated markedly. There was an outright confrontation between the Viceroy of Kush, PANEHESY, and the High Priest of Amun, AMENHOTEP. The king, RAMESSES XI, ordered the general of the army, PIANKH, to the south to restore order. This he was unable to do and eventually Egypt divided north and south and remained divided for most of its remaining history.

At this point a number of robberies occurred in the Valley of the Kings, in the perpetration of which the High Priest was implicated. Correspondence between Djehutymose, 'the Scribe of the Necropolis', and Piankh survives which indicates the extent of the damage arising from the loss of control over the Theban region, including the sacrosanct Valley.

Djehutymose and his son, BUTEHAMUN, were called in to assess the damage done to the royal tombs and to undertake their restoration and the protection of their contents. Djehutymose was evidently acknowledged as an expert in the preservation of the tombs, at least if a letter from his son is to be believed.

Wente 1967: 59–61.
Reeves and Wilkinson: 204–5.

Djehutynekht, Nomarch, Twelfth Dynasty, Middle Kingdom, 1965–1920 BC. One of the great provincial magnates of the Middle Kingdom at its height, Djehutynekht was 'Great Chief of the Hare Nome, Royal Acquaintance foremost of the South, Foremost of the *ha*-princes in the House of the King'. He was the son of Nehera and probably the uncle of the nomarch DJEHUTYHOTEP.

His tomb at El-Bersheh consists of two chambers and a shrine which originally contained a seated statue. He was obviously one of the 'Great Ones' of Egypt, as a scene in the tomb shows his coffin-sledge being drawn by representatives from all parts of Egypt, including royalty.

His wife was Hathorhotep; it appears that they had no children, and this may be the reason why his nephew eventually became nomarch.

Griffith and Newberry, *El-Bersheh II*, London, 1895: 13–14, 17–26.

Djer (alt. Zer, Ity), King, First Dynasty, Archaic Period, *c.* 3000 BC. The successor and probably the son of AHA by his wife Khenthap, Djer was the second king of the First Dynasty. In the Palermo Stone annals he is recorded as having led an expedition against 'Setjet', the term often used to denote Western Asia but which in his time probably meant Sinai. In a large mastaba tomb at Saqqara, dating to Djer's reign and belonging to a high official called SABU, a large quantity of copper objects was recovered. The copper in all likelihood came from the Sinai peninsula, as did the turquoise which was found in the king's probable tomb at Abydos, in the form of amulets, decorated with gold, on a mummified arm, which has led some scholars to speculate that the arm (which was lost) was female, and hence raises the possibility that his queen was buried with him. He was also commemorated far to the south at Wadi Halfa. In the Middle Kingdom Djer's tomb was thought to be the burial place of the god Osiris, and a basalt figure of the god lying on a lion-bed was placed in Djer's tomb.

The practice of burying numbers of sacrificed retainers seems to have become established at the time of Djer's death. When he was buried at Abydos three hundred and seventeen went to their deaths – including one, either a scribe or an artist, who took his palette with him.

Petrie 1900.
Emery 1961: 56–64; pls 41, 42a, 43a, b.
Spencer: 64–5, 79–80; pl. 59.

Djeserkareseneb, Official, Eighteenth Dynasty, New Kingdom, *c.* 1400–1390 BC. Djeserkareseneb lived during the reign of King THUTMOSE IV. He was employed in the Temple of Amun at Thebes as Accountant of the Granary of Amun.

He was buried at Deir el-Medina (TT 38) in a tomb with a number of naturalistic and cheerful paintings, of some quality. These depict two of his daughters bearing offerings and some charming naked servant girls, very young, who are attending Djeserkareseneb's friends at a convivial party.

PM I.1: 69–70.

Djet (alt. Uadjet: 'Serpent'), King, First Dynasty, Archaic Period, *c.* 2980 BC. The reign of Djet, the third king of the First Dynasty, marked the point at which the work of AHA and DJER, began to come to fruition. The increasing level of sophistication which the society was reaching is indicated by the existence of a vineyard dedicated to the king's use.

Djet's name is spelt with a serpent sign. Although he may not have reigned for as long as some of the other early kings, he is commemorated by one of the supreme masterpieces of Egyptian art, one of the most noble works from any Egyptian period, a monumental stele with the king's name displayed in the *serekh*, a rearing cobra in the sky above the palace façade which forms the base of the *serekh*.

Djet is believed to have been buried in a great tomb at Abydos where he was attended by ranks of sacrificed retainers. At least two substantial mastaba tombs at Saqqara and Giza date from his lifetime.

Petrie 1900: 1.
Emery 1954.
Emery 1961: 69–73.
G. Dreyer, 'Umm el Qa'ab: Nachuntersuchungen im Frühzeitlichen Königsfriedhof 5/6 Vorbericht', MDAIK 49 (1993) 57.
MduL E11007.

Djoser Netjerykhet (alt. Zoser), King, Third Dynasty, Old Kingdom *c.* 2667–2648 BC. The accession of Djoser Netjerykhet to the throne was one of the most crucial events in the history of Egypt, indeed of Western civilisation. The brother of SANAKHTE (alt. Nebka), who predeceased him, Djoser was the first of Egypt's rulers, of whom we have knowledge, to be reverenced not only as king but as god. The name 'Djoser' is not in fact attested until long after his lifetime; during his reign his Horus name was employed, 'Netjerykhet'.

Djoser's reign is immortalised by the building of the Step Pyramid complex at Saqqara, his eventual burial place, constructed under the supervision of his vizier and architect, IMHOTEP. This was the first monumental stone building in the history of the world, and represented a deployment of the country's resources on an immense and unprecedented scale, as well as being a miracle of technology. Djoser was served by an efficient and highly developed civil service, with the names of a number of his great ministers being preserved. He also presided over the increasing sophistication of Egypt's theological systems, in particular that associated with Heliopolis. Djoser built a great temple there which contained many fine reliefs, including portraits of the king.

The arts also advanced rapidly in Djoser's reign, and a number of elegant portraits of the king survive, including what must be recognised as one of the supreme masterpieces of the world's art, the statue of the king found in the *serdab* at Saqqara.

The character of the Third Dynasty, deriving in particular from Djoser's reign, is one of grace, elegance and light. The king's memory, and that of his minister, Imhotep, were honoured throughout the next two and a half millennia of Egypt's existence.

C. M. Frith and J. E. Quibell with J-P. Lauer, *The Step Pyramid*, 2 vols, Cairo, 1935–6.
Hayes 1953: 59–60; fig. 37.
Lauer 1976: 90–136.
Edwards 1973: 34–58.
Lehner 1997: 84–93.
EMC JE 49158 MMA 11.150.30.

Djoser, Priest, Ptolemaic Period, *c.* 333–330 BC. Djoser was a priest of the cat-goddess Bastet at Memphis, during the reign of the Ptolemaic kings. He was buried with a papyrus of the 'Book of the Dead' (*The Book of He Who is in the Underworld*) which contains a version of the 'negative confession' in which the deceased denies that he has committed any wrongdoing during his lifetime, whilst undergoing the process of judgement before the goddess Ma'at and the gods Horus, Thoth and Anubis.

EMC 6335.

Djoserti, King (?), Third Dynasty, Old Kingdom, *c.* 2648 BC. According to one of the king lists, DJOSER NETJERYKHET was succeeded by one Djoserti. However, the discovery of the tomb of King SEKHEMKHET, who *was* Djoser's heir, appeared to dispose of Djoserti as a separate individual; it is possible that the name was one of those belonging to Sekhemkhet.

Grimal: 63.

Djutmose (alt. Thutmose), Crown Prince, Eighteenth Dynasty, New Kingdom, 1390–1352 BC. The eldest son of King AMENHOTEP III and his principal wife, Queen TIY, Djutmose was his father's intended successor; he was Overseer of the Priests of Upper and Lower Egypt and High Priest of Ptah in Memphis. He died before his father, however, and was replaced as heir by his brother, Amenhotep, who eventually followed his father as AMENHOTEP IV-AKHENATEN.

Aldred 1988: 259, 298 (as Thutmosis).
A. Dodson, 'Crown Prince Dhutmose and the Royal Sons of the Eighteenth Dynasty', JEA 76 (1990) 87–96, pl. V.

Dua-Khety, Scribe, Middle Kingdom, *c.* 2055–1650 BC. A much-admired text, known as 'The Satire of the Trades', is said to be the work of a scribe, living during the Middle Kingdom, who appears to have written it as an 'instruction' to his son as he takes him from their home in the Delta, to become a pupil at the School of Scribes in the capital. He describes the unsatisfactory character of most of the alternative forms of available employment to his son, presumably to encourage him to persist with his studies at the school. The Satire loses no opportunity to denigrate professions other than the scribal and, in particular, mocks any employment which involves physical effort or manual labour. The fact that Dua-Khety, coming from a remote part of the country, is irremediably provincial, lends particular point to the Satire.

Lichtheim 1: 184–92.

E

Erasistratus, Philosopher and Physician, Ptolemaic Period, third century BC. Erasistratus lived and flourished in Alexandria in the practice of medicine. He proposed that the body consisted of numerous disparate atoms. He developed understanding of the sensory and motor nerves and advocated dieting.

G. E. R. Lloyd, *Greek Science after Aristotle*, London, 1973.

[**Eratosthenes**], Scholar, Ptolemaic Period, third/second centuries BC. A native of Cyrene, Eratosthenes was invited by PTOLEMY III, who had heard of his reputation as a polymath, to Alexandria where he succeeded CALLIMACHUS as librarian. He was especially in command of the scientific knowledge of his day; he was effectively the father of scientific geography. His *Geographica* was widely known and provides the basis of understanding of what was known of the world. He discovered the measurement of degrees of longitude. He wrote a star catalogue and some poetry.

Eratosthenes calculated the circumference of the earth by observation of the sun's rays at Alexandria and near Aswan.

J. O. Thompson, *History of Ancient Geography*, 1948: 158ff.

[**Esarhaddon**], Assyrian King (= Twenty-Fifth Dynasty), Late Period, *c.* 680–669 BC. The son and successor of King SENNACHERIB, who succeeded to the Assyrian throne after his father's murder, Esarhaddon was to prove a persistent and dangerous enemy to Egypt. The Egyptians had maintained an uneasy but generally non-confrontational relationship in the early years of the Assyrians rise to prominence in the Near East, but after SARGON II attempted to annex parts of southern Palestine, which the Egyptians considered their domain, relations cooled. In 674 BC Esarhaddon, fearing the influence of the Egyptian King TAHARQA on the Palestinian rulers, led an attack into Egypt but this was repulsed. In 671 BC he launched another foray, this time more successful, and after three victorious battles he took Memphis and captured the son and Crown Prince of King Taharqa, Prince URSHANAHURU.

He died in 669 BC on his way to lead another attack against Egypt.

CAH III.2: 122–41.
Kitchen 1986: §117.

[**Eti**], Queen of Punt, Eighteenth Dynasty, New Kingdom, *c.* 1470 BC. In the magnificent mortuary temple of Queen HATSHEPSUT at Deir el-Bahri a famous relief records an Egyptian expedition to Punt in year nine of the queen's reign. It provides a vivid depiction of the 'Great One of Punt' and his entourage.

The Great One was named Pereh but interest has always focused on his mountainous wife, Eti, the Queen of Punt, who is depicted as being barely able to walk, the consequence of the extreme steatopygia from which she suffered.

Punt lay to the south and east of Egypt, and was a source of much of its exotic materials, animals and plants.

Terrace and Fischer 1970: 21.
EMC JE 14276, JE 89661.

Euclides (Euclid), Mathematician, Ptolemaic Period, fourth/third centuries BC. Euclid taught in Alexandria during the lifetime of PTOLEMY I. His book, *Elements of Mathematics*, remained the most influential study of geometry until modern times.

G. E. R. Lloyd, *Greek Science after Aristotle*, 1973.

Eudoxus, Navigator, Ptolemaic Period, second century BC. In the service of PTOLEMY III EUERGETES, Eudoxus was sent twice to explore the sea route to India. He was said to have been lost during an exploration of the coast of West Africa.

E. Hyde, *Ancient Greek Mariners*, 1947.

G

Gemnefherbak, Temple Official, Thirtieth Dynasty, Late Period, *c.* 350 BC. Gemnefherbak lived during the days of Egypt's final flowering, after the expulsion of the Persians. As a result he was able to benefit from the high skills of the masons of the time, in the carving of his fine funerary statue.

Its inscription is florid and self-congratulatory, even for such dedications. He was 'One who is Eloquent, who knows the Right Answer to give, Son of the Chief Scribe from the Southern sanctuary, Merneithiotes'. He describes himself as 'Most excellent, one who never leaves his place in his industriousness, who never takes away the property of the poor, and never leaves the pressing undone [?]. His sin before God and his blemish before man do not exist.'[1]

Gemnefherbak's statue was acquired in Constantinople in the sixteenth century by an Austrian diplomat. It had originally been placed in the temple at Sais, by his brother.

W. Seipel, *Gott: Mensch: Pharao*, Künsterhaus 1992: 395.
H. Satzinger, *Die Ägyptische Kunst in Wien*, Vienna, n.d.: 61–2.
Kunsthistorisches Museum, Vienna, no. 62.

[Ghilukhepa], Princess, Eighteenth Dynasty, New Kingdom, *c.* 1390–1352 BC. King AMENHOTEP III was a diligent diplomatist who employed the device of marrying foreign princesses to consolidate Egypt's relations with its neighbours. In persuit of this policy, in his tenth regnal year he married Ghilukhepa, the sister of King Tushratta of Mitanni in northern Mesopotamia. She arrived in Egypt attended by a suite of more than three hundred women, soldiers and retainers.

Amenhotep produced a number of large scarabs commemorating his marriage to Ghilukhepa.

Aldred 1988: 124, 152, 192.
Redford 1984: 36, 41.
C. Blankenberg-van Delden, *The Large Commemorative Scarabs of Amenhotep III*, Leiden, 1969: 129–33.

Gua, Physician, Twelfth Dynasty, Middle Kingdom, *c.* 1850 BC. The provincial magnates, the nomarchs, of the Twelfth Dynasty maintained a nearly royal state and their administrations mirrored that of the king. Thus DJEHUTYHOTEP, nomarch of Khnum (Ashmunein) had in his service Gua, as Chief Physician, evidently himself a man of substance. A fine ivory headrest, sculpted in a form to convey protection to the sleeper, is said to have come from his burial, probably at El-Bersheh, where the nomarch was buried. His coffin was inscribed with texts from *The Book of Two Ways*, a guide for the dead particular to El-Bersheh; it includes a helpful map for the deceased to find his way to the Underworld. He was the possessor of a complete set of canopic jars, one of the earliest known.

Quirke and Spencer: 92, 97, 104; pl. 147.
BM EA 30727.

1 From Wilfried Seipel, *Bilder Für die Ewigkeit, (3,000 Years of Egyptian Art)*, exhibition catalogue, Verlag Friedr. Stadler, Konstanz, 1983.

H

[Hadrian] (Publius Aelius Hadrianus), Emperor, King of Egypt, Roman Period, 117–138 AD. Hadrian succeeded the enlightened Trajan as ruler of the Roman Empire. His background was as a soldier, with the experience of ruling imperial provinces. He possessed a distinctly mystical component to his very complex personality, and his enduring interest in his Egyptian possession seems mainly to have stemmed from this. He visited Egypt in 130 AD in the company of his young lover, ANTINOUS; in the manner of tourists before and since, the Emperor had his name and the record of his visit inscribed on one of Egypt's most notable monuments, one of the statues of 'Memnon', in reality of AMENHOTEP III, at Thebes.

Antinous was found drowned in circumstances which suggest he may have given himself as a sacrifice in place of the Emperor. Hadrian continued to mourn him throughout the remaining years of his life and ordered the establishment of a cult in Antinous' memory, proclaiming him a god. He founded the city of Antinoopolis, near Hermopolis; it was largely Greek in inspiration and was particularly handsomely appointed. Its remains were standing in the eighteenth century and were described by European travellers.

A. Levy, 'Hadrian as King of Egypt', *Num. Chr. VIII* (1948) 30–8.

J. Lindsay, *Men and Gods on the Roman Nile*, London, 1981.

Lambert 1984.

Hakare Ibi, King, Seventh/Eighth Dynasties, First Intermediate Period, *c.* 2200 BC. Hakare Ibi was one of the shadowy, short-lived kings who occupied the throne uneasily after the end of the Sixth Dynasty. They tried to maintain the appearance of a relationship with the Sixth Dynasty kings, and the earliest of them may indeed have been their descendants. Hakare Ibi built a pyramid at Saqqara, the necropolis of the Sixth Dynasty kings, which contained a recension of the Pyramid Texts. The texts in his tomb were eventually passed on to the Coffin Texts which were popular in the Middle Kingdom.

Hakare Ibi reigned only for about two years.

Grimal: 126, 140–1.

J. Jéquier, *Fouilles à Saqqarah: La Pyramide d'Aba*, Cairo, 1935.

Hakor (alt. Achoris), King, Twenty-Ninth Dynasty, Late Period, 393–380 BC. Little is known of the origins of Hakor, who secured the throne after the death of NEFAARUD I, and the struggle for control of Egypt by the latter's son, an attempt to take power which failed. Hakor undertook a range of building projects and interested himself in the politics of the

Mediterranean, for a time allying himself with the Athenians against the Persians. Then the Greeks came to an understanding with the Persians without reference to Hakor, who was left exposed. He did, however, face the Persians and defeated several attempts by the Persian navy to attack Egypt.

After Hakor's death in 380 BC his son was expelled by Nakhtnebef (NECTANEBO I), who came to the throne as the founder of the last native Egyptian dynasty.

Grimal: 373–5.

Hapuseneb, High Priest, Eighteenth Dynasty, New Kingdom, *c.* 1473–1458 BC. One of the principal protagonists of Queen HATSHEPSUT, Hapuseneb for a time combined the most powerful religious and secular offices of the state in his person. He was High Priest of Amun and also Royal Treasurer. He seems to have seen himself as pontiff, and was the first to bring the priesthoods of Egypt under one authority – his own.

His monuments and memorials are largely ruinous, the consequence no doubt of the wish of THUTMOSE III to eliminate all reference to Hatshepsut and those who supported her when he was sole ruler of Egypt.

W. C. Hayes, 'Royal Sarcophagi of the XVIII Dynasty', *Princeton Monographs in Art and Archaeology: Quarto Series 19*, Princeton NJ, 1935: 17–19.
CAH II.1: 316, 326, 328, 399, 402.
Grimal: 212.

Harhotep, Chancellor, Twelfth Dynasty, Middle Kingdom, *c.* 1965–1920 BC. Harhotep was one of King SENWOSRET I's chancellors. His burial chamber in his tomb at Deir el-Bahri contained ten seated statues of the king.

Lambelet 1978: 54.
EMC 301.

Harkhebi, Astronomer, Ptolemaic Period, third century BC. On his funerary statue Harkhebi, who enjoyed the ancient titles 'Hereditary Prince and Count, Sole Companion', describes his work as an astronomer, recording that he was 'clear-eyed in the observation of the stars' and that he analysed their times of rising and setting. He was able to predict the beginning of the year in the ancient manner, by forecasting the heliacal rising of Sirius. It is probable that he gained much of his contemporary astronomical grounding from the work of Babylonian star-gazers.

O. Neugerbauer and R. A. Parker, *Egyptian Astronomical Texts III: Decans, Planets, Constellations and Zodiacs*, Brown University Press, Newport RI, 1969.

Harkhuf, Nomarch and Traveller, Sixth Dynasty, Old Kingdom, *c.* 2278 BC. In his autobiography, set up in his tomb (A8) at Qubbet el-Hawa in the cliffs opposite Elephantine, of which region he was the governor, Harkhuf records the journeys which he took under the instructions of MERENRE and PEPY II, the latter being still a boy when he came to the throne. Altogether Harkhuf undertook four journeys into Nubia, principally to secure the trading routes and to bring back to Egypt the products which were always sought from the south.

Pepy II in particular was evidently fascinated by the tales of Harkhuf's adventures, and the latter's procurement of a dancing pygmy especially excited him; the king gave orders for the pygmy's safe conduct to the court at Memphis. Harkhuf appears to have been one of the king's principal supporters in the early years of his reign.

H. Goedicke, 'Harkhuf's Travels', JNES 40 (1981) 1–20.
Lichtheim 1: 23–7.

Harmesaf, Priest, Twenty-Second Dynasty, Third Intermediate Period, *c.* 945–924 BC. During the reign of King SHESHONQ I it was decided to record the king's triumphant campaign in Palestine on a new gate to be erected at Karnak. He sent a senior priest, Harmesaf, who held the appointments of Master of Secret Things and Chief of Works, to Silsileh to obtain stone for the new gate. Harmesaf carried out his commission satisfactorily, was praised by the king and rewarded with 'things of silver and gold'.

Breasted 4: §§706–8.

Harmose, Musician, Eighteenth Dynasty, New Kingdom, 1473–1458 BC. Harmose was the minstrel of SENENMUT the Minister and favourite courtier of Queen HATSHEPSUT; given his profession he was happily named, to English ears.

Harmose was buried amongst the members of Senenmut's family in the Minister's own burial complex. Harmose's lute, with which no doubt he used to entertain his master, was buried beside him.

Hayes 1959: 111.
L. Manniche, *Music and Musicians in Ancient Egypt*, London, 1991, 11.

Harnakhte, High Priest, Twenty-Second Dynasty, Third Intermediate Period, *c*. 870 BC. Not infrequently, rather in the manner of the appointments of the more nepotistic medieval Popes, Egyptian kings appointed sons, and sometimes other relatives, to high offices in the Two Lands at very tender ages. Such a one was Harnakhte, son of King OSORKON II. He became High Priest of Amun at Thebes when very young; he was only eight or nine years old when he died and was buried by his grieving parents with great pomp, at the back of the tomb which his father was eventually to occupy.

Kitchen 1986: §282.

Harsiese, King, Twenty-Second Dynasty, Third Intermediate Period, *c*. 874–850 BC. A member of a powerful family in Thebes, Harsiese was for five years acknowledged as king in the Thebaid, taking the name Pinujdem, at the time of King OSORKON II. His assumption of royal honours emphasises the power, both secular and religious, which families like Harsiese's wielded at the time, which was one of great confusion in Egypt.

His great-grandson, also HARSIESE, was Northern Vizier to King TAHARQA and High Priest of Heliopolis.

I. E. S. Edwards, 'Egypt from the 22nd to the 24th Dynasty', CAH III.1.

Harsiese, Priest, Twenty-Second Dynasty, Third Intermediate Period, *c*. 840 BC. The High Priest of Amun at Thebes, Osorkon, took up his office in the eleventh year of the reign of King TAKELOT II. A priest, Harsiese, took the opportunity of petitioning the newly inducted High Priest to grant him what he represented as hereditary offices attached to his family, in the temple administration. These appear to have been connected with the provisioning and cleansing of the temple, doubtless profitable enterprises. The High Priest agreed to Harsiese's claim and the lesser priest engraved the record of his agreement on the roof of the temple, to ensure that his rights to the offices which he claimed were known to all.

Breasted 4: §§752–4.

Harsiese, Vizier, High Priest, Twenty-Fifth Dynasty, Late Period, *c*. 675–660 BC. Harsiese was Northern Vizier to King TAHARQA; he was also 'Greatest of Seers in Heliopolis', in other words, High Priest of one of Egypt's most powerful temple communities. He was *sem* priest of Ptah, Chief of Prophets of Osiris in the Thinite province and 'Great Chief' of Djufy.

He was great-grandson of the Harsiese who for five years held the title of king in Thebes, under the name Pinudjem, at the time of OSORKON II.

Edwards, 'Egypt from the 22nd to the 24th Dynasty', CAH III.1.

Kitchen 1986: §§490–1.

Harwa, High Steward, Twenty-Fifth Dynasty, Late Period, *c.* 750 BC. Harwa was the High Steward of the Divine Adoratrice AMENIRDIS I, the daughter of KASHTA, the ancestor of the Kushite dynasty. With her appointment to this office in Thebes, the Nubian house consolidated its control of the south and Harwa was an important official in the region's administration. He was the son of Padimut, a high official in the temple of Amun at Thebes who early on identified with the line of Kushite kings of the Twenty-Sixth Dynasty. Harwa evidently benefited similarly by allying himself with the Kushites. He is portrayed with royal attributes on a shabti found in the tomb, suggesting that he held a high administrative rank, perhaps as the effective governor of the Theban region – and hence much of the south – on the king's behalf.

He was to be buried at Thebes in a vast subterranean tomb (TT37), work on which was never completed. It has recently been re-excavated.

Lichtheim 3: 24–5.
F. Tirandnitti, EA 13: 3–6.
EMB 8163.

Hat, Cavalry Officer, Eighteenth Dynasty, New Kingdom, *c.* 1350 BC. An adjutant in the chariotry, Hat lived during the early part of the reign of King AMENHOTEP IV-AKHENATEN. His grave is unknown but it may well have been in the vicinity of the royal city of Akhetaten.

Saleh and Sourouzian: 172.
EMC JE 39590.

Hatshepsut, Queen, Eighteenth Dynasty, New Kingdom, *c.* 1473–1458 BC. An example of the dominant women produced by the family of King AHMOSE, Hatshepsut was the most successful of Egypt's reigning queens. The daughter of THUTMOSE I, Hatshepsut married her half-brother who became THUTMOSE II; the marriage produced no sons, only a daughter, NEFERURE. However, Thutmose II had a son by a lesser wife, and on his death THUTMOSE III came to the throne whilst still a boy. Hatshepsut became regent during his minority and not long after assuming this responsibility proclaimed herself 'Female Horus', the only occasion when a woman adopted what was otherwise an exclusively male title. She invented a period of joint rule for herself with her dead father, to warrant her assumption of the kingship.

Hatshepsut's time on the throne seems generally to have been one of prosperity for Egypt. She was assisted in the government of Egypt by a number of highly competent officials including SENENMUT, an architect of genius and an official of great ability who, despite modest origins, became immensely powerful. Hatshepsut clearly permitted Senenmut a degree of intimacy which transcended the purely official nature of their relationship.

Campaigns against Egypt's enemies were conducted during Hatshepsut's reign, under the command of Thutmose, admirable experience for one who was to become the greatest of Egypt's warrior kings.

The monuments of Hatshepsut's reign are characterised by a lightness and elegance of design which are exceptional. The carving of the rose quartz blocks of her chapel at Karnak are amongst the most engaging works of architecture produced in the New Kingdom. Her great funerary monument at Deir el-Bahri, close to the equally original structure built by King NEBHEPETRE MONTUHOTEP II is one of the supreme masterpieces of Egyptian architecture. It contains the famous scene of the visit of an Egyptian expedition to the ruler of Punt and his Queen, ETI.

The queen disappeared after the twentieth year of her reign, when she was replaced by Thutmose III as sole ruler. Some time after her death, which is not thought to have been other than by natural causes, her memory was execrated and her monuments carefully defaced.

P. Der Manuelian and C. E. Loeben, 'New Light on the Recarved Sarcophagus of Hatshepsut and Thutmose I in the Museum of Fine Arts, Boston', JEA 79 (1994) 121–56.
Hayes 1959: 83–106.
Robins 1993: 45–52.
J. Tyndersley, *Hateshepsut*, London, 1996.
MMA 31.3.156, 31.3.163, 28.3.18, 29.3.1, 29.3.2, 29.3.3.

[Hattusil III], King of the Hittites, (= Nineteenth Dynasty), New Kingdom, *c.* 1264–1240 BC. The battle of Qadesh, one of the most crucial events of the reign of King RAMESSES II and one which was long celebrated by him as a notable vistory, had long-enduring reverberations in the politics of the Near East. His opponent on this occasion, King MUWATALLIS, had faced his father King SETI I at Qadesh in the past, and an uneasy truce had prevailed between Egypt and the Hittites until broken by the outbreak of hostilities between the two great powers in the fourth year of Ramesses' reign.

King Muwatallis left no legitimate heir and the kingship passed to his only son, the child of a concubine, who succeeded as Mursilis III. He was under the tutelege of his uncle, Hattusil, who gradually built up a power base in his own principality and eventually deposed his nephew and replaced him, becoming king as Hattusil III.

Hattusil was an alert politician who recognised the dangers to his kingdom by the rise of powers in Mesopotamia, notably the Assyrians and Babylonians. In Ramesses' twenty-first year Egypt and the Hittite empire signed the first known treaty between sovereign states, and one which led to the development of peaceful and cordial relations between the two powers. So cordial were they indeed, that Ramesses married two Hittite princesses and the two royal families exchanged presents and frequent contact. Ramesses journeyed to Damascus to collect one of his brides, and the Crown Prince of the Hittites visited Egypt. It is possible that Hattusil himself did so as well; if so, the visits by the two kings were the first such exchanges in history.

The relationship forged between Ramesses and Hattusil endured throughout the Egyptian king's reign and through the reigns of two of the Hittite king's successors.

Kitchen 1982: 83–8, 92–5.
Grimal 1992: 257.
Kuhrt 1995: I, 207–9, 258–60.

Hecataeus (of Miletus), Greek Geographer, *c.* 550–476 BC. A scholar of aristocratic background, Hecataeus travelled extensively throughout the Mediterranean world, including Egypt. He was greatly influenced by what he observed there and by what he was told by the priests; those of Thebes evidently convinced him that, contrary to his earlier belief, he was not descended from a god in the sixteenth generation.

Herodotus was influenced by him and frequently quoted his work, though he did not always agree with his analyses.

L. Pearson, *The Early Ionian Historians*, Oxford, 1939.

Hecataeus (of Abdera), Historian, Ptolemaic Dynasty, *c.* 320–315 BC. Hecataeus was a pupil of the sceptic Pyrrho, who wrote a number of well received philosophical and historical studies. Amongst the latter was a book *On the Hyperboreans*, and that for which he is chiefly remembered, on Egypt. This was written during the rulership of PTOLEMY I SOTER, who supported him when he moved to Egypt. He recorded the death of the reigning Apis bull as having occurred soon after Ptolemy had become ruler of Egypt following the death of ALEXANDER THE GREAT.

Hecataeus is also remembered as the first Greek historian known to have mentioned the Jews. His comments were not altogether sympathetic, thus eliciting critical reactions from Jewish writers.

O. Murray, 'Hecataeus of Abdera and Pharaonic Kingship', JEA 56 (1970) 141–71.

Hednakht, Scribe, Nineteenth Dynasty, New Kingdom, *c.* 1232 BC. Hednakht was employed as a scribe in the Treasury during the latter part of the reign of King RAMESSES II. In the company of his brother Panakht, the Scribe of the Vizier, he records in a graffito at Saqqara that they had taken a stroll there together, to enjoy themselves, in January 1232, the forty-seventh year of the king's reign. His graffito includes a plea for a long life to the 'Gods of the West of Memphis'.

Kitchen 1982: 148.

Hekaemsaf, Naval Officer, Twenty-Sixth Dynasty, Late Period, 570–525 BC. Hekaemsaf was a contemporary of King AMASIS; his appointment was that of 'Chief of the Royal Boats'. His intact burial was found at Saqqara; his mummy was covered with a mask of beaten gold and a richly embroidered cloth wrapping. That such a burial could be provided for someone who was not a very great official indicates the opulance of the period of Egypt's revival under the Saite kings.

PM III.2: 650.
Saleh and Sourouzian: 249.
EMC JE 35923 = CG 53668.

Hekaib (alt. Pepynakht), Nomarch and God, Sixth Dynasty, Old Kingdom, *c.* 2200 BC. Hekaib was one of the supporters of King PEPY II in the later years of his reign, serving as Nomarch of Elephantine and, effectively, Viceroy of Upper Egypt. He was proclaimed a god and his cult established on Elephantine where it flourished for several hundred years. 'Hekaib' appears to have been a nickname given to him by the king, as a term of endearment and affection. His temple was restored by later kings ruling in the south.

Breasted 1: §§355–60.
L. Habachi, 'The Sanctuary of Heqaib', AV 33: 1985.
——'Identification of Heqaib and Sabni with Owners of Tombs in Qubbet el-Hawa and their Relationship with Nubia', in L. Habachi (ed.) *Sixteen Studies on Lower Nubia*, CASAE 23, 11–27.

Hekanakhte, Funerary Priest and Landowner, Eleventh Dynasty, Middle Kingdom, *c.* 2000 BC. Though he occupied only the relatively modest appointment of funerary priest of the Vizier IPY at Thebes, Hekanakhte was a man of substance, owning extensive farm lands from which his duties obliged him to absent himself. His letters, found in a tomb of another of Ipy's officials, are instructions to his family, particularly to his son, MERISU, on the management of his properties. They contain much information about the system of taxation of the time, the laws relating to property and inheritance and the situation pertaining in the Theban region at the end of the Eleventh Dynasty. They provide remarkable insights into the preoccupations of an ordinary Egyptian family of the time – and are also notable for the perpetual note of complaint which they sustain.

James 1962: 1–45, pls 1–7.
K. Baer, 'An Eleventh Dynasty Farmer's Letters to his Family', *Journal of the American Oriental Society*, 83 (1963) 1–19.
H. Goedicke, *Studies in the Heqanakhte Papers*, Baltimore, 1984: *passim*, 13–37, 38–76.
Wente 1990.
Parkinson 1991: 103–7.

Hekanakhte, Viceroy, Nineteenth Dynasty, New Kingdom, *c.* 1279–1213 BC. The Viceroy of Kush (Nubia) during the reign of King RAMESSES II Hekanakhte was a Royal Scribe, Fan-Bearer on the Right of the King, Overseer of the Southern Lands.

He was also 'King's Messenger to Every Land'.

G. A. Reisner, 'The Viceroys of Ethiopia', JEA VI, 1 and 2 (1920).
L. Habachi, 'The Owner of Tomb no. 282 in the Theban Necropolis', JEA 54 (1968) 107–8.

Hekanefer, Nubian Prince, Eighteenth Dynasty, New Kingdom, *c.* 1336–1327 BC. Hekanefer was a 'Page of the Harem', a child of the *kap*, having been taken as a boy to Thebes to be educated amongst noble Egyptian children so that on returning to his country he would be supportive of Egyptian interests. He was a contemporary of King TUTANKHAMUN and is commemorated in a series of handsome paintings showing him with other Nubian nobles paying homage to the King of Egypt. Their dress and deportment suggests that by Hekanefer's lifetime the Nubian chiefs had become thoroughly Egyptianised. Hekanefer was hereditary Prince of Miam (modern Aniba) and was buried at Tushka.

N. de Garis Davis and A. H. Gardiner, *The Tomb of Huy, Viceroy of Nubia in the Reign of Tutankhamun*, London, 1926.
W. K. Simpson, *Heka-Nefer and the Dynastic Material from Toshka and Arminna*, New Haven CT and Philadelphia PA, 1963.
Scott 1986: 110, no. 61.
YAG 222265.

Hekare Aba, *see* Hakare Ibi

Hemaka, Chancellor, First Dynasty, Archaic Period, *c.* 2950 BC. Hemaka was the principal minister of the sixth king of the First Dynasty, DEN. He bore a title which is usually rendered 'Chancellor'. He was the owner of one of the great mastaba tombs at Saqqara (3035), a masterpiece of architecture from so early a period. His tomb, though pillaged and burned, contained a number of rich and important objects which show that already the lives of great officials, close to the king, were supported by lavish appointments; one of the most important of the finds was a roll of papyrus which, though it was unused, indicated that this material was already being used in the First Dynasty, presumably for the purpose of writing. Hemaka's mortuary objects include an ivory label, now in the Cairo Museum, which records important events in the king's reign, and a circular disc showing hunting dogs pursuing a gazelle.

W. B. Emery, *The Tomb of Hemaka (Services des Antiquités de l'Égypte: Excavations à Saqqarah 1935–6)*, Cairo, 1939–61: 75–6.
EMC.

Hemionu, Prince, Vizier, Fourth Dynasty, Old Kingdom, *c.* 2589–2570 BC. The son of Prince NEFERMAAT, Vizier of King SNEFERU, Hemionu was Vizier to King KHNUM-KHUFU, and thus a senior member of the Royal family. He is traditionally said to have been the architect of Khnum-Khufu's pyramid which, if correct, makes him one of the most remarkable men ever to have lived, of the quality of his forerunner IMHOTEP. He was said to have died in the nineteenth year of Khnum-Khufu's reign and to have been buried in a large and splendid tomb at Saqqara in the royal necropolis. His celebrated statue suggests a powerful and determined personality, characteristic of the highest officials of the early Fourth Dynasty.

H. Junker, *Giza, I–XII*, Vienna and Leipzig, 1929–55, vol. I, 148–61.
W. Stevenson Smith, 'The Origin of Some Unidentified Old Kingdom Reliefs', *American Journal of Archaeology*, 46 (1942) 1946–9, pl. 48.
Hildesheim, Pelizaeus Museum.

Hem-Min, Governor, Sixth Dynasty, Old Kingdom, *c.* 2345–2323 BC. Hem-Min was the Governor of Upper Egypt, one of the earliest known to hold the appointment and the first to reside outside the capital, Memphis. He lived at the beginning of the Sixth Dynasty, during the reign of King TETI.

His tomb in the mountain of El Hawawish, near the capital of the ninth nome of Upper Egypt, Akhmim, contains the largest rock-cut chapel known to survive from the Old Kingdom.

Kanawati 1980.

Henhenet, Royal Consort, Eleventh Dynasty, Middle Kingdom, *c.* 2055–2004 BC. Henhenet was one of the royal ladies buried in the temple platform of what was to be the mortuary temple of King NEBHEPETRE MONTUHOTEP II at Deir el-Bahri. Like her companions who were similarly provided with a tomb, Henhenet was described, optimistically, as 'Sole Favourite'.

Each of the ladies was given a limestone sarcophagus and a little shrine for her *ka* statue. Henhenet's sarcophagus was covered with a lid which was originally intended for the burial of KAWIT, who seems to have been particularly favoured by the king. Kawit's name and titles were carved on the lid but Henhenet had to be content with hers being written in green paint. Two eyes were painted on the exterior of the sarcophagus to allow Henhenet to look out on the world around her.

Hayes 1953: 160–1; figs 97–8.
MMA 07.230.1d, 07.230.1ab.

Henutsen, Queen, Fourth Dynasty, Old Kingdom, *c.* 2589–2566 BC. The third wife of King KHNUM-KHUFU, Henutsen was the mother of his eventual successor KHAFRE and of several of the influential high officials of the later Fourth Dynasty. She was the occupant of the southernmost of the pyramids subsidiary to the Great Pyramid.

Breasted 1: §180.
G. Daressy, 'La Stèle de la Fille de Cheops', *Recueil de Traveaux Égyptologiques à la Philogie et à la Archéologie Égyptiennes et Assyriennes*, 30 (1908) 1.

Henuttauineb (alt. Red), Singer, Twenty-First Dynasty, Third Intermediate Period, *c.* 950 BC. A singer in the train of Amun, King of the Gods, in his temple at Thebes, Henuttauineb was declared a 'female Osiris' on her death and was thus recorded in her funerary inscriptions. She also appears to have borne the name 'Red'.

G. Kueny and J. Yoyotte, *Grenoble, Musée des Beaux-Arts, Collection Égyptienne*, Paris, 1979: cat. 117; 96–7.

Henuttawy, Priestess, Twenty-First Dynasty, Third Intermediate Period, *c.* 1030 BC. 'The Songstress of Amun-Re', Henuttawy was the daughter of the High Priest MENKHEPERRE and the grand-daughter of Queen HENUTTAWY. She was buried in Deir el-Bahri, reusing the Eighteenth Dynasty tomb of MINMOSE.

H. Winlock, *Metropolitan Museum of Art Bulletin*, Part ii, 1924: 22–4.
PM I.2: 628–9.
MMA 25.3.182–4.

Henuttawy, Queen, Twenty-First Dynasty, Third Intermediate Period, *c.* 1070 BC. A royal princess, Henuttawy was married to PINUDJEM I, the High Priest of Amun who proclaimed himself king and founded the Twenty-First Dynasty. Henuttawy was the mother of PSEUSENNES I. Her much damaged mummy was found in the Deir el-Bahri cache; the embalmers had employed plaited black string to supplement her sparse hair. She is thought to have been around thirty-five when she died.

PM I.2: 663.
C. El Mahdy, *Mummies, Myth and Magic*, London, 1989: 22, 37.

Henuttawy, Priestess and Temple Singer, Twenty-First Dynasty, New Kingdom, *c.* 1000 BC. A singer in the Temple of Amun at Thebes, Henuttawy was buried in the necropolis of Deir el-Bahri. A suggestion that her mummy, now in Munich, contains traces of substances such as cocaine and tobacco, has been received with surprise by Egyptologists and historians of chemistry alike.

G. Daressy, ASAE 8: 13.
PM I.2: 639.
C. El Mahdy, *Mummies, Myth and Magic*, London, 1989: 22, 37.
Staatliche Sammlung Ägyptischer Kunst, München, ÄS 57.

Heny, Chamberlain, Eleventh Dynasty, Middle Kingdom, *c.* 2112–2063 BC. During the long reign of King INYOTEF II, one of the family of Theban princes who eventually brought about the reunification of Egypt under his descendant, King NEBHEPETRE MONTUHOTEP II, Heny was in the confidence of the king, with the probably honorary title of 'Treasurer of the King of Lower Egypt'; he also had the rank of Chamberlain. He claims to have had immediate and untrammelled access to the king at all times.

The carvings from his tomb at Thebes are of considerable merit, especially for a private individual, indicating that at this time the work of Egyptian artists and craftsmen was regaining its standards of high quality, after a period of some decline.

Hodjash and Berlev 1982: nos 25, 64–7.

Hepzefa (alt. Hapidjefa), Nomarch, Twelfth Dynasty, Middle Kingdom, *c.* 1965–1920 BC. Hepzefa was the Governor of Assiut in Middle Egypt during the reign of SENWOSRET I, but remnants of a statue of himself and an entire one of his wife Sennuwy, were found at Kerma, deep into Nubia. Hepzefa had prepared a magnificent tomb for them both in Assiut but for some reason large statues of the couple were erected so far to the south.

Hepzefa was long thought to be the owner of a huge tomb buried under a massive mound at Kerma, in which the remains of many apparently sacrificed retainers were found. This practice had died out in Egypt in the Archaic Period but evidently survived in Nubia much later. It is now thought unlikely that the Kerma tomb was Hepzefa's.

B. G. Trigger, 'Kerma; The Rise of an African Civilization', *The International Journal of African Historical Studies*, 9 (1976) 1–21.
W. Y. Adams, *Nubia: Corridor to Africa*, London, 1977: 195–216.
MFA [Sennuwy].

Hereubekhet, Temple Singer, Twenty-First Dynasty, Third Intermediate Period, *c.* 1000 BC. A singer in the temple of Amun at Thebes at the time when the priests and their attendants exercised far more than simply religious influence in Upper Egypt, Hereubekhet was the granddaughter of the High Priest of Amun, MENKHEPERRE. She was the recipient of a particularly lavishly produced copy of the 'Book of the Dead', which contains very beautiful paintings of the various procedures which Hereubekhet must perform to ensure her acceptance into the Fields of Rushes, the Land of the Blessed Dead.

Hereubekhet was also a priestess in the temple of Mut at Karnak.

Terrace and Fischer: 35, 153–6.
EMC14–7/35–6.

Herihor, High Priest, Vizier, General of the Armies, Twentieth Dynasty, Third Intermediate Period, *c.* 1080–1070 BC. The office of High Priest of Amun in Thebes had become one of great power as the royal rule declined at the end of the Twentieth Dynasty. The High Priestdom had ceased to be primarily a religious office and had acquired considerable temporal authority, including the generalship of the armies. Herihor was Vizier of the last Ramessid king, RAMESSES XI, from whom he had extracted control of much of the south, a position which was to be retained by his descendants who bore the royal titles.

The cession of Herihor was to have long-lasting consequences for the integrity of Egypt. The High Priesthood reached its apogee with Herihor. After his assumption of near-sovereignty in the south and his adoption of many of the accoutrements and symbols of royalty, Egypt was never again to be wholly or permanently unified, other than for very brief periods.

It has, however, been suggested that it may be necessary to reverse the previously accepted order of Herihor and Piankh.

M-A. Bonhème, 'Herihor, fut-il effectivement Roi?', BIFAO 79 (1979) 267–84.
Kitchen 1986: §§14–20, §269, §§435–8.
A. Leahy, 'Abydos in the Libyan Period', in A. Leahy (ed) *Libya and Egypt c. 1300–750 BC*, London, 1990: 155–200.
K. Jansen-Winkeln, 'Das Ende des Neuen Reichen', *ZÄS* 119 (1992): 22ff.
Kuhrt 1995: I, 290–310.

Herneith, Queen, First Dynasty, Archaic Period, *c.* 3000 BC. Herneith is considered to have been the wife of King DJER. She was given a huge tomb (3507) at Saqqara, which was notable for a number of features. It is one of the earliest buildings in Egypt to reveal the use of stone in its construction, with limestone slabs being laid across the wooden ceilings of the tomb's chambers. A limestone lintel was also found, on which were carved recumbent lions. The tomb was one of the earliest to contain the stepped mound structure in its interior, which later led to the pyramid form.

One of the particular aspects of Herneith's burial was that unlike the other royal and noble burials of the time, hers does not contain the burials of sacrificed retainers. The only other occupant of her tomb, lying across the threshhold, was her dog, one of the breed of elegant, prick-eared hounds which attended the Great Ones of Egypt throughout its history.

Herneith's tomb was one of only two in the necropolis to be distinguished by over three hundred auroch skulls, mounted on platforms on each side of her mastaba.

Emery 1958: 73–97.

[Herodotus], Historian, Twenty-Seventh Dynasty, Late Period, *c.* 484–420 BC. Born at Halicarnassus *c.* 480 BC, Herodotus was for many centuries the principal, sometimes the only source for the early history of Egypt. He visited the country *c.* 450 BC and spent some considerable time there. Of an intensely enquiring disposition, he set about recording his impressions of the landscape, the people and, to the extent that he was able to assemble information from the priests of the temples who were his principal source, the history of Egypt.

Although Herodotus' accuracy as much as his credulity has been the subject of the sort of criticism which deplores his falling below the standards expected of a modern scholar, his understanding of the essential *mores* of Egypt is remarkable. Many of the most deeply entrenched ideas, both accurate and mythical, about the Nile civilisation owe their origins to Herodotus.

A. B. Lloyd, *Herodotus Book II: An Introduction*, Leiden, 1975.
——*Herodotus Book II.1: Commentary 1–98*, Leiden, 1976.
——*Herodotus Book II.2: Commentary 99–182*, Leiden, 1988.
J. L. Meyer, *Herodotus, Father of History*, 1953.
J. Wilson, *Herodotus in Egypt*, Leiden, 1970.

Hesy, Trumpeter, Nineteenth Dynasty, New Kingdom, *c.* 1279–1213 BC. Hesy appears on a dedicatory stela, standing before a statue of King RAMESSES II, which he is worshipping. He carries his trumpet under his left arm, the long, slender mouthpiece to the front, the 'bell' to the rear. Hesy's trumpet is very similar to those found in the tomb of Tutankhamun.

Trumpeters were important amongst both the musicians who played at the court and and in the temple ceremonies. They also served in the army where they were responsible for transmitting the commander's orders. A scene contemporary with Hesy shows a trumpeter leading a squad of men into battle.

Pelizaeus-Museum, Hildesheim.

Hesyre (alt. Hesy), Vizier, Third Dynasty, Old Kingdom, *c.* 2667–2648 BC. The minister of King DJOSER NETJERYKHET, Hesyre was the owner of a large and brilliantly decorated tomb at Saqqara (no. 2405). The quality of the workmanship of his tomb, demonstrated by the survival of exquisitely carved wooden panels which include Hesyre's portrait, shows how far the arts had progressed in the relatively short time from the end of the Second Dynasty to the early years of the Third. Hesyre's tomb also contains some very early examples of painting, which are also of high quality, anticipating the finest work of the succeeding Fourth Dynasty.

Amongst Hesyre's titles was 'Chief Dentist', a qualification suggesting a remarkable degree of medical specialisation at so early a period.

J. E. Quibell, *The Tomb of Hesy: Excavations at Saqqara*, Cairo, 1913.
Terrace and Fischer 1970: no. 4, 33–6.
W. Wood, 'A Reconstruction of the Reliefs of Hesy-Re', JARCE 15 (1978) 9–24.
Saleh and Sourouzian: 21.
EMC CG 1426.

Hetepes, Priest, Sixth Dynasty, Old Kingdom, *c.* 2278–2180 BC. Hetepes was a *wa'b* priest, in charge of purification ceremonies in the temple and also for the ritual purification of the king. He is described as the king's 'personal servant' and the 'Gardener of the Great House' (the royal palace), though this may be an honorific. His son, Meri, is also described as a gardener.

Hodjash and Berlev 1982: nos 17, 48, 52–3.

Hetepheres I, Queen, Fourth Dynasty, Old Kingdom, *c.* 2600 BC. Probably the daughter of the last king of the Third Dynasty, HUNI, Hetepheres was the sister-wife of SNEFERU and the mother of KHNUM-KHUFU. She was thus one of the greatest figures of her time and when she died, probably during the reign of her son, she was no doubt interred in an appropriate splendour. However, it would appear that her tomb was pillaged soon after her burial. The remnants of her tomb furnishings and equipment were buried in a shaft near her son's presumed pyramid where they were discovered during this century. They are remarkable for their combination of the most sumptuous materials and exceptional purity and elegance of design.

A particularly appealing portrait of the Queen survives, a seated figure, made up of pieces of beaten gold, part of the overlays of her richly equipped furniture, which includes a canopy, her bed and chair. She holds a lotus flower to her nose, which appears engagingly retroussé, a feature which probably owes more to damage to the gold overlay than to nature.

Stevenson Smith 1946 (1949): 46, fig. 55.
Reisner and Stevenson Smith 1955.
M. Lehner, *The Pyramid Tomb of Hetep-heres and the Satellite Pyramid of Khufu*, Mainz, 1985.
Saleh and Sourouzian: no. 29.
Edwards 1993: 117–20.
EMC JE 52372.

Hetepheres II, Queen, Fourth Dynasty, Old Kingdom, *c.* 2566–2500 BC. King KHNUM-KHUFU's eldest son was Prince KAWAB, the Crown Prince. He was married to the Princess Hetepheres, Khnum-Khufu's daughter by Queen MERITITES. Kawab died before his father and Hetepheres then married another of Khnum-Khufu's sons, DJEDEFRE, who eventually succeeded him. Djedefre's succession was evidently not achieved without some degree of dissension in the royal family. He died, perhaps rather suddenly, and KHAFRE, who was favoured by some of the other powerful princes in the family, became king. Hetepheres managed to make her peace with the new regime and lived on to a great age, dying at the very end of the dynasty. She was buried in a great mastaba tomb, with her first husband, Kawab.

Hetepheres had a daughter, MERESANKH III, who married King MENKAURE, Khafre's successor. Meresankh died before Hetepheres, who built the tomb at Giza for her daughter, in which mother and daughter are shown together. By Djedefre she had NEFERHETEPERES, who may have been the mother of King USERKAF, the founder of the Fifth Dynasty. If this is so, then the kings of the Fifth Dynasty were the natural heirs of the family of King SNEFERU.

Stevenson Smith 1946 (1949): 42–4; pl. 16.
Grimal: 68, 72, 75.
MFA 30.1456.

Hetephernebti and Intkaes, Princesses, Third Dynasty, Old Kingdom, *c.* 2667–2648 BC. Hetephernebti and Intkaes were the daughters of King DJOSER NETJERYKHET. It was once thought that two large rectangular buildings in the Step Pyramid complex, lying to the east of the *serdab* in which Djoser's statue was found and of the pyramid itself, were the princesses' tombs as their names were found carved on stelae nearby; there is, however, no other evidence that the buildings ever served a funerary purpose and this explanation is now no longer held.

Edwards 1985: 44–5.

Hetepni, Tax Collector, Sixth Dynasty, Old Kingdom, *c.* 2200 BC. Hetepni was an official with an exalted opinion of the importance of his employment in the revenue office of the king, at a time of decline in the royal status. Hetepni was an accountant by profession, responsible, as he recorded in his mortuary inscriptions, 'for the counting of everything that crawled or flew in the water and in the marshland'. He owned a fine ebony chair on which he is portrayed seated, with a somewhat tense expression on his face.

J. Settgast, 'Das Sitzbild des Hetep-ni', *Jahrbuch Preussicher Kulturbesitz*, Bd XX (1983) 163–8.
EMB 1/83, cat. no. 13.

Hor, Bowman, Eighteenth/Nineteenth Dynasties, New Kingdom, *c.* 1320–1280 BC. The organisation of the Egyptian military forces developed considerably during the New Kingdom, under the patronage of kings who were warriors and who needed a modern trained army to secure their possessions beyond the frontiers.

Hor was 'Director of the Bow Workshop', where fighting bows were manufactured. His workshop also made chariots, which had appeared in Egypt after the introduction of the horse during the preceding Hyksos period. On his funerary stela, Hor is shown supervising the work of two assistants who are making arrows and the trappings for the chariots. Hor himself is shown repairing a bow, having completed work on two others.

S. Sauneron, *Villes et légendes d'Égypte*, Cairo, 1983: 44 *et seq*.
MduL C 259.

Hor, Priest, Late Period. Hor was buried with a version of the Book of the Dead painted on linen. It contains a representation of the mummy being conveyed to the tomb on a wheeled car or barque. The drawing on the linen has been intentionally distorted to suggest movement. The linen was acquired in a group of textiles in the last century, which has no provenance.

Hor was a 'God's Father, beloved of the God', *sem*-priest, priest of Ptah and Scribe of Offerings in the temple of the domain of Ptah.

James 1985: 69–70; ill. 83.
S. Quirke, *Owners of Funerary Papyri in the British Museum*, London, 1993: 39.
BM 10265.

Hor, Priest, Twenty-Sixth Dynasty, Late Period, *c.* 664–589 BC. Hor lived during the reign of PSAMETIK I and in all probability died during the reign of his grandson, PSAMETIK II. He was 'Chief of the Mysteries of Rostau', an immensely ancient office, known at least from Old-Kingdom times; he also held the title 'Father of the God'. He was buried at Saqqara with amulets and jewellery of lapis lazuli, jasper, haematite and gold.

Saad 1947: 11–13; pls III–V.

Hor, Priest, Ptolemaic Period, *c.* 200–147 BC. A minor priest in the service of the goddess Isis, Hor was a native of the Sebennytos nome in the Delta, probably from Hermopolis. He was employed in 'the town of Isis'. He acted as *pastophoros*, a junior order of the priesthood which seems principally to have been concerned with pastoral work among the public who frequented the temples. He was for a time attached to the sanctuary of Isis at Saqqara.

He is remembered for writing what has come to be known as 'The Archive of Hor'. This reveals him as a seer, even being consulted directly by the king, PTOLEMY VI Philometor. He records an audience with the king and queen in the Alexandrian Serapaeum in August 168 BC.

Part of Hor's practice seems to have been the interpretation of dreams; he evidently himself dreamed prophetically. He also writes of the historic events of his lifetime, including the Sixth Syrian war, when Antiochus IV invaded Egypt.

J. D. Ray, *The Archive of Hor*, London, 1976.

Hor and Suty, Architects, Eighteenth Dynasty, New Kingdom, *c.* 1390–1352 BC. Hor and Suty were architects, possibly twin brothers, practising at the court of AMENHOTEP III, who chose to be remembered together, their careers described in the same inscription. Their stela states that they came out of the womb on the same day and declared 'My brother, my likeness'.

The inscription itself is of interest in that it contains a prayer to the Aten, in addition to a prayer to Re, showing that already the worship of the Aten had permeated the upper levels of Egyptian society during Amenhotep's reign, particularly perhaps, having in mind the profession of the two men, in the arts.

Hor and Suty did not, however, escape the attentions of the priests of Amun who, after their orthodox paramountcy was restored following the eclipse of the Aten, took their revenge on all who were identified with the now-persecuted god. Their stele was defaced and their own portraits removed.

J. H. Breasted, *The Dawn of Conscience*, New York, 1933, 275–6.
James and Davies 49–50; ill. 56.
BM 826.

Hordedef (alt. Hordjedef), Prince, Fourth Dynasty, Old Kingdom, *c.* 2550 BC. Hordedef was a son of King KHNUM-KHUFU and long enjoyed a reputation as a wise man. In the early Middle Kingdom, centuries after his lifetime, he was bracketed with IMHOTEP in the song of a harper-singer, who cited their reputations as evidence of the transience of life and the illusions of fame.

Hordedef features in one of the 'Tales of Wonder' (Papyrus Westcar) a story about a magician, Djedi, whom he procures to entertain his father when the king was bored. He was buried at Giza, in a tomb near his father's pyramid, close to the burials of other princes, Hordedef's brothers.

'The Instructions of Prince Hordjedef' have been attributed to him but are thought to be of a later date.

CAH I.2: 145, 164, 171.
Lichtheim 1: 215–22.

Horemheb, General of the Armies, King, Eighteenth Dynasty, New Kingdom, *c.* 1323–1295 BC. From an obscure family originally coming from Heracleopolis, Horemheb is an example of the man who rose to the ultimate heights of Egyptian society by his talents and qualities of leadership. He was evidently rising during the reign of King AMENHOTEP IV-AKHENATEN, and further consolidated his military responsibilities during King SMENKHKARE'S brief reign.

It was under TUTANKHAMUN that Horemheb made his most impressive advance, becoming in effect commanding General of the armies of Egypt. He accompanied the king on his campaigns in Nubia and the north when, because of Tutankamun's youth, he directed all the operations in his name. He was effectively regent during Tutankhamun's minority.

Although Horemheb had risen under Akhenaten he was evidently one of those high officials who favoured a return to the cults of Amun. After Tutankhamun's death he presumably did not oppose AY'S accession, for the latter was already old and was not likely to rule for long.

Horemheb was proclaimed king on the death of Ay. His reign was vigorous and highly productive. He set about the suppression of the corruption and incompetence which had been allowed to flourish during the preceeding reigns; he was a keen proponent of the king's duty to impose order, *Ma'at*, on the Two Lands.

Horemheb was an enthusiastic builder, and many of the great sites benefited by his endowments. He built two tombs; the first, at Saqqara, was planned when he was still a private person. It contains reliefs of exceptional quality and delicacy. Amongst the scenes depicted are various of Horemheb's campaigns and the occasions of his being decorated by the king. In one sequence a young man, Sementawy, described as Horemheb's secretary, is shown seated immediately behind him. Later his name was erased, for whatever reason, and the name of Ramose inserted in its place.

Horemheb probably reigned for twenty-eight years. He appears to have had no surviving son; a mummy of a high-ranking female in his tomb (KV 57) together with the mummy of a newborn child has led to the speculation that his Queen Mutnodjmet may have died in childbirth, attempting to provide him with an heir. Horemheb's mummy has not been found. He was succeeded by another soldier, RAMESSES I, who founded the Nineteenth Dynasty, who was possibly the Ramose identified in Horemheb's first tomb.

R. Hari, *Horemhab et la Reine Mounedjmet, ou la Fin d'une Dynastie*, Geneva, 1965.
G. T. Martin, *The Memphite Tomb of Horemhab*, London 1989, 19.
Redford 1984: 65–8, 216–24.

Horemkhaef, Priest, Thirteenth Dynasty, Middle Kingdom, *c.* 1700 (?) BC . Horemkhaef, the son of Thuty and Tanetyeby, was Chief Inspector of the Priests of Horus at his temple at Nekhen (Hierakonpolis), the centre from which the Horus kings had set out originally to unite the Valley at the end of the fourth millennium. Horemkhaef records that he undertook a journey from Nekhen to Itjtowy, to the residence of the king, to bring back statues of Horus and his mother Isis which had been made specially in the royal workshops for the temple.

Horemkhaef's autobigraphy is of particular interest in that it shows that at this time the king (who is unnamed in his inscription) ruled much of Egypt from his capital near Memphis, as far south at least as Hierakonpolis.

Hayes 1953: 346–7; fig. 227.
——'Horemkhaef of Nekhen and his Trip to Ittowe', JEA 33: 3–11.
Lichtheim 1: 129–30.
MMA 21.2.69.

Hori, Scribe, Nineteenth Dynasty, New Kingdom, *c.* 1213–1203 BC. The apparent author of a particularly vitriolic letter addressed to one of his fellow-scribes, AMENEMOPE, whom he abuses roundly, questioning his literacy, intelligence and competance to act as a scribe or as a courier entrusted with undertaking journeys to courts in Asia. The letter contains the well known comparison of Amenemope's allegedly confused language with the incomprehension of the speech of a man from the Delta marshes with a man from Elephantine.

It is not unlikely that the letter is a training exercise for budding scribes.

Papyrus Anastasi I (BM 10247).
ANET: 475–9.
Gardiner 1942: pls XXXV–LXII.

Hori, High Priest, Nineteenth Dynasty, New Kingdom, *c.* 1225 BC. Hori was the son of Prince KHAEMWASET and thus the grandson of King RAMESSES II. He served in the temple of Ptah at Memphis, during his father's pontificate and on his death in the fifty-fifth year of Ramesses' reign, succeeded him as High Priest. His own son, also Hori, was first the northern, then the southern (Theban) vizier.

Kitchen 1982: 108, 170.

Hori, Priest, Scribe, Twenty-First Dynasty, Third Intermediate Period, *c.* 1070 BC. Hori began his career, probably during the reign of PINUDJEM I, as the bearer of the image of Amun in the processions of the god held at his temple in Thebes. He then progressed to 'Cupbearer to the King', Royal Scribe and 'Chief of the Harem of the God's Wife of Amun'. He was the son of PANEHESY, who had held similar appointments.

Kitchen 1986: §500.

Horpaa (alt. Horos), Incense-grinder, Ptolemaic period, *c.* 150 BC. Horpaa describes himself as 'a slave' of the ithyphallic god of Koptos, Min. He states that he spent nineteen years grinding incense and died at the age of thirty-two.

Hodjash and Berlev 1982: no. 133, 198–9.

Horsiesnest Meritaten, Princess, Twenty-Fifth Dynasty, Late Period *c.* 747–656 BC. The skull of Princess Horsiesnest Meritaten's mummy shows that it was trephined during her lifetime. The edges of the wound are well healed, indicating that she must have lived on after the operation. It appears that the operation was effected with the use of a hammer and chisel.

P. Ghalioungui, *Magic and Medical Science in Ancient Egypt*, 2nd edn, Amsterdam, 1973.
——*La Médecine des Pharaons*, Paris, 1973, 111–12.
Nunn 1996: 169.

Horurre (alt. Horwerre), Official, Twelfth Dynasty, Middle Kingdom, *c.* 1840 BC. A 'Seal-Bearer' and Director of Gangs, Horurre was sent to Sinai in charge of a mining expedition in the sixth regnal year of King AMENEMHET III. He recorded the success of his mission with the customary self-assurance but less usually also listed the other members of his expedition with descriptions of their various duties. These included specialist quarrymen, a cup-bearer and a magician to ward off scorpions.

Gardiner *et al.* 1952–5: I, pl. 25 a, b; II, 97–9.
Parkinson 1991: 97–9, 'Commemorating a Mining Expedition'.

Horwennefer, King, Ptolemaic Period, *c.* 206 BC. Frequently, during the rule of the Ptolemies over Egypt, the native population rebelled against their corruption, cruelty and licentiousness, and not least the extortions of the Greek administrators. Indigenous kings were proclaimed in opposition to the Ptolemies; one such was Horwennefer who, in 206 BC, during the reign of PTOLEMY IV PHILOPATOR, established a rival state in Upper Egypt.

Quirke and Spencer: 51.

Hotepdief, Official, Third Dynasty, Old Kingdom, *c.* 2650 BC. The son of

Mery-Djehuty, Hotepdief served as a priest of the royal cults of three of the Second Dynasty kings, HOTEPSEKHEMWY, RANEB and NYNETJER, whose Horus names are inscribed on the shoulder of his statue in the Cairo Museum, dating from the late Third Dynasty.

Borchardt, *Statuen und Statuetten (CG) 1*, 1–3, pl. 1.
Terrace and Fischer 1970: no. 2.
Saleh and Sourouzian: no. 22.
EMC JE 34557 (= CG 1).

Hotepsekhemwy, King, Second Dynasty, Archaic Period, *c.* 2890 BC. Little is known of this, the first king of the Second Dynasty. His name means 'The Two Powers are at Peace', suggesting that he came to the throne after a time of unrest or division, thwarting the attempts at union of the First Dynasty kings. His name, together with those of his two successors, RANEB and NYNETJER are inscribed on the shoulder of a stone statuette of the official HOTEPDIEF, probably of late Third Dynasty date. His name was misread in antiquity as Bedjau (and variants) and these sometimes appear in older texts. Unlike his predecessors, with whom his connection is unknown, he appears to have had himself buried at Saqqara rather than in the by now traditional necropolis of the kings at Abydos. His tomb is probably somewhere near the pyramid complex built for King UNAS.

Manetho records that during his reign a chasm appeared at Bubastis in the Delta, which swallowed up many people.

Emery 1961: 92.
Lehner 1997: 82.

Hui, Painter, Twentieth Dynasty, New Kingdom, *c.* 1184–1153 BC. Hui was one of the few painters who signed his work, which he produced during the reign of king RAMESSES III. He also left a portrait of himself, engaged in his work with brush and paints, amongst a procession of deified kings and queens in a tomb at Deir el-Medina. As if anticipating the conventional view of the artist, Hui shows himself very casually dressed, his appearance indeed rather louche, with his hair unbound, long and flowing down his back.

This portrait is repeated on an ostracon in the Egyptian Museum, Berlin.

P. Montet, *Eternal Egypt*, London, 1964: 244, fig. 55.
EMB, Ostracon 21447.

Huni, King, Third Dynasty, Old Kingdom, *c.* 2637–2613 BC. The last king of the greatly innovative Third Dynasty, Huni's burial place is unknown and his reign is obscure. It is likely that one of his lesser wives, MERESANKH, was the ancestress of the following Fourth Dynasty. He was possibly the builder of the Meidum pyramid which is thought to have been finished for him by SNEFERU, his son and successor; however, there is no direct evidence at Meidum to identify Huni with the pyramid. Huni is credited with a reign of twenty-four years.

It is possible that he is to be identified with a king, QAHEDJET, who is known only by one inscription.

L. Borchardt, 'König Huni (?)', ZÄS 46 (1909) 12–13.
J. Vandier, 'Une Stèle Égyptienne Portant un Nouveau Nom Royal de la Troisième Dynastie', CRAIB, Jan–Mars 1968: 16–22.
Edwards 1993: 92–3.
Berman and Letellier 1996: 36, no. 2.
Brooklyn Museum, Charles Edwin Wilbur Fund 46.167.

Huy, Viceroy, Eighteenth Dynasty, New Kingdom, *c.* 1336–1327 BC. The office of Viceroy, responsible for the government of Egypt's southerly dominions in Nubia, was one of great status in the later Eighteenth Dynasty and the beginning of the Nineteenth. The Viceroy was titled 'King's Son of Kush' and ruled in the king's place. Huy was TUTANKHAMUN'S Viceroy, and in his tomb is shown receiving the homage of the

Nubian princes, including HEKANEFER, on the king's behalf. He is also shown accepting Nubian slaves in payment of taxes.

N. De Garis Davis and A. H. Gardiner, *The Tomb of Huy, Viceroy of Nubia in the Reign of Tutankhamun*, no. 40, London, 1926.
D. O'Connor, 'New Kingdom and Third Intermediate Period, 1552–664 BC', in Trigger *et al.* 1983: 260–5.

Huya, Steward, Eighteenth Dynasty, New Kingdom, *c.* 1350 BC. Huya was a high official in the service of Queen TIY, the mother of King AMENHOTEP IV-AKHENATEN. He was 'Superintendent of the Royal Harem', 'Superintendent of the Treasury' and 'Major-domo in the House of the King's Mother'. His tomb at Akhetaten is notable for the inclusion of one of the 'Hymns to the Aten' and for the wealth of material relating to the solar cult and to the royal family.

De Garis Davis 1903–8.
Redford 1984: 150.

Huya, Royal Scribe, Nineteenth Dynasty, New Kingdom, *c.* 1279–1213 BC. An official of some standing in the reign of King RAMESSES II, Huya rejoiced in the rather unusual title, amongst others, of 'Chief Over the Fattened Fowl', as well as 'Scribe of the King'. Huya's title indicates the extraordinary specialisations in the titles of officials in the New Kingdom, which were often as recherché as those of the Old Kingdom.

G. A. Gaballa, 'Monuments of Prominent Men of Memphis, Abydos and Thebes', in Ruffle *et al.* 1979: 42–3.

I

Iahmes (alt. Neferibra-Nakht), Army Officer, Twenty-Sixth Dynasty, Late Period, *c.* 585 BC. A contemporary of General POTASIMTO, Iahmes was a senior Army officer during the reign of PSAMETIK II. During this time an inscription was carved in Greek on the left leg of the colossal statue of King RAMESSES II at Abu Simbel, which names Iahmes. He was particularly proud of the campaigns which he fought in Nubia, and the inscription was carved, doubtless by a Greek mercenary, on the way to or returning from one of his Nubian engagements.

Bothmer 1961 (1969): 60, nos 52 a, b, pls 48–9.
MMA 66.99.68.
EMC CG 895.

[Iankhamu], Governor, Eighteenth Dynasty, New Kingdom, *c.* 1352–1336 BC. The control of the extensive possessions in Palestine and Syria won by the warrior kings like THUTMOSE III and AMENHOTEP II put considerable strain on the Egyptian administration. Egypt adopted a policy of taking the sons of local rulers and other dignitaries and educating them with the royal princes in the academy known as the *kap* so that, on their return to their homelands, they would be suitably Egyptianised. In other cases Egypt appointed local men to act as royal agents, responsible for the governing of a particular territory. Typical of this process was Iankhamu, who was governor of Canaan. He appears, by his name, himself to have been a Syrian. He held the appointment of 'Fan-Bearer on the Right of the King', a high honour, especially for a foreigner.

CAH II.1: 470–3.

Ibe (alt. Ibi), Steward, Twenty-Sixth Dynasty, Late Period, *c.* 664–610 BC. The Chief Steward of Princess NITIQRET, the daughter of King PSAMETIK I, Ibe was instructed by her father to restore and equip the palace of the princess on her appointment as Divine Adoratrice (God's Wife of Amun), at Thebes and hieress to Princess SHEPENUPET. Ibe records the arrival of the princess in considerable state, borne in her palanquin, to inspect her papers and to discuss the restoration plans with him. He claims to have built one part of the palace to a height of more than one hundred and seventy feet.

He was buried at Thebes (TT 36).

Breasted 4: §958A.
Grimal: 356.

Ibi, Nomarch, Sixth Dynasty, Old Kingdom, *c.* 2320–2220 BC. Ibi was the son of DJAU, the brother-in-law and Vizier of King PEPY I; he was also of great influence in the reigns of MERENRE and PEPY II. Ibi was placed in various offices of considerable significance; in addition to his more or less hereditary position as Nomarch of Hierakonpolis he also acquired control of the Cerastes-Mountain nome, by marriage to its heiress.

Breasted 1: §§375–9.
N. De Garis Davis, *The Rock Tombs of Deir El-Gabrawi*, London, 1902: 5.

Ibi (Twenty-Sixth Dynasty), *see* **Ibe**

Ibiya, King, Thirteenth Dynasty, Middle Kingdom, *c.* 1715–1704 BC. One of the rulers of the Thirteenth Dynasty who managed to hold his office for a significant period, Ibiya reigned for about eleven years, according to the King List in Turin. He is known by only one monument, however, a memorial stele left by one SIHATHOR, an army officer in the king's service, which was found at Thebes. It is likely that Ibiya's rule was confined to the south and to Nubia.

Bourriau 1988: 58–9, no. 45.
BM EA 1348.

Idu, Overseer of Priests, Sixth Dynasty, Old Kingdom, *c.* 2300 BC. The owner of a tomb in the Giza necropolis, Idu was the Overseer of Priests of the pyramids of the kings KHNUM-KHUFU and KHAFRE. He was also described as the 'tenant' of the pyramid of PEPY I. His tomb contains scenes of mourning at the dead man's house and the funeral processions which accompanied him to his burial. There is also a curious representation of Idu in his tomb, shown from the waist up, rising out of the ground.

W. K. Simpson, *The Mastaba of Qar and Idu*, Boston, 1976.

Ihy, Noble, Fifth/Sixth Dynasties, Old Kingdom, *c.* 2375–2345 BC. Ihy was a courtier in the service of the kings of the latter part of the Old Kingdom and was given a mastaba tomb at Saqqara; he may have been the son of METHETHY. He provides an example of the nature of Egyptian names; one of his names was Ni-tawi-Izezi, commemorating King Izezi, (DJEDKARE ISESI) but he also had a 'good [or 'beautiful'] name' which was given to him at birth. In this instance Ni-tawi-Izezi's 'good name' was Ihy.

He held a number of appointments and titles of honour including 'Instructor of Gardeners' and 'Overseer of the Gardeners' Bureau'. He was 'Inspector of Gardeners of the Great House', the palace of the king. Ihy was probably not obliged to concern himself in detail with the work of the gardeners attached to the palace, however; there is no evidence that he was an horticulturalist.

Hodjash and Berlev 1982: no. 7, 42–5.

Ii-seneb, Official, Thirteenth Dynasty, Middle Kingdom, *c.* 1795–1650 BC. Ii-seneb was one of 'The Great Ones of the Tens of the South', a florid title which at this time denoted one attached to the office of the Vizier. Members of his family, including his father, Montuhotep, were soldiers, serving in the 'town's regiment', probably in Abydos.

Hodjash and Berlev 1982: no. 35, 79–81.

Ika, Priest, Fifth Dynasty, Old Kingdom, *c.* 2350 BC. Ika was a *wab* priest, Royal Acquaintance and Chief of the Great House. His tomb at Saqqara contained a fine false door in wood in which he is shown with his wife, a priestess of Hathor, and their children. He wears a distinctive kilt with a strong zigzag pattern. His tomb was buried when the causeway for King UNAS' pyramid was built.

PM III.2: 637.
Z. Saad, ASAE 40 (1940) 675–80, pls 73, 74.
Saleh and Sourouzian: no. 58.
EMC JE 77201.

Ikhernofret, Treasurer, Festival Organiser, Twelfth Dynasty, Middle Kingdom, *c.* 1874–1855 BC. Ikhernofret was the

Chief Treasurer to King SENWOSRET III. He was commanded by the king to direct the festival at the sacred city of Abydos, held in honour of Osiris. He organised the round of mystery plays which attended the cults of the god and was appointed to a special priestly rank to permit him to do so; he even himself took the place of the king in the role of Horus in the ceremonies. He organised 'The Coming Forth of Wepwawet', a canine god with one of whose manifestations, Khentiamentiu, Osiris was identified. He records that he was educated in the palace, presumably with the royal children.

Kees: 242–3.
Schäfer: 'Die Mysterien des Osiris in Abydos unter König Sesostris III'.
R. Anthes, 'Die Berichte des Neferhotep und des Ichernofret über Osirisfest in Abydos', *Festschrift zum 150 Jahrigen Bestehen des Berliner Ägyptischen Museums*, Berlin, 1974.
Lichtheim I: 123–5.

Iki, Overseer of Priests, Twelfth Dynasty, Middle Kingdom, *c.* 1850 BC. Iki was the Overseer of Priests at Abydos and in this capacity had in his employment a harpist, NEFERHOTEP. Iki and his wife, Nesankh, were buried in 'The Terrace of the Great God' at Abydos. A stele in their tomb shows them being entertained by the excessively portly Neferhotep.

Neferhotep was commemorated himself on another stele, with a touching inscription by his friend who dedicated it, and by the sculptor who produced it.

W. K. Simpson, 'The Terrace of the Great God at Abydos: The Offering Chapels of Dynasties 12 and 13', *Publications of the Pennsylvania-Yale Expedition to Egypt*, 5, 1974: pl. 84.
W. A. Ward, 'Neferhotep and his Friends: A Glimpse of the Life of Ordinary Men', JEA 63 (1977) 64–6.
Rijksmuseum van Oudheden, Leiden, Stela v. 68.

Ikui, Nomarch, Tenth Dynasty, First Intermediate Period, *c.* 2125 BC. Ikui was the ancestor of the INYOTEF kings whose descendants in turn provided the kings of the Eleventh Dynasty, including the great NEBHEPETRE MONTUHOTEP II. Ikui was awarded the status of a king posthumously, though without his name being enclosed in a cartouche.

CAH I.2: 473.

Imeru-Neferkare, Vizier, Thirteenth Dynasty, Middle Kingdom, *c.* 1725 BC. In the latter stages of the Middle Kingdom, as the Thirteenth Dynasty staggered to its evidently inglorious conclusion, the office of vizier increased in importance as the power of the king declined. Imeru-Neferkare was vizier to King SOBEKHOTEP IV. He was a noble of high rank, the possessor, it was said, 'of six great castles'. He built a canal and was also the builder of the King's funerary temple.

E. Delange, *Catalogue des statues égyptiennes du Moyen Empire au musée du Louvre*, Paris, 1987: 66–8.
MduL A 125.

Imhotep, Vizier and Architect, Third Dynasty, Old Kingdom, *c.* 2667–2648 BC. Perhaps the most original creative genius that Egypt ever produced and certainly the greatest known, Imhotep was Chief Minister and Superintendent of All the King's Works to King DJOSER NETJERYKHET, the second king of the Third Dynasty and one of the most significant men to occupy the thrones of the Two Lands. Imhotep's father was said to be Kanofer, also the Royal Superintendent of Works. The family was believed to come from Upper Egypt.

Imhotep was responsible for the design and construction of the Step Pyramid complex at Saqqara, the first monumental set of buildings made entirely from stone in the history of the world. The technical and logistical problems inherent in constructing a monument requiring the quarrying, transportation, dressing, decoration and erection of nearly one million tons of limestone with no precedents which are known, are phenomenal, as was Imhotep's response to the challenges which he and the king set themselves. It is very touching – and profoundly impressive – to see the often-tentative approaches which Imhotep brings to his work, as though he is unsure of the properties of stone, for example, or of the stresses which the structure might be expected to bear.

The Third Dynasty was a time of exceptionally rapid techological advances, of which Imhotep was in the vanguard. His resounding titles are recorded on the pedestal of a statue of the king, where Imhotep's name is directly associated with that of Djoser Netjerykhet. It reads: 'The Chancellor of the King of Lower Egypt, the first after the King of Upper Egypt, administrator of the Great Palace, hereditary Lord, High Priest of Heliopolis, Imhotep, the builder, the sculptor, the maker of stone vases.'

He lived to a great age, apparently dying in the reign of King HUNI, the last of the dynasty. His burial place has not been found but it has been speculated that it may be at Saqqara.

J. B. Hurry, *Imhotep*, Oxford, 1928.
Lauer 1976: 12, 19, 92, 98, 217–8; ill. 170.
Firth *et al.* 1935.

Imhotep, Chancellor and High Priest, Twelfth Dynasty, Middle Kingdom, *c.* 1965–1920 BC. Imhotep was Chancellor of Egypt during the reign of King SENWOSRET I. Relatively little is known of his career, but he must have been especially favoured by the king, for in his mastaba tomb at Lisht, the location also for the burials of the dynasty, were found two magnificent carved wooden statues, apparently representing Senwosret as King, respectively, of Upper and Lower Egypt. It has been suggested that the statues are of divinities in manifested in the person of the king and that they may have been placed in Imhotep's tomb after the death of the king. The statues are are painted and are exceptionally life-like.

Like his earlier namesake, Imhotep was also High Priest of Heliopolis.

Stevenson Smith 1958 (1981): 179; 446 n15.
EMC JE 44951.
MMA 143.17.

Impy, Official, Sixth Dynasty, Old Kingdom, *c.* 2345–2181 BC. The son of NEKHEBU, a royal architect, Impy was buried in a tomb at Giza, which remained unplundered until excavated in the early years of the present century. The tomb contained a very fine cedarwood sarcophagus, and Impy himself was richly accoutred with a gold and faience collar, necklaces and a gilded copper bracelet and belt.

His tomb also contained an array of vessels and model offering tables and stands, also manufactured in copper of an exceptionally high purity.

W. Stevenson Smith, *Ancient Egypt as Represented in the Museum of Fine Arts, Boston*, Boston MA, 1960: 64–7, fig. 38.
Thomas 1995: 47, 137.

Inaros, Prince, Twenty-Sixth Dynasty, Late Period, *c.* 525 BC. Inaros was perhaps the son of King PSAMETIK III; he was destined to become a figure of legend as much as he was of historical reality. He opposed the Persian occupation of Egypt and drew together all the nationalist forces who were prepared to resist the invaders. He proclaimed himself King of Egypt and managed to impose his control on much of the northern part of the country.

He defeated the son of XERXES, Achaemenes, who was killed at Papremis. However, the Persians recovered from their defeat and in turn defeated Inaros. He was first imprisoned and then executed in 454 BC, thus suffering the same fate at the hands of the Persians as probably befell his father.

He had been supported in his rebellion by AMYRTAEUS, who eventually himself became King, founding the Twenty Eighth Dynasty, of which he was the sole representative.

Inaros was celebrated as the hero of a cycle of heroic tales, *The Pedubastis Cycle*, though in this guise his story differs from that of the putative son of Psametik III.

Grimal: 370–1.

Indy, Noble, Eighth Dynasty, First Intermediate Period, *c.* 2170–2125 BC. Indy was Count of Thinis, the first capital of the kings of Egypt after they left Hierakonpolis. He was a soldier 'excellent in battle', and a Lector-Priest; he held the rank of Chancellor of the King of Lower Egypt. His wife was the Royal Acquaintance and Priestess of Hathor, Mut-Mauty.

Hayes 1953: 139, fig. 83.
MMA 1925 25.2.3.

Inebni, Army Officer, Eighteenth Dynasty, New Kingdom, *c.* 1450 BC. The Infantry Commander Inebni served under the joint sovereigns Queen HATSHEPSUT and King THUTMOSE III. His richly painted and inscribed block statue declares that it was made 'by favour' of the sovereigns, but part of the inscription relating to Hatshepsut has been deleted, following her death when mention of her was erased from many of her monuments.

Quirke and Spencer: 43; pl. 28.
BM EA 1131.

Ineni, Architect, Eighteenth Dynasty, New Kingdom, *c.* 1510–1470 BC. Ineni served five of the kings of the Eighteenth Dynasty, beginning with AMENHOTEP I. He was promoted under THUTMOSE I for whom he may have built the Great Hall at Karnak; he built the king's tomb at Thebes, the first royal entombment in the Valley of the Kings. When THUTMOSE II became king, Ineni's fortunes continued to flourish, reaching the height of royal favour under the joint rule of THUTMOSE III and Queen HATSHEPSUT. The latter in particular showered gifts and honours on him and 'filled his house with gold and silver'.

Ineni seems to have been especially interested in garden design. In his own tomb (TT 81) he listed and illustrated some of the trees he had planted, including thirty-one fruit trees; an orchard for which he was responsible had 451 trees. He is shown, sitting in his orchard, drinking water from the pool in the garden and accepting offerings from his servants, a procedure which he intended should be continued throughout eternity.

He was Steward of the Granaries of Amun, from the reign of Amenhotep I to Thutmose III. He was buried at Abd el-Qurna (TT81).

Breasted 2: §§43–6, §§99–108, §§115–18, §§340–3.
Grimal: 207, 300.
Wilkinson 1998: 28, 42–3, 97, 102, 130; fig. 48.

Ini, Nomarch, Eleventh Dynasty, First Intermediate Period/Early Middle Kingdom, *c.* 2060 BC. Ini was Treasurer, Sole Companion, Nomarch, Overseer of the Priests of the Temple of Sobek, Lord of Sumenu. He was the owner of a tomb at Gebelein which contained a pair of white leather sandals, in addition to more usual fittings. It also was supplied with about three hundred models of donkey packsaddles and two funerary boats.

E. Brovarski, 'Two Monuments in the First Intermediate Period from the Theban Nome', Studies in Honor of George R. Hughes, *Studies in Ancient Oriental Civilization*, XXXIX: 31–41.
Robins 1990: 26.

Iniamunnayefnebu, Libyan Noble, Twenty-Second Dynasty, Third Intermediate Period, *c.* 825–773 BC. The child of one of the 'Great Chiefs of the Libu', from whom several of the kings of this period traced their descent, Iniamunnayefnebu lived during the reign of King SHESHONQ III. In the thirty-first year of the reign he donated some arable land under the charge of the Divine Father, Ankh-Hor. He set up a stele to commemorate his donation and rounded off the inscription with a series of vigorous curses against anyone who displaced it, asking that they shall be pursued by fire, that the name of their family shall be cut down and their line become extinct.

Hodjash and Berlev 1982: no. 106, 157–8, 160, 165.
Kitchen 1986: §306, §311.

Inini, Butler, Twentieth Dynasty, New Kingdom, *c.* 1150 BC. The Butler, a relatively high rank, of King RAMESSES III, Inini was a Libyan and was implicated in the attempt on the king's life towards the end of his reign. In common with most of the other accused Inini was found guilty and sentenced to death.

A. Buck, 'The Judicial Papyrus of Turin', JEA 23 (1927) 152ff.
CAH II.2: 246.

Iniuia, Scribe, Eighteenth Dynasty, New Kingdom, *c.* 1330–1300 BC. Iniuia was Overseer of the Cattle of Amun and High Steward. He was also Scribe of the Treasury of Gold and Silver. He lived during the reigns of TUTANKHAMUN, AY and HOREMHEB, near whose tomb he was eventually buried with his wife Iuy.

H. Schneider, EA 3: 3–6.

Inkaf, Sculptor, Fourth Dynasty, Old Kingdom, *c.* 2558–2532 BC. Inkaf evidently worked on the tomb of the great Queen MERESANKH III at Giza. He is shown putting the finishing touches to a seated figure of the queen, on a relief in the tomb. Working with him is a painter whose name has been read as Rahay, who is applying paint to a statue of Meresankh.

A second Inkaf, also a sculptor, is known. He may be the son or nephew of the elder Inkaf. He worked on the tomb of one Red-ka.

Stevenson Smith 1946 (1949): 351–2, 353; figs 232–3.

Intef, Great Herald, Eighteenth Dynasty, New Kingdom *c.* 1450 BC. The duties which devolved upon the holder of the office of Great Herald were those of a Minister of Communications, Master of Ceremonies and Chief of Protocol. His responsibilities kept him virtually in daily touch with the king. He was responsible for keeping the king informed of the mood of the people and of their needs and preoccupations; he was also given the task of informing the people of the king's decisions and wishes.

Intef's titles were very splendid: 'Hereditary Prince and Count', 'Sole Companion', 'Great in Love', 'Count of Thinis', 'Lord of the Entire Oasis Region', 'Great Herald of the King'. He was buried at Thebes (TT 155).

Breasted 2: §§763–71.

Intefoker, *see* **Antefoker**

Inti, Vizier, Fifth Dynasty, Old Kingdom, *c.* 2410 BC. The founder of a dynasty of high-ranking state servants, Inti himself was Vizier to King DJEDKARE ISESI. He was responsible for all the building works of the king and mentions various structures which he planned for the court, which the king evidently much approved, according to the letters to Inti which the vizier reproduces.

His son MEHY was Vizier to King UNAS, the last ruler of the Fifth Dynasty, and like his father was Overseer of All the King's Works. He probably shared his responsibilities with his brother Khnumenty, who continued in office under King TETI of the Sixth Dynasty.

Mehy's son, NEKHEBU, followed his father in the Office of Public Works but not in the vizierate. He built canals and a substantial monument for King PEPY I at Heliopolis.

Nekhebu's son, IMPY, was also Overseer of All the King's Works.

CAH I.2: 186–7.

Inti, Soldier, Sixth Dynasty, Old Kingdom, *c.* 2345–2181 BC. The owner of a tomb at Deshasha, the wall-reliefs of which show an attack on an Asiatic town, possibly in Palestine, and the misfortunes of its inhabitants. One episode in the attack shows Egyptian soldiers undermining the city's walls.

W. M. F. Petrie, *Deshashah*, London, 1898.
CAH I.2: 235, 358–9.

Inyotef, Nomarch, Eighth Dynasty, First Intermediate Period, *c.* 2180 BC. Inyotef was the son of MONTUHOTEP, the son of IKUI, a noble from Thebes of which he was nomarch. He was known from the Eighth Dynasty and was regarded as the ancestor of the line from which the later Inyotefs, and hence the Eleventh Dynasty kings, were descended; he was the father of MONTUHOTEP I (Tepya'a, 'The Ancestor'). He was the subject of a religious cult in the reign of King SENWOSRET I.

P. E. Newberry, 'On the Parentage of the Intef kings of the Eleventh Dynasty', ZÄS 72 (1936): 118–20.
Winlock 1947: 5, 6.
CAH I.2: 473.

Inyotef I, Noble, Tenth/Eleventh Dynasties, First Intermediate Period/Middle Kingdom, *c.* 2125–2112 BC. Inyotef I was considered the actual founder of the Eleventh Dynasty, though not numbered amongst its kings. However, he proclaimed himself King of Upper and Lower Egypt. He opposed ANKHTIFY, the nomarch of Hierakoapolis who was loyal to the dynasty of Heracleopolitan kings whom the Inyotefs confronted. Inyotef I defeated Ankhtify and then consolidated his power over much of the south.

P. E. Newberry, 'On the Parentage of the Intef Kings of the Eleventh Dynasty', ZÄS 72 (1936): 118–20.

Inyotef II Wahankh, King, Eleventh Dynasty (Thebes) Middle Kingdom, *c.* 2112–2063 BC. Inyotef II Wahankh succeeded INYOTEF I and continued his family's opposition to the Heracleopolitans, led by their king, AKHTOY III. In later years it is likely that the two houses existed together in a sustained if uneasy state of peace.

Inyotef seems to have been exceptionally fond of dogs. He is portrayed on a stela in his funerary shrine in Western Thebes with five of his dogs, the names of which are carefully recorded. One of these, Behhek (probably a Libyan name) seems especially favoured as she is shown sitting between her master's legs.

Inyotef II Wahankh's choice of Western Thebes as the location for his burial was to be significant for it marked the beginning of its rise to the prominence which was to make it the centre of Egypt's religious cults from the Middle Kingdom onwards.

Winlock 1947: 12–17.
A. Dodson, *Monarchs of the Nile*, London, 1995: 46–9.
EMC.

Inyotef III, King, Eleventh Dynasty (Thebes) Middle Kingdom, *c.* 2063–2055 BC. Inyotef III succeeded his father, and during his reign imposed his family's control over most of Upper Egypt. His son, King NEBHEPETRE MONTUHOTEP II was to reunite the Two Lands and establish the Eleventh Dynasty as the rulers of all Egypt.

P. E. Newberry, 'On the Parentage of the Intef Kings of the Eleventh Dynasty', ZÄS 72 (1936) 118–120.
Winlock 1947.

Inyotef, Official, Twelfth Dynasty, Middle Kingdom, 1965–1920 BC. Inyotef endowed a chapel at Abydos that he might be commemorated close to the supposed burial place of Osiris, during the reign of King SENWOSRET I. A statue was placed in the chapel; Inyotef is seated, his throne-like chair placed on a high plinth. Three stelae were also dedicated by him.

James and Davies: 25–6; ill. 25.
BM 461.

Inyotef VI, King, Seventeenth Dynasty, Second Intermediate Period, *c.* 1650–1550 BC. One of the transitory kings ruling from Thebes towards the end of the Hyksos period. He was buried at Thebes but his tomb is now lost, although two of his coffins survive.

Winlock 1947: 104–8.
MduL E 3019 (as Antef).
Ryholt 1997: 266, 393.

Inyotef VII, King, Seventeenth Dynasty, Second Intermediate Period, *c.* 1650–1550 BC. Inyotef seems to have been one of the more effective rulers during what was an exceptionally disturbed period, after the invasions of the Hyksos rulers from Palestine had fractured Egypt's unity. His use of the Horus name *Nebhepetre* may be an attempt at suggesting (or perhaps recalling) a connection with the founder of the Middle Kingdom, three hundred and fifty years before his time. His wife, Queen SOBEKEMSAF, possessed a piece of gold jewellery of fine workmanship, inscribed with the names of the king and herself. Inyotef's tomb at Thebes, now lost, was one of those inspected during the reign of Ramesses IX.

Inyotef asserted his authority vigorously and is regarded as one of the founding princes of the Theban line which was to come so spectacularly to power in the following dynasty. He built extensively and evidently had some reputation as a warrior; he was buried with two bows and six flint-tipped arrowheads beside him in his coffin. He seems also to have believed in the merits of diplomacy as during his reign Thebes maintained peaceful relations with the Hyksos rulers in the north.

CAH II.1: 70–1.
J. von Beckerath, *Antef (Anjotef) V–VII, Lexikon der Ägyptologie*, I, Wiesbaden, 1975: 301–2.
Grimal: 187–9.
BM.
MduL E 3020 (as Antef).
Ryholt 1997: 266, 309, 394–5.

Ipuia, Noblewoman, Eighteenth Dynasty, New Kingdom, *c.* 1352–1336 BC. Ipuia was the mother of the distinguished vizier RAMOSE, who served both King AMENHOTEP III and his son, AMENHOTEP IV-AKHENATEN. In Ramose's beautifully decorated tomb at Thebes (TT 55) she is depicted in the reliefs, together with other members of Ramose's family, including the Overseer of the Royal Horses, MAIY, and his wife Werel.

N. De Garis Davis, *The Tomb of the Vizier Ramose*, London, 1941.

Ipuwer, Sage, Author (?), Middle Kingdom, *c.* 2000 BC. Ipuwer is the presumed author of a series of 'Admonitions' which purport to describe the chaos which overtook Egypt at the end of the Old Kingdom, *c.* 2200 BC. The language is vivid and deeply pessimistic; but it is widely doubted today if the text is anything other than a literary exercise produced long after the events which it purports to describe. Other than the 'Admonitions' attributed to him there is no independent evidence of Ipuwer's existence.

A. Erman, *The Literature of the Ancient Egyptians*, trans., London, 1927: 92.
Pritchard (ed.) 1955: 441.
Lichtheim 1: 149–63.

Ipy (alt. Ipuy), Sculptor, Nineteenth Dynasty, New Kingdom, *c.* 1279–1213 BC. Ipy lived in the reign of King RAMESSES II and, in contrast with that monarch's immense buildings, was buried in a small and engaging tomb at Deir el-Medina (TT 217). It is decorated with scenes in a garden, presumably Ipy's, and with the small tomb chapel in which part of his funeral cermonies were conducted, also in the garden. A gardener is at work (it may be Ipy himself) whilst his dog sits beside him.

Ipy was obviously an enthusiastic horticulturalist; one of his trees was a pollarded willow, and he also grew snake cucumber. In the garden pool, a boat carrying a statue of Ipy was drawn across the water, allowing Ipy to savour the air and to participate in the 'Beautiful Festival of the Valley'. The prow of the boat is ram-headed.

The tomb also contains pastoral scenes of shepherd boys with their goats; one of them plays his flute. The shepherds are also accompanied by their dogs. Ipy has himself represented with a kitten on his lap, the mother cat sitting watchfully under a chair. Part of his responsibility to the court was to provide furniture for the chapel of King AMENHOTEP I, and he shows scenes from his workshop, with incidents of mishap and humour, unusual in the decoration of what was intended to be a house for eternity.

N. De Garis Davis, *Two Ramesside Tombs at Thebes*, New York, 1927: pl. XXIX.
Stevenson Smith 1958 (1981): pls 370–1, 488.
Wilkinson 1998: 48, 59, 103, 105; pl. XIX.

[**Iripaankhkenkenef**] (**alt. Pegtjetrer**), Nubian Prince, Twenty-Fifth Dynasty, Late Period, *c*. 747–716 BC. Iripaankhkenkenef was a Nubian prince, possibly the son of the wife of King KASHTA; if he was then he was a brother of King PIANKHY, the conqueror of Egypt. He records that he came up to Egypt from Nubia at the age of twenty when his mother had died and he sought permission for her to be buried at the sacred necropolis at Abydos.

Hodjash and Berlev 1982: no. 109, 165–71.

Irtisen, Sculptor, Eleventh Dynasty, Middle Kingdom, *c*. 2055–2004 BC. A contemporary of King NEBHEPETRE MONTUHOTEP II, Irtisen prepared a famous inscription in which he delights in his proficiency in his art. He was, he says,

> Pre-eminent in my learning....I knew how to represent the movements of the image of a man and the carriage of a woman...the poising of the arm to bring the hippopotamus low and the movements of the runner. No one succeeds in this task but only I and the eldest son of my body.

The latter had been initiated and entrusted with the secrets of his craft by his father.

Irtisen was fortunate to live at a time when the arts were once again highly valued in Egypt, after the troubled years which followed the end of the Old Kingdom. His generously inscribed stela was recovered from Abydos where it was no doubt placed in the land sacred to Osiris, to ensure Irtisen's prosperity in the afterlife.

Stevenson Smith 1946 (1949): 356.
Edwards 1985: 209.
Andreu *et al*. 1997: no. 28.
MduL C14.

Irukaptah, Embalmer, Sixth Dynasty, Old Kingdom, *c*. 2250 BC. Irukaptah shared his tomb at Giza with his wife, Neferhetpes. He was 'Assistant Superintendent of the Embalming Works of the Necropolis', a responsible and doubtless busy occupation at one of the most important royal necropoleis in Egypt.

Pelizaeus-Museum, Hildesheim, nos 417, 418.

Iry, Physician, Fourth Dynasty, Old Kingdom, *c*. 2613–2494 BC. The Chief of the Court Physicians, Iry was a specialist in conditions of the abdomen and bowels as well as in opthalmics. He was also regarded as an expert in the treatment of conditions relating to the bodily fluids.

His status is indicated by the fact that he was buried at Giza in the company of the kings of the dynasty who were his patients.

H. Junker, 'Die Stele des Hofarztes "Iry" ', ZÄS 63 (1928) 53–70.

Iryenakhty, Physician, Tenth Dynasty, First Intermediate Period, *c.* 2125 BC. Iryenakhty was Court Physician at a time of relative decline in the fortunes of the monarchy. He practised in a number of specialisations, including gastroenterology, proctology and opthalmology.

H. Junker, 'Die Stele des Hofarztes "Iry" ', ZÄS 63 (1928) 53–70.
Nunn 1996: 126–7.

Iryhor, King, Late Predynastic Period, *c.* 3150 BC. Few of the names of the kings who ruled in Egypt before the First Dynasty have survived for certain. Iryhor may have been one of the immediate predecessors of NAR-MER; a tomb at Abydos has recently (1992) been identified as his on the evidence of sealings found in it. However, this interpretation has been questioned, and Iryhor's very existence doubted.

Spencer: 76–7.
T. A. H. Wilkinson, 'The Identification of Tomb B1 at Abydos: Refuting the Existence of King Ro/Iry-Hor', JEA 79 (1993) 241–3.

Isesi (alt. Izezi), *see* **Djedkare Isesi**

Isi, Official, Fifth/Sixth Dynasties, Old Kingdom, *c.* 2414–2321 BC. A high official who lived during the reign of King DJEDKARE ISESI of the Fifth Dynasty and on into that of King PEPY I of the Sixth, Isi was an administrator, judge, chief of the royal archives and a 'Great One Amongst the Tens of the South'. He was buried at Edfu where he was nomarch under Pepy I. Several notable statues were recovered from his tomb, together with copper vessels and toilet articles belonging to his wife, Sech-Sechet.

M. Alliot, *Rapport sur les Fouilles de Tell Edfou*, IFAO t.x., Cairo, 1935–9.
E. Edel, 'Inschriften des Alten Reiches, 1. Die Biographie des Gaufhursten von Edfu', ZÄS 79: 11–17.
IFAO 1981: 58–74.

Istnofret (alt. Isinope), Queen, Nineteenth Dynasty, New Kingdom, *c.* 1279–1213 BC. One of the wives of King RAMESSES II, Istnofret probably succeeded NEFERTARI as the king's principal consort. She was the mother of his second son, Prince Ramesses, for many years his father's nominated successor and of the fourth, Prince KHAEMWASET, who was also for a time Crown Prince but who, like his brother, predeceased his father, in his case late in the reign. Istnofret also gave birth to Ramesses' thirteenth son and eventual successor, King MERENPTAH.

After the death of Nefertari she became the Chief Queen; she was the mother also of Princess-Queen Bint-Anath, who eventually succeeded her on her death.

Istnofret was buried in the Valley of Queens, but her tomb has been lost.

CAH II.2: 232.
Kitchen 1982: 39, 98, 100, 103.

Isis, King's Consort, Eighteenth Dynasty, New Kingdom, *c.* 1492–1479 BC. Isis was the wife or concubine of King THUTMOSE II. Although she was evidently not his principal consort, her son succeeded to the throne as THUTMOSE III.

Lambelet 1978: 72, no. 424.
EMC.

Iti, Official, Sixth Dynasty, Old Kingdom, *c.* 2321–2287 BC. The tomb of Iti, a favourite courtier of King PEPY I, was found intact at Gebelein. In addition to a statue of the tomb's owner it contained a splendid cedar-wood coffin, a painting of seven vases containing the sacred oils and 'a very beautiful bronze water font'.

Robins 1990: 26; pl. 3.2.

Iti, Treasurer, Eleventh Dynasty, First Intermediate Period, *c.* 2130 BC. Iti was the 'King's Treasurer and Head of His Troops', a Royal Seal Bearer and the owner of a tomb at Gebelein which was extensively painted, an example of an art form which seems particularly to have flourished during this time of some political confusion. In addition to customary scenes relating to Iti's life and the ceremonies attending his funeral, there are less usual sequences, including one featuring a large sailing ship armed with shields. There is also a scene of a bullfight, an event which was evidently popular during this period.

Breasted 1: §§457–9.
Lichtheim 1: 88–9.
Robins 1990: 26–7; figs 3.6, 3.7.
EMC 20001.

Iuput, High Priest, General, Viceroy, Twenty-Second Dynasty, Third Intermediate Period, *c.* 945–924 BC. The son of SHESHONQ I, the founder of the Twenty-Second Dynasty, Iuput was appointed by his father as High Priest of Amun, a responsibility which carried with it the command of the Army and the political control of Upper Egypt. When the king returned from a victorious campaign in Palestine in 925 BC, he charged Iuput with important building works at the temple of Karnak in Thebes. Its inscriptions included references to the defeat of the kingdoms of Judea and Israel.

Sheshonq's successor, OSORKON I, removed Iuput from his office, giving it to one of his own sons.

Grimal: 322, 324, 328.

Iuput II (of Leontopolis), King, Twenty-Third Dynasty, Third Intermediate Period, 754–715 BC. During the disturbed period of the late Twenty-Third Dynasty King TAKELOT III was followed, briefly, by RUDAMUN whose influence was largely restricted to Leontopolis in the Delta. Other provincial princes proclaimed themselves 'kings', and when PIANKHY-PIYE, the Nubian king, invaded Egypt, Iuput allied himself with the ruler of Sais, TEFNAKHTE.

Iuput appears to have been recognised as king in Thebes, but ultimately Piankhy was able to assert his authority over most of the country. Iuput was subsequently appointed as Governor of Leontopolis.

Grimal: 331, 335, 339.

Iurudef, Retainer, Nineteenth Dynasty, New Kingdom, *c.* 1220 BC. Iurudef was only a retainer of the Princess TJIA, the sister of King RAMESSES II, and her husband, TIA, but nonetheless was accorded a tomb in the same necropolis of some scale. He was evidently highly regarded by his employers, for he directed their obsequies. His tomb contained a number of other burials, some of which may have been of members of his family, though others were intrusive, of later periods. His father's name was Pekhou, 'The Syrian'.

Martin 1991: 134–9; ills 93, 94.

Iuu, Vizier, Seventh/Eighth Dynasties, First Intermediate Period, *c.* 2181–2150 BC. Iuu was Vizier at the time of the breakup of the royal administration at the end of the Old Kingdom. He held the ancient title 'He of the Curtain' and was 'Overseer of the Scribes of the King's Documents'. He was a devotee of Anubis and was buried at Abydos. He was to be provided with the seven sacred unguents necessary for the preservation of the spirit in the afterlife.

Hodjash and Barev 1982: no. 20, 57.

Iuwelot, Prince, High Priest, Twenty-Second Dynasty, Third Intermediate Period, *c.* 889–804 BC. Iuwelot was the son of OSORKON I. He succeeded his brother SHESHONQ II as High Priest of Amun, and Commander of the Army, thus effectively becoming ruler of Upper Egypt.

Kitchen 1986: §89, §96, §184.
BM 1224.

Iwty, Physician, Nineteenth Dynasty, New Kingdom, *c.* 1320 BC. Iwty was an expert in the preparation of drugs and medicines, and was familiar with the immense library of those who had preceeded him in medical practice in Egypt. The pharmacopaea which was available to medical practitioners, based on the use of natural substances and plant extracts, was very extensive. Iwty maintained his own library in which were contained many of the treatises on the preparation of his materials as well as instructions on the treatment of the various conditions which he might expect to encounter.

F. Jonckheere, *Les Médecins de l'Égypte Pharaonique*, Brussels, 1958: 18–20, 91, 105, 109.
P. Ghalioungui, *The Ebers Papyrus*, Cairo, 1987.
Rijksmuseum van Oudheden, Leiden AST 110.

K

Ka (alt. Sekhem Ka), King, Late Predynastic Period, *c.* 3150 BC. Ka is one of the latest of the acknowledged kings of the Predynastic period; his name is recorded on pottery and inscribed on rocks in the desert. His is one of the first royal names to be displayed in the *serekh*, the heraldic 'badge' which was used to record the king's Horus name. He may have been buried at Abydos, in what was later to become the royal cemetery of the First Dynasty.

Trigger *et al.* 1983: 70.
Spencer: 51, 60, 76.

Ka, Official, Fifteenth Dynasty, Second Intermediate Period, *c.* 1650–1550 BC. During the Second Intermediate Period Egyptians took service with the King of Kush. One of these was Ka who lived, or was based, at Buhen in Nubia. He declared that 'he washed his feet in the waters of Kush in the retinue of the ruler Nedjeh and returned safely to his family'. He describes himself as 'capable servant of the ruler of Kush'.

T. Säve-Söderbergh, 'A Buhen Stela from the Second Intermediate Period', JEA 35 (1949) 50–8.
B. Trigger, *Nubia under the Pharaohs*, London, 1976: 97.

Ka'a (alt. Qa'a), King, First Dynasty, Archaic Period, *c.* 2890 BC. Ka'a was the last king of the First Dynasty. Although he is said to have reigned for almost forty years and celebrated two jubilees, little is known of the events of his reign. The circumstances of the end of the First Dynasty and its replacement by the Second, with which it does not seem to have had any very close relationship, are obscure. Ka'a was the possessor of a fine stele, displaying his Horus name in the *serekh*.

The tomb of Ka'a at Abydos has recently been re-excavated. It was a complex structure, showing a number of additions, alterations and changes of plan during its construction.

Petrie 1900.
Emery 1958.
——1961: 86–91.
Spencer: 83–4.
Dreyer 1993.
Thomas 1995: 31.
University of Pennsylvania Museum of Archaeology and Anthropology E.6878.

Ka'aper, Scribe and Lector-Priest, Late Fourth/Early Fifth Dynasties, Old Kingdom, *c.* 2500 BC. An otherwise relatively minor official, Ka'aper is remembered by the very fine and exceptionally lifelike statue, carved in acacia wood, recovered from his burial (Saqqara C8). The quality of the carving is an eloquent testimony to the standards achieved by the craftsmen of the late Fourth Dynasty; the naturalistic treatment is achieved in part by the eyes which are of rock crystal, with copper surrounds. Ka'aper is frequently called 'Sheikh el-Beled', a consequence of his statue's supposed similarity of appearance with the sheikh of the village from which the workers who excavated his tomb came.

Ka'aper was Chief Lector-Priest and 'army scribe of the king'; in the latter capacity he seems to have been concerned with the army's campaigns in Palestine.

Borchardt 1911–36 (= CG 1): 32–3.
C. I. Vandersleyen, 'La Date du Cheikh el-Beled', JEA 69 (1983) 61–5.
Saleh and Sourouzian: 40.
EMC CG 34.

Kaemked, Priest, Fifth Dynasty, Old Kingdom, *c.* 2400 BC. The funerary (*ka*) priest of Uriren (Wa-ir-en) at Saqqara, Kaemked's memory is perpetuated by a statue of an exceptionally lifelike quality, in painted limestone, the eyes encrusted. He is shown in an unusual posture, kneeling tranquilly with his hands clasped on his lap. The statue was recovered from Uriren's mastaba at Saqqara (D20).

EMC 119.
Stevenson Smith 1946 (1949): 79–80 (as *Ka-m-qed*).

Kagemni, Vizier, Sixth Dynasty, Old Kingdom, *c.* 2350 BC. Kagemni was appointed to the royal service in the reign of King UNAS and achieved high rank under King TETI, having been appointed Vizier. He was buried in a tomb in Saqqara, on the walls of which he is shown in the company of pet monkeys and members of the ancient breed of prick-eared hounds.

Kagemni, who may or may not be the same person as the Vizier, is also remembered for a literary text, a series of 'Admonitions' in which he is offered, by an unknown author, practical, even cynical advice on how to succeed in life. The text, as it survives, was probably written during the Middle Kingdom. Some authorities would have it that the authorship of the 'Admonitions' is by a different hand.

Stevenson Smith 1946 (1949): 205, 207–9.
Lichtheim 1: 58–60.

Kahay, Singer, Fifth Dynasty, Old Kingdom, *c.* 2460–2420 BC. Kahay came from a family of professional musicians and was a singer at the king's court, probably during the reign of the later kings of the Fifth Dynasty, such as NEFERIRKARE, SHEPSESKARE and NIUSERRE, the last being, in all probability, the king during whose reign the tomb of Kahay and his son NEFER was constructed at Saqqara.

Kahay first attracted the attention of the king by the quality of his singing. He was appointed Inspector of Singers, later promoted to Controller of Singers and priest of the goddess who was the patron of temple music. He was a 'Keeper of the Secrets of the King' and 'Inspector of the Great House' and of the 'Artisans Workshop'.

Kahay's friendship with the king resulted in his eldest son, Nefer, rising even higher in the royal service than he did and enjoying a most distinguished career.

A. M. Moussa and H. Altenmüller, *The Tomb of Nefer and Ka-Hay*, Cairo and Mainz-am-Rhein, 1971.

Kahotep, Craftsman, First Dynasty, Archaic Period, *c.* 3000 BC. Kahotep was a craftsman working during the reign of King DEN, the fourth king of the First Dynasty. On the king's death Kahotep was sacrificed and buried with him. His name was inscribed on a copper axe, which he took with him, presumably to enable him to follow his trade in the afterlife, in the service of the king.

W. M. F. Petrie, *The Tombs of the Courtiers and Oxyrhynkhos*, London, 1925: 5.
Adams and Ciałowicz 1997: pl. 29.
Petrie Museum of Egyptology, University College London, UC 16173.

Kai, Army Commander, Twelfth Dynasty, Middle Kingdom, *c.* 1985–1795 BC. Kai described himself as 'Chief Hunter of the Desert and Commander of the Western Desert'. He led an attack on fugitives in the Western Oases and secured the routes through the desert. He congratulates himself on having brought his army back without loss.

Wilson 1951: 140.

Kai-Aper, Military Scribe, Fifth Dynasty, Old Kingdom, *c.* 2490 BC. Kai-Aper was an officer serving in the 'Turquoise Terraces' in the Sinai peninsula. He was also involved in the fortification of a number of strongholds along the 'Ways of Horus', the route which ran to the north-east out of the Delta.

CAH I.2: 358.

Kaihep, Nomarch, Sixth Dynasty, Old Kingdom, *c.* 2287–2278 BC. Kaihep was the first of the nomarchs of Akhmim, the capital of the ninth, Panopolite nome of Upper Egypt. He was appointed during the reign of King MERENRE, the son of King PEPY I and the elder brother of the long-lived King PEPY II.

He was also High Priest of Re at Memphis and in addition held important offices at the court. Members of his family ruled the nome for more than a hundred years, an example of the virtually hereditary status which the great provincial nobles acquired in the late Old Kingdom and which eventually contributed to the collapse of the central authority.

He was succeeded as nomarch by Nehewet, who died prematurely.

Kanawati 1980.

Kama, Queen, Twenty-Second/Twenty-Third Dynasties, Third Intermediate Period, *c.* 790–749 BC. A queen of the Libyan dynasties, Kama had her tomb built at Leontopolis, a city near Bubastis where the cult of the cat-goddess Bastet was powerful. Her tomb was unrobbed when it was found and contained some exceptionally fine jewellery. She was the mother of King OSORKON III.

Kitchen 1986: §74.
EMC CG 52715.

Kameni, High Priest, Fourth Dynasty, Old Kingdom, *c.* 2550 BC. Kameni was the High Priest of the temple of the ancient vulture goddess Nekhbet at El-Kab on the Nile, opposite the city of Hierakonpolis which was always associated with the origins of the kingship. Kameni was unusual in having apparently held no other offices than his priestly appointment. Parts of a statue found in Kameni's tomb are important in showing the development of the style of private statuary in the Fourth Dynasty.

Stevenson Smith 1946 (1949): 45, 142.

Kamose, King, Seventeenth Dynasty, Second Intermediate Period, *c.* 1555–1550 BC. The son of King SEQENENRE TAO II, Kamose succeeded his father after the latter was killed in battle. He took on the task of driving out the Hyksos invaders with enthusiasm and purpose, and appears to have forced them back to their stronghold in Avaris. The Hyksos king APEPI wrote to the king of Kush urging him to attack Kamose, but his message was intercepted and the Kushites remained quiescent.

Kamose's reign, though influential in contributing to the expulsion of the Hyksos, was comparatively brief. He was succeeded by his brother, AHMOSE, who was a child at the time of his accession. When he reached his majority, however, he completed the work begun by his father and elder brother, driving the Hyksos out of Egypt and inaugurating the Eighteenth Dynasty.

H. A. Winlock, 'The Tombs of the Kings of the Seventeenth Dynasty at Thebes', JEA 10 (1924) 217–77.

L. Habachi, 'The second stela of Kamose and his struggle against the Hyksos ruler and his capital', *ADAIK* 8.
H. S. Smith and A. Smith, 'A reconsideration of the Kamose texts', *ZÄS* 103: 43–76.
PM II: 37.
Luxor Museum J.43; cat. no. 43, figs 32–3 ('The Great Stela of King Kamose').

Kaninisut I, Prince, Late Fourth/Early Fifth Dynasties, Old Kingdom, *c*. 2500 BC. The patriarch of a noble family, Kaninisut I was a 'Son of the King, of his Body'; but it is not clear to which king this refers. Kaninisut and four generations of his descendants were buried at Giza, in sight of King KHNUM-KHUFU's pyramid. Although the family continued to hold official positions over the years their status declined, a situation frequently encountered amongst descendants of high-ranking persons of previous generations, which allowed for the promotion of new families to the service of the king or the state.

H. Junker, *The Offering Room of Prince Kaninisut*, Vienna, 1931.
Kunsthistorisches Museum, Vienna.

Kanufer, Prince, Fourth Dynasty, Old Kingdom, 2613–2589 BC. The eldest son of King SNEFERU, the founder of the Fourth Dynasty, Kanufer was appointed High Priest of Re in Heliopolis, one of the greatest appointments in the land. In this office he was also proclaimed 'Greatest of Seers' and given charge of the king's public works. As such he may have been one of those responsible for the immense undertakings involved in the construction of Sneferu's three, or possibly four pyramids.

Kanufer held other high offices: he was a General, in command of enlisted men, in which capacity he extended Egypt's control over the Sinai peninsula, and Treasurer of the God. He was also his father's vizier. It is to be presumed that he predeceased his father, thus depriving Egypt of someone who would evidently have been an excellent king.

Kees 1961: 162–3.

Karef, General, Twenty-Sixth Dynasty, Late Period, *c*. 664–610 BC. Although the Egyptians tended always to vilify the Libyans they were not above employing them, from time to time, in positions of importance. Such a one was Karef, a Libyan by birth, who served King PSAMETIK I loyally, as General of the Armies.

Bothmer 1961 (1969): 37, no. 31, pls 28–9.
Musées Royaux d'Art et Histoire, Brussels, E. 7526.

Karem, Scribe, Eighteenth Dynasty, New Kingdom, *c*. 1465–1455 BC. Karem and his wife Abykhy were not native Egyptians but were probably, to judge by their names, originally from a Semitic-speaking community. But they were evidently accepted into Egyptian society, for Karem was also given an Egyptian name, indicating that he was recognised as a resident of Thebes. It is possible that he was originally a prisoner of war, but in any event he flourished and became Door-keeper of the Chapel of the goddess Hathor in the mortuary temple of King THUTMOSE III.

The five children of Karem and Abykhy were all given orthodox Egyptian names.

S. Quirke, 'Karem in the Fitzwilliam Museum', JEA 76 (1990) 170–4.
E. Vassilika (ed) *Egyptian Art*, Cambridge, 1995: 48.
Fitzwilliam Museum, E. 21. 1882.

Karomama Merymut II, Queen, Twenty-Second Dynasty, Third Intermediate Period, *c*. 850–825 BC. Karomama II, the wife of King TAKELOT II (her uncle) and granddaughter of King OSORKON II, is remembered by a superb bronze and gilded statuette in which she is shown wearing a broad collar of gold.

J. Capart, *Documents pour Servir à l'Étude de l'Art Égyptien*, II, Paris, 1931: 77, pl. 85.

Kitchen 1986: §181, n111, §290.
MduL N500.

[Kashta], King, Twenty-Fifth Dynasty, Late Period, *c*. 760 BC. Kashta was King of Kush, one of a long line of Nubian kings who were the contemporaries and frequently the opponents of the kings of Egypt during the times of uncertainty which followed the end of the New Kingdom. Kashta moved against the Libyan dynasties then ruling Egypt *c*. 760 BC and the south fell to him; he moved northwards down the Valley, leaving evidence of his presence in, for example, Elephantine. He proclaimed himself King of Egypt and assumed the full royal regalia and titulary. He appointed his daughter AMENIRDIS I as 'God Wife of Amun' in Thebes, where she remained, exercising considerable political influence over the South for many years.

Kashta was the ancestor of the Kushite kings who formed the Twenty-Fifth Dynasty. His son PIANKHY was the most powerful of the Nubian kings of Egypt.

Grimal: 334–5.
Africa in Antiquity: 78.

Kawab, Prince, Fourth Dynasty, Old Kingdom, *c*. 2580 BC. Kawab was the son and nominated successor of King KHNUM-KHUFU; his mother was Queen MERITITES, one of Khnum-Khufu's principal wives. However, he died before his father, a circumstance which was greatly to destabilise the Fourth Dynasty for the remainder of its existence. Khnum-Khufu was succeeded by DJEDEFRE who married Kawab's widow HETEPHERES II, an evidently opportunistic lady. By Kawab Hetepheres had a daughter, MERESANKH III, who was married to Djedefre's successor, KHAFRE. Kawab's mastaba tomb at Giza (G7110–G7120) contains some very fine reliefs.

Reisner 1942: 115, 118, 125, 149, 151, 205, 307.
Stevenson Smith 1971: 165–74.
W. K. Simpson, *The Mastabas of Kawab and Khafkhufu*, I, II, Boston MA, 1978.

Kawit, Queen, Eleventh Dynasty, Middle Kingdom, *c*. 2055–2004 BC. Kawit was one of the queens of King NEBHEPETRE MONTUHOTEP. She was buried, with some of his other consorts, near his tomb at Deir el-Bahri. In common with the others, she was given a finely decorated sarcophagus, on which she is depicted having her hair dressed by her serving women.

E. Naville, *The XIth Dynasty Temple at Deir el-Bahri*, London, 1907: 48–9, 53–6, pls 19, 20.
Saleh and Sourouzian: 68a, b.
EMC JE 47397.

Kemsit, Royal Concubine, Eleventh Dynasty, Middle Kingdom, *c*. 2023–2004 BC. Although Kemsit is described as a Royal Concubine, she seems to have enjoyed a position of honour in the entourage of King NEBHEPETRE MONTUHOTEP II, though she is not ranked as one of his queens. They are portrayed together in scenes of almost domestic intimacy, and Kemsit is represented, most unusually for royal portraiture, almost on the same scale as Montuhotep.

The portraits of Kemsit, from her shrine at Deir el-Bahri in the temple of the king, suggest that she was a strong-featured woman.

E. Naville, *The XIth Dynasty Temple at Deir el-Bahri*, London, 1907: I, 50–1, pl. XVII, C; II, pl. XX.
Bourriau 1988: 14–17, nos 3, 4.
BM EA 1450.

Kenamun (alt. Qenamun), Priest, Eighteenth Dynasty, New Kingdom, *c*. 1546–1504 BC. Kenamun was a 'cult servant', a *wa'b* priest responsible for the purification of the statues of divinities. He is shown on a stela commemorating his life making offerings to two dead and deified kings, AMENHOTEP I and SENWOSRET I.

Hayes 1959: 51, fig. 24.
MMA: 28.9.6.

Kenamun, Royal Steward, Eighteenth Dynasty, New Kingdom, *c.* 1427–1400 BC. The Steward of King AMENHOTEP II, Kenamun was buried at Thebes (TT93). His tomb contains scenes of the presentation to the king of the products of the various *ateliers* under his control made during the year. These included 'chariots of silver and gold, statues of ivory and ebony, collars of various hardstones of value, and weapons'.

He was described as the foster-brother of the king, most probably Amenhotep II himself. Kenamun's mother, Amenemopet, was the king's nurse and the boys would therefore in all probability have been brought up together. Kenamun's mother is shown nursing the king.

The tomb contains scenes of the presentation of statues to the king of his ancestor King THUTMOSE I, and of his mother. It also shows scenes of hunting in the desert, from the earliest times a particular pleasure of well founded Egyptians, and one to which King Amenhotep himself was especially addicted.

N. De Garis Davis, *The Tomb of Ken-Amon at Thebes*, London, 1930.

Kenamun, Mayor, Eighteenth Dynasty, New Kingdom, *c.* 1390–1352 BC. Kenamun (the younger) was Mayor of Thebes during the reign of AMENHOTEP III. In this capacity he was responsible for the purchase, probably on behalf of the temple of Amun, of the merchandise brought by foreign ships. This is portrayed in his tomb (TT 162), a scene which is otherwise unique.

CAH II.1: 386.

Kenherkhopshef, Scribe, Nineteenth/Twentieth Dynasties, New Kingdom, *c.* 1220–1190 BC. Kenherkhopshef, a scribe working in the necropolis of Deir el-Medina, lived during the reign of RAMESSES II and probably died during SIPTAH's reign. He was a keen collector of manuscripts, as befitted one of his calling, though it was unusual for a private individual to pursue such an interest. His collection of papyri, which was added to by members of his family in subsequent generations, is especially strong in medical treatises, though none of the family seems to have been a doctor.

He was an early conservationist of papyri, giving instructions that a manuscript that had been affected by water should be dried in the sun.

J. Černý, *A Community of Workmen at Thebes in the Ramesside Period*, Cairo, 1973: 331–2.
P. W. Pestman, 'Who were the Owners in the "Community of Workmen" of the Chester Beatty Papyri?', in *Gleanings from Deir el-Medina*, eds R. J. Demarée and J. J. Jansen, Leiden, 1982: 155ff.
M. L. Brierbrier, *Tomb Builders of the Pharaohs*, London, 1982: 33–5.
L. H. Lesko, 'Literature, Literacy and Literati', in L. H. Lesko (ed.) *Pharaoh's Workers; the Villagers of Deir el-Medina*, Ithaca NY, 1994: 131–44.
Nunn 1996: 36–7.
BM EA 278.

Kha (alt. Khai), Official, Eighteeenth Dynasty, *c.* 1430–1370 BC. One of the batallions of middle-rank officials in the royal service at the time of Egypt's heightened prosperity, Kha was Director of Works in Deir el-Medina, the village of the Theban necropolis. With his wife he occupied a rock-cut tomb (TT8) in the mountainous part of the necropolis. Its contents were witness to the wealth which even an official of Kha's relatively modest status might enjoy at the height of the New Kingdom. Obviously he had access to the finest craftsmen of his day, and his intact tomb was full of their products. These included implements plated with gold (perhaps the gift of the king), bronze and silver vases donated by Kha's friends and family, and a considerable range of personal possessions, including a painter's palette and brushes. Amongst the linen which he was careful to take with him into the afterlife were fifty pairs of underpants.

Scamuzzi: pls XLI–XLIX.
S. Curtio and M. Mancini, 'News of Kha and Meryt', JEA 54 (1968) 77–81, figs 1–4, pls XII, XIII.
Museo Egizio, Turin.

Khaba, King, Third Dynasty, Old Kingdom, *c.* 2640–2637 BC. A somewhat shadowy figure whose existence was at one time doubted, Khaba was probably the penultimate king of the dynasty, preceeding King HUNI. In some lists Khaba is shown as succeeding DJOSER NETJERYKHET. It is possible that the Layer Pyramid at Zawiyet el-Aryan may be his.

Stevenson Smith 1965 (1981): 55, 437 n3, n7.
J-P. Lauer, *Observations sur les Pyramides*, Cairo, 1960: fig. 17, pl. 10.
Dows Dunham, *Zawiyet el Aryan: The Cemeteries Adjacent to the Layer Pyramid*, Boston, 1978: 34.
CAH I.2: 150, 156, 158.

Khababash, King (?), Second Persian Period, *c.* 335 BC. It is possible that Khababash led a revolt against the Persians in the last years of their rule of Egypt and was recognised as King of Egypt by his followers. If this be so then he was one of the last native-born rulers of the country. He appears to have attempted to secure the frontiers, but little else is known of him.

Grimal: 381.

Khabausoker, High Priest, Third Dynasty, Old Kingdom, *c.* 2630 BC. Khabausoker is a representative of the influential, practical executive who emerged in the Third Dynasty, of whom IMHOTEP is the leading example, who played so important a part in establishing the mechanism of the Egyptian state's administration. He was a great officer of state in the latter part of the dynasty, and he must have been one of those who contributed much to the development of the sacred kingship in Egypt and the ceremonies and rituals which accompanied it. He is a somewhat enigmatic figure, commemorated, with his wife, Hathorneferhetepes, in a handsome tomb at Saqqara which seems to be transitional in style between the mastabas of the early Third Dynasty and those of the later Old Kingdom.

Khabausoker was High Priest of Anubis and hence concerned with the cults of the dead. He also served the god of the Western Oases and the ancient Upper Egyptian god, Set. His duties towards the goddess of writing and architecture, Seshat, probably meant that he was a follower of IMHOTEP.

His interests were many and diverse, ranging from the direction of the court dancers to the management of breweresses. He was especially responsible for the direction of the carpenters and craftsmen who served the king.

Khabausoker was entitled to wear a curious collar peculiar to the office of High Priest of Ptah in Memphis, which comprises an elongated Anubis dog and a complex series of chains and necklaces. One scholar has seen this feature of his regalia as indicating that Khabausoker was the death-priest who announced to the king when his allotted term had been realised. The idea of the sacrifice of the king, especially in Predynastic times, was once widely accepted by Egyptologists but is now generally discarded. Certainly no evidence exists of the ritual killing of the king in the historic period. Khabausoker is a somewhat enigmatic figure, but forecasting the death of kings is unlikely to have been one of his duties.

Terrace and Fischer 1970: 37–40.

M. A. Murray, *Saqqarah Mastabas*, London, 1904: I, 3, pls 1–2; II, 1–12, pl. 1.
Stevenson Smith 1958 (1981): 61–7, ills 49, 50.
EMC CG 1385.

Khaemetnu, Funerary Priest, Fourth Dynasty, Old Kingdom, *c.* 2550 BC. Khaemetnu was a priest in the service of Queen MERESANKH III. She required him to continue his service to her in the afterlife, and therefore had him represented by his portrait and his name and titles in her tomb, thus ensuring his own immortality.

Wilson 1951: 65.
G. A. Reisner, *Bulletin of the Museum of Fine Arts, Boston*, Boston MA, 1927: XXV, 76.

Khaemhese, Architect, Fifth Dynasty, Old Kingdom, *c.* 2300 BC. Khaemhese was buried in a tomb at Saqqara, where his wife and young son were also commemorated. He was Royal Architect and Chief of Sculptors; a fine statue shows him wearing a small moustache, rather in the fashion of the Fourth Dynasty. The statue's high quality is presumably a consequence of his access to the finest available talent amongst the sculptors of the day. It has retained virtually all of its original, vivid colour.

J. E. Quibell and A. G. K. Hayter, *The Teti Pyramid, Cairo, North Side, Excavations at Saqqara*, Cairo, 1927: 18, 44, pl. 29.
PM III.2: 542.
Saleh and Sourouzian: 54.
EMC JE 44174.

Khaemhor, Vizier, Twenty-Fourth Dynasty, Third Intermediate Period, *c.* 728–715 BC. A member of a family of high-ranking state servants, Khaemhor probably served King OSORKON III and King TAKELOT III as Vizier. However, he evidently accommodated himself to the Kushite King PIANKHY when he occupied the country and dismissed the several minor kings who had ruled small territories, especially in the north.

He was the grandfather of the remarkable MONTUEMHET, who was effectively the ruler of the South from Thebes during the reign of King PSAMETIK I.

Kitchen 1986: §330, §344.

Khaemipet, Scribe, Nineteenth Dynasty, New Kingdom, *c.* 1270 BC. Khaemipet's office is somewhat grandiosely titled 'Scribe of the Book of God of the Lord of the Two Lands, who Records the Annals of All the Gods in the House of Life', a function in which he evidently succeeded his father. His family was an old and distinguished one, with its origins in Thebes. His son became a scribe in the temple of Mont in Hermopolis.

Württembergisches Landesmuseum, Stuttgart, no. 32.

Khaemwaset, Prince, Magus, Antiquarian, Nineteenth Dynasty, New Kingdom, *c.* 1270 BC. The fourth son of King RAMESSES II by one of his principal queens in the early years of his reign, ISTNOFRET, Khaemwaset exercised a considerable influence during the earlier periods of his father's reign, later holding the rank of Crown Prince and the appointments of High Priest of Ptah and Governor of Memphis. Long after his lifetime he enjoyed a considerable reputation as a magician and as one who knew the secrets of the origins of the kingship. He was concerned to restore the monuments of earlier kings, and carried out conservation work on the the tombs of King SHEPSESKHAF, of King SAHURE and King NIUSERRE; he restored the pyramid of King UNAS of the Fifth Dynasty. In each case he left an inscription at the site recording the work carried out and identifying the building. He also rebuilt the temple of Ptah, of which he was the High Priest. He was a bibliophile and compiled catalogues of the royal and temple libraries.

Khaemwaset predeceased his father, in the fifty-fifth year of the reign, his death probably depriving Egypt of an excellent king. Although he possessed a handsome tomb, commensurate with his rank, he is said to have chosen, most remarkably, to be buried amongst the sacred Apis bulls in Saqqara. This was perhaps because of his High Priesthood of Ptah, of whom the Apis was a manifestation; he was thus entombed with the god he had served. During his lifetime he was considered a sage; he was paid divine honours after his death, his cult surviving until Hellenistic times. A number of marvellous tales grew up around him in the Late Period, collected as the 'Stories of Setne Khamwas'.

Kitchen 1982: 40, 89, 102, 103, 170.
Lichtheim 3: 125–51.
Saleh and Sourouzian: 209.
EMC JE 36720 = CG 42147.
BM 947.

Khaemwaset, Prince, Twentieth Dynasty, New Kingdom, 1184–1183 BC. The son of King RAMESSES III, Khaemwaset bore the same name as the son and nominated successor of King RAMESSES II. Unlike his namesake, however, this Khaemwaset was not Crown Prince, though he is described as 'Eldest Son of the King', probably an honorific. Like his brothers he was also 'Standard-Bearer on the Right Hand of the King'. He was probably buried during the reign of his brother King RAMESSES IV.

His splendid tomb, QV 44, is one of the group prepared by Ramesses for his sons, who gave orders for them to be built in the twenty-eighth year of his reign.The princes are all shown as young boys, though their ages at death are unknown; the king himself was careful to ensure that he is represented in all the reliefs, in which he is shown presenting his sons to the gods.

Khaemwaset's tomb is especially sumptuous, the paintings extensively preserved and much of the colour still brilliant.

E. Schiaparelli, *Relazione dei lavori della missione archeologica italiana in Egitto II: l'esplorazione della Valle delle Regine*. Turin, 1922–7.

Khafre (alt. Chephren), King, Fourth Dynasty, Old Kingdom, *c*. 2558–2532 BC. The son and eventual successor of King KHNUM-KHUFU, Khafre seems to have been set aside from the succession initially by the party which supported DJEDEFRE, who conducted Khufu's obsequies and was therefore, it may reasonably be supposed, his son, as indeed was Khafre. After eight years of Djedefre's reign, which may have ended abruptly, Khafre came to the throne and ruled Egypt for twenty-four years.

Khafre is associated with the second of the pyramids at Giza, which is only slightly smaller than Khufu's. It is the more remarkable for the survival of the Mortuary Temple, the Causeway and the architecturally singular Valley Temple. Traditionally it is Khafre's face which is said to be borne by the Great Sphinx of Giza.

Khafre probably represented the senior line in the royal family; he was supported by powerful princes such as MINKHAF, ANKHAF and NEFERMAAT, all of whom held the office of Vizier. Khafre is remembered by the superb diorite statue, larger than lifesize, of the king enthroned protected by the Horus Falcon, the eternally reincarnated embodiment of the kingship.

Terrace and Fischer 1970: no. 6, 41–44.
Grimal: 72–4.
Edwards 1993: 121–37.
Lehner 1997: 122–33.
Saleh and Sourouzian: no. 31.
EMC JE 10062 (= CG 14).

Khaihapi, Privy Councillor, Twentieth Dynasty, New Kingdom, *c*. 1150 BC. Khaihapi is particularly notable for the circumstances of the discovery of his block-statue, a somewhat archaicising form for the period. He was an important figure in latter years of King RAMESSES III and during the reign of King RAMESSES IV. In addition to his rank as Privy Councillor he was 'God's Father', a title of honour in the court, and Temple Scribe of Re. This last, together with his expressed wish to be buried at Heliopolis and that he might live to be 110 years old, suggest that he served in the great temple of Re in that city.

His statue was discovered in Vienna around 1800, in excavations in the third Vienna district, which in Roman times had been the location of the city of Vindobona. It is not known how Khaihapi's statue found its resting place so far from Heliopolis.

Kunsthistorisches Museum, Vienna, no. 64.

Khakhara, Hairdresser and Wigmaker, Fifth/Sixth Dynasties, Old Kingdom, *c.* 2400 BC. Khakhara had himself immortalised in a statue together with his son, Ankhremenes. He was a Hairdresser and Wigmaker, though not of the first rank in the court but employed to attend to the needs of lesser officials. He was, however, buried at Giza.

Thomas 1995: no. 43 (131).
Phoebe A. Hearst Museum of Anthropology, University of Berkeley, California, 6–19780.

Khasekhem/Khasekhemwy, King, Second Dynasty, Archaic Period, *c.* 2686 BC. One of the greatest of Egypt's kings, Khasekhemwy's life rapidly assumed the proportions of legend which endured throughout the history of Egypt. It is likely that he adopted the second form of his name, 'In Him the Two Powers are at Peace', after achieving the pacification of the various factions in the country which arose after the end of the First Dynasty, continuing throughout much of the Second. Khasekhemwy is one of the true unifiers of the Egyptian state. Unique amongst the kings of Egypt, Khasekhemwy adopted a dual *serekh*, surmounting his sacred name with both the Horus Falcon and the Seth Hound, indicating thereby his reconciliation of the opposing powers in the state.

His reign was long and was marked by advances both in the sumptuous appointments of life at the court and in architecture. Carved stone vessels were decorated with golden mounts – perhaps a little exquisite in taste – and the king's funerary complex at Abydos was notable for the use of dressed stone blocks, laid in regular courses, in the interior. In 1991, a remarkable discovery near Khasekhemwy's burial place uncovered a fleet of twelve large boats, buried in shallow trenches in the desert. Soon after that, work on an otherwise unexcavated part of the tomb produced sealings of King DJOSER NETJERYKHET. This suggests that Djoser conducted Khasekhemwy's obsequies, a duty which devolved upon a king's successor. It therefore appears that Djoser followed Khasekhemwy to the thrones of Egypt.

NEMAATHAP, Khasekhemwy's daughter (and possibly also his wife) was revered as the ancestress of the succeeding Third Dynasty; she was mother of the great king DJOSER NETJERYKHET, but it is not known whether Khasekhemwy was his natural father.

P. E. Newberry, *The Set Rebellion of the Second Dynasty, Ancient Egypt*, London, 1922: part 2, 40–6.
Emery 1961: 98–103, 116, 162, 169, 193.
M. Hoffman, *Egypt before the Pharaohs*, London, 1980: 348–54.
D. O'Connor, 'The Earliest Royal Boat Graves', EA 6 (1995) 3–7.
EMC JE 32161.
Ashmolean Museum E 517.

Khay, Gold-worker, Nineteenth Dynasty, New Kingdom, *c.* 1279–1243 BC. Khay was a metalworker employed in the service of RAMESSES II, whose duties were to supervise the extraction and refining of gold brought from Nubia. His tomb contains scenes of the various processes involved. His own coffin was decorated with gold leaf.

Martin 1991: 131–2.

Khayan, King, Fifteenth Dynasty, Second Intermediate Period, *c.* 1600 BC. One of the more accommodating, and in consequence more successful, of the 'Great Hyksos', Khayan maintained contact with a wide range of Egypt's contemporaries in the Near East throughout his reign. He does not, however, seem to have been able to maintain Egypt's control of Nubia, as an independent kingship appears to have been established there during his reign.

CAH II.1: 42–76.
Ryholt 1997: 306, 383–5.

Khekheretnebty, Princess, Fifth Dynasty, Old Kingdom, *c.* 2445–2420 BC. The princess was buried in a mastaba tomb at Abusir, and her funerary equipment included a set of miniature copper tools, particularly chisels, and copper vessels. The copper contained quantities of naturally occurring arsenic, bismuth, iron, tin, silver, nickel and antimony. These agents would have had the effect of substantially toughening the copper.

It is not clear why the princess should have wished to take tools more suitable for a craftsman with her into the afterlife.

Verner 1994: 82–7.

Khenetetenka, Queen, Fourth Dynasty, Old Kingdom, 2566–2558 BC. The lower part of a royal seated statue which probably is to be attributed to King DJEDEFRE, has a small figure of the king's consort, Khenetetenka, kneeling beside him, one arm locked companionably around his left leg.

Chassinat, *Monuments Piot XXV*, 1921–2: 53–75.
MduL E 12627.

Kheni, Nomarch, Sixth Dynasty, Old Kingdom, *c.* 2278–2184 BC. The son of the nomarch of Ahkmim, TJETI-IKER, Kheni built a fine tomb for his father at El Hawawish. It was decorated by the painter SENI, one of the first Egyptian artists to 'sign' his work. Indeed, Seni went further and showed himself in the familiar company of his patrons.

Kheni ruled his province during the reign of King PEPY II. In his tomb he is shown enjoying a sport popular in this region of Egypt in the late Old Kingdom and the succeeding First Intermediate Period – bull-fighting. In Akhmim it appears that the bulls sometimes fought to the death, an outcome which was generally discouraged in Egypt.

Kanawati 1980.

Khentika (alt. Ikhekhi), Vizier, Sixth Dynasty, Old Kingdom, *c.* 2345–2323 BC. Like his near contemporary and fellow vizier, MERERUKA, Khentika is depicted seated before a sort of easel, painting the three seasons. He has a brush and a shell-shaped dish, presumably for his paints. The board on which he is actually painting has a form of ratchet to allow it to be set at different heights. Khentika is attended by three assistants.

T. G. H. James, *The Mastaba of Khentika called Ikhekhi*, London, 1953.
James and Davies: 9–10; ill. 7.
BM 52947.

Khentkawes I, Queen, Fourth Dynasty, Old Kingdom, *c.* 2560–2490 BC. The daughter of King DJEDEFRE, the son and immediate successor of King KHNUM-KHUFU, Khentkawes was one of the greatest of the royal ladies of the Old Kingdom. She was married to King SHEPSESKHAF, the last king of the Fourth Dynasty.

Her particular importance arises from the fact of her giving birth to the first two kings of the Fifth Dynasty, SAHURE and NEFERIRKARE. She was in consequence honoured as the ancestress of the dynasty.

Khentkawes was the owner of a large and unusually designed monument at Giza, part mastaba, part pyramid. Her first husband, Shepseskhaf, was similarly entombed in a structure of unusual form, the so-called 'Mastabat Fara'un'.

S. Hassan, *Excavations at Giza IV (1932–3)*, Cairo, 1943: 1–62.
CAH I.2: 176–9.

Khentkawes II, Queen, Fifth Dynasty, Old Kingdom, *c.* 2475–2445 BC. Queen Khentkawes II was the wife of King NEFERIRKARE and the mother of Kings NEFEREFRE and NIUSERRE. She may have ruled independently for a time. She was provided with a pyramid at Abusir, where a cult to her memory long continued.

M. Verner, *The Pyramid Complex of the Royal Mother Khentkaus*, Prague, 1994.
Lehner 1997: 146.

Khentkawes, Princess (?), Sixth Dynasty, Old Kingdom, *c.* 2345–2181 BC. A tomb at Saqqara, excavated during the middle years of the Second World War and which appeared to be unplundered, indicated by its inscriptions that it was the burial place of a Princess Khentkawes, a Royal Princess, the elder daughter of the king. On examining the body, however, the excavator came to the conclusion that Khentkawes was in fact a man, hence a Prince and not a Princess. The face had been covered by a plaster mask. Khentkawes had apparently chosen to live as a woman, though he had taken with him into the tomb equipment for hunting in the afterlife, suggesting that whatever had been his mortal status, he intended to follow masculine pursuits after death.

Z. Y. Saad, 'Preliminary Report on the Royal excavations at Saqqara, 1942–3', *Annales de Service des Antiquités de l'Égypte*, cahier 3, 62–7.
——*Royal excavations at Saqqara and Helwan (1941–5)*, Cairo, 1947: 62–7; pls XXVI–XXXII.

Kheruef, Royal Steward, Eighteenth Dynasty, New Kingdom, *c.* 1390–1352 BC. Kheruef was a man of influence and importance at the court of AMENHOTEP III; he was a Royal Scribe and First Herald of the king. Later, he was appointed Steward of Queen TIY, in the Estate of Amun. He was given a tomb (TT 192) in the necropolis but it does not appear to have been occupied. The decorations were unfinished and Kheruef's name had been excised, suggesting that he had fallen from favour. The decoration which does remain shows the celebrations of the jubilees of King Amenhotep, with which Kheruef was involved. These were organised at the king's festival site at Malkata and were exceptionally elaborate and splendid, drawing on ancient precedents for the details of the ceremonies.

Kheruef's tomb was enlivened by scenes of near-nude dancing girls and sports, including bare-knuckle boxing.

Aldred 1988: 161–3.
C. F. Nims, *The Tomb of Kheruef*, Chicago IL, 1980.
Redford 1984: 49–51.
Kuhrt 1995: I, 215–6.

Khety I, II, III, *see* **Akhtoy I, II, III**

Khety, Chancellor, Eleventh Dynasty, Middle Kingdom, *c.* 2020 BC. Khety was Chancellor to King NEBHEPETRE MONTUHOTEP II for upwards of forty years. His career is widely recorded in inscriptions in many parts of Egypt, a testimony to the extensive travels which he undertook as part of his duties. He was buried at Deir el-Bahri, in a large and sumptuous tomb, which was later used as a quarry for its fine limestone decoration.

Grimal: 157.
MMA 26.3 104A.

Khnemetneferhedjet Weret (alt. Khnemet), Queen, Twelfth Dynasty, Middle Kingdom, *c.* 1908–1878 BC. Khnemetneferhedjet was the wife of King SENWOSRET II and mother of King SENWOSRET III. She evidently died early in his reign, and was buried with a splendid set of royal jewellery, which is typical of the finest work of the Middle Kingdom goldsmiths; her golden diadems are especially splendid. She was buried in a mastaba at Dahshur, near the pyramid in which her son was later interred.

Two other queens of the Royal Family at this time were named Khnemetneferhedjet; one was a princess of AMENEMHET II and the other, Khnemetneferhedjet Khered, was the wife of SENWOSRET III.

J. de Morgan, *Fouilles à Dahchour II*, Vienna, 1894: 65–8, pl. 12.
Terrace and Fischer 1970: no. 13, 69–72.
O. Perdu, 'Khenemet-Nefer-Hedjet: Une Princesse et Deux Reines du Moyen Empire', Rd'E 29 (1977) 68–85.
A. M. Dodson, 'The Tombs of the Queens of the Middle Kingdom', ZÄS 115: 123–36.
A. Oppenheim, EA 9: 26.
EMC JE 31113–6. CG 52975–52979.

Khnum-baf, Official (Prince ?), Fourth Dynasty, 2558–2532 BC. Khnum-baf was buried in an immense mastaba tomb at Giza, appropriate for one who bore the title 'Overseer of All the King's Works' and, to judge by his name, was probably a member of the royal family; he may have been a grandson of King KHNUM-KHUFU. The tomb contained a large number of statues of the owner. However, for reasons which are obscure, many of these appear to have been deliberately broken up, to provide material for the manufacture of stone vessels.

Reisner 1942: 248.
Stevenson Smith 1946 (1949): 33, 46, 50–52, 358, pl. 19.

Khnumhotep and Niankhkhnum, Royal Manicurists and Hairdressers, Fifth Dynasty, Old Kingdom, *c.* 2350 BC. The excavation of the Causeway for the Pyramid of King UNAS of the late Fifth Dynasty resulted in the tomb of these two priests of the sun temple of King NIUSERRE being buried and preserved until recent times (see also the tomb of NEFER and KAHAY). Khnumhotep and Niankhkhnum, who may have been twins, wished to be buried together; they are shown in scenes of considerable and rather touching intimacy, though they are attended by their respective wives and children.

In addition to their priestly duties they were the principal manicurists and hairdressers to the king ('Overseers of Manicurists of the Palace'), positions evidently of honour since they were empowered, in the course of their duties, to touch the body of a living god. The two men occupy the innermost part of the tomb alone, unencumbered by their families.

A. M. Moussa and H. Altenmüller, *Des Grab des Nianchnum und Chnumhotep*, Mainz, 1977.

Khnumhotep I, Nomarch, Twelfth Dynasty, Middle Kingdom, *c.* 1985 BC. The accession of AMENEMHET I to the kingship at the commencement of the Twelfth Dynasty marked the beginning of a marked decline in the power of the provincial magnates, many of whom had acquired virtual independence following the end of the Old Kingdom. Amongst the greatest of such magnates were the rulers of the Oryx Nome, centred on Beni Hasan, in Middle Egypt. Khnumhotep I evidently was a partisan of Amenemhet I and assisted him in his bid for the throne; in consequence he remained in possession of the full powers of his principality, though deferring to the king and mounting expeditions in his name against remaining pockets of resistence to the resurgent royal authority. As a reward Amenemhet made Khnumhotep Count of Menet-Khufu; he was also appointed Hereditary Prince and Count, Seal-Bearer, Sole Companion, and confirmed as Great Lord of the Oryx Nome.

Breasted I: §§463–5.

Khnumhotep II, Nomarch, Twelfth Dynasty, Middle Kingdom, *c.* 1890 BC. The biography of the second Khnumhotep, the grandson of Khnumhotep I, reveals in interesting detail how it was still possible for a family of provincial princes to maintain and augment their power, even under the sovereignty of such experienced and watchful kings as those of the latter part of the Twelfth Dynasty. In the case of Khnumhotep II, this aggregation of status and power was achieved by the twin processes of inheritance and a strategic marriage to the heiress of a nearby nome.

Khnumhotep is particularly remembered (in part the consequence of the Biblical orientation of early Egyptology) by the scene on the walls of his tomb at Beni Hasan showing him receiving a visit from Asiatics bearing gifts. As he lived at the time conventionally ascribed to the life of the prophet Abraham, this scene was frequently cited in support of the idea of the journey into Egypt which Abraham was supposed to have made and for which, outside the Biblical story, there is no evidence whatsoever.

Breasted 1: §§619–39.

Khnumhotep, Steward, Twelfth Dynasty, Middle Kingdom, *c.* 1985–1795 BC. Khnumhotep was buried with a sarcophagus in the form of a 'house', protected by the painted representations of divinities. He was buried at Meir, facing the east, with his head to the north.

Hayes 1953: 310; fig. 201.
MMA 12.183.131c.

Khnum-Khufu (alt. Cheops), King, Fourth Dynasty, Old Kingdom, *c.* 2589–2566 BC. The son of King SNEFERU and his Queen, HETEPHERES I, Khnum-Khufu succeeded his father and is immortalised by his presumed tenancy of the Great Pyramid. Little is actually known of his reign, which probably lasted about twenty-three years, though he is recorded as having despatched expeditions to the mines in the north and south and to have ordered raids on the troublesome inhabitants of the Sinai peninsula.

Only one known portrait of Khnum-Khufu survives, a tiny ivory figurine, of the king enthroned, found at Abydos. He appears in the story of DJADJAEMANKH, in the Westcar papyrus, which relates an attempt to divert Khnum-Khufu's father, Sneferu, when he was depressed, by entertaining him with the spectacle of scantily clad girls rowing on the lake. Khnum-Khufu fathered numerous sons and daughters, including two of his immediate successors, the first of whom, King DJEDEFRE, conducted his funeral ceremonies. He was eventually followed to the throne by King KHAFRE, another of his sons, who is associated with the Second Pyramid at Giza.

Khnum-Khufu's memory appears to have been execrated by later generations, though there is no evidence to justify so dire a reputation. In fact a cult in his memory continued for at least a thousand years after his death, in which he was invoked as a benefactor of his people (see entry for MEMI).

Petrie 1903: 30; pls 13, 14.
Z. Hawass, *Mélanges Gamal Moukhtar I*, Cairo, 1985: 379–94.
Edwards 1993: 98–121.
Lehner 1997: 108–19.
Saleh and Sourouzian: no. 28.
EMC JE 36143.

Khufu-ankh, Architect, Fourth Dynasty, Old Kingdom, *c.* 2600–2500 BC. Khufu-ankh was 'Overseer of All the Building Works of the King', a position of great responsibility in the Fourth Dynasty. He was provided with a magnificent rose-granite sarcophagus, the design of which echoed the recessed panelling of the mastabas of the First Dynasty.

Lambelet 1978: no 44.

Khufu-Khaf, Prince, Fourth Dynasty, Old Kingdom, *c.* 2580 BC. Khufu-Khaf was the son of King KHNUM-KHUFU by a lesser wife, Queen HENUTSEN. He was a senior prince, however, and was provided with monuments at Giza during his lifetime. In one of these he is shown, in a exceptionally elegant relief, with his wife. He is also depicted in the company of his mother.

CAH I.2: 165–7.
Stevenson Smith 1958 (1981): 108–9, 111; ills 105, 106.
W. K. Simpson, *The Mastabas of Kawab and Khafkhufu*, I, II.
MFAB G 7140 [91].

Khunere, Prince, Fourth Dynasty, Old Kingdom, *c.* 2532–2503 BC. Khunere was the son of King MENKAURE by his chief wife, Queen Khamerernebty, and therefore of the highest rank. As seems to have been the case so frequently in the Fourth Dynasty, however, he died before his father.

He was buried at Giza in one of the finest tombs, even when judged by the elevated standards of the Fourth Dynasty. It was one of the first to be decorated with scenes of the life of the owner, including performances by musicians and dancers and, on a more practical plane, boat building. Khunere himself appears as a seated scribe, in a handsome yellow quartzite statue.

Stevenson Smith 1946 (1949): 31, pl. 10.
MFAB.
CAH I.2: 176.

Khusobek, General, Twelfth Dynasty, Middle Kingdom, *c.* 1874–1855 BC. In the reign of King SENWOSRET III, Khusobek served in campaigns in Palestine. On one occasion, deep into alien territory, he commanded the rearguard which was attacked by bands of marauding *badu*. Khusobek records with pride that he killed one of them.

CAH I.2: 508, 538.

Kiya, Queen, Eighteenth Dynasty, New Kingdom, *c.* 1350 BC. One of the wives of AMENHOTEP IV-AKHENATEN, Kiya occupies a somewhat ambiguous place in the Amarnan family. She may have been a foreign princess, her name originally Tudukhepa; it has been suggested, though not generally accepted, that she was the mother of King TUTANKHAMUN. She apparently fell into disfavour and disappears from view in the middle of Akhenaten's reign. The coffin made for her was later appropriated for the burial of King SMENKHKARE.

It is believed that tomb KV 55 was originally prepared for her, later used for the Theban burial of AKHENATEN and Queen TIY.

Aldred: 285–9.
Redford 1984: 190–2.
J. R. Harris, 'Kiya', C d'E 97: 25–30.

['The Prince of Kush'], Nubian Ruler, Seventeenth Dynasty, Second Intermediate Period, *c.* 1550 BC. Towards the end of the Hyksos period of rule over the northern part of Egypt, whilst the Princes of Thebes were beginning to mount their campaign to drive the invaders out of the country, a family of Nubian chieftains established an independent state, much to the annoyance of King KAMOSE, the father of King AHMOSE, the founder of the Eighteenth Dynasty. The names of the Princes of Kush are uncertain but they sustained a distinctly Egyptianised system of government and state. The Prince maintained contact with the Hyksos, however, and the two parties sought, unsuccessfully, to unite against the Egyptian king.

The Princedom of Kush was overthrown by Kamose; later, the Viceroy of Nubia was known by the title 'King's Son of Kush', thus linking the earlier title firmly with the King of Egypt.

CAH II.1: 298.
L. Habachi, *The Second Stela of Kamose and His Struggle against the Hyksos Ruler and His Capital*, Gluckstadt, 1972.

Kynebu, Priest, Twentieth Dynasty, New Kingdom, *c*. 1129–1126 BC. Kynebu was a priest during the reign of Ramesses VIII, and was responsible for 'the Secrets of the Estate of Amun' in the temple in Thebes. Paintings in his tomb show him adoring Osiris and King AMENHOTEP I and his mother Queen AHMOSE NEFERTIRY, whose cult had thus survived from the early Eighteenth Dynasty, especially in the Theban necropolis.

James 1985: 35–6; ills 36–7.
BM 37995, 37993, 37994.

L

Lamintu, Shield-Bearer, Twenty-Second Dynasty, Third Intermediate Period, *c.* 822 BC. In the third year of the reign of King SHESHONQ III, Lamintu, the royal shield-bearer, made a festive donation of land to the god Osiris. The donation included a pool, which is described as *birket*, a word which is still extant in Arabic.

Hodjash and Berlev 1982: no. 107, 164–5.

Lycophron, Poet and Scholar, Ptolemaic Period, fourth/third centuries BC. Lycophron was one of the first generation of enterprising Greek scholars who made their way to Alexandria when the first Ptol-emies began to develop it as the intellectual capital of the world. His speciality was tragedy, of which he is said to have written either forty-six or sixty-four examples. However, he also compiled a catalogue of comedies. Much of his writing is notable for its obscurity.

W. A. Mair, *Callimachus, Lycophron, Aratus*, New York, Loeb, 1921.

M

Maanakhtef, Chamberlain, Eighteenth Dynasty, New Kingdom, *c.* 1427–1400 BC. One of the great officers of state under King AMENHOTEP II, Maanakhtef was responsible for the direction of Egypt's agricultural production and the overall control of the royal estates. A fine cube statue of Maanakhtef, now in the Louvre, was found in the excavations of the temple at Medamud.

His titles included Grand Intendent and Royal Chamberlain, Master of the Double Granary, and Master of the Peasants and Serfs of the King; his duties were perhaps equivalent to those of a Minister of Agriculture.

PM V: 148.
IFAO 1981: 254.
MduL E12926.

Maatkare, Princess, Twenty-First Dynasty, Third Intermediate Period, *c.* 1065–1045 BC. The 'Divine Adoratrice' and 'God's Wife of Amun', Maatkare was probably the daughter of PINUDJEM I. She was installed in the office of what was effectively a High Priestesshood of Thebes by her father, who was himself High Priest before naming himself king. Maatkare apparently chose to be buried with her pet monkey, whose mummy was for long mistakenly thought to be that of a child. As the 'God's Wife' was dedicated to celibacy, the presence of the mummy had provoked not a little, though as it transpired, quite unwarranted, comment.

Kitchen 1986: §548.
G. Daressy, 'Cercuils des Cachettes Royales' (CG) 82–4, pl. 39.
Saleh and Sourouzian: 237.
EMC JE 26200 = CG 61028.

Maaty, Treasury Official, Eleventh Dynasty, Middle Kingdom, *c.* 2055–2004 BC. Maaty was the Gate Keeper of the Royal Treasury during the reign of King NEBHEPETRE MONTUHOTEP II. He was evidently an adherant of Bebi, a Chancellor of the time. He lived during the early years of Nebhepetre Montuhotep's restoration, and the quality of his stela, carved in fine quartzite, testifies to the return of high artistic standards in Egypt after the uncertainties of the First Intermediate Period.

Hayes 1953: 153; fig. 91.
MMA 14.2.7.

Machon, Poet, Ptolemaic Period, 3rd century BC. A comic dramatist, born in Greece, Machon spent much of his life in Alexandria. A collection of anecdotes written by him about Athenian lowlife is preserved.

A. S. F. Grow, *Machon, the Fragments*, Cambridge, 1964.

P. M. Fraser, *Ptolemaic Alexandria*, Oxford, 1972.

Madja, 'Mistress of the House', Eighteenth Dynasty, New Kingdom, 479–1425 BC. The wife of an artisan working in the necropolis of Deir el-Medina, Madja's intact tomb yielded a well painted sarcophagus and the mummy of an unnamed man. With her in the tomb was a quantity of offerings, indicating a degree of prosperity for someone who was a relatively modest individual. Several scarab seals bore the name of THUTMOSE III; one had also been used to seal a jar which had been found in the tomb unopened.

B. Bruyère, IFAO XV, 217–22, Cairo, 1937.
MduL 14543 etc.

Mahu, Chief of Police, Eighteenth Dynasty, New Kingdom, *c.* 1352–1336 BC. Mahu was Chief of Police in Akhetaten, the new capital city of Egypt which AMENHOTEP IV-AKHENATEN created when he elevated the Aten above all the other divinities of Egypt. He died before the collapse of the Amarna experiment and the withdrawal of the new king, TUTANKHAMUN, from the city. The decorations of his tomb (no. 9) illustrate his working life in the city – pursuing his enquiries as to the whereabouts of fugitives, escorting arrested robbers for trial before the Mayor of Akhetaten. He also records the return to their palace of Akhetaten and his queen, NEFERTITI, from one of the temple ceremonies at which they officiated, the king driving his chariot whilst the queen embraces him fondly.

De Garis Davis, *The Rock Tombs of El Amarna*, 6 vols, 1903–8: IV, pl. XXVI; VI, pls XXIV–XXVI.
Stevenson Smith 1958 (1981): 302, 462, n14; ill. 295.
Aldred 1988: 22, 64, 277.

Maïa, Noble, Eighteenth Dynasty, New Kingdom, *c.* 1345 BC. A dramatic discovery in 1997 in the New Kingdom cemetery at Saqqara revealed the burial place of the Lady Maïa, the royal nurse of King TUTANKHAMUN. Maïa was evidently herself of high birth for she was considered suitable to act as wet-nurse to the future king. He is shown, sitting on her lap, though fully accoutred in his royal regalia.

A. Zivie, 'The tomb of the Lady Maïa, wet-nurse of Tutankhamun', *EA* 13: 7–8 (preliminary report).

Maiherperi, Fan-Bearer, Eighteenth Dynasty, New Kingdom, *c.* 1450 BC. A much favoured friend of the king, Maiherperi is depicted in the splendid papyrus which accompanied him into his tomb. In it he is shown to have been dark-skinned. He was probably the child of a Nubian mother and one of the kings of the early part of the dynasty. His particular status may have been the consequence of having been the foster brother of one of the king's sons, in all probability THUTMOSE III, although THUTMOSE IV has also been suggested as the king reigning when Maiherperi was buried.

He bore the title 'Fan-Bearer on the Right Hand of the King', a position of great honour. He was also a royal page. He was given the singular privilege of burial in the royal necropolis (KV 36).

Maiherperi's tomb was robbed but nontheless many of the sumptuous offerings buried with him survived. Amongst them were two finely chased dog collars. The name of one of his dogs is recorded in the tomb: Tantanouet.

G. Daressy, 'Fouilles de la Vallée des Rois', 1898–9, CG, 38–57; pls 13, 15.
Reeves and Wilkinson: 179–81.
Saleh and Sourouzian: 142.
EMC CG 24095.

Maiy, Official, Eighteenth Dynasty, New Kingdom, *c.* 1390–1336 BC. RAMOSE was the vizier who served the kings AMENHOTEP III and his son AMENHOTEP IV-AKHENATEN and recorded various of his relations in his fine tomb at Thebes (TT 55). Amongst those whom he sought to have with him in the afterlife were his mother IPUIA and Maiy, the Overseer of the Royal Horses and his wife, Werel.

The reliefs and paintings from Ramose's tomb are probably the finest surviving from the Amarna period. They record much of the life at court and the rituals associated with the newly introduced worship of the Aten.

N. De Garis Davis, *The Tomb of the Vizier Ramose*, London, 1941.
PM I.1: 105–11.

Mami, Royal Scribe, Eighteenth Dynasty, New Kingdom, *c.* 1427–1400 BC. In the course of administering their extensive imperial possessions to the north of Egypt, especially in Palestine and Syria, the Egyptians frequently despatched trusted officials on diplomatic journeys, which might require them to remain in a foreign land for quite long periods. Mami was a treasury official, 'the Overseer of the House of Silver', who lived for some time in Ugarit on the Eastern Mediterranean coast. He evidently absorbed the local culture as he dedicated a stele, inscribed in Egyptian hieroglyphs, to the city god, a manifestation of the Syrian god Ba'al. He was probably stationed there to ensure the transfer of 'tribute' from Ugarit back to Egypt.

CAH II.2: 133, 152.

Manetho, High Priest and Chronicler, Ptolemaic Period, *c.* 305–285 BC. The High Priest of Re in Heliopolis during the reigns of the first two Ptolemies, Manetho was concerned that his sovereigns should be aware of the course of Egyptian history and of the quality of those kings who had preceeded them on the throne. The original text of his chronicle is lost, but it was greatly respected in antiquity and a number of authors quoted from it extensively. In consequence it has been very largely possible to restore the sequence of kings as defined by him. He was 'Scribe of the Sacred' and as such had a special responsibility for the preservation of the temple records.

Manetho organised the listing of the kings into 'Dynasties', presuming some form of familial relationship between the members of the same dynasty, though this might sometimes, indeed quite often, be effected by marriage, a likely prince marrying the daughter of the previous incumbent. In each case he seems to have given a version of the king's name, an indication of the principal events of his reign, observations on his character and an assessment of the duration of his reign. He finally provides an estimate of the length of time that the dynasty ruled Egypt.

Generally speaking, Manetho's system has stood the test of time and still forms the basis of the listing of the kings. His work has beeen supplemented by the discovery of other king lists, some descending from the Old Kingdom and others from the New Kingdom.

Manetho, *Aegyptiaca*, ed. and trans. W. G. Waddell, London, 1940.
J. Málek, 'The original version of the Royal Canon of Turin', JEA, 68 (1982): 93–106.
G. P. Verbrugghe and J. M. Wickersham, 'Berossos and Manetho', in *Native Traditions in Mesopotamia and Egypt*, Michigan, 1996.

May, Painter, Eighteenth Dynasty, New Kingdom, *c.* 1300 BC. May was employed in the necropolis of Thebes, Deir el-Medina, as 'Outline-draughtsman of Amun'. The wall paintings in his tomb (TT 338), executed in tempera, were detached and removed to the Egyptian Museum, Turin.

The paintings shown May's sarcophagus being dragged to its tomb by men and oxen, and May and his wife Tamyt making offerings. They also represent the pilgrimage to Abydos, which the 'justified' Egyptian, deemed worthy of enjoying eternal life, sought to make after death.

PM I.1: 406.
Scamuzzi: pls L–LII.

Maya, Painter, Eighteeenth Dynasty, New Kingdom, *c.* 1350 BC. Although he is described merely as a painter, Maya must have been well-connected for his tomb at Deir el-Medina, the Theban necropolis, contained some of the finest and most elegant statuary attributed to a private individual (and to his wife, Merit) at any period of Egyptian history.

Leiden Museum, *Artefact*, review of collection, Leiden 1968: 36; pls 49–51.
Rijksmuseum Van Oudheden, Leiden, AST 1–3.

Maya, Courtier, Eighteenth Dynasty, New Kingdom, *c.* 1350 BC. 'Fan Bearer at the King's Right Hand', Maya was one of the influential nobles of AMENHOTEP IV-AKHENATEN'S court and a proponent of the cult of Atenism. He was rewarded with a tomb at Akhetaten, though its decoration was never finished.

It is likely that this Maya went on to occupy an important place in the court of King HOREMHEB. He was King's Scribe, Overseer of the Treasury, Overseer of Works in the Place of Eternity and leader of the festival of Amun in Karnak. He was given the responsibility of restoring the burial of King THUTMOSE IV. He is mentioned in an inscription of the eighth year of Horemheb's reign with his assistant, DJEHUTYMOSE. Maya was the son of 'the noble Iawy' and 'the lady of the house Weret'. He was buried at Memphis.

Reeves and Wilkinson: 108.

Maya, Official, Eighteenth Dynasty, New Kingdom, *c.* 1327 BC. Maya made an offering of a model of King TUTANKHAMUN lying on a bier, which was placed in the king's tomb.

Reeves and Wilkinson: 41.

Mehetenwesket, Queen, Twenty-Sixth Dynasty, Late Period, *c.* 664–610 BC. Mehetenwesket was the wife of King PSAMETIK I, the longest reigning of the Saite kings. She was the mother of the Princess NITIQRET, who was appointed God's Wife of Amun at Thebes.

Grimal: 354 (as Mehytemwaskhet).

Mehu, Vizier, Sixth Dynasty, Old Kingdom, *c.* 2375–2345 BC. Mehu was Chief Minister to the king at the end of the Fifth Dynasty, at the time of King UNAS, to whom he may have been related. He was provided with a mastaba tomb at Saqqara, which contains well executed if conventional scenes of hunting and the provision of offerings for Mehu's eternity.

One of the chambers in Mehu's tomb was later taken over by one MERYREANKH, a priest of the pyramid of King PEPY I, and used as his own offerings chamber.

Z. Y. Saad, 'A Preliminary Report on the Excavations at Saqqara', ASAE XL: 687–92, pls LXXX, LXXXI.

Mehy, Vizier, Fifth Dynasty, Old Kingdom, *c.* 2375–2345 BC. Mehy was the son of King DJEDKARE ISESI's Vizier, INTI. He also achieved the vizierate, serving King UNAS in that capacity. He was Overseer of All the King's Works, as were his father before him and his brother with whom he shared the office. His son NEKHEBU succeeded him in this appointment but not in the vizierate.

CAH I.2: 186–7.

Meketaten, Princess, Eighteenth Dynasty, New Kingdom, *c.* 1352–1336 BC. The second daughter of King AMENHOTEP IV-AKHENATEN and Queen NEFERTITI, it would appear that Meketaten died in childbirth. It is probable that the father of her child was her own father; a famous relief in the royal wadi at Amarna shows the royal family mourning her death, pouring dust on their heads as they stand before what is either her corpse or her mummy. It is unlikely that her child survived for very long, although a nurse appears to be carrying a baby at the mourning ceremony.

Aldred 1988: 283–4.
Reeves and Wilkinson: 118–19.

Meketre, Chancellor, Eleventh Dynasty, Middle Kingdom, *c.* 2000 BC. Meketre was one of the great officials who served the kings of the Eleventh Dynasty, first the great Nebhepetre MONTUHOTEP II in the last years of his reign, and then his son and successor, Sa'ankhkare MONTUHOTEP III. Meketre had a grand tomb prepared for himself close to a temple built by Montuhotep III near Deir el-Bahri. The tomb contained many beautifully made models, carved in wood and painted very naturalistically, of daily life on a great estate of the period. All aspects of the daily round of managing a large property are included, as is Meketre's house itself.

H. E. Winlock, *Models of Daily Life in Ancient Egypt*, Cambridge MA, 1955.
Saleh and Sourouzian: 74–8.
EMC JE 46725, 46715, 46724, 46723, 46722.
MMA 20.3.13., 20.3.10., 20.3.12., 20.3.7., 20.3.1,3., 20.3.6., 20.3.4.

Memi, Priest, Thirteenth Dynasty, Middle Kingdom, *c.* 1795–1650 BC. Memi was a *wa'b* priest in the cult of King KHNUM-KHUFU, probably at Giza. The inscription on a statue of Memi and his wife Aku invokes Khufu to provide all the necessities of the afterlife for the couple. It is interesting that Khufu's cult was operating nearly a thousand years after his death and that his aid is still invoked for the welfare of his people. HERODOTUS reported that Khufu's memory was execrated but the evidence of Memi's office and his prayer would seem to contradict so harsh a judgement.

Hodjash and Berlev 1982: no. 42, 93–5.

Menelaus, Mathematician and Astronomer, Ptolemaic Period, 1st century BC. Menelaus, a native of Alexandria, was the first known mathematician to write a text on spherical trigonometry. He also conducted a number of astronomical observations which were recorded by Claudius Ptolemy. Only one of his works survives, the *Spherica*, which was preserved in an Arabic translation.

T. L. Heath, *History of Greek Mathematics*, vol. 2, Oxford, 1921.

Menes, King (?), Late Predynastic Period, *c.* 3100 BC. Probably to be identified with NAR-MER, the last predynastic king before the establishment of the First Dynasty, or with AHA, the first king of the First Dynasty, Menes was regarded by the Egyptians of later times as the country's original unifier. It is now thought that 'Menes' may be some sort of descriptive title, attributed to the earliest of the kings and related to the idea of unification.

Emery 1961: 33–7, 49.
Hoffman 1980: 289, 292–305.

Menhet, Merti, Menwi, Queens, Eighteenth Dynasty, New Kingdom, *c.* 1479–1425 BC. Three of the wives of King THUTMOSE III, whose jewellery was found in a rock-cut tomb near Deir el-Bahri. The three women were not Egyptians, but probably Syrians taken into Thutmose's harem as part of his dealings with foreign powers, a practice which flourished throughout the New Kingdom.

They were buried with some exceptionally elegant possessions, including pairs of sheet gold sandals which imitated leatherwork, an elaborate gold-encrusted headdress and fine jewellery.

Hayes 1959: 114–30.
Shaw and Nicholson: 144–5.
MMA 26.8.117, 26.8.99, 26.8.92, 26.8.66–8, 26.8.135,26.8.121,26.8.63,26.8.86,26.8.60–1.

Menkauhor-Akauhor, King, Fifth Dynasty, Old Kingdom, *c.* 2421–2414 BC. The successor of King NIUSERRE is known by a rock inscription at Sinai. He built a pyramid and a sun-temple but their location is uncertain. At one time it was thought possible that they might lie near the pyramid of King SNEFERU; it is now believed that the 'Headless Pyramid' at Saqqara may be that of Menkauhor-Akauhor. A small alabaster statue of the king survives.

Although little is known of his reign he was well regarded by later generations as distant in time as the New Kingdom, when a cult to him still flourished at Saqqara. He is said to have reigned for eight years.

Gardiner *et al.* 1952: pts I and II, 55: 12, pl. v.
Vandier 1958: 31, pl. vi, 3.
CAH I.2: 185–6.
Lehner 1997: 153, 165.

Menkaure (alt. Mycerinos), King, Fourth Dynasty, Old Kingdom, *c.* 2532–2503 BC. The succession after the death of KHNUM-KHUFU appears to have been disputed with a junior branch of the royal family assuming the throne during the reign of DJEDEFRE. KHAFRE, Khnum-Khufu's son, eventually succeeded, reigning for some twenty-four years. He in turn was followed by his son, Menkaure, to whom is attributed the building of the third and smallest pyramid at Giza.

Menkaure is commemorated by a number of exceptionally fine sculptures, some of which are by any standards to be acknowledged as supreme masterpieces. Several which show Menkaure in the company of his wife or attended by divinities, are carved in an extremely hard schist, which is also very friable. The technique developed by the artists of the time achieves a degree of plasticity and verisimilitude in the hardest stones which is remarkable.

G. A. Reisner, *The Temples of the Third Pyramid at Giza*, Cambridge MA, 1931.
Terrace and Fischer 1970: no. 7, 45–8.
Edwards 1993: 137–51.
Lehner 1997: 134–7.
EMC CG 647.
JE 40679.

Menkheperre, High Priest, Twenty-First Dynasty, Third Intermediate Period, *c.* 1045–992 BC. The end of the Twentieth Dynasty was marked by the rise to power of a separate dynasty, virtually independent of the king, of High Priests of Amun in Thebes. As they were also army commanders they dominated the politics of the south.

Amongst the most skilful of this line of warrior-priests was Menkheperre, the son of PINUDJEM I, who himself only relinquished the pontificate on assuming royal titles. He passed on the office to two of his sons, the second of whom was Menkheperre, also a skilled politician who, when first acceding to his high office, encountered vigorous opposition; this he firmly suppressed, but later seems to have promoted a policy of conciliation towards his one-time opponents which won them over to his support.

In the later years of his reign he seems to have brought about a pacification of the warring factions which had come to disrupt the southlands. He enhanced his position by marrying the daughter of King PSEUSENNES I. Occasionally his name is enclosed in a cartouche, a format reserved for a king. He appears to have been a great builder of walls to protect and enhance the temple structures.

He was also an important magnate in the north of Egypt, with a stronghold at El-Hibeh; this too he fortified considerably.

He was in his late eighties when he died.

Kitchen 1986: §43, §65, §218, §226, §228.
Grimal: 312, 314–15.

Menkheperreseneb, High Priest, Eighteenth Dynasty, New Kingdom, *c.* 1479–1425 BC. The High Priest of Amun at Thebes during the reign of King THUTMOSE III, Menkheperreseneb was buried at Thebes (TT 86). In his tomb, in addition to scenes of metalworking, Menkheperreseneb is shown supervising the presentation of a visiting delegation from Crete, who bring the king gifts of pottery and stoneware vessels and a rhyton in the form of the head of a piebald bull. He also supervises the presentation of gifts from Hittites, Syrians, farmers and carpenters.

Stevenson Smith 1965: 33, fig. 91.
Gardiner 1961: 196–7.
CAH II.1: 326.

Menna, Royal Charioteer, Nineteenth Dynasty, New Kingdom, *c*. 1274 BC. Menna was Shield-bearer and Royal Charioteer to King RAMESSES II and fought alongside the king at the battle of Qadesh. In the famous description of the battle which the king caused to be inscribed at Thebes, Menna is reported as being fearful of the odds which the Egyptian forces were facing but is encouraged by the king: 'Stand fast, steady yourself, my shield-bearer'. Ramesses goes on to record the names of his two noble horses, 'Victory-in-Thebes' and 'Mut-is-Content', who he says 'alone helped me, together with the charioteer Menna, my Shield-bearer and my Palace Cup-bearers'.

Kitchen 1982: 59, 61.

Menna, Royal Scribe, Eighteenth Dynasty, New Kingdom, *c*. 1400–1390 BC. Menna was the Scribe of the Royal Fields and as such was responsible for the accounting and control of the king's herds and plantations. His tomb at Thebes (TT 69) is celebrated for its scenes of harvest, of girls fighting, and of hunting in the marshes, a pastime evidently much enjoyed by Menna and his family.

PM I.1: 134–9.

Mentuherkhepshef, Prince, Twentieth Dynasty, New Kingdom, *c*. 1126–1108 BC. The tomb KV 19 is associated with the son of King RAMESSES IX, though it was originally intended for another prince, Ramesses Sethherkhepshef, before he ascended the throne as Ramesses VIII and therefore was entitled to a grander burial place. However, KV 19 is acknowledged as containing some of the finest paintings in the Valley of Kings, and the occupant, who is represented as being quite young, though he probably died during the reign following that of his father, is portrayed with great elegance.

The tomb is revealing in that many of the paintings are unfinished, thus permitting the examination of the techniques of late New Kingdom painters.

Reeves and Wilkinson: 170–1.

Mentuhotep, Official, Twelfth Dynasty, Middle Kingdom, *c*. 1840 BC. The 'Overseer of the House', Mentuhotep was buried at Thebes, from whence the ruling dynasty had moved the capital to Lisht. His burial yielded a quantity of high quality grave goods.

Most notable was a statue in wood of Mentuhotep standing and holding in his right hand a libation vessel. He wears a tripartite wig which is more usually associated with women, rather than men. He wears also a long, kilt-like garment knotted at the waist. Montuhotep has a distinctive, sensitive and intelligent face, suggesting that the statue is intended to be a portrait.

He was buried with a model of the ships which would have served to carry him on the posthumous pilgimage to Abydos.

G. Steindorff, 'Das Grab des Mentuhotep', in *Mittheilungen aus den Orientalischen Sammlungen*, Heft VIII, 'Grabfunde des Mittleren Reichs in den königlichen Museen zu Berlin', Berlin, 1896.
EMB inv. no. 4650. 12. cat. nos 18, 70.

Mentuhotep, Queen, Seventeenth Dynasty, Second Intermediate Period, *c*. 1650–1550 BC. Queen Mentuhotep lived during the late Hyksos Period, a member of the family which eventually achieved their expulsion from Egypt. Her coffin contains the earliest known version of the Book of the Dead.

E. A. W. Budge, *Facsimilies of Egyptian Hieratic Papyri in the British Museum*, first series, London, 1910: pl. XLVII, line 16ff.

Merefnebef, Vizier, Sixth Dynasty, Old Kingdom, *c.* 2345–2323 BC. The mastaba tomb of a hitherto unknown vizier, Merefnebef, was found at Saqqara in 1997. The owner of the tomb was connected with the funerary temple of King TETI.

Merefnebef, who also bore the names Fefi and Unasankh, had five wives. His tomb contains vividly coloured panels of inscriptions, overlaid on a white plaster surface. Much of the colour is also retained on the painted reliefs in the tomb.

The several sons of the vizier whose portraits were included in the tomb have all had their likenesses defaced; only one, named Fefi like his father, is unscathed.

Karol Mysliwiec, 'A new mastaba, a new vizier', *EA* 13: 37–8 (preliminary report).

Merenptah, King, Nineteenth Dynasty, New Kingdom, *c.* 1213–1203 BC. The thirteenth son, by Queen ISTNOFRET, and the eventual successsor of King RAMESSES II, Merenptah was already elderly when he came to the throne. He was a conscientious ruler, if less dazzling than his very much larger-than-life father, in whose last years he had acted as regent. In addition to the almost mandatory temple building which he undertook he was particularly preoccupied with Egypt's foreign relations. His generousity of spirit is indicated by his supplying grain to the Hittite empire, once Egypt's enemy, during a famine.

Merenptah used to be identified as 'the Pharaoh of the Exodus'. As there is no certain historical or archaeological evidence that such an event ever took place or that a large Semitic-speaking community was ever captive in Egypt, this identification is now generally disregarded. However, the first historical reference to 'Israel' appears on a stela from Merenptah's mortuary chapel, where it is named as one of the peoples conquered during his Asiatic campaign, when he advanced into Canaan and crushed the local tribes and small states which were resentful of Egyptian hegemony.

He was buried in the royal necropolis at Thebes (KV 8).

W. M. F. Petrie, *Six Temples at Thebes*, London, 1897.
Lichtheim 2: 73–8.
EMC 34025.

Merenre I, King, Sixth Dynasty, Old Kingdom, *c.* 2287–2278 BC. The son and successor of the long reigning PEPY I, Merenre was the product of the king's old age by one of his two queens who shared the same name, ANKHENESMERYRE. Merenre was probably co-regent with his father towards the end of the latter's reign; it is likely also that it is Merenre who is the youthful figure in the double copper statue with the king found at Hierakonpolis.

Merenre recorded the occasion of a state visit by Nubian chiefs when they came to the frontier to pay their respects to him, 'kissing the ground before the king'.

During his reign Merenre was supported by a group of powerful nobles, including his uncle, the Vizier DJAU, and HARKHUF, the governor of Elephantine. Merenre had a particular concern for his southern dominions, and built a canal at Aswan which was probably the one later excavated by SENWOSRET III.

When Merenre's pyramid was opened the mummy of a young man was found in a sarcophagus. It is unclear, however, whether this was Merenre, though he was said still to be a youth on his death, and it is possible that the mummy is of a later date.

Stevenson Smith 1971: 192–4, 506.

Merenre II, King, Sixth Dynasty, Old Kingdom, *c.* 2184 BC. The probable son of PEPY II's old age and his eventual successor. Evidence of his reign is exceedingly sparse and it is thought that he did not survive on the throne for more than a year.

According to legend he was killed by a rioting mob and his sister and wife NITIQRET (Nitocris) avenged his death fiercely before killing herself.

CAH I.2: 196–7.
Grimal: 89.

Merer, Scribe, Tenth Dynasty, First Intermediate Period, 2050 BC. Merer, the Scribe of the Divine Offerings, was buried with a number of wooden statues, representing him dressed in his kilt, each of which is inscribed with extracts from the Coffin Texts, written in cursive hieroglyphs. In the dedications Merer is hailed as 'Osiris Merer', an early example of the practice of nominating the deceased as an Osiris, which was to become universal.

Hayes 1953: 211; fig. 129.
MMA 10.176.59.

Merer, Gardener, Twelfth/Thirteenth Dynasties, Middle Kingdom, *c.* 1840–1640 BC. Merer's statue bears an inscription which suggests that it was the gift of the king that Merer might be remembered by the god. It is possible, however, that the statue was usurped as its quality suggests that it was made for an official more important than a gardener.

Thomas 1995: no. 65 (158).
University of Pennsylvania Museum of Archaeology and Anthropology, E 10751.

Merery, Priest, Eighth Dynasty, First Intermediate Period, *c.* 2181–2125 BC. Merery was a senior priest in the temple of Hathor at Denderah. To judge by the size of his mastaba tomb he was a man of importance, more than would be indicated by his role of priest alone. He called himself 'Count, Chancellor of the King of Lower Egypt and Sole Companion'. He was also Keeper of the Cattle of Hathor. He records that his predecessor was one Bebi, Nomarch of the Sixth Nome of which Denderah was the capital. Although Merery does not appear to have been nomarch, his status was evidently such that he might be compared with Bebi. His autobiography was contained in a narrow frieze extending across the front of his mastaba, the hieroglyphs carved in high relief.

Hayes 1953: 138–9; fig. 81.
MMA 98.4.2.

Mereruka, Vizier, Sixth Dynasty, Old Kingdom, *c.* 2345–2323 BC. Mereruka was one of the great nobles of the reign of King Teti, to whose daughter he was married. In addition to his rank as Vizier he was Governor of Memphis and the Inspector of Prophets. His tomb at Saqqara is a source of reference for the exceptionally agreeable lifestyle of a princely Egyptian of the late Old Kingdom.

In one relief Mereruka sits before an easel, painting a representation of the seasons in the form of three figures. As Mereruka was a great noble and not a professional painter, his practice of the art suggests a degree of culture and sophistication amongst Old Kingdom magnates which permitted them to undertake tasks which were more usually the province of the artists in their employment.

P. Duell, *The Mastaba of Mereruka*, Chicago IL, 1938.
Stevenson Smith 1946 (1949): 355; fig. 231.

Meresamun, Priestess, Twenty-Second Dynasty, Third Intermediate Period, *c.* 850 BC. Meresamun was a singer in the temple of Amun and hence a member of the suite of the God's Wife of Amun, the Divine Adoratrice at a time when the temple exercised considerable political power in Upper Egypt, in addition to its more conventional religious duties.

EMB (Westerman-Reihe Museum) 1981: 91.
EMB 71/71. cat. no. 58.

Meresankh I, Queen, Third Dynasty, Old Kingdom, 2637–2613 BC. Meresankh was a minor wife of King HUNI, the last king of the Third Dynasty. Her son, SNEFERU, married Huni's daughter, HETEPHERES I and thus obtained the kingship. Despite her relatively minor status, Meresankh was evidently greatly respected and her memory was long venerated. She was regarded as ancestress of the Fourth Dynasty.

CAH I.2: 159, 164–5.
Grimal: 67–8.

Meresankh III, Queen, Fourth Dynasty, Old Kingdom, *c.* 2558–2500 BC. Meresankh III was the great-granddaughter of MERESANKH I and granddaughter of King KHNUM-KHUFU. She was the daughter of the Crown Prince, KAWAB, and HETEPHERES II, but her father died before succeeding to the throne. The last years of the dynasty seem to have been fraught with dissent in the royal family and Meresankh's mother, Hetepheres II, appears to have allied herself with what proved to be the losing faction, marrying Khufu's immediate successor, DJEDEFRE. However, after his death Hetepheres made her peace with the ruling faction and married Meresankh to the king, KHAFRE. Meresankh was the mother of Prince NEBMAKHET.

Meresankh was buried in a pretty rock-cut tomb under her mother's mastaba; she died before Hetepheres who provided the tomb for her daughter and is shown in it in her company. She lived on into the reign of SHEPSESKHAF, the last king of the dynasty.

Reisner and Stevenson Smith 1955: 5.
CAH I.2: 169–79.
Dows Dunham and W. K. Simpson, 'The Mastaba of Queen Meresankh III', *Giza Mastabas*, vol. I, Boston MA, 1971.
MFA Boston.

Meresankh, Official, Fifth Dynasty, Old Kingdom, *c.* 2345 BC. Meresankh was the Director of Funerary Priests in his lifetime and thus responsible for the ceremonies conducted at the time of the burials of important members of the society. He is commemorated by a series of rather unsophisticated but engaging statues, of himself, his wife, children and servants in his tomb at Saqqara.

S. Hassan, *Excavations at Giza (I), 1929–30*, Oxford, 1932: 115–16; pl. 73.
Saleh and Sourouzian: 50, 51.
EMC JE 66619, 66617.

Meri, High Priest, Eighteenth Dynasty, New Kingdom, *c.* 1427–1400 BC. The High Priest of Amun during the reign of AMENHOTEP II, Meri was buried in a splendid tomb at Thebes (TT 95), having also usurped the tomb of Amonezeh (TT 84). His parents were Nebpehitre, First Prophet (High Priest) of Min of Koptos and Hunay 'Chief Nurse of the Lord of the Two Lands'.

PM I.2: 195–6.
G. Lefebvre, *Historie de Grands Prêtres D'Amon de Karnak Jusqu'à La XXIe Dynastie*, Paris, 1929: 56, 92, 235.

Meribastet, Royal Steward, Twentieth Dynasty, New Kingdom, *c.* 1184–1153 BC. Meribastet was Chief Steward in Hermopolis in Middle Egypt. He was the patriarch of a remarkable family which acquired great power in Thebes, in the years after the death of King RAMESSES III, when a succession of generally indifferent kings held the throne, making the High Priesthood of Amun virtually an hereditary office. His son, RAMESSES-NAKHTE, was the first of these; other of his descendants inherited offices which enabled them to control much of the region's tax revenue and, in the process, to acquire very extensive landholdings.

Kees 1961: 280.
Kitchen 1986: §207.

Merikare, King, Tenth Dynasty, First Intermediate Period, *c.* 2160–2125 BC. In the confused times following the end of the Sixth Dynasty the reigns of the Heracleopolitan kings of the Tenth Dynasty provide some continuity with the past. One of the more successful rulers was Merikare, the successor and probably the son of Wahkare AKHTOY III. He is remembered chiefly for an *Instruction*, left by the old king and addressed to him. It urges the proper conduct for a king and the priorities which he should establish for his rule.

Egypt seems to have enjoyed considerable prosperity during Merikare's reign. He was supported by magnates such as TEFIBI and AKHTOY II whom he installed as governor of the Asiut nome.

CAH I.2: 467–8.
A. H. Gardiner, JEA 1 (1914) 20–36.
Lichtheim 1: 79–109.

Merisu, Landowner, Eleventh Dynasty, Middle Kingdom, *c.* 2004–1992 BC. Merisu was the son of HEKANAKHTE, the landowner and priest who left an archive of letters of instructions to his family during his absences from home. He instructs him to care particularly for his youngest sons, the more junior of whom is to be indulged with anything that he wants. One of the maids is to be dismissed and Hekanakhte is scathing about Merisu's relations with his wife-to-be. It appears that the letters, none of which appeared to have been read, were discarded near the tomb of IPY and were found there four thousand years later.

It seems that Merisu was awaiting the delivery of a bolt of linen, of high value (24 deben) and that robbers intercepted it. The robbers evidently discarded the letters which were with the cloth, and they were found by the priests who had charge of Ipy's burial.

CAH I.2: 489.
T. G. H. James, *The Hekanakhte Papers and other Early Middle Kingdom Documents*, London, 1962.
H. Goedicke, *Studies in the Hekanakhte Papers*, Baltimore MD, 1984.

Meritaten, Princess, Eighteenth Dynasty, New Kingdom, *c.* 1350 BC. The eldest of the six daughters of AMENHOTEP IV-AKHENATEN and NEFERTITI, Meritaten was associated with her father after the disappearance of Nefertiti. She was also shown in the company of the king's immediate successor, SMENKHKARE, to whom she may have been married. It is probable that she died before her father.

Aldred 1973: 176, no. 103.
Redford 1984: 190–3.
EMB 21245, cat. no. 44.

Meritites, Queen, Fourth Dynasty, Old Kingdom, *c.* 2589–2566 BC. A consort of King KHNUM-KHUFU, Meritites was the mother of the the Crown Prince, KAWAB. He died before his father and the succession seems to have been disputed. Queen Meritites lived on into the reign of King KHAFRE, but may have been discredited, having supported one of the losing factions in the family feuding which followed the death of Khnum-Khufu.

CAH I.2: 165, 170–4.

Merka, Noble, First Dynasty, Archaic Period, *c.* 2890 BC. Merka was buried in mastaba tomb no. 3505 at Saqqara. He was commemorated by a very large funerary stele found in the mastaba. A contemporary of King KA'A, Merka was a *sem*-priest with the title of 'Prince'. He held a number of other offices including 'Controller of the Palace', 'Captain of the Boat of the King of Upper Egypt', 'Administrator' and 'Head of the Singers'.

Emery 1961: 90, 168, 193.

Spencer: 93, 96; ill. 71.
Lehner 1997: 79–80.

Merneferre Iy, King, Thirteenth Dynasty, Middle Kingdom, *c.* 1700 BC. Athough he was a member of the generally insecure Thirteenth Dynasty during the years when the Hyksos invaders entered Egypt, Merneferre Iy managed to hold his throne for twenty-four years. He seems to have accepted the role of vassal to the Hyksos rulers.

CAH II.1: 52.

Merneith (alt. Meryet-nit), Queen, First Dynasty, Archaic Period, *c.* 2950 BC. Probably the daughter of King DJER, the second king of the First Dynasty, Merneith was the wife of DJET and the mother of DEN; she was thus of great importance in the formative years of the Egyptian state. There is some indication that Merneith was accorded sovereign status, perhaps because she acted as regent during the minority of her son. She was given a great tomb at Abydos, where she was buried with a number of her retainers, including several who, in later times, would have stood firmly – and more securely – in the middle ranks of society: her shipmaster, artists and her vase maker. She was provided with a solar barque to enable her to sail across the sky to join the gods.

Merneith's name is a compound with that of the goddess of Sais, Neith, but there is no evidence that she had any special affiliations with the north. A mastaba tomb at Saqqara (3503) which was associated with her was supported by the burials of a number of craftsmen who were sent to serve the queen in the afterlife.

Sealings of a high official, Seshemka, were found in tomb 3503 and it has been speculated that the tomb may be his.

Emery 1961: 32, 65–9.
Spencer: 64, 80; ills 60–1.
Stevenson Smith 1981: 35, ills 16a, b.
Lehner 1997: 78–80.

Mery, Priest, Twelfth Dynasty, Middle Kingdom, *c.* 1805 BC. Mery was the son of Intef, and in the thirty-ninth year of the reign of King AMENEMHET III he drew up his will. In it he bequeathed his office of controller of the 'phyle', the monthly 'watches' into which the lower orders of the temple priests were organised, to his son, also called Intef. The office carried with it a share in the temple income, staff and an estate.

From Kahun. University College 32037 (= P. Kahun VII.I).
F. Ll. Griffith, *Kahun Papyri II*, London, 1897–8: pl. XI, lines 10–27.
Bourriau 1988: 80, no. 63.

Mery-Atum, Prince, Nineteenth Dynasty, New Kingdom, *c.* 1255 BC. The sixteenth child of King RAMESSES II, borne by Queen NEFERTARI, Mery-Atum was for a time recognised as his father's heir, being proclaimed Crown Prince. When a boy he had visited Sinai in the care of his guardian ASHA-HEBSED, one of his father's most trusted confidants. He was appointed High Priest of Re in Heliopolis, further confirming his status as the king's successor. He seems to have lived for another twenty years but died before his father.

He was buried in the large tomb in the Valley of the Kings prepared for Ramesses' son, KV 5.

Kitchen 1982: 111.

Merymose, Viceroy, Eighteenth Dynasty, New Kingdom, *c.* 1390–1352 BC. One of the longest serving of the Viceroys of Kush, Merymose occupied his post for thirty years during the reign of King AMENHOTEP III. He commanded the soldiery during the only military expedition of Amenhotep's reign, when a troublesome coalition of Bedu tribes rebelled in the region of Ibhet. Merymose recruited an army of Nubians and the rebellion was suppressed. Amenhotep then undertook a triumphal tour deep into the south of Nubia, bringing back quantities of gold for the adornment of his pylon in the temple of Amun at Karnak. Merymose's victory is commemorated on the reverse of a standing rock near the village of Tombos; on the front is a stela proclaiming a similiar victory, in the same region, of King THUTMOSE I, a century earlier.

Merymose ruled the south from his capital at Mi'am, modern Aniba. No doubt because of his close relationship with the king, he was granted a tomb (TT 383) at Thebes. He was also provided with three magnificent sarcophagi, carved in diorite and covered with ritual scenes and inscriptions; such provision was highly unusual for a non-royal official, no matter how high his rank.

CAH II.1: 347–8.
BM EA 1001.

Meryreankh, Priest, Sixth Dynasty, Old Kingdom, post-*c.* 2187 BC. Meryreankh served as priest of the pyramid of King PEPY I at Saqqara. He appropriated one of the rooms in the tomb of the Vizier MEHU and converted it to his own use as his offering chamber. He is represented in a brightly coloured painted relief seated in a lion-clawed chair, drinking elegantly from a beaker whilst deferential servants present offerings to him.

Lauer 1976: 153, pl. XVIII.

Meryrehashtef, Noble, Sixth Dynasty, Old Kingdom, *c.* 2345–2181 BC. Meryrehashtef was buried at Sedment. His tomb contained a number of wooden statues of him, showing him at different stages of his life, a funerary custom which prevailed at this time. The statues are highly naturalistic; the most striking shows him as a young man, striding forward with energy and an expression of determination on his face, which is in no way diminished by the fact that Meryrehashtef is completely naked, probably a cultic convention of the time.

James and Davies: 23; ill. 22.

Quirke and Spencer: 186–7.

Meryrenufer Qa, Official, Sixth Dynasty, Old Kingdom, 2345–2181 BC. Meryrenufer Qa was responsible for the management of the pyramid towns of Kings KHNUM-KHUFU and MENKAURE. He was also 'Inspector of the Priests' of the pyramid of KHAFRE. As a reward for his services to the Fourth Dynasty kings he was buried with them at Giza.

J. Malek and W. Forman, *In the Shadow of the Pyramids*, London, 1986: 52–3.

Mesheti, Noble, Eleventh Dynasty, Middle Kingdom, *c.* 2000 BC. Like his near contemporary MEKETRE, Mesheti had placed in his tomb at Asiut in Middle Egypt a series of lifelike models. The most celebrated of these are two groups of soldiers, marching in formation and carrying their weapons. The two groups are indicated as racially distinct: a Nubian formation and a lighter-pigmented platoon. Each advances with firm, disciplined steps; the lighter-skinned troops carry shields made from the hides of oryxes.

Mesheti was a 'Seal-Bearer', hence a noble; he was Overseer of the Priests of Wepwawet, the ancient god of Abydos.

PM IV: 265.
M. Bietak, *Mélanges Gamal Eddin Moukhtar I*, Cairo, 1985: 87–97, pls I–IV.
Saleh and Sourouzian: 72, 73.
EMC JE 30969, 30986.

Methen, Royal Steward, Fourth Dynasty, Old Kingdom, *c.* 2550 BC. The Steward of the royal estates in the Pyramid age, Methen was a man of consequence and was buried in the great necropolis at Saqqara. His statue is clearly an attempt at portraiture, despite the rather massive, block-like treatment of the seated figure. Methen's face is very distinctive, with what appear to be prominent upper teeth which he keeps concealed behind his closed lips.

H. Fechteimer, *Die Klein Plastik der Äegypte*, Berlin, 1922: Tf. 6,7.
Breasted: §§170–5.
EMB 1106, cat. no. 7.

Methethy, Official, Fifth Dynasty, Old Kingdom, *c.* 2400 BC. An important official of the Fifth Dynasty, 'Overseer of the King's Tenants', Methethy was buried at Saqqara. He is portrayed striding masterfully forward, grasping his wand of office, wearing a white starched skirt and a coloured necklace.

J. D. Cooney, *Bulletin of the Brooklyn Museum*, 15 (1953) 1–25.
Stevenson Smith 1958 (1981): 139–41; figs 135–6.
P. Kaplony, *Studien zum Grab des Metheti*, Berne, 1976.
Kansas City, William Rockhill Nelson Gallery of Art.
Brooklyn Museum.

Metjen, Nomarch, Third/Fourth Dynasties, Old Kingdom, *c.* 2613–2589 BC. Metjen lived during the Third Dynasty and died during the reign of King SNEFERU, the first king of the Fourth Dynasty. His tomb contains the earliest surviving autobiography of an Egyptian noble.

Breasted 1: §§170–5.
Hayes 1953: 121.

Min, Provincial Magnate, Royal Tutor and Festival Director, Eighteenth Dynasty, New Kingdom, 1427–1400 BC. Min bore the titles Count of This and Count of the Oasis; he was a powerful figure in the region of Abydos and governed it much in the manner of the old nomarchs of the past. He was tutor to King AMENHOTEP II and also his Master of Arms. Like IKHERNOFRET in the Twelfth Dynasty, he was director of the festivals at Abydos and acted for the king in the temple ceremonies.

Kees 1961: 244–5.

Minbaef (alt. Antiu), Royal Treasurer, Late Sixth Dynasty/Early Twelfth Dynasty, Old Kingdom/Middle Kingdom, *c.* 2250–1955 BC. The 'Treasurer of the King of Lower Egypt', Minbaef was buried in a wooden coffin decorated with the Eyes of Horus, to allow him to observe the world outside, and with the ancient design of the palace facade, which first appeared in the First Dynasty, flanked by vessels of holy oils. Minbaef was 'Overseer of Reports on Land and Serfs'.

P. E. Newberry, *Liverpool Annals of Archaeoogy and Anthropology IV* (1912) 100, 119–20.
PM V: 19.
Ashmolean Museum.

Minkhaf, Prince, Vizier, Fourth Dynasty, Old Kingdom, *c.* 2589–2532 BC. One of remarkable group of princes who led the court of King KHNUM-KHUFU and who determined much of the diversity and splendour of the Pyramid Age, Minkhaf was probably a son of Khnum-Khufu by his queen, HENUTSEN and was Vizier to his brother, KHAFRE.

Minkhaf was evidently one of the princes who opposed the succession of DJEDEFRE after Khnum-Khufu's death and who were responsible for the eventual succession to the sovereignty of Khafre.

Reisner and Stevenson Smith 1955: 7–8, 11.

Minmose, Architect, Eighteenth Dynasty, New Kingdom, *c.* 1427–1400 BC. When news of the death of King THUTMOSE III reached the dependant territories in Palestine and Syria, some of the local dynasts rebelled against Egyptian rule. Minmose was Royal Overseer of Works and was responsible for setting up records of King AMENHOTEP II's swift and decisive action to put the rebellion down. He states that the king's first campaign to the country around Qadesh resulted in the capture and plundering of thirty towns. Minmose was later responsible for erecting boundary stele in the north and south, to mark the frontiers of the land of Egypt.

CAH II.1: 459–60.
Gardiner 1961: 197–200.

Minnakhte, Merchant, Eighteenth Dynasty, New Kingdom, *c.* 1550–1295 BC. Minnakhte is one of the relatively few merchants to be known by name from Ancient Egypt. He, and one of his fellow traders, Sherybin, are recorded as receiving rather modest deliveries of meat, wine and cakes. Much of Egypt's trade was in the hands of the government and the great temples, and there were comparatively few opportunities for private enterprise, although transactions involving slaves, cattle and land are known.

CAH II.1: 388–9.

Minnakhte, Official, Eighteenth Dynasty, New Kingdom, 1479–1425 BC. During the long and glorious reign of King THUTMOSE III Minnakhte was Superintendent of Granaries of Upper and Lower Egypt, an appointment of prestige and importance in the state. He was also Overseer of Horses of the Lord of the Two Lands. He was buried at Thebes (TT 87) and the decorations of his tomb are interesting in that they depict his villa, to which he was presumably attached during his lifetime. His garden is shown with the lotus pool which would have contained fish and on which a boat is depicted, carrying his coffin, a metaphor perhaps for the sacred journey by river which the spirit was believed to take to Abydos, the city consecrated to Osiris. Minnakhte's garden is full of birds.

PM I.1: 178–9.

Mitry, Governor, Fifth Dynasty, Old Kingdom, *c.* 2490 BC. Mitry was a Provincial Administrator, a Priest of Maat and a Privy Councillor, living early in the Fifth Dynasty. Wooden statues of he and his wife, a priestess of Hathor, are preserved; Mitry is shown carrying his sceptre of office and the long cane of a noble or person of authority.

Hayes 1953: 110–11; fig. 64.
MMA 26.2.2.

Miut (alt. Miit), Princess, Eleventh Dynasty, Middle Kingdom, *c.* 2055–2004 BC. Miut was a child of about five years old when she died and was buried in the great tomb which King Nebhepetre MONTUHOTEP II had prepared for himself, his queens and his daughters, at Deir el-Bahri. It is not known what relation Miut was to the king; she had been buried in a coffin which was much too big for her, probably because her death was unexpected and no arrangements had been made for the burial of one so young. Although she was only a child Miut was buried with a set of typically fine Middle Kingdom royal jewellery, appropriate to her rank.

Her name is the feminine form of the word for 'cat'. In view of her age a more apt translation for Miut might be 'kitten'.

H. E. Winlock, *Excavations at Deir el-Bahri, 1911–31*, New York, 1942.
J. Málek, *The Cat in Ancient Egypt*, London, 1996: 48.

Montuemhet, Noble, Twenty-Fifth Dynasty, Late Period, *c.* 700–650 BC. Montuemhet was a contemporary of King TAHARQA and was effectively Mayor of Thebes. He exercised considerable power in Upper Egypt, though his only official rank seems to have been Fourth Prophet of Amun. He was one of the most important builders of the Theban temples in the Late Period, both on behalf of Taharqa and on his own account.

Montuemhet was caught up in the troubles of the latter part of Taharqa's reign when the Theban region was invaded and pillaged by the Assyrians. By this time Montuemhet was virtually an independent ruler and he seems to have reached some sort of understanding with the Assyrians.

Montuemhet was provided with an immense tomb (TT 34) at Deir el-Bahri which, amongst other features, has a huge sun-court.

J. Leclant, *Montuemhet*, Cairo, 1961: 3–20, pls 1, 2.
Terrace and Fischer 1970: no. 37, 161–4.
Saleh and Sourouzian: 246.
EMC JE 36933 = CG 42236.

Montuhotep I, Prince (of Thebes), Tenth/Eleventh Dynasties, First Intermediate Period, *c.* 2130 BC. The son of the first INYOTEF to be known as nomarch of the Theban region, Montuhotep was acknowledged as the ancestor of the Eleventh Dynasty and was called 'The Horus Tepya'a', ('The Ancestor') and 'the Father of the Gods'. Montuhotep's son, also INYOTEF (I), proclaimed himself King of Egypt, though at the time the Herakleopolite kings were still ruling.

A. H. Gardiner, 'The First King Montuhotep of the Eleventh Dynasty', MDAIK 14 (1956) 42–51.

(Nebhepetre) Montuhotep II, King, Eleventh Dynasty, Middle Kingdom, *c.* 2055–2004 BC. One of the greatest of Egypt's kings, Nebhepetre Montuhotep II effected the reunification of the Two Kingdoms after the divisions which followed the end of the Old Kingdom. He was the son of INYOTEF III.

He imposed a firmly centralised control over the country, reducing the power of the provincial nobles which had grown great during the period of disunity. As the scion of an ancient and noble family, Montuhotep evidently had a strong sense of destiny. He changed his Horus name three times during his reign. First he was Horus Sankhibtowy, 'Giving Heart to the Two Lands'. Then he was Horus Netjeryhedjet, 'Lord of the White Crown'; finally he was Horus Smatowy, 'Uniting the Two Lands'. Montuhotep's adoption of these different styles during his lifetime was unprecedented.

Nebhepetre Montuhotep II built for himself a magnificent funerary palace as individual as his choice of Horus names. This was sited at Deir el-Bahri, in a natural amphitheatre and his tomb was built beneath a series of terraces, planted with trees and gardens (suggesting perhaps that he liked nature tamed) and probably surmounted with a pyramid. A number of his wives and consorts were buried nearby. Despite the rather formidable appearance of some of his surviving portraiture, Nebhepetre Montuhotep was evidently a king who appreciated the sacrifices of those who supported him. Close to his own tomb was found the burials of some sixty young soldiers who had evidently been killed in one of his campaigns to restore the central authority of the kingship. Nebhepetre Montuhotep ordered their bodies to be collected, shrouded and buried where he would eventually lie, thus ensuring that they would be rewarded by sharing his immortality. The names of many of them were recorded on their mummy wrappings.

H. E. Winlock, *Excavations at Deir el-Bahri, 1911–31*, New York, 1942.
——*The Slain Soldiers of Nebhepetre Montuhotep*, New York, 1945.
L. Habachi, 'King Nebhepetre Montuhotep: His Monuments, Place in History, Deification and Unusual Representation in the Form of Gods', MDAIK 19 (1963) 16–52.
D. Arnold, *The Temple of Montuhotep at Deir el-Bahri*, New York, 1979.
EMC JE 36195.

(Sa'ankhkare) Montuhotep III, Eleventh Dynasty, Middle Kingdom, *c.* 2004–1992 BC. The son of King Nebhepetre MONTUHOTEP II, Sa'ankhkare succeeded to the throne after the long reign of his father; he was already well advanced in years. He was a builder on a scale remarkable even for a Middle Kingdom ruler despite his comparatively short reign, which was otherwise peaceful and prosperous. His buildings are noticeable for the delicacy and elegance of their reliefs.

Sa'ankhkare Montuhotep was served by a number of outstanding ministers, including his Steward, Henenu, and his Chancellor, MEKETRE. The former led an expedition to open the route to the Red Sea, through the Wadi Hammamat on the king's orders. He sent a ship to Punt with goods for barter. The expedition provided access to the mines of the Wadi Hammamat, from which some of the finest and rarest stone was quarried in the following centuries.

Winlock 1947: 48–51.
CAH I.2: 488–92.
Luxor Museum: 18, fig. 12; cat. no. J 69.

Montuhotep IV, King, Eleventh Dynasty, Middle Kingdom, *c.* 1992–1984 BC. Nebtawyre Montuhotep is the last of the kings of the Eleventh Dynasty, and his exact relationship with his predecessors is not clear. He emerges quite suddenly as the successor of Sa'ankhkare MONTUHOTEP III, but his parentage is unknown, other than his mother.

He is remembered chiefly for the activities of his energetic and forceful Vizier, AMENEMHET, who recorded a journey to the quarries in the Wadi Hammamat to extract stone for a sarcophagus, to dig wells and to find a suitable location for a new port. During Amenemhet's campaign a number of prodigies appeared – a pregnant gazelle dropped her young on the block of stone which had been chosen and she was immediately sacrificed in the sight of all Amenemhet's soldiers. Then rain fell.

Such omens do not seem to have boded well for Montuhotep. He disappears, and Amenemhet the Vizier is proclaimed King of Upper and Lower Egypt, the first of the line of Twelfth Dynasty sovereigns who were to restore the ancient glory of Egypt.

Winlock 1947: 54–7.
Grimal: 158.

Montuhotep, Prince and Vizier, Twelfth Dynasty, Middle Kingdom, *c.* 1830 BC. The Middle Kingdom enthusiasm for elaborate literary expression may account for the popularity of the inscriptions which Montuhotep left, describing his life as a most active and influential member of the nobility. He lists the many offices which he held and the wide variety of the duties which he undertook for the king and for the welfare of the state and its people. Montuhotep's self-lauditory declarations were borrowed by others long after his lifetime, as late as the New Kingdom, who evidently found the adoption of his encomia fulfilling of their own needs for self-expression.

Breasted 1: §§530–4.

Montuwosre, Royal Steward, Twelfth Dynasty, Middle Kingdom, *c.* 1965–1920 BC. King SENWOSRET I caused to be set up a fine stele commemorating the life and loyal service of his Steward Montuwosre, 'to the spirit of the honoured one'. Montuwosre is unstinting in recording his virtues and the nobility of his life, in the customary manner of such dedications. He describes himself as 'rich and fortunate in luxury: I was the possessor of bulls, rich in goats, a possessor of donkeys and abounding in sheep. ... I was well provided with boats and great in vineyards'. The stele is a particularly fine piece of carving, with a portrait of Montuwosre with his children and a well provisioned feast before him, to sustain him through eternity.

Hayes 1953: 182, 290–300, fig. 195.
MMA 12.184.

Mose, Litigant, Nineteenth Dynasty, New Kingdom, *c.* 1279–1213 BC. The hearing of a case in the Temple of Ptah brought by a scribe, Mose, is important for the light which it throws on the principle of law in Egypt and on the existence of a body of law which protected even quite modest citizens from injustice, though the process of obtaining it might be long-drawn-out.

The case derived from what Mose claimed was a gift of land to an ancestor, a sea-captain, by King AHMOSE at the beginning of the Eighteenth Dynasty. The case lingered on over the generations; in King HOREMHEB's time a court was presided over by no less an official than the Vizier. This found against Mose's family, represented by his father, who died in the course of the litigation.

The defendents in the case resorted both to intimidation, forcibly evicting Mose's mother from the disputed property, and to the forgery of documents. The latter practice resulted in Mose's family once again losing their claim.

Mose was determined to persist, however, and his determination eventually resulted in a still higher court deciding in his family's favour during the reign of King RAMESSES II. The sequence of events is recorded in Mose's tomb.

Gardiner 1961: 268–9.
S. Allam, 'Some Remarks on the Trial of Mose', JEA 75 (1989) 103–12.

Mutemwiya, Queen, Eighteenth Dynasty, New Kingdom, *c.* 1400 BC. The wife of King THUTMOSE IV, Mutemwiya features in reliefs on the walls of the 'Birth Room' at Luxor, where she is shown in the company of the king whose form for the occasion has been assumed by the god Amun. The baby who will become the splendid AMENHOTEP III is fashioned by the god Khnum; he is then born to the queen in the company of rejoicing goddesses. His divine ancestry is confirmed when he is presented to Amun, his father, who kisses him affectionately.

Aldred 1988: 140–1.

[**Muwatallis**], Hittite King, (= Nineteenth Dynasty), New Kingdom, *c.* 1295–1271 BC. When King SETI I ascended the throne, he set about energetically restoring Egypt's standing in the Near East, which had been severely depleted by the episode of the Amarna period; in this he was continuing the policies of King HOREMHEB, of whom he was the effective successor. The Hittite empire was a particular threat and, after he had restored Egypt's control of its vassals in Palestine and the Levant, he turned to dealing with the Hittites. Little is known of his campaign, but both sides seem to have come out of the conflict relatively unscathed and the king of Hatti, Muwatallis, made his peace with Seti.

On King RAMESSES II's succession to his father's throne he was obliged to face a renewed threat from the Hittites. This culminated in the famous battle of Qadesh, one of the most crucial events in Ramesses' long reign. Both sides claimed victory; Muwatallis died not long afterwards and was succeeded by his illegimate son, Urhi-Teshub. His reign was marked by a continuing conflict with his uncle, HATTUSIL, who eventually deposed him, proclaiming himself king. From this point relations between Egypt and the Hittite empire greatly improved, with a close friendship between the two royal families being signalled by Ramesses' marriage to two Hittite princesses.

Kitchen 1982: 51, 56–64, 68.
Kuhrt 1995: I, 204–8, 254–63.

Mycerinos, *see* **Menkaure**

N

[Nabopolassar], King of Babylon (= Twenty-Sixth Dynasty), Late Period, *c.* 616–605 BC. The long and generally peaceful reign of King PSAMETIK I was disturbed in its later years by the rise of powers in Western Asia, notably the Assyrians, to whom at one point Psametik deferred, and later the Babylonians under the one-time king of Chaldaea, Nabopolassar. The disintegration of the Assyrian empire provided Nabopolassar with the opportunity for aggrandisement. Psametik was alarmed at this prospect and he sought to aid his one erstwhile enemy, Assyria, in resisting the Babylonian advance. The Assyrians were defeated, however, and the Egyptians were not able to halt Nabopolassar's advance. Psametik, and after his death, his son NECHO II, maintained the policy of aiding the Assyrians, though their empire was reduced to remnants of its past power. In his later years Nabopolassar devoted himself to consolidating his empire and handed much of the leadership of his armies to his son NEBUCHADREZZAR. As the old king was dying his son secured a major victory over the Egyptian forces at Carchemish.

Kitchen 1986: §§369–70.
Grimal: 358–60.

Nakht (alt. Nakhti), Chancellor, Twelfth Dynasty, Middle Kingdom, *c.* 1980 BC. Nakht was Chancellor of Egypt, probably in the Twelfth Dynasty. He was the owner of a well appointed tomb at Asiut, in Middle Egypt, which yielded a quantity of models of daily life and a particularly handsome carved wooded statue of Nakht himself.

E. Chassinat and C. Palanque, 'Une Campaigne des Fouilles dans la Nécropole d'Assiout', MIFAO 24 (1911) 78–110, pls XVI, XXI.
IFAO 1981: 106–32.
MduL E 11937.

Nakht, Gardener, Eighteenth Dynasty, New Kingdom, *c.* 1479–1425 BC. Throughout their history the Egyptians loved and cultivated flowers; gardens were places of pleasure, foreshadowing paradise. Professional gardeners were employed at the courts, by the magnates and in the temples: Nakht was 'Gardener of the Divine Offerings of Amun' in the temple of Amun at Thebes. As such he and other members of his family were responsible for the provision of flowers to decorate the temples at great festivals and also for the preparation of the bouquets which were presented to the gods, a duty shown being performed by Nakht's 'beloved son'.

L. Manniche, 'Tomb of Nakht, the Gardener, at Thebes (no. 161) as Copied by Robert Hay', JEA 72 (1986) 55–78; figs 1–13.
S. Quirke, 'The Hieratic Texts in the Tomb of Nakht the Gardener, at Thebes (no. 161) as

Copied by Robert Hay', JEA 72 (1986) 79–90; figs 1–5.

Nakht, Astronomer, Eighteenth Dynasty, New Kingdom, *c.* 1400 BC. The Egyptians were accomplished observers and recorders of the night sky and Nakht, a priest during the reign of THUTMOSE IV, was one such, part of the priesthood of Amun, trained in the observation of the stars and heavenly bodies. The knowledge obtained by the astronomers was used in establishing the calendar, in determining the seasons for planting and harvesting, and in the programming of the great temple ceremonies.

Nakht's pleasant and handsomely appointed tomb in the Theban necropolis (TT 52) contains a famous depiction of a blind harp-player and scenes of the hunt. It also features a repertory of agricultural, horticultural and viticultural activities. In Nakht's vineyard the workers pick the grapes and tread them, holding on to ropes to preserve their balance and counteract the effects of the vapours rising from the grape juice, then filling jars with the fermenting liquor from a tap in the cask in which they are treading.

N. De Garis Davis, *The Tomb of Nakht at Thebes*, New York, 1917.

Nakht, Noble, Eighteenth Dynasty, New Kingdom, *c.* 1320–1290 BC. Nakht, a Royal Scribe and Army Commander, was the possessor a particularly finely produced copy of the Book of the Dead, one of the last to be written in part on leather. One of the scenes shows Nakht and his wife Tjuiu leaving their house in the early morning and entering their garden, to greet the rising sun god Re. Osiris is also in the garden, seated on a throne, attended by the goddess Maat. Osiris' throne is set before a pool, surrounded by trees, from one corner of which a vine is growing outwards, seemingly reaching towards the god. The drawing of the papyrus is delicate and beautifully executed; the colours are fresh and subtle, less vivid than those generally favoured for funerary texts. Other expertly drawn vignettes show Nakht paddling his small skiff, harvesting flax, adoring the phoenix and making offerings to the god Thoth, who records Nakht's acts of piety.

James 1985: 52–3; ills 57–8.
BM 10471.

Nakhthorheb, Official, Twenty-Sixth Dynasty, Late Period, *c.* 590 BC. A high officer of state in the service of King PSAMETIK II and a member of a noble family of great influence, Nakhthorheb was able to employ a sculptor of considerable skill to make his funerary statue. Showing Nakhthorheb kneeling with his hands folded in front of him, it is one of the masterpieces of private sculpture of the Saitic period.

He is described as 'Prince, Count, Friend, Director of the Teams, Officer to the Crowns, Director of Every Divine Function ... Orator for the Whole Town of Pe, Responsible for the Secrets of the House of the Morning'.

He was a devotee of the god Thoth, of Hermopolis in Middle Egypt.

A.P. Zivie, *Hermopolis et le nome d'Ibis I*, Cairo 1975: 98ff.
Andreu *et al.* 1997: 185, no. 92.
MduL A94.

Nakhtmin, Prince, Eighteenth Dynasty, New Kingdom, *c.* 1390–1352 BC. The inscription identifying Nakhtmin as the son of a king is incomplete and it is not certain who his father was. It is possible that it was King AMENHOTEP III. During the king's reign he bore the title 'Commander-in-Chief of the Army'. He presumably predeceased the king.

CAH II.1: 370.

Nakhtmin (alt. Minnakht), Officer, Eighteenth Dynasty, New Kingdom, *c.* 1336–1327 BC. Nakhtmin was a serving officer in the Army who was also a significant figure at the court during the reign of TUTANKHAMUN. He presented a group of five large wooden *shabti* figures to the burial of the King. It has been suggested that he was a partisan of AY, who succeeded Tutankhamun to the throne, and that it may have been Ay's intention that Nakhtmin should in turn succeed him. In the event, Ay was followed to the throne by General HOREMHEB, and nothing further is known of Nakhtmin.

Reeves 1990a: 30.

Nakhtdjehuty, Craftsman, Nineteenth Dynasty, New Kingdom, *c.* 1279–1213 BC. Nakhtdjehuty flourished during the closing years of the long reign of King RAMESSES II, when he was Superintendent of Carpenters and Chief of Goldworkers. He specialised in the renovation of the gold inlays and the goldleaf decoration applied to high-quality woodwork in the temples, particularly the doorways and door leaves in the precinct of Amun at Karnak, in the temples of Khons and Mut (where one of his sons was a priest), and possibly the Ramesseum.

He also specialised in the embellishment of the sacred barques which were carried in the processions of the gods. He refers to the use of 'gold, silver, lapis lazuli and turquoise', in the inscription in his funerary chapel which he had built into the wall of the courtyard of the tomb of KHERUEF.

K. Kitchen, 'Nakht-Thuty – Servitor of Sacred Barques and Golden Portals', JEA 60 (1974) 168–72; figs 1, 2a, 2b.
——1982: 172.

Nar-Mer, King, Late Predynastic Period, *c.* 3100 BC. It is now generally accepted that there were men who ruled much if not all of the Valley before the First Dynasty acknowledged by MANETHO. Nar-Mer, who used to be described as the first King of Egypt, is now thought to be a late-Predynastic king, perhaps succeeding 'SCORPION' and preceeding AHA.

His name, enclosed in the *serekh*, has been found in several late-Predynastic contexts, including some inscribed on ceremonial maceheads. His tomb, a massive structure, has been identified at Abydos.

His most enduring legacy – apart, perhaps, from Egypt itself – is the great schist palette from Hierakonpolis in which he is portrayed on one face wearing the crown of Upper Egypt and on the other that of Lower Egypt. This used to be advanced as evidence that Nar-Mer was the original unifier of the country and the first acknowledged King of the Two Lands. There is, however, the suggestion that the Nar-Mer Palette is a production of a later period, a pious memorial to a respected figure of the past. Whilst there is no doubt about Nar-Mer's historical existence, it is now generally believed that the first actual ruler of a reasonably unified Egypt was AHA, probably Nar-Mer's son.

Quibell 1900: pl. XXIX.
Emery 1961; 42–7.
W. A. Fairservis Jr, 'A Revised View of the Na'rmr Palette', JARCE 28 (1991) 1–20.
Spencer: 49, 53–6, 64; ills 32, 43.
Saleh and Sourouzian: 8.
EMC JE 32169 = CG 14716.

Nashuyu, Scribe, Nineteenth Dynasty, New Kingdom, *c.* 1246 BC. The scribe Nashuyu visited the ancient necropolis at Saqqara in July 1246 BC, near the pyramid of King TETI of the Sixth Dynasty, and the Step Pyramid complex of the Third Dynasty king, DJOSER NETJERYKHET, who was evidently known in Nashuyu's time as 'Djoser-Discoverer-of-Stoneworking'. He left behind him a graffito recording his visit near the Middle Kingdom pyramid of King USERKARE KHENDJER of the Thirteenth Dynasty. He invokes the beneficence of the gods of the West of Memphis, in much the same way that the scribes HEDNAKHT and Panakht were to do sixteen years later.

Kitchen 1982: 148.

Nebamun, Physician, Eighteenth Dynasty, New Kingdom, *c.* 1427–1400 BC. Nebamun was Chief Physician to King AMENHOTEP II. His reputation was evidently international, for in his tomb at Thebes (TT 17) he records the visit of a Prince from Mesopotamia who by his dress might be Syrian or from one of Egypt's Palestinian dependencies, who consulted him about an unspecified medical condition. The prince is seated and Nebamun stands behind him. An assistant appears to be offering the prince a potion which, with a graceful gesture, he seems to be declining.

W. Wreszinski, *Atlas zur altägyptischen Kulturgeschichte*, pl. 115, Leipzig, 1923.
T. Säve-Söderbergh, *Private Tombs at Thebes*, I, pl. XXIII.
Stevenson Smith 1965: 29; pl. 41.

Nebamun, Scribe, Eighteenth Dynasty, New Kingdom, *c.* 1390–1352 BC. The owner of some of the finest paintings ever recovered from a New-Kingdom tomb is something of a mystery. He is thought to have been Nebamun, a Scribe and 'Counter of Grain', who lived during the reigns of King THUTMOSE IV and King AMENHOTEP III. The paintings were brought to Britain in the early nineteenth century, but the circumstances of their discovery and the location of the tomb from which they were taken are unknown.

The paintings relate vividly the life and pursuits of an Egyptian official, well-to-do though by no means of the highest class, during a period of the country's greatest prosperity. Nebamun and his wife and their young daughter are sailing in the marshes and to enable Nebamun to hunt birds – which he does with a throwing stick – he has the assistance of the family cat, who brings down the birds which fall prey to Nebamun. His wife, perhaps a little overdressed for a day in the marshes, stands in the stern of their light skiff looking, as well she might, distinctly uneasy.

Nebamun is also represented, with his family and friends, enjoying a party which he has hosted for them, with musicians and dancing girls. His garden has an elegantly designed pool, well stocked with fowl and fish. Other pursuits are not forgotten, for Nebamun is shown inspecting the counting of his cattle, the substance no doubt of his fortune, and conducting a census of his geese. He even shows the assessment of his wealth for the benefit of the tax collectors; these include the quite recently introduced horse, a pair of which are harnessed to a light chariot.

James 1985: 26–33; ills 25–32.
BM 37977, 37983, 37976, 37978, 37982.

Nebamun and Ipuky, Sculptors, Eighteenth Dynasty, New Kingdom, *c.* 1390–1350 BC. Nebamun and Ipuky were craftsmen-sculptors working in the royal necropolis at Thebes who prepared for themselves a tomb (TT 181), the decoration of which bears comparison with the best of the nobles' tombs nearby. The tomb contains scenes of the worship of AMENHOTEP II and his mother, Queen AHMOSE NEFERTIRY, who were honoured as patrons of the necropolis.

N. de Garis Davis, *The Tomb of Two Sculptors at Thebes*, New York, 1925.
PM I: 286–9.

Nebenkeme, Army Officer, Nineteenth Dynasty, New Kingdom, *c.* 1279–1213 BC. Nebenkeme was buried at Heracleopolis (modern Ihnasyah el-Medina) which, in the time of RAMESSES II and later, was an important garrison town. Nebenkeme was Captain of Bowmen and Fan-Bearer of the Royal Boat.

Kees 1961: 218.

Nebenmaat, Temple Official, Nineteenth/ Twentieth Dynasties, New Kingdom, *c.* 1310–1290 BC. A 'Servant in the Place of Truth', Nebenmaat, the son of Amennakht and Iymway (TT 218), was provided with a tomb at Thebes (TT 219). In it he is shown playing draughts with his wife, Meretseger.

PM I.1: 320–2.

Nebet, Queen, Sixth Dynasty, Old Kingdom, *c.* 2375–2345 BC. Nebet was the principal wife of King UNAS. She was buried near her husband in a large and elaborate tomb, with a row of two-storied store rooms and a commodious vestibule with large-scale reliefs. These include a portrait of the queen, seated on her throne.

CAH I.2: 188.
Lauer 1976: 146.

Nebetka, Noble, First Dynasty, Archaic Period, *c.* 2925 BC. A high official in the reign of King ANEDJIB, Nebetka was the owner of mastaba tomb no. 3038 at Saqqara. Its interior contains an early example of the stepped structure which was to reach its climax in DJOSER NETJERYKHET's pyramid complex, several hundred years later.

Emery 1949: 82–94.

Nebhepetre Montuhotep, *see* **Montuhotep II**

Nebipusenwosret, Courtier, Twelfth Dynasty, Middle Kingdom, *c.* 1860 BC. Nebipusenwosret, whose name incorporates that of the King SENWOSRET III, was attached to the royal court. However, he wished to participate in the festivals of Osiris and Wepwawet which were held at Abydos. As was frequently the case with such journeys, as much spiritual as real, it seems that he never reached Abydos in person, but sent a fine limestone stela in his stead, in the charge of one of his colleagues, the priest Ibi.

The stela contains a long description of Nebipusenwosret's duties at the court, in which he is impressively described as 'Keeper of the Diadem' and Priest of the Royal Toilet.

Parkinson 1991: 139–42.

Nebit(ef), Chief of Police, Thirteenth Dynasty, Middle Kingdom, *c.* 1780 BC. Nebit was Chief of Police in the early part of the Thirteenth Dynasty, when the central administration was undergoing one of its periods of crisis at the end of the Middle Kingdom. Nebit is represented as a man of severe countenance, appropriate perhaps to his profession. His statue was found in the mastaba of ISI, a celebrated official and sage of the late Old Kingdom who was honoured as a god in Edfu. His mastaba tomb became a place of worship in the Middle Kingdom.

M. Alliot, *Rapport des Fouilles de Tell Edfou*, IFAO t.X. 2e partie, Cairo, 1935: 15.
J. Vandier, 'La Statuaire', *Manuel d'Archeologie Égyptienne*, t. III, Paris, 1957: 279, fig. XCIV-3.
IFAO 212.
MduL E 14330.

Nebka, *see* **Sanakhte**

Nebkheperre Inyotef, *see* **Inyotef VII**

Nebmakhet, Prince, Fourth Dynasty, Old Kingdom, *c.* 2558–2532 BC. Nebmakhet was the son of King KHAFRE and his principal wife, Queen MERESANKH III. He died before his father and was buried in a large mastaba tomb, befitting a prince of his status. The tomb is notable for a number of considerations, several of which throw light on the character of the prince himself.

Much of the decoration of Nebmakhet's tomb anticipates themes which are to become commonplace in the embellishment of the tombs of the magnates of the Old Kingdom; a number of them appear here for the first time.

The tomb's reliefs shown the interests and pastimes which the prince enjoyed during his life and which he was disposed to continue in the afterlife. Trapping birds in the marshes, cattle crossing water, craftsmen at work at their trades, young animals being suckled and a reluctant bull being slaughtered – all these show the prince following the way of life to which all well-to-do Egyptians in the Old Kingdom aspired. He enjoys his own funerary meal and is seated in a pavilion being entertained by musicians as he watches a performance by dancers, who are rewarded with gold ornaments.

From an inscription in the tomb it appears that Semer-ka, a painter, designed it as a gift to the prince and that INKAF, the sculptor, supervised its construction and decoration, also as a gift to Nebmakhet. It is possible that Inkaf is the same sculptor who worked on the decoration of the tomb of Queen Meresankh.

Nebmakhet was provided with a second tomb, to the west of his father's pyramid.

Stevenson Smith 1946 (1949): 42, 166, 169–71, 178, 296, 352–3, 358, 360; fig. 68.

Nebmertuef, Royal Scribe, Eighteenth Dynasty, New Kingdom, *c.* 1391–1353 BC. An important functionary during the reign of King AMENHOTEP III, Nebmertuef is known from reliefs in which he is shown participating in rituals in close association with the king. He is particularly celebrated, however, for two statuettes, one in schist, the other in alabaster, in which he is represented in his scribal function, sitting cross-legged and taking down the words of his divine patron and protector, the god Thoth in the form of a cynocephalous baboon. The god is dictating to Nebmertuef a summary of the principles which should govern service to the king, so that all of his servants should know their duties.

G. Bénédite, 'Scribe et babouin, au sujet de deux petits groupes de sculpture exposée au Musée du Louvre', *Monuments Piot* 1911 t. XIX: 3–42; pls I, II.

Nebnakhtu, Priest, Eighteenth Dynasty, New Kingdom, *c.* 1550 BC. One of a family of priests resident in Heracleopolis, Nebnakhtu was attached to the temple consecrated to the ram god Heryshef (Gk. Harsaphes), the patron of the city. He was also priest of Sekhmet, a divinity particularly concerned with healing, a royal scribe, and the Overseer of Cattle.

His wife was the daughter of SENNEFER, the High Priest of Heliopolis, and hence a very great man. He is recorded in Nebnakhtu's tomb together with his parents and his son, Amenhotep, who also followed the family profession of priestly duties.

W. M. F. Petrie, G. Brunton, *Sedment II*, London, 1924: 23–4, pls 49, 50.
EMC JE 46993.
Saleh and Sourouzian: 128.

Nebneteru, High Priest, Nineteenth Dynasty, New Kingdom, *c.* 1320–1290 BC. Nebenteru was High Priest of Amun in Thebes in the reign of King SETI I, having been appointed to his office at the end of the preceding Eighteenth Dynasty. He was an aristocrat by birth, said to be a descendant of the Heracleopolitan nomarchs who became kings in the Ninth and Tenth Dynasties. His son was the Vizier PASER; his wife, Meritre, was Chief of the Harem of Amun at Karnak.

Lefebvre 1929: 115–17, 246–7.

Nebneteru, Royal Scribe, Twenty-Second Dynasty, Third Intermediate Period, *c.* 874–850 BC. Nebneteru was a member of an important Theban family, with connections with the royal family. A contemporary of King OSORKON II, he was a 'Royal Secretary', with a number of other high-ranking appointments. He was the son of the Southern Vizier Neseramun, who was himself the son of Nebneteru, a Royal Scribe who became High Priest of Montu. Neseramun named his own son Nebneteru, after his father. Nebneteru the Younger records with satisfaction that he enjoyed a long and well fulfilled life – he lived to ninety-six – and urges all those who read his inscriptions to enjoy life to the full whilst they are able to do so.

Kitchen 1986: §§177–8, §266.
Lichtheim 3: 18–24.

Nebre, Draughtsman, Nineteenth/Twentieth Dynasties, New Kingdom, *c.* 1295–1186/1069 BC. Nebre was an artist, his official designation 'Outline Scribe'. He was responsible for providing the drawings for reliefs or the hand-drawn hieroglyphs for inscriptions. He would have been crucial in determining the design and proportions of the finished work. When his task was completed the craftsman who carried out the actual carving of the relief or inscription would cut it out, and a third practitioner would apply the paint.

James 1985: 8–9; fig. 5.
Lichtheim 2: 105–7.
BM 2292.

Nebt, Princess, Eleventh Dynasty, Middle Kingdom, *c.* 2050 BC. A noblewoman of considerable authority and status, Nebt was the heiress of estates on Elephantine Island, at Aswan in the far south of Egypt. She was a patroness of the arts and maintained a band of scholars in her service. Her daughter, who shared her interests and who established an important collection of works of art, was one of the wives of King Nebhepetre MONTUHOTEP II.

[**Nebuchadrezzar II**], King of Babylonia (= Twenty-Sixth Dynasty), Late Period, 605–562 BC. The son of King NABOPOLASSAR of Babylon, Nebuchadrezzar was his father's Crown Prince, and in the latter part of his reign was given responsibility for Babylon's military campaigns. As his father lay dying, Nebuchadrezzar captured the strategically important city of Carchemish, where the Egyptian forces were spending the winter, during their attempts to secure their possessions in Syria. He pursued the Egyptians as they hastened back to their own territory and inflicted heavy losses on them.

Nabopolassar's death meant that Nebuchadrezzar had to return hastily to Babylon, where he was proclaimed king in 605 BC. The King of Egypt, NECHO II, dealt circumspectly with the Babylonians and managed to contain their threat of incursions on the eastern frontier. However, Nebuchadrezzar famously menaced Egypt's hold over Palestine by the capture of Jerusalem in 597 BC, which was followed by its sack in 587–6 BC

Nebuchadrezzar's long reign coincided with the kingships of NECHO II, PSAMETIK II, APRIES (who withdrew from Jerusalem, leaving it to be sacked by the Babylonians) and AMASIS.

Nebuchadrezzar was a man of considerable culture, and has earned a reputation as an early conservator of the past of his country. He died in 562 BC and was succeeded by his son Nabonidus, who was the last king of Babylon, eventually to be defeated by the Persians, who were emerging, to Egypt's misfortune as well, as the dominant power in the Near East.

Kitchen 1982: §§369–70.
Grimal: 359–60.

Nebunenef, High Priest, Nineteenth Dynasty, New Kingdom, *c.* 1279–8 BC. In the first year of his reign, King RAMESSES II paid a formal visit to Thebes to attend the festival of Opet, one of the most important in the ecclesiastical calendar of the South. On his way from the North, which his family seem always to have preferred, he stopped at the holy city of Abydos. There he met, no doubt among other dignitaries, Nebunenef, the High Priest of Osiris at nearby This.

In Thebes, Ramesses was angered by the dilapidated state of many of the temples and the lack of completion of some of the monuments of King SETI I, his recently deceased father. He appointed Nebunenef to the great office of High Priest of Amun, presumably having been impressed by him and believing him to have the energy and will to restore Thebes' ancient authority as the Kingdom's principal religious centre.

Hayes 2: 346 (as Nebwenenef).
Kees 1961: 279.
CAH II.2: 225.

Necho I, King, Twenty-Sixth Dynasty, Late Period, 672–664 BC. The ruler of the city of Sais at the time when Egypt was being harried by the Assyrians and the country had fragmented into many small, competing statelets, Necho came to an understanding with the invaders and as a result substantially improved the influence and prosperity of his state, which incorporated the Western Delta and lands around Heliopolis and Memphis. In subsequent reigns, Sais was to achieve great prosperity and give rise to the archaicising style of late Egyptian art which is identified with it.

Necho was killed by the Kushite king, TANUTAMANI, who invaded Egypt in an attempt to reimpose Nubian rule over the country. He in turn was driven out by the Assyrians, who installed Necho's son, PSAMETIK I, as king.

Kitchen 1986: §116, §117, §118, §124.

Necho II, King, Twenty-Sixth Dynasty, Late Period, 610–595 BC. After the half-century during which Egypt was ruled by his father, PSAMETIK I, Necho inherited a prosperous and stable kingdom. He turned his mind to the expansion of Egypt's interests and influence abroad, seeking, in true Saite fashion, to return to the days of the country's ancient dignity as the greatest power in the Near East. He entered Syria-Palestine and killed the king of Judah; Jerusalem then paid tribute to Egypt.

Necho, unusually for an Egyptian king, was an enthusiastic protagonist of maritime power. He developed Egypt's navy and made it a considerable factor in the Eastern Mediterranean's trading networks. It is said that in his reign Egyptian seamen circumnavigated Africa, which, if true, was a considerable achievement for the time.

J. Yoyotte, 'Néchao', *Supplément au Dictionnaire de la Bible, VI*, Paris, 1960: 363–94.
Grimal: 145–6, 359–61.

Nectanebo I (Nakhtnebef), King, Thirtieth Dynasty, Late Period, 380–362 BC. In one of the typically troubled times in the terminal centuries of Egypt's history a ruler of the relatively small kingdom of Sebennytos, Nectanebo, son of Teos, was declared King of Egypt. He founded the Thirtieth Dynasty, which was to prove to be the last native Egyptian family of kings.

Nectanebo was opposed by the formidable might of the Persian Empire, which employed Greek mercenaries, always skilled and tenacious soldiers, in its army. However, when in 373 BC the Persians and their allies attacked Egypt, Nectanebo, against all the odds, repelled them.

Nectanebo's reign was the final moment of Egypt's creative existence. He was responsible for an upsurge in the arts and in building; many of his works survive. He was succeeded by his son, TEOS.

Grimal: 375–81.

Nectanebo II (Nakhtharheb), King, Thirtieth Dynasty, Late Period, 360–343 BC. After deposing King TEOS, Nectanebo II, the great-grandson of NECTANEBO I, ruled for eighteen years, during a time when the Persian Empire was beginning to disintegrate. His policies in the management of Egypt brought back prosperity to the country, once again signalled by much increased building programmes, particularly of the temples. The priests extended their wealth and power greatly.

ARTAXERXES III, the Persian Great King, attacked Egypt in 351–350 BC but was roundly defeated by Nectanebo. Artaxerxes returned to the attack in 343 BC, this time assisted by Greek mercenaries, whose generals were the leading stategists of the day. Nectanebo fought valiantly but was outnumbered by a more enterprising enemy. Eventually he recognised that he was defeated, and the last native king of Egypt fled southwards into Nubia taking, it was alleged, much of the royal treasure with him.

Nectanebo disappears at this point, though he may have continued some sort of independent status in Nubia for a while. The shadowy rebel leader, KHABABASH, may have supported him before himself being proclaimed king for a brief period.

One final legend clings to Nectanebo's name. According to some ancient sources it was believed that he was the true father of ALEXANDER THE GREAT, having visited OLYMPIAS, Alexander's mother, during one of PHILIP II's frequent absences; both Olympias and Alexander preferred to claim Amun as Alexander's father. However, the precedent of Amun having adopted the person, the king, as witnessed by his assumption of the physical form of King THUTMOSE II to engender AMENHOTEP III, should not be forgotten.

Grimal: 375–81.

Nefaarud I (alt. Nepherites), King, Twenty-Ninth Dynasty, Late Period, 399–393 BC. Nefaarud became king after the death of AMYRTAEUS, though the manner of his succession is obscure; one story has it that Nefaarud executed Amyrtaeus after defeating him in battle. He moved the capital to Mendes, from which city his family presumably originated. He attempted to identify his rule with the Saitic kings, and like them he built extensively, especially in northern Egypt.

Grimal: 372–3.

Nefer, Official, Fifth Dynasty, Old Kingdom, *c.* 2400 BC. Nefer was the eldest son of KAHAY, a singer in the royal court who attracted the attention of the king who, to show him favour, had his son educated with the young princes. This had the effect of placing Nefer most advantageously for the advancement of his career.

Nefer came from a family of musicians and inherited many of his father's duties in directing the music for the court ceremonies. In addition he was appointed to high offices in the service of the royal administration. These included 'Controller of the Singers' and 'Inspector of the Great House and the Artisans' Workshop', and Nefer was also honoured with the title 'Keeper of the Secrets of the King'. The ultimate mark of favour shown to him by the king, probably NIUSERRE, with whom he had grown up, was the provision of a fine rock-cut tomb for himself and his family at Saqqara.

The tomb is a delightful compendium of the pleasures of the lifestyle of a well placed Egyptian of the late Old Kingdom, of which there can have been few more favoured existences. In the cheerfully decorated chambers Nefer and the members of his family are shown enjoying country pursuits on their farm in Upper Egypt, being entertained, appropriately enough, by a small orchestra and with their family pets, including their dog, an Egyptian hound, and a handsome baboon which assists with the wine-harvest and directs the sailors loading Nefer's boat.

Nefer probably died *c.* 2400 BC. Since his tomb was not one of the first importance it was buried during the building of the Causeway for King UNAS' pyramid, thus resulting in its preservation until modern times. Various members of his family were buried in the tomb, which contains one of the oldest and best preserved mummies in Egypt.

A. M. Moussa and H. Altenmüller, *The Tomb of Nefer and Ka-Hay*, Mainz-am-Rhein, 1971.

Neferabu, Temple Draughtsman, Nineteenth Dynasty, New Kingdom, *c.* 1295–1186 BC. Neferabu was an employee in the 'Place of Truth' in the necropolis of Deir el-Medina. He records his distress that, for swearing falsely in the name of the god Ptah, he was struck blind. 'Beware of Ptah', he urges those who visit his otherwise pleasant and well appointed tomb.

He also apparently fell foul of the goddess Meretseger ('She who loves Silence'), whom he thanks for restoring his health after some unnamed transgression against 'The Peak', the pyramidal-shaped mountain, sacred to the goddess, which stood above the necropolis.

Lichtheim 2: 107–10.

Neferamun, Pageant Master, Eighteenth Dynasty, New Kingdom, *c.* 1350 BC. Neferamun flourished during the latter part of the Eighteenth Dynasty, on the evidence of his funerary monuments; no king's name appears on them to determine during which reign he lived. He bore two unusual titles, indicating his fields of responsibility: by the first he was designated 'Governor of the River' (the river, of course, being the Nile). This title reveals that he was what might be termed 'the River Pageant Master', in charge of the festivals of the gods which were held on the water; one such was the annual journey which the god Amun made from his principal shrine at Karnak.

Neferamun was also 'Chief of the *megas* of His Majesty with the children of the *kap*'. The word *megas* may be Nubian and probably applies to young soldiers (cadets?) recruited from Nubia and educated with Egyptian nobles in the *kap*, the 'nursery' as it was regarded, which trained young men of good family from Egypt's dominions who could return to their homelands as administrators or army officers.

Musée Calvet: §§41–4, fig. 12.

Neferefre (alt. Raneferef), King, Fifth Dynasty, Old Kingdom, *c.* 2448–2445 BC. This king was little known until the excavations at Abusir revealed that, although he died young, he enjoyed a relatively rich and prosperous reign. His pyramid was, however, never finished, although the excavations of the site produced an important cache of papyrus documents, which appear to include records of royal decrees.

Neferefre was served by a remarkable Vizier, PTAHSHEPSES, who was also buried at Abusir, in a mastaba tomb containing much lively relief carving.

M. Verner, 'Excavations at Abousir, Season 1982 – Preliminary Report: The Pyramid Temple of Raneferef', ZÄS III: 70–8.
Verner 1994, especially Ch. 5.
Lehner 1997: 146–8.
Saleh and Sourouzian: 38.
EMC JE 98171.

Neferherenptah, Official, Fifth Dynasty, Old Kingdom, *c.* 2380 BC. Neferherenptah died shortly before the accession of King UNAS. He was a 'Royal Acquaintance', 'Inspector of Artisans' and 'Overseer of the Carpenters'. When work began on the king's pyramid and the causeway leading to it, Neferherenptah's tomb was incomplete. It contains, however, drawings which, had they been carved as reliefs, would have been of exceptional quality. They show the tomb owner hunting, observing birdlife, enjoying his garden, watching the harvest and the vintage.

A. M. Abu-Bakr, *Excavations at Giza, 1949–50*, Cairo, 1953: 121–4; pl. LXVIb.

Neferherenptah, called Fifi, Priest, Fifth/Sixth Dynasties, Old Kingdom, *c.* 2345 BC. Neferherenptah was a purification priest and prophet of the mortuary cults of the kings KHAFRE and MENKAURE. He was thus of considerable influence in Giza, where he was buried in his own mastaba.

His tomb contained statues, rather simple in character and now in the Cairo Museum, of himself, of his wife, 'the Royal Acquaintance' Sat-Meret; his son Tesen, a butcher in the palace slaughter-house; and his daughter Meretites.

S. Hassan, *Excavations at Giza V, 1933–4*, Cairo, 1944: 279–87, figs 143–50.
EMC JE 87804, 87806, 87805, 87807.

Neferheteperes, Princess (Queen?), Fourth Dynasty, Old Kingdom, *c.* 2566–2558 BC. Neferheteperes was the daughter of King DJEDEFRE, the successor of King KHNUM-KHUFU. It has been speculated that she was also a queen, the mother of King USERKAF, the founder of the Fifth Dynasty, whose mother bore the same name. If this were the case, she would be especially significant in the promotion of the solar religion, which became markedly more important in the Fifth Dynasty under the influence of the priests of Heliopolis. A story, current in the late Old Kingdom, attributed the paternity of the first kings of the Fifth Dynasty to the god Ra by a mortal woman, Radjedet.

Part of a statue of Neferheteperes was found at Abu Roash.

Chassinat, *Monuments Piot XXV, 1921–2*, 67–8, pl. X.
IFAO 56.
MduL E 12628.

Neferhotep, Harpist, Twelfth Dynasty, Middle Kingdom, *c.* 1850 BC. Neferhotep was a harpist employed in the household of Iky, the Overseer of Priests at Abydos. He was grossly overweight; in one of his two surviving stelae, which were allowed to be placed in Iky's cenotaph, he is shown reaching forward, in gluttonous anticipation, for the great pile of fruits, meat and sweetmeats which have been provided for his afterlife.

He has a second stela which gives an insight into the course of a humble Egyptian's life around the beginning of the second millennium BC. Neferhotep was provided with the stela, which calls on the gods to be merciful to him, by 'his beloved friend, the Carrier of Bricks, Nebsumenu'. The stela itself has been carved, not especially skilfully, by 'The Draughtsman Rensonb's son Sonbau'.

Neferhotep is depicted playing for the pleasure of his employer and his wife on their funerary stela. The offerings piled before them must have been a sore temptation.

W. A. Ward, 'Neferhotep and his Friends: A Glimpse of the Life of Ordinary Men', JEA 63 (1967) 63–6.
Parkinson 1991: 'A Monument for a Favourite Harpist', 114–16.
W. K. Simpson, *The Terrace of the Great God at Abydos: The Offering Chapels of Dynasties 12 and 13*, Pennsylvania, 1974: pl. 84.
Rijksmuseum van Oudheden, Leiden.

Neferhotep I, King, Thirteenth Dynasty, Middle Kingdom, *c.* 1740 BC. One of the marginally more successful and longer-lasting of the Thirteenth Dynasty rulers, Neferhotep reigned for about nine years and built a pyramid for himself at El-Lisht. He may not have been of the royal line but he attracted the respect of succeeding generations. Despite the uncertainties of the times, Neferhotep maintained contact with the Lebanon and Nubia, two poles of the Egyptian trading and diplomatic network. He paid special attention to the cult of Osiris at Abydos, where he himself directed the ceremonies and sacred plays in honour of the god at the festivals which were important features of the religious round in Abydos.

He was particularly concerned to ensure that the religious ceremonies followed the correct form, 'as instructed by the gods at the beginning of time'.

Breasted 1: 332–7.

M. De Wachter, 'Le Roi Sahathor et La famille de Neferhotep 1er', R d'E 28 (1976) 66–73.
Grimal: 184–5, 188.
Ryholt 1997: 226–8.

Neferhotep, Temple Official, Eighteenth Dynasty, New Kingdom, *c.* 1327–1323 BC. Neferhotep was the incumbent of the important office of Chief Scribe of Amun at Thebes during the reign of King AY. He was buried at Thebes (TT 49) and his tomb displays a number of episodes in his life which are of some interest. He is portrayed being presented with a bouquet of flowers in the porch of the Temple of Amun and subsequently offering the bouquet to his wife in their garden.

Neferhotep seems to have been close to the royal family and records the king presenting him with gold from the 'Window of Appearances' of the palace; similarly his wife is presented with jewellery by the queen in her garden.

Gardens evidently appealed to Neferhotep, and several incidents in the tomb record his pleasure in them. One scene shows an employee of Neferhotep using a *shaduf*, the first occasion in which this device for raising water to irrigate a planted area appears in Egyptian art.

Wilkinson 1998: 32, 124, 131–3; figs 61, 66–8.

Neferhotep, Priest, Eighteenth Dynasty, New Kingdom, *c.* 1300 BC. A contemporary of King HOREMHEB, Neferhotep was a priest of the Temple of Amun in Thebes. His tomb (TT 50) contains an example of a 'Harper's Song', a literary genre of which there are a number of surviving examples. The harpist-singer, presumably of Neferhotep's household, is unnamed. His song is rather sceptical in attitude, suggesting that life is a dream.

Lichtheim 2: 115–16.

Neferhotep, Royal Scribe, Nineteenth Dynasty, New Kingdom, *c.* 1279–1213 BC. An official employed in the main royal palace at Memphis in the reign of King RAMESSES II, Neferhotep was responsible for the care of the decanters and goblets made of precious metal used at the royal table.

D. A. Lowie, 'A Nineteenth Dynasty Stela in the Louvre', in Ruffle *et al.* 1979: 50–4.

Neferibre Psametik II, *see* **Psametik II Neferibre**

Neferibrenofer, Noble, Twenty-Sixth Dynasty, Late Period, *c.* 595–589 BC. A high official in the reign of King PSAMETIK II, Neferibrenofer, in addition to bearing the customary honorifics of 'Prince', 'Count' and 'Seal-Bearer', was also tutor and guardian to the king. He also supervised various of the king's building projects, including the construction of temples in the capital, Sais.

Breasted 4: §§981–3.
A. B. Lloyd, 'The Late Period', in Trigger *et al.* 1983: 292.

Neferirkare (alt. Kakai), King, Fifth Dynasty, Old Kingdom, *c.* 2475–2455 BC. Neferirkare was the brother of King SAHURE, the founder of the Fifth Dynasty, and succeeded him on the throne. Their mother was Queen KHENTKAWES.

Neferirkare is recalled in anecdotes which show him in a kindly light. A priest attending the king in a temple ceremony was accidentally struck by him. Such an event might have seemed ill-omened but the king hastened to assure him that, if anything, it must be thought of as an honour.

Another notable occasion was when the Vizier WESHPTAH had what was probably a stroke and collapsed in the king's presence. The king sent for his own physicians to attend him but the vizier died.

The High Priest of Memphis, PTAHSHEPSES, recorded that Neferirkare showed him so much favour that he was permitted to kiss the royal foot rather than the ground before the king.

Neferirkare's mortuary temple at Abusir contained an important cache of hieratic papyri which throws light on the royal funerary cult; they comprise the reigns of DJEDKARE ISESI to PEPY II.

L. Borchardt, *Das Grabdenkmal das Königs Nefer-ir-ka-re*, Leipzig, 1907.
P. Posener-Kriéger, *Les Archives du Temple Funéraire de Neferirkare (Les Papyrus d'Abousir)*, 2 vols, Cairo, 1976.
Stevenson Smith 1971: 183–4, 201, 204.

Neferkahor, King, Eighth Dynasty, First Intermediate Period, *c.* 2180–2170 BC. Although the central authority of the kings had broken down in the immediate aftermath of the end of the Sixth Dynasty, some of the forms were still maintained. Neferkahor, an early monarch of the Eighth Dynasty, and marginally less transient than his fellow kings in the dynasty in that a fourth year of his reign is recorded, issued a series of decrees directing the Governor of Upper Egypt, Shemay, in the manner of offerings to be made in the temples in the South, on the occasion of the king's accession. He also decreed the titles to be given to his daughter, Nebyet, who was married to Shemay.

Another of Neferkahor's decrees appoined Idu, Shemay's son, to his father's office.

Hayes 1: 137; fig. 80.
MMA 14.7.11.

Neferkare (Sixth Dynasty), *see* **Pepy II**

Neferkare, King, Tenth Dynasty, First Intermediate Period, *c.* 2130 BC. In the confused times which prevailed in Egypt towards the end of the Tenth Dynasty, Neferkare seems to have been able to impose some sort of control over much of the north of the country and perhaps over parts of the south, too. ANKHTIFY, the nomarch of Hierakonpolis, was an adherent of Neferkare's.

CAH I.2: 464, 474.

Nefermaat, Prince, Fourth Dynasty, Old Kingdom, *c.* 2613–2589 BC. The Egyptian genius for innovation and technical experiment is well demonstrated by the tomb of Prince Nefermaat, a very great personage of the early Fourth Dynasty who was Vizier to King SNEFERU; he bore the title 'Great Son of the King'. In his mastaba tomb at Meidum lively scenes of life on his estates are depicted in a technique of coloured pastes inlaid into hollowed-out bas-reliefs, which is said to have been developed by the prince himself. Unfortunately the exceptionally dry climate of Egypt meant that the inlays became desiccated and crumbled; the original effect, however, must have been striking.

Nefermaat also had at his disposal the finest painters of his day. His tomb, and that of his wife ATET, are famous for the wonderful paintings which decorated them. These include the famous geese (from Atet's tomb), sequences of bird-trapping, and an antelope being led by a handler. There are also engaging scenes of the sons of Nefermaat and Atet playing with their household pets, monkeys, geese and dogs.

Nefermaat was a partisan of Prince KHAFRE and was one of those senior members of the royal family who ensured his eventual succession to the kingship. One of his sons was HEMIONU, the Vizier, who is credited with the direction of the construction of King KHNUM-KHUFU'S Great Pyramid.

W. M. F. Petrie, *Meidum*, London, 1892.
EMC JE 43809. JE 34571 = CG 1742.
Saleh and Sourouzian: 25a, 25b.
BM 69014/5.

Neferneferuaten, Queen, King, Princess, Eighteenth Dynasty, New Kingdom, *c.* 1350–1336 BC. The principal wife of

AMENHOTEP IV-AKHENATEN, NEFERTITI was also known by the name Neferneferuaten. On her death or eclipse in the latter part of the king's reign the name seems to have been transferred to his eventual if brief successor, King SMENKHKARE. A daughter of Akhenaten and Nefertiti was also called Neferneferuaten-ta-sherit.

Aldred 1988: 227–9.
Redford 1984: 149.
J. R. Harris, 'Nefernefruaten', GM 4 (1973) 15–18.
——'Nefernefruaten Regnans', Ac Or 36: 11–21.

Neferronpet, Vizier, Nineteenth Dynasty, New Kingdom, *c.* 1225 BC. During the last years of the reign of King RAMESSES II his son and ultimate heir, MERENPTAH, was effectively regent, ruling Egypt in his father's name. He was assisted by a number of able advisers of whom Neferronpet, the Theban Vizier, was the most senior. In token of his standing he was permitted to proclaim the later jubilees of the old king, a considerable honour.

Neferronpet was the last official to bear the title of Theban Vizier.

Kitchen 1982: 112, 182, 206.

Neferseshemseshat, Prince, Vizier, Fifth/Sixth Dynasties, Old Kingdom, *c.* 2375–2345 BC. One of a group of princes who occupied offices of differing status who were buried at Saqqara, Neferseshemseshat seems to have been one of the more important; he held the office of Vizier and was Overseer of the King's Works. He was represented among the portraits of King UNAS' courtiers in the reliefs carved on the walls of the causeway leading to his pyramid.

K. Baer, *Rank and Title in the Old Kingdom*, Chicago IL, 1960: no. 275.
H. Gauthier, *Le Livre des Rois d'Égypte, vol. 1: Des Origines à la Fin de la XIIe Dynastie*, Cairo, 1907: 198.

Nefertari, Queen, Nineteenth Dynasty, New Kingdom, *c.* 1279–1250 BC. The first and most favoured wife of King RAMESSES II, Nefertari was honoured by him with her own temple at Abu Simbel, next to the great temple which he consecrated to himself and to Amun, Ptah and Ra-Horakhty. The queen was identified with the goddess Hathor and one scene in the temple shows her coronation, attended by ministering goddesses. She was the mother of several of Ramesses' elder children; however, they seem all to have predeceased him.

She was given a large and beautifully decorated rock-cut tomb in the Valley of the Queens, the fine paintings of which have now largely been restored.

C. Desroches Noblecourt and C. Kuentz, *Le Petit Temple d'Abou Simbel*, 2 vols, Cairo, 1968.
M. A. Corzo and M. Afshar (eds) *Art and Eternity: The Nefertari Wall Paintings Conservation Project*.

Nefertiabet, Princess, Fourth Dynasty, Old Kingdom, *c.* 2589–2566 BC. This princess, a contemporary of King KHNUM-KHUFU, was buried in a mastaba at Giza, amongst the other members of the royal family. She was provided with a beautifully designed and carved stela, now in the Musée du Louvre, which displays all the offerings which she wished to ensure would be provided for her in the afterlife.

H. Junker, *Giza, I–XII, Vienna and Leipzig, 1929–55*, vol. I, Vienna, 1929.
Reisner 1942: pls 19, 39, 57.
Stevenson Smith 1946 (1949): 160, 302.
MduL E 22745.

Nefertiry, *see* **Ahmose Nefertiry**

Nefertiti, Queen, Eighteenth Dynasty, New Kingdom, *c.* 1352–?1340 BC. Possibly the daughter of the courtier AY, brother of Queen TIY, Nefertiti was married to King AMENHOTEP IV-AKHENATEN and bore him six daughters. She was closely involved with her husband's royal duties, seeming to share them in a public fashion unusual in Egypt. She was depicted in various stages of *deshabillé* with the king and her children and, more formally attired, participating in the ceremonies which concerned the cult of the Aten, of which she appears to have been a keen protagonist. She was also shown, even more unusually, in the act of smiting Egypt's enemies.

Nefertiti is renowned as one of the supreme examples of beauty, from any culture in any time. Her painted portrait bust is one of the acknowledged masterpieces of Egyptian, or indeed any, art. It was probably executed by the sculptor THUTMOSE, who succeeded BEK in the position of Chief Sculptor to the king.

Nefertiti was very much part of the public face of the Amarna episode; it is the more remarkable therefore that after the fourteenth year of Akhenaten's reign she is heard of no more. Some of her titles seem to have been conferred on Prince, later briefly King, SMENKHKARE. (See NEFERNEFERUATEN.)

R. Anthes, *Die Büste des Köningin Nofretete*, Berlin, 1953.
D. Radford, *Akhenaten the Heretic King*, Princeton NJ, 1984.
J. Sampson, *Nefertiti and Cleopatra, Great Monarchs of Ancient Egypt*, London, 1985.
Aldred 1988: 196.
EMB 21300, cat. no. 50.

Neferty, Priest and Sage, Twelfth Dynasty, Middle Kingdom, *c.* 1980 BC. A priest of the temple at Bubastis, Neferty – who has been somewhat harshly described as 'the propagandist and pseudo-prophet' (CAH) – was recruited to his service by King AMENEMHET I, who had recently assumed the kingship. Neferty most fortunately discovered a prophecy which foretold the accession of a king from the Southland who could only be Amenemhet. The prophecy was said to have been derived from the reign of the revered founder of the Fourth Dynasty, SNEFERU. The only surviving copy is P. Leningrad 1116 B, of Eighteenth Dynasty date.

Amenemhet is known to have extended the temple at Bubastis, an action which may have been intended to provide Neferty with a reward for all eternity.

CAH I.2: 495.
ANET: 444–6.
H. Goedicke, *The Prophecy of Neferty*, Baltimore MD, 1977.
Lichtheim 1: 139–45.

Neferu I, Queen, Eleventh Dynasty, First Intermediate Period, *c.* 2125 BC. The mother of King INYOTEF II WAHANKH, whom she bore to MONTUHOTEP I, Neferu was greatly honoured by her son, who ensured that her name was perpetuated in many of his inscriptions.

P. E. Newberry, 'On the Parentage of the Intef Kings of the Eleventh Dynasty', ZÄS 72 (1936) 118–20.
L. Habachi, 'God's Fathers and the Role they Played in the History of the First Intermediate Period', ASAE 55 (1958) 167–90.

Neferu II, Queen, Eleventh Dynasty, First Intermediate Period, *c.* 2063–2055 BC. Neferu II was the mother of INYOTEF III, the successor of INYOTEF II, who reigned only briefly.

Winlock 1947: 44.

Neferu III, Queen, Eleventh Dynasty, Middle Kingdom, *c.* 2055–2004 BC. Neferu III was a wife of King Nebhepetre MONTUHOTEP II and the mother of King Sa'ankhkare MONTUHOTEP III. She was given a large and imposing tomb near that of her husband at Deir el-Bahri. Like her colleague KAWIT, she was evidently much concerned with her appearance and she had the foresight to depict at least two of her hairdressers on the reliefs in her tomb. In earlier times, in the First Dynasty, they would no doubt have been sacrificed to join her on her death.

Winlock 1947: 24, 27.

Neferuptah, Princess, Twelfth Dynasty, Middle Kingdom, *c.* 1855–1808 BC. Neferuptah was the daughter of King AMENEMHET III and like many of the princesses of the Twelfth Dynasty was well endowed with jewellery and offerings for her burial. It was intended that she should be buried with her father, but for an unknown reason she was in fact buried some two kilometres away.

Grimal: 179.
Edwards 1993: 223–6.

Neferure, Princess, Eighteenth Dynasty, New Kingdom, *c.* 1492–1470 BC. Neferure was the daughter of King THUTMOSE II and Queen HATSHEPSUT. After her father's death and her mother's assumption of the kingly titles and authority, Neferure, still a child, is often portrayed in scenes of an almost familial intimacy with the Queen's minister and close associate, SENENMUT, to the extent that some commentators have speculated about Neferure's paternity. Senenmut was the princess's tutor, in which responsibility he was succeeded by his brother SENIMEN.

Neferure appears during her mother's reign officiating as 'God's Wife of Amun', an anomaly occasioned by Hatshepsut's assumption of kingly status, which prevented her from assuming the office herself.

It appears that Neferure was married to the young King THUTMOSE III, despite his apparent antipathy towards her mother, but that she died prematurely. The last reference to her is in the eleventh year of the queen's reign.

Grimal: 207, 210–11.
Tyldesley: 86–90.

Neferyu, Chancellor, Eighth Dynasty, First Intermediate Period, *c.* 2170 BC. Neferyu lived in the early years of the Eighth Dynasty, in the turbulent times after the end of the Old Kingdom. He came from Denderah in the south, and is commemorated by a funerary stela, well carved in limestone and painted in bright colours. It is notable for perpetuating the ancient 'Palace Facade' design, which appeared early in the First Dynasty, on the royal *serekh*, and in the walls of the huge mastaba tombs built for the nobles of the dynasty. Neferyu's stela shows the double doors leading into the 'palace', with sliding bolts and a pair of eyes to enable the owner to look out on the world of the living. In addition, the interior of the 'palace' is also shown, revealing Neferyu enjoying his funerary banquet.

Hayes 1: 139; fig. 82.
MMA 12.183.8.

Neheri, Vizier and Nomarch, Tenth/Eleventh Dynasties, First Intermediate Period, *c.* 2125 BC. Neheri was the son of prince THUTNAKHTE IV, nomarch of Hermopolis in the latter years of the Heracleopolitan kings. He was given command of two divisions of soldiers by his king but seems to have concentrated rather on protecting the people of his nome from the depredations of the impendingly victorious Theban forces, loyal to the princes who founded the Eleventh Dynasty. He made his peace with the Thebans and remained in office until his death when he was succeeded by his son, THUTNAKHTE V.

CAH I.2: 467, 469–70.

Nehesy, Prince, Thirteenth Dynasty, Middle Kingdom, *c.* 1720 BC. Nehesy was probably the son of an ephemeral Thirteenth Dynasty king, during a period of Egypt's history when reigns were many and generally brief: his name means 'Nubian'. He lived at what was to become the Hyksos capital Avaris during the occupation of Egypt and contributed to the building of a temple to Seth.

Kuhrt 1995: I, 178.
CAH II.1: 53.

Nehi, Viceroy, Eighteenth Dynasty, New Kingdom, *c.* 1479–1425 BC. Nehi was appointed Viceroy of Nubia by King THUTMOSE III, as part of his masterful organisation of his foreign dominions. Nehi was a most competant administrator, and Egyptian rule, if not entirely welcomed, brought both prosperity and peace to the southlands. He ensured the profitable working of the gold mines and he repaired the canal, first opened by King SENWOSRET III at the First Cataract, giving instructions for its annual maintenance. He rebuilt the ruined brick-built temple of Senwosret at Semna and restored it in stone. He erected the great stela at the fortress of Buhen which records Thutmose's victories. Nehi was succeeded in his office by Wesersatet.

PM I: 461.

Neith, Queen, Sixth Dynasty, Old Kingdom, *c.* 2278–2200 BC. A wife of King PEPY II, Neith was the daughter of PEPY I and the sister of MERENRE I. She was perhaps the mother of his ephemeral successor, MERENRE II. Her pyramid at Saqqara contains one of the recensions of the Pyramid Texts.

G. Jéquier, *Les Pyramides des Reines Neit et Apouit*, Cairo, 1933.
Stevenson Smith 1971: 196–7.
Lehner 1997: 163.

Neithhotep, Queen, First Dynasty, Archaic Period, *c.* 3100 BC. The name of the wife of King AHA, the first king of the First Dynasty, has prompted speculation that it indicates a royal marriage as an act of policy in promoting the unification of Upper and Lower Egypt; Neith was a goddess especially associated with northern Egypt, with her principal temple located at Sais. There is nothing to indicate that such an event ever occurred, however. Neithhotep was probably buried in an immense tomb at Abydos, which is one of the earliest decorated with the 'palace facade' recessed panelling on its exterior walls.

Emery 1961: 25, 47–9.
Spencer: 60–1.

Nekaure, Prince, Fourth Dynasty, Old Kingdom, *c.* 2550 BC. The son of King KHAFRE, Nekaure left a will in which he set out his bequests to his heirs. Most of his wealth was represented by the towns which he controlled and which were in his gift. His heirs included his wife, sons, a deceased daughter and 'the king's confidant', Nekennebti, whose relationship to the prince is unknown.

Breasted 1: §§190–9.

Nekhebu, Architect, Fifth/Sixth Dynasties, Old Kingdom, *c.* 2321–2287 BC. The record of his career which Nekhebu contrived to leave for posterity appears to demonstrate the manner in which a man of humble origins could attain high office and responsibility in Ancient Egypt, especially in the early centuries of its history. Starting his working life as a clerk 'carrying the scribe's palette', he rose through the ranks, becoming successively journeyman builder, master builder, Royal Constructor, Royal Attaché and, ultimately, Royal Architect. In his funerary dedication he remarks: 'I never went to bed angry against anybody'.

But Nekhebu is disingenuous, at least so far as his progress through the upper levels of the Egyptian bureaucracy is concerned. His father was MEHY, Vizier to King UNAS; his father before him was INTI, Vizier to King DJEDKARE ISESI. His father and grandfather therefore were successively the most powerful men in the state after the king.

Nekhebu had a second name, Meryremerptahankh, under which he led an expedition to the quarries of the Wadi Hammamat during the reign of PEPY I. He devoted six years to building a monument for King Pepy at Heliopolis.

Two of his sons are known; they followed in the distinguished public careers of their family. The tomb of one of them, IMPY, was found intact.

Wilson 1951: 89–90.
Dows Dunham, JEA XXIV (1938) 1ff.
CAH I.2: 186–7.

Nekhonekh, High Steward, Fifth Dynasty, Old Kingdom, *c.* 2490 BC. In addition to his role as High Steward, Nekhonekh was 'Governor of New Towns', a priest of Hathor and a mortuary priest. His will distributes his wealth and hereditary offices amongst his children. He left instructions that each of his children was to serve for one month in each office; as he had thirteen heirs this instruction meant that the last two had to divide their month's occupancy of the priesthood between them.

Breasted 1: §§216–17.

Nekmertaf, Scribe, Eighteenth Dynasty, New Kingdom, *c.* 1360 BC. Nekmertaf is commemorated by a statue group depicting him in his capacity of scribe, receiving dictation from the god Thoth, manifested as a cynocephalus baboon.

MduL E11154.

Nemaathap, Queen, Second Dynasty, Archaic Period, *c.* 2686 BC. Nemaathap was probably the daughter and the wife of the great Second-Dynasty king, KHASEKHEMWY, and the mother of the equally remarkable DJOSER NETJERYKHET, the second king of the Third Dynasty. She was titled 'Mother of the King's Children' and a cult in her memory was still being observed in the reign of King SNEFERU.

Stevenson Smith 1971: 151–2.
Emery 1961: 103.

Nemtyemweskhet, High Steward, Thirteenth Dynasty, Middle Kingdom, 1786–1650 BC. The 'Seal-Bearer of the King' and 'High Steward', Nemtyemweskhet was commemorated in a stela which was set up in an offering chapel at Abydos, a practice popular among high state officials and others during the Thirteenth Dynasty. At the foot of the stela a model stone sarcophagus was buried which contained a miniature coffin, representing a dummy burial at Abydos which would enable the deceased Nemtyemweskhet to take part in the mysteries of Osiris.

Nemtyemweskhet was buried elsewhere. Although a high official, his dummy coffin's decoration and inscriptions are summarily carried out. Originally it contained a figure representing the deceased.

Bourriau 1988: 93–4, no. 74.

Nesipakashuty, Vizier, Twenty-Sixth Dynasty, Late Period, *c.* 644–610 BC. Nesipakashuty was Vizier to King PSAMETIK I, who built his tomb in an earlier, Eleventh Dynasty tomb near Deir el-Bahri. The tomb contained reliefs of the mourners at Nesipakashuty's funeral.

PM II: 149.
Kitchen 1986: §169, §§171–2, §296.
EMC CG 42232 = JE 36662.
BM 32.
Luxor Museum J 152, cat. no. 260, fig. 140.

Neska, Royal Treasurer, First Dynasty, Archaic Period, *c.* 2950 BC. The owner of mastaba Tomb X at Saqqara, Neska was Treasurer of Upper Egypt in the reign of King DEN. His tomb contained a number of fine objects, including a handsome table on four legs.

Emery 1949: 107–15.

Nesmin, Priest, Ptolemaic Period, *c.* 305 BC. Despite his profession, Nesmin, a 'God's Father' and priest of Amonrasonther, chose to be buried with a variety of texts, particularly secular ones, including the 'Secret Books of the Treasure which No-one has Seen'.

He was the son of Pediamennebesut-tawy and Tasheretentaihet Irtyru; it is probable that the family was Theban.

F. Haikal, *Two Hieratic Papyri of Nesmin, I and II*, Brussels, 1970–2.
S. Quirke, *Owners of Funerary Papyri in the British Museum*, London, 1993: 49, 78–9.
British Museum: Bremner Rhind Papyrus, BM 10208–9.

Nesmont, General, Twelfth Dynasty, Middle Kingdom, *c.* 1970 BC. A senior army officer, Nesmont served under both King AMENEMHET I and his son, SENWOSRET I.

Staatliche Sammlung Äegyptischer Kunst, Munich.

Nesuhor, Army Commander, Twenty-Sixth Dynasty, Late Period, *c.* 589–570 BC. Nesuhor was commander of King APRIES' army at Elephantine and custodian of the Gateway to the South. He was faced with a mutiny by some of his mercenary soldiers but appears to have succeeded in defusing it. The army was, however, once more to revolt against Apries and on that occasion to dethrone and kill him. Nesuhor's tomb is at Aswan.

Kuhrt 1995: I, 642–3.
Breasted 4: §§989–95.

Niankhamon and Khnumhotep, *see* **Khnumhotep and Niankhkhnum**

Niankhpepi, Governor, Sixth Dynasty, Old Kingdom, *c.* 2278–2184 BC. Niankhpepi was known as 'Hepi the Black' and held the important office of Chief of Upper Egypt. He was buried at Meir and his tomb contains a quantity of models of servants, musicians, brewers and all the persons of his household.

PM IV: pl. 247.
Blackman 1914: pl. 14.
Saleh and Sourouzian: 65 ('The Porter of Niankh-pepi').
EMC JE 30810 = CG 241.

Niankhpepiken, Chancellor, Sixth Dynasty, Old Kingdom, *c.* 2321–2287 BC. The Chancellor of King PEPY I, Niankhpepiken was buried in one of the fine tombs of the nomarchs at Meir.

Blackman 1914–53.

Niankhsekhmet, Physician, Fifth Dynasty, Old Kingdom, *c.* 2487–2475 BC. The Chief Physician to King SAHURE, Niankhsekhmet asked the king to give him a well made 'false-door' for his tomb. The king was pleased to comply, commanding that fine limestone be brought from Tura and that the false door should be carved and inscribed in his presence. He gave instructions that it should be painted blue.

The king was gratified by his good health – presumably the consequence of Nianhksekhmet's care – and expressed the wish that his physician might depart into his tomb 'at an advanced old age'.

Breasted 1: §§237–40 (as 'Nenekhsekhmet').
Ghalioungui 1983: 19.

Niankhre, Physician, Fifth Dynasty, Old Kingdom, *c.* 2300 BC. Niankhre was Court Physician during the Fifth Dynasty when the clinical and medical sciences flourished. His statue suggests that he himself was crippled. He was, perhaps, a priest of Heka, the god of magic; he was also concerned with Selket, the scorpion goddess, who was invoked as a protector against her creatures' stings.

H. Junker, *Giza, I–XII*, Vienna and Leipzig, 1929–55.
Nunn: 99–100.
EMC 6138.

Niankhptah, Sculptor, Fifth Dynasty, Old Kingdom, *c.* 2414–2375 BC. PTAHHOTEP, the Vizier to King DJEDKARE ISESI was buried in a splendid mastaba tomb at Saqqara. The reliefs on the walls of the tomb are particularly rich and fine; they are carved in high relief and, in common with the best of Egyptian wall carvings, have the fluency and immediacy of drawings.

The sculptor of Ptahhotep's tomb was Niankhptah, one of the comparatively few major artists to have their signature appended, as it were, to their work. Niankhptah is further favoured by actually being portrayed in the tomb with his master. He is shown seated in a small skiff, in the middle of what appears to be a particularly vigorous contest between competing teams of boatmen on the river. A quantity of food has been placed in the skiff in which Niankhptah is sitting, and he is being encouraged to drink beer offered to him in a pottery vessel by a young boy.

R. F. E. Paget and A. A. Pirie, *The Tomb of Ptah-Hetep*, London, 1898: 29 (ref. 'Ankh-n Ptah'), pl. XXXII.
Stevenson Smith 1946 (1949): 354, 360 (as Ny-ankh-ptah).

Nimaatsed, Priest, Judge, Fifth Dynasty, Old Kingdom, *c.* 2445–2421 BC. Nimaatsed was a priest in the solar temple of King NEFERIRKARE and served as a judge and as priest of the king's pyramid and those of King NEFEREFRE and King NIUSERRE. He is commemorated by a double statue in which his figure is duplicated. The statues are virtually identical except that one is very slightly smaller than the other.

PM III.2: 584–5.
Borchardt: 99–100, pl. 130.
Saleh and Sourouzian: 48.
EMC CG133.

Nimlot, General and High Priest, Twenty-Second Dynasty, Third Intermediate Period, *c.* 940 BC. Originally appointed commander of the army at Herakleopolis, Nimlot subsequently became High Priest of Amun at Thebes.

Grimal: 322.

Nimlot, Ruler, Twenty-Fifth Dynasty, Third Intermediate Period, *c.* 747–716 BC. Although King PIANKHY was angry with the way in which Nimlot had allowed his horses to suffer during the seige of the city of which he was the Ruler – Piankhy was inordinately fond of horses – he nonetheless favoured him above the other Egyptian rulers when he accepted their submission. He permitted Nimlot to remain in control of Ashmunein.

Grimal: 331, 339.

Nitiqret (alt. Nitocris), Queen, Sixth Dynasty, Old Kingdom, *c.* 2184–2181 BC. A woman whose very existence has been doubted, Nitiqret was probably the last ruler of the Sixth Dynasty, standing between its end and the confused situation which persisted in the country at the commencement of the First Intermediate Period. HERODOTUS described her as having assumed the royal titles after the murder of the king her brother, whose death she avenged. If she is an historical personage then she was one of the first women to assume the full powers of the kingship, although MERNEITH of the First Dynasty may have ruled independently before her, prior to the accession of her son.

Nitiqret is listed in the Turin Canon after MERENRE II, who was probably the son of the aged King PEPY II and whose reign was brief. There is nothing in fact to indicate that Nitiqret and he were related, though legend had it that she was his sister and avenged his death after he was killed by a mob.

Grimal: 89, 93, 128.

Nitiqret (alt. Nitocris), Princess, Twenty-Sixth Dynasty, Late Period, *c.* 664–610 BC. Nitiqret was the daughter of King PSAMETIK I. She was sent by her father to become the hieress of the reigning God's Wives of Amun in Thebes, SHEPENUPET II and AMENIRDIS II, and eventually succeeded them. The incumbent God's Wives adopted Nitiqret, thus ensuring the continuation of the north's domination of the politics of Upper Egypt.

R. A. Caminos, 'The Nitocris Adoption Stela', JEA 50: 71–101.

Niuserre, King, Fifth Dynasty, Old Kingdom, *c.* 2445–2421 BC. One of the successors of King SAHURE, Niuserre was the son of King NEFERIRKARE and Queen KHENTKAWES. He reigned for some twenty-five years, his occupancy of the throne representing one of the high points of the later Old Kingdom.

He was a devotee of the solar cult associated with the Fifth Dynasty kings and built the sun temple at Abu Ghurob, the only example to survive in anything like a complete state. It contained several fine series of carvings, including one sequence depicting the seasons.

He also was the first Egyptian king to record the division of the country into nomes, the administrative units which were to remain part of the fabric of Egypt throughout its remaining history. Niuserre was honoured even in so distant a time as the reign of SENWOSRET II, when he was one of the early kings singled out for a commemorative statue.

Niuserre built a pyramid at Abusir and completed those begun by his father, his mother and his brother King NEFEREFRE.

L. Borchardt, *Das Grabdenkmal des Königs Ne-user-Re*, Leipzig, 1907.
W. H. Kaiser, 'Zu den Sonnenheiligtumern des 5 Dynastie', MDAIK 14 (1956) 104–16.
Vandier 1952: 582.
B. V. Bothmer, 'The Karnak Statue of Ny-user-ra', MDAIK 30 (1974) 165–70.
E. Edel and S. Wenig, *Die Jahrenszeitenreliefs aus dem Sonnenheiligtum des Königs Ne-User-Re*, Berlin, 1974.

Nofret, *see* **Rahotep and Nofret**

Nofret (alt. Nefret), Queen, Twelfth Dynasty, Middle Kingdom, *c.* 1880–1874 BC. The wife of King SENWOSRET II, Nofret was Queen of Egypt at a time of the country's greatest prosperity and power. She is represented as a stately, rather formidable lady, wearing an immense wig, very fashionable in her day. She is described as 'the noblewoman, favourite and highly praised one, beloved of Senwosret'.

Nofret's sarcophagus and jewels have recently (1994) been discovered and excavated.

Terrace and Fischer 1970: no. 14, 73–6.
H. Sourouzian, MDAIK 37 (1981) 448–9, pl. 71b.
EMC JE 37487 (= CE 381).
Saleh and Sourouzian: 93.

Nubkhas, Queen, Seventeenth Dynasty, Second Intermediate Period, *c.* 1650–1550 BC. The wife of King SOBEKEMSAF, Queen Nubkhas was one of the victims of the outbreak of tomb robbing in the reign of King RAMESSES IX, when a number of royal tombs were found to have been pillaged. The sacrilege came to light during the process brought against the Mayor of Western Thebes, PAWERAA, initiated by his rival, the Mayor of the East Bank, PASER.

J. Capart, A. H. Gardiner and B. Van der Walle, 'New Light on the Ramesside Tomb-Robberies', JEA 22 (1936): 169–93.

Nykuhor, Judge, Fifth Dynasty, Old Kingdom, *c.* 2470 BC. A judge (*sab*) who also held a number of other high offices, Nykuhor was a priest of the sun temple of King USERKAF and hence responsible for the cult of the deified king. He was Inspector of Scribes and a Privy Councillor. His tomb contains reliefs of a small group of instrumentalists and singers, and of his retainers whiling away eternity playing draughts.

Hayes I: 102–3; figs 58–9.
MMA 08.201.2.

Nynetjer, King, Second Dynasty, Archaic Period, *c*. 2850 BC. A ruler of considerable obscurity, Nynetjer may nonetheless have reigned for thirty-eight years; some incidents relating to his reign are recorded in the Palermo Stone. During that time he is said to have built extensively and to have celebrated numerous festivals. He was probably the third king of the Dynasty, following RANEB to the throne. He may have been buried at Saqqara though his tomb has not been found; it may be one of those thought to have been buried or destroyed during the building of the pyramid of King UNAS.

S. Hassan, 'Excavations at Saqqara 1937–8', *ASAE*, 38 (1938) 521.
CAH I.2: 20, 31–2.

O

Octavian, *see* **Augustus Caesar**

[Olympias], Queen, Macedonian Dynasty, *c.* 370–316 BC. The princess of Epirus, daughter of King Neoptolemos I, Olympias was married to PHILIP II, the King of Macedon. At first their marriage was satisfactory but after the birth of her son, ALEXANDER (THE GREAT), Olympias became increasingly wilful. When her husband was murdered by an officer in his guard, a discarded lover, she had his new wife and her child put to death.

Her relationship with her son was profoundly possessive. She encouraged the rumour that Alexander had been conceived as the result of her impregnation by the Egyptian god Amun, in the form of a snake. There was also a story, derived from 'The Romance of Alexander', that his true father was NECTANEBO II, the last native Egyptian king.

During her son's lifetime she harassed him unmercifully, intriguing against his officers whom he had left in charge of affairs in Macedon. After his death she attempted to consolidate her position by causing the murder of anyone whom she sensed was a rival. She was executed by Cassander, son of Antipater, in 316 BC, seven years after the death of her son, having been tried by the army.

Lane Fox 1973: 57–9, 90, 214–15, 413, 469, 475.

Osorkon I, King, Twenty-Second Dynasty, Third Intermediate Period, *c.* 924–889 BC. Osorkon I was the son and successor of SHESHONQ I who died *c.* 924 BC. He enjoyed a long and placid reign, marked by considerable political manoeuvering around the office of High Priest of Amun in Thebes, a process which was to have long-lasting repercussions on the stability of the state.

Egypt was exceptionally rich during the reign of Osorkon, who endowed the temples with prodigal generosity. He built extensively. In his old age he appointed his son, the High Priest of Amun, SHESHONQ II, as joint sovereign. Sheshonq died suddenly, however, and thus never reigned independently. When he died not long afterwards, Osorkon was succeeded by TAKELOT I.

R. Dessau, 'Dedicace d'une statue d'Osorkon I par Eliba'al, roi de Byblos', *Syria*, 6: 101–17. Kitchen 1986: §§261–9.

Osorkon II, King, Twenty-Second Dynasty, Third Intermediate Period, *c.* 874–850 BC. Oskorkon II was TAKELOT I's son and hence OSORKON I's grandson. The problems associated with the Theban ponti-ficate continued, which Osorkon II attempted to alleviate by following the generally accepted practice of appointing a son to an office when it fell vacant, a situation which occurred not infrequently in a family that, with a few exceptions, does not seem to have been especially long-lived.

The king soon proved himself an energetic ruler. He was ruthless in suppressing the aspirations of rival claimants to the High Priesthood in Thebes; HARSIESE in particular troubled him and, on the latter's death, Osorkon appointed one of his sons, NIMLOT, as High Priest in Thebes. He built very widely and was responsible for many works of high quality. He celebrated his jubilee in his twenty-second regnal year, an occasion of rejoicing throughout all Egypt. This jubilee was proclaimed by one of the leading clerics, BAKENKHONS, who was deeply conscious of the honour done to him.

Osorkon II was active in promoting closer relations with Egypt's neighbours and in seeking alliances against the rising power of Assyria. One such alliance was with the kings of Israel.

Nonetheless, Osorkon II maintained reasonable relations with the Assyrians; in the last years of his reign other claimants to the kingship of Egypt appeared, with whom Osorkon does not appear to have been inclined to quarrel.

Osorkon is commemorated in one of the smaller though undoubted masterpieces of Egyptian craftsmanship, the so-called 'Osorkon Triad', a jewel-like object comprising the god Osiris (possibly a portrait of Osorkon) crouching on a lapis lazuli column, supported by Horus and Isis. The gods are all fashioned in gold.

P. Montet, *La Nécropole royale de Tanis I: les constructions et le tombeau de Osorkon II à Tanis*, Paris, 1951.
W. Barta, 'Die Sedfest-Darstellung Osorkons II im Tempel von Bubastis', SAK 6: 25–42.
J. Leclant (ed.), *L'Égypte en crépuscule: collection 'Univers des formes'*, Paris, 1980.
Kitchen 1986: §§271–88.
Andreu *et al.* 1997: no. 87.
MduL E 6204.

Osorkon III, King, Twenty-Third Dynasty, Third Intermediate Period, *c.* 777–749 BC. Osorkon III was the great-grandson of the second of the name. He was initially High Priest of Amun at Thebes, an office which, despite its apparently religious character, also required its incumbent to lead the armies. He became king in Leontopolis (though some commentators rather see him as king in Tanis) in the Delta on the death of SHESHONQ IV; his mother was Queen Kamama. In a time of extreme insecurity in the kingship in Egypt, Osorkon contrived to contain the influence of his rivals in the south by the skilful manipulation of ecclesiastical appointments, one of the marks of the age. Two of his sons, TAKELOT III, who succeeded him, and RUDAMUN became kings. He died a very old man.

Kitchen 1986: §309, §§312–14, §§317–18.

Osorkon IV, King, Twenty-Second Dynasty, Third Intermediate Period, *c.* 730–715 BC. Osorkon came to the throne at an extremely low point in the fortunes of the Egyptian monarchy. His power was limited to the area around Tanis and Bubastis. By his time there were four rival kings in the north and Osorkon was the most exposed to the menaces of the powers to the north-east, notably Assyria. He tried to assist the Israelite kings and the Palestinians, but the renewed threats from the Assyrians made him seek to conciliate their king, SARGON II, with gifts, notably of twelve fine horses. Osorkon disappeared soon after this episode and the Twenty-Second Dynasty was extinguished.

Kitchen 1986: §§333–6.

P

Pabes, Tradesman, Nineteenth Dynasty, New Kingdom, *c.* 1245 BC. Pabes was the son of the gold-worker KHAY, but seems to have been engaged in trade, one of the comparatively few businessmen known from Ancient Egypt. On his tomb walls are scenes of ships at the port of Memphis being unloaded on to the quay.

Martin 1991: 132–4; ill. 92.

Pahemnetjer, High Priest, Nineteenth Dynasty, New Kingdom, *c.* 1295–1186 BC. Pahemnetjer was High Priest of Ptah in Memphis. He usurped the sarcophagus belonging to Paser, a troop commander, after it had apparently been carried north from Thebes.

James and Davies 1983: 57.

Paneb, Worker, Nineteenth Dynasty, New Kingdom, *c.* 1260 BC. During the reign of RAMESSES II a series of robberies occurred in Thebes, at Deir el-Medina and the Valley of the Kings; the work apparently of one Paneb, the foreman of the Right Side of the gang. He stole some statues from the temple of King SETI I, with the intention of decorating his own tomb. He then went on to murder his gang foreman and adoptive father, Neferhotep, in the hope of securing his position. Arrested and then sent for trial before the Vizier AMENMOSE, he nonetheless, by the exercise of who knows what influence or chicanery, was able to secure his acquittal, obtained Neferhotep's position, and eventually had himself buried in a handsome tomb (TT 211).

Paneb seems generally to have been of deplorable character. He is recorded as having had illicit affairs with five women, and was accused of failing to pay for clothes which had been made for him, and of drunkenness and assault.

J. Černý, 'Papyrus Salt 124 (BM 10055)', JEA 15: 243–58.
——*A Community of Workmen at Thebes during the Ramesside Period*, Cairo, 1973: 351.
Grimal 1992: 287.

Panehesy, Viceroy, Twentieth Dynasty, New Kingdom, 1099–1069 BC. Panehesy was appointed Viceroy of Kush in the reign of RAMESSES XI, the last king of the Twentieth Dynasty. He first came to prominence when he was required to curtail the pretensions to near-royal power of AMENHOTEP, the High Priest of Amun at Karnak; Amenhotep was sent into exile.

Panehesy extended his power over much of the south of Egypt but he was opposed by HERIHOR and eventually driven back into Nubia. He appears to have survived there into old age undefeated. After his time Kush was never again to be a province of Egypt nor under the control of its kings.

Kitchen 1986: §14, §208, §209.
Grimal 1992: 292, 312.

Panemerit, Governor, Ptolemaic Period, *c*. 80–47 BC. Panemerit was Governor of Tanis during the reigns of PTOLEMY XI and PTOLEMY XIII. A fine portrait head of Panemerit is in the Cairo Museum whilst the body of the statue is in the Louvre.

EMC CG 27493 (head).
MduL E15683 (statue).

Parennefer, Architect, Eighteenth Dynasty, New Kingdom, *c*. 1352–1336 BC. Parennefer was one of King AMENHOTEP IV-AKHENATEN's chief assistants in imposing the 'Amarna Style' on Egypt's architecture as successfully – short-term – as it was applied to the other arts. As 'Overseer of All the Works in the Mansion of Aten', he was probably responsible for a great new shrine which was to be built at Karnak.

He was a Royal Butler and Overseer of the Prophets of All the Gods. He was in charge of all temple offerings to Aten.

He was buried at Thebes (TT 188).

De Garis Davis 1903–8.
Stevenson Smith 1958 (1981): 299.
Aldred 1988: 16, 91.
Redford 1984: 60, 137, 151.

Pariamakhu, Physician, Nineteenth Dynasty, New Kingdom, *c*. 1240–1230 BC. The fame of Egypt reached its widest extent during the years in which King RAMESSES II was consolidating the control of his kingdoms. The reputation of all sorts of specialists from Egypt was unrivalled, amongst them the medical practitioners who had been a feature of Egyptian society at least since the time of the Old Kingdom. One such practitioner was Pariamakhu; Ramesses received a request from one of the vassals of the Hittite king, Kurunta, king of Tarhuntas, for medical assistance. Ramesses sent word that he had given orders for Pariamakhu, a specialist in herbal remedies, to visit the Hittite court. He was similarly employed on other occasions, specifically in the preparation of herbal medications.

Kitchen 1982: 91.
Jonckheere 1958: 36–7, 105.

Pasenhor, Priest, Twenty-Second Dynasty, Third Intermediate Period, *c*. 767–730 BC. A priest in the Serapeum at Memphis, Pasenhor was the scion of a long line of aristocrats, originally from Libya, who traced their descent from a son of King OSORKON II, whose own ancestors could be followed for a further nine generations. Pasenhor's family was an example of the often considerable lineages which senior temple clergy could demonstrate.

He was in office during the reign of King Sheshonq V, when the incumbent Apis bull died, at the age of fifteen.

Kitchen 1986: §74, §85, table 19.

Paser, Vizier, Nineteenth Dynasty, New Kingdom, *c*. 1294–1279 BC. Paser was the son of NEBNETERU, called Theri, the High Priest of Amun, and Merytre. He was one of the companions of his youth to Prince Ramesses, later King RAMESSES II. His first important post was as Chief Chamberlain to Ramesses' father, King SETI I, when he was still in his twenties. He was appointed 'High Priest of the Goddess Great of Magic' and 'Chief of the Secrets of the Two Goddesses'. In this capacity he was responsible for the care of the Two Crowns, of Upper and Lower Egypt respectively, which were themselves divine. He became Vizier of the South to SETI I when he was thirty and continued in his office into the reign of RAMESSES II, to whom he was initially chief adviser. It may have been Paser who actually placed the Double Crown on Ramesses' head at his coronation.

He served Ramesses as Vizier for some twenty-five years, and for ten years he held the same office as did his father, the High Priest of Amun.

Paser was responsible for many important building projects for both the kings he served. He was especially proud of the fact that he cared for the workers under his charge. He was responsible for the construction of Seti I's magnificent tomb in the Valley of the Kings. He left a scribbled comment, 'very beautiful', on the scene of the girl dancers in the tomb of KENAMUN.

Paser's wife was Tiy, Chief of the Harem of Amun. He was interred at Thebes (TT 106).

PM I.1: 219–24.
Kitchen 1982: 28, 36, 39, 44, 103, 125–6, 148, 169, 171.
Reeves and Wilkinson: 24.

Paser, Mayor, Twentieth Dynasty, New Kingdom, *c.* 1126–1108 BC. A contemporary of PAWERAA, Paser was the Mayor of Eastern Thebes and Paweraa's superior. He accused his junior colleague of neglect – or worse – when the robbing of tombs in the Valley, including that of RAMESSES VI, came to light late in the reign of RAMESSES IX. Ramesses reported his concern to the vizier Khaemwaset, who ordered an enquiry, as a result of which a number of arrests were made amongst the workmen engaged in the construction or maintenance of the tombs.

Paser's suspicions were initially dismissed, but he persisted and a year later several of the workmen were convicted. Paser himself, however, disappears from the record at this point; Paweraa continued in office and the pillaging of the tombs continued unabated.

Grimal 1992: 289–90.
Reeves and Wilkinson 1996: 193.

Pashedu, Royal Craftsman, Nineteenth Dynasty, New Kingdom, *c.* 1294–1279 BC. One of the officials of the 'Place of Truth', the Theban necropolis at Deir el-Medina, during the reign of King SETI I, Pashedu was responsible for the construction of the royal tombs. His own (TT 3) contains paintings of an exceptionally high quality.

Grimal 1992: 285–6.

Paweraa, Mayor, Twentieth Dynasty, New Kingdom, *c.* 1126–1108 BC. Paweraa was the Mayor of Western Thebes and as such responsible for the security of the Royal Tombs in the necropolis. His colleague PASER, the Mayor of Eastern Thebes, accused him of neglecting his duties when a series of robberies of royal tombs came to light in the later years of the reign of King RAMESSES IX. An inquiry was held and a number of workmen in the necropolis were tried; however, no evidence appears to have been offered which would implicate Paweraa, though there is some suggestion that it may have been suppressed. Certainly, Paweraa survived, and the robberies continued.

Wilson 1951: 283–6.
Reeves and Wilkinson: 193.

Pay, Royal Official, Eighteenth Dynasty, New Kingdom, *c.* 1336–1327 BC. A contemporary of King TUTANKHAMUN, Pay was a high official at the court, holding offices which must have brought him close to the king. He was Overseer of the Royal Harem in Memphis, Overseer of the Royal Private Apartments and, a temple appointment, Overseer of the Cattle of Amun-Re. He was buried at Saqqara in a tomb which was adorned with a superb stela. It has been suggested, on the basis of representations in his tomb, that he was especially fond of figs. His sons succeeded him in a number of his offices.

G. T. Martin, EA 5: 3–6.

Pediamonet, Priest, Twenty-Second Dynasty, Third Intermediate Period, *c.* 850–825 BC. A priest in the temple of the god Montu, Pediamonet lived during the reign of King TAKELOT II. His father was the Vizier NESIPAKASHUTY. A wooden box containing the four 'canopic' jars, which held the internal organs after mummification, belonging to Pediamonet, were found beneath the pavement of the temple of Queen HATSHEPSUT at Deir el-Bahri.

Kitchen 1986: §290.
Luxor Museum J 75, cat. no. 263; fig. 141.

Pediamunranebwaset, Priest, Twenty-Sixth Dynasty, Late Period, *c.* 650–610 BC. The Second Prophet of Khonsu-in-Thebes, Pediamunranebwaset had the misfortune of having his statue thrown into a pit at Karnak, where it was broken in two pieces. He claims, in the inscription on his statue, to have served his lord for eighty years.

Bothmer 1961 (1969): 45, no. 38 A/B, pls 35–6.
A: Metropolitan Museum of Art 07. 228. 33; B: EMC JE 37442.

Pediese, Prince, Twenty-Second Dynasty, Third Intermediate Period, *c.* 798 BC. Pediese was 'Great Chief of Ma' and thus a powerful Libyan chieftain. He took part in the search for a replacement for the sacred bull, Apis, whose incarnation had died in the twenty-eighth year of King SHESHONQ III's reign. Having found the new incarnation, Pediese was evidently in some way involved in its career as a living god. He supervised its burial at its death twenty-six years later.

His son, PEFTJAUAWYBAST, was High Priest of Ptah at Memphis.

Breasted 4: §§771–4.
Kitchen 1986: §§81–2, 155, 301.

Pedubastis I, King, Twenty-Third Dynasty, Third Intermediate Period, *c.* 818–793 BC. Pedubastis' origins are obscure, but as soon as he proclaimed himself king in 818 BC he was recognised as King of Upper and Lower Egypt, including by the rulers of the south, from their stronghold in Thebes. His family was originally Libyan and he was no doubt connected with one of the small royal houses which had emerged at this time. He nominated Iuput I as his co-regent and successor. Pedubastis reigned for nearly twenty-five years.

Kitchen 1986: §§297–301.
Kuhrt 1995: I, 628.

Pefnefdineit, Physician, Twenty-Sixth Dynasty, Late Period, *c.* 589–526 BC. The Chief Physician to King APRIES, Pefnefdineit switched his allegiance to General AMASIS when he deposed the king, taking the throne in his place. Pefnefdineit was confirmed as Chief Physician to the new king and used his influence to promote the interests of the god Osiris and his priests at their temple at Abydos. He was responsible for the dispossession of one of the last of the ancient line of the Counts of This, diverting his remaining wealth to providing facilities for the proper burial of the people of Abydos.

Breasted 4: §§1015–25.

Peftjauawybast, High Priest, Twenty-Second Dynasty, Third Intermediate Period, *c.* 780 BC. Peftjauawybast came from a prominent family of Libyan chieftains; his father was PEDIESE, 'Great Chief of Ma'. He was High Priest of Ptah at Memphis and the great-grandson of King OSORKON II.

Kitchen 1986: §81, §§155–6; table 18.

Peftjauawybast, King, Twenty-Third/Twenty-Fifth Dynasties, Third Intermediate Period, *c.* 747–716 BC. One of the small 'kinglets' who seized a very localised power in the confused period before the invasion of Egypt by the Kushite kings. Peftjauawybast's seat was at Heracleopolis. He was married to a daughter of the briefly reigning King RUDAMUN, and so may have had some title to royalty. He surrendered Heracleopolis to King PIANKHY and his speech is recorded in Piankhy's Victory Stele. He may originally have been High Priest in Heracleopolis and, not for the first time amongst his order, have adopted royal pretensions.

Kitchen 1986: §101, §318.
Lichtheim 3: 66–84, specifically 73ff.
Grimal: 331, 337–8.

Peftuaneith, Temple Official, Twenty-Sixth Dynasty, Late Period, *c.* 589–526 BC. Peftuaneith was an important member of the administrations of two kings, APRIES and AMASIS. He had the appointments of Chief Physician, Chief Treasurer and High Steward. He was involved with the reorganisation undertaken in the city of Abydos, in the Temple of Osiris and, earlier, at Heliopolis. His funerary inscriptions detail the work which he carried out and the responsibilities which he assumed, including the suppression of crime.

Lichtheim 3: 33–6.

Penbuy, Craftsman, Official, Nineteenth Dynasty, New Kingdom, *c.* 1250 BC. Penbuy was evidently a man of no very great standing, but nonetheless was commemorated by a handsome carved wooden statuette in which he is shown perhaps taking part in some temple ceremony in the Theban necropolis, 'The Place of Truth', where he was employed. His wife is represented, much reduced in scale, engraved on the plinth which supports Penbuy's statuette. He carries two large staffs, surmounted with sacred images, of Amun-Re and Ptah respectively. He was buried in TT 10.

Scamuzzi: pl. LXXIV.
Quirke and Spencer: 26.
Museo Egizio, Turin 3048.

Penmaat, Archivist, Twenty-First Dynasty, Third Intermediate Period, *c.* 950 BC. The principal archivist in the treasury of the temple of Amun at Thebes, Penmaat was provided with a handsome recension of the Book of the Dead, appropriate to the standing of a senior scribal official.

Quirke and Spencer: pl. 54.
BM EA 1002/1.

Penno, Official, Twentieth Dynasty, New Kingdom, *c.* 1143–1136 BC. Penno was an important administrator at Derr, in Nubia, during the reign of King RAMESSES VI. He was Deputy Governor of Lower Nubia and Controller of the Temple of Horus at Derr.

He evidently saw to it that his relatives occupied similarly valuable posts in the same province. Two of them were Treasurers, another a scribe and Mayor of Derr.

Breasted 4: §§474–83.
Gardiner 1961: 298 (as Penne).

Pentaweret, Prince, Twentieth Dynasty, New Kingdom, *c.* 1153 BC. At the end of the reign of King RAMESSES III a conspiracy in the royal harem was hatched against him, led by a minor wife, TIY. She evidently hoped to propel her son Pentaweret to the throne but, although Ramesses died, the conspiracy failed. A trial of the principal conspirators was held. Despite collusion with the defendants on the part of some of the judges, the accused were found guilty. The lower ranking of them were executed; Pentaweret and those of more exalted rank were permitted to commit suicide.

Wilson 1951: 268–9.
Grimal: 276.

Pentu, Courtier, Eighteenth Dynasty, New Kingdom, *c.* 1352–1323 BC. The career of Pentu, one of the principal courtiers of King AMENHOTEP IV-AKHENATEN illustrates both the ability of one man to hold a variety of official appointments and the value of the political skills which enabled a high official to trim his convictions – at least in public – and so survive drastic political change.

Pentu appears originally as Chief Physician to Akhenaten. As such he was provided with a tomb at Amarna (no. 5) in which he praises the king as 'the god who fashions mankind, and who makes the Two Lands live'. After the king's death or disappearance, Pentu survived in high office in the subsequent reigns when the ideologies of the Amarna 'heresy' were disowned and the supremacy of the priesthood of Amun was restored. Pentu seems to have been an associate of AY who, like him, abandoned the cult of the Aten and eventually became king. Pentu was Southern Vizier during the reign of King TUTANKHAMUN, which saw the vigorous pursuit and execration of anything which recalled the Amarna period.

Aldred 1988: 23, 221, 241, 248, 295.

Pepy I, King, Sixth Dynasty, Old Kingdom, *c*. 2321–2287 BC. The successor of King USERKARE, who ruled for only a short time having himself succeeded King TETI, who according to MANETHO was assassinated and whose reign seems certainly to have ended abruptly, Pepy evidently inherited the throne at a time of some discord in Egypt's internal affairs. It is likely that he was the son of Teti and was probably a child at his accession.

Pepy's reign was full of incident and challenge. He was required to deal with an uprising of the tribes in Palestine for which a substantial army was raised under the command of WENI. He was also active in the south, in Nubia.

His domestic life was complicated by what may have been a plot to assassinate him hatched by one of his queens; Weni records that he was given the sole responsibility for hearing the case against the queen and her son, also implicated.

Later in his life Pepy married the two daughters of a provincial magnate, Khui. Both queens were named ANKHENESMERYRE and each produced a son who was to be king, MERENRE and PEPY II. The queens' brother, DJAU, was Vizier to Pepy I, Merenre and Pepy II.

Pepy I is commemorated by a striking portrait in the form of a copper statue, somewhat larger than lifesize, accompanied by a similar statue of one of his sons, probably Merenre. The statues, that of the elder king being a remarkable and early example of work in copper on a large scale, was recovered from the temple in the home of the Egyptian kingship, Hierakonpolis.

Pepy I reigned for more than forty years.

J. Leclant, *Recherches dans la Pyramide et au Temple Haut du Pharaon Pepi I à Saqqarah*, Leiden, 1979.

——'A la Quête des Pyramides des Reines de Pepi Ier', BSFE 113 (1988) 20–31.

Pepy II, King, Sixth Dynasty, Old Kingdom, *c*. 2278–2184 BC. Pepy II followed his brother, MERENRE, to the throne when he was about six years old. In his early years he was supported by a number of powerful officials including his uncle, the vizier DJAU and HARKHUF who went on several expeditions to the south, from one of which he brought back a dancing dwarf, probably a pygmy, much to the delight of the young king.

As Pepy grew to manhood the country grew more prosperous than it had been in recent reigns. He seems to have been a generally conciliatory ruler, giving himself to the customary practice of monumental building on a generous scale. He paid attention to the situation in Nubia, where he was aided by one of his officials, HEKAIB, who seems particularly to have earned the king's affections. Throughout his reign he mounted large-scale expeditions to Nubia and Sinai to obtain gold and fine stones for the embellishment of his palaces and court.

During Pepy's reign the practice of granting estates to the great nobles and tax exemptions to temples, favoured individuals and towns, considerably increased. By this means the king presumably hoped to ensure the loyalty of those who benefited from his generosity. This policy was to cause great difficulties after his death, and brought on a period of considerable instability in Egypt, with the weakening of the central authority.

Pepy married frequently and outlived most, if not all, of his queens. According to a story circulating during the Middle Kingdom he also pursued a homosexual affair with one of his generals, SASENET. The king was said to have been observed creeping surreptitiously out of his palace at night and climbing over the wall of the general's house, returning in the dawn.

Pepy is said to have been the longest-reigning monarch in history, occupying the throne of Egypt for ninety-four years. If this is so, he was a hundred years old when he died. He was buried in a pyramid at Saqqara inscribed with the Pyramid Texts.

C. Jéquier, *Le Monument Funéraire de Pepi II*, 3 vols, Cairo, 1936–41.
Grimal 1992: 81–9.
Edwards 1993: 179–94.
Parkinson 1991: 54–6.

Pepyankh, Nomarch, Sixth Dynasty, Old Kingdom, *c.* 2100 BC. Pepyankh was a near contemporary and namesake of King PEPY II. He was a provincial governor with his seat at Meir. Another connection between himself and the king was that both apparently lived to be centenarians.

CAH I.2: 195.

Pepynakht, *see* **Hekaib**

Peribsen (alt. Sekhemib), King, Second Dynasty, Archaic Period, *c.* 2700 BC. Towards the end of the Second Dynasty there is evidence of marked unrest in Egypt, suggesting that the unification of the country, so earnestly sought by the early kings, was still vulnerable to local loyalties and ambitions. The situation is revealed in the life of King Peribsen, who is probably the penultimate ruler of the dynasty.

At the outset of his reign he adopted the Horus-name Sekhemib; some authorities would have it that this represents a contemporaneous but ephemeral ruler. Later he proclaimed himself the Seth-king Peribsen, apparently changing his own loyalty from the god hitherto associated with the kingship, Horus, to Seth, who was especially linked with Upper Egypt.

Peribsen indicated his change of affiliation by removing the falcon which surmounted his Horus-name in the *serekh*, which he displayed in the earlier part of his reign, and replacing it with the animal (hound) of Seth. In the next reign Peribsen's successor, KHASEKHEMWY, demonstrated the resolution of the division in the state and the bringing together of the opposing parties by proclaiming himself 'Horus and Seth' and adopting both the Horus Falcon and the Seth Hound on his badge, a unique phenomenon in the history of the Egyptian kingship.

The Seth Peribsen is amongst the most enigmatic of Egypt's early kings. He was buried at Abydos, and the ritual enclosure of his burial place has been identified by sealings found by the excavators. His cult was still being maintained in the Fourth Dynasty, indicating that his memory was honoured long after his death.

Petrie 1901: 11–12, pls LVIII, LXI.
P. E. Newberry, 'The Set Rebellion of the Second Dynasty', *Ancient Egypt* (1922) 40–6.
Gardiner 1961: 416–20.
Spencer 1993: 67, 72, 80, 84–5.

Peryneb, Chancellor, Fifth Dynasty, Old Kingdom, *c.* 2414–2370 BC. The son of the Vizier Shepsesre, Peryneb built a mastaba for himself not far from the pyramid of King USERKAF. He served, in all probability, King DJEDKARE and King UNAS, in whose reign he died.

His tomb, now reassembled in the Metropolitan Museum of Art, New York, was placed close to that of his father. His titles were imposing but largely domestic: 'Keeper of the Crowns', 'Arranger of the King's Parure', 'Intimate of the Royal Bathing and Dressing Rooms'. He was also Chamberlain and Privy Councillor.

His tomb is notable for the fact that some of the reliefs are unfinished, thus allowing the early stages of their preparation, including the designers' sketches, to be visible. However, the 'false door' of the tomb is highly finished and displays the quality of the decoration which an important man would expect to find in his burial place at the height of the Old Kingdom.

C. Ransom Williams, *Decoration of the Tomb of Per-Neb*, New York, 1932.
Hayes 1: 90–4; figs 50–3.
MMA 13.183.3.

Peseshet, Director of Female Physicians, Fifth/Sixth Dynasties, Old Kingdom, *c.* 2350–2320 BC. Peseshet held an appointment unique in the annals of the Old Kingdom. She was 'Overseer of Female Doctors'. She was given a stela in the tomb of Akhethotep, who may have been her son. Whilst it is not certain that Peseshet was herself a doctor, her appointment indicates that there were women practising medicine at least as early as the latter part of the Old Kingdom.

P. Ghalioungui, *The House of Life: Magic and Medical Science in Ancient Egypt*, Amsterdam, 1973: 72.
Nunn 1996: 124–5.

Pesshuper, Chamberlain, Twenty-Fifth Dynasty, Late Period, *c.* 742–716 BC. Pesshuper was Chamberlain to Princess AMENIRDIS, the Divine Adoratrice or God's Wife of Amun in Thebes. He had himself portrayed as a scribe, seated cross-legged with a papyrus scroll open before him. The statue, carved in purple quartzite, shows marked archaicising characteristics, which would become especially popular in the next dynasty.

James and Davies 1983: 7, 13, 14, 62; ill. 11.
BM EA 1514.

Petamenope, Priest, Twenty-Sixth Dynasty, Late Period, *c.* 650 BC. Petamenope was a Chief Lector Priest and a man of substance and consequence at Karnak. His statue, showing him seated cross-legged as a scribe, is a characteristic product of the Saite period, harking back to Old Kingdom forms.

Another figure of Petamenope has given him a modest place in the history of Egyptology as the inscriptions on a block statue of the priest were published in the seventeenth century in an attempt to decipher the hieroglyphs. The attempt was not successful.

Petamenope was buried in a large subterranean tomb at Thebes (TT 33).

G. Herwart von Hohenberg, *Thesaurus Hieroglyphicum*, Munich, 1920: 13.
EMC JE 37341.

Petosiris, High Priest, Ptolemaic Period, *c.* 300 BC. A High Priest of Thoth at Hermopolis in Middle Egypt, Petosiris was buried in a tomb of some magnificence at Tuna el-Gebal. It was built in the style of a small temple and is decorated with reliefs which deliberately combine Hellenistic with early Egyptian designs, apparently inspired by the work of Old Kingdom sculptors. In this it provides echoes of the archaicising techniques of the artists of the Saite period.

The tomb also contains literary passages which probably derive from the much earlier 'Admonitions' or 'Instructions'.

G. Lefebvre, *Petosiris*, 3 vols, Cairo, 1923–4.
Lichtheim 3: 44–9.
Saleh and Sourouzian: 260.
EMC JE 46592.

[Pharnabazes], Persian Satrap, Twenty-Seventh Dynasty, Late Period, 400–380 BC. The politics of the later years of the Persian Empire were marked by changes of policy direction and the often opportunistic grasping of apparent chances of consolidation or advance. The relationship of Persia and Egypt was always fraught, and it was further complicated by the involvement of the Greeks, who changed their alliances with rapidity and insouciance.

In 380 the Persians determined on the

conquest of Egypt. Led by Pharnabazes and the Greek general Iphicrates, a powerful army was assembled but it was beset with dissension, particularly amongst the Greeks.

The invasion was finally underway in the spring of 373. At first it was entirely successful and the path to Memphis seemed open to the invaders. Then the mutual distrust of the Persians and the Greeks supervened, and the march on Memphis was delayed until the main Persian forces arrived. This gave the Egyptians time to regroup, and in the ensuing battle the Persian-Greek forces were defeated.

Kuhrt 1995: I, 697–8.

[Philip II], King of Macedon, reigned 359–336 BC. Philip's principal, indeed perhaps his only, contribution to Egyptian history was his fathering of ALEXANDER THE GREAT. Even this was disputed, on the one hand by his wife OLYMPIAS who maintained that Alexander's true father was the god Amun in the form of a snake, and on the other by the author of the apochryphal 'Romance of Alexander', who gave the credit to NECTANEBO II, the last Egyptian king.

A rumour, current in Philip's lifetime, suggested that PTOLEMY, Alexander's companion, later one of his generals and ultimately King of Egypt and founder of the Ptolemaic dynasty, was Philip's son by his mistress Arsinoë, the wife of Ptolemy's supposed father, Lagus. Her name was borne by several queens of Ptolemy's dynasty.

Lane Fox 1973: 30–40, 46–53.
P. Green, *Philip II, Alexander the Great and the Macedonian Heritage*, Washington, 1982.
M. Andronicos, *Vergina – The Royal Tombs*, Athens, 1984.

Philip Arrhidaeus, King, Macedonian Dynasty, 323–317 BC. The reputedly half-witted half-brother of Alexander the Great, son of PHILIP II by a lesser wife or a mistress of peasant stock, Philip succeeded his half-brother as the nominee of some of the factions of the Macedonian soldiery after Alexander's death. He is commemorated in reliefs in Karnak, in the temples which his half-brother had also embellished, in which he is portrayed in the full regalia of a king of Egypt, in familiar association with the gods. He was murdered on the orders of Alexander's mother, OLYMPIAS.

Lane Fox 1973: 473, 475.

Philiscus (of Corcyra), Tragedian, Ptolemaic Period, third century BC. Philiscus was the priest of Dionysos in Alexandria and thus head of the guild of Dionysiac actors in the city. He was a member of the group of seven tragic poets who were celebrated under the name of *The Pleiad*, after the seven stars of the Pleiades. He was the author of a number of tragedies and a hymn to Demeter.

P. M. Fraser, *Ptolemaic Alexandria. 1. Text*, Oxford, 1972: 608–9, 619, 650–2.
The Lateran Museum.

Pia, High Priest, Eighteenth Dynasty, New Kingdom, *c.* 1450–1400 BC. Pia was the High Priest of the crocodile god Sobek at the god's temple at Dahamsha, probably during the reigns of Queen HATSHEPSUT and King THUTMOSE III.

Luxor Museum J. 149; cat. no. 79; fig. 49.

Piankh, High Priest and General of the Army, Twenty-First Dynasty, Third Intermediate Period, *c.* 1060 BC. Piankh was the successor of HERIHOR, who broke away from the control of the central government and established virtually an independent fiefdom in Thebes, based on the High Priesthood of Amun. Piankh was his son or son-in-law. He was the commander of the armies of Upper Egypt and in this capacity set out against PANEHESY, the Viceroy of Kush who, taking advantage of the troubled times, had made himself independent, as much as Herihor was, of the king. The campaign was long drawn-out and ultimately indecisive.

It has been suggested that the generally accepted order of Piankh and Herihor should be reversed.

Piankh was succeeded in his office by his son, PINUDJEM I.

R. El-Sayed, 'Piankhi, fils de Herihor: documents sur sa vie et sur son rôle', BIFAO 78 (1978) 197–218.
Grimal 1992: 311–12.
K. Jansen-Winkeln, 'Das Ende des Neuen Reichen', ZÄS 119 (1992): 22ff.

Piankhy (alt. Piankhy-Piye, Piy), King, Twenty-Fifth Dynasty, Late Period, *c.* 747–716 BC. Piankhy was the first member of the dynasty of Kushite kings to be recognised as King of Upper and Lower Egypt. He was the son of KASHTA and married the daughter of ALARA, thus securing his claim to the throne in all directions.

He moved northwards through Egypt consolidating his hold on the country. In Thebes he appointed his sister AMENIRDIS I 'God's Wife of Amun' ('Divine Adoratrice'), a position of great political as much as of sacerdotal power. He then defeated a coalition of princes from the northern towns, thus completing his conquests.

However, the northern princes, some of them claiming royal honours, still intrigued to oppose Piankhy. He met his opponents at Memphis, lay seige to the city and captured it.

Piankhy required all the 'kings' to come before him and make their submission; some he excluded from his presence as they were uncircumcised and, having recently eaten fish were, in his view, unclean.

Piankhy was a great lover of horses. Although he gave some authority to NIMLOT, one of the defeated rulers, he was shocked at the way in which Nimlot treated his horses, allowing them to go hungry during the seige.

He died and was buried in a pyramid at El-Kurru in his native Nubia, in the company of some of his beloved horses. He was succeeded by his brother SHABAKA and then by his son, SHABATAKA.

N. Grimal, *Le Stèle Triomphale de Pi(ankhy) au Musée du Caire*, JE 8862, 47086–9, Cairo, 1981.
Kitchen 1986: §§325–32.
Grimal 1992: 335–43.

Pimay (alt. Pimiu), King, Twenty-Second Dynasty, Third Intermediate Period, *c.* 773–767 BC. One of the dynasty of kings ruling from Bubastis, a city sacred to the cat goddess Bastet, Pimay was known by the alternative name, Pimiu, 'Tom-cat'. It is not clear why or how he acquired this appellation, though he shared it with the great god Re. 'Miu' was one of the Egyptians' words for 'cat', an animal to which they were greatly attached. In Roman times, according to DIODORUS SICULUS, a foreigner was lynched by an angry crowd for accidentally killing a cat. HERODOTUS, too, recorded the Egyptians' exceptional devotion to their cats, observing that in the event of a house catching fire, it was the cats which were the first to be saved.

J. Málek, *The Cat in Ancient Egypt*, London, 1993.
BM 32747.

Pinudjem I, High Priest, Twenty-First Dynasty, Third Intermediate Period, 1070–1030 BC. Pinudjem was the son of PIANKH, and for much of his career was content to be High Priest of Amun in Thebes and thus exercise considerable military as well as sacerdotal and political power in Upper Egypt.

Eventually Pinudjem claimed royal honours, though a little tentatively until he felt sure of his position. He acquired the coffins of THUTMOSE I, which he had adapted for his own use. He and they were found in the Deir el-Bahri cache. One of his grandsons was PINUDJEM II, who was also High Priest of Amun.

Kitchen 1986: §§216–7, §436, §441.

Pinudjem II, High Priest, Twenty-First Dynasty, Third Intermediate Period, *c*. 985 BC. The son of MENKHEPERRE and grandson of PINUDJEM I, Pinudjem II was High Priest of Amun and ruler of the south. He organised the reburial of the royal mummies which had suffered desecration. He removed them to the tomb of his wife, whose coffin was used for the reburial of King RAMESSES IX; Pinudjem was also eventually placed amongst the reburied royalty in what may have been his family's tomb.

Kitchen 1986: §228, §441.

[Piryawaza], Governor, Eighteenth Dynasty, New Kingdom, *c*. 1352–1336 BC. A locally recruited noble, Piryawaza was appointed 'Prince of Damascus' during the reign of AMENHOTEP IV-AKHENATEN, when it was Egyptian practice to appoint native administrators in the territories which they ruled. Piryawaza was one such, a 'Palestinian chief', a redoubtable warrior who was one of those who wrote to the King of Egypt demanding soldiers to defend his territories. Akhenaten failed to respond.

CAH II.2: 101–2, 104.

Plotinus, Philosopher, Roman Period, 205–70 AD. The founder of the system of philosophy known as Neo-Platonism, a fusion of traditions drawn from Plato, eastern mystery religions and late-Egyptian concepts. It was to be profoundly influential in the late Middle Ages and Renaissance Europe. Plotinus lived in Rome for much of his life though he was born in Egypt.

J. M. Rist, *Plotinus*, 1967.

[Plutarch], Author, Roman Period, d. *c*. 120 AD. Like DIODORUS SICULUS, Plutarch, a native of Lycopolis, wrote an influential account of the Isis and Osiris myth, which passed into general circulation. Although Plutarch's version of the myth is even later than that of Diodorus, it has been very largely accepted as a canonical recension of an important Egyptian cult. However, there is actually no extant Egyptian version of the myth, nor any real indication of its significance in the minds of Egyptians, despite the undoubted popularity of the divinities, particularly amongst the lower orders of society in the later periods of Egyptian history.

J. Gwyn Griffiths, *Plutarch, De Iside et Osiride*, Cambridge, 1970.

Polybius, Historian, Ptolemaic Period, *c*. 200 BC. One of the most respected and influential historians of the Hellenistic period, Polybius was the son of Lycortas, a leading Achaean politician. He first visited Egypt with his father as a boy. His history is the source of much of the detailed information of the period covering the reigns of PTOLEMY V, PTOLEMY VI and PTOLEMY VIII; he also wrote, very critically, of the reign of PTOLEMY IV. He also disapproved strongly of contemporary Alexandria, especially during the reign of PTOLEMY VIII.

Frank W. Walbank, 'Polybius', in Ruffle *et al.* 1979.

Potasimto (alt. Padisemataoui), General, Twenty-Sixth Dynasty, Late Period, *c*. 590 BC. Potasimto was a contemporary of King PSAMETIK II and was a general of his army who led an expedition to Nubia in 591 BC. He was buried in the necropolis of Kom Abu Yasin, in Upper Egypt.

'Un Chaouabti du General Potasimto au Musée d'Annecy', BIFAO LXI, 1962: 43–53, pls II–IV. Musée d'Annecy inv. 1089.1.

Prehirwenmef, Prince, Nineteenth Dynasty, New Kingdom, *c*. 1279–1213 BC. The third son of the prolific King RAMESSES II, Prehirwenmef was 'Leader of the Army of the King', 'Chief of the Braves' and 'Chief Charioteer of His Majesty'.

Prehirwenmef is shown in action on a number of temple walls whose reliefs record the campaigns of King Ramesses. He died when he was twenty-six.

J. K. Thomson, 'A Statue of Prehirwenmef, Son of Ramesses II', JEA 73 (1987) 220–4; fig. 1, pls XVI–XVII.

Prehotep, Ploughman, Nineteenth Dynasty, New Kingdom, *c.* 1279–1213 BC. Prehotep owes his small, accidental immortality to the behaviour of a recalcitrant cow, depicted in a painting in the tomb of PANEHESY (TT 16). Two wild cattle are yoked together to pull the plough which is Prehotep's responsibility. One has chosen to lie down, evidently disinclined to continue a task which she found unrewarding. Prehotep shouts at her to rise, but her response is not recorded.

Kitchen 1982: 185; pl. 57.

Psametik I (alt. Psammetichus), Twenty-Sixth Dynasty, Late Period, 664–610 BC. Psametik was the son of NECHO I and after his father's death he was recognised as sole king of Egypt by the Assyrians. He was a forceful and agile ruler, whose more than fifty-year reign marked a high point in Egypt's later history. First he secured the control of the south by sending his daughter NITIQRET to be the heiress of the God's Wife of Amun in Thebes after SHEPENUPET II and AMENIRDIS II. Mentuemhet, the most powerful magnate in the Theban region, accepted Psametik's sovereignty, an important achievement for the king. When the opportunity presented itself Psametik expelled the Assyrian garrisons still remaining in Egypt.

The king then turned to the whipping-in of the little kings and chiefs who had proliferated in the Delta and to the west, encouraged very often by the Libyans. He was able to bring them to accept his sovereignty, just as had Mentuemhet.

Psametik opened up Egypt increasingly to foreign interests, particularly the Greeks, Syrians, Phoenicians and Jews who stimulated Egypt's trade with the Eastern Mediterranean to their own and Egypt's profit. The Greeks in particular became a significant community in Egypt and were encouraged by the king to found colonies along the Mediterranean coast.

It was under Psametik's influence that the remarkable renaissance of Egyptian art and architecture occurred which is associated with the Saite kings. Sais and the other centres favoured by the king were admired throughout the ancient world for the splendour of their architecture and the nobility of their works of art, which deliberately looked for their inspiration to the finest works of the Old Kingdom.

Psametik did much also to give new life to the religious cults of Egypt, which had, in some cases, become atrophied. In particular he promoted the cult of Apis and substantially enlarged the Serapeum at Saqqara.

Although Psametik owed his initial acceptance as king to the Assyrians, the problems of the Assyrian Empire meant that he was able to assert Egypt's independence from the invaders. Towards the end of his life it became clear that the Assyrian Empire was disintegrating, and Psametik sent troops to aid his old enemy.

He died in 610 BC, full of years and honour.

R. A. Caminos, 'The Nitocris Adoption Stela', JEA 50 (1964) 71–101.
Kitchen 1986: §117, §225, §§360–8.

Psametik II Neferibre, King, Twenty-Sixth Dynasty, Late Period, 595–589 BC. The grandson of the first Psametik seems deliberately to have modelled himself on his great predecessor. He became involved in the disputes of the Palestinian kingdoms and also sought glory in campaigns in Kush. He died before his policies could really achieve their full results.

J. Yoyotte, 'Le Martelage des Noms Royaux Ethiopiens par Psammétique II', R d'E 8 (1951) 215–39.
H. Goedicke, 'The Campaign of Psammetik II Against Nubia', MDAIK 37 (1981) 187–98.
Kitchen 1986: §369.

Psametik III, King, Twenty-Sixth Dynasty, Late Period, 526–525 BC. The last king of the Twenty-Sixth Dynasty succeeded to the throne when the fortunes of Egypt were terminally in decline. By this time the Persian Empire was becoming dominant in the Near East and Egypt was a natural prize for the Empire's rulers to covet. In 525 CAMBYSES II succeeded the great CYRUS on the Persian throne, marched on Egypt and annihilated Psametik's army. The unfortunate king was captured and hauled in chains to Susa. He was later executed by the Persians.

Kitchen 1986: §§369–70.

Psametik, Physician, Twenty-Sixth Dynasty, Late Period, *c.* 570–526 BC. Psametik flourished at the court of King AMASIS where he enjoyed the rank of 'Overseer of Libyans'. He was provided with a handsome anthropoid sarcophagus but his tomb was never used; it was decorated with stone removed from the pyramid of King UNAS and contained extracts from the Pyramid Texts and the Book of the Dead.

Thomas 1995: no. 16 (101).
Phoebe A. Hearst Museum of Anthropology, University of Berkeley, California, 5–522.

Psametiksaneith, Gold- and Silversmith, Twenty-Seventh Dynasty, Late Period, *c.* 500 BC. Psametiksaneith was the 'Head of All the King's Workmen in Gold and Silver'. He was provided with a statue which is exceptionally naturalistic. He describes himself as 'King's Relative', though by this time such a usage was purely honorific.

Terrace and Fischer 1970; no. 39, 169–72.
EMC JE 31335 = CG 726.

Psammetichus, *see* **Psametik I**

Psenptais III, High Priest, Ptolemaic Period, *c.* 76 BC. Psenptais was appointed to the great office of High Priest of Ptah in Memphis at the age of fourteen, during the reign of King PTOLEMY XII NEOS DIONYSOS AULETES. He was succeeded in the office in 39 BC by his son, who was seven years old, during the reign of CLEOPATRA VII.

D. J. Thompson, 'High Priests of Memphis under Ptolemaic Rule', in *Pagan Priests: Religion and Power in the Ancient World*, eds Mary Bland and John North, Cornell, 1990: 101.

Pseusennes I (Pasebakhaenniu), King, Twenty-First Dynasty, Third Intermediate Period, 1039–993 BC. The son of PINUDJEM I by his wife, a princess HENUTTAWY, Pseusennes was to reign for nearly half a century. In the beginning of his reign the secular and religious powers were effectively split, with the High Priest of Amun claiming the power to declare the king legitimate by the will of Amun. Eventually Pseusennes was to combine the offices in his own person or through the nomination of close relatives, especially sons; this was to become the practice throughout the dynasty.

Pseusennes was a native of Tanis and did much to enhance the city's prestige. He was to build his tomb there. A golden bowl from it bears the name of his daughter Esemkhebe, who married the High Priest MENKHEPERRE and was the mother of PINUDJEM II.

P. Montet, *La Nécropole Royale de Tanis I: Les Constructions et le Tombeau de Psousennes à Tanis*, Paris, 1951.
Kitchen 1986: §§283–6.
EMC JE 85912.
JE 85913 (gold mask).

Pseusennes II, King, Twenty-First Dynasty, Third Intermediate Period, *c.* 959–945 BC. Pseusennes II was the last king of the dynasty, ruling from Tanis in much reduced circumstances.

A. Dodson, 'Psusennes II', R d'E 38 (1987) 49–54.

Psherenptah, High Priest, Ptolemaic Period, d. 41 BC. The High Priest of Ptah in

Memphis in late Ptolemaic times during the reign of Queen CLEOPATRA VII, Psherenptah was married to TAIMHOTEP, who predeceased him and whose tomb bore a melancholy inscription lamenting her early death. Psherenptah died a year later, in 41 BC.

Lichtheim 3: 59–65.

Ptahemhat-Ty, High Priest, Eighteenth Dynasty, New Kingdom, *c.* 1336–1327 BC. Ptahemhat-Ty was High Priest of Ptah at Memphis during the reign of King TUTANKHAMUN.

A relief from his tomb describes how King AY introduced the future king, General HOREMHEB, to the people as his heir.

Reeves 1990a: 32.
BM AE 972.

Ptahhotep, Vizier, Fifth Dynasty, Old Kingdom, *c.* 2414–2375 BC. The minister of King DJEDKARE ISESI, the penultimate king of the Fifth Dynasty, Ptahhotep is remembered as the supposed author of a popular set of 'Maxims', a literary form especially popular in the First Intermediate Period, which sets out to provide guidance on good and proper behaviour and to recommend courses of action most likely to bring credit and profit to the recipient of the advice concerned. He is also known as the owner of a handsome tomb at Saqqara which he occupied with his son, Akhethotep.

His grandson, also Ptahhotep, known as Tshefi, has also been accredited with the authorship of the 'Maxims'.

N. de Garis Davis, *The Mastaba of Ptahhetep and Akhethetep at Saqqareh*, London, 1910: pts 1 and 2.
E. Dévaud, *Les Maxims de Ptahhotep*, Fribourg, 1916.
A. Erman, *The Literature of the Ancient Egyptians*, trans. A. M. Blackman, London, 1927: 6, 54.
Pritchard 1955: 412.
Lichtheim I: 61–80.

Ptahhotep, Treasurer, Twenty-Seventh Dynasty, Late Period, *c.* 490 BC. Ptahhotep was one of the senior Egyptian officials who served the Persian dynasty, specifically DARIUS I, after the defeat of the last of the Saite kings, PSAMETIK III. He is even depicted wearing a version of Persian dress.

Bothmer 1961 (1969): 76, no. 64, pls 60–1.
Brooklyn Museum 37. 353.

Ptahmes, High Priest and Vizier, Eighteenth Dynasty, New Kingdom, *c.* 1390–1352 BC. The High Priest of Amun at Thebes and Vizier of the South, Ptahmes was one of the principal officers of State during the richly endowed reign of AMENHOTEP III. He is accompanied on his commemorative stela by his wife Aypy and by various members of their family. He invites those who read the stela to consider the excellance of his life and achievements and urges them to conduct themselves similarly.

J.-C. Guyon, *Les Reserves de Pharaon – L'Egypte dans les Collections du Musée des Beaux-Arts de Lyon*, Lyons, 1988: 59 (exhibition catalogue).

Ptahpehen, Sculptor, Third Dynasty, Old Kingdom, *c.* 2650 BC. The sculptor and 'Maker of Vases', Ptahpehen was evidently a respected craftsman of the time of King DJOSER NETJERYKHET, for whom the Step Pyramid complex was built at Saqqara. Djoser caused to be buried beneath the pyramid a great quantity of bowls and vases (some 40,000 in all) inscribed with the names of his predecessors on the thrones of Egypt. Ptahpehen was thus honoured by vases inscribed with his name being similarly preserved beneath the king's monument.

P. Lacau and J-P. Lauer, *La Pyramide à Degrés IV: Inscriptions Gravés sur les Vases*, Cairo, 1959: 65ff., pl. 25.
IFAO 1981: 15, 'Bol de Ptahpen', cat. no. 9.
MduL E 11016.

Ptahshepses, Vizier, Fourth/Fifth Dynasties, Old Kingdom, *c.* 2530–2470 BC. Ptahshepses was born during the reign of King MENKAURE. He married the Princess Khamaat and served four kings of the Fifth Dynasty.

James and Davies 1983: 21; ill. 19.
BM 682.

Ptahshepses, Vizier, Fifth Dynasty, Old Kingdom, *c.* 2445–2421 BC. Ptahshepses, originally the royal manicurist and hairdresser, rose to the highest rank as Vizier to King NIUSERRE. He was married to the king's daughter, Khamerernebty. He was given a magnificent mastaba tomb, of royal dimensions, at Abusir. Nearby was the tomb of Niuserre's predecessor, NEFEREFRE.

Ptahshepses, like others who held the office of manicurist and hairdresser, was a priest of high rank since, to discharge his function of grooming the king, he had to touch the body of a living god.

Breasted 1: §§254–62.
PM III: 79–80.
M. Verner, *The Mastaba of Ptahshepses*, Prague, 1977.
Verner 1994: 173–4.

Ptolemaios, Donor, Ptolemaic Period, *c.* 104–5 BC. Ptolemaios paid for the erection of a stela honouring the god Thoth and in return asked for a long life. He invokes Thoth with the epithet 'Thrice Great', a designation which was to come to be applied widely in later alchemical and gnostic texts as 'Hermes Trismegistus'.

Hodjash and Berlev 1982: no. 134, 199–200.

Ptolemy I Soter, General, King, Macedonian and Ptolemaic Periods, *c.* 305–285 BC. The founder and first king of the Ptolemaic dynasty was a Macedonian, son of Lagus and Arsinoë, a former concubine of King PHILIP II. There were in consequence of his mother's relationship with the king, rumours about his actual parentage.

Ptolemy was brought up with ALEXANDER, Philip's son and one of his closest companions. When they grew to manhood Ptolemy became one of Alexander's most trusted commanders.

After Alexander's death in 323 BC and the disintegration of his empire, Ptolemy seized control of Egypt. He and his descendants were to rule it for the next three centuries.

Ptolemy was an enlightened and civilised ruler. Building on Alexander's foundations he made Alexandria the centre of the Greek presence in Egypt; it rapidly became the intellectual and cultural centre of the ancient world, and was to remain so for more than half a millennium. During his reign the Library and the Museum were founded and flourished under his support and that of his son and successor.

Ptolemy achieved an important symbolic and psychological advantage by capturing the mummified body of Alexander as it was carried from Babylon to Greece. For the remainder of Ptolemy's life it was kept in Memphis. Ptolemy proclaimed himself king in 304 BC.

Throughout his life Ptolemy was obliged to conduct a number of campaigns, some against envious companions from the past. His military prowess, however, never deserted him.

Ptolemy introduced the practice of marrying his sister (in fact, his half-sister, Berenice), which was to be a characteristic of the dynasty. Berenice was the mother of his heir.

With characteristic maturity and self-assurance, Ptolemy I abdicated power in favour of his son in 285 BC; he died in 283.

Turner 1984: 118–74.
Bowman, 1990.
W. M. Ellis, *Ptolemy of Egypt*, London, 1994.

Ptolemy II Philadelphus, King, Ptolemaic Period, 285–246 BC. Continuing the enlightened policies of his father, Ptolemy II further developed the Library and the

Museum at Alexandria, raising them to international importance. He built the Pharos which stood at the sea-entrance to Alexandria. He also gave attention to enlarging the influence of Egypt by annexing Phoenicia and parts of Syria. In Egypt itself he pursued a policy of inaugurating new towns, increasing the Greek-speaking population as he did so. He undertook an extensive irrigation programme in the Fayum, thus increasing Egypt's agricultural yield considerably.

D. J. Crawford, 'Ptolemy, Ptah and Apis', *World Archaeology*, 11, 1980: 135–45.
Turner 1984: 118–74.
D. J. Thompson, *Memphis under the Ptolemies*, Princeton NJ, 1988: 116–17, 126–32.

Ptolemy III Euergetes, King, Ptolemaic Period, 246–221 BC. Ptolemy III succeeded his father when he was around forty years old. To avenge the murder of his sister Berenice Syra and her son, he invaded Syria and captured Babylon. He developed Egypt's naval capacity considerably and expanded his domains by a profitable marriage with Berenice of Cyrene.

Turner 1984: 118–74.
Fraser 1972.
Green 1990.

Ptolemy IV Philopator, King, Ptolemaic Period, 221–203 BC. The son of PTOLEMY III, the fourth of the name was memorable for having defeated the formidable general Antiochos III in battle. He was, however, beset by dynastic and family intrigues which he attempted to resolve in the fashion which was to become a standard practice among the Ptolemies, by murdering any of his relations who stood in his way. He married his sister, Arsinöe III. He died suddenly, an event concealed by his ministers for some time.

Fraser 1972.
Green 1990.

Ptolemy V Epiphanes, King, Ptolemaic Period, 205–181 BC. The son of PTOLEMY IV, Epiphanes was a young child when he succeeded to the throne. He was much manipulated by his ministers. He was attacked by Antiochos IV and the king of Macedon, Philip V. He was saved by the intervention of Rome, an intervention which was to be ominous for Egypt's future. He then married the daughter of Antiochos. He is best remembered by the appearance of his name in a bilingual inscription on the Rosetta Stone. This was a decree which records the attainment of his majority and his coronation. Champollion's intuition that the royal names, including Ptolemy's, were contained in the inscription's cartouches, led to the eventual decipherment of Egyptian hieroglyphs.

Fraser 1972.
Green 1990.
R. M. Errington, 'Rome Against Philip and Antiochus', CAH VIII (1990) 244–89.

Ptolemy VI Philometor, King, Ptolemaic period, 181–145 BC. Coming to the throne as a child, Ptolemy VI was the subject of a regency by his mother (hence, no doubt, Philometor, 'Mother-loving') the widow of PTOLEMY V. Antiochos IV, king of Syria, invaded Egypt, capturing the king. His younger brother, also Ptolemy, proclaimed himself king in Ptolemy VI's stead. He was, however, reinstated by Antiochos and for a time the brothers reigned jointly. Ptolemy VI was forced out of Egypt by his brother, Ptolemy VIII; he appealed to Rome (where, exiled, he was given refuge by the landscape painter DEMETRIUS) and was again reinstated, his brother being expelled to Cyrene (acquired by PTOLEMY III) which he was permitted to hold as an independent kingdom. Eventually Ptolemy VI was killed in battle against Alexander Balas.

Fraser 1972.
Green 1990.

Ptolemy VII Neos Philopator, King, Ptolemaic Period, 145 BC. The heir of

PTOLEMY VI, he was murdered by his uncle, Ptolemy VIII (see PTOLEMY VI) who then seized the throne.

Fraser 1972.
Green 1990.

Ptolemy VIII Euergetes II (alt. Physcon), King, Ptolemaic Period, 170–116 BC. One of the longest-reigning of the Ptolemaic kings, Ptolemy VIII was also one of the most deplorable. He murdered PTOLEMY VII and married his mother, the widow of PTOLEMY VI, who was also his sister.

His alternative surname means 'Potbelly'. He was driven out of Alexandria by the people, who supported his queen; he returned and then murdered his own son. He married his sister-wife's daughter by her original husband, his brother.

Fraser 1972.
Green 1990.

Ptolemy IX Soter II (alt. Lathyrus), King, Ptolemaic Period, 116–107; 88–81 BC. The son of PTOLEMY VIII he was proclaimed king jointly with his mother, Cleopatra III, as queen. She expelled him from Egypt and he moved to Cyprus, which he ruled as an independent kingdom. On his mother's death in 88 BC he returned to Alexandria at the behest of its citizens. His brother had been installed by their mother as king but he was expelled by Ptolemy IX. He was eventually restored to the throne and died as King of Egypt.

Fraser 1972.
Green 1990.

Ptolemy X Alexander I, King, Ptolemaic Period, 107–88 BC. Appointed to reign jointly with his brother PTOLEMY IX by their mother, he continued to hold the throne with her after his brother's deposition. On his mother's death his brother returned, deposed him in turn and killed him fighting in Cyprus.

Fraser 1972.
Green 1990.

Ptolemy XI Alexander II, King, Ptolemaic Period, 80 BC. The son of PTOLEMY X, Ptolemy XI married PTOLEMY IX's daughter, whom he then murdered. He was torn to pieces by an outraged mob in Alexandria.

Fraser 1972.
Green 1990.

Ptolemy XII Neos Dionysos (alt. Auletes), King, Ptolemaic Period, 80–51 BC. Well exemplifying the disintegration of the line of its great founder, Ptolemy XII was the illegitimate son of PTOLEMY IX; the legitimate line was now extinct. He was expelled by the people of Alexandria in 58 BC but was reinstated by Rome, which now did not hesitate to treat the Ptolemaic kings as clients, to dispose of them as Roman interests dictated.

His daughter was CLEOPATRA VII.

Fraser 1972.
Green 1990.
A. N. Sherwin-White, *Roman Foreign Policy in the East, 168 BC–AD 1*, London, 1984.
R. D. Sullivan, *Near Eastern Royalty and Rome, 100–30 BC*, Toronto, 1990.

Ptolemy XIII, King, Ptolemaic Period, 51–47 BC. The son of PTOLEMY XII was proclaimed joint ruler with his sister CLEOPATRA VII. He expelled her in 48 BC but she sought the aid of CAESAR and by his intervention was restored. A civil war ensued and Ptolemy XIII was drowned in the Nile.

Fraser 1972.
Green 1990.
Hughes-Hallett 1990.

Ptolemy XIV, King, Ptolemaic Period, 47–44 BC. A younger brother of Cleopatra, he was married to his sister, who had him murdered so that she might rule alone with her son, supposedly sired by Caesar, CAESARION.

G. H. Macurdy, *Hellenistic Queens*, Baltimore MD, 1932.

Fraser 1972.
Green 1990.
Hughes-Hallett 1990.

Ptolemy XV Caesarion, *see* **Caesarion**

Ptolemy Claudius, Geographer and Astronomer, Roman Period, second century AD. An inhabitant of Alexandria after the extinction of the Ptolemies, Claudius was one of the most enduringly influential of the city's savants. His *Almagest* (the Arabic version of his *Mathematike Syntaxis*) remained in use for many centuries. His observations of the stars, planets and constellations were accurate, comprehensive and precise.

His *Geography* was by far the most advanced study of its kind extant; this, too, survived long after Claudius' lifetime as a work of scholarly reference. However, it suffered somewhat from its author's own failure to unite the two disciplines which he had at his disposal and to check his geographical conclusions by reference to astronomical observation.

G. J. Toomer, 'Ptolemy and his Greek Predecessors', in C. Walker (ed.) *Astronomy before the Telescope*, London, 1966: 82–91.

Puyemre, Architect, Eighteenth Dynasty, New Kingdom, *c.* 1479–1425 BC. One of the principal architects of the early part of the reign of King THUTMOSE III, when he shared power with Queen HATSHEPSUT, Puyemre records the careful selection of rare materials for the royal building projects. He also fulfilled some political duties in the reign, receiving envoys bearing gifts for the king. He was buried in Thebes (TT 39).

Breasted 2: 160.
Tyldesley 1996: 168.

[Pythagoras], Philosopher, Magus, Twenty-Sixth Dynasty, Late Period, *c.* 569–470 BC. The son of Mnesarchus, Pythagoras was a native of Samos, who spent his youth in the island during the reign of the Tyrant Polycrates, the contemporary of King AMASIS of Egypt. When still young, Pythagoras is said to have left Samos and journeyed to Egypt. There he was presented to Amasis and sought initiation by the priests of the leading temples of Egypt. He was refused admission by the hierarchs of Heliopolis and Memphis but is said to have been accepted by the priests of Diospolis.

Pythagoras was reputed to be the first Greek to learn to speak Egyptian. He was evidently much impressed by the Egyptians' use of symbolism and, like all Greeks, was much in awe of hieroglyphs. Certainly, many of the tenets which he promulgated to his followers in later years were influenced by Egypt. However, one of the most enduring concepts attributed to him, that of the transmigration of souls, seems distinctly un-Egyptian and must have its origins elsewhere. Similarly, Pythagoras' strictures against blood sacrifices would have made little sense to the Egyptians.

According to his own mythology, Pythagoras was taken prisoner by CAMBYSES the Persian when he invaded Egypt and was carried off to Babylon where he remained for a number of years. An important component of Pythagorean philosophy was the recognition of number and the underlying structure of the cosmos, a belief which may have been fortified by the astronomical studies of the Babylonian priests to which Pythagoras was no doubt exposed.

In the later years of his life Pythagoras migrated to Southern Italy, first to Croton and later to Metapontum. There he is said to have died at the age of ninety-nine.

J. L. Raven, *Pythagoras and the Eleatics*, Amsterdam, 1966.
P. Gorman, *Pythagoras: A Life*, London, Oxford and Boston, 1979.

Q

Qa'a, *see* **Ka'a**

Qahedjet (alt. Huni [?]), King, Third Dynasty, Old Kingdom, *c.* 2637–2613 BC. An entirely shadowy figure, Qahedjet is known only by one monument, an extremely finely carved stela in which he is shown wearing the White Crown of Upper Egypt, in the company of the god Horus of Heliopolis.

The king's name, Qahedjet, is compounded with the word which signifies the White Crown. He is shown face-to-face with the god, whom he equals in height, the first occasion in which an Egyptian king is represented on equal terms with one of the great divinities, in this case the god who is incarnated in the king.

Heliopolis was an important centre in the Third Dynasty, and a large temple was built there as early as the reign of King DJOSER NETJERYKHET, the second king of the dynasty. It is possible that Qahedjet is to be identified with King HUNI, the last ruler of the dynasty, who is otherwise known only by his birth name; in that case, Qahedjet would be Huni's Horus name.

J. Vandier, 'Une Stèle Égyptienne Portant un Nouveau Nom Royal de la Troisième Dynastie', CRAIB Jan–Mars 1968: 16–22.
L. M. Berman, 'Stele of Qahedjet', in Berman and Letellier 1996: 36, no. 2.
MduL E 25982.

Qenamun, *see* **Kenamun**

R

Rahotep and Nofret, Prince and Princess, Fourth Dynasty, Old Kingdom, *c.* 2613–2589 BC. The uncommonly lifelike statues, still retaining much of their original paint, of the two 'Great Ones' of the early Fourth Dynasty, Rahotep and Nofret, are amongt the most celebrated of Egyptian works of art. Rahotep was probably the son of King SNEFERU; he was High Priest of Re at Heliopolis (with the added title, which was particular to Heliopolis, of 'Greatest of Seers'), Director of Expeditions and Chief of Construction. In the latter capacity he may have been concerned with the design and building of the early pyramids.

His wife, Nofret, sits beside him; often the wife, even if she was a princess, was depicted on a much smaller scale than her husband, but Nofret is shown in the same proportions as her husband. Nofret was a 'Royal Acquaintance', a title of considerable honour in the Old Kingdom.

Borchardt 1911–36: (GG) 3–5, pl. 1.
Stevenson Smith 1958 (1981): 85.
James and Davies 1983: 21; ill. 18 (Rahotep only).
Saleh and Sourouzian: 27.
EMC CG 34.
BM 1242.

Rahotep, Royal Scribe, Fifth Dynasty, Old Kingdom, *c.* 2494–2345 BC. Rahotep was the Royal Scribe of Decrees and Keeper of the King's Document Case. His mastaba at Saqqara contained nineteen statues of himself.

Hayes 1: 109–10; fig. 61.
MMA 25.9.

Rahotep, King, Seventeenth Dynasty, Second Intermediate Period, *c.* 1650 BC. At the beginning of the occupation of much of northern Egypt by the Semitic-speaking Hyksos invaders from the region of Palestine, a line of princes emerged in the south, centred on Thebes, which claimed descent from one of the Thirteenth Dynasty royal families. The first of this line was Rahotep, who assumed the royal titulary and founded the dynasty which was, a hundred years later, to expel the Hyksos.

Rahotep restored temples in Koptos and Abydos, and his rule extended over most of the south. He was contemporary with the Hyksos king YAQUB-HOR (Yaqub-Baal) and they appear to have maintained relatively good relations. He was succeeded by Inyotef V.

Grimal 1992: 187.

Raia, Musician, Nineteenth Dynasty, New Kingdom, *c.* 1279–1213 BC. Raia was the Chief of Singers of the great temple of Ptah of Memphis; as such he must have been a key figure in the elaborate ceremonies conducted in the temple, often, no doubt, in the presence of the king himself, RAMESSES II.

Raia is depicted playing the harp in his tomb. In this scene he appears to be blind, though this may simply be a convention, when musicians are playing before the god or to emphasise the player's absorption in the music at the expense of another sense. When he died, Raia's choir, of which he had been the leader, participated in his funeral. His wife, Mutemwiya, was buried in the same tomb.

Martin 1991: 124–30; ills 84–8.
Manniche 1991: 101.

Ramesses I, King, Nineteenth Dynasty, New Kingdom, *c.* 1295–1294 BC. The founder of the Nineteenth Dynasty was chosen by King HOREMHEB to succeed him. Like Horemheb he was a soldier and had also held high civil office, including the responsibility, again like Horemheb, for Egypt's foreign relations.

Ramesses came from the north of Egypt and his family kept their loyalties to that region and its gods; his son and successor, SETI, was named in honour of Seth.

Ramesses reigned only for a short time, not more than two years. He was buried in KV 16.

See RAMOSE.

E. Cruze-Uribe, 'The Father of Ramses I', JNES 37 (1978) 237–44.
J. J. Clere, 'Notes sur la Chapelle Funéraire de Ramsès I à Abydos et sur Son Inscription Dedicatoire', R d'E 11 (1957) 1–38.

Ramesses II, King, Nineteenth Dynasty, New Kingdom, *c.* 1279–1213 BC. The son of King SETI I, with whom he had been portrayed as a boy, lassooing a sacred bull and inspecting the roll-call of the ancestors who had gone before them on the thrones of Egypt, Ramesses was trained for the kingship from an early age. He succeeded when he was in his early twenties; he was to reign for sixty-seven years.

Ramesses is chiefly recalled for his frenetic building programmes, covering the land of Egypt with gigantic structures, most of them containing huge representations of himself. He married many times, though his favourite wife seems to have been NEFERTARI, who has a small and elegant temple next to his huge one at Abu Simbel. He was the father of many children (he was said to have produced over one hundred) of whom Prince KHAEMWASET was perhaps the most notable, though many of his sons occupied high offices with distinction; most of them predeceased him, however. He was eventually succeeded by his thirteenth son, MERENPTAH, born of his other principal wife, eventually Nefertari's successor, ISTNOFRET.

Ramesses delighted in having himself portrayed as a warrior, riding into battle accompanied by his pet lion or slaying enemy hordes single-handed. He fought one major engagement against the Hittites at the city of Qadesh, the outcome of which was largely unfavourable to Ramesses; the king, however, always a skilled and persistent propagandist, had the battle depicted as an overwhelming victory. In the great inscription recording the battle, Ramesses gives his Shield-Bearer and Charioteer, MENNA, and his two horses, Victory-in-Thebes and Mut-is-Content, particular praise.

Ramesses continued the policy of the regeneration of the Egyptian economy and the improvement of its standing abroad introduced by King HOREMHEB after the disastrous years of the Amarna kingship, a policy which had been ably extended by his father, King Seti. His management of Egypt's foreign affairs was generally beneficial and his reign was in the main a time of peace and prosperity for Egypt.

Ramesses' principal monument in Western Thebes is the immense funerary temple which he built there, the Ramesseum. It was a disconnected head of one of Ramesses' statues which prompted

Shelley's poem *Ozymandias*, a corruption of Usermare, Ramesses' prenomen. The king, however, outwitted the poet; far from 'Nothing else remains…', the entire region is heavy with Ramesses' presence.

Ramesses II was buried in in the Valley of the Kings in KV 7. His mummy was recovered from the Deir el-Bahri cache and now rests in the Egyptian Museum, Cairo.

Kitchen 1982: passim.
C. Desroches Noblecourt, *The Great Pharaoh Ramesses II and His Time*, Montreal, 1985.
BM 67 (and countless others in virtually every major museum collection).

Ramesses, Prince, Nineteenth Dynasty, New Kingdom, *c.* 1280–1229 BC. The second of the sons of Prince Ramesses, born before his father ascended the throne as King RAMESSES II, the younger Ramesses became a general in the Army and for a long time was his father's nominated successor, perhaps for as long as twenty-five years. He was the eldest son of Ramesses' second principal wife, ISTNOFRET. He was the full brother of Prince KHAEMWASET, who succeeded him as Crown Prince.

Kitchen 1982: 103.

Ramesses III, King, Twentieth Dynasty, New Kingdom, *c.* 1184–1153 BC. The second king of the Twentieth Dynasty consciously modelled himself on RAMESSES II. He was a forceful and conscientious monarch, but if he lacked any particular quality, it was luck, for many of his enterprises did not mature for reasons which were often beyond his control or influence. The first recorded workers' strike – at Deir el-Medina – occurred in his reign; he was required to deal with an invasion of a coalition of opponents, known collectively as the 'Sea Peoples', drawn from the Mediterranean islands and the Syrian coastal towns, who had been troublesome in MERENPTAH'S time. Ramesses defeated them decisively and recorded the event at his temple at Medinet Habu.

Ramesses was remembered as a great benefactor of the temples of Egypt; as such he was no doubt able to conciliate the priestly faction which was growing ever more powerful. The Great Harris Papyrus, prepared by his successor after Ramesses' death, records many of the grants which he made to the temple institutions.

Towards the end of his life Ramesses III was the target of a serious conspiracy hatched in the harem. It involved one of his wives who tried to bring her son to the throne. The conspiracy was detected but Ramesses died soon after and it has been speculated that his death may have been precipitated by the plot.

Ramesses III was buried in the Valley of the Kings (KV 11). His mummy was found in the cache recovered from AMENHOTEP II's tomb; he seems to have been about sixty-five when he died. He built an immense funerary temple at Medinet Habu.

Ramesses III was the last important king of the New Kingdom. He was followed by a succession of generally short-lived kings, all of whom adopted the name Ramesses.

F. Fèvre, *Le Dernier Pharaon : Ramsès III ou la Crépuscule d'une Civilization*, Paris, 1992.
W. F. Edgerton, 'The Strikes in Ramses III's 29th Year', JNES 10 (1951) 137–45.
A. de Buck, 'The Judicial Papyrus of Turin', JEA 23 (1937) 152–67.

Ramesses IV, King, Twentieth Dynasty, New Kingdom, *c.* 1153–1147 BC. One of the first acts of Ramesses IV's reign was to settle a dispute with the workers in the royal necropolis which had bedevilled RAMESSES III's final days. The men were paid and preparations could thus go ahead for the dead king's burial. Ramesses IV appears to have had some continuing concern for the welfare of the workers at Thebes. He was a keen builder of monuments though few survive. He conducted extensive mining expeditions, seeking the finest stones for the embellishment of the temples. The Great Harris Papyrus dates from Ramesses IV's reign and lists both his many endowments to the temples and also the principal events of his father's reign.

Ramesses prayed to the gods to grant him a life as long as that of the great RAMESSES II. The gods failed to comply with this request as Ramesses IV reigned only for six years. He was buried in KV 2.

E. Erichsen, *Papyrus Harris*, Brussels, 1933.
E. Hornung, *Zwei Ramessidische Königsgräber: Ramses IV und Ramses VII*, Mainz, 1990.
A. J. Peden, *The Reign of Ramesses IV*, Warminster, 1994.

Ramesses V, King, Twentieth Dynasty, New Kingdom, *c.* 1147–1143 BC. During the brief reign of RAMESSES IV, the level of corruption which had been allowed to grow amongst the priests in the temple administrations was uncovered and an enquiry set up to determine responsibility. That Ramesses V attempted to maintain something of the quality of Egypt's administrative systems is suggested by documents which probably derive from his reign, concerned with taxation and other bureaucratic matters, especially relating to land.

The recital of Ramesses V's resounding titles indicates the complexity which the titulary of the late New Kingdom had attained, and how hollow the titles sound, given the knowledge of the political conditions which pertained in Egypt during his lifetime:

'Living Horus, Mighty Bull, Great in Victory, Sustaining the Two Lands; Favourite of the Two Goddesses: Mighty in Strength, Repulser of Millions; Golden Horus: Rich in Years, Like Ta-Tanen, Sovereign, Lord of Jubilees, Protector of Egypt, Filling Every Land with Great Monuments in His Name; King of Upper and Lower Egypt: Nibmare-Meriamon; Son of Re, of His Body, His Beloved, Lord of Diadems: Amonhirkhepeshef-Ramesses-Neterhekon, Given Life, Like Re, Forever'.

Ramesses V died after only four years on the throne, probably from smallpox, though some suspicion attaches to his successor. He was buried in KV 35, though originally KV 9 was intended for his burial.

Breasted 4: §473.
Reeves and Wilkinson 1996: 164–5, 201.

Ramesses VI, King, Twentieth Dynasty, New Kingdom, *c.* 1143–1136 BC. The successor of the relatively young RAMESSES V was most likely a son of RAMESSES III; he seems to have been ill-disposed to his immediate predecessors, presumably resenting their occupancy of the throne. It is possible that he may have deposed Ramesses V, but of that there is no certain evidence, though there is some indication that there may have been an insurrection prompted by the factions supporting rival claimants to the throne at this time. When he died he was buried in KV 9 but was later moved with Ramesses V to KV 35.

Despite the uncertainties of the reigns of the immediate successors of Ramesses III, it is notable that some senior officials continued in office throughout the period, into the reign of Ramesses VI.

A. A. Amer Amin, 'Reflexions on the Reign of Ramesses VI', JEA 71: 66–70.
Reeves and Wilkinson 1996: 164–5.
Grimal: 288–9.

Ramesses VII, King, Twentieth Dynasty, New Kingdom, *c.* 1136–1129 BC. Little is known of the reign of Ramesses VII, other than that the condition of Egypt began seriously to decline: prices rose alarmingly and there was considerable distress in the lands. KV 1 was prepared for him.

Ramesses VII reigned for seven years and was followed by Ramesses VIII, who held the kingship only for one year. He was one of the last of RAMESSES III's sons to survive.

K. Kitchen, 'Ramesses VII and the Twentieth Dynasty', JEA 58 (1972) 182–94.
Grimal: 288–9.

Ramesses IX, King, Twentieth Dynasty, New Kingdom, *c.* 1126–1108 BC. After the short and generally unproductive reigns of the successors of RAMESSES III, the seventeen-year reign of Ramesses IX promised a more coherent rule to be exerted over Egypt and for the problems which were mounting against the country's peaceful progress, both at home and abroad, to be confronted. Ramesses built extensively and gave special attention to Heliopolis and the land around it.

During his reign the first of a series of major scandals involving the pillaging of royal and private tombs in the necropolis was discovered. Ramesses IX set up a commission to investigate the allegations. The situation deteriorated to the extent that in a few years after the end of the Twentieth Dynasty the rulers of the Theban region in the Twenty First Dynasty moved the mummies of the kings, including Ramesses IX and various of his predecessors, to safety in DB 320, where they were found in the last century.

Ramesses IX was followed by Ramesses X, who reigned unremarkably for some ten years; his tomb was KV 18.

F. Guilmant, *Le Tombeau de Ramsès IX*, Cairo, 1907.
M. Bierbrier, 'The Length of the Reign of Ramesses X', JEA 61: 251.
K. Kitchen, 'Family Relationships of Ramesses IX and the Late Twentieth Dynasty', SAK 11: 127–34.
Reeves and Wilkinson 1996: 168–71.

Ramesses XI, King, Twentieth Dynasty, New Kingdom, *c.* 1097–1069 BC. The last of the Ramessid kings, the eleventh of the name, proved to be one of the longest-lasting, reigning for twenty-seven years. Early in his reign he had to deal with the increasing depredations in the north and west caused by the activities of the Meshwesh and the Libu, undisciplined tribesmen who harried the Egyptian towns in the Delta and even as far south as the region below Memphis.

The most enduring development in Ramesses XI's reign was the emergence in Thebes of powerful members of the priestly orders, the most aggressive of whom began to challenge the royal authority and prerogatives, even assuming royal titles. In the case of one such pretender, AMENHOTEP, the High Priest of Amun, Ramesses managed to outface him and the priest was sent into exile. But at the same time the situation in Thebes and the south deteriorated to the extent that the king ordered the Viceroy of Kush, PANEHESY, to move northwards and put the rebellion down. This decision was to have long-lasting consequences.

Ramesses decided upon a policy of conciliation with the Thebans, entering into an understanding with two of the great magnates of the region, SMENDES and HERIHOR. At the king's death the royal power was flouted by the southeners, and for many years to come Upper Egypt was virtually independent of the royal authority. The generally dismal cycle of the reigns of the successors of RAMESSES II had resulted in the priests of Amun becoming richer and more powerful than the kings themselves.

Ramesses' reign was marked by outbreaks of tomb robberies and a number of reports of court investigations survive. In the king's own case it was intended that Ramesses XI should be buried in KV 4, but this tomb was abandoned unfinished and he was not buried there. His tomb has not been found.

Peet 1930.
Kitchen 1986: §§209–12.
Reeves and Wilkinson 1996: 172–3, 190–2.

Ramessesnakhte, High Priest, Twentieth Dynasty, New Kingdom, *c.* 1160 BC.

During the reign of King RAMESSES IV Ramessesnakhte was appointed High Priest of Amun at Thebes. He seems to have been able to secure the succession to this most powerful of offices in the south of the country to members of his own family. Two of his sons followed him in the office, thus anticipating the situation in the Twenty-First Dynasty when the High Priesthood became truly hereditary, challenging the authority of the king in the south.

Ramessesnakhte's career demonstrates how the office of High Priest of Amun had outreached the kingship in authority and security. Ramessesnakhte saw six kings come and go, whilst he remained in office. He was a member of the powerful Merybast family.

Kitchen 1986: §207.
Kuhrt 1995: I, 205.

Ramose, Vizier, Eighteenth Dynasty, New Kingdom, *c.* 1390–1360 BC. Ramose was one of the most distinguished of the holders of the office of Chief Minister to the King, in this case the magnificent AMENHOTEP III, and later AMENHOTEP IV-AKHENATEN.

He was born of a family from Athribis and was related to other holders of high office under Amenhotep III, including AMENHOTEP, son of Hapu. His mother was IPUIA who is portrayed in Ramose's tomb, along with other of his relations, including MAIY, the Overseer of Horses, and his wife Werel. He was buried in a richly decorated tomb at Thebes (TT 55), the wall reliefs of which are among the finest to survive.

N. de Garis Davis, *The Tomb of the Vizier Ramose*, London, 1941.
W. F. Edgerton, 'The Government and the Governed in the Egyptian Empire', JNES 6 (1947) 152–60.

Ramose, Soldier, Eighteenth/Nineteenth Dynasties, New Kingdom, *c.* 1300 BC. The owner of a tomb at Memphis, close to the tomb of King HOREMHEB, Ramose's identity is something of a mystery. An officer of the same name is represented in Horemheb's tomb, where he is designated as the king's private secretary and scribe of the army; he seems to have succeeded SEMENTAWY, who was apparently much in Horemheb's affections, when he was Generalissimo of the army.

Ramose's tomb was largely depleted (KV 16), and it has been speculated that Ramose may have been transmuted, eventually and after Horemheb's death, into his successor, RAMESSES I (1295–1294 BC). If so, although his reign was brief he nonetheless was the founder of the Nineteenth Dynasty and had ten kings of Egypt who adopted his name.

Martin 1991: 60–1, 72–3, 119.

Ramose, Scribe, Nineteenth Dynasty, New Kingdom, *c.* 1279–1213 BC. One of RAMESSES II's long-serving officials, Ramose was 'Scribe in the Place of Truth'. He seems to have enjoyed considerable status and popularity in Deir el-Medina. A number of statues are known of him, and he and his wife are represented in several of the tombs of their contemporaries. He appears to have enjoyed the patronage of the Vizier of Ramesses II, which might go some way towards explaining his standing. He was buried at Deir el-Medina.

He was the adoptive father of KENHERKHOPSHEF, another scribe at Deir el-Medina.

Černý 1973.
M. Bierbrier, *Tomb Builders of the Pharaohs*, London, 1982.
IFAO 264.
MduL E 16364.
BM 243.

Raneb, King, Second Dynasty, Archaic Period, *c.* 2865 BC. The second king of the Second Dynasty, Raneb succeeded HOTEPSEKHEMWY, the dynasty's founder. Little is known of him, though some sealings have been recovered which bear his name. It is also engraved on the shoulder of a statue in the Cairo Museum.

Raneb is the first king of Egypt to have a name compounded with that of the solar god, Re. A *serekh* bearing his name is carved in a particularly bold and emphatic manner.

It is possible that Raneb was buried at Saqqara and that his tomb is concealed under later constructions.

H. G. Fischer, 'An Egyptian Royal Stela of the Second Dynasty', *Artibus Asiae*, 24 (1961) 46–8, figs 8, 9.
Emery 1961: 92–3.
Spencer: 84.
MMA 60–144.

Ranefer, High Priest, Fifth Dynasty, Old Kingdom, *c.* 2475 BC. Ranefer was the High Priest of Ptah and of Sokar at Memphis. In the former capacity he had charge of all the artists and craftsmen working for the king and the higher nobility.

Naturally enough, Ranefer had a large mastaba tomb built for himself at Saqqara. It contained two superlative statues of the High Priest, lifesize, showing him to have been a most imposing figure; their quality indicates what it meant to have the finest artistic talent in Egypt at one's disposal.

He is portrayed in the immortal Egyptian pose, striding forward with his left foot advanced. Two thousand years later the same posture would characterise the Greek statues of the *kouros*.

A. Mariette, *Les Mastabas de l'Ancien Empire*, Paris, 1889, 123.
Borchardt 1911–36: 19–20.
Stevenson Smith 1946 (1949): 49, pl. 18.
Terrace and Fischer: 10, 57–60 (as 'Ranofer').
Saleh and Sourouzian 1987: 45–6.
EMC JE10063/CG19.
EMC JE10064/CG18.

Redyzet, Princess, Third Dynasty, Old Kingdom, *c.* 2660 BC. The Princess Redyzet is remembered by a fine statue of herself, seated, which is typical of the monumental, assertive style of statuary in the Third Dynasty, when so many of the expressions and characteristics of Egyptian art were evolving towards their canonical forms. It has been suggested that Redyzet has something of the look of King DJOSER NETJERYKHET about her.

Stevenson Smith 1958 (1981): 67–8, ill. 55.
Scamuzzi: pl. IX.
Museo Egizio, Turin.

Redjedef, *see* **Djedefre**

Reemkuy, Prince, Fifth Dynasty, Old Kingdom, *c.* 2414–2375 BC. Reemkuy was the eldest son and heir apparent of King DJEDKARE ISESI. As was so often the case he did not outlive his father and he was buried in a tomb originally intended for another, whose name and titles were erased to allow for those of the prince to be substituted.

The reliefs in the tomb are nonetheless of a high quality. They show Reemkuy engaged in his favourite pastimes, the representation of which would ensure their continuation in the afterlife. Hunting scenes, the review of animal stocks, sailing on the river, and even the names of favoured servants are all recorded.

Reemkuy's titles are very florid, as befits his rank. They include 'Hereditary Prince', 'King's Eldest Son Whom He Loved', 'Scribe of the Sacred Writings', 'Magnate of the Incense', 'Servant of the Throne' and 'Sole Companion'.

Hayes 1: 94–102, figs 54–7.
MMA 08.20.1.

Rehu, Official, Eighth/Ninth Dynasties, First Intermediate Period, *c.* 2181–2055 BC. Rehu was an official residing at Akhmim, the capital of the ninth Upper Egyptian nome, at the end of the Old Kingdom. His tomb, cut into the mountain at El Hawawish, is attractively decorated, though the painters' techniques are not as accomplished as the best Old Kingdom work in the region.

Rehu lived into the uncertain years of the First Intermediate Period, when the central authority of the state effectively collapsed. His tomb records fighting between rival forces from the north and south of Egypt (Akhmim was close to the centre of the Valley) in addition to the more usual representations of bullfighting, a pastime especially popular in the province.

Kanawati 1980.

Rehuerdjersen, Chancellor, Twelfth Dynasty, Middle Kingdom, *c.* 1985–1955 BC. One of those officials whom King AMENEMHET I took with him when he assumed the throne after the end of the Eleventh Dynasty, Rehuerdjersen had a stela dedicated at Abydos, the centre of the cult of Osiris. In its inscription he was named as 'Overseer of Sealers'. The stela was set up by the Lector Priest Hekayotef in the king's name. It contains the names of Rehuerdjersen's large family whom he obviously wanted to share his immortality, including his mother, his brothers and their children.

Rehuerdjersen possessed a mastaba tomb at El-Lisht, the capital to which King Amenemhet moved on assuming the throne. A relief from the mastaba shows Rehuerdjersen boating on the Nile in the company of his son, Nefry.

Hayes 1: 333–4, figs 108, 221.
MMA 22.1.5.

Rekhmire, Vizier, Eighteenth Dynasty, New Kingdom, *c.* 1479–1400 BC. Rekhmire came from a family which had produced a number of civil servants of the highest rank. He was Vizier of the South to King THUTMOSE III and King AMENHOTEP II, thus being responsible for the administration of Upper Egypt at a time of Egypt's greatest power and prosperity. To judge by his tomb and funerary chapel, Rekhmire was a man of taste and high culture; the reliefs and paintings are of a superlative quality.

Rekhmire also incorporated into his funerary apartments descriptions of the duties of a vizier and the responsibility for right-doing and honourable conduct that the office demanded. He was buried in the Valley of the Nobles at Thebes (TT 100).

The paintings in his tomb show much of the daily life of the highest official in the state. Rekhmire is shown receiving tribute from Nubian envoys, leading giraffes and long-horned cattle; a monkey is depicted climbing up the neck of one of the giraffes. Other tribute bearers, from Syria, are shown bringing horses, elephants and panthers to the Vizier.

N. de Garis Davis, *The Tomb of Rekh-mi-re at Thebes*, New York, 1943.

Rewer, Vizier, Sixth Dynasty, Old Kingdom, *c.* 2300 BC. The king's First Minister either in the reign of PEPY I or of his heirs, Rewer seems to have been disgraced, or at least to have fallen from favour, to judge by the fact that everywhere in his tomb in Saqqara his name has been erased. Equally enigmatic is the fact that nowhere does he mention any relative or companion, a very un-Egyptian omission, nor are there provisions for mortuary priests to attend to his cult after his death. Rewer appears to be entirely alone.

Said Amer el-Fikey, *The Tomb of Vizier Re-wer at Saqqara*, Warminster, 1980.

Roma-Roy, High Priest, Nineteenth Dynasty, New Kingdom, *c.* 1212 BC. The son of the long-lived High Priest of Amun, BAKENKHONS, Roma-Roy was appointed to his father's office after his death, in the last months of the reign of King RAMESSES II. Roma-Roy was in turn succeeded by his son, ROY.

Kitchen 1982: 174.

Roy, High Priest, Nineteenth Dynasty, New Kingdom, *c.* 1213–1194 BC. The

High Priest of Amun at Thebes, Roy was the son of a previous incumbent of the office, ROMA-ROY. The latter succeeded BAKENKHONS and it is probable that Roy was Bakenkhons' grandson. He was High Priest during the reign of King MERENPTAH and lived on, a very old man, into the reign of King SETI II at the end of the Nineteenth Dynasty. His portrait statue suggests a proud and forceful man. He is represented holding a sistrum, sacred to the goddess Hathor.

Breasted 3: §§618–28.
BM 8.

Ruaben, Chancellor, Second Dynasty, Archaic Period, *c.* post-2865 BC. Ruaben is one of the comparatively few high officials from the Second Dynasty whose name is known; despite the fact that the dynasty survived for two centuries its history is very obscure.

The tomb at Saqqara (no. 2302) which is attributed to Ruaben is huge, with many chambers and halls; it is probably fair to assume that he would have been buried with great riches. His tomb is evidence that, despite the obscurity of the times, Egypt even at this very early period could produce funerary buildings of size and complexity. On the evidence of the sealings in the tomb Ruaben was a contemporary of King NYNETJER, the third king of the dynasty.

J. E. Quibell, *Excavations at Saqqara (1912–14): Archaic Mastabas*, Cairo, 1923: 30; pl. XXX.
Reisner 1936: 138; fig. 60.

Rudamun, King, Twenty-Third Dynasty, Third Intermediate Period, *c.* 757–754 BC. Rudamun was the brother of King TAKELOT III and he followed him to the throne. He appears to have reigned in almost total obscurity, with only some relatively minor building works to recall him. His daughter, Nesitperauty, married one of the 'kinglets' who emerged in various parts of Lower Egypt at this time, PEFTJAUAWYBAST, who later declared himself 'king' in Heracleopolis. As Rudamun was a legitimate if very restricted king, Peftjauawybast gained a degree of legitimacy himself as the result of his marriage.

Rudamun was succeeded after a reign of about four years by IUPUT II.

J. Berlandini, 'Une Stèle de Donation du Dynastie Libyen Roudamon', BIFAO 78 (1978) 147–64.
Kitchen 1986: §322.
Grimal: 331.

S

Sa'ankhkare Montuhotep, *see* **Montuhotep III.**

Sabef, Noble, First Dynasty, Archaic Period, *c.* 2890 BC. Sabef is one of the earliest Egyptians to be portrayed on a commemorative stela; it comes from Abydos and Sabef is depicted in what was to become one of the immemorial stances of Egyptians of high status, striding forward, grasping his wand of office.

He lived during the reign of King KA'A, the last ruler of the First Dynasty. Sabef was 'Governor of the Residence', 'Keeper of the Secrets of the Decrees' and a priest of Anubis. He was also Overseer of the Sed Festival, one of the most important and ancient ceremonies associated with the kingship, whose origin thus goes back to the very beginning of Egyptian history, and very possibly into the Predynastic period. The stela commemorating Sabef was found in Ka'a's tomb.

Petrie 1900: 44; pls XXX, XXXI.
Emery 1961: 168, 193.

Sabu, High Priest, Fifth Dynasty, Old Kingdom, *c.* 2375–2345 BC. Sabu was the High Priest of Ptah at Memphis and so had charge of the principal artists and craftsmen of the Two Kingdoms. He was one of the favourite courtiers of King UNAS, the last king of the Fifth Dynasty.

Breasted 1: §§1282–8.

Sa-Hathor, Official, Twelfth Dynasty, Middle Kingdom, *c.* 1880 BC. During the Middle Kingdom favoured officials were sometimes particularly honoured by being permitted to install a statue of themselves in the temple courtyard, where they could spend eternity in the presence of the king and share in the temple offerings. Sa-Hathor was one who enjoyed this privilege; he was 'Granary Superintendent of the Divine Offering'.

Pelizaeus-Museum, Hildesheim, no. 10.

Sahure, King, Fifth Dynasty, Old Kingdom, *c.* 2487–2475 BC. The succession of Sahure, the second king of the Fifth Dynasty, was secured through his mother, Queen KHENTKAWES, the heiress of King MENKAURE, who had earlier been married to King SHEPSESKHAF. She evidently brought the kingship to her new husband, USERKAF, and then to her sons, Sahure and NEFERIRKARE, who followed him on the throne.

Sahure and his successors gave particular prominence to the cults of the sun-god Re; their names are all compounded with that of the god.

Sahure moved the royal necropolis to Abusir. He built a pyramid there, of relatively modest proportions; it is now very much deflated. He continued the practice, inaugurated by the founder of the dynasty, Userkaf, of building a sun-temple in addition to his pyramid; thus did he and other kings of the dynasty demonstrate their attachment to Re. Sahure's sun-temple at Abusir has not been found; it is known only from references in papryus inscriptions.

Sahure's reign was notable for considerable trading activity and for various expeditions against the marauding tribes which had always harried Egypt's frontiers. At the Wadi Maghara in the Sinai, Sahure left a warning of the fate which awaited those who rebelled against his authority: the immemorial propaganda image in the form of a relief of the king smiting a desert chieftain.

L. Borchardt, *Das Grabdenkmal des Königs Sa'hu-re*, 2 vols, Leipzig, 1910–13.
Hayes 1: 71; fig. 46.
Lehner 1997: 142–4.
MMA 18.2.4.

Saiset, Official, Nineteenth Dynasty, New Kingdom, *c*. 1279–1213 BC. Saiset was Overseer of the Granaries during the reign of King RAMESSES II. Though his was a relatively modest post he was able to commission a handsome red granite sarcophagus, much of the detailed carving of which was enlivened with colour.

J. Settgast, 'Ein anthropoider Sarkophagdeckel der 19. Dynastie', *Jahrbuch Preußsischen Kulturbesitz*, Bd.X (1972) S. 254–9.
EMB inv. no. 1/72, cat. no. 1.

Salitis, King, Fifteenth Dynasty, Second Intermediate Period, *c*. 1650 BC. The Hyksos invaders of Egypt gained their name from an Egyptian term meaning 'rulers of foreign lands'. One of these was Salitis, who was amongst the original leaders of the Semitic-speaking hordes who entered northern Egypt at the end of the Thirteenth Dynasty (the Fourteenth was ephemeral and shadowy). He was evidently chosen by his fellow shaikhs (to employ an anachronistic terminology), initially no doubt as *primus inter pares*, as king. He established himself in Memphis, the ancient capital, but sought a stronghold in the north where the Hyksos might stay in contact with their ancestral lands in Palestine and the Levant. He chose the city of Avaris, which he rebuilt and refortified, establishing, it is said, a garrison of 240,000 men to guard the frontiers.

CAH II.1: 52, 58–9.
Grimal: 185–7.

Sa-Mont, Official, Twelfth Dynasty, Middle Kingdom, *c*. 1950 BC. Sa-Mont held the appointment of 'Scribe of the Great Prison', perhaps the equivalent of a prison director or governor. He was the son of the Granary Superintendent, Seneb, and the Lady of the House, Renseneb. His commemorative stele was dedicated by his brother, another Seneb, who occupied the important office of Royal Treasurer.

W. Seipel, *Bilder Für Die Ewigkeit: 3000 Jahre Ägyptische Kunst*, Konstanz, 1983: no. 48, 80–1.
Württembergisches Landesmuseum, Stuttgart, no. 1710.

Sanakhte (alt. Zanakht, Nebka), King, Third Dynasty, Old Kingdom, *c*. 2686–2667 BC. The first king of the Third Dynasty followed King KHASEKHEMWY, the last of the Second, without any indication of a break in the succession though MANETHO and other Egyptian chroniclers indicate a change of dynasty. It may be that Khasekhemwy was without a son; his daughter NEMAATHAP, the mother of Sanakhte's successor DJOSER NETJERYKHET, may also have been the mother of Sanakhte, since it is likely that he and Djoser were brothers.

Sanakhte was responsible for innovations in connection with the kingship. He was the first king to enclose his name in a cartouche; also in the Third Dynasty the Golden Horus name was added to the king's titulary.

The king's name appears on a rock outcrop from the Wadi Meghara in Sinai (now in the Cairo Museum) where he is shown in the timeless royal stance, smiting Egypt's enemies.

The burial place of Sanakhte is unknown but it was probably at Saqqara.

J. Garstang and K. Sethe, *Mahâsna and Bet Khallâf (ERA)*, London, 1903: 9, 25 pl. XIX.
BM EA 691.

Sanehet (alt. Sinuhe), Official, Twelfth Dynasty, Middle Kingdom, *c.* 1965 BC. A popular story, well known from a variety of texts and which originated in the Middle Kingdom, purports to tell of Sanehet (more widely known as Sinuhe), an official in the royal household, evidently favoured and well trusted. By some ill chance, he learned something of the circumstances attending the assassination of King AMENEMHET I and, fearing that he might be implicated, fled the court and ultimately, Egypt.

He made his way to Sinai, where he was befriended by a powerful Badu sheikh. Sanehet married the sheikh's daughter and prospered exceedingly, becoming the owner of many flocks and herds.

He hankered for Egypt, however, and, as he grew older, he evidently put out feelers to know if he might return. The king, SENWOSRET I, indicated that he would be entirely welcome, and Sanehet went home, to be welcomed by the king's children who, it was reported, jumped about and shouted with joy at his return.

The story ends with the death of Sanehet and his burial in a tomb given to him by the king. His story gained wide currency, though whether or not it is entirely fictional is still disputed.

A. F. Rainer, 'The World of Sinhue', *Israel Orient. Studies*, 2: 369–408.
A. M. Blackman, *Bibliotheca Aegyptiaca II*, Brussels, 1932: 1–41.
——'Some Notes on the Story of Sinuhe and Other Egyptian Texts', JEA 22 (1936) 35–44.
Lichtheim 1: 222–35.
H. Goedicke, 'The Route of Sinuhe's Flight', JEA 43 (1957) 77–85.

[Sargon II], Assyrian King, (= Twenty-Second/Twenty-Fifth Dynasties), Third Intermediate/Late Periods, *c.* 722–705 BC. The king of Assyria, Tiglath Pileser III, fomented considerable unrest in the Levant and Palestine in the eighth century, thus representing a threat to Egypt's interests and the security of the client states which looked to her for protection. Egypt was still weakened by the fragmentation of the kingship but an Egyptian expeditionary force was sent in support of the King of Gaza. Sargon, however, defeated the Gazans and was left in possession of an area dangerously close to Egypt's northern frontier. The last king of the Libyan dynasty, the Twenty-Second, OSORKON IV, adopted diplomacy and presented Sargon with 'twelve great horses, unrivalled in the whole country'. His gesture seems to have worked.

King PIANKHY, of the Kushite Twenty-Fifth Dynasty, also followed a policy of moderation towards the Assyrians, a policy followed too by his successor King SHABAKA. Sargon was succeeded by SENNACHERIB.

Grimal: 342, 343, 344, 346.

Sasenet, General, Sixth Dynasty, Old Kingdom, *c.* 2250 BC. Sasenet was a Commander of soldiers under King PEPY II, whose lover he was said to be, despite the king having been much married. A story current in the Middle Kingdom relates how the king was observed surreptitiously leaving his palace at night and climbing into Sasenet's house, leaving before the dawn. The story makes the point that Sasenet had no wife, a condition unusual for an Egyptian of the time.

Parkinson 1991: 54–6, 'The Tale of King Neferkare and General Sasenet'.

Sawadjenre Nebiryerawet I, King, Seventeenth (?) Dynasty, Second Intermediate

Period, *c.* 1650–1550 BC. One of the Theban princes to be recognised as King during the latter days of Hyksos rule in Egypt, Sawadjenre Nebiryerawet I was involved with the otherwise unprecedented sale of the office of nomarch in satisfaction of a debt. The agreement was recorded at the royal court where the Nomarch of Elkab disposed of his office to his brother in respect of a debt amounting to some twelve pounds (weight) of gold.

CAH II.1: 69.
Ryholt 1997: 389–90 (as Sixteenth Dynasty).

'Scorpion', King, Late Predynastic Period, *c.* 3150 BC. Few of the Predynastic 'kings' of Egypt have any documented historical existence. The king known as 'Scorpion', from the glyph which represents his name, is an exception. His most celebrated remembrance is from a large, ceremonial mace-head where he is shown opening a canal with, in the background, a scene which is thought to symbolise the killing of Egypt's enemies. His name has also been found on pottery from the late Predynastic period.

'Scorpion' was probably the last Egyptian prince to rule from Hierakonpolis; his monuments have been found there. His successors moved downriver, to This near Abydos and then to Memphis, though Hierakonpolis always remained sacred as the place of origins of the kingship.

It is possible that there was a second ruler of the same name, which may have been articulated 'Zekhen'. An important tomb at Abydos has recently been attributed to a Scorpion King, who is not thought to be the same as the king depicted on the mace-head.

J. E. Quibell and F. W. Green, *Hierakonpolis I and II*, London, 1900–02.
A. J. Arkell, 'Was King Scorpion Menes?', *Antiquity*, 46 (1963) 221–2.
Hoffman 1980: 312–17.
Dreyer 1993: 23–62.
Spencer: 49, 56–7, ill. 36.
Ashmolean Museum, Oxford.

Se'ankh, General, Eleventh Dynasty, Middle Kingdom, *c.* 1985 BC. Se'ankh was commander of the Army of the Eastern Desert. He was responsible for building the frontier defences, which he constructed based on fortified walls; the northernmost boundary of the defences was at Menat-Khufu (modern El-Minya). The most southerly of his defence systems was possibly located in the Wadi Hammamat, the ancient route through the Eastern Desert which ran from the Nile to the Red Sea coast.

J Couyat and P. Montet, *Inscriptions Hiéroglyphiques du Ouadi Hammâmât*, no. 1, Cairo, 1912.
Blackman 1947: 56.
Kees: 120.

Sebastet, Hairdresser, Eighteenth Dynasty, New Kingdom, *c.* 1452 BC. Sebastet was a hairdresser in the entourage of King THUTMOSE III. In one of the king's campaigns Sebastet captured a slave, Ameniuy, who was given to him. Sebastet gave Ameniuy his niece, Takemet, as his wife and adopted Ameniuy as his son.

Robins 1993: 56.

Sebekemhet, Treasury Official, Thirteenth/Fifteenth Dynasties, Second Intermediate Period, *c.* 1720 BC. An official in the Royal Treasury in the disturbed period at the end of the calamitous Thirteenth Dynasty, Sebekemhet had connections with the great temple at Heliopolis. It appears that he was a devotee of the equivocal god Seth, who was associated with the principal god of Heliopolis as Seth-Re. Although the later cults connected with Osiris cast Seth in the role of villain, the murderer of his brother, he was in fact a very ancient divinity of the desert and storm. In an inscription on a standing figure of Sebekemhet the 'animal of Seth' appears, by which the manifestation of the god is announced, indicating that Sebekemhet was an adherant of the god.

The significance of Seth appearing in a formal context at this time, is that the statue derives from immediately before the invasion of the Hyksos princes from beyond Egypt's northern frontiers. The Hyksos venerated Seth, whom they identified with their own god of storms.

W. K. Simpson, 'A Statuette of a Devotee of Seth', JEA 62 (1976) 41–4; pl. VIII.

Sebni, Noble, Sixth Dynasty, Old Kingdom, *c.* 2278–2184 BC. Sebni left a dramatic account of an expedition which he undertook to recover the body of his father, Mekhu, who had died whilst campaigning in Lower Nubia, at Wawat. Sebni obtained embalming materials and had his father's body borne home, attended by soldiers from the family's estates.

The king, PEPY II, and his ministers were greatly impressed by Sebni's devotion and made him a grant of land in reward.

Breasted 1: §§362–74.

Sedjememoaou, Priest, Nineteenth Dynasty, New Kingdom, *c.* 1279–1213 BC. Certain priests in Ancient Egypt were tonsured in the manner of Christian monks many hundreds of years later. Sedjememoaou dressed his hair in this manner. He was a priest of the goddess Hathor and the Keeper of the Gate of her temple. One of his sons, Ihy, was a musician.

J. J. Clère, 'Deux Statues "Gardiennes de porte" d'époque Ramesside', JEA 54 (1968) 135–48.

Sehetepibre, Official, Twelfth Dynasty, Middle Kingdom, *c.* 1860–1800 BC. Sehetepibre was a Treasurer and Scribe, living during the reigns of King SENWOSRET III and King AMENEMHET III. He is one of the earliest individuals, certainly amongst private persons, who is recorded as having been a collector of written texts.

Lichtheim 1: 125–9.
EMC CG 20538.

Sekhemib, *see* **Peribsen**

Sekhem-Ka, Royal Treasurer, First Dynasty, Archaic Period, *c.* 2980 BC. Sekhem-Ka was one of the 'Great Ones' of the early First Dynasty, at the time when the royal administration of Egypt was being defined and established. He lived during the reign of King Djet (Uadji), the fourth king of the Dynasty. He was probably the proprietor of Tomb 3504, one of the huge mastabas at Saqqara which were built for the principal officers of the dynasty.

Sekhem-Ka's burial was very rich, in accordance with his high rank. He was buried with a large quantity of finely made artefacts, stone vessels, furniture, pottery, flint implements, games and weapons. The uniformly high quality of their manufacture and the exceptional sophistication of the tomb's architecture are compelling witnesses to the abundant skills which the magnates of Egypt could summon to their service at this very early time.

A most remarkable element in the architecture of Sekhem-Ka's tomb is the presence of over three hundred clay skulls of wild bulls, to which the horns have been fixed, which surround the mastaba, mounted on raised platforms around the tomb. This particular feature is known from only one other of the Saqqara tombs, that of Queen HERNEITH.

Sekhem-Ka was buried with sixty-two of his retainers, who joined him in his tomb so that they could continue their service to him in the afterlife.

Emery 1954: 5–127; pls I–XVI.

Sekhemka, Official, Fifth Dynasty, Old Kingdom, *c.* 2400 BC. Sekhemka was the 'Inspector of Scribes of the House of the Master of Largesse, One Revered before the Great God'. He commissioned a number of very finely carved statues for his tomb, which was probably located at Saqqara. His wife was Sitmeret, 'She who is concerned with the affairs of the King'. She too was 'Revered before the Great God'.

T. G. H. James, 'The Northampton Statue of Sekhemka', JEA 53 (1967) 5–12; fig. 1, pls I–III.

Sekhemkhet, King, Third Dynasty, Old Kingdom, *c.* 2648–2640 BC. Sekhemkhet was for long confused with the First Dynasty king, SEMERKHET, a consequence of the similarity of the hieroglyphs which comprise their names. He was the successor of King DJOSER NETJERYKHET, though his relationship to the king is unknown. Only the names of Djoser's daughters have been recovered, and if this means that he had no surviving son, then probably Sekhemkhet married one of them.

Sekhemkhet's posthumous claim to celebrity arises from the strange circumstances attending the burial in the Step Pyramid at Saqqara which is attributed to him. A large, ruined step-pyramid complex surrounded, like Djoser's, with a great wall, was identified with the king. There was great excitement when, in what appeared to be the pyramid's burial chamber, a magnificent alabastar sarcophagus was found which was still sealed and intact, with the remains of the flowers which had been lain on it, presumably during the funeral ceremonies.

The sarcophagus was sealed extremely tightly. When it was opened it was found to be empty and it was clear that it had never contained a body. In the burial chamber, however, some exquisitely made gold objects were recovered, indicating that it was, or was intended to be, associated with a burial of the highest status.

The enigma of the empty sarcophagus remains unresolved; it may be that the king still waits discovery in one of the rabbit-warren of corridors and chambers which are particular features of the tomb. Many of them are in an extremely unstable condition.

M. Goneim, *The Buried Pyramid*, London, 1956.

——*Excavations at Saqqara: Horus Sekhem-Khet: The Unfinished Step Pyramid at Saqqara I*, Cairo, 1957.

J-P. Lauer, 'Recherche et Decouverte du Tombeau Sud de l'Horus Sekhem-Khet dans son Complex Funéraire B Saqqarah', BIE 48–9 (1969) 121–3.

Edwards 1985: 60–6.

Lehner 1997: 94.

Sekhemre Wahkhau, King, Seventeenth Dynasty, Second Intermediate Period, *c.* 1650 BC. Although relatively little is known of his reign, Sekhemre Wahkhau, ruler of Thebes during the Hyksos period when Egypt was under the yoke of invaders from the north, is one of those credited with the foundation of the Seventeenth Dynasty. This was eventually to deliver Egypt from the alien Hyksos and from which the Eighteenth Dynasty, one of the most brilliant in Egypt's history, was descended. He is known to have rebuilt the temples of Min at Koptos and of Osiris at Abydos.

CAH II.1: 66.

Sekwaskhet, Priest, Tenth/Eleventh Dynasties, First Intermediate Period, *c.* 2060 BC. There were several members of the same priestly family who bore the name Sekwaskhet. The Sekwaskhet who was memorialised (by his son, Ipysahathor, whose name incorporates that of a hippopotamus goddess of the Saqqara region) was the administrator of the funerary temple, pyramid and estates of King TETI, the founder of the Sixth Dynasty, who had died nearly three hundred years earlier. Sekwaskhet was responsible for the maintenance of the dead king's cult, which was long enduring.

The responsibility for Teti's cult had evidently been in the family for several generations. In one generation there appear to have been three Sekwaskhets – the elder, middle and younger – one of whom was the grandfather of the present Sekwaskhet.

A. Abdallah, 'The Cenotaph of the Sekwaskhet Family from Saqqara', JEA 78 (1992) 93–112; pls XIX–XXIII.

Semenkhkare-Mermenfitu, King, Thirteenth Dynasty, Middle Kingdom, *c.* 1750 BC. Near the ruined pyramid of King USERKARE KHENDJER, one of the few reasonably well documented rulers of the Thirteenth Dynasty, the excavator found another, larger monument similar to Userkare Khendjer's. The interior of the pyramid, the superstructure of which was entirely ruined, was remarkable, of exceptional complexity and sophistication. A series of internal portcullises barred access to the burial chamber subsidiary to the principal burial; one would have locked on to the lid of the sarcophagus when it was in position, but it appears never to have been used.

What the excavator concluded was intended as the king's tomb was made out of a single quartzite monolith, weighing forty-five tons. This had been positioned at the bottom of a pit twelve metres deep and was set exactly level and perfectly oriented.

The excavator believed that the monument belonged to Semenkhkare-Mermentifu, who was probably Userkare Khendjer's immediate successor and a usurper. By the second component in his name it was proposed that he was some sort of military leader who seized the throne after Userkare Khendjer's death. Semenkhkare-Mermentifu is known by two colossal statues, found at Tanis, which were later usurped by APEPI II.

It is very remarkable that at a time of such general disruption and apparent lack of resources a monument of the quality of Semenkhkare-Mermentifu's pyramid tomb could be built at Saqqara, showing that the spectacular skills of the architects and builders of Egypt had survived even in such troubled times.

G. Jéquier, *Deux pyramides du Moyen Empire*, Cairo, 1938.
Lauer 1976: 173–4, fig. 14.
Ryholt 1997: 221.

Sementawy, Scribe, Eighteenth Dynasty, New Kingdom, *c.* 1320 BC. Sementawy was Private Secretary to HOREMHEB whilst he was still the Commander of the Armies. He seems to have been particularly close to Horemheb and was represented in the tomb which the general prepared for himself before he succeeded to the kingship. Sementawy is shown seated immediately behind Horemheb, a very youthful, rather delicate figure. Later he disappeared to be replaced in his office by an army officer, RAMOSE, who may have been Horemheb's eventual successor as RAMESSES I.

Martin 1991: 60, 72–2, fig. 24.

Semerkhet, King, First Dynasty, Archaic Period, *c.* 2900 BC. Semerkhet came to the throne after ANEDJIB, whose legitimacy as king has been questioned. Semerkhet himself is not recorded in all the extant king lists, evidence perhaps of the uncertainties which attended the latter years of the dynasty.

An important document from Semerkhet's reign is an ivory label containing his name which is associated with one of his high officials, Henuka. It records a ceremony related to the worship of 'The Great White', a baboon god.

Semerkhet was succeeded by the last king of the First Dynasty, KA'A, who was probably his son.

Petrie 1900.
Emery 1961: 84–6.
Spencer: 83–4.

Senakhtenre Tao I, King, Seventeenth Dynasty, Second Intermediate Period, *c.*

1570 BC. During the reign of the Hyksos king APEPI, Senakhtenre Tao succeeded King INYOTEF VII in Thebes. It was at this point that the smouldering opposition to the Hyksos presence exploded into open conflict. Senakhtenre Tao was married to Queen TETISHERI, one of the formidable women who dominated the affairs of the dynasty and of Egypt at the end of the Hyksos period. Their son, SEQENENRE TAO (identified as 'the Second', to distinguish him from his father) succeeded and began the process of expelling the invaders, in the course of which he was killed.

Senakhtenre Tao's daughter was Queen AHHOTEP, who was the mother of King AHMOSE and possibly of King KAMOSE.

Grimal 1992: 189–90.

Senba, Courtier, First Dynasty, Archaic Period, *c.* 3000 BC. Senba was buried in a tomb subsidiary to the 'Funerary Palace', the immense tomb complex erected for King DJER at Abydos. His stela, giving his name and titles, contains very early forms of hieroglyphic inscriptions.

Hayes 1: 37; fig. 25.
MMA 01.4.93.

Senbi (alt. Sonebi), Nomarch, Twelfth Dynasty, Middle Kingdom, *c.* 1985 BC. The son of the nomarch UKHHOTEP I, Senbi was governor of the Fourteenth Upper Egyptian nome, centred on Meir where he was buried. His tomb depicts the life of a provincial magnate of the time and the entertainment, provided by his retainers, which he wished to translate to the afterlife. Senbi was evidently a notable dog-fancier, and one of his dogs, 'Breath of Life of Senbi', a representative of the ancient breed of Egyptian hounds, is portrayed in the tomb with his master.

Blackman 1914: 22–7, pls 2, 3.
Parkinson 1991: 79–81, 114.

Seneb, Priest, Fourth Dynasty, Old Kingdom, *c.* 2530 BC. Seneb was a priest in the service of the king, responsible for the care of the royal wardrobe. He was a dwarf and had charge of others like him who traditionally looked after the king's costumes and regalia. He was also attached to the funerary cults of Kings KHNUM-KHUFU and DJEDEFRE.

Seneb was well rewarded by his employers, in this life and in the next. He was given lands and cattle and a well furnished tomb which he shared with his wife Senetites. She was evidently well connected and herself held priestly offices. Their statue, with two of their children, is one of the most celebrated and touching examples of private sculpture of the period.

O. El-Aguiz, 'Dwarfs and Pygmies in Ancient Egypt', ASAE 71 (1987) 53–60.
Terrace and Fischer 1970: no. 12, 65–68, pl. III.
Saleh and Sourouzian: 39.
V. Dasen, *Dwarfs in Ancient Egypt and Greece*, Oxford, 1993.
EMC JE 51280.

Senebsuema, Seal-Bearer, Thirteenth Dynasty, Middle Kingdom, *c.* 1740–1720 BC. Despite the generally disturbed times which characterised Egypt in the middle years of the Thirteenth Dynasty and despite the perilous state of the kingship, the administration of Egypt somehow managed to continue relatively consistently. That this was so must be due to the quality and dedication of the high officials who continued to discharge their offices with kings coming and going around them. Senebsuema was 'Royal Seal-bearer, Sole Companion and Treasurer'. Many of his seals, in the familiar Egyptian form of the scarab beetle, have been found, though only two come from excavations; both of these were close to the Royal Residence at Itj-Tawy.

The scaraboid seal had become universal in Egypt by this time, having replaced the earlier cylinder seals, which are known from the late Predynastic period.

The form of the scarboid seal may have been influenced by Western Asiatic and Near Eastern precedents, which would have been known to the Egyptians as a consequence of the wide-ranging trade which was a feature of the times.

Senebsuema is thought to have been a contemporary of King NEFERHOTEP I and his brother SOBEKHOTEP IV.

Bourriau 1988: 158–9; no. 182.

Senebtyfy (alt. Ptahmes), Chancellor, Thirteenth Dynasty, Middle Kingdom, *c.* 1750 BC. The late Thirteenth Dynasty, though it flourished at a time when Egypt was under both internal and external pressures, still managed to produce works of art of a quality which bears comparison with those produced in the the more secure times of the Old Kingdom. The statue of Senebtyfy, which is carved in quartzite, an extremely hard stone, demonstrates this, for the figure of the Chancellor and Royal Scribe has all the authority and proud bearing that would go with his offices. Such craftsmanship became not uncommon in the period in which he lived.

James and Davies 1983: 26; ill. 28.
BM 24385.

Senebtysy, Land and Factory Owner, Thirteenth Dynasty, Middle Kingdom, *c.* 1750–1725 BC. Despite the generally fraught times in which she lived, Senebtysy owned an estate in her own right, which included a textile factory among its assets, which apparently she managed.

She is recorded as being in dispute over the ownership of slaves with her husband's daughter, Tehenwet, who claimed that the slaves had been given to her by *her* husband, so her father had no right to give them to Senebtysy. It is probable that she was buried at Thebes.

W. C. Hayes, *A Papyrus of the Late Middle Kingdom in the Brooklyn Museum*, New York, 1955.
S. Quirke, *The Administration of Egypt in the Late Middle Kingdom*, New Malden, 1990.
Robins 1993: 128–9.
Quirke and Spencer: 22.

Sened, King, Second Dynasty, Archaic Period, *c.* 2730 BC. The probable predecessor of King PERIBSEN towards the end of the Second Dynasty, Sened would be entirely unknown were it not for an inscription of the Fourth Dynasty recording that a priest, SHERI, served his cult at Saqqara, as he did that of Peribsen. That Sened's cult survived until the Pyramid Age suggests that he was considered to be of some status in the line of kings. It is possible that his tomb may have been obliterated by the building of the Causeway and Mortuary Temple of King UNAS at the end of the Fifth Dynasty.

CAH I.2: 20, 31, 35.
Ashmolean Museum, Oxford.

Senedjemibmehy, Vizier and Architect, Fifth Dynasty, Old Kingdom, *c.* 2375–2345 BC. An architect in the service of King UNAS, the last king of the Fifth Dynasty, Senedjemibmehy was Overseer of All the King's Works; he was also the king's Vizier. He had a handsome statue of himself carved in hard wood which, unusually but not uniquely, presents him nude. It may be that originally the statue was clothed or that its nudity has a particular cultic significance, but its state now reveals Senedjemibmehy as a commanding figure; he is shown as being circumcised, a condition which was by no means universal in Egypt. His tomb at Giza contains many scenes and inscriptions related to his service with the king.

PM V: 87–9.
C. R. Lepsius, *Denkmäler aus Aegypten and Aethiopien Ergänzungsband*, Leipzig, 1913: XI–XII.
Y. Harpur, *Decoration in Egyptian Tombs of the Old Kingdom: Studies in Orientation and Scene Content*, London and New York, 1987: 214–15, 252.

Senenmut, Royal Steward, Architect, Eighteenth Dynasty, New Kingdom, *c.* 1473–1458 BC. Although of comparatively humble origins, Senenmut figures prominently throughout much of Queen HATSHEPSUT's reign, when she effectively usurped the kingship from her stepson THUTMOSE III. He held the office of Steward of the Royal Family and was the Queen's spokesman. As architect he supervised the erection of Hatshepsut's obelisks in the temple of Amun-Re at Karnak and, most particularly, designed the splendid mortuary temple which the queen built at Deir el-Bahri. He is often portrayed, in the form of a block statue, holding the queen's little daughter NEFERURE on his lap, suggesting a degree of informality and intimacy which has led to speculation that he might have been the princess's father. He was permitted a small presence of his own in the queen's mortuary chapel; his own tomb at Deir el-Bahri is remarkable for a fine astronomical ceiling, suggesting that a concern for the stars was one of Senenmut's interests, which seem to have been many and diverse. A number of Senenmut's companions were buried in his tomb, presumably so that they might share eternity with him. They included one of his horses, a little mare, said to be barely twelve and a half hands high, and a cyncephalous ape. Both had been carefully mummified and placed in coffins.

Senenmut disappears from sight in the nineteenth year of Hatshepsut's reign.

W. C. Hayes, *Ostraca and Name Stones from the Tomb of Sen-Mut (no. 71) at Thebes*, New York, 1942.
Hayes 2: 105–13.
A. R. Schulman, 'Some Remarks on the Alleged "Fall" of Senmut', JARCE 8: 29–48.
Terrace and Fischer 1970: no. 24, 113–16.
P. Dorman, *The Monuments of Senenmut: Problems in Historical Methodology*, London, 1988.
Tyldesley 1996: 177–209.
EMC CG 42116.

Senenu, Priest, Sixth Dynasty, Old Kingdom, *c.* 2345–2181 BC. Senenu was Inspector of *wab* priests and Prophet of Khufu. His memorial was set up by his son, Akhethetep.

A. M. Abu-Bakr, *Excavations at Giza 1949–50*, Cairo. 1953.
H. Fischer, *Varia: Egyptian Studies 1*, New York, 1976: 19–21; fig. 4.

Senet, Noblewoman, Twelfth Dynasty, Middle Kingdom, *c.* 1985–1955 BC. Senet was the mother of ANTEFOKER, the Vizier of King AMENEMHET I, the founder of the Twelfth Dynasty. She was buried at Thebes, in what was to become the most important necropolis in Egypt (TT 60). Her tomb may have been intended originally for Antefoker, but he was buried at Lisht, near the burial place of the king. The fact that his name and titles have been excised from Senet's tomb and his portraits defaced have led to the speculation that King SENWOSRET I, Amenemhet's son and successor, may have suspected that he was implicated in some way in Amenemhet's assassination.

Robins 1993: 100, 165, 168.

Seni, Painter, Sixth Dynasty, Old Kingdom, *c.* 2278–2184 BC. The rulers of the ninth nome of Upper Egypt, the Panopolite, with its capital at Akhmim, were buried in tombs cut into the rock of a mountain at El Hawawish, to the southeast of the capital. Seni was responsible for the decoration of at least two of the tombs, those of the nomarchs TJETI-IKER and his son, KHENI. He was evidently highly regarded, for he identified himself as the tombs' decorator in their inscriptions and had himself represented in the company of his patrons.

Seni's work, painted on to the mud-lined walls of the tombs, is very distinctive. Though it is much depleted, the high quality and the originality of Seni's paintings and inscriptions are still sparkling and evident.

Kanawati 1980.

Senimen, Steward, Eighteenth Dynasty, New Kingdom, 1473–1458 BC. A close associate of Queen HATSHEPSUT'S great Minister, SENENMUT (it has been suggested that they shared the same father), Senimen also served the queen, as her Steward. He was said to have begun his career as page to King AHMOSE (presumably posthumously); he was the administrator of Hatshepsut's estates and at one time her daughter's tutor.

Hayes 2: 44, 81, 105, 106, 111.
Tyldesley 1996: 181, 196.
C. H. Roehrig and P. F. Dorman, 'Senimen and Senenmut: A Question of Brothers', *Varia Aegyptiaca*, 3, 1987: 127–34.

[Sennacherib], Assyrian King, (= Twenty-Fifth Dynasty) Late Period, *c.* 722–705 BC. The son and successor of King SARGON II faced a rebellion by his Palestinian vassals on his assumption of the kingship. They sought the aid of Egypt but Sennacherib, by dint of his forces' exceptional mobility and the ferocity of his campaign, defeated the Egyptians. There was an engagement between Sennacherib's army and the Egyptians near Lachish. The Egyptian king, Taharqa, withdrew and Sennacherib did not pursue him beyond the frontier as he was faced with a serious threat in his own dominions from the Babylonians.

Eventually Sennacherib was assassinated, probably by his own son, at Nineveh.

CAH III.2: 103–22.
Kitchen 1982: §§128–9, §346.
Grimal: 344, 346–7.

Sennedjem, Official, Nineteenth Dynasty, New Kingdom, *c.* 1270 BC. A royal servant in 'The Place of Truth', Sennedjem was rewarded with a beautifully decorated tomb at Deir el-Medina, on the Theban West Bank (TT 1). Because of the relative unimportance of its owner the tomb was not disturbed until it was found in this century. The tomb contained objects connected with the funerals of Sennedjem, his wife and family, including the sledge on which their coffins were transported for burial. Sennedjem is portrayed playing draughts and, with his wife, worshipping the gods associated with death and the afterlife.

The tomb's paintings include scenes of mummification, conducted by a priest wearing an Anubis mask. In a nearby tomb Sennedjem's son, Khabekhet, was buried and the Anubis-priest is there shown, mummifying a large fish. Sennedjem's tomb contained twenty coffins.

EMC JE 27303.
Saleh and Sourouzian: 215.

Sennefer, Chancellor, Eighteenth Dynasty, New Kingdom, *c.* 1490–1450 BC. A long-serving high official in the reigns of THUTMOSE II, HATSHEPSUT and THUTMOSE III, Sennefer was one of a group of senior civil servants given a shrine in the region from which the kings of the New Kingdom quarried much of the stone for their building projects. This is situated at Es-Sibaiya, forty-five miles upriver from Thebes.

Sennefer was 'Overseer of the Seal' and 'Overseer of the Gold-Land of Amun'. His mother was Sitdhout and his wife Taimau. He was buried at Abd el-Qurna (TT 99).

PM I: 204–6.
BM 48.

Sennefer, Mayor, Eighteenth Dynasty, New Kingdom, *c.* 1427–1400 BC. Sennefer was honoured by King AMENHOTEP II, who permitted the presentation of a double statue of Sennefer and his wife, to be placed in the temple at Karnak. This was evidently in return for Sennefer's service as Mayor of Thebes, itself an important position. Unusually, the sculpture of Sennefer and his wife is signed by the sculptors who made it: Amenmes and Djed-Khonsu.

Sennefer recorded two wives in his tomb at Thebes (TT 96), the first Senetnay, a royal wetnurse, and the second Meryt. With the latter he is shown sailing to Abydos on the pilgrimage which justified spirits were believed to take after death, to the temple of Osiris.

Sennefer wears a double, heart-shaped amulet collar. He is shown wearing the same collar in paintings in his tomb. Some are inscribed with the name of his king, AMENHOTEP II; one, however, is inscribed with the name 'Alexander', added many hundred years after Sennefer's death by a presumably admiring or affectionate Greek visitor.

H. Carter, 'Report on the Tomb of Sen-nefer Found at Biban el Molouk near the Tomb of Thotmes III, no. 34', ASAE 2 (1901) 196–200.
G. Legrain, *Statues et Statuettes de Rois et de Particuliers*, 3 vols (CG) Cairo, 1906–14. I, 76–8, pl. 75.
PM I.1: 197–203.
Terrace and Fischer 1970: n24, 113–16.
Saleh and Sourouzian: 140.
EMC JE 36574 (CG 42126).

Sennu, Architect, Ptolemaic Period, *c.* 285–246 BC. During the reign of PTOLEMY II PHILADELPHUS, Sennu built the king a temple, dedicated to Min and Isis, on a site in Koptos (modern Kift) which had been similarly used by kings of the Middle Kingdom and by King THUTMOSE III. Sennu's temple was added to by PTOLEMY IV PHILOPATOR and by the Roman Emperors, Caligula and Nero.

Koptos had been the site of important religious foundations since Old Kingdom times.

W. M. F. Petrie, *Koptos*, London, 1896.

Senpu, Official, Twelfth/Thirteenth Dynasties, Middle Kingdom, *c.* 1785 BC. Senpu was the Chamberlain of the Chamber of Offerings. He had himself portrayed in a family group, standing before a table of offerings, with himself wrapped in a voluminous cloak.

PM V, 1937: 99.
MduL E11253.

Senu, Soldier, Ninth/Tenth Dynasties, First Intermediate Period, *c.* 2160–2125 BC. Senu was a Nubian mercenary serving in the Egyptian army; he lived and was buried at Gebelein, where a contingent of Nubian troops was for a long time garrisoned. The Nubians evidently intermarried with the local population. Senu's wife is portrayed as fair-skinned whilst his son and the family's servants are all shown as dark-complexioned.

In addition to the members of his household Senu included two of his dogs on his stele; they sit obediently before him, ears pricked.

See also entry for SOBEKNEKHT RENEFSONB

H. G. Fischer, 'The Nubian Mercenaries of Gebelein during the First Intermediate Period', *Kush*, 9 (1961) 44–80.

Senu, Royal Scribe and Herald, Eighteenth Dynasty, New Kingdom, *c.* 1390–1352 BC. Senu was Royal Scribe and King's First Herald during the lifetime of King AMENHOTEP III; as such he must have participated in the great ceremonies which marked the king's sumptuous reign. As Herald he was responsible for aspects of foreign affairs and for keeping the king informed of opinion in the country. His funerary stelae, dedicated by his son, Pawahy, are exceptionally finely and elegantly carved. He was buried in a richly appointed tomb at Tuneh, ancient Hermopolis.

He was succeeded as King's First Herald by AMENHOTEP son of Hapu.

Hayes 2: 272–4.
MMA 12.182.39, 18.2.5.
MduL C140–142.

Senusret, Overseer of Priests, Twelfth Dynasty, Middle Kingdom, *c.* 1985–1955 BC. Senusret, the son of Ip, was the Overseer of Priests in five shrines or temples dedicated to Uadjet, Hathor, Anubis, Min and Khnum. He was Mayor of the City of the Horizon of King SENWOSRET I at Lisht. It is probable that his funerary statue was originally set up in the king's mortuary temple at Lisht, an honour to which Senusret's responsibilities evidently entitled him.

S. Birch, *Catalogue of the Collection of Egyptian Antiquities at Alnwick Castle*, London, 1880: 60ff.
Bourriau 1988: 28–9, no. 19.
Oriental Museum, University of Durham, no. 501.

Senwosret, Priest, Eleventh Dynasty, Middle Kingdom, *c.* 2000 BC. A priest who married a woman from Upper Egypt, Nofret, Senwosret was regarded as the ancestor of the Twelfth Dynasty as his son became AMENEMHET I, the first king of the dynasty. Senwosret was awarded the posthumous title of 'God's Father'.

Winlock 1947.
A. Dodson, *Monarchs of the Nile*, London, 1995: 56.

Senwosret I (alt. Senusret, Sesostris), King, Twelfth Dynasty, Middle Kingdom, *c.* 1965–1920 BC. When AMENEMHET I was assassinated his heir and co-regent, Senwosret, was campaigning in Libya. He received the news of his father's death, and without informing his entourage of the event, hastened back to Egypt to claim the throne. His succession seems to have been undisputed though he encouraged the invention and promulgation (by the priest AMENTY) of what purported to be a message from his father beyond the grave confirming his legitimacy and urging him to be distrustful of his associates.

Senwosret was one of Egypt's greatest kings. The speed and decisiveness which marked his accession were repeated in the frequent and far-ranging military campaigns which he undertook. He was a great builder and was responsible for one of the most beautiful of all Egypt's buildings, the so-called White Kiosk at Karnak, a small chapel which served as a 'way-station' for the god and his priests as they processed round the temple. He also built what may have been the first 'new town' in history, Itj-tawy. His immense pyramid complex at El-Lisht was surrounded by the tombs, many of them of considerable splendour, of his great officers of state.

For centuries after his death Senwosret was worshipped as a god. His reputation grew and was conflated with that of his descendant, SENWOSRET III (and with later kings such as THUTMOSE III and RAMESSES II) to produce the composite mythical king Sesostris, whose legend has persisted to the present day.

P. Lacau and H. Chevrier, *Une Chapelle de Sésostris Ier à Karnak*, 2 vols, Paris, 1956–69.
Hayes 1: 182–5; fig. 117.
MMA 14.3.17.
EMC JE 44951.

Senwosret II, King, Twelfth Dynasty, Middle Kingdom, 1880–1874 BC. The grandson of the great SENWOSRET I followed his father AMENEMHET II on the throne. If he did not earn the same mythical posterity as his grandfather, he was nonetheless a worthy successor. He was particularly active in securing Egypt's reputation internationally and in making the country the dominant power in the Near East of the day.

Senwosret II demonstrated his character as a progressive ruler in carrying out large-scale environmental and reclamation projects. These included the land reclamation and control of the Nile flood and, like his predecessor Senwosret I, he created one of the first 'new towns' recorded in history, Hotep-Senwosret, in the Faiyum.

W. K. Simpson, 'Sesostris II und Sesostris III',

Lexikon der Ägyptologie V, Weisbaden, 1984: 889–906.

Senwosret III, King, Twelfth Dynasty, Middle Kingdom, *c.* 1874–1855 BC. The third Senwosret was the most remarkable of all the kings of his family and outstanding amongst all of Egypt's sovereigns. He was an inspired administrator who reorganised Egypt's bureaucracy, making the royal control of affairs virtually total. He was, like his father SENWOSRET II, much concerned with the management of Egypt's physical resources, including the re-opening of the channel first excavated by Kings PEPY I and MERENRE at Aswan; Egypt's relations with its southern neighbours were important aspects of Senwosret's policy, and he conducted many campaigns against 'the wretched Kush'. He built a number of fortresses in the south to secure Egypt's frontiers there and set up boundary stelae at Semna.

Senwosret III is remembered particularly for a remarkable series of portraits of him, showing him at various ages. The statues of him as an old man are notable for their expression of profound melancholy. It is he, more than his predecessors, who is the prototype of the mystical king, Sesostris.

W. K. Simpson, 'Sesostris II and Sesostris III', *Lexikon der Ägyptologie V*, Weisbaden, 1984: 889–906.
Hayes 1: 198–201; fig. 119.
Lichtheim 1: 118–20.
MMA 17.9.2.
Luxor Museum J 34.

Senwosretankh, High Priest, Twelfth Dynasty, Middle Kingdom, *c.* 1965–1920 BC. Senwosretankh was High Priest of Ptah in Memphis during the reign of King SENWOSRET I. He was buried in a huge mastaba tomb near the king's burial, at El-Lisht.

Hayes 1: 206; fig. 124.
MMA 33.1.2.

Senwosretankh, Vizier, Twelfth Dynasty, Middle Kingdom, *c.* 1870 BC. A Minister serving the kings of the later Middle Kingdom, Senwosretankh's statue, with his wife and daughter, was found at Ras Shamra in Syria. It seems likely that he was sent on some form of mission, perhaps actually posted there, to represent the king's affairs at a distant outpost of Egyptian interests.

PM VII 1951: 37, 394.

Sepa and Nesa, Nobles, Third Dynasty, Old Kingdom, *c.* 2680 BC. The statues of Sepa and Nesa are amongst the earliest attempts at portraying standing figures at almost life size. The sculptor had difficulty in managing the staffs which the figures are holding, and the stance was not repeated in later work.

Vandier 1958: 985–6.
Ziegler 1990: 21–4.
Andreu *et al.* 1997: no. 11.
MduL A36, A38.

Seqenenre Tao II, King, Seventeenth Dynasty, Second Intermediate Period, *c.* 1560 BC. A warrior prince of an ancient Theban family, the son of King SENAKHTENRE TAO I, Seqenenre Tao was married to Queen AHHOTEP and was the father of Kings KAMOSE and AHMOSE. He was revered as one of the ancestors of the Eighteenth Dynasty.

He died in one of the campaigns against the Hyksos invaders; his mummy, found in the Deir el-Bahri, bears terrible wounds, which clearly caused his death. His sons, aided by his formidable wife, avenged him and drove the Hyksos out of Egypt.

H. Winlock, 'The Tombs of the Kings of the Seventeenth Dynasty at Thebes', JEA 10 (1924) 217–77.

Serenput, Nomarch, Twelfth Dynasty, Middle Kingdom, *c.* 1985–1795 BC. The owner of a fine rock-cut tomb on the escarpment at Elephantine, Serenput is shown, on the lintel of his tomb, seated, with an air of great assurance, on his chair of state, attended by his pet dogs, a bitch of a rather squat terrier-type and a handsome Egyptian hound.

J. J. Clere, 'Notes sur l'Inscription Biographique de Serenput Ier à Assouan', R d'E 22 (1970) 41–9.

Seshemnefer, Official, Sixth Dynasty, Old Kingdom, *c.* 2375–2345 BC. Seshemnefer was a contemporary of King UNAS, whom he served as 'Overseer of the Tenants of the Great House', and 'Master Butcher of the Great House'. His wife was Kerfet. He was buried in a small, elegantly appointed mastaba to the north-west of the king's pyramid at Saqqara.

PM (J. Málek) 1977, 2.2: 614.
Saad 1947: 56–7; pl. XVIII.

Setau, High Priest, Twentieth Dynasty, New Kingdom, *c.* 1160–1126 BC. Setau was the High Priest of Nekhbet, the cobra goddess, at her ancient shrine at Elkab; he recorded the visit of King RAMESSES III's Vizier, Ta, to the temple in connection with the organisation of the king's jubilee.

Setau was to hold his office for an exceedingly long time, from the reign of Ramesses III to the beginning of the reign of RAMESSES IX, half a century later.

He was buried at Elkab (EK 4).

J. E. Quibell, *El-Kab*, London, 1898.
Breasted 4: §§413–15.
Gott, Mensch und Pharaonen, Vienna 1992: 317ff., no. 23 (exhibition catalogue).
Andreu *et al.* 1997: no. 49.
MduL 4196.

Sethirkhopshef, Prince, Nineteenth Dynasty, New Kingdom, *c.* 1279–1227 BC. The son of Queen NEFERTARI, the principal wife of King RAMESSES II, Prince Sethirkhopshef was his father's heir apparent and the priest of the king's cult as a god. He was also appointed a minister of state responsible for northern affairs. He was Crown Prince in year twenty-one of his father's reign but he had evidently been dead for some time by year fifty-three when his burial at Thebes required attention.

Kitchen 1982: 102.

Sethnakhte, King, Twentieth Dynasty, New Kingdom, *c.* 1186–1184 BC. The founder of the Twentieth Dynasty is an obscure figure, though it is possible that he had some familial connection with the kings of the Nineteenth Dynasty. He came to power in the aftermath of the unsatisfactory period marked by the presence of the Chancellor BAY and Queen TWOSRET, the widow of King SETI II, as the rulers of Egypt. He evidently died suddenly as no tomb was ready for him. Twosret's tomb, (KV 14) was made ready for him, the renegade queen being removed to make room for him. His mummy was eventually found in the cache in KV 35.

His brief reign is referred to in the Great Harris Papyrus, dated to the end of the reign of RAMESSES III and prepared by RAMESSES IV.

Reeves and Wilkinson 1996: 157–9.

Seti I, King, Nineteenth Dynasty, New Kingdom, *c.* 1294–1279 BC. The son and co-regent of RAMESSES I, Seti succeeded after his father's brief reign which inaugurated the Nineteenth Dynasty. Prior to Ramesses' accession Seti had been a high-ranking officer in the Army; under his father, and also possibly during the latter part of the reign of King HOREMHEB, he was especially concerned with Egypt's foreign relations.

It was Seti, more than any other, who restored Egypt's status in the world, after the uncertainties of the Amarna period and its immediate aftermath. In the early years of his reign he led a number of campaigns into the lands beyond Egypt's frontiers. He was particularly active against the Hittites, a power which was to play an important part in the foreign relations of his son, RAMESSES II.

In Egypt itself Seti continued Horemheb's policy of repairing the ravages of the Amarnan period. Although the family was from the Delta (Seti's name indicates their adherance to the cult of the god Set, who at this time was associated with the north of Egypt), Seti and his successors maintained the position of Thebes as the religious and secular capital of the country.

Seti's funerary temple at Abydos is one of the supreme masterpieces of New Kingdom architecture. The exceptional richness of the wall reliefs and the brilliance of colour in the interior make the temple an outstanding example of the Egyptian creative genius. Seti commissioned a list of his predecessors (the 'Abydos King-List') to be displayed in his temple at Abydos; he is depicted showing his son, the future Ramesses II, the names of those kings who had gone before them on the thrones of Egypt. His tomb (KV 17) is also one of the largest and most magnificent in the Valley of the Kings with, amongst other notable features, a superb astronomical ceiling.

E. Hornung, *The Tomb of Seti I*, Zurich and Munich, 1991.
M. L. Bierbrier, 'The Length of the Reign of Sethos I', JEA 58: 303.

Seti II, King, Nineteenth Dynasty, New Kingdom, *c.* 1200–1194 BC. The rightful successor of King MERENPTAH, Seti II was usurped by AMENMESSE, also a grandson of RAMESSES II. Seti succeeded after Amenmesse had occupied the throne for five years; the circumstances both of the usurpation and Seti's accession are obscure. Seti was originally buried in KV 15 but was later moved to KV 35, the tomb of AMENHOTEP II. He was succeeded by his son SIPTAH.

H. Chevrier, *Le Temple Reposoir de Seti II*, Cairo, 1940.
Reeves and Wilkinson 1996: 152–3.
BM 26.

Setka, Prince, Fourth Dynasty, Old Kingdom, *c.* 2550 BC. Although Setka was the son of the evidently ill-fated King DJEDEFRE, like other royal sons he was not above having himself portrayed in the relatively humble posture of a scribe, seated cross-legged, waiting to write down the instructions of his master, the king. He was 'Master of the Secrets of the House of Morning', a Lector-Priest and an Administrator of the Palace.

Chassinat, *Monuments Piot XXV*, 1921–2: 66.
IFAO 50 (1981) cat. no. 55.
MduL E 12629.

Setka, Priest, Eighth/Ninth Dynasties, First Intermediate Period, *c.* 2170 BC. Setka was a mortuary priest with particular concern for the pyramid of King PEPY II. He enjoyed the rank of Count and the appointment of 'Overseer of the Phyles of Upper Egypt'. He had a tomb of his own at Aswan, overlooking the island of Elephantine, which contains some fine paintings, a fact which indicates that standards did not all collapse after the end of the Old Kingdom.

Baines and Málek 1980: 72.
E. Edel, *Die Falsengräber der Qubbet el-Hawa bei Assuan*, Wiesbaden, 1967.

Shabaka, King, Twenty-Fifth Dynasty, Late Period, 716–702 BC. When King PIANKHY died in 716 BC and was buried at Napata, he was succeeded by his brother, Shabaka. He established himself early in his reign at Memphis and from there systematically imposed his rule over the entire country.

Shabaka, like his brother, was a believer in the old ways and sought diligently to find evidence from the past on which he could base his reform of everything which he saw around him. His search confirmed to him the view that such reform was overdue. The so-called 'Memphite Theology', dates from this time although it purports to be a text from the most distant past and was carved in stone by Shabaka in this belief.

When Shabaka died, like his brother he was buried in Napata, amongst his horses. He was succeeded by his nephew, SHABATAKA.

Kitchen 1986; §§339–44 (as Shabako).

Shabataka (alt. Shabitku), King, Twenty-Fifth Dynasty, Late Period, *c.* 702–690 BC. The son of King PIANKHY, Djedkaure Shabataka followed his uncle SHABAKA on the throne. He was in turn succeeded by his younger brother, TAHARQA, after a relatively undistinguished reign when he seems to have sustained the policies of his predecessors without introducing any innovations of his own.

Like other members of his family, Shabataka was buried at the Nubian pyramid complex of El-Kurru with a number of sacrificed horses. They had been decapitated, dressed with beads and buried standing up.

Kitchen 1986: §§132–7, §§345–8, §462, §466, §§468–9 (as Shabitku).
Lehner 1997: 194–5.

[Shanakdakhete], Queen, Meroitic Period (= Ptolemaic Period), 2nd century BC. Shanakdakhete was the first woman to be a ruler of the Nubian kingdom of Meroe. A pyramid at Meroe is thought to have belonged to her.

Quirke and Spencer: 214–15.
BM EA 719.

Shedsunefertem, High Priest, Twenty-Second Dynasty, Third Intermediate Period, *c.* 940–920 BC. Shedsunefertem was High Priest of Memphis during the reign of King SHESHONQ I, who was probably his brother-in-law. His name appears with the king's on a ceremonial table used for the embalming of the Apis bull. He was married to a Princess Tentsepeh, possibly a daughter of King PSEUSENNES II.

His father had been High Priest of Memphis before him. Shedsunefertem also enjoyed the offices of the Chief of the Secrets of Ptah and Prophet of Ptah. His son, Pahemneter, succeeded him in these offices.

Kitchen 1986: §§151–4, §248, §275, §474; tables 10, 12, 18.

Shepenupet I (alt. Shepenwepet), Princess, Twenty-Third Dynasty, Third Intermediate Period, *c.* 777–749 BC. The daughter of King OSORKON III, Shepenupet was appointed by her father as God's Wife of Amun in Thebes, thus strengthening the influence of the Tanite dynasty in the south; Shepenupet was to be the last Libyan God's Wife. She was awarded full royal titles, her names being enclosed in cartouches. Her titles included 'Lady of the Two Lands' and 'Lady of Epiphanies'.

With her father, King Osorkon and King TAKELOT III she was associated with the building and decoration of the small temple of Osiris-Ruler-of-Eternity at Karnak.

When the Kushite princes of the Twenty-Fifth Dynasty seized power in Egypt Shepenupet was obliged to adopt the Princess AMENIRDIS I, whose brother, King PIANKHY, wished her to succeed to the office on Shepenupet's death.

Kitchen 1982: §72, §§143–5, §164, §312, §§317–18.

Shepenupet II (alt. Shepenwepet), Princess, Twenty-Fifth Dynasty, Late Period, 747–746 BC. Shepenupet II was God's Wife of Amun, appointed by her father King PIANKHY, the first king of the Kushite Dynasty. She was the sister of the kings TAHARQA and SHABAKA; she was also a contemporary of the redoubtable MONTUEMHET, the Mayor of Thebes with whom, in her later years she shared the rule of the south. The Princess AMENIRDIS II, the daughter of King Taharqa and hence Shepenupet's niece, was given to her as her heiress.

Shepenupet lived on into the reign of King PSAMETIK I and is known to be living *c.* 656 BC. Another princess, NITIQRET, the daughter of King Psametik, became heiress and a relief from Karnak shows Shepenupet receiving her as she arrives by river, attended by a great concourse, her arrival celebrated by elaborate festivities.

Shepenupet enjoyed the soubriquet 'Mistress of Beauty'.

Kitchen 1982: §120, §§143–5, §§204–5, §347, §§350–1, §355, §359, §364.

Shepseskare Isi, King, Fifth Dynasty, Old Kingdom, *c.* 2455–2448 BC. Shepseskare was probably the immediate successor of King NEFERIRKARE. His reign, which possibly lasted seven years, is entirely obscure.

CAH I.2: 184.

Shepseskhaf, King, Fourth Dynasty, Old Kingdom, *c.* 2503–2498 BC. The dynastic in-fighting amongst the factions of the royal family in the latter part of the Fourth Dynasty complicated the succession. The arrival of King MENKAURE on the throne restored the senior line; his successor and presumed son was Shepseskhaf.

He was married to his sister, KHENTKAWES, by whom he had a daughter but evidently no son.

Shepseskhaf seems deliberately to have set out to break with the immediate past in the matter of the design of his own tomb. Eschewing the pyramid form, he built for himself a huge sarcophagus-shaped mastaba in South Saqqara, the 'Mastabat Fara'un'. He reigned only for four years and his funeral ceremonies appear to have been conducted by another queen, BUNEFER.

Vandier 1954: 89.
A. Badawy, *A History of Egyptian Architecture I*, Giza, 1954: 142.
Grimal: 114–15.

Sheri, Priest, Fourth Dynasty, Old Kingdom, *c.* 2613–2498 BC. A mortuary priest responsible for maintaining the cults of the dead kings in the royal necropolis at Saqqara, Sheri was the Overseer of the Priests of PERIBSEN (whose tomb was at Abydos) and an otherwise entirely obscure king of the Second Dynasty, SENED. Were it not for an inscription commemorating Sheri, Sened's name would have remained unknown.

CAH I.2.: 20, 31.
PM III: 101–2.
Ashmolean Museum 1836.479.

Sheshonq I, King, Twenty-Second Dynasty, Third Intermediate Period, 945–924 BC. Sheshonq inaugurated a dynasty which had its origins in Libya; his family came from Tanis in the Delta, which continued to be their stronghold. Sheshonq's own status was derived from his position as 'Great Chief of the Ma' and son-in-law of King PSEUSENNES II, whom he succeeded to the throne of Egypt. He was a most skilful political operator, consolidating his family's power throughout Egypt by a series of carefully plotted marriages and appointments of his sons to positions of power.

In pursuit of a vigorous foreign policy, he conducted campaigns in Palestine where he appears to have subdued the kingdoms of Israel and Judah; he gave refuge to the rebellious Jeroboam until he returned to set up the Kingdom of Israel once more. However, Jeroboam betrayed Sheshonq's trust.

Sheshonq also invaded Nubia in an attempt, not wholly successful, to re-establish Egyptian control over the southern extremity of the empire.

Kitchen 1986: §§241–60.
Grimal: 319–30.

Sheshonq II, King, Twenty-Second Dynasty, Third Intermediate Period, 890–889 BC. Sheshonq II reigned briefly in a co-regency with OSORKON I, of whom he was the heir. He died before the older king, however. The careful restructuring of the state introduced by his grandfather, SHESHONQ I, was beginning to come apart, a situation which Sheshonq II attempted to rectify, but without success. A virtual civil war ensued, with factions within the royal family and those who had installed themselves as magnates in the provinces fighting amongst themselves and against the central authority.

Sheshonq was buried sumptuously by his sorrowing father, and with him were consigned a number of heirlooms and objects of family piety. Amongst these objects was a Mesopotamian cylinder seal, evidently a prized if somewhat unlikely possession of an Egyptian royal family.

Kitchen 1986: §§93–4, §§264–5, §452.

Sheshonq III, King, Twenty-Second Dynasty, Third Intermediate Period, 825–773 BC. By the time the third Sheshonq reached the throne a competing dynasty, the Twenty-Third, was established, which refused to recognise the claims of the Libyan family to sovereignty over all Egypt. Sheshonq found himself ruling a smaller and smaller territory in the company of two or more competing kings. Notable amongst these was PEDUBASTIS, who was acknowledged as the founder of the Twenty-Third Dynasty, ruling from Leontopolis in the Delta.

Despite the confusions and pressures of the time, Sheshonq III managed to reign for more than fifty years. By the time of his death he was undisputed ruler of only a small part of the Delta.

P. Montet, *Le Nécropole Royale de Tanis: Les Constructions et la Tombeau de Chechonq III*, B. Tanis, Paris, 1960.
Kitchen, 1986: §§287–354, §§575–6.
D. A. Aston, 'Takelot II: A King of the 23rd Dynasty', JEA 75 (1989) 139–53.
Grimal: 319–30.
I. E. S. Edwards, 'Egypt from the 22nd to the 23rd Dynasty', CAH III.1.

Sheshonq IV, King, Twenty-Third Dynasty, Third Intermediate Dynasty, *c.* 783–777 BC. The successor of King IUPUT, Sheshonq IV reigned unremarkably, to judge by the few evidences which survive of his time on the throne. It is likely that the vigorous OSORKON III was his son, by Queen Kamama.

Kitchen 1986: §303.

Siamun, King, Twenty-First Dynasty, Third Intermediate Period, *c.* 978–959 BC. One of the Tanite kings, Siamun pursued a vigorous policy abroad in an attempt to re-establish Egypt's foreign relations and her prestige; at home he was faced with another serious outbreak of tomb-looting. He organised the removal of royal mummies from the Valley of the Kings in his tenth regnal year. Eventually they were taken to to the tomb of the High Priest of Amun, PINUDJEM II (DB 320), where they comprised 'the Deir el-Bahri cache'.

He built extensively at Tanis, and also at Memphis where he seems particularly to have favoured the temple of Ptah. He was succeeded by PSEUSENNES II, the last king of the dynasty.

Kitchen: 1986: §§232–6, §431, §433.
Grimal: 318–19.
Reeves and Wilkinson 1996: 207.

Sihathor, Treasurer, Twelfth Dynasty, Middle Kingdom, *c.* 1922–1878 BC. The Treasurer of King AMENEMHET II, Sihathor was responsible for the control of the king's largesse and thus a particularly trusted official. He is commemorated by an early example of the 'block statue', a conventional sculptural form which portrays the subject seated on the ground, wrapped in an enveloping cloak. In Sihathor's case his statue was found in the inscribed niche in which it was placed in his tomb. Sihathor has very distinctive features, to the extent that it is difficult not to believe that it is a portrait from the life. He appears surprisingly youthful, boyish even, for so high an official and, in the way that he is represented, very much at ease.

Hieroglyphic Texts from Egyptian Stelae etc. in the British Museum II, London, 1912: pls 19–20.
D. O'Connor, 'The "Cenotaphs" of the Middle Kingdom at Abydos', in 'Mélanges Gamal Eddin Mokhtar', B d'E 97 (1985) 161–77.
Parkinson 1991: 137–9.
BM 569, 570.

Sihathor, Army Officer, Thirteenth Dynasty, Middle Kingdom, *c.* 1715–1704 BC. Despite the generally uncertain conditions which prevailed throughout Egypt in the Thirteenth Dynasty, nonetheless the royal bureaucracy continued in place, though perhaps on a somewhat less lavish scale than during times of political stability and prosperity. Sihathor was a senior army officer in the service of a little known king of the dynasty, IBIYA. He is described as 'Commander of the Crew of the Ruler', and his wife Senebseni as 'Handmaiden among the First of the King'. It is possible that Sihathor's particular area of responsibility was in Upper Egypt which Ibiya, ruling from Thebes, probably controlled.

Bourriau 1988: 57–8, no. 45.

Si-Montu, Prince, Nineteenth Dynasty, New Kingdom, *c.* 1260–50 BC. The twenty-third son of King RAMESSES II, Si-Montu was employed in a relatively modest position, in charge of his father's vineyard. He was married to the daughter of a Syrian sea-captain, Ben-Anath.

Kitchen 1982: 111–12.

Sinuhe, *see* **Sanehet**

Sipa and Neset, *see* **Sepa and Nesa**

Sipair, Chamberlain, Seventeenth/Eighteenth Dynasties, Second Intermediate Period/New Kingdom, *c.* 1550 BC. A royal servant during the momentous years which saw the expulsion of the Hyksos invaders and the establishment of the New Kingdom, thus inaugurating a period of unexampled power and splendour for Egypt, Sipair held a number of important offices, probably under King AHMOSE, the effective founder of the Eighteenth Dynasty. He enjoyed the great advantage of being a 'child of the nursery', the *kap*, the academy in which the royal children were educated with the sons of particularly favoured noble or official families. As well as the familiar titles of Hereditary Prince, Count, and Sole Companion, Sipair was a Royal Chamberlain, Spokesman of the Army, 'One who Introduces Courtiers to the King', 'Stablemaster who Provides the Chariotry with Silver and Gold' and 'Overseer of the Gate of Ebony of the King's House'.

He was the holder of an office translated as 'Bearer of the Branding Iron to the Lord of the Two Lands'. This was perhaps associated with his most important appointment, Overseer of the Treasury; traditionally the nation's wealth was reckoned in cattle, which were the subject of a bi-annual count.

Sipair's involvement in rewarding the chariotry with gold and silver produced the earliest known hieroglyphic representation of a horse. The horse had been introduced to Egypt during the Hyksos period.

Sipair's father was Wedehu-senbu; he was buried at Saqqara.

PM III.2: 732.
J. Málek, 'An Early Eighteenth Dynasty Monument of Sipair from Saqqara', JEA 75 (1989) 61–76; pls VII.2, VIII.

Siptah, King, Nineteenth Dynasty, New Kingdom, *c.* 1194–1188 BC. At the end of the Nineteenth Dynasty the succession was disputed and confused, the consequence, in part at least, of the large number of RAMESSES II's descendants; SETI II produced a son (evidently a cripple, to judge by his portrait, and confirmed by his mummy which shows that he was club-footed or that his leg was withered due to poliomyelitis) who succeeded to the throne as Siptah. He was a minor when he became king and his stepmother, TWOSRET, acted as regent, in collusion with the Chancellor, the Syrian BAY. Siptah's mummy was amongst those found in Amenhotep II's tomb in the Valley of the Kings (KV 35), where it had been moved for safety.

E. R. Ayrton, 'Discovery of the tomb of Si-ptah in the Bibân el Molûk, Thebes', PSBA 28 (1906) 96.
C. Aldred, 'The Parentage of King Siptah', JEA 49 (1963) 41ff.
J. von Beckerath, 'Twosre as Guardian of Siptah', JEA 48 (1962) 70ff.
Reeves and Wilkinson 1996: 155–6.

Sitepehu, High Priest, Eighteenth Dynasty, New Kingdom, *c.* 1473–1458 BC. Sitepehu was High Priest in the Thinite nome, near Abydos, during the reign of Queen HATSHEPSUT. He is recorded in an inscription of the queen, relating to the setting up of one of her obelisks. He is represented by a fine block statue.

Thomas 1995: no. 81 (180).
University of Pennsylvania, Museum of Archaeology and Anthropology E 9217.

Sithathor Iunet, Princess, Twelfth Dynasty, Middle Kingdom, *c.* 1880–1874 BC. The daughter of King SENWOSRET II, Sithathor Iunet was buried near her father's pyramid at El-Lahun. In her tomb was found an exceptional collection of very finely designed and crafted jewellery, which testifies to the taste and discernment of the courts of the Middle Kingdom at its height. Her diadems and an exceptionally elegant mirror are compelling examples of the quality of craftsmanship available to Middle Kingdom magnates.

G. Brunton, *Lahun I, The Treasure*, London, 1920.
Saleh and Sourouzian: 112, 113.
EMC JE 44919 (= CG 52611), JE 44920 (= CG 52663).

Sit-Sneferu, Nurse, Twelfth Dynasty, Middle Kingdom, *c.* 1985–1795 BC. During the reigns of the great kings of the Twelfth Dynasty Egyptian interest and influence extended as far as Turkey, with Egyptian travellers being present there. One such enterprising individual was the nurse Sit-Sneferu, who journeyed to Adana, taking with her her diorite tomb statuette; another Egyptian left a statue of himself at a place some thirty miles east of modern Ankara.

Hayes 1: 235; fig. 132.
CAH I.2: 504.
MMA 18.2.2.

Smendes (Nesbanebdjedet), King, Twenty-First Dynasty, Third Intermediate Period, *c.* 1069–1043 BC. After the death of RAMESSES XI, with whom he had shared power together with HERIHOR, Smendes, the High Priest in Thebes, proclaimed himself king. Smendes drew his influence from the north and, on his assumption of the kingship, established himself at Tanis, which was to remain the power-base of the dynasty which he founded, and its successor. His queen was Tentamun.

Smendes is mentioned in the chronicle of WENAMUN, whose ill-omened journey to the Levant in search of timber for the temple of Amun is one of the classics of later Egyptian literature. Wenamun reports to Smendes, and it is he who arranges for the payment for Wenamun's eventually successful negotiations.

Even during the reign of Ramesses IX Smendes controlled much of the Delta. According to the Wenamun text Smendes was appointed king by the direct intervention of Amun, through the god's oracle, thus demonstrating that Thebes acknowledged his position.

Smendes outlived both Ramesses IX and Herihor.

G. Daressy, 'Les Carrières de Gebelein et le roi Smendés', *Receuil de Travaux Relatifs à la Philologie et à l'Archeologie Égyptiennes et Assyriennes*, 10 (1988) 133–8.
Grimal: 292, 311–12.
Kitchen 1986: §§209–12, §§213–17.
Lichtheim 2: 224–30.

Smenkhkare (alt. Neferneferuaten), King, Eighteenth Dynasty, New Kingdom, *c.* 1338–1336 BC. The relationships of the principal members of the Amarnan family are obscure. Smenkhkare was possibly the son, certainly the immediate if short-lived successor, of King AMENHOTEP IV-AKHENATEN. He was married to the king's daughter, MERITATEN.

He was co-ruler with Akhenaten for a time before the latter's death. After the apparent eclipse of NEFERTITI, the king's principal wife, Smenkhkare seems to have inherited some of her titles, including *Neferneferuaten* ('Beautiful are the beauties of the Aten'), which has occasioned speculation about the nature of Smenkhkare's relationship with the king. It is possible, however, that Smenkhkare was the king's son.

Smenkhkare died after only some three years as king. He was succeeded by TUTANKHAMUN, possibly his brother. At the latter's death a gold coffin, originally intended for Smenkhkare, was adapted for his use.

C. Aldred, 'The Amarna Period and the End of the Eighteenth Dynasty', CAH II.2: 63–6, 79–80.
J. E. Samson, ' "Nefernefruaten" Nefertiti, "Beloved of Akhenaten": Ankhkheperrure Nefernefruaten, "Beloved of Akhenaten", Ankhkheperure Smenkhkare', GM 57 (1982) 61–8.
——'Akhenaten's Coregent Ankheperure-Nefernefruaten', GM 53 (1981–2) 51–4.
M. Eaton-Krauss, 'The Sarcophagus in the Tomb of Tutankhamun', JEA 84 (1998): 210–12.

Sneferu (alt. Snofru), King, Fourth Dynasty, Old Kingdom, *c.* 2613–2589 BC. King HUNI, the last king of the Third Dynasty, appears to have been succeeded by Sneferu, the first king of the Fourth Dynasty, who is now thought to have been the elder king's son by MERESANKH I. Huni's daughter HETEPHERES I, who bore the title 'Daughter of the God', married Sneferu, thus ensuring him a double right to the succession.

Sneferu was long remembered as a kindly and beneficent king. His reign was long and prosperous made especially notable by the building of two, possibly three, conceivably four, great pyramids. The two pyramids which are certainly to be ascribed to him are both sited at Dahshur: the Red Pyramid to the north and the Bent Pyramid to the south. He is also believed to have completed the pyramid at Meidum which was dedicated to his father-in-law, Huni.

The work involved in the excavation and building of Sneferu's pyramids was colossal. Some nine million tons of stone were quarried, shaped and laid in place, an undertaking of a magnitude which makes even the building of the Great Pyramid, identified with Sneferu's son, KHNUM-KHUFU, seem modest by comparison. He may have been responsible for a fourth pyramid, a relatively small one at Seila.

Sneferu was commemorated in many literary texts which were popular long after his reign. He was worshipped as a god for many centuries.

W. M. F. Petrie, *Researches in Sinai*, London, 1906; 44, fig. 50.
A. Fakhry, *The Monuments of Sneferu at Dahshur*, 2 vols, Cairo, 1959–61.
Edwards 1993; 70–96.
Lehner 1997: 97–105.
Saleh and Sourouzian: 24.
EMC JE 38568.

Sneferunefer, Impresario, Fifth/Sixth Dynasties, Old Kingdom, *c.* 2350 BC. Complex and elaborate professionally produced performances were part of the spectacle of royal ceremonies in the Old Kingdom and important occasions in the life of the court. The king and his close associates were offered brilliant entertainments at which music and dancing featured prominently. Sneferunefer was 'Overseer of the Court Singers' and 'Director of Entertainments'. He was responsible for productions at funerals, temple ceremonies and state occasions. He was also in charge of the recruitment and training of musicians, singers and dancers.

Two other Snefereunefers are known: two of the three may have been father and son; both were overseers of the court singers and they were buried at Saqqara. The statue of the third Sneferunefer was found at Giza. He was 'Instructor of Singers in the Great House'.

L. Manniche, *Music and Musicians in Ancient Egypt*, London, 1991: 121–2.
Kunsthistorisches Museum, Vienna, no. 7506.

Sobekemsaf II, King, Seventeenth Dynasty, Second Intermediate Period (Hyksos), *c.* 1600 BC. A king about whom little is known, Sobekemsaf was nonetheless surnamed 'The Great' by his contemporaries and apparently reigned in Thebes for some sixteen years during the Hyksos occupation of northern Egypt.

His tomb, in which his queen, NUBKHAS, was also buried, was one of the first to be found to have been violated when the official inspection of royal tombs was conducted in the Twentieth Dynasty.

Grimal: 188, 290.
Peet 1930.
J. Capart, A. H. Gardiner and B. van der Walle, 'New Light on the Ramesside Tomb-Robberies', JEA 22 (1936): 169–93.
BM 871.
Ryholt 1997: 272, 395–7.

Sobekemsaf, Queen, Seventeenth Dynasty, Second Intermediate Period, *c.* 1575 BC. Names compounded with that of the crocodile god Sobek were popular amongst the family ruling in Thebes during the latter part of the Hyksos period, as indeed had been the case during the Thirteenth Dynasty. The wife of King NEBKHEPERRE INYOTEF VII bore the name; she came from Edfu, to the south of Thebes. She was considered to be of the highest royal birth and her cult was associated with that of Queen AHHOTEP, the mother of King AHMOSE who finally drove out the invading Hyksos.

Despite the uncertainties of the times, the kings and queens of the Seventeenth Dynasty could still call on the services of highly skilled craftsmen, capable of producing works of elegance, even of luxury. Such was the case with jewellery made for Queen Sobekemsaf, who possessed a bracelet or necklace which had gold spacebars surmounted with reclining cats; each bar is inscribed with her name and that of the king.

Sobekemsaf was honoured as one of the ancestresses of the Eighteenth Dynasty.

CAH II.1: 71.
BM EA 57699, EA 57700.

Sobekhotep I, King, Thirteenth Dynasty, Middle Kingdom, *c.* post-1795 BC. The first of the line of often shadowy kings of the Thirteenth Dynasty who identified themselves with the crocodile god, Sobek, may have had some familial connection with the last kings of the Twelfth Dynasty. During his reign of some five years, much of the customary administration of the Two Kingdoms seems to have remained in place.

A. Spalinger, LÄ V (1984) 1036–7.
Ryholt 1997: 209.

Sobekhotep II, King Thirteenth Dynasty, Middle Kingdom, *c.* post-1795 BC. The second Sobekhotep was perhaps not of royal blood. He copied, not very expertly, a relief of SENWOSRET III enthroned, showing himself similarly seated in state.

A. Spalinger, LÄ V (1984) 1038–9.
Ryholt 1997: 215.

Sobekhotep III, King, Thirteenth Dynasty, Middle Kingdom, *c.* 1750 BC. Like SOBEKHOTEP II, the third of the name was not of royal blood, but was of noble birth. He survived for about three years though his monuments are widespread. He was able to make extensive grants to the temples and to favourite courtiers. He built extensively and had a large family, the members of which he ensured occupied positions of influence in the state.

A. Spalinger, LÄ V (1984) 1039–41.
Ryholt 1997: 222–4, 343–5.

Sobekhotep IV, King, Thirteenth Dynasty, Middle Kingdom, *c.* 1725 BC. Sobekhotep IV followed his brother NEFERHOTEP I on the throne and attempted to continue his predecessor's active policies. During his reign, however, Egypt lost control of Avaris, in the north of the country, to the Hyksos, allowing the intruders to establish a stronghold there. He was king for about eight years.

Sobekhotep V and Sobekhotep VI reigned briefly and unremarkably.

S. Quirke, 'Royal Power in the 13th Dynasty', in *Middle Kingdom Studies*, ed. S. Quirke, New Malden, 1991: 123–39.
Ryholt 1997: 229–31, 348–52.

Sobekhotep, Chancellor, Eighteenth Dynasty, New Kingdom, *c.* 1400–1390 BC. In addition to his office of Chancellor to King THUTMOSE IV, Sobekhotep was also Mayor of the Southern Lake and the Lake of Sobek, where he was the king's Chief Huntsman; he was 'Companion of His Majesty in the Middle Island of the Lake Country' and 'Overseer of the Bird-Pond of Pleasure'. More prosaically Sobekhotep was also also Overseer of the Royal Treasurers. His tomb in the Theban necropolis (TT 63) contains a number of paintings of considerable interest for the evidence which they provide of the management of affairs at the court. In one scene foreign envoys, by their dress and appearance from a Semitic-speaking land, bring offerings to the king, products of Asiatic craftsmen. In another scene Africans are brought before the king with their gifts, including gold from the mines in the south, ebony logs, a bunch of giraffes' tails (for fly whisks), and a leopardskin carried by an African who has a monkey sitting on his shoulder.

It was evidently the artist's intention to portray as accurately as possible the different character of the nationalities and races that that he described. Another sequence in the tomb shows various trades at work, including jewellers who are using an abrasive substance in the drilling of hardstones.

James 1985: 23–4; ills 22–3.
BM 43467, 922, 920.

Sobekhotep, Royal Butler, Nineteenth/Twentieth Dynasties, New Kingdom, *c.* 1180 BC. In addition to his rank as Royal Butler, Sobekhotep was 'Overseer of the Treasury of Silver and Gold' and was accustomed to leading expeditions to the mines of Sinai. He was sent to supervise the extraction of copper for one of the Ramessid kings. His stela was erected in the forecourt of the temple at Serabit el-Khadim.

A. H. Gardiner, T. E. Peet and J. Černý, *Inscriptions of Sinai*, London, 1952: 15, no. 302, pl. LXXV.
Scott 1986: 127, no. 72.

Sobekneferu, Queen, Twelfth Dynasty, Middle Kingdom, *c.* 1799–1795 BC. The Twelfth Dynasty, once so vibrant and creative, petered out in the short, ineffectual reigns of its final kings. Paradoxically, one of these was in fact a queen, though she adopted the style and titles of a king. This was Sobekneferu, the sister-wife of the last king, AMENEMHET IV. Her name was included in the Saqqara King List. She ruled as king for three years and ten months.

She may have been responsible for the completion of the mortuary temple of AMENEMHET III at Hawara, 'The Labyrinth', one of the few events reliably attributed to her short reign.

W. M. F. Petrie, G. A. Wainwright and E. Mackay, *The Labyrinth, Gerzeh and Mazghuneh*, London, 1912.
Edwards 1993: 227.
Tyldesley 1996: 18.

Sobeknekht Rinefsonb, Army Officer, Thirteenth Dynasty, Middle Kingdom, *c.* 1795–1650 BC. Sobeknekht Rinefsonb was 'Inspector of the King's Bodyguard'. He was evidently a Nubian – as were many of the kings' military entourage. He is depicted on his stela as being of dark pigmentation, where he is attended by his wife, Ikhekhet, who is of a pale complexion; with them is a diminutive maidservant, Nehku. Sobeknekht Rinefsonb was buried at Gebelein, where there was a long established Nubian garrison.

See also entry for SENU.

Hodjash and Berlev 1982: no. 40, 86–9.

Somtutefnakht, High Priest, Thirtieth, Persian/Macedonian Dynasties, *c.*350–330 BC. The holder of many great offices including the High Priesthood of the goddess Sekhmet, and named for the god Somtus, Somtutefnakht was a Royal Treasurer, Sole Companion, a priest of Horus, a prince and count. It is likely that he began his career under King NECTANEBO II. After the Persian victory in 341 BC and Nectanebo's flight to the south, Somtutefnakht switched his alliegence to the Persians. In the Persian service he witnessed the great battles which ALEXANDER THE GREAT fought against DARIUS III, which culminated in the Great King's murder and Alexander becoming ruler of the Persian Empire and King of Upper and Lower Egypt. Somtutefnakht, fortunately enough, was advised in a dream by the tutelary god of his home town to return there and to resume his priestly offices under Alexander and his successors. As Somtutefnakht observed in his funerary inscription addressed to his god, 'So have you made my end complete. You gave me a long lifetime in gladness.'

Lichtheim 3: 41–4.

Sotades (of Maroneia), Poet, Ptolemaic Period, early third century BC. A Greek who moved to Alexandria, Sotades lived there during the reign of PTOLEMY II PHILADELPHUS. He was reputed to have been locked in a leaden box and drowned at sea, the consequence of a sarcastic remark that he was said to have made on the occasion of the king's marriage to his sister, Arsinoë. He apparently commented 'You have thrust your prick into an unholy opening'. To no one's surprise, Philadelphus imprisoned him, though previously he had ignored his remarks. Sotades escaped to a small island near Crete. There he was found by the admiral, Patroclus, who executed him in the manner described. His poetry included salacious verses, mocking the gods.

Fraser 1972: 117–18, 620, 734.

Strabo, Historian and Geographer, Roman Period, *c.* 63 BC–21 AD. Strabo visited Egypt and evidently spent some years in Alexandria; he described the country extensively in *The Geography*. He examined the Theban monuments and went as far south as Aswan, where he recorded the Nilometer.

Strabo, *The Geography*, trans. H. L. Jones, London, 1932.

Suemniuet (alt. Suemnut), Royal Butler, Eighteenth Dynasty, New Kingdom, *c.* 1427–1400 BC. The office of Royal Butler in the New Kingdom was often one of considerable influence and responsibility. Suemniuet served King AMENHOTEP II in this capacity and was sent on sensitive diplomatic missions by the king. He was buried in one of the élite Eighteenth-Dynasty tombs at Thebes (TT 92); two of his wives, Kat and Iunna, were also commemorated in the tomb. The tomb has recently been the subject of study, which has revealed that several hands were involved in its decoration, some of them distinctly less competent than others. The decoration of the tomb is unfinished.

Suemniuet is also shown in what might be thought to be the more usual duties of a butler, even of a grand domestic of his rank: supervising the preparation of food for the palace and directing the laying-out of a state banquet.

PM I.1: 187–9.
B. M. Bryan, EA 6: 14–16.

Suemnut, Admiral, Eighteenth Dynasty, New Kingdom, *c.* 1427–1400 BC. During the New Kingdom, military officers were accustomed to serve in various arms as well as taking on the duties of civilian administration. Suemnut was a Standard-Bearer of Infantry, then Stablemaster of Chariotry. He was appointed Admiral of the Fleet by King AMENHOTEP II. Ships under his command were manned by 200 marines, as well as the sailors and the officers who were responsible for them.

CAH II.1: 369.

[**Suppiluliumas I**], King (of Hatti), Eighteenth Dynasty, New Kingdom, 1327 BC. Suppiluliumas became King of Hatti in Anatolia during the later years of the reign of King AMENHOTEP III. Hatti enjoyed a somewhat uneasy relationship with Egypt, as its kings saw themselves as the more natural overlords of the northern limits of Egyptian interests than the Egyptians themselves. Suppiluliumas was an energtic and forceful ruler who quickly spread the influence of his state. Although he attacked some of Egypt's allies in Syria and Palestine, some degree of diplomatic relations were sustained between them and Suppiluliumas was one of the foreign kings who corresponded with the King of Egypt, a correspondence which has survived. He was engaged in a seige in the Bekaa Valley, in modern Lebanon, when word was received of the death of TUTANKHAMUN ('Nibhururiya' to the Hittites) to be followed swiftly by a letter, in a form unprecedented in royal exchanges of the time, from Tutankhamun's widow, ANKHESENAMUN, begging Suppiluliumas to send one of his 'many sons' to become king of Egypt. Suppiluliumas was evidently taken aback by the queen's request and sent a chamberlain to establish whether her approach was genuine. He was reassured and despatched Prince ZENNANZA, but he was murdered on the way to Egypt.

Aldred 1968: 240–1, 252.
——1988: 228–9.
K. A. Kitchen: *Suppiluliuma and the Amarna Pharaohs*, Liverpool, 1961.
Redford 1984: 197–203, 217–21.
H. G. Güterbock, 'The Deeds of Suppiluliuma as Told by His Son Mursili II', *Journal of Cuneiform Studies*, 10 (1956) 41–68, 75–98, 107–30.

T

Ta, Vizier, Twentieth Dynasty, New Kingdom, *c.* 1153 BC. Towards the end of his life King RAMESSES III planned to celebrate his jubilee. Responsibility for the arrangements was given to his Vizier, Ta, who travelled to the south of the country to organise the celebrations and the attendant rituals. He visited Elkab, the site of the ancient temple of the cobra goddess Nekhbet, where he was received by the High Priest, SETAU, who recorded the event as one of the high points of his career.

Breasted 4: §§413–14.

Tadimut, Singer, Twenty-First Dynasty, Third Intermediate Period, *c.* 1069–945 BC. Tadimut was a singer in the Temple of Amun at Thebes. He and his wife Herub were the possessors of a particularly fine funerary papyrus, painted with scenes related to the chapters of the Book of the Dead. Herub is shown worshipping the rising sun in the company of Thoth, the cynocephalus baboon, honouring the earth god Geb in the form of a crocodile and, in company with her husband, working in the fields of the paradise land.

Lambelet 1978: 276.
EMC 2512.

[**Tadukhepa**], Princess, Eighteenth Dynasty, New Kingdom, *c.* 1390–1352 BC. In addition to the Princess GHILUKHEPA, King AMENHOTEP III brought another Mitannian princess into his harem. However, Tadukhepa seems to have arrived late in his life, when he was old and ill. She was transferred to the harem of his son and successor King AMENHOTEP IV-AKHENATEN.

Aldred 1968: 48, 91, 208, 240.

Taharqa, King, Twenty-Fifth Dynasty, Late Period, 690–664 BC. Taharqa was perhaps the brother of King SHABATAKA and, after his death, succeeded him on the throne of Egypt. His reign was the most successful of all the Kushite kings. He was an enthusiast for the old ways and sought always to emulate the greatness of Egypt's past. He encouraged artists and craftsmen to bring their skills to the service of the court and the temples. In his concern for past glories he anticipated the archaicising tendencies which were to become so significant an influence in the art and architecture of the Twenty-Sixth Dynasty.

However, Taharqa's pursuit of peaceful enterprises was threatened by the ambitions of the Assyrian kings. ASSURBANIPAL invaded Egypt and drove Taharqa from Memphis. He pursued him to Thebes, where he had retreated. Taharqa was again defeated and withdrew from Egypt to his Nubian kingdom. He died in 664 BC, leaving his kingdom to his cousin or nephew, TANUTAMANI. Like many Nubian kings he was buried in a pyramid; in it, 1,070 shabti figurines were found.

M. F. Laming Macadam, *The Temples of Kawa*, 2 vols, Oxford, 1949–55.
James and Davies 1983: 45–6; ill. 53.
W. Y. Adams, *Nubia: Corridor to Africa*, Princeton NJ and London, 1984: 246–93.
BM 1770.

Taimhotep, Noble, Ptolemaic Period, 73–42 BC. Taimhotep was married at the age of fourteen to PSHERENPTAH, the High Priest of Ptah in Memphis, one of the most powerful offices in the state. She bore him three daughters and then a son; she died at the age of thirty.

Taimhotep left a long inscription in which she records her life and laments the fact that it was cut short; the inscription belongs to a genre of such memorial dedications which are notable for their mood of pessimism and anxiety, in contrast to the generally sunnier and more optimistic terms of earlier memorials. Taimhotep died on 15 February 42 BC and was buried by her husband the High Priest, who died the following year.

Lichtheim 3: 59–65.

Takelot I, King, Twenty-Second Dynasty, Third Intermediate Period, *c.* 889–874 BC. The son of OSORKON I, Takelot reigned, apparently unremarkably, for fifteen years. He seems to have had difficulty controlling his family; his son, the High Priest at Thebes, refused to accept his authority. He was succeeded by another son, who reigned as OSORKON II.

Kitchen 1986: §270, §453, §456, §460.
Grimal: 324.

Takelot II, King, Twenty-Second Dynasty, Third Intermediate Period, *c.* 850–825 BC. Another obscure figure, Takelot II succeeded OSORKON II, though his power base appears to have been Thebes, where the High Priests had effectively established a rival dynasty to the Tanite kings; this division in the country was to have long-lasting effects, and during Takelot II's reign a state approaching civil war broke out in Egypt.

Kitchen 1986: §§287–94, §454.
Grimal: 326–8.
D. A. Aston, 'Takelot II–A King of the "Theban" 23rd Dynasty', JEA 75 (1989) 139–53.

Takelot III, King, Twenty-Third Dynasty, Third Intermediate Period, *c.* 764–757 BC. The son of OSORKON III, Takelot III was High Priest in Thebes and was nominated as Crown Prince by his father. By this time Egypt was hopelessly fragmented; the reign of Takelot III did nothing to improve the situation. The time was ripe for radical change, and this was provided by the Kushite kings of the Twenty-Fifth dynasty who, under their king, PIANKHY, invaded Egypt and imposed order on the Two Lands.

Kitchen 1986: §§317–21, §521.
D. A. Aston and J. H. Taylor, 'The Family of Takelot III and the "Theban" 23rd Dynasty', in A. Leahy (ed.) *Libya and Egypt c. 1300–750 BC*, London, 1990: 135–54.
Grimal 1992: 324, 326–8, 330.

Tanutamani (alt. Tantamun), King, Twenty-Fifth Dynasty, Late Period, 664–656 BC. The successor of King TAHARQA, his uncle or cousin, Tanutamani pursued the policy of opposition to the Assyrians' aggrandisement at Egypt's expense. Initially he was successful, travelling down river and subduing or conciliating those who had supported the Assyrians or who still resented Kushite rule. He eliminated those in the Delta who had compromised with the Assyrians, and the chiefs of the region surrendered to him.

But calamity was imminent; the Assyrians, after an initial defeat, regrouped and poured into Egypt. They sacked the sacred city of Thebes and pillaged its legendary treasure. Tanutamani fought back but was driven further and further south until he had no recourse but to withdraw to Nubia; there he remained. He was the last king of the Kushite dynasty to rule Egypt, though members of his family were kings in Nubia for many years to come.

Kitchen 1986: §§345–55.
A. A. Gasm El-Seed, 'La Tombe de Tanoutamon à El-Kurru (Ku 16)', R d'E 36 (1985) 67–72.

Tefibi, Nomarch, Ninth/Tenth Dynasties, First Intermediate Period, *c.* 2150 BC. In the uncertain political conditions which followed the end of the Sixth Dynasty and the ephemeral Seventh and Eighth, an element of stability was maintained in some of the provinces by determined nobles who became, in effect, independent rulers. One such family of princes was ruling in Asiut, in Middle Egypt, in the Lycopolite nome.

The elder of these princes was Tefibi, 'Hereditary Prince, Count, Seal-Bearer, Sole Companion, Superior Prophet of Wepwawet, Lord of Asiut.' Although the titles were derived from the Old Kingdom they were largely empty, though the Lycopolite nomarchs did provide some support for the kings ruling in Heracleopolis, who claimed sovereignty over all Egypt.

The Lycopolite nomarchs acted as a buffer against rebels from the south who menaced the Heracleopolitans and who eventually were to overthrow them.

Tefibi was succeeded as nomarch by his son, AKHTOY II.

F. L. Griffith, *The Inscriptions of Siut and Der Rifeh III*, London, 1889: 1–16.
Breasted 1: §§393–7.
H. Brunner, *Die Texte aus den Gräben der Herakleopolitzeit von Siut* (Ägyptol. Forsch 5) Gluckstadt, Hamburg and New York, 1937: 2, 17, 43–4.

Tefnakhte, King, Twenty-Fourth Dynasty, Third Intermediate Period, *c.* 727–716 BC. Tefnakhte was the Prince of Sais, in the Western Delta, a member of an ancient family who constituted the 'Great Chiefs of Ma'. Following the confusions which beset Egypt at the end of the Twenty-First and throughout much of the Twenty-Second Dynasties, the country fragmented into a mosaic of small competing states, none of which could exercise authority over all the country. Tefnakhte, an ambitious and able man, saw an opportunity for aggrandisement and moved south, capturing Memphis. He opposed the rulers of Leontopolis and Tanis but his expansion was firmly halted by the Kushite king, PIANKHY. Alone among the rebellious princes, Tefnakhte did not come to pay homage to Piankhy and seems to have maintained some sort of independent state in Sais.

Eventually Tefnakhte seized the opportunity provided by Piankhy's return to his Nubian kingdom to proclaim himself King of Egypt. He reigned for about eight years and was succeeded by his son, BAKENRENEF, who was overthrown by Piankhy's successor, SHABAKA. However, the family of Tefnakhte was to regain royal status in the Twenty-Sixth, Saite, Dynasty.

Lichtheim 3: 79–80.
Kitchen 1986: §§324–8.
Grimal 1992: 336, 338, 340–1.

Tenry (alt. Tjuneroy), Priest, Nineteenth Dynasty, New Kingdom, *c.* 1279–1213 BC. Tenry was a priest and a Royal Scribe of no special distinction other than the fact that in his tomb at Saqqara a list of the kings of Egypt was found inscribed on its walls. The list, now known as the 'Table of Saqqara', records fifty-eight names of kings, from ANEDJIB of the First Dynasty to RAMESSES II, in whose reign Tenry lived and died. Tenry's list has served to confirm other king lists which have survived; like the famous inscription dedicated by King SETI I at Abydos which Tenry's list in part resembles, it omits any reference to the Hyksos invaders or AMENHOTEP IV-AKHENATEN and his immediate successors.

Tenry was Overseer of Works on All Monuments of the King. He served King RAMESSES II and was responsible for all the artists in the king's employment. One of his canopic jars, that of the human-headed divinity Imsety, has highly individual features and it has been speculated that it may be a portrait of Tenry.

PM III.2 (J. Málek): 575–776.
Brooklyn 1979: 56, pl. 24.
J. Málek, 'The Special Features of the "Saqqara King List" ', *Journal de la SSGA*, 12 (1982) 21–8.
EMC CG 34516.
Brooklyn Museum.

Teos (alt. Tachos), King, Thirtieth Dynasty, Late Period, 362–360 BC. Teos was the son of NECTANEBO I, whom he succeed in 362 BC. He was deposed by his nephew NECTANEBO II two years later and fled to the Persian court.

A. B. Lloyd, in Trigger *et al.* 1985: 302–3.
Grimal 1992: 375–81.

Tepemankh, Noble, Fifth Dynasty, Old Kingdom, *c.* 2490 BC. One of the great nobles of Egypt when the Old Kingdom was at its height, Tepemankh was provided with a mastaba at Saqqara which has yielded a number of reliefs. These are of high quality and have been compared with those from the mastaba of TI, one of the exemplars of Old Kingdom funerary decoration. Tepemankh's tomb contained a range of lively scenes of the market place, with tradesmen, farmers and stockmen promoting their wares; one craftsman is engaged to engrave a bowl, probably to be dedicated in a tomb by its donor, a woman. Elements of humour appear, as when leashed baboons reach out to steal the fruit piled in great baskets and one of them tries to grasp his handler, a young boy, by the leg.

Smith 1949: 182, 186, fig. 225c.
Hodjash and Berlev 1982: nos 3, 33, 36, 38–9.

Teti, King, Sixth Dynasty, Old Kingdom, *c.* 2345–2323 BC. At the death of King UNAS, the last king of the Fifth Dynasty, a new line was proclaimed by the coronation of King Teti, the founder of the Sixth Dynasty. Once again, the title to the throne was probably acquired by marriage to the heiress of the previous family of kings.

Teti reigned for at least twelve years. His principal queen was Iput, the mother of his eventual successor, King PEPY I; he was married also to Khuit. Throughout much of his reign Teti was served by the great viziers KAGEMNI and MERERUKA.

It is possible that Teti organised an expedition to the land of Punt, a country distant from Egypt, probably lying in East Africa, which was a source of rare spices, woods, exotic animals and other sought-after products.

According to the historian MANETHO, Teti was assassinated; certainly the succession seems to have been disputed after his death. He had provided himself with a pyramid at Saqqara, which was embellished with the Pyramid Texts. A cult in his memory was maintained into the Middle Kingdom.

C. M. Firth and B. Gunn, *The Teti Pyramid Cemeteries*, 2 vols, Cairo, 1926.
J-P. Lauer and J. Leclant, *Le Temple Haut du Complexe Funéraire du Roi Téti*, Cairo, 1972.
Grimal 1992: 80–1.
Edwards 1993: 179–80.

[Teti], Nubian Noble, Eighteenth Dynasty, New Kingdom, *c.* 1550–1520 BC. Teti was the ancestor of a line of Nubian princes ruling a principality north of the Second Cataract, Tikekhti. The inscription recording his name and titles was set up by his son, Ruyu, who was the first to be acknowledged as a ruling prince. He was succeeded by his son, DJEHUTYHOTEP, who lived during the reign of Queen HATSHEPSUT. By reason of the principality's location its rulers were particularly committed to the cult of the god Khnum, who was identified with Elephantine and the extreme south of Egypt.

Hodjash and Berlev 1982: nos 45, 98–101.

Teti, Priest, Eighteenth Dynasty, New Kingdom, *c.* 1500 BC. Teti was the Lector Priest of Queen Senseneb, mother of King THUTMOSE I. He was provided with an inscribed pyramidion by his son, Djehuti.

P. E. Newberry, *Proc. Bib. Assoc*, XXVII: 102.
Ashmolean Museum 3926.

Tetiseneb, Theban Woman, Seventeenth Dynasty, Second Intermediate Period, *c.* 1550 BC. Tetiseneb lived during the troubled times which saw the expulsion of the Hyksos invaders from Egypt and the restoration of the Dual Monarchy, centred on Thebes, whose princes brought about the final defeat of the foreigners. Her statue was dedicated as an act of piety by her son, Sa-Imen, the 'Royal Sandal-Maker and Doorman'.

Kestner Museum, Hannover, nos 1935, 200, 106.

Tetisheri, Queen, Seventeenth Dynasty, Hyksos Period, *c.* 1580 BC. The wife of King SENAKHTENRE TAO I, Tetisheri was the mother of SEQENENRE TAO II, who was killed fighting the Hyksos invaders. She was the grandmother of King AHMOSE, who eventually effected the expulsion of the Hyksos after the death of his brother King KAMOSE. She was venerated as the ancestress of the Eighteenth Dynasty.

M. H. Gauthier, *Livre des Rois d'Égypte II*, Paris, 1907–17: 159–60.
W. V. Davies, *A Royal Statue Reattributed*, London, 1981.

Thaasetimun, Royal Herald, Thirtieth Dynasty, *c.* 378–360 BC. A Royal Herald and King's Secretary, Thaasetimun was a contemporary of King NECTANEBO I. In his funerary inscription he mentions Iahmes-sa-neith, who lived a century and a half before him.

Bothmer 1961 (1969): 92, no. 74, pls 70–1.
Brooklyn Museum, 56, 152.

Thaenwaset, Priest, Twenty-Third Dynasty, Third Intermediate Period, *c.* 818–715 BC. A priest in the temple of Amun at Thebes, Thaenwaset was buried in the forecourt of the tomb of KHERUEF, a courtier in the reign of King AMENHOTEP III, whose tomb (TT 192), served as a convenient location for the burials of later Thebans, generally of lesser standing than Kheruef himself. Thaenwaset was buried with his wife Shepenkhonsu and their daughter Kapathau, who was a singer in the temple.

Luxor Museum J 106; cat. no. 257, figs 138–9 (Cartonnage of Shepen-Khonsu).

Thenuna, Courtier, Eighteenth Dynasty, New Kingdom, *c.* 1400–1390 BC. Thenuna was 'Fan-Bearer to the Right of the King', an appointment of considerable honour. He was also Superintendent of Royal Property and Treasurer of the King in the reign of King THUTMOSE IV. At some point he seems to have fallen into disfavour; his tomb (TT 76) was vandalised and his name and titles erased, though not totally.

PM I.1: 103.
Kunsthistorisches Museum, Vienna, no. 63.

Theocritus, Poet, Ptolemaic Period, third century BC. Theocritus was a native of Sicily but settled in Alexandria, under the patronage of PTOLEMY II PHILADELPHUS. He was a pastoral poet, whose work was to have a long-lasting influence on the poetic forms of later European verse. He wrote much of love and his powers of vivid description are considerable. He wrote with elegance and wit.

A. S. F. Gow, *Theocritus*, 1952.

Thothhotep, Official, Twelfth Dynasty, Middle Kingdom, *c.* (?)1985–(?)1796 BC. The Twelfth Dynasty kings paid particular attention to Egypt's relations with the states which were emerging beyond their northern frontiers, for example, in Palestine. Thothhotep was sent to Megiddo, where he established himself with the purpose of acquiring cattle to be taken back to Egypt. In his tomb at Ashmunein (ancient Khmun, Greek Hermopolis) he had the journey of the cattle represented, emphasising the care which he exercised in ensuring that they were properly tended.

A. M. Blackman, JEA 2 (1915).

Thutmose I, King, Eighteenth Dynasty, New Kingdom, *c.* 1504–1492 BC. AMENHOTEP I died apparently without a son; he was succeeded by a General of the Army, Thutmose, who was, in all probability, his son- or brother-in-law. It may be that he also had some direct familial connection with the Theban royal family. He campaigned vigorously in Syria and Nubia. He reigned for about thirteen years. He was buried in the Valley of the kings (KV 38) and is thought to have been the first king to be entombed there.

CAH II.1: 313–18.
D. B. Redford, *History and Chronology of the Eighteenth Dynasty of Egypt: Seven Studies*, Toronto, 1967.
Kuhrt 1995: II, 191.

Thutmose II, King, Eighteenth Dynasty, New Kingdom, *c.* 1492–1479 BC. The son and successor of King THUTMOSE I was the child of one of his father's lesser wives, his elder half-brothers having predeceased him. His reign lasted for some thirteen years, perhaps ended by the king's sudden illness and death.

Thutmose II married his sister, HATSHEPSUT by whom he had a daughter. By a lesser wife, the Lady ISIS, he had a son who was to follow him on the throne as THUTMOSE III.

CAH II.1: 316, 317, 318.
Kuhrt 1995: I, 191.

Thutmose III, King, Eighteenth Dynasty, New Kingdom, *c.* 1479–1425 BC. THUTMOSE II appears to have secured the succession of his young son before his untimely death. According to the stories attached to his selection, Thutmose, during his education in the temple of Amun in Thebes, was publicly identified as the chosen king by the god himself. THUTMOSE III was a boy on his accession and his aunt and stepmother, HATSHEPSUT, became regent. She then secured acceptance by the principal interests in the kingdom, remarkably enough, as king, reigning as 'Female Horus', jointly with Thutmose, who remained in obscurity for much of the next twenty years, though he gained much valuable experience as a soldier.

Eventually – probably on the death of Hatshepsut – he asserted himself and became sole ruler of Egypt; Hatshepsut disappears from the record and although Thutmose was in the later years of his reign diligently to eradicate as much reference to her as he could from her monuments, there is no indication that she died other than by natural causes.

Thutmose was to enjoy one of the most brilliant reigns of an Egyptian king, and brought the country to an unexampled level of prosperity and prestige. On assuming full power he began a series of military campaigns which extended the bounds of Egypt's influence throughout the Near East. Well served by commanders such as DJEHUTY, Thutmose outshone even the kings of the Middle Kingdom and in the process created an empire for Egypt. His military exploits, though so extensive, were conducted with compassion for those whom he had defeated in battle, with whom he dealt mercifully.

Thutmose is, in the eyes of some commentators, the greatest of Egypt's kings. Certainly he was a man of immense and multi-faceted talent; in addition to his prowess as a warrior he was a superb athlete. He was also a man of taste and discrimination in the arts, which he encouraged throughout his reign, not only the conventional occupation of a great king in building splendid monuments but in the lesser arts, including, it was said, the designing of furnishings for the temple of Amun.

Thutmose was a scholar who studied hieroglyphs, in the use of which he was as proficient as any scribe; he loved plants and flowers and caused one of the rooms of his Festival Hall at Karnak to be decorated with examples of flora and fauna from his dominions.

Thutmose III was rewarded by years of tranquility as his reign drew to its end. He died after fifty-four years as King of Egypt.

Thutmose was buried in the Valley of the Kings in KV 43. His mummy was one of those found in the tomb of AMENHOTEP II (KV 35).

Hayes 2: 130–40; figs 69–75.
CAH II.1: 313–416 (ch. IX).
A. Tullhoff, *Tuthmosis III*, Munich, 1984.
MMA 26.8.117.

Thutmose IV, King, Eighteenth Dynasty, New Kingdom, *c.* 1400–1390 BC. Thutmose IV was the son of AMENHOTEP II and grandson of THUTMOSE III. He reigned only for about nine years and was still young when he died, suggesting that he may have been a younger son whose elder brother, the heir, predeceased him.

Although he followed the military and sporting traditions of his family, he is remembered principally for a story on a stela which he set up between the paws of the Sphinx at Giza. According to this, as a young prince he was hunting one day in the desert when he rested between the Sphinx's paws. At this time – as so often – the sand had buried much of the monument. In a dream the god spoke to Thutmose and promised him the crowns of Egypt if he would clear away the encroaching sand. This the young prince did and in due course succeeded, thus earning both the throne and an undying reputation as a conservationist.

B. M. Bryan, *The Reign of Thuthmose IV*, Baltimore MD and London, 1991.
D. B. Redford, *History and Chronology of the Eighteenth Dynasty of Egypt: Seven Studies*, Toronto, 1967.
Grimal: 207–21.

Thutmose, Sculptor, Eighteenth Dynasty, New Kingdom, *c.* 1352–1336 BC. The Chief Sculptor to King AMENHOTEP IV-AKHENATEN at the beginning of the Amarna period, Thutmose must have been responsible for the implementation of much of the artistic style which is associated with the king's reign and which was evidently inspired directly by him. He was responsible for the production of the celebrated bust of NEFERTITI, Akhenaten's queen, which was found in the ruins of his atelier at Amarna. Thutmose succeeded BAK in his office.

T. E. Peet, L. Woolley and B. Gunn, *The City of Akhenaten I*, London, 1923: 118, pls XXXVII–XXXIX.
R. Krauss, 'Der Bildhauer Thutmose in Amarna', *Jahrbuch der Preussischer Kulturbeditz*, 20, 1983: 119–32.

Thutnakht, Nomarchs, Eighth to Twelfth Dynasties, First Intermediate Period/Middle Kingdom, *c.* 2181–1860 BC. A remarkable family of princes, five of whom bore the name Thutnakht, ruled the Hare nome from the Eighth Dynasty to the reign of King SENWOSRET III, in the Twelfth. Their rule embraced the thirteenth, fifteenth and sixteenth nomes of Upper Egypt, and their capital was at Hermopolis.

The family appears in the reign of King AKHTOY II, in the person of Prince AHA (IHA) II. Two Princes Thutnakht, II and III, followed in later generations, at the time of the Tenth Dynasty of Heracleopolitan kings. Ahanakht and Thutnakht IV ruled the nomes during the reigns of King Wahkare AKHTOY III and King MERIKARE.

Thutnakht IV's son was the nomarch and vizier NEHERI, who contrived, with great skill, to protect his possessions and their people during the disturbed times when the princes of Thebes were fighting with the kings in Heracleopolis, to whom the Hare nomarchs were loyal.

The victory of Nebhepetre MONTUHOTEP II, who became king of all Egypt *c.* 2055 BC, was a challenge to the family but they remained in office; Neheri was succeeded by Prince Thutnakht V, who became a close associate and supporter of the new ruling dynasty. It was his descendants who were still ruling in the later years of the following dynasty, during the reign of King SENWOSRET III.

CAH I.2: 470–1.
Grimal: 144.

Thuwre, Viceroy, Eighteenth Dynasty, New Kingdom, *c.* 1525–1492 BC. Thuwre was appointed commander of the important fortress at Buhen, far to the south, which guarded the access of the Nubians to Egypt, in the reign of King AMENHOTEP I. He was subsequently promoted to the highest rank in the imperial administration, 'Governor of the South', the first Egyptian Viceroy of Kush. He was energetic in the discharge of his duties and evidently highly competent. On the death of King Amenhotep his successor, King THUTMOSE I (a soldier by profession, whatever may have been his relationship to the royal family) sent a message to Thuwre announcing his accession. Thuwre erected a stela both at Buhen and at Kubban which proclaimed Thutmose's coronation, incorporating the decree which the king had sent him.

W. B. Emery, *Egypt in Nubia*, London, 1965: 172–5.

Ti, Official, Fifth Dynasty, Old Kingdom, *c.* 2445–2421 BC. The life of a high official of the latter part of the Old Kingdom was, by any standards, agreeable. Although not of the highest rank, despite the fact that his wife was a princess, Ti held responsible offices at the court, particularly in the service of King NIUSERRE, including the direction of the funerary complexes of past kings, especially the sun temples which the Fifth Dynasty favoured, and the management of the royal estates.

Ti himself had extensive holdings throughout Egypt, and these are recorded, in exceptional detail, in the splendid mastaba tomb which he built for himself at Saqqara. He was able to employ the finest craftsmen of his time; his statue in the Cairo Museum is one of the masterpieces of the period.

Ti had himself portrayed, with his family and their pet animals, engaged in all the pleasant activities of a grandee of the time. He was concerned to identify all those aspects of the good life which he hoped to take with him to the afterlife, thus to preserve the good fortune which had been his, for all eternity.

G. Steindorff, *Das Grab des Ti*, Leipzig, 1913.
L. Epron and F. Daumas, *Le Tombeau de Ti*, Cairo, 1936.
H. Wild, *Le Tombeau de Ti*, Cairo, 1953.
Saleh and Sourouzian: cat. no. 49.
EMC JE 10065 (= CG 20).

Tity, Overseer of Sealers, Thirteenth Dynasty, Middle Kingdom, *c.* 1740–1720 BC. Although he was an official of some rank, albeit at a time of relative decline in the fortunes of Egypt, Tity chose to have himself commemorated with members of his staff who worked with him in the Palace. Tity's colleagues included the Keeper of the Chamber and Cupbearer, the Scribe of the House of Life and various other scribes, cupbearers and upper servants. Tity sits before his assembled staff, receiving their offerings, and has provideed for their immortality and for the provision of his own sustenance in the afterlife by thus identifying them on his stela.

E. A. W. Budge, *A Catalogue of the Egyptian Collection in the Fitzwilliam Museum, Cambridge*, Cambridge, 1893: no. 76.
Bourriau 1988: 64–5, no. 49.
Fitzwilliam Museum, E.I. 1840.

Tiy, Queen, Eighteenth Dynasty, New Kingdom, *c*. 1390–1340 BC. The daughter of the influential courtiers, YUYA AND TUYU, Tiy was married at an early age to AMENHOTEP III and appears to have remained his chief wife. She was the mother of King AMENHOTEP IV-AKHENATEN, and retained her influence in the early years of her son's reign. She is frequently credited with having exerted an influence on the development of the cult of the Aten, which was certainly current during her husband's reign.

It is likely that Tiy was buried at Akhetaten, though her mummy was probably later taken to Thebes. It has not been positively identified.

Tiy's brother, AY, succeeded TUTANKHAMUN as king, possibly as a consequence of having married Tiy's granddaughter, ANKHESENAMUN.

Hayes 2: 259–61.
Aldred 1988: 146–52, 219–22.
Robins 1993: 21–55.
Saleh and Sourouzian: 144.
EMC JE 38257.

Tjahepimu, Prince, Thirtieth Dynasty, Late Period, *c*. 362–360 BC. When TEOS was named as successor to his grandfather, NECTANEBO I, he at once determined on full-scale opposition to the Persians, who were threatening Egypt at this time. He devoted himself to this task, imposing unpopular taxes on the population to finance the coming conflict. These were deeply resented and, taking advantage of the situation, Tjahepimu, the son of Teos, manoeuvred his own son, NECTANEBO II, into the kingship, deposing his father in the process.

Grimal 1992: 377.

Tjaneni, Military Scribe and Propagandist, Eighteenth Dynasty, New Kingdom, *c*. 1455 BC. Tjaneni was a Military Scribe who accompanied King THUTMOSE III on his campaigns in Palestine and Syria in the twenty-second year of the king's reign. His responsibility was to keep a journal of the campaigns' progress; in particular he was required to record the king's part in them. This he did evidently with enthusiasm; not only did he describe the valour and heroic deeds of the king but he wrote tellingly of his wisdom and his abilities as a strategist, often reporting him overruling the advice of his staff officers. As Thutmose was undoubtedly Egypt's foremost warrior king, it is unlikely that Tjaneni was required to exaggerate the royal prowess unduly.

The king was greatly pleased by Tjaneni's work and caused extracts from his journal to be inscribed on the walls of temples throughout the kingdom. The original, written on a papyrus scroll, was deposited in the temple of Amun at Karnak.

Breasted 2: §392.
CAH II.1: 445–6.

Tjauti, Nomarch, Tenth Dynasty, First Intermediate Period, 2160–2125 BC. Tjauti was governor of the Coptite nome during the uncertain period towards the end of the Tenth (Heracleopolitan) Dynasty, when the princes of Thebes were beginning successfully to assert their control over more and more of the Valley, eventually leading to the foundation of the Middle Kingdom by their descendants, the kings of the Eleventh Dynasty. Tjauti tried to keep control of the vital routes into the Thebaid and he did manage to build new roads, no small achievement at the time. He sought to secure the routes into the Western Desert on behalf of the Heracleopolitans, but he was evidently defeated by one of the INYOTEFS of Thebes.

At an earlier time another Tjauti was Nomarch of the Sixth nome, centred on Denderah.

D. and J. Darnell, EA 10: 24–6.
Hayes 1: 106.

Tjay, Stablemaster, Eighteenth Dynasty, New Kingdom, *c.* 1390–1352 BC. The stablemaster Tjay was responsible for the management of the horses and chariots of King AMENHOTEP III who, in the earlier years of his reign at least, was an enthusiastic sportsman. Although Tjay was a relatively minor official he is commemorated by one of the finest ebony statues from New Kingdom Egypt; he is depicted as a most graceful figure, young and very elegant. He was also a Royal Scribe.

Stevenson Smith 1958 (1981): 277, ill. 273.
Saleh and Sourouzian: 153.
EMC JE 33255.

[**Tjehemau**], Nubian Soldier, Eleventh Dynasty, Middle Kingdom, *c.* 2055–2004 BC. A Nubian mercenary in the service of King Nebhepetre MONTUHOTEP II, Tjehemau left a series of graffiti inscriptions on the rocks near Abisko in Lower Nubia, recording a visit to the region by the king, perhaps to recruit Nubians for his forces. Tjehemau and his son served with the king, accompanying him on a number of his journeys on the river and fighting in campaigns to subdue recalcitrant 'Asiatics'. Tjehemau was unimpressed by the courage of his Theban fellow soldiers, an opinion formed during a visit which he made to Thebes itself.

CAH 1.2: 487.

Tjeti-iker, Nomarch, Sixth Dynasty, Old Kingdom, *c.* 2278–2184 BC. Tjeti-iker was ruler of the Panopolite nome, the ninth of Upper Egypt, in the late Old Kingdom, during the reign of King PEPY II. He was the father of the nomarch KHENI, who employed the artist SENI to decorate his tomb at El Hawawish, the mountain near the nome's capital city. Seni had himself included amongst the nomarch's companions in the tomb and 'signed' his work, declaring 'It was I who decorated this tomb, I being alone'.

Tjeti-iker is also known from a handsome wooden statue showing him striding forward purposefully, his wand of office grasped in his hand. He is depicted nude, which may have been a convention of the time.

Kanawati 1980.
BM 25954.

Tjetji, Official, Eleventh Dynasty, First Intermediate Period/Middle Kingdom, *c.* 2125–2063 BC. When the INYOTEF princes of Thebes were beginning to extend their area of control to much of the south they were still thwarted in asserting their rule over the whole country by the Heracleopolitan kings in the north. Tjetji served INYOTEF I and INYOTEF II and described the conflicts in the politics of Egypt in his monumental stela, which was set up in Thebes. His long and florid inscription suggests a royal administration more secure than it probably was in reality. He says that the southern limits of the Inyotefs' rule was set at Elephantine and extended to This in the north. He was Chief Treasurer to the two kings whom he served.

Breasted 1: §§423A–423G.
James and Davies 1983: 23; fig. 23.
Lichtheim 1: 90–3.

Tjia and Tia, Princess and Official, Nineteenth Dynasty, New Kingdom, *c.* 1279–1213 BC. The Princess Tjia was the granddaughter of RAMESSES I, the daughter of SETI I and the sister of RAMESSES II. Her husband, who does not seem to have been of the same rank as she and was the son of a relatively minor official, was Tia, whose name was almost a homonym of his wife's.

At their extensive but not particularly well built tomb at Memphis the remains of a pyramid were found; although not unknown in the New Kingdom, the pyramid was evidently a deliberate recalling of a royal funerary symbol of a much earlier age. A pyramidion (the capstone of the pyramid) was known in the eighteenth century but was subsequently lost.

The burial of the Tjia and Tia was arranged by their retainer, IURUDEF.

Kitchen 1982: 18, 28, 98.
Martin 1991: 101–16 (both named as Tia).

Tjuneroy, Royal Scribe, Nineteenth Dynasty, New Kingdom, *c.* 1280 BC. Tjuneroy was brother to PASER the builder, but was a man of far greater importance: Overseer of All the Works of the King, Chief Lector Priest, Royal Scribe, Chief Scribe, Master of Largesse. But his tomb, unlike his brother's, has not been found, though memorial stelae have been recovered which record his career and titles.

Martin 1991: 123–4.

Tjutju, Physician, Eighteenth Dynasty, New Kingdom, *c.* 1335–1300 BC. A doctor in practice during the reign of King TUTANKHAMUN, Tjutju was prosperous enough to endow a chapel at Saqqara. His importance lies in the fact that the chapel was dedicated to the cult of King MENKAUHOR-AKAUHOR of the Fifth Dynasty, who had lived a thousand years before Tjutju's lifetime. Relatively little is known of Menkauhor-Akauhor's reign, but that his cult persisted for a millennium suggests that something in his life was considered to be worthy of honour. It is possible that he was buried at Saqqara, though his tomb has not been discovered.

Tjutju's wife Nemau and his sister Naia join with him in worshipping Menkauhor-Akauhor on a relief from the chapel, which was preserved by being re-used in the construction of the Serapeum at Memphis, long after Tjutju's act of piety in consecrating it to the dead king's cult.

B. Letellier, in Berman and Letellier 1996: 66–7, no. 17.
MduL E 3028.

To, High Priest, Nineteenth Dynasty, New Kingdom, *c.* 1323–1294 BC. The High Priesthood of Osiris at Abydos was a particularly rich endowment as a consequence of the temple's importance in the cult of the dead king, and as the focus of a nationwide cult of the god of the underworld, Osiris. In the reign of King HOREMHEB the office of High Priest was held by To, who was effectively to found a dynasty, for five members of his family followed him in the High Priesthood. He was succeeded by his brother-in-law, Hat, in the reign of King SETI I, who was followed by his son, Mery, who lived into the reign of King RAMESSES II. The most distinguished member of the family then appeared, the son of Mery, WENNUFER. By his time the family had extended its involvement in the higher bureaucracy of Egypt prodigiously.

Wennufer's son, HORI, succeeded his father after the latter's long pontificate. He in turn was followed by his son, Yuyu.

Kitchen 1982: 170–1.

Tryphiodorus, Poet, Twenty-Sixth Dynasty, Late Period, sixth century BC. An Egyptian poet who composed *The Conquest of Ilium*, in hexameters, a work said to be of very indifferent quality.

Tutankhamun, King, Eighteenth Dynasty, New Kingdom, *c.* 1336–1327 BC. A boy of about nine years old when he succeeded King SMENKHKARE (who may have been his brother), Tutankhamun was brought back to Thebes by the priests of Amun who sought to eliminate all traces of the 'Amarnan heresy' associated with King AMENHOTEP IV-AKHENATEN, who may have been Tutankhamun's father by a lesser wife, the Lady KIYA. The young king's name was changed to its familiar form from its original, Tutankhaten, as part of this process.

Tutankhamun was married to the daughter of Akhenaten and NEFERTITI, the princess ANKHESENAMUN (Ankhesenpaaten). Two female foetuses were found in the king's tomb who may have been the couple's stillborn daughters.

Tutankhamun's reign seems generally to have been tranquil, though he apparently went campaigning in Syria where the military command was exercised by General HOREMHEB, who was later to become king.

Throughout his reign Tutankhamun was supported by the powerful family of YUYA AND TUYU whose son, AY, was Master of the Horse and an influential courtier. It was he who conducted Tutankhamun's funeral ceremonies when the young king died around his nineteenth year. The cause of his death is obscure, though a wound to his skull, behind the ear, has suggested that he might have been murdered.

Tutankhamun's tomb (KV 62) was almost intact when it was opened in 1922. Its contents indicate the splendour which attended even a relatively unimportant King of Egypt in death as in life.

H. Carter, *The Tomb of Tut-Ankh-Amun*, 3 vols, London, 1923–33.
Desroches Noblecourt 1963.
I. E. S. Edwards, *Tutankhamun* (Exhibition Catalogue).
The Griffith Institute, *Tutankhamun's Tomb Series*, 10 vols, Oxford, 1963–90.
Reeves 1990.
EMC.

Tutu, Chamberlain, Eighteenth Dynasty, New Kingdom, *c.* 1352–1336 BC. Tutu was a Syrian by origin and exercised considerable influence over affairs in the reign of AMENHOTEP IV-AKHENATEN. He was 'First Prophet of the Divine King', thus doubtless something of a High Priest of the royal cult, and 'The Mouth of the Whole Land'. It has been speculated, perhaps unjustly, that his influence was pernicious. He was involved with the correspondence in cuneiform with the Egyptian king's vassal states in the Levant, who complained so bitterly of Egypt's neglect of their welfare and defence.

He is not heard of after the death of Akhenaten.

De Garis Davis 1903–8.
Aldred 1988: 189, 241.

Tuyi, Queen, Nineteenth Dynasty, New Kingdom, *c.* 1294–1279 BC. Tuyi was the wife of King SETI I and the mother of RAMESSES II. She was buried in the Valley of the Queens at Thebes.

L. Habachi, 'La Reine Touy, Femme de Sethi I et ses Proches Parents Inconnus', R d'E 21 (1969) 27–47.

Tuyu and Yuya, *see* **Yuya and Tuyu**

Twosret, Queen, Nineteenth Dynasty, New Kingdom, 1188–1186 BC. The exceptionally long reign of King RAMESSES II resulted in a highly confused succession amongst his descendants. SETI II was the heir of Merenptah, Ramesses II's son; he married several times and on his death his second wife, Twosret, became regent for his successor, her stepson SIPTAH. Twosret was closely involved with the Chancellor BAY, probably of Syrian origin, who has enjoyed a singularly unfavourable reputation.

The last years of the Nineteenth Dynasty were a time of repression and hardship for the people, if the contemporary and later reports are to be believed. The distress which the country experienced was laid to the account of Twosret and Bay.

On Siptah's death Twosret reigned on her own account for a short time. She built a grandiose tomb for herself (KV

14), from which she was ejected by her successor.

H. Altenmüller, 'Tausret and Sethnakhte', JEA 68: 107–15.

Tyti, Queen, Twentieth Dynasty, New Kingdom, *c.* 1184–1153 BC. Tyti was probably both the daughter and the consort of King RAMESSES III. As such, she was probably the mother of his successor, King RAMESSES IV.

J. Grist, 'The Identity of the Ramesside Queen Tyti', JEA 71 (1985) 71–81; figs 1–6.

U

Udjahorresnet, Priest, Physician, Official, Twenty-Seventh Dynasty, *c.* 525–486 BC. The Egyptian attitude to some of their Persian conquerors was ambivalent, a fact demonstrated by the career of Udjahorresnet. He was a naval officer who also became a doctor; he was also a priest at the temple in Sais. He became chief physician to CAMBYSES II and saw it as part of his role to educate the king in Egyptian ways and Egyptian history. He was especially concerned to protect his own city of Sais, an objective which he apparently succeeded.

Udjahorresnet also served DARIUS I, whom he accompanied to the royal capital at Susa. On his return to Egypt he was able to restore the monuments and ensure that the temples were properly staffed.

A. B. Lloyd, 'The Inscription of Udjahorresnet: A Collaborator's Testament', JEA 68 (1982) 166–80.
Verner 1994: 195–210.

Udjebten, Queen, Sixth Dynasty, Old Kingdom, *c.* 2278–2184 BC. One of the several queens whom King PEPY II married in the course of his exceptionally long life, Udjebten was buried in a small pyramid, close to the king's. It appears that it once had a gilded capstone, according to an inscription found when the pyramid was excavated.

G. Jéquier, 'Les Femmes de Pépi II', in S. R. K. Glanville (ed.) *Studies Presented to F. L. Griffith*, Oxford, 1932: 9–12.
Edwards 1993: 203, 285; fig. 42.9.

Ukhhotep I, Nomarch, Twelfth Dynasty, Middle Kingdom, *c.* 1965–1920 BC. Ukhhotep I was a member of a family of great magnates who were the Princes of the Fourteenth Upper Egyptian nome ('the Atef-nome'). He also held the rank of Chancellor of the King of Lower Egypt, and was one of those high officials of the Twelfth Dynasty who were provided with handsome tombs at Meir. The nome was rich and it rulers maintained a considerable state which is reflected in their burials.

Ukhhotep was buried with two funerary boat models. On one of them Uhkhotep lies on his bier, in the form of Osiris, mourned by the goddesses Isis and Nephthys. The canopy erected over the bier is painted with a leopardskin, indicating perhaps that Ukhhotep was a priest and hence entitled to wear the skin. The second boat contains a number of representations of Ukhhotep, seated as a statue, two figures standing amidships and a funerary statuette, very much larger in scale than the others. The boat itself is very finely made and decorated.

Ukhhotep was probably the son of the nomarch Senbi and lived during the reign of King SENWOSRET I.

Blackman 1915: part ii.

Hayes 1: 272–3; fig. 179 (as Wekhhotep).
PM IV: 250.
MMA 12.183.4.

Ukhhotep II, Nomarch, Twelfth Dynasty, Middle Kingdom, *c.* 1965–1878 BC. Ukhhotep II possessed a tomb which is notable for the quality of the drawing which underlays the designs, but the reliefs are less skilfully executed. Its designs hark back to the work of the Old Kingdom. He was ' Overseer of Sealers' and he lived during the reigns of King SENWOSRET I and King AMENEMHET II. It is probable that the dog-loving nomarch SENBI was his son.

PM IV: 249.
Blackman 1914: 8, 11–12.

Ukhhotep III, Nomarch, Twelfth Dynasty, Middle Kingdom, *c.* 1922–1878 BC. Ukhhotep III was buried in a tomb whose decoration is much more refined than that of his predecessor. It contained a ceiling painted with stars and is typical of high quality work of the Middle Kingdom.

He lived during the reign of King AMENEMHET II. He was Overseer of the Prophets of Hathor, Mistress of Cusae and 'Director of Every Divine Office'. His wife was Thuthotep. His tomb contains scenes of family and everyday life of a very high quality, which has led to the suggestion that he may have been able to employ court artists. The ceiling of the outer room of the tomb was painted blue and studded with yellow stars.

Blackman 1915: part iii.
PM IV: 251.

Ukhhotep IV, Nomarch, Twelfth Dynasty, Middle Kingdom, *c.* 1880–1874 BC. Ukhhotep IV was a contemporary of King SENWOSRET II and was one of the important magnates of the time. The kings of the Twelfth Dynasty determined to reduce the power and wealth of the nomarchs. However, Ukhhotep was able to prepare a sumptuous burial place for himself which is innovative in its use of high-quality painted scenes, rather than reliefs. His coffin is notable for its exceptionally lifelike mask, the product particularly of the inlaid eyes which, unusually, are still in place.

Stevenson Smith 1946 (1949): 241, 243, 264, 337.
Blackman 1915: part i: 9, 12–13, 17.
PM IV: 253.

Unas (alt. Wenis), King, Fifth Dynasty, Old Kingdom, *c.* 2375–2345 BC. The last king of the Fifth Dynasty Unas enjoyed a thirty-year reign and general tranquility, though not without some challenges to the royal prerogatives. In his funerary complex at Saqqara, scenes of what appear to be near-starvation conditions amongst the people are matched by one of the earliest battle sequences to be depicted in a king's funerary monuments.

Unas is chiefly remembered, however, as the first king for whom the majestic Pyramid Texts were inscribed on the interior walls of his pyramid. Exquisitely incised hieroglyphs, once filled with a vivid blue paste, contained the spells, incantations and liturgies which would ensure the king's translation to the afterlife and his continued existence as a star.

The building of his pyramid at Saqqara and of the causeway which led to it, up which his sarcophagus would have been drawn, resulted in the tombs of a number of Old Kingdom officials being buried and, in consequence, preserved. The causeway, originally roofed over, contained dramatic scenes of famine in Egypt.

S. Hassan, 'The Causeway of Wnis at Sakkara', ZÄS 80 (1955) 136–44.
A. Piankoff, *The Pyramids of Unas*, Bollingen Series, Princeton NJ, 1968.
A. Labrousse, J.-P. Lauer and J. Leclant, *Le Temple Haut du Complexe Funéraire du Roi Ounas*, Cairo, 1977.
Edwards 1993: 173–6.
Lehner 1997: 154–5.

Unas-Ankh, Prince, Fifth Dynasty, Old Kingdom, *c.* 2375–2345 BC. The son of King UNAS and his principal Queen, NEBET, was provided with a mastaba tomb at Saqqara, not far from his parents' burials. Much of it was sold to the Oriental Institute in Chicago.

CAH I.2: 188, 199.
Lauer 1976: 147.

Urhiya, General, Nineteenth Dynasty, New Kingdom, *c.* 1294–1270 BC. During the later New Kingdom, when relations between Egypt and her neighbours were generally placid, several of the 'client' states in Palestine and the Levant contributed able young men to the service of the king of Egypt. One such was Urhiya, by his name a Syrian or Canaanite, who became a general under King SETI I, and who became thoroughly Egyptianised.

After his career in the Army, Urhiya joined the royal administration, becoming High Steward to King RAMESSES II. His son Yupa (the bearer of an orthodox Canaanite name) followed him in this office.

Kitchen 1982: 30, 70, 139.

Urshanahuru, Crown Prince, Twenty-Fifth Dynasty, Late Period, *c.* 664 BC. When the Assyrians invaded Egypt towards the end of the Twenty-Fifth (Kushite) Dynasty, King TAHARQA waged a courageous defence against the Assyrian king ESARHADDON, but was overcome by more powerful forces. He was driven out of the capital, Memphis, whose treasure was pillaged. In the process, Urshanahura the Crown Prince and Taharqa's queen were captured.

Stevenson Smith 1965 (1981): 404.

User, Vizier, Eighteenth Dynasty, New Kingdom, *c.* 1473–1458 BC. User was a great official living in the reigns of Queen HATSHEPSUT and King THUTMOSE III. He is described, amongst his other titles, as 'Noble, Prince, Prophet of Ma'at, Supervisor of the Treasuries of the Two Lands, Head of the Secrets of the Palace, Judge'.

It has been remarked that the inscriptions in his tomb at Thebes are those more usually found in connection with royal burials.

G. Kueny and J. Yoyotte, *Grenoble Musée des Beaux-Arts, Collection Egyptienne*, Paris, 1979: cat. 18; 35–6.
Urk 10: inv. 1954.
Cat. Tresson.

Userenre (alt. Seuserenre), King, Seventeenth Dynasty, Second Intermediate Period, *c.* 1650–1550 BC. One of the Seventeenth Dynasty rulers of Thebes about whom little is known, Userenre nonetheless evidently managed to hold the throne for twelve years, according to the chronicles.

CAH II.1: 69.

Userhat, High Priest, Eighteenth Dynasty, New Kingdom, *c.* 1336–1327 BC. Although he reigned only for a short time and was a very minor king, TUTANKHAMUN after death was given the rites appropriate to a dead King of Egypt, returning to the underworld to reign as Osiris. Userhat was High Priest of his cult in Thebes.

He has left an engaging record of his life, less encumbered with bombast than most funerary inscriptions. 'I was one calm, one patient and careful in my language. I was one content with his lot and not rapacious. I went on my way without deviating from it.'

His stela, on which he is portrayed with his wife, is particularly delicately carved.

Hayes 2: 306; fig. 191.
Reeves 1990: 28.
MMA 05.4.2.

Userhet, Noble, Eighteenth Dynasty, New Kingdom, *c.* 1430–1400 BC. A noble who served King THUTMOSE III and King AMENHOTEP II, Userhet was a Royal Scribe and also a royal tutor, responsible for the upbringing of the princes; he himself was a child of the *kap*, the royal nursery and academy. He was buried in one of a series of handsome tombs at Thebes (TT 56) provided for high officials at this period. It contains scenes of the chase, a lavish banquet and the owner of the tomb being shaved by his barber.

PM I.1: 111–13.

Userkaf, King, Fifth Dynasty, Old Kingdom, *c.* 2494–2487 BC. After the death of the last king of the Fourth Dynasty, SHEPSESKHAF, Userkaf came to the throne, his accession perhaps representing a return to the secondary branch of King KHNUM-KHUFU'S line. It is likely that his mother was the daughter of King DJEDEFRE, Khufu's immediate successor. He may have reinforced his claim to the kingship by marrying Queen KHENTKAWES, the daughter of King MENKAURE.

Userkaf is immortalised by the work of his sculptors. Two magnificent portrait heads of the king demonstrate how the finest quality of the work of the Fourth Dynasty was securely carried on into the Fifth. A cup inscribed with the name of Userkaf's sun temple was found on the island of Kythera in the Aegean.

Userkaf built a pyramid at Saqqara. His sun temple, part of a funerary complex which he built at Abusir, was the first example of a construction which was to become one of the hallmarks of the Fifth-Dynasty kings.

J-P. Lauer, 'Le Temple Haut de la Pyramide du Roi Ouserkaf à Saqqarah', ASAE 53 (1955) 119–33.
H. Ricke, *Das Sonnenheiligtum des Königs Userkaf*, Wiesbaden, 1965–9.
Terrace and Fischer: 9, 53–6.
EMC JE 90220.

Userkare, King, Sixth Dynasty, Old Kingdom, *c.* 2321 BC. This ephemeral ruler is thought to have occupied the throne for about a year, immediately before the accession of King PEPY I, perhaps during the king's minority. He is believed to have been a descendant of the ruling family of the Fifth Dynasty.

CAH I.2: 189–90.
Grimal: 81.

Userkare Khendjer, King, Thirteenth Dynasty, Middle Kingdom, *c.* 1750 BC. This king is but little known from the Egyptian annals, though it appears that he ruled successfully and was able to command the loyalty of much of the country in the troubled times which followed the end of the Twelfth Dynasty. He was buried in a mud-brick pyramid faced with limestone. Fragments of a black granite pyramidion have been found recording his name and titles.

G. Jéquier, *Deux Pyramides du Moyen Empire*, Cairo, 1938: 8, pl. 7; pl. v, b, c.
——*Douze Ans des Fouilles dans la Nécropole Memfite, 1924–36*, Neufchâtel, 1940.

Usermont, Vizier, Eighteenth Dynasty, New Kingdom, *c.* 1336–1327 BC. Usermont served King TUTANKHAMUN as Vizier. A member of a leading Theban family he was a Priest of Ma'at, a provincial governor, a judge and an hereditary prince.

L. Habachi, 'Unknown or Little Known Monuments of Tutankhamun and of his Viziers', in Ruffle *et al.* 1979: 32–41.

Usertatet, Viceroy, Eighteenth Dynasty, New Kingdom, *c.* 1427–1400 BC. Usertatet was appointed Viceroy of Nubia by King AMENHOTEP II, one of the warrior kings of the early years of the dynasty, with whom Usertatet had previously served and with whom he was evidently on terms of friendship. He carried out a number of building projects in Nubia whilst he was in office.

Grimal 1992: 219.

Userwer, Sculptor, Twelfth Dynasty, Middle Kingdom, *c.* 1963–1862 BC. Userwer was the recipient of a funerary stela which shows himself, his wives, his parents, brother, sons and daughters receiving offerings. The principal interest of Userwer's stela, however, is not so much its form and content (both fairly conventional) but rather that it is unfinished and, given Userwer's profession, it is valuable in tracing the stages in the making of such a memorial. First, an assured repertoire of black-ink drawings indicate the content of the stele. At least two stone cutters were, it is thought, involved in the excision of the hieroglyphs and the figures of the family. It is not known which of the various functions involved in the stele's production would have been undertaken by Userwer himself. It appears that it may have been finished off by a less experienced artist whose work was certainly not of the first quality.

Bourriau 1988: 29–31; pl. 20; no. 20.

Usimarenakhte, High Steward, Twentieth Dynasty, New Kingdom, *c.* 1130–1120 BC. The son of the powerful High Priest of Amun, RAMESSESNAKHTE, Usimarenakhte, unlike his brothers who inherited their father's office, achieved a high place in the secular administration of the south. By virtue of its authority he as able to acquire for himself large landholdings in Upper Egypt at the expense of the peasants and small farmers. He appointed himself assessor of claims and he was one of those whose machinations led to the impoverishment of the monarchy, the eventual collapse of the central authority and the division of Egypt effectively into two separate entities, the division which the early kings had striven so diligently to overcome.

Kees 1961: 68.
Kitchen 1986: §207, n21.

Wah, Estate Manager, Eleventh Dynasty, Middle Kingdom, *c.* 2055–2004 BC. Convincing evidence of the prosperity enjoyed by even modest officials in the Middle Kingdom is provided by the intact burial at Thebes of the Estate Manager Wah, an employee of the great Chancellor, MEKETRE, during the reign of King NEBHEPETRE MONTUHOTEP II. He evidently died young, and he was buried in finely woven wrappings and a splendid mummy case. He was decked in his jewellery and his mummy made ready for its burial in the tomb where it remained for four thousand years. He was buried with his mummy turned to the east, his head to the north.

He bore the title 'Overseer of Sealers'.

Hayes 1953: 203, 303–5; fig. 196.
MMA 20.3.203.

Wah, Priest, Twelfth Dynasty, Middle Kingdom, *c.* 1806 BC. Wah entered into a contract designed to protect his wife and heirs and to ensure that they succeeded to his property. The contract initially made provision for his wife; a codicil was added later, evidently after the birth of a son. It appears that Wah may not have expected to live to see his son grow to maturity, as he appointed a guardian for the boy.

Wah owned property formerly belonging to his brother, Ankhreni, a man evidently of some substance who had several Asiatic servants in his employ. They, together with several properties, had been made over by Ankhreni to Wah some years earlier. The servants are mentioned in Wah's 'will', when he bequeathed them to his wife.

Wah's instructions for the management of his wife's inheritance display some unease, as though he were unsure of his brother's reliability in respecting his wishes. In particular he asks that his wife shall be allowed to live in the rooms which Ankhreni had built for him.

Wah's contract was found, still sealed, in an archive at El-Lahun.

F. L. Griffith, *The Petrie Papyri: Hieratic Papyri from Kahun and Gurob*, London, 1898: 31–5, pls 12–13.
Parkinson 1991: 108–9, no. 36.

Wahankh Intef, *see* **Inyotef II**

Wahka, Nomarchs, Twelfth Dynasty, Middle Kingdom, *c.* 1920–1808 BC. Wahka I was a member of a powerful family of provincial magnates who governed the region of Anteopolis (Qaw el-Kabir) in the latter years of the Middle Kingdom. He was buried in a finely built and decorated tomb in which his titles are recorded as Noble, Prince and Overseer of Priests.

His successor, Wahka II, sems to have maintained a still larger state and to have flourished during the reigns of

AMENEMHET II, SENWOSRET III and AMENEMHET III. Later, nobles of the status of the Wahkas appear to have been deprived of the title of 'prince' which they had previously borne, perhaps because it implied a status approaching the king's.

M. C. Carlos Hall, in Robins 1990: 30–2.

Wahkare, *see* **Akhtoy III**

Wahneferhotep, Prince, Thirteenth Dynasty, Middle Kingdom, *c.* 1740 BC. The son of King NEFERHOTEP I, Wahneferhotep was probably buried near the pyramid of King SENWOSRET I at El-Lisht. A funerary figure of the prince was found near the king's pyramid.

D. Arnold, *The Pyramid of Senwosret I: The South Cemeteries of Lisht, vol. 1*, New York, 1988: 37–40, 147–9.

Wedjankhdjes, Governor, Fourth Dynasty, Old Kingdom, *c.* 2613–2494 BC. A 'pair statue' of the Governor Wedjankhdjes and his wife Inefertef from the early years of the Fourth Dynasty is significant as one of the earliest family groups related to a private individual, a form which was to become characteristic of much Egyptian funerary art. The group retains much of its original colour, though Inefertef has lost her head; she stands, deferentially, a little behind her seated husband, her arm protectively across his shoulders, a posture which was also to be repeated throughout Egytptian history.

B. Piotrovsky (ed.) *Egyptian Antiquities in the Hermitage Museum*, Leningrad (St Petersburg), 1974: no 14.
The Hermitage Museum, St Petersburg, inv. no. 18107.

Wegaf, King, Thirteenth Dynasty, Middle Kingdom, *c.* 1795 BC. The first recorded king of the Thirteenth Dynasty and its putative founder, Wegaf set the pattern for his successors by reigning not more than a couple of years. He is recorded in the Karnak King List, however, and was followed over the next two centuries by a flood of ephemeral kings. Such authority as Wegaf had was probably confined to Thebes and the south.

J. von Beckerath, 'Ugaef', LÄ VI (1986) 838.

Wenamun, Priest, Twentieth/Twenty-First Dynasties, New Kingdom/Third Intermediate Period, *c.* 1065 BC. Wenamun was a priest in the Temple of Amun of Thebes. In the twenty-third year of the reign of King RAMESSES XI, Egypt had effectively been divided into two parts, the south being dominated by the High Priest of Amun, HERIHOR, whilst SMENDES was ruling in the Delta. Wenamon was sent to Byblos to negotiate the purchase of timber for the construction of the sacred barque of Amun.

Egypt's prestige at this time was low. In consequence Wenamun found himself mocked, he was robbed, and the Prince of Byblos treated him in a most unworthy manner. The record of Wenamun's attempts to assert the status of Egypt and the cavalier treatment that he received makes painful reading.

Finally, Wenamun, whose competance as an envoy must be seriously doubted, secured his timber and set out, sadly and with his pride severely dented, to return to Egypt.

Even then his troubles were not over. His ship, which he had had great difficulty in securing, was blown off course to Cyprus where he was shipwrecked. Hauled before the queen, he was nearly sent for execution. The record of his misfortunes breaks off here. It survives on a papyrus, and it is always possible that the whole story was in fact a literary invention.

Gardiner 1961: 306–13.
Lichtheim 2: 224–30.

Wendjebaendjed, Courtier, Twenty-First Dynasty, Third Intermediate Period, *c.* 1000 BC. Wendjebaendjed was the

Steward of Khonsu and the Prophet in his temple at Tanis. He was a leading figure at the court of King PSEUSENNES I; he was 'Hereditary Prince', 'Seal-Bearer', 'General and Leader of the Army'. He was also 'Superintendent of the Prophets of All the Gods', an office somewhat equivalent to the High Priesthood. He was provided with a burial chamber in the tomb of King Pseusennes, where he was buried with an exceptionally rich complement of funerary goods, many of fine workmanship, crafted in gold. Amongst the most notable objects were vessels of great purity of design, a magnificent pectoral and a model shrine, fabricated in lapis lazuli and gold, with the ram god standing in it. He was provided too with statues of gods and goddesses, also in gold.

P. Montet, *La Nécropole Royale de Tanis*, 3 vols, Paris, 1947–60.
G. Goyon, *La Découverte des Trésors de Tanis*, Éditions Persea, 1987.
Kitchen 1986: §8, §45, §222, §228, §395.
EMC.

Weneg (alt. Wadjnes, Tlas), King, Second Dynasty, Archaic Period, *c.* 2800 BC. A king of almost unreserved obscurity whose name is known only as a consequence of King DJOSER NETJERYKHET'S antiquarian interests, for a bowl inscribed with his name was placed under the Step Pyramid complex. According to the king lists he reigned in the middle of the dynasty; it is possible that his power did not extend much beyond the area of Memphis.

CAH I.2: 31.
Spencer 1993: 67.

Weni (alt. Uni), Noble, Sixth Dynasty, Old Kingdom, *c.* 2340–2280 BC. Weni was a member of a family with close affiliations with the court. In a long and distinguished career he served several kings, probably starting with King TETI, the first king of the Dynasty, when he must have been little more than a boy. He then rose through the upper reaches of the royal bureaucracy. He was a soldier, leading expeditions against the nomads, who always represented trouble to the settled people of the Valley; in this capacity he commanded the first recorded invasion by an Egyptian army against marauders in Palestine. He was a judge who gained much satisfaction from the fact that he was ordered by the king, PEPY I, to conduct an enquiry into the behaviour of one of the queens, WERETYAMTES. He was, as he said of his relationship with the king in his long autobiographical inscription at Abydos, 'rooted in his heart'.

He was responsible for a number of important civil engineering projects, including the cutting of canals at the First Cataract.

After the death of King Pepy he was one of the chief supporters of the young King MERENRE I. The culmination of his career was his appointment as Governor of Upper Egypt, a position equivalent to Viceroy. There, he carried out public works in the south, including building canals at the First Cataract, the first ever made. He received the homage of the Nubian chieftains on the king's behalf. He appears to have died during Merenre's reign.

Weni had a tomb (or perhaps a cenotaph) at Abydos.

A. Mariette, *Abydos II*, 2 vols, Paris, 1869–80.
Breasted 1: §§292–4, §§306–15, §§319–24 (as Uni).
L. Borchardt, *Denkmaler des Alten Reiches I*, Berlin, 1937: 18ff, pls 29–30.
Lichtheim 1; 18–23.

Wennufer, High Priest, Nineteenth Dynasty, New Kingdom, *c.* 1279–1213 BC. From the Eighteenth to the Twentieth Dynasties, the office of High Priest of Osiris at Abydos, one of the great temple appointments of the age, was frequently held by members of the same family. Wennufer was the son of MERY, who held the office during the reign of SETI I; he was High Priest during the reign of Seti's son, RAMESSES II.

He reigned as pontiff for thirty-five years. He was succeeded by his son HORI and his grandson Yuya.

G. A. Gaballa, 'Monuments of Prominent Men of Abydos, Memphis and Thebes', in Ruffle *et al.*: 43–6.
Kitchen 1982: 170–1.

Wepwawetemsaf, King, Thirteenth Dynasty, Middle Kingdom, *c.* 1650 BC. An obscure figure even when judged by the general obscurity of the later part of the Thirteenth Dynasty, King Sekhemneferkhaure Wepwawetemsaf is known only by a rather forlorn stela, rudely executed, in which he is shown standing before his patron divinity, Wepwawet-re, lord of Abydos. The dismal quality of Wepwawetemsaf's one monument is eloquent testimony to the poverty of the royal house at this time.

Bourriau 1988: 72, no. 58.
BM EA 969.

'Weretyamtes', Queen, Sixth Dynasty, Old Kingdom, *c.* 2231–2287 BC. One of the consorts of King PEPY I, Weretyamtes (now thought to be a queen's title rather than a name) was implicated in a harem conspiracy directed against the king. A discreet investigation was ordered into the Queen's conduct, and was carried out by WENI, one of the king's trusted companions. The outcome of the investigation is not recorded.

Lichtheim 1: 19.

Wermai, Priest, Twentieth Dynasty, New Kingdom, *c.* 1100 BC. Wermai was a priest in Heliopolis who, according to an inscription which represents itself as biographical, appears to have fallen foul of the authorities and was, as it were, 'defrocked'. He had a miserable existence, trying to make a living for himself by farming some unproductive land in the 'Great Oasis', west of the Nile. He fell behind in his taxes and was punished as a result.

It is suspected that this story is fictional.

R. A. Caminos, *A Tale of Woe from a Hieratic Papyrus in the A. S. Pushkin Museum of Fine Arts in Moscow*, Oxford, 1977: 70–2.

Wesersatet, Viceroy, Eighteenth Dynasty, New Kingdom, *c.* 1427–1400 BC. The Viceroy of Nubia during the reign of AMENHOTEP II and therefore one of the most powerful men in Egypt, Wesersatet was evidently an intimate of the king, from the days of their youth. A letter from the king survives, evidently written spontaneously, in which he recalls their days together and the time they spent together campaigning in Syria. The king reminds his friend of the women who were taken as booty during the wars.

Dows Dunham and J. M. A. Janssen, 'Second Cataract Forts', JNES 14 (1955) 22–31, pl. 82.

Weshptah, Vizier, Fifth Dynasty, Old Kingdom, *c.* 2475–2455 BC. In addition to being Vizier to King NEFERIRKARE, Weshptah was a judge and Chief Architect; he was thus one of the most important men of his time. The king and his courtiers were one day inspecting a new building which was being constructed under Weshptah's direction, when he suffered what appears to have been a stroke. The king was much distressed and at once sent for his principal physicians whilst he himself withdrew to pray to Re for the recovery of Weshptah. All was in vain however; the king then turned to supervising the funeral and burial of his servant.

Breasted 1: §§242–9.

X

[Xerxes], King, Twenty-Seventh Dynasty, First Persian Period, 486–465 BC. The successor of DARIUS I, Xerxes was determined to assert Persian control of Egypt when he achieved the throne. He imposed a particularly repressive regime to the rule of Egypt, and consequently his name was execrated by the Egyptians. He was assassinated in 465 BC.

E. Bresciani, 'The Persian Occupation of Egypt', CHI 2.

Y

Yah, Queen, Eleventh Dynasty, Middle Kingdom, *c.* 2063–2055 BC. The wife of King INYOTEF III, Yah was the mother of the real founder of the Middle Kingdom, NEBHEPETRE MONTUHOTEP II. Another of her children was the princess Neferu, who as NEFERU III became the principal wife of her brother Nebhepetre Montuhotep.

CAH I.2: 478.

Yamu-nedjeh, First Herald, Eighteenth Dynasty, New Kingdom, *c.* 1479–1425 BC. One of THUTMOSE III's senior officers and much favoured by him, Yamu-nedjeh accompanied the king on his campaigns in Western Asia and crossed the Euphrates with him. In civilian life Yamu-nedjeh was responsible for supervising the erection of three pairs of obelisks for the king, two at Karnak and one at Heliopolis. He was honoured by having his statue set up in the king's mortuary temple.

W. C. Hayes, ASAE 33 (1933) 6–16.
The Luxor Museum of Ancient Egyptian Art, J3.
EMC JE 59190.

Yaqub-Hor, King, Fifteenth Dynasty, Second Intermediate Period, *c.* 1650–1550 BC. The successor of King SALITIS, the first king of the dynasty and the first of the Hyksos to rule Egypt, Yaqub-Hor reigned for eighteen years. His reign was notable for the fact that he maintained good working relations with the rulers of Thebes, the founders of the Seventeenth Dynasty which was ultimately to bring about the Hyksos' expulsion from Egypt. Yaqub-Hor is represented by seals which have been found from Gaza to Kerma.

CAH II.1: 59–60 ('Meruserre Yak-Baal or Yekeb-Baal').
R. Giveon, 'Ya'aqob-har', GM 83 (1981) 27–30.
Grimal: 187–8.

Yewelot (alt. Iuwelot), High Priest, Twenty-Third Dynasty, Third Intermediate Period, *c.* 777 BC. Yewelot was the son of King OSORKON I, and his duties as High Priest of Amun at Thebes entailed the political control of much of Upper Egypt and the command of the army. He had an estate in the west of Thebes, called 'Beautiful Region', which he bequeathed to his son, Khamwase.

Kitchen 1986: §96, §184, §270 (as Iuwelot).

Yii, Priest, Scribe, Eighteenth Dynasty, New Kingdom, *c.* 1327–1323 BC. Yii was Second Prophet of Amun, First Prophet of Mut and a Royal Scribe. He was evidently an officer of King AY's short-lived court, as the king's name apppears on Yii's statue.

B. V. Bothmer, 'Private Sculpture of Dynasty

XVIII in Brooklyn', *The Brooklyn Museum Annual VIII* (1966–7) 55ff; figs 30–4.

Yupa, Mayor, Nineteenth Dynasty, New Kingdom, *c.* 1279–1213 BC. Yupa is thought to have lived during the reign of King RAMESSES II and was, according to his commemorative stela, mayor of 'The Glorious City', the whereabouts of which is unknown but was probably in the region of Memphis and Heliopolis.

Yupa was Overseer of the Priests 'of the Gods, Lords of the Sea'. The reference to 'Lords of the Sea' is unusual in Egyptian liturgies and possibly refers to the divinities of a region near Heliopolis who were thought to control the flooding of the Nile in the Delta, and all aquatic matters generally.

Hodjash and Berlev 1982: no. 85, 142–4.

Yuya, Steward, Nineteenth Dynasty, New Kingdom, *c.* 1279–1213 BC. A member of a family – his father was General URHIYA – which occupied many high offices during the early Nineteenth Dynasty, Yuya began his career as a stable master; he served RAMESSES II as High Steward of the Ramesseum, the king's massive funerary temple, an office which his father had also held. He proclaimed the king's ninth jubilee, a very great honour, sometimes discharged by royal princes. He also held high military rank.

J. Ruffle and K. A. Kitchen, 'The Family of Urhiya and Yuya, High Stewards of the Ramesseum', in Ruffle *et al.*: 55–74.

Yuya and Tuyu, Nobles, Eighteenth Dynasty, New Kingdom, *c.* 1390–1352 BC. This couple were the grandparents of AMENHOTEP IV-AKHENATEN by virtue of their daughter TIY having been married to AMENHOTEP III and borne his successor. They were to exercise a considerable influence on the affairs of the dynasty and the court throughout the two kings' reigns.

Yuya came from Akhmim, where he had estates and was a priest of the principal divinity, Min. He was Master of the Horse and hence held important military responsibilities.

The title 'Father of the God' was conferred on Yuya, and his prestige and standing at court was correspondingly enhanced. When Akhenaten became Crown Prince his power was augmented correspondingly.

It is probable that AY, who eventually succeeded TUTANKHAMUN as king, was the son of Yuya and Tuyu; he certainly held the same offices as Yuya and had estates in Akhmim. Another son, ANEN, was appointed High Priest of Re in Karnak.

Yuya and Tuyu were buried together in a tomb in the Valley of the Kings, KV 46. It was intact when discovered and contained a wealth of splendid funerary offerings. The double statue of Yuya and Tuyu, seated side by side, is one of the finest from the latter part of the Eighteenth Dynasty.

T. M. Davies *et al.*, *The Tomb of Iouiya and Touiyou*, London, 1907.
J. E. Quibell, *The Tomb of Yuaa and Thuiu*, Cairo, 1908.

Z

Zekhonsefankh, Noble, Twenty-Second Dynasty, Third Intermediate Period, 825–773 BC. During the reign of SHESHONQ III, disturbances in the south led to the High Priest of Amun in Thebes, the king's son Osorkon, leaving the city and withdrawing to the south with a number of courtiers and his family. His sister was married to Zekhonsefankh, a powerful Theban noble who may have been the cause, or the occasion, for the opposition to the king and his son. Eventually, peace appears to have been restored.

Breasted 4: §§757–9.

[Zennanza], Prince, Eighteenth Dynasty, New Kingdom, d. post-*c.* 1327 BC. When TUTANKHAMUN died, the line of AHMOSE, the founder of the Eighteenth Dynasty, was extinct. The circumstances of Tutankhamun's death are ambiguous; it appears that it precipitated a crisis in the court which was demonstrated, most remarkably, by Tutankhamun's widow ANKHESENAMUN pleading with the King of the Hittites, SUPPILULIUMAS, to send her one of his sons so that she might marry him and, as the daughter of a king, convey the kingship to him.

Such a proposal was without precedent and must have been deeply shocking to the more conservatively minded of the courtiers and the religious establishment. Suppiluliumas, however, saw the political advantage of being the father of the King of Egypt, and on Ankhesenamun repeating her request he despatched Zennanza, one of his sons, to the queen.

Zennanza was murdered before he reached Egypt.

H. G. Güterbock, 'The Deeds of Suppiluliuma as told by his son Mursili II', *Journal of Cuneiform Studies*, 10 (1956) 41–68, 75–98, 107–30.

[Zenodotus], Critic and Librarian, Ptolemaic Period, early third century BC. Zenodotus was an Ephesan by birth but came to Alexandria as tutor to the sons of PTOLEMY II PHILADELPHUS. He became superintendent of the royal library. He produced a critical editon of Homer's works, including a *Homeric Glossary*, and of Aristarchus. He lived to a great age.

Diogenes Laertius, *Lives of the Eminent Philosophers*, trans. R. D. Hicks, Cambridge, Mass. and London, 1925: 5.58.
W. M. Ellis, *Ptolemy of Egypt*, London, 1994: 47.

Zenon, Administrator, Ptolemaic Period, *c.* 280 BC. An associate of the brilliant Ptolemaic Minister of Finance, APOLLONIUS, Zenon was involved in many of his ambitious schemes to improve the economy of Egypt. He was particularly concerned with extending

Egypt's irrigated areas and, although not all his plans were realised, he was responsible for the reclamation of large tracts of land which had been allowed to fall into disuse. A substantial archive of his correspondence with Apollonius survives, and throws much light both on the economy and on the administration of the state in the early Ptolemaic period.

Kees 1961: 210, 228–9.

P. W. Pestaran, *A Guide to the Zenon Archive*, 2 vols, Leiden, 1981.

Zer, *see* **Djer**

Zet, *see* **Djet**

Zoser, *see* **Djoser Netjerykhet**

Glossary

Note: Transliterations of Egyptian words are italicised.

Admonitions or Instructions A literary genre whereby an ancestor or previous holder of the kingship, for example, purportedly left to a successor a series of observations, often of a very practical not to say cynical nature, on life and the exercise of high office.

Akh The justified spirit of the dead; the power of the gods.

Akhu The spirits of dead predynastic kings of Hierakonpolis, Buto and Heliopolis; also the Companions of Horus (see also ***Shemsu Hor***).

Amarna The location (Tel El-Amarna) of the new capital of Egypt, Akhetaten, built downriver from Thebes by AMENHOTEP IV-AKHENATEN. Also used adjectivally to describe the style of art promoted by the king.

Amratian (El-Amra) A site in Upper Egypt where an important predynastic culture was first identifed; frequently classified as NAQADA I.

Amulets Magical jewels or ornaments often placed inside the mummy wrappings to protect various of the organs and parts of the body of the deceased. Also worn by the living as protection against sickness or misfortune.

Astronomy The Egyptians were skilled observational astronomers who used stellar alignments to orient their buildings, notably the Giza and nearby pyramids and, later, numerous of the great temples, notably those in Upper Egypt.

Ba The psychic power inherent in all beings, living or dead; a psychic double of the deceased which, in the form of a bird, flew away at the moment of death, to return after mummification.

Badarian El-Badari, a site in Upper Egypt, where the earliest predynastic culture in Egypt was identifed; hence Badarian.

Benben A conical OBELISK, standing on a podium or platform, symbolising the 'DIVINE EMERGING ISLAND'. It was particularly associated with Heliopolis and represented the petrification of the sun's rays.

Book of Caverns A New-Kingdom text, employed in royal tombs, illustrating the journey of RE through the caverns of the Underworld. The texts deal with the rewarding of good deeds and the punishment of wickedness.

Book of the Dead A guide to the perils of the journey to the afterlife, attention to which would obviate the dangers which the spirit would otherwise face. The Book descended from the PYRAMID TEXTS and the COFFIN TEXTS, called by the Egyptians 'The Book of Going Forth by Day'.

Book of Gates A funerary text, first introduced in the reign of King HOREMHEB, describing RE's journey through the gates of the Underworld.

Book of He Who is in the Underworld Originally, royal funerary texts describing the Underworld (the '*Amduat*') and the nocturnal journey of the sun, providing advice to the spirit on its own journey to the Underworld.

Calendars Egypt employed several calendars, the earliest of which was probably based on phases of the moon. This was replaced by a more accurate solar calendar, determined by the 'heliacal rising' of the star Sirius (*Sopdet*) which marked the beginning of the 365-day year. As the true solar year is 365 days and 6 hours, a discrepancy arose, amounting to one day in every four years; this could only be corrected after a lapse of 1,460 years, known as the 'Sothic Cycle', after the Greek term for Sirius-Sopdet.

Canopic Jar Vessels in which the internal organs of the deceased were placed after their removal during the process of mummification. The four jars were surmounted with the heads of the 'Sons of Horus'.

Cartouche A design of an oval coil of rope in which two of the principal names of the king were displayed.

Cataracts Rapids in the southern reaches of the Nile, six in all, which prevented craft sailing its length, unless transported overland.

Chronology The Egyptians recorded time from the accession of each king. Various KING LISTS were compiled recording the names and titles of the kings and, sometimes, the principal events of their reigns. MANETHO, the Egyptian-Hellenistic historian, provided the framework for the sequence of the kings, divided into dynasties, which is still largely valid (see also **Calendars**).

Coffin Texts Funerary texts, descending from the PYRAMID TEXTS, inscribed on the interiors of the coffins and sarcophagi of well-to-do Egyptians of the Middle Kingdom period.

Crowns See **Red Crown, White Crown, Double Crown.**

Decans Divisions of the day and night into twelve hours each. Each decan was the responsibility of a minor divinity. The progress of the decans was frequently represented in New Kingdom tombs.

Demotic A form of 'speed-writing', developed principally for commercial and legal documents in the Late Period. Its use became more general in Ptolemaic times.

Deshret See **Red Crown.**

Divine Adoratrice The highest religious office open to a woman, whereby she became 'Great Wife of Amun' (as the office was originally named) in the Temple in Thebes, from whence she exercised great political influence in the south. Frequently the Divine Adoratrice was a royal princess. She was required to remain celibate.

'Divine Emerging Island' The place of creation, the first ground to emerge from the watery chaos which preceded it. The birthplace of the first generations of gods.

Djed A fetish, probably originating in predynastic times in Abydos, its form based on the spinal column or a tree particularly associated with the later worship of Osiris.

Double Crown The combined crowns of Upper and Lower Egypt, the White and the Red, worn by the king in his capacity as Dual King; in this form the crown was known as *pschent*.

El-Omari A site in Lower (northern) Egypt where an important predynastic culture was identified and named for it.

Ennead The Company of the Great Gods, nine (or sometimes more) in number. The oldest and most important of the Enneads was that of Heliopolis, led by Atum and followed by three generations of his progeny.

Gerza An Upper Egyptian site originally used to type the third or latest predynastic culture in the south, the Gerzean. This phase is now more usually classified as NAQADA II.

Heb-Sed The jubilee celebrated to mark the anniversary of the king's accession, usually held in the thirtieth year of his reign, designed to renew his vitality and fitness to rule. It was once thought that the *Heb-Sed* was a substitute for the ritual death of the king in remote times but there is no evidence for this belief.

Hedjet See **White Crown.**

Hieratic A cursive form of HIEROGLYPHIC writing, more formal than DEMOTIC. The earliest examples of hieratic writing date from the Old Kingdom.

Hieroglyphs The 'sacred letters' of Egypt, pictorial signs, laid out in lines, either horizontal or vertical, used in monumental inscriptions and formal documents. Over 600 individual signs in common use are known.

Hyksos 'The Rulers of Foreign Lands' (*Hekaw-khasut*), Semitic-speaking invaders from Syro-Palestine, who entered Egypt during the Thirteenth Dynasty. They are recorded as the Fifteenth and Sixteenth Dynasties of kings. They were eventually expelled by the princes of Thebes who formed the Seventeenth and Eighteenth Dynasties.

Hypostile Hall The great hall at the entrance to the major temples of the New Kingdom and later. The term is derived from the forest of columns, often very massive, which supports the temple roof. The columns are symbolic of the primeval reeds which surrounded 'The Divine Emerging Island' at the creation; they are also a symbol of the unconscious, in later interpretations.

Jubilee See ***Heb-Sed.***

Ka The 'etheric double' of the individual created at the same time as the physical body. It was considered the life-force of the individual and survived death. The *ka* was represented by the hieroglyph of two raised arms.

Kap The academy, often referred to as 'the nursery', where the sons of Egypt's client princes and the leading families of vassal states were educated in Egyptian manners and customs with the children of the royal family. The *kap* was particularly important during Egypt's imperial period, in the Eighteenth and Nineteenth dynasties.

King List Lists of past monarchs were compiled throughout Egyptian history. The Palermo Stone, the earliest known, the Turin Canon, written on PAPYRUS, the Saqqara List and the great wall reliefs in Abydos and Karnak are examples. In general they provide an accurate, if sometimes sharply edited record of the past kings at the time of their compilation.

Kohl A substance obtained by grinding malachite and making it into a paste for application around the eyes to cut down sun-glare and to treat opthalmic conditions. Kohl was frequently mixed on greywacke, slate or steatite PALETTES, especially in late Predynastic times.

Ma'at The concept of order, truth and rectitude, personified by a young girl (also a very ancient goddess). The king was said to rule by Ma'at, hence in truth, thus sustaining the divine order of the Universe.

Mastaba (Ar.) A rectangular brick-built tomb, first appearing at the beginning of the First Dynasty (*c.* 3100 BC) which continued in use throughout the Old Kingdom, particularly for great officials and nobles. The later examples, built in stone, have elaborate scenes of daily life carved on their walls.

Merimde The site of a Predynastic culture in Lower Egypt.

Mortuary Temple In the Old Kingdom, erected beside the Pyramids in which the funerary rites and the cult of the dead king were celebrated. In later times large and imposing buildings which perhaps represented the palace of the king in life.

Naqada A location in Upper Egypt where several late Predynastic cultures were identified. These had borne earlier type-site names but these, AMRATIAN and GERZEAN, have generally been discarded and the terms Naqada I and Naqada II employed. The phase which is generally regarded as transitional between the Predynastic and the Dynastic periods is classified as Naqada III.

Nemes A cloth head- or wig-covering, the more elaborate of which were worn by the kings.

Nome (Greek *nomos*) Egypt was traditionally divided into administrative districts, ultimately forty-two in number, which may recall the divisions of the country in Predynastic times. The governors of the nomes, royal appointments in the Old Kingdom, and by convention known as *nomarchs*, gradually transformed themselves into hereditary rulers by the end of the Sixth Dynasty, until stripped of their power by the Middle Kingdom monarchs.

Obelisk Slender, upright standing stone column, capped with a PYRAMIDION or ***benben***, associated originally with the sun cult in the Fifth Dynasty, later adopted as architectural features set up at the entrance of a temple or mortuary chapel.

Ogdoad Groups of eight divinities, associated with the primordial forces which effected creation.

Ostraca (sing. Ostracon) Fragments of pottery or stone flakes, used by artists and craftsmen, their pupils and the producers of graffiti, for sketches and rough drawings, frequently as sketches for larger-scale projects.

Palace Facade An architectural device of recessed panelling which appears on the exterior walls of MASTABAS in the Archaic Period and the Old Kingdom and as the ***serekh***, the armorial badge on which the king's most sacred name was displayed. It appears to have originated in south-west Asia, probably in Elam (south-western Iran).

Palette A stone plate, rectangular or oval in shape, sometimes in the form of an animal, popular in predynastic and early historic times, originally used for the grinding of KOHL, for protecting the eyes from infection and sun-glare. The palettes are often decorated with engraved or relief scenes, sometimes of great complexity and significance.

Papyrus The Ancient Egyptians' writing material, made from the bark of the flowering marsh reed *Cyperus papyrus L.* It had been manufactured in Egypt as early as Archaic times. The word is probably derived from the Greek *papyros.*

Pharaoh From *per-o*, 'Great House', a circumlocution which first appeared in the New Kingdom and referred to the royal palace as the centre of government. It became more frequently used in the Late Period and then was adopted specifically to mean the King of Egypt, often pejoratively, in the Old Testament; from this well publicised source it came into general use, even adjectivally to describe Egyptian civilisation. It is wholly anachronistic if used in any context prior to the late New Kingdom.

Priest A term conventionally applied to holders of cultic or temple appointments. A *High Priest* ('First Prophet') stood at the head of a temple congregation, dedicated to the cult of a particular divinity. Lesser 'prophets' were responsible for the maintenance of the god's image. The *wab* priest was responsible for the purification of the vessels and instruments used in the ceremonies, whilst the *Lector-Priest* recited the sacred texts. A special rank, often held by princes who officiated at the funeral ceremonies of a dead king, was *sem-priest*, his rank indicated by the panther skin and the 'side-lock of youth' that he wore. The priest responsible for supervising mummification was known as the *Overseer of the Mysteries.*

Pschent See **Double Crown.**

Pylon Monumental masonry gateway, set up at the entrances to the principal temples.

Pyramidion A four-sided, triangular stone placed at the apex of a PYRAMID and on the top of OBELISKS. The form is thought to have been derived from the ***benben.***

Pyramid Texts A collection of incantations and recitations, some in antiphonal and dramatic form, displayed on the inner walls of late Old Kingdom pyramids, but perhaps descending from Predynastic times. They are the oldest ritual texts extant and inspired the COFFIN TEXTS in the Middle Kingdom and the various BOOKS associated in the New Kingdom and later times with the spirit's journey to the afterlife.

Red Crown The *deshret*, the CROWN of Lower Egypt, worn by the king when appearing as sovereign of the northern of the Two Lands and in combination with the WHITE CROWN, forming the DOUBLE CROWN (*pschent*), as King of Upper and Lower Egypt.

Reserve Head A 'portrait' head of the deceased, placed in Old Kingdom tombs, as a form of insurance against the loss of the mummy or the principal statues of the tomb owner. The presence of the reserve head would enable the ***ba*** to find its way back to the tomb and to provide life to the person represented by the reserve head.

Royal Names The King of Egypt originally had three names; by the Fourth Dynasty the number of his names had increased to five. These were:

1 the *Horus-name*, by which he was proclaimed the Divine King;
2 the *Two Ladies* name, denoted by the hieroglyphic group *Nebty*, representing the two goddesses of Upper and Lower Egypt who protected him;
3 the *Golden Horus* name, represented by *Bik Nebu*, Falcon of Gold;
4 the *Coronation* or *Throne* name, represented either by the group *Nesubit*, King of Upper and Lower Egypt, or by *Netjer Nefer*, the Good God. This name was customarily enclosed in a CARTOUCHE; as was
5 the name which identified him as Son of Re, *Sa Re.*

Sacred Lake A body of water in the largest temples across which the king or chief priests might sail in ceremonies symbolising the sky journeys of the gods.

Sarcophagus The coffin, made of stone or of painted and decorated wood, in which the mummy of the deceased was placed in the tomb.

Scarab The scarabeus beetle represented the hieroglyph *Kheper*, one meaning of which is 'become'. The beetle, by virtue of its practice of laying its eggs in a ball of dung and rolling it to where it would hatch out, became a symbol of the sun god's journey across the sky and of rebirth.

Sed* Festival** See ***Heb-Sed.

Serdab Literally, 'cellar' (Ar.), a small chamber in which a statue of the deceased would be placed, entirely enclosed except for an opening for the eyes.

Serekh The armorial badge of the king on which is displayed his most sacred name, as the incarnate HORUS, from the Archaic Period onwards. The design of the badge is based on the PALACE FACADE, which appears to have had its origin in south-western Iran (Elam).

Shabti (*shawabti*, *ushabti*) Literally, 'answerer', a small figurine often with features of the deceased, placed in the tomb to answer for him or her and to carry out any disagreeable tasks which might be required during the journey to the afterlife.

Shemsu Hor The 'Followers of Horus', the 'Spirits of the Dead' thought to be Predynastic kings, ruling Egypt before the appearance of the incarnate HORUS.

Sphinx Human-headed or ram-headed zoomorphic statues set up to guard sacred sites or to line processional ways. Occasionally, as in the Middle Kingdom, the king would be portrayed as a crouching human-headed lion, similar to the Great Sphinx at Giza.

Stela A stone or wooden slab, sometimes of monumental dimensions, of a funerary or commemorative nature, or for the display of royal names and titles or the record of the achievements of the deceased.

Sun Temple Structures associated with the kings of the Fifth Dynasty, when the solar cult was predominant, dedicated to the sun-god and incorporating an OBELISK, bearing a ***benben*** at its crown.

Triad A group of three divinities – god, goddess-consort and son – of whom one was often the king.

Uraeus The rearing cobra, the manifestation of the goddess UADJET of the south, who protected the king, worn as a diadem as part of the royal regalia.

Valley Temple A monumental building in the Old Kingdom PYRAMID complexes in which parts of the funerary ceremonies for the king were performed. The valley temple was often connected to the pyramid by a stone causeway, up which the king's sarcophagus was drawn during his funeral ceremonies.

Vizier Conventional rendering of the Egyptian term for the king's Chief Minister. Sometimes, as was the case in the Old Kingdom, there were two viziers, of the South and the North.

White Crown The *hedjet*, the tall white linen cap which formed the crown of Upper Egypt. When combined with the RED CROWN the two formed the *pschent*, the crown of Upper and Lower Egypt.

Abbreviations

Ac Or	*Acta Orientalia*, Leiden, Netherlands
ANET	*Ancient Near Eastern Texts Relating to the Old Testament*, third edition with supplement, ed. J.B. Pritchard, Princeton, 1969.
ASAE	*Annales du Service des Antiquités de l'Égypte*, Cairo
AV	*Archäologische Veröffentlichungen des Deutschen Archäologischen Instituts*, Cairo
B d'E	*Bibliothèque d'Études*, IFAO, Cairo
BIE	*Bulletin de l'Institut de l'Égypte*, Cairo
BIFAO	*Bulletin de l'IFAO*, Cairo
BM	British Museum
BMFAB	*Boston Museum Fine Arts Bulletin*
BSFE	*Bulletin de la Société Française de l'Égyptologie*
Brooklyn	Brooklyn Museum
CAH	*Cambridge Ancient History*
C d'E	*Chronique d'Égypte*, Brussels
CG	*Catalogue Général*, Egyptian Museum, Cairo
CHI	*Cambridge History of Iran*
CRAIBL	*Comptes Rendus de l'Académie des Inscriptions et Belles-Lettres*, Paris
DB	Deir el-Bahri
EA	*Egyptian Archaeology*, London
EMB	Egyptian Museum, Berlin
EMC	Egyptian Museum, Cairo
GM	*Göttingen Miszellen*, Göttingen
IFAO	Institut Français d'Archéologie Orientale, Cairo
JARCE	*Journal of the American Research Centre in Egypt*, Cairo
JE	*Journal d'Entrée*, Egyptian Museum, Cairo
JEA	*Journal of Egyptian Archaeology*, London
JNES	*Journal of Near Eastern Studies*, Chicago
KV	Valley of the Kings Tomb [followed by number]
LÄ	*Lexikon der Ägyptolgie*, Wiesbaden
MDAIK	*Mitteilungen des Deutschen Archäolgischen Instituts*, Cairo
MFA	Museum of Fine Arts, Boston
MMA	Metropolitan Museum of Art, New York
MduL	Musée du Louvre, Paris
PMFA	Pushkin Museum of Fine Arts, Moscow

PM	Porter, B. and Moss, R. L. B. (1939–88) *Topographical Bibliography of Ancient Egyptian Hieroglyphic Texts, Reliefs and Paintings*, 8 vols, Oxford
PSBA	*Proceedings of the Society of Biblical Archaeology*, London
R d'E	*Revue d'Égyptologie*, Paris
SAK	*Studien zur Altägyptischen Kultur*, Hamburg
SSEA	Society for the Study of Egyptian Antiquities, Toronto
TT	Theban Tomb [followed by number]
Urk	Sethe, K. (1906) *Urkunden des Aegyptischen Altertums*, Leipzig
Vienna	Kunsthistorischer Museum, Vienna
WV	Western Valley
YAG	Yale Art Gallery
ZÄS	*Zeitschrift fur Äegyptische Sprache und Altertumskunde*, Leipzig and Berlin

Bibliography

Note: Many of the works identified here are illustrated. Those marked * in particular provide an overview of Egyptian art.

Adams, B. and Cialowicz, K. M. (1997) *Protodynastic Egypt*, Princes Risborough.

Aldred, C. (1968) *Akhenaten, Pharaoh of Egypt: A New Study*, London.

——(1973) *Akhenaten and Nefertiti*, Brooklyn.

——(1975) 'The Amarna Period and the End of the Eighteenth Dynasty', CAH II.2.

——(1988) *Akhenaten: King of Egypt*, London.

Andreu, G., Rutschowscaya, M.-H. and Zeigler, C. (1997) *Ancient Art at the Louvre*, Paris.

Baines, J. and Málek, S. (1980) *Atlas of Ancient Egypt*, Oxford.

Berman, L. M. and Letellier, B. (eds) (1996) *Pharaohs: Treasures of Egyptian Art from the Louvre*, Cleveland and Oxford.*

Bierbrier, M. (1978) *The Late New Kingdom in Egypt*, Warminster.

Blackman, A. M. (1914) 'The Rock Tombs of Meir: The Tomb Chapel of Ukh-hotep's son Senbi', ASAE 22.

——(1914–53) *The Rock Tombs of Meir*, 6 vols, London.

Borchardt, L. (1911–36) *Statuen und Statuetten von Königen und Privattenten*, I–V, Berlin.

Bothmer, B. V. (1969) *Egyptian Sculpture of the Late Period 700 BC–100 AD*, 2nd edn, Brooklyn.

Bourriau, J. (1988) *Pharaohs and Mortals*, Cambridge.

Bowman, A. K. (1990) *Egypt after the Pharaohs, 332 BC–AD 642*, 2nd edn, London.

Breasted, J. E. (1906) *Ancient Records of Egypt*, 4 vols, Chicago.

Bresciani, E. (1985) 'The Persian Occupation of Egypt', CHI. 2: 502–528.

British Museum (1964) *A General Introductory Guide to the Egyptian Collection in the British Museum*, London.

Brooklyn Museum (1979) *Ancient Egyptian Sculpture from the Brooklyn Museum*, catalogue, Puerto Rico.

——(1978) *Africa in Antiquity: The Arts of Ancient Nubia and the Sudan*, catalogue.

Budge, E. A. W. (1923) *Facsimilies of Egyptian Hieratic Papyri in the British Museum*, London.

——(1926) *The Teaching of Amen-en-apt, son of Kanekt*, London.

Butzer, K. W. (1976) *Early Hydraulic Civilization in Egypt*, Chicago.

Capart, J. (1907) *Une Rue de Tombeaux à Saqqarah*, Brussels.

Černý, J. (1973) *A Community of Workmen at Thebes in the Ramesside Period*, Cairo.

Davis, N. de Garis (1903–8) *Rock Tombs of el-Amarna*, 6 vols, London.

Desroches Noblecourt, C. (1963) *Tutankhamen: Life and Death of a Pharaoh*, London.
Dodson, A. (1995) *Monarchs of the Nile*, London.
Dreyer, G. (1993) 'Umm el-Qa'ab: Nachuntersuchungen im Frühzeitlichen Königsfriedhof 5/6 Vorbericht', MDAIK 49: 23–62
Edwards, I. E. S. (1969/1973/1985/1993) *The Pyramids of Egypt*, London.
Egerton, W. (1951) 'The Strikes of Ramesses III's 23rd Year', JNES 10: 137–45
Emery, W. B. (1949) *Great Tombs of the First Dynasty, I*, Cairo.
——(1954) *Great Tombs of the First Dynasty, II*, Cairo.
——(1958) *Great Tombs of the First Dynasty, III*, Cairo.
——(1961) *Archaic Egypt*, London.
Fakhry, A. (1961) *The Pyramids*, Chicago.
Faulkner, R. O. (1975) 'Egypt: From the Inception of the Nineteenth Dynasty to the Death of Ramesses III', CAH II.2.
Firth, C. M., Quibell, J. E., with Lauer, J-P. (1935–6) *The Step Pyramid: Excavations at Saqqara*, 2 vols, Cairo.
Fraser, P. M. (1972) *Ptolemaic Alexandria*, 3 vols, Oxford.
Frey, B. (ed.) (1982) *Egyptian Museum Berlin*, Mainz.
Friedman, R. and Adams, B. (eds) (1992) *The Followers of Horus: Studies Dedicated to Michael Allen Hoffman*, Oxford.
Gardiner, A. H. (1942) *Select Papyri in the Hieratic Character from the Collections of the British Museum, vol. II*, London.
——(1961) *Egypt of the Pharaohs*, Oxford.
Gardiner, A. H., Peet, T. E. and Černý, J. (1952–55) *The Inscriptions of Sinai, Parts I and II*, London.
Ghalioungui (1983) *The Physicians of Pharaonic Egypt*, Cairo.
——(1987) *The Ebers Papyrus*, Cairo.
Gitton, M. (1984) *Les Divines Épouses de la 18e Dynastie*, Paris.
Grant, M. (1982) *From Alexander to Cleopatra*, London.
Green, P. (1990) *Alexander to Actium: The Historical Evolution of the Hellenistic Age*, Berkeley and Los Angeles.
Grimal, N. (1992) *A History of Ancient Egypt*, trans. I. Shaw, Oxford.
Hassan, S. (1944) *Excavations at Giza (V) 1933–4*, Cairo.
——(1938) 'Excavations at Saqqara 1937–8', ASAE 38.
Hayes, W. C. (1953) [1990] *The Scepter of Egypt, I: Before 1600 BC*, Boston.
——(1955) *A Papyrus of the Late Middle Kingdom*, Boston.
——(1959) [1990] *The Scepter of Egypt, II: 1675–1080 BC*, fifth printing, revised 1990 with accession numbers for all objects illustrated, Cambridge, Mass.
Herodotus (1972) *The Histories*, trans. A. de Selincourt, London.
Hodjash, S. and Berlev, O. (1982) *The Egyptian Reliefs and Stelae in the Pushkin Museum of Fine Art, Moscow*, trans. O. Berlev, St Petersburg (Leningrad).
Hoffman, M. (1980) *Egypt Before the Pharaohs*, London.
Hornung, E. (1983) *Conceptions of God in Ancient Egypt: The One and the Many*, London.
Hughes-Hallett, L. (1990) *Cleopatra*, London.
IFAO (1981) *Un Siècle de Fouilles Françaises en Egypte*, catalogue, Cairo and Paris.
James, T. G. H. (1962) *The Hekanakhte Papers and Other Middle Kingdom Documents*, New York.
——(1985) *Egyptian Painting*, London.
James, T. G. H. and Davies, W. V. (1983) *Egyptian Sculpture*, London.
Jonckheere, F. (1958) *Les Medicins de l'Egypte Pharaonique*, Brussels.

Kees, H. (1961) *Ancient Egypt: A Cultural Topography* (trans) London.
Kitchen, K. A. (1982) *Pharaoh Triumphant: The Life and Times of Ramesses II*, new edn, Warminster.
——(1986) *The Third Intermediate Period in Egypt (1100–650 BC)*, 2nd edn, Warminster.
Kueny, G. and Yoyotte, J. (1979) *Grenoble, Musée des Beaux-Arts, Collection Égytpienne*, Paris.
Kuhrt, A. (1995) *The Ancient Near East c. 3000–330 BC*, 2 vols, London.
Lambelet, E. (1978) *Orbis Terrae Aegiptiae: Illustrated Guide of the Egyptian Museum, Cairo*, Cairo.
Lambert, R. (1984) *Beloved and God: The Story of Hadrian and Antinous*, London.
Lane Fox, R. (1973) *Alexander the Great*, London.
Lauer, J.-P. (1976) *Saqqara, the Royal Cemetery of Memphis: Excavations and Discoveries since 1850*, London.
Lefebvre, G. (1929) *Histoire des Grands Prêtres d'Amon de Karnak jusqu'a la XXIe Dynastie*, Paris.
Lehner, M. (1997) *The Complete Pyramids*, London.
Lichtheim, M. (1975–80) *Ancient Egyptian Literature: A Book of Readings*. I (1975): 'The Old and Middle Kingdoms'; II (1976): 'The New Kingdom'; III (1980): 'The Late Period'; Berkeley, Calif.
Manniche, L. (1991) *Music and Musicians in Ancient Egypt*, London.
Martin, G. T. (1974–89) *The Royal Tombs at El-Amarna*, 2 vols, London.
——(1991) *The Hidden Tombs of Memphis: New Discoveries from the Time of Tutankhamun and Ramesses the Great*, London.
Michalowski, K. (1969) *The Arts of Ancient Egypt*, London.*
Montet, P. (1964) *Eternal Egypt*, London.
Moran, W. L. (1992) *The Amarna Letters*, Baltimore.
Newberry, P. E. (1893–1900) *Beni Hasan*, 4 parts, Archaeological Survey of Egypt, London.
Nunn, J. F. (1996) *Ancient Egyptian Medicine*, London.
Parkinson, R. B. (1991) *Voices from Ancient Egypt: An Anthology of Middle Kingdom Writings*, London.
Peet, T. E. (1930) *The Great Tomb Robberies of the 20th Egyptian Dynasty*, Oxford.
Petrie, W. M. F. (1900) *The Royal Tombs of the First Dynasty, I*, London.
——(1901) *The Royal Tombs of the First Dynasty, II*, London.
——(1903) *Abydos, II*, London.
Pritchard, J. B. (ed.) (1955) *Ancient Near Eastern Texts Relating to the Old Testament*, Princeton, N.J.
Quibell, J. E. (1900) *Hierakonpolis, I*, London.
Quirke, S. and Spencer, J. (1992) *The British Museum Book of Ancient Egypt*, London.
Redford, D. B. (1984) *Akhenaten the Heretic King*, Princeton, N.J.
Reeves, C. N. (1990a) *The Complete Tutankhamen*, London.
——(1990b) *The Valley of the Kings*, London.
Reeves, N. and Wilkinson, R. H. (1996) *The Complete Valley of the Kings: Tombs and Treasures of Egypt's Greatest Pharaohs*, London.
Reisner, G. A. (1936) *The Development of the Egyptian Tomb down to the Accession of Cheops*, Cambridge, Mass. and London.
——(1942) *Giza Necropolis, I*, Cambridge, Mass.
Reisner, G. A. and Smith, W. S. (1955) *A History of the Giza Necropolis, II: The Tomb of Hetepheres, The Mother of Cheops*, Cambridge, Mass.
Rice, Michael (1990) *Egypt's Making: The Origins of the Egyptian State, 5000–2000 BC*, London.

——(1997) *Egypt's Legacy: The Archetypes of Western Civilization, 3000–30 BC*, London.
Robins, G. (ed.) (1990) *Beyond the Pyramids: Egyptian Regional Art from the Museo Egizio, Turin*, catalogue, Turin.
——(1993) *Women in Ancient Egypt*, London.
Ruffle, J., Gaballa, G. A. and Kitchen, K. A. (eds) (1979) *Glimpses of Ancient Egypt: Studies in Honour of H. W. Fairman*, Warminster.
Ryholt, K. S. B. (1997) *The Political Situation in Egypt during the Second Intermediate Period*, c. *1800–1550 BC*. Copenhagen, 1997.
Saad, Z. Y. (1947) *Royal Excavations at Saqqara and Helwan (1941–5)*, Cairo.
Saleh, M., and Sourouzian, H. (1987) *The Egyptian Museum, Cairo: The Official Catalogue*, Mainz.*
Scamuzzi, E. (n.d.) *Egyptian Art in the Egyptian Museum, Turin*, New York.*
Scott III, G. D. (1986) *Ancient Egyptian Art at Yale*, catalogue, New Haven, Conn.
Shafer, B. E. (ed.) (1991) *Religion in Ancient Egypt: Gods, Myth and Personal Practice*, London.
Shaw, I. and Nicholson, P. (1995) *The British Museum Dictionary of Ancient Egypt*, London.
Spencer, A. J. (1993) *Early Egypt: The Rise of Civilization in the Nile Valley*, London.
Stevenson Smith, W. (1946) [1949] *A History of Egyptian Sculpture and Painting in the Old Kingdom*, Oxford.*
——(1958) [1981] *Art and Architecture in Ancient Egypt*, New Haven, Conn. and London.*
——(1965) *Interconnections in the Ancient Near East: A Study of the Relationships Between the Arts of Egypt, the Aegean, and Western Asia*, New Haven, Conn.
——(1971) 'The Old Kingdom in Egypt and the Beginning of the First Intermediate Period', CAH I.2.
Strouhal, E. (1989/1992) *Life in Ancient Egypt*, Cambridge.*
Terrace, E. L. B. (1968) *Egyptian Painting of the Middle Kingdom: The Tomb of Djehutynekht*, New York.
Terrace, E. L. B. and Fischer, H. G. (1970) *Treasures of the Cairo Museum*, catalogue, London.*
Thomas, N. (ed) (1995) *The American Discovery of Ancient Egypt*, Los Angeles.*
Trigger, B. G., Kemp, B. J., O'Connor, D. and Lloyd, A. B. (1983) *Ancient Egypt: A Social History*, Cambridge.
Turner, E. (1984) 'Ptolemaic Egypt', CAH VII: 118–74.
Tyldesley, J. (1996) *Hatshepsut: The Female Pharaoh*, London.
Vandier, J. (1952) *Manuel d'Archéologie Égyptienne, I*, Paris.
——(1954) *Manuel d'Archéologie Égyptienne, II*, Paris.
——(1958) *Manuel d'Archéologie Égyptienne, III*, Paris.
Vassilika, E. (ed) (1995) *Egyptian Art*, catalogue, Cambridge.
Verner, M. (1994) *Forgotten Pharaohs, Lost Pyramids*, Prague.
Waddell, W. G. (1948) *Manetho*, Cambridge, Mass.
Wente, E.F. (1967) *Late Ramesside Letters*, Chicago.
——(1990) *Letters from Ancient Egypt*, Atlanta.
Wilkinson, A. (1998) *The Garden in Ancient Egypt*, London.
Wilson, J. A. (1951) *The Burden of Egypt*, London.
Winlock, H. E. (1917) 'A Restoration of the Reliefs from the Mortuary Temple of Amenhotep I', JEA 4: 11–15.
——(1947) *The Rise and Fall of the Middle Kingdom in Thebes*, New York.
Ziegler, C. (1990) *Le Louvre. Les Antiquités Égyptiennes*, Paris.

Appendices

The appendices which follow are intended to show

1 the grouping of entries by the occupations of the subjects;
2 the subjects in chronological context; and
3 the distribution of material relating to entries in leading museum collections.

In the case of the Appendix 1, it should be remembered that many of the titles which indicate the subject's principal activity changed over the centuries: 'Official', for example, probably meant more in the early periods than it did later; 'Priest' only acquired a *specifically* religious connotation, in any sense which might apply in the contemporary world, in later times.

Similarly, 'Scribe' might refer to one who employed his skills in writing, either in an official, governmental context or as a specialist in a temple administration. 'Scribe' might also denote a writer, in the sense of one who wrote creatively. 'Warrior' has been used generally to include those who served in the Army, on board ship or as suppliers of weapons and equipment.

The title 'Prince' is one which is found throughout all the centuries that Egypt survived. It may indicate a direct descendant of a king or be conferred as a mark of honour on a high official.

In many instances, particularly amongst the higher echelons of Egyptian society, a man might occupy a diversity of appointments. Where these are relevant, a cross-reference is provided.

The numbers in parenthesis indicate the dynasty during which the subject lived. These are expressed in Roman numerals.

The names of non-Egyptian subjects, other than those who were recognised as kings of Egypt, are enclosed in square brackets. Individuals whose status is suspect (for example, ephemeral or disputed kingships) are shown in italic.

The holders of several offices will generally be listed under their principal appointment. In some cases (a royal prince who is also a priest, for example) multiple entries will be listed. Where a subject's career spanned more than one dynasty, his or her name will recorded in Appendix 2 under the dynasty in which he or she is presumed to have been born or in which he or she first came to prominence.

Abbreviations

CP	Crown Prince
HP	High Priest [A = Amun (Thebes), O = Osiris (Abydos), P = Ptah (Memphis), R = Re (Heliopolis)]
Ptol.	Ptolemaic Period
Rom.	Roman Period

Appendix 1

Entries by occupation

Kings

[Abdi Khebar] (XVIII), Aha (I), Ahmose (XVIII), Akhtoy I (IX/X), Akhtoy II (IX/X), Akhtoy III (X), [Alara] (XXV), Alexander III (Mac.), Alexander IV (Mac.), Amasis (XXVI), Amenemhet I (XII), Amenemhet II (XII), Amenemhet III (XII), Amenemhet IV (XII), Amenemnisu (XXI), Amenemope (XXI), Amenhotep I (XVIII), Amenhotep II (XVIII), Amenhotep III (XVIII), Amenhotep IV-Akhenaten (XVIII), Amenmesse (XIX), Amyrtaeus (XXVIII), Anedjib (I), Apepi I (XV), Apepi II (XV), Apries (XXVI), [Arnekhamani] (Pt.), [Artaxerxes I] (XXVII), [Artaxerxes II] (XXVII), [Artaxerxes III] (XXVII), [Assurbanipal] (XXVI), [Augustus Caesar] (Rom.), Awibre Hor (XIII), Ay (XVIII)

Bakare (IV), Bakenrenef (XXIV)

Caesarion-Ptolemy XV (Ptol.), [Cambyses II] (XXVII), [Cyrus II]

[Darius I] (XXVII), [Darius II] (XXVII), [Darius III] (XXVII), Demedjibtawy (VIII), Den (I), Djedefre (IV), Djedkare Isesi (V), Djedneferre Dudimose (XIII), Djer (I), Djet (I), Djoser Netjerykhet (III), *Djoserti* (III)

[Esarhaddon] (XXV)

Hadrian (Rom.), Hakor (XXIX), Hakare Ibi (VIII), Hariese (XXII), [Hattusil III] (XIX), Horemheb (XVIII), Horwennefer (Ptol.), Hotepsekhemwy (II), Huni (III)

Ibiya (XIII), Inyotef I (XI),[1] Inyotef II Wahankh (XI), Inyotef III (XI), Inyotef VI (XVII), Inyotef VII (XVII), Iryhor (PreD.), Iuput II (XXIII)[2]

Ka (PreD), Ka'a (I), Kamose (XVII), [Kashta] (XXV), Khaba (III), *Khababash* (XXVII), Khafre (IV), Khasekhem-Khasekhemwy (II), Khayan (XV), Khnum-Khufu (IV)

Menes (PreD.), Menkauhor Akhauhor (V), Menkaure (IV), Merenptah (XIX), Merenre I (VI), Merenre II (VI), Merikare (X), Merneferre Iy (XIII), Montuhotep I,[3] (XI), (Nebhepetre)Montuhotep II (XI), (Sa'ankhkare) Montuhotep III (XI), Montuhotep IV (XI), [Muwatallis] (XIX)

[Nabopolassar] (XXVI), Nar-Mer (PreD.), [Nebuchadrezzar] (XXVI), Necho I (XXVI), Necho II (XXVI), Nectanebo I (XXX), Nectanebo II (XXX), Nefaarud I (XXIX), Neferefre (V), Neferhotep I (XIII), Neferirkare (V), Neferkahor (VIII), Neferkare (X), Neferneferuaten (XVIII),[4] Niuserre (V), (Nimlot) (XXV), Nynetjer (II)

Osorkon I (XXII), Osorkon II (XXII), Osorkon III (XXIII), Osorkon IV (XXII)

Pedubastis (XXIII), Peftjauawy-Bast (XXIII), Pepy I (VI), Pepy II (VI), Peribsen (II), [Philip II] (Mac.), Philip Arrhidaeus (Mac.), Piankhy (XXV), Pimay (XXII), Pinudjem I (XXI)[5] Psametik I (XXVI), Psametik II (XXVI), Psametik III (XXVI),

Pseusennes I (XXI), Pseusennes II (XXI), Ptolemy I–XV (Pt.)

Qahedjet (III)

Rahotep (XVII), Ramesses I (XIX), Ramesses II (XIX), Ramesses III (XX), Ramesses IV (XX), Ramesses V (XX), Ramesses VI (XX), Ramesses VII (XX), Ramesses VIII (XX), Ramesses IX (XX), Ramesses X (XX), Ramesses XI (XX), Raneb (II), Rudamun (XXIII)

Sahure (V), Salitis (XV), Sanakhte (III), [Sargon II] (XXII/XXV), Sawadjenre Nebiryerawet I (XVII), 'Scorpion' (PreD.), Sekhemkhet (III), Sekhemre Wahkau (XVII), Semenkhakare Mermentifu (XIII), Semerkhet (I), [Sennacherib] (XXV), Sened (II), Senwosret I (XII), Senwosret II (XII), Senwosret III (XII), Senakhtenre Tao I (XVII), Seqenenre Tao II (XVII), Sethnakhte (XX), Seti I (XIX), Seti II (XIX), Shabaka (XXV), Shabataka (XXV), Shepseskare Isi (V), Shepseskhaf (IV), Sheshonq I (XXII), Sheshonq II (XXII), Sheshonq III (XXII), Sheshonq IV (XXIII), Siamun (XXI), Siptah (XIX), Smendes (XXI), Smenkhkare (XVIII),[6] Sneferu (IV), Sobekemsaf II (XVII), Sobekhotep I (XIII), Sobekhotep II (XIII), Sobekhotep III (XIII), Sobekhotep IV (XIII), [Suppiluliumas] (XVIII)

Taharqa (XXV), Takelot I (XXII), Takelot II (XXII), Takelot III (XXIII), Tanutamani (XXV), Tefnakhte (XXIV), Teos (XXX), Teti (VI), Thutmose I (XVIII), Thutmose II (XVIII), Thutmose III (XVIII), Thutmose IV (XVIII), Tutankhamun (XVIII)

Unas (V), Userkaf (V), Userkare (VI), Userkare Khendjer (XIII), Userenre (XVII)

Wegef (XIII), Weneg (II), Wepwawetemsaf (XIII)

[Xerxes] (XXVII)

Yaqub-Hor (XV)

Notes

1 Posthumously ranked as king
2 'Ruler'
3 'Prince of Thebes'
4 See also 'Queens', 'Princes and Princesses'
5 Originally HPA
6 See also 'Neferneferuaten'

Queens

Ahhotep I (XVII/XVIII), Ahhotep II (XVIII), Ahmose-Meryatum (XVIII), Ahmose Nefertiry (XVIII), Ankhenesmeryre (VI), Ankhesenamun (XVIII), Arsinoe II (Ptol.), Arsinoe III (Ptol.), Artatama (XVIII)

Bener-ib (I), Berenice I (Ptol.), Betrest (I), Bint-Anath (XIX), Bunefer (IV)

Cleopatra VII (Ptol.)

[Eti] (XVIII)

Hatshepsut (XVIII), Henutsen (IV), Henuttawy (XXI), Herneith (I), Hetepheres I (IV), Hetepheres II (IV)

Isinofret (XIX)

Kama (XXII/XXIII), Karomama Merymut II (XXII), Kawit (XI), Khentkawes I (IV), Khentkawes II (V), Khnemetneferhedjet Weret (XI), Khnetetenka (IV), Kiya (XVIII)

Mehetenwesket (XXVI), Menhet, Merti, Menwi (XI), Mentuhotep (XVII), Meresankh I (III), Meresankh III (IV), Meritites, (IV), Merneith (I), Mutemwiya (XVIII)

Nebet (VI), Neferheteperes (IV),[1] Neferneferuaten (XVIII),[2] Nefertari (XIX), Nefertiti (XVIII), Neferu I (XI), Neferu II (XI), Neferu III (XI), Neith (VI), Neithhotep (I), Nitiqret (VI), Nofret (XII), Nubkhas (XVII), Nemaathap (II)

[Olympias] (Mac.)

[Shanakdakhte] (Pt.), Sobekneferu (XII), Sobekemsaf (XVII)

Tetisheri (XVII), Tiy (XVIII), Tuyi (XIX), Tyti (XX), Twosret (XIX)

Udjebten (VI)

'Weretyamtes' (VI)

Yah (XI)

Notes
1 Status as queen uncertain
2 See also 'King' and 'Princess'

Princes and princesses

Amenhirwonmef CP (XIX), Amenhirkhepshef CP (XX), Amenirdis I (XXIII), Amenirdis II (XXV), Ankhaf (IV), Ankhesenamun (XVIII), Ankhnesneferibre (XXVI), Anu (X/XI), Atet (IV)

Bakare (IV),[1] Baketaten (XVIII)

Djutmose CP (XVIII), [Djehutyhotep] (XVIII),[2] [Djehutyhotep] (XVIII)[2]

[Ghilukhepa] (XVIII)[3]

Hekanefer (XVIII),[2] Hemionu (IV),[4] Hetephernebti and Intkes (III), Hordedef (IV), Horsiesnet Meritaten (XXV)

Inaros (XXVI), [Iriamunnayefnebu] (XXII),[5] [Iripaankhkenkenef] (XXV),[2] Iuwelot (XXII)[6]

Kaninisut (IV/V), Kanufer CP (IV), Karomama I (XXII), Kawab (IV), Khaemwaset (XIX),[7] Khaemwaset (XX), Khekheretnebty (V), Khent-kaw-Es (VI),[13] Khnum-baf (IV),[4] Khunmet (XII), Khufu-Kaf (IV), Khunere (IV), ['The Prince of Kush'] (XVII)

Maatkare (XXI), Meketaten (XVIII), Mentuherkhepshef (XX), Merka (I),[4] Meritaten (XVIII), Mery-Atum CP (XIX), Minkhaf (IV), Miut (XI), Montuhotep I (XI), Montuhotep (XII)

Nakhtmin (XVIII), Nebmakhet (IV), Nebt (XI), Neferhetepes (IV),[8] Neferibrenofer (XXVI), Nefermaat (IV), Neferneferuaten (XVIII),[9] Nefershesemshat (V/VI),[4] Nefertiabet (IV), Neferuptah (XII), Neferure (XVIII), Nehesy (XIII/XIV), Nekaure (IV), Nitiqret (XXVI)

Pediese (XXII), Pentaweret (XX), Prehirwenmef (XIX)

Rahotep,[10] and Nofret (IV), Ramesses CP (XIX), Redyzet (III), Reemkuy (V)

Setka (IV), Sethirkhopshef CP (XIX), Shepenupet I (XXIII),[11] Shepenupet II XXV),[11] Si-Montu (XIX), Sithathor Iunet (XII)

[Tadukhipa] (XVIII), Tjia (XIX), Tjahepimu (XXX)

Unas-Ankh (V), Urshanahuru CP (XXV)[12]

Wahneferhotep (XIII)

[Zennanza] (XVIII)

Notes
1 Perhaps king
2 A Nubian prince
3 A Mittannian princess
4 Also Overseer of All the King's Works
5 A Libyan prince
6 Also HPA
7 Also HPP
8 Perhaps queen
9 See also 'King', 'Queen'
10 Also HPR
11 God's Wife of Amun
12 Probably CP
13 Prince living as princess

Viziers and great officers of state: viceroys,[b] chancellors,[c] chamberlains,[d] royal heralds[e]

Akhtoy (XI), Amenemope (XIX), Amenemopet (XVIII), Amenemopet (XIX), Amenhotep Son of Hapu (XVIII),[1] Amenhotep (XVIII), Amenmose (XIX), Ankhaf (IV),[2] Ankhefenamun (XXI),[d] Ankhenmer (XIII),[e] Ankh-Ka (I),[c] Ankhmahor (VI), Ankhu (XIII), Antefoker (XII), Aper-El (XVIII), Apollonius (Ptol.)[3]

Bawi (VI),[12] Bay (XIX), Ben-Ozen (XIX)[e], Bes (XXVI)

Cleomenes (Ptol.)[3]

Dagi (XI), Djau (VI)

Harhotep (XII), Harsiese (XXV),[4] Hekanakhte (XIX),[b] Hemaka (I),[c] Hemionu (IV),[2] Heny (XI),[d] Herihor (XXI),[5] Hesyre (III), Huy (XVIII),[b]

Ikhernofret (XII),[6] Imeru-Neferkare (XIII), Imhotep (III),[7] Imhotep (XII),[c] Intef (XVIII),[e] Inti (V), Iuu (VII/VIII)

Khnum-baf (IV),[2] Kagemni (VI), Kaihep (VI), Khaihapi (XX),[8] Khaemhor (XXIV), Khentika (VI), Khety (XI)

Maanakhtef (XVIII),[c] Mehu (VI), Mehy (V), Meketre (XI),[c] Merefnebef (VI), Mereruka (VI), Merka (I),[2] Merymose (XVIII),[b] Minkhaf (IV),[2] Montuhotep (XII)

Nakht,[c](XII), Nebetka (I), Neferibre-Nofer (XXVI), Nefersheshemseshat (V/VI),[2] Neferronpet (XIX), Neferyu (VIII),[c] Nehi (XVIII),[b] Neheri (X/XI),[9] Neska (I),[10] Nesipakashuty (XXVI), Niankhpepiken (VI), Nykuhor (V)[9]

Panehesy (XX),[b] Panemerit (Pt.), Paser (XIX), Pentu (XVIII), Peryneb (V),[c] Pesshuper (XXV),[d] [Pharnabazes] (XXVII), Ptahhotep (V), Ptahmes (XVIII),[4] Ptahshepses (IV/V), Ptahshepses (V)

Ramose (XVIII), Rehuerdjersen (XII), Rekhmire (XVIII), Rewer (VI), Ruaben (II)[c]

Senebtyfy (XIII),[c], Senedjemibmehy (V),[7] Sennefer (XVIII),[c] Senu (XVIII),[e] Senwosretankh (XII), Sipair (XVII/XVIII),[d] Sobekhotep (XVIII)[c]

Ta (XX), Thaasetimun (XXX),[e] Thuwre (XVIII),[b] Tutu (XVIII)[d]

Ukhhotep (XII), User (XVIII), Usermont (XVIII), Usertatet (XVIII),[b] Usimarenakhte (XX)[11]

Wedjankhdjes (IV), Wesertatet (XVIII),[b] Weshptah (V)[b]

Yamunedjeh (XVIII)[e]

Notes

1 Chief Steward
2 Prince
3 'Minister of Finance'
4 HPA
5 HPA
6 Festival Organiser
7 Architect Physician
8 Privy Councillor
9 Nomarch
10 Treasurer
11 High Steward
12 Father and son

High priests

Amenemopet (XIX) HPR, Amenhotep (XX) HPA, Anen (XVIII) HPA, Anhurmose (XIX) HP Thinis

Bak (XIX) HPR, Bakenkhons (XIX) HPA

Didia (XIX) HPM, Djedkhonsuefankh (XXI) HPA, Djedkhonsuefankh (XXVI) HP Montu

Hapuseneb (XVIII) HPA, Harnakhte (XXII) HPA, Harsiese (XXV) HPR, Herihor (XXI) HPA,[1] Hori (XIX) HPM

Imhotep (III) HPP, Imhotep (XII) HPR, Iuput (XXII) HPA, Iuwelot (XXII) HPA

Kaihep,[2] Kameni (IV) HP Nekhbet, Kanufer (IV) HPR, Khabausoker (III) HP Anubis, HPP, Khaemwaset (XIX) HPP, CP

Manetho (Pt.) HPR, Menkheperre (XXI) HP, Menkheperresenb (XVIII), Meri (XVIII) HPA

Nebenteru (XIX) HPA, Nebunenef (XVIII) HPA, Nimlot (XXII) HPA

Peftjauawybast (XXII) HPP, Petosiris (Pt.) HP Thoth, Pahemnetjer (XIX) HPM, Pia (XVIII) HP Sobek, Piankh (XXI) HPA, Pinudjem I (XXI) HPA,[3] Pinudjem II (XXI) HPA, Psenptah (Rom.), HPP, Psenptais III (Rom.) HPP, Psherenptah (Pt.) HPR, Ptahemhat-Ty (XVIII) HPP, Ptahmes (XVIII) HPA[4]

Rahotep (IV) HPR, Ramessesnakhte (XX) HPA, Ranefer (V) HPP, Roma-Roy (XIX) HPA, Roy (XIX) HPA

Sabu (V) HPP, Setau (XX) HP Nekhbet, Senwosretankh (XII) HPM, Shedsunefertem (XXII) HPP, Sitepehu (XVIII) HP Abydos, Somtutefnakhte (XXX) HP Sakhmet

To (XIX) HPO

Userhat (XVIII) HP Tutankhamun

Wennufer (XIX) HPO

Yewelot (XXIII) HPA

Notes
1 Vizier
2 Nomarch
3 Later king
4 Vizier of the South

Nomarchs and governors

Ahanakht (IX/X), Akhtoy I (X), Akhtoy II (X), Ankhtify (X)

Baket III (XI), Bes (XXVI)

Dedu (XVIII), Djehutyhotep (XII), Djehutynekht (XII)

Harkhuf (VI), Hekaib (VI), Hem-Min (VI), Hepzefa (XII)

[Iankhamu] (XVIII), Ibi (VI), Ikui (X), Ini (XI), Inyotef (VIII)

Kaihep (VI) HPR, Kheni (VI), Khnumhotep I (XII), Khnumhotep II (XII)

Min (XVIII),[1] Metjen (III/IV), Mitry (V)

Neheri (X/XI),[2] Niankhpepi (VI), Nimlot (XXV)

Panemerit (Ptol.), Pepyankh (VI), [Piryawaza] (XVIII)[3]

Senbi (XII), Serenput (XII)

Tefibi (IX/X), Thutnakht I (VIII/IX), Thutnakht II, Thutnakht III, Thutnakht IV(X), Thutnakht V (XI), Tjauti (X), Tjetiiker (VI)

Ukhhotep I (XII), Ukhhotep II (XII), Ukhhotep III (XII), Ukhhotep IV (XII)

Wahka I (XII), Wahka II (XII), Wedjankhdjes (IV)

Notes
1 Festival Director, Royal Tutor
2 Vizier
3 'Prince of Damascus'

Nobles and courtiers

[Amenemhet] (XVIII), Amenemhe Siste (XIII), Amenhotep (XVIII), Anhernakhte (XIX), Ankh (III), Antinous (Rom.), Ashahebsed (XIX), Ay (XVIII)[1]

Debhen (IV)

Henhenet (XI)

Idu (VI), Ihy (V/VI), Indy (VIII), Ini (XI),[2] Iniamunayefnabu (XXII), Inyotef I (X/XI), Ipuia (XVIII), Isis (XVIII), Iti (XI)

Kemsit (XI), Kenamun (XVIII)[3]

Maïa (XVIII), Maiherperi (XVIII), Maya (XVIII), Merka (I), Meryrehashtef (VI), Mesheti (XI), Methethy (V), Min (XVIII),[2] Montuemhet (XXV)

Nakht (XVIII), Nakhtmin (XVIII), Nebetka (I), Nebipusenwosret (XII), Nefer (V), Neferibrenofer (XXII), Nemtyemweskhet (XIII),[3] Neska (I), Nykuhor (V)

Pasenhor (XXII), Pentu (XVIII)[4]

Sabef (I), Sabu (I), Sebni (VI), Sekhem-Ka (I), Senba (I), Senebsuema (XIII), Senet (XII), Senu, (XVIII),[5] Senusret (XII),[6] Sihathor (XII), Sipair (XVII/XVIII), Sipa and Neset (III), Sobekhotep (XIX/XX)[7]

Taimhotep (Pt.), Tepemankh (V), [Teti] (XVIII), Ti (VI), Thenuna (XVIII)

Userhet (XVIII)

Wendjebaendjed (XXI), Weni (VI)

Yamu-nedjeh (XVIII), Yuya and Tuyu (XVIII)

Zekhonsefankh (XXII)

Notes
1 Later king
2 Nomarch, Royal Tutor, Festival Director
3 Royal Steward
4 Physician, Vizier
5 Royal Herald
6 Mayor
7 Royal Butler

Officials

Aba (XXVI), Amenemhe Siste (XIII),[1] Amenemhat (XIII), Ameneminet (XIX)

Bebi (V/VI), Bener (XII), Bes (XXVI)[1]

Djadaemankh (VI), Djar (XI), Djari (XI), Djefai-nisut (III), Djserkaresoneb (XVIII)

Hetepni (VI), Horurre (XII), Hotepdief (III)

Ii-seneb (XIII), Impy (VI), Inyotef (XII), Isi (V/VI), Iti (VI), Iti (XI)

Ka (XV), Ka'aper (IV/V), Kenamun (XVIII),[1] Kha (XVIII)

Maaty (XI), Maiy (XVIII), Maya (XVIII), Mentuhotep (XII), Meresankh (V), Meryrenufer Qa (VI), Methethy (V), Minbaef (VI/XII), Minnakhte (XVIII), Montuemhet (XXV)

Nakhthorheb (XXVI), Nefer (V), Neferherenptah (V)

Paser (XX),[1] Paweraa (XX),[1] Penbuy (XIX), Penno (XX), Ptahhotep (XXVII)

Rehu (VIII/IX), Rehuerdjersen (XII)

Sa-Hathor (XII), Saiset (XIX), Seshemnefer (VI), Sa-Mont (XII), Sebekemhet (XIII/XV), Sehetepibre (XII), Sekhemka (V), Senenmut (XVIII),[2] Senimen (XVIII), Sennedjem (XIX), Sennefer (XVIII),[1] Senpu (XII/XIII), Senusret (XII),[1] Senehet (XII), Sihathor (XII)

Theti (XI), Thothhotep (XII), Ti (V), Tia (XVIII), Tity (XIII), Tjay (XVIII), Tjetji (XI)

Wah (XI),[3] Weni (VI)

Yupa (XIX)[1]

Zenon (Ptol.)

Notes
1 Mayor
2 Architect
3 Estate Manager

Scribes

Aba (XX), Akhpet (XIX), Aakhesperkaresenb (XVIII), Amenemhet (XVIII), Amenemope (XX), Amenemope(t) (XIX), Amenmose (XIX), Amennakhte (XX), Ani (XIX)

Butehamun (XX/XXI)[1]

Djehutymose (XVIII),[1] Djehutymose (XX), Dua-Khety (MK)

Hednakht (XIX), Hori (XIX), Hori (XXI), Huya (XIX)[2]

Iniuia (XVIII), Ipuwer (MK)

Ka'aper (IV/V), Kaiaper (V),[3] Karem (XVIII), Khaemipet (XIX), Kenherkhopshef (XIX/XX)

Mami (XVIII),[4] Menna (XVIII),[2] Merer (X)

Nashuyu (XIX), Nebamun (XVIII), Nebneteru (XXII),[2] Nebre (XVIII), Neferhotep (XIX),[2] Nekmertaf (XVIII)

Penmaat (XIX)

Rahotep (V), Ramose (XVIII)

Sementawy (XVIII)

Tjaneni (XVIII),[3] Tjuneroy (XIX)[2]

Yii (XVIII)

Notes
1 Restorer, Conservator
2 Royal Scribe
3 Military Scribe
4 'Diplomat'

Poets, writers, philosophers, scientists

Agatharchides (Ptol.), Apion (Rom.), Appianus (Rom.), Apollonius Rhodius (Ptol.)

Callimachus (Ptol.)

[Diodorus Siculus] (Rom.)

Eratosthenes (Ptol.), Euclides (Ptol.)

Hecataeus (of Abdera) (Pt.), Hecataeus (of Miletus) (= XXVI), [Herodotus] (XXVII)

Ipuwer (MK)

Lycophron (Ptol.)

Machon (Ptol.), Manetho (Ptol.)[1]

Philiscus (Ptol.),[2] Plutarch (Rom.), Plotinus (Ptol.), Polybius (Ptol.), [Pythagoras] (XXVI)

Sotades (Ptol.), Strabo (Rom.)

Theocritus (Ptol.), Tryphiodorus (sixth century)

Zenodotus (Ptol.)

Notes

1 HPR
2 Tragedian and Priest

Priests and temple officials

Anen (XVIII), Amenemhat Nebuy (XII), Amenhotep (XVIII), Amenmose (XXII),[1] Amenwahsu (XVIII), Amenyseneb (XIII), Ankhpakered (XXV), Ankhsheshonq (Ptol.)

Chaeremon (Rom.)

Djadjaemankh (IV), Djedkhonsuefankh (XXVI), Djoser (Ptol.)

Gemnefherbak (XXX)

Harmesaf (XXII),[2] Harsiese (XXII), Henuttawy (XXI),[3] Hetepes (VI), Hekanakhte (XI), Hor (XXVI), Hor (Ptol.) Horemkhaef (XIII), Hori (XXI), Horpaa (Pt.)

Idu (VI), Ika (V), Iki (XII), Inkaptah (V), Irukaptah (VI)[4]

Kaemked (V), Kenamun (XVIII), Khaemetnu (IV), Kynebu (XX)

Memi (XIII), Merery (VIII), Mery (XII), Meryreankh (VI)

Nakht (XVIII),[5] Nebenmaat (XIX), Nebnakhtu (XVIII), Neferabu (XIX),[6] Neferherenptah (V), Neferherenptah (V/VI), Neferhotep (XVIII), Neferhotep (XVIII),[7] Neferty (XII), Nekhonekh (V),[8] Nesmin (Ptol.), Nimaatsed (V), Nykuhor (V)[9]

Pediamonet (XXII), Pasenhor (XXII), Pedyamunranebwaset (XXVI), Peftuaneith (XXV/XXVI), Penmaat (XXI),[10] Pentamenope (XXVI), Philiscus (Pt.)[11]

Sedjememoaou (XIX), Sekweskhet (X/XI), Seneb (IV), Senenu (VI), Senusret (XII),[12] Senwosret (XI), Setka (VIII/IX), Sheri (IV)

Tenry (XIX), Teti (XVIII), Thaenwaset (XXIII)

Udjahornesret (XXVII)

Wah (XII), Wenamun (XX/XXI), Wermai (XX)

Yii (XVIII)

Notes

1 Physician
2 Architect
3 Singer
4 Embalmer
5 Gardener
6 Temple Draughtsman
7 Chief Scribe of Amun
8 Royal Steward
9 Judge
10 Archivist
11 Tragedian
12 Mayor

Royal officials and servants

Amenhotep (XVIII)

Djar (XI)

Harwa (XXV), Huya (XVIII)

Ibe (XXVI), Inini (XX),[1] Iurudef (XIX)

Kenamun (XVIII),[2] Kheruef (XVIII), Khnumhotep and Niankhkhnum (V), Khnumhotep (XII)

Meribastet (XX), Methen (IV), Methethy (V), Montuwosre (XII)

Nebmertuef (XVIII), Nekhonekh (V)[2]

Pay (XVIII), Pesshuper (XXV)

Sebastet (XVIII), Sihathor (XII), Suemniuet (XVIII), Sobekhotep (XIX/XX)[3]

Tjay (XVIII)

Urhiya (XIX)[4]

Yuya (XIX)

Notes
1 Criminal
2 Royal Steward
3 Royal Butler
4 General, later High Steward

Warriors – army officers, soldiers, military scribes, naval officers, charioteers

Ahmose (XVIII), Ahmose Pennekheb (XVIII), Amenemheb (XVIII), Amentefnakhte (XXVI), Anhernakhte (XIX), [Marcus Antonius] (Ptol.)

Bayenemwast (XX)[1]

[Gaius Julius Caesar] (Ptol.), [Chabrias] (XXX)

Dedu (XVIII), Djehuty (XVIII), Djehutyemhab (XX)

Hat (XVIII), Hekaemsaf (XXVI), Herihor (XXI),[2] Hor (XVIII/XIX), Horemheb (XVIII)[3]

Iahames (XXVI), Indy (VIII), Inebni (XVIII), Inti (VI), Iti (XI), Iuput (XXII),[4] Iuwelot (XXII)[4]

Kai (XII), Kaiaper (V),[5,] Karef (XXVI), Khusobek (XII)

Lamintu (XXII)

Menna (XIX)

Nakhtmin (XVIII),[6] Nakhtmin (XVIII),[7] Nebenkeme (XIX), Nemtyemweskhet (XIII), Nesmont (XII), Nesuhor (XXVI), Nimlot (XXII)[2]

[Pharnabazes] (XXVII), Piankh (XXI),[2] Potasimto (XXVI), Prehirwenmef (XIX)[8]

Ramose (XVIII/XIX)

Sasenet (VI), Se'ankh (XI), Senu (IX/X), Sihathor (XIII), Sobeknekht Rinefsonb (XIII), Suemnut (XVIII)

Tjaneni (XVIII), Tjay (XVIII), [Tjehemau] (XI)

Udjahorresnet (XXVII),[9] Urhiya (XIX)[10]

Yamu-nedjeh (XVIII), Yuya (XIX)

Notes
1 Criminal
2 Vizier, HPA
3 Later king
4 HPA
5 Military Scribe
6 Reign of Amenhotep III
7 Reign of Tutankhamun
8 Prince
9 Physician, Priest
10 Later High Steward

Medical practitioners

Aha-Nakht (XII),[1] Amenmose (XXII)

Eratistratus (Pt.)

Gua (XII)

Imhotep (III),[2] Iry (IV), Iryenakhty (X), Iwty (XIX)

Nebamun (XVIII), Niankh-re (V), Niankhsekhmet (V)

Pariamakhu (XIX), Pefnefdineit (XXVI), Pentu (XVIII),[5] Peseshet (V/VI), Psametik (XXVI)

Sit-Sneferu (XII)[3]

Tjutju (XVIII)

Udjahorresnet (XXVII)[4]

Notes
1 Veterinarian
2 Vizier, Architect
3 Nurse
4 Soldier, Priest
5 Vizier

Architects: builders, overseers of public works, engineers

Bakenkhons (XIX)[1]

Ctesibus (Ptol.)

Deinocrates (Mac./Ptol.)

Harmesaf (XXII),[2] Hemionu (IV),[3] Hor and Suty (XVIII)

Imhotep (III),[4] Ineni (XVIII)

Khaemhese (V), Khnum-baf (IV),[5] Khufu-Ankh (IV)

Minmose (XVIII)

Nekhebu (V/VI)

Parennefer (XVIII), Pashedu (XIX), Puyemre (XVIII)

Sennedjemibmehy (V),[6] Senenmut (XVIII), Sennu (Ptol.)

Thenry (XIX)

Notes
1 HPA
2 Priest
3 Prince, Vizier
4 Vizier, Physician
5 Prince?
6 Vizier

Astronomers

Aristachus (Ptol.)

Harkhebi (Ptol.)

Menelaus (Ptol.)[1]

Nakht (XVIII)

Ptolemy, Claudius (Rom.)[2]

Notes
1 and Mathematician
2 and Geographer

Musicians and singers

Harmose (XVIII), Hennuttawy (XXI), Hennutauineb (XIX), Hereubekhet (XXI), Hesy (XIX)

Kahay (V)

Meresamun (XXII)

Neferhotep (XII)

Raia (XIX)

Tadimut (XXI)

Painters and draughtsmen

Amenaankhu (XII), Antiphilus (Ptol.)

Dedia (XIX), Demetrius (Ptol.)

Hui (XX)

May (XVIII), Maya (XVIII)

Nebre (XVIII),[1] Neferabu (XIX)

Seni (VI)

Note
1 'Outline Scribe'

Sculptors

Auta (XVIII)

Bek (XVIII)

Imhotep (III)

Inkaf I (IV), Inkaf II (IV), Ipy (XIX), Irtisen (XI)

Nebamun and Ipuky (XVIII), Niankhptah (V)

Ptahpehen (III)

Thutmose (XVIII)

Userwer (XII)

Craftsmen and tradesmen

Amenemopet (XVIII),[1] Amenpanufer (XX),[2] Ankhwah (III)[3]

Bekh (I)[4]

Horpaa (Pt.)

Kahotep (I),[5] Khakhara (V/VI),[6] Khay (XIX)[7]

Merer (XII/XIII)[8]

Nakht (XVIII),[9] Nakhtdjehuty (XIX)[10]

Pabes (XIX),[11] Paneb (XIX), Penbuy (XIX), Psametiksaneith (XXVII)[12]

Sebastet (XVIII)[13]

Notes
1 Jeweller
2 Robber
3 Shipbuilder
4 Artisan (sacrificed)
5 Copper-worker (sacrificed)
6 Hairdresser and Wigmaker
7 Goldsmith
8 Temple Gardener
9 Gardener
10 Craftsman in gold inlays
11 Tradesman
12 Gold- and silver-smith
13 Hairdresser

Festival organisers

Ikhernofret (XII)[1]

Min (XVIII)

Nebamun (XVIII), Neferamun (XVIII)

Sneferunefer (V)

Note
1 Royal Treasurer

Police and security services

Bakenwerel (XX)

Dedu (XVIII)

Mahu (XVIII)

Nebit(ef) (XIII)

Criminals

Amenpanufer (XX),[1] Amenwah (XX)

Bayenemwast (XX)[2]

Inini (XX)[3]

Paneb (XIX)[4]

Notes
1 Stone Carver
2 Army Officer
3 Royal Steward
4 Unconvicted

Unclassified

Demetrius Phalereus (Ptol.)[1]

Eudoxus (Pt.)[2]

Madja (XVIII),[3] Merisu (XII),[4] Minnakhte (XVIII),[5] Mose (XIX)[6]

Prehotep (XIX),[7] Ptolemaios (Ptol.)[8]

Senebtysy (XIII)[9]

Tetiseneb (XVII)[10]

Notes
1 Statesman
2 Navigator
3 'Mistress of the House'
4 Landowner
5 Merchant
6 Litigant
7 Ploughman
8 Donor
9 Land and Factory Owner
10 Theban Woman

Appendix 2

Entries in chronological sequence

Predynastic Period

Iryhor, Menes, Nar-Mer, 'Scorpion', Ka.

Archaic Period

Dynasty I

Aha, Anedjib, Ankhka, Bekh, Bener-ib, Betrest, Den, Djer, Djet, Hemaka, Herneith, Ka'a, Kahotep, Merka, Merneith, Nebetka, Neithhotep, Neska, Sabef, Sabu, Sekhem-Ka, Semerkhet, Senba.

Dynasty II

Hotepsekhemwy, Khasekhem-Khasekhemwy, Nemaathap, Nynetjer, Peribsen, Raneb, Ruaben, Sened, Weneg.

The Old Kingdom

Dynasty III

Ankh, Ankhwah, Djefai-nisut, Djoser Netjerykhet, *Djoserti*, Hesyre, Hetephernebti and Intkaes, Hotepdief, Huni, Imhotep, Khaba, Khabausoker, Meresankh I, Ptahpehen, *Qahedjet*, Redyzet, Sanakhte, Sekhemkhet, Sipa and Neset.

Dynasty IV

Ankhaf, Atet, *Bakare,* Bunefer, Debhen, Djadjaemankh, Djedefre, Hemionu, Henutsen, Hetepheres I, Hetepheres II, Hordedef, Inkaf (I), Inkaf (II), Iry, Ka'aper, Kameni, Kaninisut, Kanufer, Kawab, Khaemetnu, Khafre, Khentkawes I, Khnum-baf, Khnum-Khufu, Khufu-ankh, Khufu-kaf, Khnetetenka, Khunere, Menkaure, Meresankh III, Meritites, Methen, Metjen, Minkaf, Nebmakhet, Neferheteperes, Nefermaat, Nefertiabet, Nekaure, Nyku-Hor, Ptahshepses, Rahotep and Nofret, Seneb, Setka, Shepseskhaf, Sheri, Sneferu, Wedjankhdjes.

Dynasty V

Bebi, Djedkare Isesi, Ihy, Ika, Inkaptah, Inti, Isi, Kaemked, Kahay, Kaiaper, Khaemhese, Khakhara, Khekheretnebty, Khentkawes II, Khnumhotep and Niankhkhum, Mehy, Menkauhor Akauhor, Meresankh, Methethy, Mitry, Nefer, Neferefre, Neferherenptah,[1] Neferherenptah,[2] Neferirkare, Neferseshemseshat, Nekhebu, Nekhonekh, Niankhsekhmet, Niankhptah, Nimaatsed, Niankhre, Niuserre, Nykuhor, Peryneb, Peseshet, Ptahhotep, Ptahshepses, Rahotep, Ranefer, Reemkuy, Sabu, Sahure, Sekhemka, Senedjemibmehy, Shepseskare Isi, Sneferu-nefer, Tepemankh, Ti, Unas, Unas-Ankh, Userkaf, Weshptah.

Notes

1 Official
2 Priest 'Fifi'

Dynasty VI

Ankhenesmeryre,[1] Ankhmahor, Bawi, Djadaemankh, Djau, Djedkhonsuiefankh, Harkhuf, Hekaib, Hem-Min, Hepzefa, Hetepes, Hetepni, Ibi, Idu, Impy, Inti, Irukaptah, Iti, Kagemni, Kaihep, Kheni, Khentika, Khentkawes, Khnumhotep, Mehu, Merefnebef, Merenre I, Merenre II, Mereruka, Meryreankh, Meryrehashtef, Meryrenufer Qa, Minbaef, Nebet, Neith, Niankhpepi, Niankhpepiken, Nitiqret, Pepy I, Pepy II, Pepyankh, Rewer, Sasenet, Seni, Sennefer, Sebni, Senenu, Seshemnefer, Teti, Tjeti-iker, Udjebten, Unas-Ankh, Userkare, Weni, 'Weretyamtes'.

Note

1 Two Queens of Pepy I of the same name

First Intermediate Period

Dynasties VII/VIII

Demedjibtawy, Hakare Ibi, Indy, Inyotef, Iuu, Merery, Neferkahor, Neferyu, Rehu, Setka.

Dynasties IX/X

Ahanakht, Akhtoy I,[1] Akhtoy II,[1] Akhtoy I,[2] Akhtoy II,[2] Ankhtify, Anu, Ikui, Inyotef I, Iryenakhty, Merer, Merikare, Neferkare, Neheri, Sekwasket, Senu, Tefibi, Thutnakht I, II, III, IV, Tjauti.

Notes

1 King

2 Nomarch

The Middle Kingdom

Dynasty XI

(Wahkare) Akhtoy III, Baket III, Dagi, Djar, Djari, Dua-Khety, Hekanakht, Henhenet, Heny, Ini, Inyotef, Inyotef II, Inyotef III, Ipuwer, Irtisen, Iti, Kawit, Kemsit, Khety, Khemetneferhedjet Weret, Maaty, Meketre, Menhet, Merti, Menwi, Merisu, Mesheti, Miut, Montuhotep I, (Nebhepetre) Montuhotep II, (Sa'ankhkare) Montuhotep III, Montuhotep IV, Nebt, Neferu I, Neferu II, Neferu III, Se'ankh, Senwosret, Tjetji, Thutnakht V, [Tjehemau], Wah, Yah.

Dynasty XII

Aha-nakht, Amenaankhu, Amenemhat Nebuy, Amenemhet I, Amenemhet II, Amenemhet III, Amenemhet IV, Antefoker, Bener, Djehutyhotep, Djehutynekht, Gua, Harhotep, Hepzefa, Horurre, Iki, Ikhernofret, Imhotep, Inyotef, Kai, Khnemetneferhedjet Weret, Khnumhotep I, Khnumhotep II, Khnumhotep,[1] Khusobek, Mentuhotep, Merer, Mery, Merisu, Montuhotep, Montuwosre, Nakht, Nebipusenwosret, Neferhotep, Neferty, Neferuptah, Nesmont, Nofret, Rehuerdjesen, Sa-Hathor, Sa-Mont, Sehetepibre, Senbi, Senehet, Senet, Senpu, Senusret, Senwosret,[2] Senwosret I, Senwosret II, Senwosret III, Senwosretankh,[3] Senwosretankh,[4] Serenput, Sihathor, Sithathor Iunet, Sit-Sneferu, Sobekneferu, Thothhotep, Ukhhotep I, Ukhhotep II, Ukhhotep III, Ukhhotep IV, Userwer, Wah, Wahka I, Wahka II.

Notes

1 Steward

2 Priest

3 Vizier

4 HPM

Dynasty XIII

Amenemhe Siste, Amenemhat, Amenyseneb, Ankhenmer, Ankhu, Awibre Hor, Djedneferre Dudimose, Horemkhaef, Ibiya, Ii-seneb, Imeru-Neferkare, Memi, Merneferre Iy, Mery, Nebit(ef), Neferhotep I, Nehesy, Nemtyemweskhet, Sebekemhet, Semenkhkare-Mermentifu, Senebsuema, Senebtyfy, Senebtysy, Sihathor, Sobekhotep I, Sobekhotep II, Sobekhotep III, Sobekhotep IV, Sobeknekht Rinefsonb, Tity, Userkare Khendjer, Wahneferhotep, Wegaf, Wepwawetemsaf.

Second Intermediate Period

Dynasties XIV/XV

Ka, Khayan, Nehesy, Salitis, Yaqub-Hor.

Dynasty XVI

Apepi I, Apepi II-Aqenienre.

Dynasty XVII

Ahhotep, Inyotef VI, Inyotef VII, Kamose, ['The Prince of Kush'], Madja, Mentuhotep, Nubkhas, Rahotep, Sawadjenre Nebiryerawet, Sekhemre Wahkhau, Sanakhtenre Tao I, Seqenenre Tao II, Sipair, Sobekemsaf II,[1] Sobekemsaf,[2] Tetiseneb, Tetisheri, Userenre.

Notes

1 King
2 Queen

The New Kingdom

Dynasty XVIII

Aakheperkare-seneb, Abdi Kheba, Ahhotep I, Ahhotep II, Ahmose-Meritamun, Ahmose,[1] Ahmose,[2] Ahmose Nefertiry, Ahmose-Pennekheb, Amenemheb, Amenemhet, Amenemope,[3] Amenemope,[1] Amenemope,[4] Amenemopet,[5] Amenemopet,[6] Amenhotep I, Amenhotep II, Amenhotep III, Amenhotep IV-Akhenaten, Amenhotep Son of Hapu, Amenhotep,[7] Amenhotep,[8] Amenhotep,[5] Amenhotep,[13] Amenmose, Amenwahsu, Anen, Ankhesenamun, Aper-El, Artatama, Auta, Ay, Bek, Baketaten, Beknekhonsu, Dedu, Dhutmose, Djehuty, Djehutyhotep,[9] Djehutyhotep,[10] Djehutymose, Djeserkaresoneb, [Eti], [Ghilukhepa], Hapuseneb, Harmose, Hat, Hatshepsut, Hekanefer, Hor, Hor and Suty, Horemheb, Huy, [Iankhamu], Inebni, Ineni, Iniuia, Intef, Ipuia, Ipy, Isis, Karem, Kenamun,[7] Kenamun,[8] Kenamun,[11] Kha, Kheruef, Kiya, Maanekhtef, Madja, Mahu, Maïa, Maiherperi, Maiy, Mami, May, Maya,[12] Maya,[13] Maya,[8] Meketaten, Menkheperreseneb, Menna,[8] Meri, Meritaten, Merymose, Min, Minmose, Minnakhte,[15] Minnakhte,[8] Mutemwiya, Nakht,[16] Nakht,[17] Nakht,[18] Nakhtmin,[19] Nakhtmin,[20] Nebamun,[21] Nebamun,[4] Nebamun and Ipuky, Nebmertuef, Nebnakhtu, Nebre, Nebunenef, Neferamun, Neferhotep,[29] Neferhotep,[7] Neferneferuaten,[22] Nefertiti, Neferure, Nehi, Nekmertaf, Parennefer, Pay, Pia, Pentu,[13] [Piryawaza], Ptahemhat-ty, Ptahmes, Puyemre, Ramose,[5] Ramose,[23] Rehkmire,[24] Sebastet,[14] Sementawy, Senenmut, Senimen, Sennefer,[25] Sennefer,[26] Senu, Sitepehu, Smenkhkare, Sobekhotep, Suemniuet, Suemnut, [Suppiluliumas], [Tadukhipa], Teti,[7] [Teti],[27] Thenuna, Thutmose I, Thutmose II, Thutmose III, Thutmose IV, Thutmose,[28] Thuwre, Tiy, Tjaneni, Tjay, Tjutju, Tutankhamun, Tutu, User, Userhat, Userhet, Usermont, Usertatet, Wesersatet, Yamu-nedjeh, Yii, Yuya and Tuyu, [Zennanza].

Notes

1 King
2 Army Officer
3 Viceroy
4 Scribe
5 Vizier
6 Jeweller
7 Priest
8 Royal Scribe
9 tem. Hatshepsut
10 tem. Tutankhamun
11 Mayor
12 Painter
13 Courtier
14 Hairdresser
15 Merchant
16 Gardener
17 Astronomer
18 Noble
19 Prince
20 Officer
21 Physician
22 Queen, King, Princess
23 Soldier
24 Chancellor
25 Mayor
26 Priest
27 Nubian noble

28 Sculptor
29 Chief Scribe of Amun

Dynasty XIX

Akhpet, Ameneminet, Amenemope, Amenemopet, Amenmesse, Amenmose,[1] Amenmose,[2] Amenhiwonmef (Amenhirkhopshef), Anhernakhte, Anhurmose, Ani, Asha-hebsed, Bak, Bay, Bakenkhons, Ben-Ozen, Bint-Anath, Dedia, Didia, [Hattusil], Hednakht, Hekanakhte, Henuttauineb, Hesy, Hori, Hori, Huya, Ipy, Istnofret, Iurudef, Iwty, Kenherkhopshef, Khaemipet, Khaemwaset, Khay, Menna, Merenptah, Mery-Atum, Mose, [Muwatallis], Nakhtdjehuty, Nashuyu, Nebemkeme, Nebenmaat, Nebenteru, Nebre, Nebunenef, Neferabu, Neferhotep, Neferronpet, Nefertari, Pabes, Pahemnetjer, Paneb, Pariamakhu, Paser,[2] Paser,[3] Pashedu, Penbuy, Penmaat, Prehirwenmef, Prehotep, Raia, Ramesses I, Ramesses II, Ramesses,[4] Ramose, Roma-Roy, Roy, Saiset, Sedjememoaou, Sennedjem, Sethirkhopshef, Seti, Seti I, Seti II, Si-Montu, Siptah, Sobekhotep, Tenry, Thenry, Tjia and Tia, Tjuneroy, To, Tuyi, Twosret, Urhiya, Wennufer, Yamunedjeh, Yupa, Yuya.

Notes
1 Royal Scribe
2 Vizier
3 Mayor
4 Crown Prince

Dynasty XX

Aba, Amenemope, Amenhirkhepshef, Amenhotep, Amennakhte, Amenpanufer, Amenwah, Bakenwerel, Bayenemwast, Butehamun, Djehutyemhab, Herihor, Hui, Inini, Khaemwaset, Khaihapi, Kynebu, Mentuherkhepshef, Meribastet, Panehesy, Paser, Paweraa, Penno, Pentaweret, Ramessesnakhte, Ramesses III, Ramesses IV, Ramesses V, Ramesses VI, Ramesses VII, Ramesses VIII, Ramesses IX, Ramesses X, Ramesses XI, Setau, Sethnakhte, Ta, Tyti, Usimarenakhte, Wenamun, Wermai.

Third Intermediate Period

Dynasty XXI

Amenemnisu, Amenemope, Ankhefenamun, Djedkhonsuefankh, Henuttauineb, Henuttawy,[1] Henuttawy,[2] Henuttawy,[3] Hereubekhet, Herihor, Hori, Maatkare, Menkheperre, Penmaat, Pesshuper, Piankh, Pinudjem I, Pinudjem II, Pseusennes I, Pseusennes II, Siamun, Smendes, Tadimut, Wendjebaendjed.

Notes
1 Queen
2 Priestess
3 Priestess and temple singer

Dynasty XXII

Amenmose, Harmesaf, Harnakhte, Harsiese, Harsiese,[1] Iniamunnayefnabu, Iuput, Iuwelot, Kama, Karomama Merymut II, Khnumhotep, Lamintu, Meresamun, Nebneteru, Nimlot, Osorkon I, Osorkon II, Osorkon IV, Pasenhor, Pediamonet, Pediese, Peftjauawybast, Peftuaneith, Pimay, [Sargon II] Shedsunefertem, Sheshonq I, Sheshonq II, Sheshonq III, Takelot I, Takelot II, Zekhonsefankh.

Note
1 King

Dynasty XXIII

Amenirdis I, Iuput II, Osorkon III, Pedubastis I, Peftjauawy-Bast, Rudamun, Sheshonq IV, Shepenupet I, Takelot III, Thaenwaset, Yewelot.

Dynasty XXIV

Bakenrenef, Khaemhor, Tefnakhte.

Late Period

Dynasty XXV

[Alara], Amenirdis II, Ankhpakhered, [Esarhaddon], Harsiese, Harwa, Hecataeus, Horsiesnest Meritaten, Hor, [Irypaankhkenekenef], [Kashta], Montuemhet, Nimlot, Piankhy, [Sennacherib], Shabaka, Shabataka, Shepenupet II, Taharqa, Tanutamani, Urshanahuru.

Note
1 Nubian king

Dynasty XXVI

Aba, Amasis, Amentefnakhte, Ankhnesneferibre, Apries, [Assurbanipal], Bes,[1] Bes,[2] [Cyrus II], Djedkhonsuefankh, Hakaemsaf, Hor, Hecataeus (of Miletus), Iahmes, Ibe, Inaros, Karef, Mehetenwesket, [Nabopolassar], Nakhthorheb, [Nebuchadrezzar II], Necho I, Necho II, Neferibrenofer, Nesipakashuty, Nesuhor, Nitiqret, Pediamunraneb Waset, Pefnefdineit, Peftuaneith, Petamenope, Potasimto, Psametik,[3] Psametik I, Psametik II, Psametik III, [Pythagoras], Tryphiodorus.

Notes
1 Nomarch
2 Mayor
3 Physician

Dynasty XXVII

[Artaxerxes I], [Artaxerxes II], [Artaxerxes III Ochos], [Cambyses], [Darius I], [Darius II], [Darius III Codoman], [Herodotus], Khababash, [Pharnabazes], Psamteksaneith, Ptah-hotep, Udjahorresnet, [Xerxes].

Dynasty XXVIII

Amyrtaeus.

Dynasty XXIX

Hakor, Nefaarud I.

Dynasty XXX

[Chabrias], Gemnefherbak, Nectanebo I, Nectanebo II, Somtutefnakht, Teos, Thaasetimu, Tjahepimu.

Macedonian Dynasty

Alexander III, Alexander IV, [Deinocrates], [Olympias], [Philip II], Philip Arrhidaeus.

Ptolemaic Period

Agatharchides, Ankhsheshonq, Antiphilus, Apollonius, Apollonius Rhodius, Aristachus, [Arnehkamani], Arsinoe II, Arsinoe III Philopator, Berenice I, [Gaius Julius Caesar], Caesarion,[1] Callimachus, Cleomenes, Cleopatra VII, Ctesibus, Demetrius, Demetrius Phaleraeus, Djoser, Eristratus, Eratosthenes, Euclides, Eudoxus, Harkhebi, Hecataeus (of Abdera), Hor, Horpaa, Horwennefer, Lycophron, Machon, Manetho, Menelaus, Nesmin, Panemerit, Petosiris, Philiscus, Polybius, Psenptais III, Psherenptah, Ptolemaios, Ptolemy I Soter, Ptolemy II Philadelphus, Ptolemy III Euergetes, Ptolemy IV Philopator, Ptolemy V Epiphanes, Ptolemy VI Philometor, Ptolemy VII Neos Philopator, Ptolemy VIII Euergetes II, Ptolemy IX Soter II, Ptolemy X Alexander I, Ptolemy XI Alexander II, Ptolemy XII Neos Dionysos, Ptolemy XIII, Ptolemy XIV, Ptolemy XV Caesarion, Sennu, [Shaknadakhete], Sotades, Taimhotep, Theocritus, [Zenodotus], Zenon.

Note
1 Ptolemy XV

Roman Period

Antinous, Marcus Antonius, Apion, Appianus, Augustus Caesar, Chaeremon, Diodorus Siculus, Hadrian, Plotinus, Plutarch, Psenptah, Claudius Ptolemy, Strabo.

Appendix 3

Ancient Egypt in museum collections

The world's great museums are exceptionally rich in the heritage of Ancient Egypt, in the work of her sculptors, painters and craftsmen. No past society has left so extensive, diverse and representative an overview of itself; none has depicted with such obvious delight the life of the people, from the ceremonies surrounding the king and the great magnates to the everyday concerns of the inhabitants of the Nile Valley. So immediate is the impact of Egyptian art, especially when it looks to the life of the individual and his preoccupations, that the centuries dissolve and the Egyptians whom we observe become, as it were, our contemporaries.

Who's Who in Ancient Egypt has drawn on the resources of many of the important collections of Egyptian artefacts which are housed in the museums of the world. Once again it must be said that such a survey cannot pretend to be be exhaustive; here, the references to museum collections indicate where an object or inscription throws light on the life of the subject of the biographical entry.

In many cases, particularly of the most celebrated figures in Egyptian history, there are many portraits and it would be invidious to select a particular example in a book which is not primarily concerned with the artistic heritage and which is not illustrated. The references, therefore, are selective and are given where a statue, relief, painting or artefact may throw particular light on the individual concerned. The bibliography contains a number of works which provide a comprehensive survey of Egyptian art; these are indicated by an asterisk. Although it is largely composed of English-language sources, it should enable the reader to follow up aspects if the entries which might be of special or further interest.

The list which follows itemises some of the most important and extensive collections which contain portraits or other material relevant to the biographical entries.

Musée d'Annecy

Potasimto

Musée Calvet, Avignon

Bes, Neferamun

Phoebe A. Hearst Museum of Anthropology, University of Berkeley, California

Khakhara, Psametik

Egyptian Museum, Berlin

Amenmope(t), Bek, Harwa, Hetepni, Hui, Mentuhotep, Meresamun, Meritaten, Nefertiti

Museum of Fine Arts, Boston

Ankhaf, Impy, Khaemneteru, Khufu-Kaf, Khunere, Meresankh III

Brooklyn Museum

Ankhenesmeryre, Huni, Methethy, Ptahhotep, Thaasetimun, Tenry, Yii

Musées Royaux d'Art et Histoire, Brussels

Karef

Egyptian Museum, Cairo

Ahhotep I, Ahmose, Akhenaten, Amenirdis, Ankhpakhered, Atet, Awibre Hor, Djoser Netjerykhet, Djoser, [Eti], Harhotep, Hat, Hekaemsaf, Hemaka, Hereubekhet, Hesyre, Hetepheres I, Hotepdief, Iahmes, Ika, Imhotep, Inyotef II Wahankh, Isis, Iti, Ka'aper, Kaemked, Kama, Kawit, Khabausoker, Khaemhesi, Khaemwaset, Khafre, Khasekhem-Khasekhemy, Khnumet, Khnumetneferhedjet Weret, Khnumhotep, Khnum-Khufu, Maatkare, Maiherperi, Meketre, Menkaure, Merenptah, Meresamon, Meresankh, Mesheti, Montuemhet, Nebhepetre Montuhotep II, Nar-Mer, Nebnakhtu, Neferefre, Neferherenptah, Nefer-Maat, Niankhpepi, Nesipakashuty, Nimaatsed, Niankhre, Nofret, Panemerit, Pediamunranebwaset, Pepy I, Pepy II, Petamenope, Petosiris, Piankhy, Psamtek-Sa-Neith, Pseusennes I, Rahotep and Nofret, Saiset, Sehetepibre, Seneb, Senenmut, Sennedjem, Sennefer, Senwosret I, Sithathor Iunet, Sneferu, Tadimut and Herub, Ti, Tiy, Tjay, Tutankhamun, Userkaf, Wendjebaendjed, Yamunedjeh

Fitzwilliam Museum, Cambridge

Amenemhet III, Amenemhet Nebuy, Karem, Ramesses III, Tity

Oriental Institute, University of Chicago

Bakenwerel

Oriental Museum of the University of Durham

Amenemhat, Senusret

Musée des Beaux Arts, Grenoble

Hennuttauineb, User

Kestner Museum, Hannover

Tetiseneb

Pelizaeus-Museum, Hildesheim

Djadaemankh, Hemionu, Hesy, Irukaptah, Sahathor

Sudan National Museum, Khartoum

Djehutyhotep

Rijksmuseum van Oudheden, Leiden

Ankh, Iki, Intef, Iwty, Maya, Neferhotep

British Museum, London

Aha, Ahmose, Ahmose-Meritatum, Amenemhet III, Amenemope, Amenhotep, Amenirdis, Ani, Ankhnesneferibre, Ankhwah, Bener-ib, Gua, Harhotep, Hat, Heqanakhte, Hor, Hor and Suty, Ibiya, Inebni, Inyotef, Inyotef VII, Iuwelot, Kemsit, Kenherkhopshef, Khaemwaset, Merymose, Nebhepetre Montuhotep II, Neithhotep, Nesmin, Pesshuper, Pimay, Ptahemhat, Ptahshepses, Qenherkhopshef, Ramose, Roy, Sanakhte, Semerkhet, Senebtify, Sennefer, Seti I, Seti II, [Shakdakhete], Sihathor, Sihathor, Sobekemsaf II, Sobekemsaf, Sobekhotep, Taraqa, Tjeti-iker, Wepwawetemsaf

The Luxor Museum of Egyptian Art

Amenhotep II, Amenhotep III, Amenmose, Kamose, Sa'ankhkare Montuhotep III, Nesipakashuty, Pediamonet, Pia, Senwosret III, Thaenwaset

Liverpool Museum

Ankhmahor

Petrie Museum of Egyptian Archaeology, University College, London

Kahotep, Mery

Pushkin Museum of Fine Arts, Moscow

Amenemhe Siste, Heny, Hepes, Horpaa, Ihy, Iiseneb, Iniamunnayefnebu, Irypaankhkenkenef, Iuu, Memi, Ptolemaios, Sobeknekht Rinefsonb, Tepemankh, Teti, Yupa

Staatliche Sammlung Ägyptischen Kunst, Munich

Bakenkhons, Amenemopet, Henuttawy, Nesmont

Metropolitan Museum of Art, New York

Amenhotep, Bener, Djedkhonsuefankh, Hatshepsut, Henhenet, Hepzefa, Hetepheres II, Horemkhaef, Imhotep, Indy, Kenamun, Khety, Khnumhotep, Meketre, Menhet, Merery, Merti and Menidi, Mitry, Montuwosre, Neferkahor, Neferyu, Nykuhor, Pediamunranebwaset, Peryneb, Raneb, Reemkuy, Rehuerdjersen, Sahure, Senba, Sennuwy, Senu, Senwosretankh, Sit-Sneferu, Thutmose III, Userhat, Wah

Ashmolean Museum, Oxford

Bawi, Khasekhem-Khasekhemwy, Minbaef, 'Scorpion', Sened, Sheri, Teti

Museo Nationale, Palermo

Bes

Musée du Louvre, Paris

Amenyseneb, Ankh, Dedia, Djedefre, Djehuty, Djet, Hor, Imeru-Neferkare, Inyotef VI, Inyotef VII, [Irypaankhkenkenef], Irtisen, Karomama Merymut II, Khenetetenka, Maankhetef, Nakht, Nakhthorneb, Neferheteperes, Nefertiabet, Nekmertaf, Osorkon II, Panemerit, Ptahpehen, Qahedjet, Ramose, Senpu, Senu, Sepa and Neset, Setau, Setka, Tjutju

University of Pennsylvania Museum of Archaeology and Anthropology

Amenemhet, Merer, Qa'a, Sitepehu

Hermitage Museum, St Petersburg

Wedjankhdjes

Würtembergisches Landesmuseum, Stuttgart

Khaemipet, Sa-Mont

Museo Egizio, Turin

Anen, Butehamun, Kha, May, Penbuy, Redyzet

Kunsthistorisches Museum, Vienna

Gemnefherbak, Kaninisut, Khaihapi, Sneferunefer, Tjenuna

Yale University Art Gallery

Bebi, Hekanefer